McGRAW-HILL ELECTRICAL AND ELECTRONIC ENGINEERING SERIES

Frederick Emmons Terman, *Consulting Editor*
W. W. Harman and J. G. Truxal,
Associate Consulting Editors

RALPH J. SCHWARZ

Professor of Electrical Engineering
Columbia University

BERNARD FRIEDLAND

Principal Staff Scientist
General Precision, Inc.
Little Falls, New Jersey

McGRAW-HILL BOOK COMPANY

New York • St. Louis • San Francisco
Toronto • London • Sydney

LINEAR SYSTEMS

PREFACE

The purpose of this book is to provide a unified treatment of the main techniques for the analysis of linear systems. Differential equations for studying the behavior of linear systems were largely superseded in some branches of engineering by "operational" methods which make use of the Laplace transform. During the 1950s, however, interest in nonlinear systems increased significantly. Since transform methods are not generally applicable to nonlinear problems, many investigators returned to the use of differential equations in the state-variable form. The significant results achieved have validated this approach even in problems to which transform methods can be applied and have caused reduced emphasis on transform methods. Preoccupation with any single method, however, may not lead to the most direct or perceptive analysis of a problem. We have, therefore, endeavored to provide a balanced treatment of both transform methods and differential equations in the state-variable form and to discuss the relationship between them.

The presentation is intended to be intuitively appealing, yet not entirely without mathematical sophistication. Much of the book can be read with a typical undergraduate-mathematics background of calculus, differential equations, and the elements of matrix algebra. Some familiarity with functions of a complex variable is needed for parts of Chapters 6, 8, 12, and 13, and elementary probability theory is needed for Chapters 9 and 10. Since good treatments of these subjects are widely available, it was not considered necessary to discuss these topics in the text or in appendices.

Discrete-time signals and systems, which are increasing in importance because of the widespread use of digital computers, are treated along with their continuous-time counterparts. Difference equations in vector-matrix form and the Z transform are both studied, and are both compared with differential equations and the Laplace transform. This parallel treatment is also carried through in the study of random signals and stability.

The basic definitions of linear-system theory, such as linearity, time-invariance, and causality, are introduced in Chapter 1 at a level consistent with the rest of the text. The next three chapters deal with the analysis of linear systems by time-domain methods. Chapter 2 is a review of the representation of the dynamics of linear lumped systems by ordinary differential equations and introduces vector-matrix notation. The parallel development for discrete-time systems, including their representation by difference equations, is initiated here. The basic techniques of time-domain analysis are introduced in Chapter 3, in which the general form of the superposition integrals for continuous-time systems, as well as the analogous superposition summations for discrete-time systems, are derived. The *fundamental matrix* of a finite-order, lumped system is defined in Chapter 4 for both continuous- and discrete-time systems; expressions for the superposition integral or summation are obtained in terms of this fundamental matrix.

Frequency-domain methods are introduced in Chapter 5. Fourier series and their properties are discussed; then the Fourier transform is developed as a heuristic extension of Fourier series. The Laplace transform is introduced in Chapter 6 as a formal generalization of the Fourier transform. The Laplace transform inversion theorem, however, is demonstrated independently and is thus established on a more rigorous basis than provided by the formal generalization. Properties of the Laplace transform are discussed, together with techniques for finding the inverse Laplace transform, including contour integration. In Chapter 7, general expressions for the Laplace transform of the fundamental matrix of lumped time-invariant systems are obtained. Chapter 8 treats the Z transform and its use in discrete-time systems.

Chapters 9 and 10 deal, respectively, with statistical properties of random

signals and with linear systems excited by random signals. A discussion of least-squares filtering is included in Chapter 10.

Various definitions and theorems concerning stability, particularly in linear systems, and a discussion of Lyapunov's second method are presented in Chapter 11. Several practical methods for determining the stability of fixed linear systems are treated in Chapter 12. Derivations of the Routh-Hurwitz stability algorithms by the classical techniques of complex variables and by the use of Lyapunov's second method are included, and the graphical methods (Nyquist criterion, root loci) are briefly discussed.

Chapter 13, which concludes the book, deals with distributed-parameter systems such as electrical transmission lines, vibrating beams, and thermal systems and employs the frequency-domain method of analysis.

The first eight chapters, in preliminary form, have been used for several years as the text for a one-semester course in linear-system theory for senior undergraduate and first-year graduate students at Columbia University. The material in the last five chapters could serve as the basis for the second semester of such a course. Alternatively, by the omission of some of the material which may already be familiar (most likely Chapters 3 and 5 and the first part of Chapter 6), it would be possible to include some of the contents of the last five chapters in a one-semester course. For students in mechanical engineering, Chapters 1 to 7 and 13 could be included in a one-semester course.

Numerous examples illustrating the application of the techniques are included. In order to compare various approaches, we have made use of several "running examples," which are started at one point and then taken up one or more times subsequently as new ideas are introduced.

A variety of problems to be worked out are given at the end of each chapter. Some are simply numerical exercises; some test the thoroughness of the reader's grasp of the material; others extend the results of the text.

Our students and colleagues have made numerous valuable suggestions, which we have incorporated in the book. In particular, we are indebted to Professor Philip E. Sarachik of New York University, Professors Christos Halkias and Paul Diament of Columbia University, and Mr. Peter Oden, who have read the preliminary versions of the first eight chapters of the text. Mrs. Gay Oden, who typed the manuscript, deserves our special gratitude.

Ralph J. Schwarz
Bernard Friedland

CONTENTS

CHAPTER ONE

FUNDAMENTAL CONCEPTS

1.1 INTRODUCTION

A knowledge of the theory of linear systems is indispensable for an understanding of the behavior of dynamic processes. Although very few systems, in practice, are *exactly* linear, they often are adequately approximated by linear models. Moreover, it is difficult to begin a study of nonlinear systems until the fundamentals of linear systems have been mastered.

The systems which arise in modern technology frequently involve a variety of physical quantities such as electrical voltages and currents, mechanical forces and displacements, volumes, flow rates, temperatures, and so forth. This book aims at developing general abstract models which aid in the study of such systems; it is concerned with the specific nature of the quantities only by way of illustration. The methods are thus applicable to any system which is linear.

A system is a collection of interconnected components in which there is

specified a set of dynamic variables called *inputs*, or *excitations*, and another set called *responses*, or *outputs*.   The objective of system *analysis* is to determine how such a collection of components behaves when subjected to a specified excitation or set of excitations.   The analysis starts with the known characteristics of the individual components, represented by mathematical expressions (models), and combines these to obtain a convenient characterization of the system by means of which the required response may be calculated.

Most practical systems are too complicated to permit the exact calculation of the response, and one must usually settle for qualitative information.   Fortunately, this qualitative information is often adequate. For example, all one might need to know is whether a system is stable, its steady-state response (to sinusoidal excitations at different frequencies), and its *rise time*, or *bandwidth*.

When the problem requires more detailed information, it is often necessary to enlist the aid of electronic computers.   In particular, it might be desirable to simulate the system on an analog computer.   For this purpose it is necessary to represent the system in terms of the components available in these computers.   We shall develop methods by which this representation may be accomplished.

The techniques for system *design*, whose objective is the construction, by use of available components, of a system which performs in some specified manner, are quite different in different fields.   When the systems involved are linear, however, the analytical techniques used in design are generally based on the theory developed in this book.

1.2   TERMINOLOGY

Since our main concern is with the mathematical relations governing a linear system rather than with the details of its physical structure, it is often convenient to represent a system† schematically by means of a box as shown in Fig. 1.1.   On the left-hand side of the box are a group of arrows labeled $x_1, x_2, \ldots, x_n$ which designate the inputs (excitations, stimuli) to the system, and on the right-hand side are arrows labeled $y_1, y_2, \ldots, y_m$, the outputs (responses).   The inputs and outputs, which may be any physical quantities, generally vary with time.   In general, the number of inputs and outputs are not equal.   (It is readily appreciated that a single input may affect a number of physical quantities designated as outputs and that a single output may be influenced by various inputs.) The input and output time functions are called *signals*.

† Systems will in general be denoted by capital letters such as G, H, K, etc.

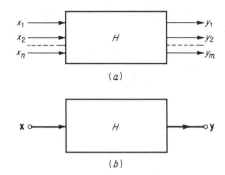

FIG. 1.1   Schematic representation of a system.   (a) Individual signals shown; (b) signals in "cables."

For economy of notation it is often convenient to designate the *sets* of inputs $x_1, x_2, \ldots, x_n$ and outputs $y_1, y_2, \ldots, y_m$ by single symbols; i.e.,

$$\mathbf{x} = \begin{bmatrix} x_1 \\ x_2 \\ \cdot \\ \cdot \\ \cdot \\ x_n \end{bmatrix} \qquad \mathbf{y} = \begin{bmatrix} y_1 \\ y_2 \\ \cdot \\ \cdot \\ \cdot \\ y_m \end{bmatrix}$$

In conformity with mathematical terminology we call $\mathbf{x}$ and $\mathbf{y}$ the input and output *vectors*, respectively, and the individual inputs and outputs x_i, y_i the *components* of the vectors.   The number of components contained in a vector is called the *dimension* of the vector.   Since each component of such a vector may be a function of time, the vector is, in general, a function of time.   In the schematic diagram a vector is connected to the system by a single line which may be regarded as a "cable" comprising connections for each component of the vector.

It is assumed, unless otherwise stated, that the input vector $\mathbf{x}(t)$ is applied at $t = -\infty$ and that the system is at rest or unexcited at that time, i.e., that no energy is stored in the system.   In most problems of practical interest, the input is first applied at a known time instant; then the energy stored in all energy-storing elements of the system must be specified at that instant if the future behavior of the system is to be determined.

A very simple example of a system is the electric circuit with two elements shown in Fig. 1.2a.   The voltage $e(t)$ is the (only) input; the current $i(t)$ may be the only output.   A more complicated example is the automobile of Fig. 1.2b.   The inputs are the force exerted by the driver on the gas pedal, the wind and air friction forces (two components), road friction, vertical displacements due to road unevenness, and rotation of the steering wheel by the driver.   The outputs may be the horizontal dis-

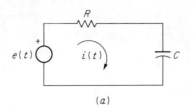

(a)

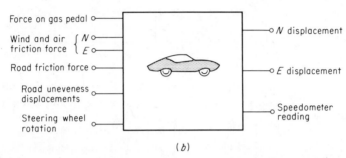

Force on gas pedal

Wind and air { N
friction force { E

Road friction force

Road unevenness
displacements

Steering wheel
rotation

N displacement

E displacement

Speedometer
reading

(b)

*FIG. 1.2   Examples of systems.   (a) An electric circuit;
(b) an automobile.*

placement of the car (two components) and the speedometer reading. Additional quantities might be designated as outputs if there is any interest in them.

The relation between the input vector and the output vector (*input-output relation*) is written in the generic form

$$\mathbf{y} = H\mathbf{x} \tag{1.1}$$

which should be read

$$\mathbf{y} \text{ is the response of } H \text{ to } \mathbf{x}$$

The symbol H serves to identify a system as well as its associated *operator*.† When H precedes a signal such as $\mathbf{x}$ in (1.1), it is an operator which operates on the input $\mathbf{x}$ to produce the output $\mathbf{y}$.

1.3   CLASSIFICATION OF SYSTEMS

CONTINUOUS-TIME, DISCRETE-TIME, AND QUANTIZED SIGNALS AND SYSTEMS

In most cases we shall be concerned with the effects of changing (time-varying) input(s) on the output(s).   If the inputs to and the outputs from

† An operator assigns a member y of a set $\mathcal{Y}$ of functions to each member x of the set $\mathcal{X}$ of functions.

a system are capable of changing at any instant of time, the system is called a *continuous-time signal system*, or *continuous-time system* for short. We make the fact of continuous change evident by writing the input and output as functions of the continuous-time variable t; that is,

$$\mathbf{x} = \mathbf{x}(t) = \begin{bmatrix} x_1(t) \\ x_2(t) \\ \cdot \\ \cdot \\ \cdot \\ x_n(t) \end{bmatrix}$$

and similarly for $\mathbf{y} = \mathbf{y}(t)$. It is important to note that the designation "continuous-time" does not imply that all inputs and outputs are mathematically continuous functions, but rather that they are functions of a *continuous variable*.

In some systems the signals change only at discrete instants, say every second, or year, or perhaps irregularly. Between the instants at which the variables may change value, the signals may not be defined or they may be constant. In either case, the behavior of the signals during these time intervals is of no interest. Mathematically, these signals are functions of *discrete* variables. Systems with such inputs and outputs are called *discrete-time signal systems*, or *discrete-time systems* for short. We make the discrete nature of the system evident by writing the signals as functions of a discrete variable t_k, where the t_k ($k = 1, 2, 3, \ldots$) are the instants at which the functions may change their values. Thus, for a discrete-time system,

$$\mathbf{x} = \mathbf{x}(t_k) = \begin{bmatrix} x_1(t_k) \\ x_2(t_k) \\ \cdot \\ \cdot \\ \cdot \\ x_n(t_k) \end{bmatrix}$$

or, more simply,

$$\mathbf{x} = \mathbf{x}(k) = \begin{bmatrix} x_1(k) \\ x_2(k) \\ \cdot \\ \cdot \\ \cdot \\ x_n(k) \end{bmatrix}$$

A distinction must be made between *discrete-time* systems and *quantized* systems. In quantized (signal) systems the variables may assume only a

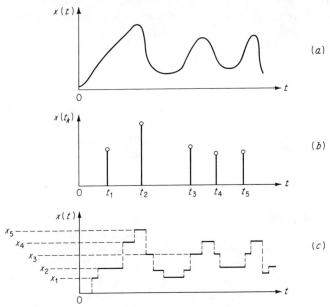

FIG. 1.3   Types of signals.   (a) Continuous-time signal;
(b) discrete-time signal; (c) quantized signal.

countable number of values (levels) but the changes from level to level may occur at any time.   Figure 1.3 illustrates the different types of signals.

ILLUSTRATIONS

1. The electric circuit of Fig. 1.2a is a continuous-time system.
2. The prices of stocks printed in the daily newspapers are discrete-time signals, since they are subject to change only when a new edition of the paper goes to press.   The prices are also quantized, usually at levels differing by one-eighth of a dollar.
3. The signals in digital computers are quantized discrete-time signals.
4. A person's body temperature is a continuous-time signal; however, a patient's temperature on a hospital chart is a discrete-time signal, since it is measured and recorded several times a day and not continuously.

It is worth noting that some continuous-time systems may be treated as if they were discrete by observing the input and output only intermittently.   An important mathematical distinction between continuous-

time and discrete-time systems is the fact that the former are characterized by *differential* equations whereas the latter are characterized by *difference* equations.

FIXED AND TIME-VARYING SYSTEMS

Another way of classifying systems is by the property of *time invariance* (*stationarity*). Loosely defined, a system is *time-invariant* (*stationary, fixed*) if its input-output relations do not change with time. More precisely, a continuous-time system having the input-output relation†

$$\mathbf{y}(t) = H\mathbf{x}(t)$$

is fixed if and only if

$$H\mathbf{x}(t - \tau) = \mathbf{y}(t - \tau) \tag{1.2}$$

for any $\mathbf{x}(t)$ and any τ. The system must be at rest prior to the application of $\mathbf{x}(t)$. Likewise, a discrete-time system having the input-output relation

$$\mathbf{y}(k) = H\mathbf{x}(k)$$

is fixed if and only if

$$H\mathbf{x}(k - n) = \mathbf{y}(k - n) \tag{1.3}$$

for any $\mathbf{x}(k)$ and any n. These definitions indicate that the shape of the response to an input applied at any instant *depends only on the shape of the input*, and not on the time of application, as shown in Fig. 1.4.

† It should be noted that in the relation $\mathbf{y}(t) = H\mathbf{x}(t)$, the value of the output, or response, $\mathbf{y}$ at the time t indicated as the argument generally depends on the values of the input $\mathbf{x}$ during a finite or infinite interval, not only on the value of $\mathbf{x}$ at time t. The symbol H indicates an operation on the *signal* $\mathbf{x}$, not on the value of $\mathbf{x}$ at time t. The signal is written $\mathbf{x}(t)$ to indicate that it is a continuous-time signal.

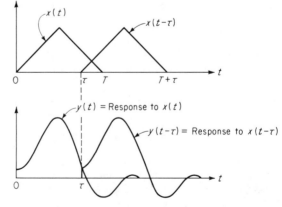

FIG. 1.4 *Inputs and outputs in a fixed system.*

A system for which (1.2) or (1.3) does not hold is called *time-varying, variable,* or *nonstationary.*

ILLUSTRATIONS

1. A system characterized by a linear differential (or difference) equation with constant coefficients is fixed. (This will be demonstrated subsequently.)
2. A system characterized by a linear differential (or difference) equation with time-dependent coefficients is generally time-varying.† The Bessel equation

$$\frac{d^2y}{dt^2} + \frac{1}{t}\frac{dy}{dt} + y = 0$$

   is such an equation.
3. An amplifier whose gain varies as the result of ambient-temperature changes is a time-varying system (provided the ambient temperature is not itself considered an input of the system).
4. A lumped- or distributed-parameter network whose elements or parameters are constant is a fixed system.
5. A traffic-control system in which relays actuate traffic lights periodically is a variable system.

Example 1.1   Suppose the response of a system H to an input $x(t)$ is

$$y(t) \equiv Hx(t) = x(t^2)$$

i.e., the output at time t equals the input at time t^2. If the input is delayed by τ sec, the response is

$$Hx(t - \tau) = x(t^2 - \tau)$$

The delayed response to $x(t)$ is, however,

$$y(t - \tau) = x[(t - \tau)^2] = x(t^2 - 2t\tau + \tau^2)$$

which clearly differs from $Hx(t - \tau)$. Hence the system is time-varying.

CAUSAL SYSTEMS

A *causal* (or *physical*, or *nonanticipatory*) system is one whose response to an input does not depend on future values of the input. More precisely,

† A system may be governed by time-varying differential equations and nevertheless have an output-input relation which is that of a time-invariant system; see Prob. 3.30.

a continuous-time system is causal (physical) if and only if

$$\mathbf{x}_1(t) = \mathbf{x}_2(t) \qquad \text{for } t \leq t_0$$

implies

$$H\mathbf{x}_1 = H\mathbf{x}_2 \qquad \text{for } t \leq t_0$$

for all t_0, where $\mathbf{x}_1$ and $\mathbf{x}_2$ are any two input vectors. (For a discrete-time system, t is replaced by t_k.) Note that if the two inputs are identical for all $t \leq t_0$ and the system is at rest at $t = -\infty$, the conditions in the system at any $t \leq t_0$ cannot differ for the two inputs.

Example 1.2 Suppose the response of a system to the step function of Fig. 1.5a is the ramp of Fig. 1.5b, which begins before the step input occurs. For values of t_0 slightly less than t_1, the two inputs x_1 and x_2 are equal for $t \leq t_0$ but the responses are not equal. The system is thus not causal. If, on the other hand, the response begins after the step is applied (Fig. 1.6),

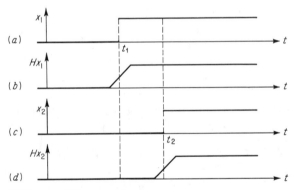

FIG. 1.5   Noncausal system.

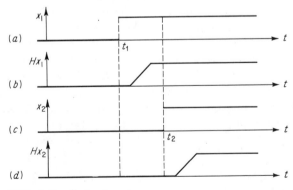

FIG. 1.6   Causal system.

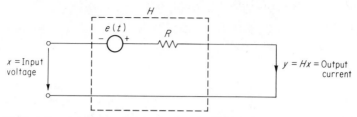

FIG. 1.7   Active circuit in which $Hx \neq 0$ when $x = 0$.

the definition shows that the system may be causal, since for any $t_0 \leq t_1$, the two inputs are equal and the two outputs are equal.   The system of Example 1.1 is noncausal, since for any $t > 1$, the output anticipates the input.

It should be noted that the definition of a causal system given above states that if the *difference* between two inputs is zero, the *difference* between the respective responses must be zero.   It is thus not necessary that the response to zero input be zero, a condition easily violated in an active circuit (Fig. 1.7).

The knowledge that we must deal with a causal system will frequently impose constraints on the mathematical formulation of system behavior.

DYNAMIC AND INSTANTANEOUS SYSTEMS

A system is classified as *instantaneous* if its output at any instant t (t_k) depends at most on the input values at the same instant but not on past or future values of the input.   Otherwise the system is said to be *dynamic*. In the latter, the output at any instant depends not only on the present input, but also on at least some of the past input values (and, in noncausal systems, on the future input values).   A system whose output at time t is completely determined by the input in the interval $t - T$ to t ($T \geq 0$) is said to have a *memory* of length T.   Thus an instantaneous system has a memory of zero length (and is sometimes called a zero-memory system). If T is finite but nonzero, the system has a *finite* memory.

The input-output relation for an instantaneous system may be expressed by

$$\mathbf{y}(t) = \mathbf{f}[\mathbf{x}(t), t]$$

where $\mathbf{f}$ is a vector-valued (possibly time-dependent) *function*, not an

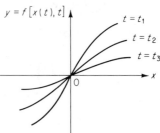

*FIG. 1.8 Representation of an instan-
taneous system.*

operator. When, for example, there is a single input and a single output,
we write

$$y(t) = f[x(t), t]$$

The function f may be represented by a set of curves in the xy plane, as
shown in Fig. 1.8. If the system is fixed, it is characterized by a single
curve.

ILLUSTRATIONS

1. A system whose output is the current $i(t)$ flowing through a resistor R
   in response to the voltage $e(t)$ applied across the resistor is instantaneous, since

$$i(t) = \frac{1}{R} e(t)$$

2. A system consisting of a capacitor whose input is the current flowing
   into and whose output is the voltage across the capacitor has infinite
   memory since

$$e(t) = \frac{1}{C} \int_{-\infty}^{t} i(\lambda) \, d\lambda$$

   which depends on the values of $i(t)$ at all time instants up to time t.
   [It is assumed that $e(-\infty) = 0$.]

3. Any system whose output is the first difference of the input (e.g., the
   change in the price of a share of stock, giving the differences between
   today's price and yesterday's price) has a finite memory equal to the
   time interval between inputs.

4. Simple data-smoothing systems often indicate the average of several,
   say five, successive inputs or readings. If the inputs occur 1 sec apart,
   such a system has a memory of 5 sec.

LINEAR AND NONLINEAR SYSTEMS

In this book the principal distinction between systems is made on the basis of linearity.   A system is linear if it satisfies the principle of superposition.   More precisely, a system is *linear* if and only if

$$H(\alpha \mathbf{x}_1 + \beta \mathbf{x}_2) = \alpha H \mathbf{x}_1 + \beta H \mathbf{x}_2$$

where α and β are any constants, and $\mathbf{x}_1$ and $\mathbf{x}_2$ are any input signals.[†] It is important to remember our assumption that $\mathbf{x}_1$ and $\mathbf{x}_2$ are applied at $t = -\infty$ and that the system is unexcited at that time.

The foregoing definition, with $\alpha = \beta = 1$, becomes

$$H(\mathbf{x}_1 + \mathbf{x}_2) = H \mathbf{x}_1 + H \mathbf{x}_2$$

which is called the property of *additivity*, and asserts that the response to a sum of two inputs is equal to the sum of the two responses.   With $\mathbf{x}_2 \equiv \mathbf{0}$, the definition becomes

$$H(\alpha \mathbf{x}_1) = \alpha H \mathbf{x}_1$$

which is called the property of *homogeneity*, and asserts that the response to a constant multiple of any input is equal to the response to the input multiplied by the same constant.   Thus a linear system possesses both the property of additivity and the property of homogeneity.   It is easy to show that any system which possesses these properties is linear.   Hence a system is linear if and only if it is both additive and homogeneous.   It can be shown that, for rational α, additivity implies homogeneity (Prob. 1.15).

By induction we can demonstrate that in a linear system

$$H \left(\sum_{i=1}^{n} \alpha_i \mathbf{x}_i \right) = \sum_{i=1}^{n} \alpha_i H \mathbf{x}_i$$

provided that the upper index n is finite.   We shall assume that the property is valid in linear systems for infinite sums and also for integrals; i.e.,

$$H \left(\sum_{i=1}^{\infty} \alpha_i \mathbf{x}_i \right) = \sum_{i=1}^{\infty} \alpha_i H \mathbf{x}_i$$

and

$$H \int_{a}^{b} \alpha(\lambda) \mathbf{x}(t, \lambda) \, d\lambda = \int_{a}^{b} \alpha(\lambda) H \mathbf{x}(t, \lambda) \, d\lambda$$

[†] For a more precise definition, which is not needed here, see L. A. Zadeh, An Extended Definition of Linearity, *Proc. IRE*, vol. 49, p. 1452, September, 1961, and vol. 50, p. 200, February, 1962.

ILLUSTRATIONS

1. Any system characterized by linear differential or difference equations is linear. (This will be demonstrated subsequently.)
2. A square-law device has the input-output relation

$$y(t) = Hx(t) = x^2(t)$$

This device is not linear since

$$H(x_1 + x_2) = (x_1 + x_2)^2 \neq Hx_1 + Hx_2 = x_1^2 + x_2^2$$

3. A multiplier (whose output is the product of two inputs) has the input-output relation

$$y = H \begin{bmatrix} x_1 \\ x_2 \end{bmatrix} = x_1 x_2$$

This device is not linear since

$$y = Ha \begin{bmatrix} x_1 \\ x_2 \end{bmatrix} = H \begin{bmatrix} ax_1 \\ ax_2 \end{bmatrix} = a^2 x_1 x_2 \neq a x_1 x_2$$

4. An instantaneous device whose output y is a linear function of the input x,

$$y = mx + b$$

where m and b are constants, is not linear since

$$H(x_1 + x_2) = mx_1 + mx_2 + b \neq Hx_1 + Hx_2$$

The system is linear, however, if the changes Δx and Δy about an "operating point" x_0, y_0 are considered the input and output, respectively. Then $x = x_0 + \Delta x$, $y = y_0 + \Delta y$, and

$$\Delta y = m \, \Delta x$$

Every linear instantaneous system may be characterized by a relation of the form

$$\mathbf{y}(t) = \mathbf{A}(t)\mathbf{x}(t)$$

where $\mathbf{A}(t)$ is an $m \times n$ matrix (for a system with m outputs and n inputs). If $\mathbf{A}(t)$ is constant, the system is fixed.

1.4 ALGEBRA OF INTERCONNECTED LINEAR SYSTEMS: FLOW DIAGRAMS

A system comprising a collection of subsystems may be conveniently represented by means of a flow diagram or block diagram, which illustrates

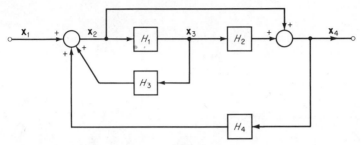

FIG. 1.9   Example of a flow diagram.

the interconnections between the subsystems.   As an example, consider a system characterized by the following set of input-output relations:

$$\mathbf{x}_2 = \mathbf{x}_1 + H_3\mathbf{x}_3 + H_4\mathbf{x}_4$$
$$\mathbf{x}_3 = H_1\mathbf{x}_2 \tag{1.4}$$
$$\mathbf{x}_4 = \mathbf{x}_2 + H_2\mathbf{x}_3$$

These relations correspond to the system shown in Fig. 1.9.   In addition to the boxes representing the subsystems H_1, H_2, H_3, and H_4, we have introduced *summers*, indicated by circles, which are instantaneous devices whose output vector is the vector sum of the input vectors.   Evidently this representation is meaningful only when the input vectors to a summer all have the same dimension.

In this example the input to the overall system may be taken to be $\mathbf{x}_1$ and the output may be taken as $\mathbf{x}_4$.   The system could have $\mathbf{x}_2$ or $\mathbf{x}_3$ as the output, in which case the diagram would usually be redrawn.   If the input-output characteristics of each subsystem were known, it would be possible to combine these to obtain the overall characteristic of the system, which is symbolically represented by

$$\mathbf{x}_4 = H\mathbf{x}_1$$

We shall now develop a *flow-diagram algebra* for systems which will enable us to develop a symbolic expression for H in terms of (1.4).   As we shall see, this algebra follows rules of matrix algebra; i.e., it is associative and distributive but in general not commutative.   We start with two systems in cascade as shown in Fig. 1.10a.   We have

$$\mathbf{z} = H_1\mathbf{y} = H_1(H_2\mathbf{x})$$

Hence, if we denote the overall input-output relation by

$$\mathbf{z} = H\mathbf{x}$$

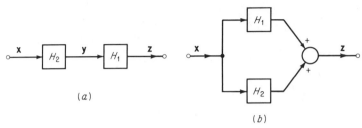

FIG. 1.10   *Systems in cascade and parallel.   (a) Cascade combination; (b) parallel combination.*

we can represent the overall system symbolically by

$$H = H_1 H_2$$

which is a symbolic statement of the fact that the action of H is the same as passing the input through H_2 and the resulting output through H_1. Likewise, if we have two systems in parallel (Fig. 1.10b), we can write

$$H = H_1 + H_2$$

as a symbolic representation of the fact that the output is obtained by passing the input through H_1 and H_2 separately and adding the respective responses.

If we have three systems in cascade as shown in Fig. 1.11, we can combine H_2 and H_3 first as in Fig. 1.11a or H_1 and H_2 first as in Fig. 1.11b. Thus we have

$$H = (H_3 H_2) H_1 = H_3 (H_2 H_1) \tag{1.5}$$

which establishes the *associative property* for system operators (including those representing linear systems).   To demonstrate the *distributive property*, consider Fig. 1.12.   We have

$$\mathbf{z} = H_3(\mathbf{y}_1 + \mathbf{y}_2) = H_3(H_1 \mathbf{x} + H_2 \mathbf{x}) = H_3(H_1 + H_2)\mathbf{x}$$

but if the system H_3 is linear, it follows from the property of additivity

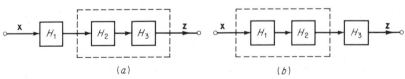

FIG. 1.11   *Three systems in cascade.*

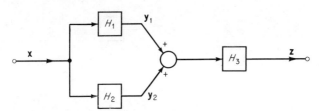

FIG. 1.12 *Demonstration of distributive property.*

that

$$\mathbf{z} = H_3\mathbf{y}_1 + H_3\mathbf{y}_2 = H_3H_1\mathbf{x} + H_3H_2\mathbf{x} = (H_3H_1 + H_3H_2)\mathbf{x}$$

Hence, for linear systems,

$$H_3(H_1 + H_2) = H_3H_1 + H_3H_2 \tag{1.6}$$

The *commutative property* does not hold for linear systems in general. As an example, consider the system comprising a differentiator and an amplifier having a gain proportional to time as shown in Fig. 1.13 (both of these are linear). If the two systems are connected as shown in Fig. 1.13a, the response to a signal $x(t) = t$ is $z_1(t) = 2t$; if they are connected as shown in Fig. 1.13b, the response is $z_2(t) = t$. Thus $H_1H_2 \neq H_2H_1$.

The identity system, or operator, is characterized by the symbol I, defined by

$$I\mathbf{x} = \mathbf{x} \tag{1.7}$$

This is the system whose output is identical with the input. It follows that

$$HI = IH \tag{1.8}$$

If two systems are connected in cascade so that the second cancels the effect of the first and the first cancels that of the second as shown in Fig.

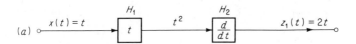

FIG. 1.13 *Demonstration that linear systems are not always commutative.*

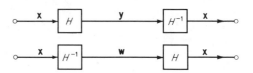

FIG. 1.14   Inverse systems.

1.14, then the systems are said to be inverses of each other.   The inverse
of a system H is denoted by H^{-1}.   We have

$$H^{-1}H = I = HH^{-1} \qquad (1.9)$$

It should be noted that there is no assurance that the inverse of an arbitrary causal system is causal; it usually is not.   For example, the inverse
of a system which delays the input signal by Δ sec is a predictor which
advances the input signal in time by Δ sec.   Such a system clearly violates
the definition of a causal system (Example 1.2).
    A system G for which

$$GH = I$$

but

$$HG \neq I$$

is called the left inverse of H since it behaves like an inverse only
when the signals are passed through H first.   In a similar manner, G is
the right inverse of H if

$$HG = I$$

but

$$GH \neq I$$

Example 1.3   Consider the modulator and detector of Fig. 1.15a.   The
modulator multiplies the input $x(t)$ by $\cos \omega_0 t$.   The detector recovers the
input signal $x(t)$ provided $x(t)$ varies slowly compared with $\cos \omega_0 t$; that is,
the frequencies contained in $x(t)$ must be small compared with ω_0.   If the
arrangement is inverted as in Fig. 1.15b, the detector has no effect on the
slowly varying input, and the modulator output is not equal to the detector

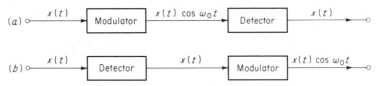

*FIG. 1.15   Example of left inverse.   (a) Normal arrangement
of modulator and detector; (b) inverted arrangement of modulator
and detector.*

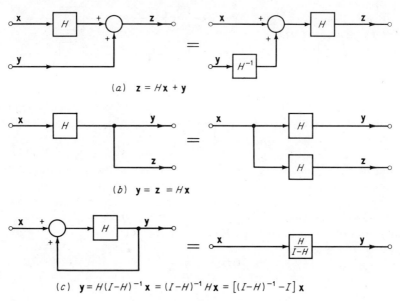

(a) $\mathbf{z} = H\mathbf{x} + \mathbf{y}$

(b) $\mathbf{y} = \mathbf{z} = H\mathbf{x}$

(c) $\mathbf{y} = H(I-H)^{-1}\mathbf{x} = (I-H)^{-1}H\mathbf{x} = \left[(I-H)^{-1}-I\right]\mathbf{x}$

FIG. 1.16   Flow-diagram equivalents.

input. Thus the detector is the left inverse of the modulator, and the modulator is the right inverse of the detector, for *slowly varying inputs*. The limited inverse property is thus restricted to a particular class of inputs and is not valid for any input. It should further be noted that these systems are nonlinear.

In summary, it is seen that one can employ the rules of matrix algebra to reduce a system of input-output equations to a single equation. In particular, applications of these rules allow us to combine Eqs. (1.4) into the single expression

$$\mathbf{x}_4 = [I - (I + H_2H_1)(I - H_3H_1)^{-1}H_4]^{-1}(I + H_2H_1)(I - H_3H_1)^{-1}\mathbf{x}_1$$

assuming that the inverses exist. It is often convenient to use the flow diagram as an aid in calculation, particularly when the number of relations is relatively large and it is difficult to see which sequence of substitutions to use. For this purpose, the equivalences listed in Fig. 1.16 are useful. The third entry in Fig. 1.16 is derived by observing that

$$\mathbf{y} = H(\mathbf{x} + \mathbf{y}) = H\mathbf{x} + H\mathbf{y}$$

or

$$(I - H)\mathbf{y} = H\mathbf{x}$$

whence

$$\mathbf{y} = (I - H)^{-1}H\mathbf{x} \tag{1.10}$$

We can also obtain (Prob. 1.11)

$$\mathbf{y} = H(I - H)^{-1}\mathbf{x} \tag{1.11}$$

so that the notation $H/(I - H)$ in Fig. 1.16c is unambiguous.

By use of these rules we obtain for the system in Fig. 1.9

$$H = [I - (I + H_2H_1)(I - H_3H_1)^{-1}H_4]^{-1}(I + H_2H_1)(I - H_3H_1)^{-1}$$

The steps in the calculation are illustrated in Fig. 1.17.

An extensive list of rules for flow-diagram simplification has been developed by Mason and others,[†] but those given in Fig. 1.16 are adequate for most purposes.   Mason made use of a somewhat different convention in

† S. J. Mason and H. J. Zimmerman, "Electronic Circuits, Signals, and Systems," chaps. 4 and 5, John Wiley & Sons, Inc., New York, 1960.   The original papers on which most of the material in this reference is based are S. J. Mason, Feedback Theory: Some Properties of Signal Flow Graphs, *Proc. IRE*, vol. 41, pp. 1144–1156, September, 1953, and Feedback Theory: Further Properties of Signal Flow Graphs, *Proc. IRE*, vol. 44, pp. 920–926, July, 1956.

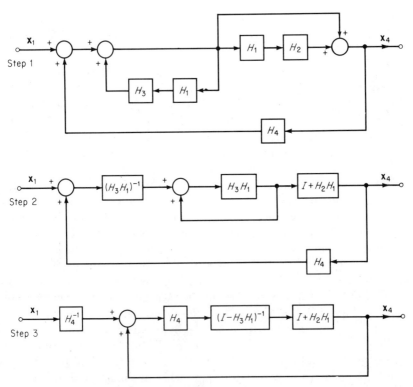

FIG. 1.17   *Example of flow-diagram reduction.*

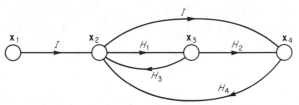

FIG. 1.18   Signal-flow graph for system of Fig. 1.9.

drawing flow diagrams and called them *signal-flow graphs*. In these, signals are represented by circles, and the linear systems by directed lines connecting the circles. All signals entering a circle are assumed to be summed. Thus the flow diagram for the system of Fig. 1.9 would have the appearance shown in Fig. 1.18. Apart from the fact that the use of the signal-flow graph results in a somewhat less cluttered picture than a block diagram, neither convention has any particular advantage over the other.

1.5   THE TECHNIQUES OF LINEAR SYSTEM ANALYSIS

There are two basic approaches to the analysis of linear systems. The first of these, which might be termed the "direct" approach, consists in directly solving the differential or difference equations relating the input and output of the system for the given input vector $x(t)$ or $x(n)$ subject to a known set of initial conditions. This amounts to searching for that vector of functions $y(t)$ or $y(n)$ which satisfies the differential or difference equation and the initial conditions for the system.

The greatest difficulty in this approach is usually the determination of the part of the output $y(t)$ due to the input function $x(t)$. Mathematically, this requires finding the "particular solution" by one of the standard methods. The second approach to linear system analysis uses an indirect approach to circumvent this difficulty. The input is resolved into a (usually infinite) set of elementary functions or components, all of which are similar in form. (The expansion of a periodic function into a Fourier series of sines and cosines or of exponentials is an example of such a resolution.) The response of the system to each elementary component is then obtained in some manner (for example, by using the differential equation of the system). Finally, the responses to all the elementary components of the input are added to obtain the output corresponding to this input. The steps followed in these two approaches are illustrated in Fig. 1.19.

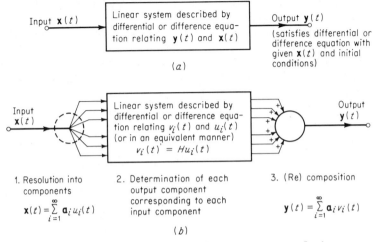

FIG. 1.19   *The two approaches to linear system analysis.*

The indirect approach will now be formulated more quantitatively in order to demonstrate its validity for linear systems. The excitation is first resolved into a set of elementary components; i.e.,

$$\mathbf{x}(t) = \sum_i \mathbf{a}_i u_i(t) \tag{1.12}$$

where $u_i(t)$ is a typical component, and $\mathbf{a}_i$ the amplitude vector of this component of $\mathbf{x}(t)$. The response $v_i(t)$ of the system to each elementary component $u_i(t)$ is then obtained from the differential equation or equivalent characterization of the system,

$$v_i(t) = H u_i(t) \tag{1.13}$$

The final step consists in summing the responses to the elementary components to obtain the response to the given excitation. Thus

$$\mathbf{y}(t) = H\mathbf{x}(t) = H \sum_i \mathbf{a}_i u_i(t)$$

By the additivity property, this becomes

$$\mathbf{y}(t) = \sum_i H[\mathbf{a}_i u_i(t)]$$

and, in view of the homogeneity property,

$$\mathbf{y}(t) = \sum_i \mathbf{a}_i H u_i(t) = \sum_i \mathbf{a}_i v_i(t) \tag{1.14}$$

which shows that $\mathbf{y}(t)$ obtained in this manner is indeed the response of the system to the excitation $\mathbf{x}(t)$.

It is frequently assumed that the initial conditions of the system are zero prior to the application of the excitation. Then the system is said to be "relaxed," or "at rest," before the excitation is applied. As will be shown subsequently, it is generally possible to account for any initial conditions by adding suitable signals to the actual input.

Equation (1.12) implies that the excitation is capable of being resolved into a denumerable† set of elementary signals. In most cases, however, a continuum (a nondenumerable set) of elementary signals must be used. Then the resolution is represented by an integral

$$\mathbf{x}(t) = \int \mathbf{a}(\lambda) \, d\lambda \, u(\lambda, t) \tag{1.15}$$

where $u(\lambda, t)$ is a typical component of the set, and $\mathbf{a}(\lambda) \, d\lambda$ is the amount or quantity of this component between λ and $\lambda + d\lambda$.

The composition of (1.14) is likewise represented by an integral,

$$\mathbf{y}(t) = \int \mathbf{a}(\lambda) \, d\lambda \, v(\lambda, t) \tag{1.16}$$

where $v(\lambda, t) = Hu(\lambda, t)$.

Any one of a number of elementary components may be used for the decomposition of the excitation function; the particular choice is a matter of convenience and depends on the nature of the excitation function of the system and the objectives of the analysis. The unit-impulse function and the unit-step function are frequently used as elementary components since the response of a system to these inputs may easily be determined experimentally and since they are convenient mathematically.

Another convenient choice for the elementary component is the complex exponential e^{st}, where s is a complex quantity whose imaginary part corresponds to the angular frequency ω used in steady-state circuit analysis. For this reason, the quantity s is frequently called "complex frequency." The exponential is a natural choice for the elementary component because it is the only function which remains unchanged in form when differentiated or integrated (its amplitude will, of course, ordinarily change). As a result, an exponential input to a fixed linear system (whose output and input are related by a linear differential equation with constant coefficients) will yield a response $H(s)e^{st}$, where $H(s)$ is *independent* of time, depends on the system, and serves as the complex amplitude of the response component relative to that of the input component. Because of its unique

---

† An infinite set whose elements may be put into a one-to-one correspondence with the positive integers is called denumerable, or enumerable, or countable. The elements $u_1(t)$, $u_2(t)$, $u_3(t)$, . . . , in the infinite sum of (1.12), may clearly be put into one-to-one correspondence with the integers 1, 2, 3, ... When this is not possible, the set is said to be nondenumerable.

Table 1.1

Step	Time domain		Frequency domain
Resolution of input	*Resolution into unit impulses* $\delta(t)$	*Resolution into unit steps* $\mu_1(t)$	*Resolution into complex exponentials* e^{st}
Response to component	*Impulse response* $h(t)$	*Step response* $a(t)$	*System transfer function* $H(s)$
Composition	*Superposition integrals*		*Multiplication and inversion*

behavior, the exponential is called a *characteristic function*, or *eigenfunction*, of a fixed linear system.

The use of the complex exponential as the elementary component thus means that all input components and all response components are complex exponentials. It is therefore sufficient, in determining the effect of the system on the input, to deal with the quantity $H(s)$; the exponential time functions need to be considered only in the resolution and recomposition processes. When this method is used, we speak of *frequency-domain* analysis since we deal largely with the complex frequencies only and not with the time functions. On the other hand, when the time functions are used explicitly (as they must be whenever the system modifies the form of these elementary components), we speak of *time-domain* analysis.

A summary of the methods of analysis is given in Table 1.1.

In conclusion, a brief comment on this three-step analysis technique is appropriate. There are unquestionably many problems in which this method will not yield results as rapidly as the direct method. The power of the method lies not so much in the ease with which simple problems can be solved through its use, but rather in the systematic manner in which all linear systems, from the simplest to the most complex, can be treated.

PROBLEMS

1.1 Determine whether each of the following systems is linear, fixed, or zero-memory.

(a) A delay line, characterized by

$$y(t) = x(t - a) \qquad a > 0$$

(b) The network shown in Fig. P 1.1b, with $x(t) = i(t)$, $y(t) = v(t)$.

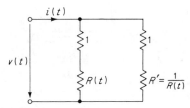

FIG. P 1.1b

(c) A system in which the output is independent of the input; e.g., $y(t) = $ constant for all t.

1.2   Determine conclusively, using the tests of additivity and homogeneity, which of the following systems are (1) linear; (2) fixed.

(a) $H \begin{bmatrix} x_1 \\ x_2 \end{bmatrix} = \max (x_1, x_2)$.

(b) $Hx(t) = \begin{cases} 0 & t < T \\ 2x & t \geq T. \end{cases}$

(c) $Hx(t) = 1 + x(t) \sin \omega_0 t$.

(d) $Hx(t) = \sin [1 + x(t)]\omega_0 t$.

1.3   Specify for each of the following systems whether it is linear, causal, fixed, or zero-memory or whether insufficient information is given. State the reasons for your answer in each case.   The response $y(t)$ to $x(t)$ is

(a) $y(t) = 3x(t) + \dfrac{dx(t)}{dt} + x(t^2) \qquad t > 0$.

(b) $y(t) = \displaystyle\int_{t}^{t+2} t^2 x(\lambda) \, d\lambda$.

(c) That of Fig. P 1.3c.

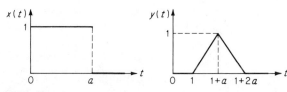

FIG. P 1.3c

(*d*) That of Fig. P 1.3*d*.

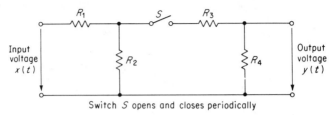

Switch *S* opens and closes periodically

FIG. P 1.3d

1.4   Specify whether the following systems are linear or nonlinear, fixed or time-varying, zero-memory or non-zero-memory, causal or noncausal.

(*a*) $Hx(t) = 3x(t + 1)$.
(*b*) Fig. P 1.4*b*.

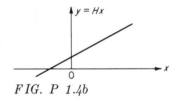

FIG. P 1.4b

1.5   Justify or disprove clearly the following statement: A zero-memory system is always causal.

1.6   A linear system is described by

$$y(t) = Hx(t)$$

If $x(t) = 0$ for all t, show that $y(t) = 0$ for all t.

1.7   A fixed linear system is subjected to the "staircase" input $x(t)$ shown in Fig. P 1.7.   The observed response to this input is $y(t)$. Determine whether or not the system is causal.

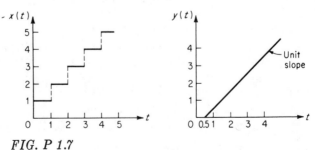

FIG. P 1.7

1.8   Given a linear zero-memory fixed system H.   It is known that $Hx_0(t) = 0$ for a particular input $x_0(t)$.   If $x_0(t)$ is not identically zero, show that

$$Hx(t) = 0 \qquad \text{for all } x(t)$$

1.9   In a signal-detection system, the phase of a sinusoidal signal $\cos \omega_0 t$ is altered as shown in Fig. P 1.9a and b.   Determine for each of the

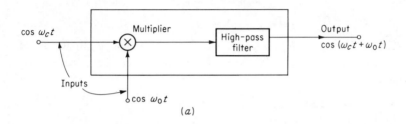

(a)

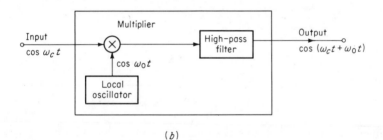

(b)

FIG. P 1.9

systems H_1 and H_2 whether it is fixed or time-varying with respect to the sinusoidal input or inputs shown (other types of inputs need not be considered).

1.10   A system H_2 consists of a multiplier, local oscillator, and high-pass filter as shown in Fig. P 1.9b.   Only inputs $\cos \omega_c t$ are of interest. The local oscillator generates a signal $\cos \omega_0 t$, where ω_0 is close to ω_c so that $0 < \omega_c - \omega_0 \ll \omega_c$.   The ideal high-pass filter has a pass-band from $\omega_c + \omega_0/2$ to $\omega_c + 3\omega_0/2$ rad/sec.   System H_3 has the same structure, except that the high-pass filter is replaced by an ideal low-pass filter whose passband extends from 0 to $\omega_c + \omega_0/2$ rad/sec.   Is H_3 the inverse of H_2?   Explain.

1.11   Derive Eq. (1.11).

1.12   Obtain a single operational expression for the systems characterized by the flow diagrams shown in Fig. P 1.12a and b.

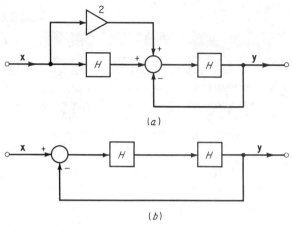

(a)

(b)

FIG. P 1.12

1.13   Show that, for the feedback system shown in Fig. P 1.13,

$$y = (I - H_1H_2)^{-1}H_1x = H_1(I - H_2H_1)^{-1}x$$

and that the notation $H_1/(I - H_1H_2)$ is therefore unambiguous if and only if H_1 and H_2 commute.

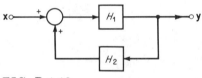

FIG. P 1.13

1.14   Extend the definition of a fixed (space-invariant) system to systems with input $x(u, v)$ and output $y(u, v)$ which are functions of two space variables.

1.15   Show that, if α is a rational number, the property of additivity implies the property of homogeneity: $H(\alpha x) = \alpha Hx$.

CHAPTER TWO

DYNAMIC EQUATIONS OF
LINEAR LUMPED SYSTEMS

2.1 DEFINITION OF A LUMPED SYSTEM

A dynamic system is said to be *lumped* if its behavior is governed by a set of *ordinary* differential (or difference) equations. Examples of such systems are electric networks comprising ideal resistors, capacitors, and inductors; mechanical systems made of rigid bars, small springs, and the like.

Systems which require the use of *partial* differential equations to describe their dynamic behavior are said to be *distributed*. Electrical transmission lines, waveguides, elastic bars, pneumatic and hydraulic lines are representative of this type of system. In the strict sense, all physical systems are distributed, but for practical purposes it is generally possible to approximate the behavior of many by means of ordinary differential equations. Consider, for example, a typical physical capacitor, constructed by winding into a roll two long strips of conducting

material, insulated from each other by dielectric material. Although this device is actually a rolled transmission line, it is usually adequate to approximate the device by an ideal capacitor whose terminal voltage and current are related by a single ordinary differential equation. The problem of determining the conditions under which it is adequate to approximate a given distributed system by means of a lumped system is often difficult. For example, the electrical engineer is accustomed to approximating physical circuits by lumped equivalents when the actual size of the components is "much smaller than the electrical wavelength." The latter is inversely proportional to frequency, so that it is said that the lumped approximation is valid at low frequencies. Many signals, however, contain a wide range of frequencies; at some the approximation may hold, at others it may not. The decision to use a lumped approximation in a specific physical problem often requires considerable experience in the technology of the problem. Some of the questions regarding lumped approximations are treated in Chap. 13; until then we deal with lumped systems, with the a priori understanding that the approximation is valid.

2.2 NORMAL FORM OF DIFFERENTIAL EQUATIONS

The differential equations which govern the behavior of a dynamic system can be written in a number of ways, and no single method can be said to be preferable in all circumstances. In general, the result required and the familiarity of the investigator with a particular method will determine the form in which the differential equations are written. The methods of *loop analysis* and *nodal analysis* are generally familiar to electrical engineers, who can rapidly write a system of differential equations which govern the dynamic behavior of a simple electric network. On the other hand, a person with less experience in the techniques of network analysis might well write the differential equations for the same network in another form.

One particularly convenient method of characterizing the behavior of a dynamic system is by a system of k first-order differential equations

$$\frac{dq_1}{dt} = f_1(q_1, q_2, \ldots, q_k, x_1, \ldots, x_n, t)$$

$$\cdots \cdots \cdots \cdots \cdots \cdots \cdots \cdots \cdots \cdots \quad (2.1)$$

$$\frac{dq_k}{dt} = f_k(q_1, q_2, \ldots, q_k, x_1, \ldots, x_n, t)$$

where $x_1, x_2, \ldots, x_n$ are the inputs, and $q_1, q_2, \ldots, q_k$ are a set of

auxiliary dynamic variables, known as the *state variables;* $f_1, f_2, \ldots, f_k$ are each nonlinear functions of $k + n + 1$ arguments. The outputs of the system are related to the state variables by means of a system of non-dynamic equations of the following form:

$$y_1 = g_1(q_1, q_2, \ldots, q_k, x_1, \ldots, x_n, t)$$
$$\cdots \cdots \cdots \cdots \cdots \cdots \cdots \cdots \cdots \cdots \cdots \cdots$$
$$y_m = g_m(q_1, q_2, \ldots, q_k, x_1, \ldots, x_n, t)$$

(2.2)

In vector notation, (2.1) and (2.2) may be written

$$\frac{d\mathbf{q}(t)}{dt} = \mathbf{f}(\mathbf{q}, \mathbf{x}, t)$$

(2.3)

and

$$\mathbf{y} = \mathbf{g}(\mathbf{q}, \mathbf{x}, t)$$

(2.4)

where $\mathbf{x}$ = input vector
$\mathbf{y}$ = output vector
$\mathbf{q}$ = state vector
$\mathbf{f}, \mathbf{g}$ = vector-valued functions

There are several reasons for the importance of this *normal form* of the system equations. An obvious advantage of writing the differential equations of a system in this form is its notational simplicity: a system of order k has the appearance of a first-order system. Thus, instead of having to write out a system of simultaneous differential equations for a specific system, one can deal with all systems by means of a compact notation. Another reason for the importance of this representation is that most of the modern literature in the theory of differential equations makes use of this representation, and one must be familiar with it in order to employ this theory. We shall find the normal form very useful in setting up diagrams for analog-computer simulation.

While the inputs and outputs of a system are generally the tangible physical quantities of interest in a problem, it is the state variables which assume the dominant role in this formulation. It might appear that we have introduced quantities which are not of interest and have thereby complicated the problem. The contrary turns out to be true, however, in most cases. We shall first give several concrete examples of this formulation and later attempt to give a physical interpretation of the state variables.

In electric networks it is natural to identify the state variables with the inductor currents and the capacitor voltages. The differential equations

can be very simply derived by a method which is illustrated in the following example.

Example 2.1   Consider the network shown in Fig. 2.1.   An arrow indicates a voltage drop in the direction of the arrow.†   By inspection, the equations for this network are

$$v_1 = L\frac{di_1}{dt} = e_1 - e_2 - v_2$$

$$i_2 = C\frac{dv_2}{dt} = i_1 - \frac{1}{R}(v_2 + e_2)$$

or after rearrangement,

$$\frac{di_1}{dt} = -\frac{1}{L}v_2 + \frac{1}{L}e_1 - \frac{1}{L}e_2$$

$$\frac{dv_2}{dt} = \frac{1}{C}i_1 - \frac{1}{RC}v_2 - \frac{1}{RC}e_2$$ (2.5)

In matrix form these equations may be written

$$\begin{bmatrix} \dfrac{di_1}{dt} \\ \dfrac{dv_2}{dt} \end{bmatrix} = \begin{bmatrix} 0 & -\dfrac{1}{L} \\ \dfrac{1}{C} & -\dfrac{1}{RC} \end{bmatrix} \begin{bmatrix} i_1 \\ v_2 \end{bmatrix} + \begin{bmatrix} \dfrac{1}{L} & -\dfrac{1}{L} \\ 0 & -\dfrac{1}{RC} \end{bmatrix} \begin{bmatrix} e_1 \\ e_2 \end{bmatrix}$$ (2.6)

Any other variables may now be expressed in terms of i_1 and v_2 and the sources.   If we are interested in i_1 and i_2 (these then become the "outputs"),

$$i_1 = i_1$$

$$i_2 = i_1 - \frac{1}{R}v_2 - \frac{1}{R}e_2$$ (2.7)

which express the outputs in terms of the state variables and the inputs.

† B. Friedland, O. Wing, and R. Ash, "Principles of Linear Networks," McGraw-Hill Book Company, New York, 1961.   This convention is used throughout this book for denoting polarities of voltages.

FIG. 2.1   Two-loop network for Example 2.1.

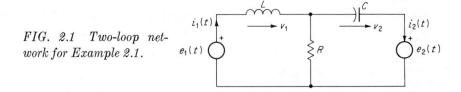

In matrix form, (2.7) may be written

$$
\begin{bmatrix} i_1 \\ i_2 \end{bmatrix} = \begin{bmatrix} 1 & 0 \\ 1 & -\dfrac{1}{R} \end{bmatrix} \begin{bmatrix} i_1 \\ v_2 \end{bmatrix} + \begin{bmatrix} 0 & 0 \\ 0 & -\dfrac{1}{R} \end{bmatrix} \begin{bmatrix} e_1 \\ e_2 \end{bmatrix}
\tag{2.8}
$$

Let us now consider a more general network having l inductors and c capacitors.† It is always possible to express the network equations in the following normal form:

$$
v_j = L_j \frac{di_j}{dt} = \sum_{k=1}^{l} R_{jk}i_k + \sum_{k=l+1}^{l+c} M_{jk}v_k + \sum_{k=1}^{n} P_{jk}x_k \qquad j = 1, 2, \ldots, l
\tag{2.9}
$$

$$
i_j = C_j \frac{dv_j}{dt} = \sum_{k=1}^{l} N_{jk}i_k + \sum_{k=l+1}^{l+c} G_{jk}v_k + \sum_{k=1}^{n} Q_{jk}x_k
$$
$$
j = l + 1, \ldots, l + c
$$

where v_j ($j = 1, 2, \ldots, l$) is the voltage across the jth inductor, i_j ($j = l + 1, \ldots, l + c$) is the current in the jth capacitor, and x_k is the kth source (current or voltage). The coefficients R_{jk} and G_{jk} have the dimensions of resistance and conductance, respectively, and the coefficients M_{jk} and N_{jk} are dimensionless.

It is evident that these coefficients can be defined as follows:

R_{jk} = ratio of v_j to i_k with all other voltages and currents (including sources) set equal to zero

M_{jk} = ratio of v_j to v_k with all other voltages and currents set equal to zero

N_{jk} = ratio of i_j to i_k with all other voltages and currents set equal to zero

G_{jk} = ratio of i_j to v_k with all other voltages and currents set equal to zero

In a similar manner the coefficients P_{jk} and Q_{jk} can be defined in terms of the ratios of the voltages across the inductors or currents in the capacitors to the source voltages or currents. Each of these coefficients can be calculated by solving a simple problem in a *purely resistive* network.

By dividing each equation in the first set of (2.9) by the corresponding L_j and each equation of the second set by the corresponding C_j and arrang-

† For a more detailed description of this subject, see T. R. Bashkow, The A Matrix: A New Network Description, *IRE Trans. Circuit Theory*, vol. CT-4, pp. 117–120, September, 1957, and P. R. Bryant, The Explicit Form of Bashkow's A Matrix, *IRE Trans. Circuit Theory*, vol. CT-9, pp. 303–306, September, 1962.

ing in the form of partitioned matrices, we obtain

$$
\begin{bmatrix} \dfrac{di_1}{dt} \\[2mm] \cdot \\ \cdot \\ \cdot \\ \dfrac{di_l}{dt} \\[1mm] \hdashline \\ \dfrac{dv_{l+1}}{dt} \\[1mm] \cdot \\ \cdot \\ \cdot \\ \dfrac{dv_{l+c}}{dt} \end{bmatrix}
=
\begin{bmatrix} \left[\dfrac{R_{jk}}{L_j}\right] & \left[\dfrac{M_{jk}}{L_j}\right] \\[3mm] \hdashline \\ \left[\dfrac{N_{jk}}{C_j}\right] & \left[\dfrac{G_{jk}}{C_j}\right] \end{bmatrix}
\begin{bmatrix} i_1 \\ \cdot \\ \cdot \\ \cdot \\ i_l \\ \hdashline \\ v_{l+1} \\ \cdot \\ \cdot \\ \cdot \\ v_{l+c} \end{bmatrix}
+
\begin{bmatrix} \left[\dfrac{P_{jk}}{L_j}\right] \\[3mm] \hdashline \\ \left[\dfrac{Q_{jk}}{C_j}\right] \end{bmatrix}
\begin{bmatrix} x_1 \\ \cdot \\ \cdot \\ \cdot \\ x_n \end{bmatrix}
\qquad (2.10)
$$

where

$\left[\dfrac{R_{jk}}{L_j}\right]$ is an $l \times l$ matrix $\qquad$ $\left[\dfrac{M_{jk}}{L_j}\right]$ is an $l \times c$ matrix

$\left[\dfrac{N_{jk}}{C_j}\right]$ is a $c \times l$ matrix $\qquad$ $\left[\dfrac{G_{jk}}{C_j}\right]$ is a $c \times c$ matrix

$\left[\dfrac{P_{jk}}{L_j}\right]$ is an $l \times n$ matrix $\qquad$ $\left[\dfrac{Q_{jk}}{C_j}\right]$ is a $c \times n$ matrix

If we define

$$
q_j = \begin{cases} i_j & j = 1, 2, \dots, l \\ v_j & j = l+1, \dots, l+c \end{cases}
$$

and

$$
\mathbf{q} = \begin{bmatrix} q_1 \\ \cdot \\ \cdot \\ \cdot \\ q_{l+c} \end{bmatrix}
$$

then (2.10) takes the normal form, which in vector notation is

$$
\frac{d\mathbf{q}}{dt} = \mathbf{A}\mathbf{q} + \mathbf{B}\mathbf{x}
$$

as required.   Note that in this case the vector function $\mathbf{f}(\mathbf{q}, \mathbf{x}, t)$ appearing in the general equation (2.3) is now linear in $\mathbf{q}$ and $\mathbf{x}$ and is independent of time.   If the inductors or capacitors were time-varying, however, (2.9) would not properly describe the behavior of the circuit, since the voltages across the inductors and the currents in the capacitors

would have to be expressed by the more general relations

$$v_j = \frac{d(L_j i_j)}{dt} = \frac{L_j di_j}{dt} + \frac{i_j dL_j}{dt}$$

$$i_j = \frac{d(C_j v_j)}{dt} = \frac{C_j dv_j}{dt} + \frac{v_j dC_j}{dt}$$

Likewise, if one of the capacitors or inductors were nonlinear, (2.9) would no longer represent the true behavior of the network. In these cases it might be preferable to use the inductor fluxes and the capacitor charges as state variables instead of the inductor voltages and capacitor currents, respectively, since it is always true that the voltage across an inductor is the derivative of the flux, and the current in a capacitor is the derivative of the charge.

It should be noted that the total stored energy in a network described by (2.9) may be expressed directly in terms of the state variables. The energy is given by

$$E = \frac{1}{2} \sum_{j=1}^{l} L_j i_j^2 + \frac{1}{2} \sum_{j=l+1}^{l+c} C_j v_j^2$$

$$= \frac{1}{2} \mathbf{q}' \mathbf{T} \mathbf{q} \tag{2.11}$$

where $\mathbf{q}$ is the state vector previously defined, a prime ($'$) denotes transposition, and $\mathbf{T}$ is a diagonal matrix with elements

$$t_{jj} = \begin{cases} L_j & j = 1, 2, \ldots, l \\ C_j & j = l + 1, \ldots, l + c \end{cases}$$

Thus the total energy for a linear network is a quadratic form in the state variables.

The relationship between the total energy and the state of a system can be exploited to obtain the equations of motion of a rigid body in classical dynamics. For this purpose the *generalized coordinates* q_i and the corresponding *conjugate momenta* p_i constitute a suitable set of state variables. The total energy of the system, if it is conservative, can be expressed in terms of these quantities, and the expression thereby obtained is called the Hamiltonian $H(q_1, \ldots, q_k, p_1, \ldots, p_k)$, where k is the number of *degrees of freedom* of the system. The equations of motion are directly obtained from the Hamiltonian and can be written†

$$\frac{dq_i}{dt} = \frac{\partial H}{\partial p_i}$$

$$\frac{dp_i}{dt} = -\frac{\partial H}{\partial q_i} \tag{2.12}$$

† See, for example, P. M. Morse and H. Feshbach, "Methods of Theoretical Physics," vol. 1, sec. 3.2, McGraw-Hill Book Company, New York, 1953.

Thus, if the state variables are taken as the coordinates and conjugate momenta, the Hamiltonian equations (2.12) are a system of $2k$ first-order equations in normal form.

Example 2.2 Consider the motion of a particle of constant mass m in a plane, under the action of a central force which varies inversely as the square of the distance from an attractive center. The generalized position coordinates are $r = q_1$ and $\theta = q_2$ in the polar coordinate system of Fig. 2.2. The corresponding conjugate momenta are the linear and angular momenta $p_1 = m\dot{r}$ and $p_2 = mr^2\dot{\theta}$, respectively. The kinetic energy of the particle in terms of the Hamiltonian variables is given by

$$T = \tfrac{1}{2}m\dot{r}^2 + \tfrac{1}{2}m(r\dot{\theta})^2$$
$$= \frac{1}{2m}\left(p_1^2 + \frac{p_2^2}{q_1^2}\right)$$

and the potential energy is given by $V = -K/q_1$. Thus the total energy is expressed by

$$H = \frac{1}{2m}\left(p_1^2 + \frac{p_2^2}{q_1^2}\right) - \frac{K}{q_1}$$

and the equations of motion are†

$$\dot{q}_1 = \frac{\partial H}{\partial p_1} = \frac{p_1}{m}$$
$$\dot{q}_2 = \frac{\partial H}{\partial p_2} = \frac{p_2}{mq_1^2}$$
$$\dot{p}_1 = -\frac{\partial H}{\partial q_1} = \frac{p_2^2}{mq_1^3} - \frac{K}{q_1^2} \tag{2.13}$$
$$\dot{p}_2 = -\frac{\partial H}{\partial q_2} = 0$$

Our objective in introducing this example is to show that the normal form (2.3) arises quite naturally in classical mechanics, although the equations generally turn out to be nonlinear. We shall have occasion to return to this example later in the chapter (Example 2.9).

Although in many problems there is a natural choice of state variables,

† See, for example, H. Lamb, "Higher Mechanics," 2d ed., sec. 82, Cambridge University Press, London, 1929.

FIG. 2.2 Motion of particle under action of central force.

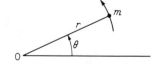

situations arise where one must select a set of state variables in some arbitrary fashion. A situation of this sort arises when the differential equation governing the behavior of the system is given in the form of a single differential equation involving the output of the system and its first k time derivatives; namely,

$$\phi(y, \dot{y}, \, \ldots \, , y^{(k)}) = x(t) \tag{2.14}$$

where $y^{(p)}$ denotes the pth time derivative of y. When it is possible to solve (2.14) for the highest derivative of y and thus to obtain

$$y^{(k)} = f(y, \dot{y}, \, \ldots \, , y^{(k-1)}) + x(t) \tag{2.15}$$

a natural, but quite arbitrary, choice of state variables would be the following:

$$q_1 = y$$
$$q_2 = \dot{y}$$
$$\cdots\cdots$$
$$q_k = y^{(k-1)}$$

From the foregoing definitions it follows that the differential equations take the form

$$\dot{q}_1 = q_2$$
$$\dot{q}_2 = q_3$$
$$\cdots\cdots$$
$$\dot{q}_{k-1} = q_k$$
$$\dot{q}_k = f(q_1, q_2, \, \ldots \, , q_k) + x(t)$$

the last line being obtained from (2.15). These equations are in the required normal form. A more complicated situation arises when the differential equations also involve derivatives of the inputs. This is illustrated for linear equations in the following section.

2.3 LINEAR DIFFERENTIAL EQUATIONS

The differential and output equations in the form of (2.3) and (2.4) are said to be *linear* if the functions $\mathbf{f}$ and $\mathbf{g}$ appearing in these equations are linear in $\mathbf{q}$ and $\mathbf{x}$, that is, if

$$\mathbf{f}(\mathbf{q}, \mathbf{x}, t) = \mathbf{A}(t)\mathbf{q} + \mathbf{B}(t)\mathbf{x}$$
$$\mathbf{g}(\mathbf{q}, \mathbf{x}, t) = \mathbf{C}(t)\mathbf{q} + \mathbf{D}(t)\mathbf{x}$$

The system equations become

$$\frac{d\mathbf{q}}{dt} = \mathbf{A}(t)\mathbf{q} + \mathbf{B}(t)\mathbf{x} \tag{2.16}$$

$$\mathbf{y} = \mathbf{C}(t)\mathbf{q} + \mathbf{D}(t)\mathbf{x} \tag{2.17}$$

where $\mathbf{A}(t)$ is a $k \times k$ matrix, $\mathbf{B}(t)$ is a $k \times n$ matrix, $\mathbf{C}(t)$ is an $m \times k$ matrix, and $\mathbf{D}(t)$ is an $m \times n$ matrix. When these matrices are independent of time, the system is said to be *fixed*, or *time-invariant*. In accordance with this definition, we note that the electric network of Example 2.1 and, more generally, all networks consisting of ideal resistors, capacitors, and inductors are linear. It is also easy to show that a system governed by any set of differential equations in which only linear combinations of the input(s) and output(s) and their derivatives are involved is a linear system. Let us first consider the reduction to normal form of linear differential equations involving derivatives of the inputs. The following example illustrates the problem and a possible solution; a more general procedure is outlined below.

Example 2.3 Consider the equation

$$(D^k + \alpha_1 D^{k-1} + \cdots + \alpha_{k-1}D + \alpha_k)y(t) = (\beta_1 D + \beta_2)x(t) \tag{2.18}$$

If we made the same choice of state variables as for (2.15), i.e.,

$$q_1 = y \qquad q_2 = Dy \qquad \cdots \qquad q_k = D^{k-1}y$$

we would obtain the dynamic equations

$$\dot{q}_1 = q_2 \qquad \dot{q}_2 = q_3 \qquad \cdots \qquad \dot{q}_{k-1} = q_k$$

but the remaining equation, in order to satisfy the differential equation (2.18), would be

$$\dot{q}_k = -\alpha_1 q_k - \alpha_2 q_{k-1} - \cdots - \alpha_k q_1 + \beta_1\, Dx + \beta_2 x$$

which is not in normal form because of the presence of the Dx term.
If we modify our choice of q_k so that

$$q_k = D^{k-1}y - bx$$

where b is a constant to be determined, and leave the other state variables unchanged, the dynamic equations become

$$\dot{q}_1 = q_2 \qquad \dot{q}_2 = q_3 \qquad \cdots \qquad \dot{q}_{k-2} = q_{k-1}$$
$$(D^{k-1}y =)\dot{q}_{k-1} = q_k + bx$$

The last equation must satisfy the original differential equation (2.16), so that

$$\dot{q}_k = \ddot{q}_{k-1} - b\,Dx = D^k y - b\,Dx$$
$$= -\alpha_1(q_k + bx) - \alpha_2 q_{k-1} - \cdots - \alpha_k q_1 + \beta_1\,Dx + \beta_2 x - b\,Dx$$

The terms involving Dx disappear if we choose $b = \beta_1$.   Then

$$\dot{q}_k = \sum_{j=1}^{k} -\alpha_{k+1-j} q_j + (\beta_2 - \alpha_1 \beta_1)x$$

which is in normal form.

GENERAL PROCEDURE FOR DETERMINING NORMAL FORM OF LINEAR DIFFERENTIAL EQUATIONS

When a good choice of state variables is not evident, a general, although cumbersome, procedure may always be used to obtain the dynamic equations in normal form.   This procedure may be used for a set of simultaneous differential equations.   The highest possible order of a system described by a set of simultaneous differential equations is the sum of the orders l_i of the highest derivatives of each of the m unknowns y_i appearing in the equations.   The number k of state variables is chosen equal to this number;[†] that is, $k = \sum_{i=1}^{m} l_i$.   Then we assume the most general form (2.17) for each output variable y_i ($i = 1, 2, \ldots, m$) and (2.16) for each state variable derivative $\dot{q}_j$ ($j = 1, 2, \ldots, k$); that is,

$$y_i = \sum_{j=1}^{k} c_{ij} q_j + \sum_{j=1}^{n} d_{ij} x_j \qquad i = 1, 2, \ldots, m$$
$$\dot{q}_j = \sum_{r=1}^{k} a_{jr} q_r + \sum_{r=1}^{n} b_{jr} x_r \qquad j = 1, 2, \ldots, k$$

The expression for each y_i is substituted in the differential equations.   A derivative dy_i/dt, for example, becomes

$$\frac{dy_i}{dt} = \sum_{j=1}^{k} c_{ij} \dot{q}_j + \sum_{j=1}^{n} d_{ij} \dot{x}_j$$
$$= \sum_{j=1}^{k} \sum_{r=1}^{k} c_{ij} a_{jr} q_r + \sum_{j=1}^{k} \sum_{r=1}^{k} c_{ij} b_{jr} x_r + \sum_{j=1}^{n} d_{ij} \dot{x}_j$$

and similarly for higher derivatives.   Thus each differential equation is

† This may result in one or more redundant state variables which are not independent of the other state variables.

expressed in terms of the state variables q_j and the inputs x_j and their derivatives. By equating coefficients of each q_j and each derivative of each input x_j, a number of simultaneous equations for the unknown constants a_{ij}, b_{ij}, c_{ij}, d_{ij} are obtained. The number N of these equations will usually be smaller than the number M of unknown constants, so that $M - N$ of the constants may be chosen arbitrarily.† The remaining N constants are then obtained by solving the N equations. The number of constants which may be chosen arbitrarily may frequently be determined by inspection of the original equations, so that the problem may often be simplified considerably. This is illustrated in the following example.

Example 2.4 If the first k derivatives of $x(t)$ appear in the kth-order differential equation for $y(t)$, we have

$$(D^k + \alpha_1 D^{k-1} + \cdots + \alpha_k)y(t)$$
$$= (\beta_0 D^k + \beta_1 D^{k-1} + \cdots + \beta_k)x(t) \quad (2.19)$$

The most general expressions for y and the dynamic equations are

$$y = \sum_{j=1}^{k} c_j q_j + dx \quad (2.20)$$

$$\dot{q}_j = \sum_{r=1}^{k} a_{jr}q_r + b_j x \qquad j = 1, 2, \ldots, k \quad (2.21)$$

The numbers of unknown constants are k^2, k, k, 1, corresponding to the a_{jr}, b_j, c_j, and d constants, respectively—a total of $k^2 + 2k + 1$. By substituting in (2.19) for y and for the derivatives $\dot{q}_j$, we obtain an equation of the form

$$K_1 q_1 + K_2 q_2 + \cdots + K_k q_k + K_{k+1}x + K_{k+2} Dx + \cdots$$
$$+ K_{2k+1}D^k x = 0$$

where $K_1, \ldots, K_{2k+1}$ are functions of the unknown constants. Thus there are $2k + 1$ equations for the $k^2 + 2k + 1$ constants, obtained by setting

$$K_i = 0 \qquad i = 1, 2, \ldots, 2k + 1$$

Hence we may choose k^2 of the unknown constants arbitrarily. In order to keep y as simple a function of the q's as possible, we may in (2.20) set

$$c_1 = 1$$
$$c_2 = c_3 = \cdots = c_k = 0$$

† The choice is not completely arbitrary since N independent equations for the other N constants must remain. Thus we may not choose all $c_{1j} = 0$, which would make y_1 a function of the inputs only.

This leaves $k^2 - k$ constants which may be chosen. In (2.21), let

$$a_{jr} = \begin{cases} 0 & \text{for } r = 1, 2, \ldots k,\ r \neq j + 1 \\ 1 & \text{for } r = j + 1 \end{cases} \Bigg\} \ j = 1, 2, \ldots, k - 1$$

With these choices, (2.20) and (2.21) reduce to

$$y = q_1 + dx$$
$$\dot{q}_1 = q_2 + b_1 x$$
$$\dot{q}_2 = q_3 + b_2 x$$
$$\cdots\cdots\cdots\cdots$$
$$\dot{q}_{k-1} = q_k + b_{k-1}x$$
$$\dot{q}_k = a_{k1}q_1 + a_{k2}q_2 + \cdots + a_{kk}q_k + b_k x$$

Using these equations we find for the terms occurring in (2.19)

$$Dy = \dot{q}_1 + d\,Dx = q_2 + b_1 x + d\,Dx$$
$$D^2 y = \dot{q}_2 + b_1\,Dx + dD^2 x = q_3 + b_2 x + b_1\,Dx + dD^2 x$$
$$\cdots\cdots\cdots\cdots\cdots\cdots\cdots\cdots\cdots\cdots$$
$$D^{k-1}y = \dot{q}_{k-1} + b_{k-2}\,Dx + \cdots + dD^{k-1}x = q_k + b_{k-1}x + b_{k-2}\,Dx +$$
$$\cdots + dD^{k-1}x$$
$$D^k y = a_{k1}q_1 + a_{k2}q_2 + \cdots + a_{kk}q_k + b_k x + b_{k-1}Dx + \cdots + dD^k x$$

We now substitute these expressions in (2.19) by multiplying y by α_k, Dy by $\alpha_{k-1}, \ldots, D^k y$ by 1, and adding. This process results in

$$(\alpha_k + \alpha_{k-1}D + \cdots + D^k)y = (\alpha_k + a_{k1})q_1$$
$$+ (\alpha_{k-1} + a_{k2})q_2 + \cdots + (\alpha_1 + a_{kk})q_k$$
$$+ (\alpha_k d + \alpha_{k-1}b_1 + \cdots + \alpha_1 b_{k-1} + b_k)x$$
$$+ (\alpha_{k-1}d + \alpha_{k-2}b_1 + \cdots + \alpha_1 b_{k-2} + b_{k-1})\,Dx$$
$$+ \cdots + (\alpha_1 d + b_1)D^{k-1}x + dD^k x$$

and this must equal $(\beta_0 D^k + \beta_1 D^{k-1} + \cdots + \beta_k)x$. Equating coefficients of q_j in the two expressions, we find

$$a_{kr} = -\alpha_{k-r+1} \qquad r = 1, 2, \ldots, k$$

Equating coefficients of x and its derivatives, we find

$$
\begin{aligned}
d &= \beta_0 \\
\alpha_1 d + b_1 &= \beta_1 \\
\alpha_2 d + \alpha_1 b_1 + b_2 &= \beta_2 \\
\cdots\cdots\cdots\cdots\cdots\cdots\cdots\cdots\cdots \\
\alpha_{k-1}d + \alpha_{k-2}b_1 + \alpha_{k-3}b_2 + \cdots + b_{k-1} &= \beta_{k-1} \\
\alpha_k d + \alpha_{k-1}b_1 + \alpha_{k-2}b_2 + \cdots + \alpha_1 b_{k-1} + b_k &= \beta_k
\end{aligned}
\tag{2.22}
$$

These equations can be solved successively to yield $d, b_1, \ldots, b_k$. As a mnemonic it is convenient to represent (2.22) in matrix form:

$$\begin{bmatrix} 1 & 0 & 0 & \cdots & 0 \\ \alpha_1 & 1 & 0 & \cdots & 0 \\ \alpha_2 & \alpha_1 & 1 & \cdots & 0 \\ \cdot & \cdot & \cdot & \cdots & \cdot \\ \alpha_k & \alpha_{k-1} & \alpha_{k-2} & \cdots & 1 \end{bmatrix} \begin{bmatrix} d \\ b_1 \\ b_2 \\ \cdot \\ b_k \end{bmatrix} = \begin{bmatrix} \beta_0 \\ \beta_1 \\ \beta_2 \\ \cdot \\ \beta_k \end{bmatrix}$$

The matrices of the normal form (2.16) and (2.17) are thus

$$\mathbf{A} = \begin{bmatrix} 0 & 1 & 0 & \cdots & 0 \\ 0 & 0 & 1 & \cdots & 0 \\ \cdot & \cdot & \cdot & \cdots & \cdot \\ 0 & 0 & 0 & \cdots & 1 \\ -\alpha_k & -\alpha_{k-1} & -\alpha_{k-2} & \cdots & -\alpha_1 \end{bmatrix} \qquad \mathbf{B} = \begin{bmatrix} b_1 \\ b_2 \\ \cdot \\ b_{k-1} \\ b_k \end{bmatrix}$$

$$\mathbf{C} = \begin{bmatrix} 1 & 0 & 0 & \cdots & 0 \end{bmatrix} \qquad \mathbf{D} = [d]$$

The choice of state variables in the preceding two examples has been motivated by a desire to facilitate the simulation of the differential equation on an analog computer, but is otherwise quite arbitrary.

The state variables may be changed even after the equations have been put into normal form. Suppose, for example, that we have a system of equations in normal form

$$\dot{\mathbf{q}} = \mathbf{A}\mathbf{q} + \mathbf{B}\mathbf{x}$$
$$\mathbf{y} = \mathbf{C}\mathbf{q} + \mathbf{D}\mathbf{x}$$

and we wish to use a different set of state variables $\xi_1, \xi_2, \ldots, \xi_k$, each of which is a linear combination of the original ones; that is,

$$\xi_i = \sum_{j=1}^{k} m_{ij} q_j \qquad i = 1, 2, \ldots, k$$

or, in vector-matrix notation,

$$\boldsymbol{\xi} = \mathbf{M}\mathbf{q} \tag{2.23}$$

where $\mathbf{M}$ is a $k \times k$ matrix whose elements are m_{ij}.

It is assumed that the components of the new state vector are linearly independent. Hence $\mathbf{M}$ is nonsingular, and its inverse $\mathbf{M}^{-1}$ exists. Thus

$$\mathbf{q} = \mathbf{M}^{-1}\boldsymbol{\xi} \qquad \dot{\mathbf{q}} = \mathbf{M}^{-1}\dot{\boldsymbol{\xi}}$$

Substitution of these relations into the normal form gives

$$\mathbf{M}^{-1}\dot{\xi}(t) = \mathbf{A}\mathbf{M}^{-1}\xi + \mathbf{B}\mathbf{x}(t)$$
$$\mathbf{y}(t) = \mathbf{C}\mathbf{M}^{-1}\xi + \mathbf{D}\mathbf{x}(t)$$

Premultiplying both sides of the first equation by $\mathbf{M}$, we obtain

$$\dot{\xi}(t) = \mathbf{M}\mathbf{A}\mathbf{M}^{-1}\xi + \mathbf{M}\mathbf{B}\mathbf{x}(t)$$

Thus the normal form in terms of the new state variables is

$$\dot{\xi} = \overline{\mathbf{A}}\xi + \overline{\mathbf{B}}\mathbf{x}$$
$$\mathbf{y} = \overline{\mathbf{C}}\xi + \overline{\mathbf{D}}\mathbf{x} \tag{2.24}$$

where the new matrices are given by

$$\overline{\mathbf{A}} = \mathbf{M}\mathbf{A}\mathbf{M}^{-1} \qquad \overline{\mathbf{B}} = \mathbf{M}\mathbf{B} \qquad \overline{\mathbf{C}} = \mathbf{C}\mathbf{M}^{-1} \qquad \overline{\mathbf{D}} = \mathbf{D} \tag{2.25}$$

We now wish to show that a system governed by (2.16) and (2.17) is linear according to the definition of Chap. 1, i.e., that it satisfies the superposition principle. To facilitate the discussion we make the assumption that the solution to (2.16) and (2.17) exists and is unique.† (This assumption is implicit in the assertion that these equations govern the behavior of a deterministic system—a given input producing a unique output—and if this assumption is not valid, the implication is that the equations do not represent any deterministic system; either an error has been made or an invalid approximation has been used.)

Let us take two arbitrary inputs $\mathbf{x}_1(t)$ and $\mathbf{x}_2(t)$, to which correspond two state vectors $\mathbf{q}_1(t)$ and $\mathbf{q}_2(t)$ and two outputs $\mathbf{y}_1(t)$ and $\mathbf{y}_2(t)$, respectively. We must show that if the input is $\mathbf{x}(t) = \alpha\mathbf{x}_1(t) + \beta\mathbf{x}_2(t)$, where α, β are constants, then the corresponding output is $\mathbf{y}(t) = \alpha\mathbf{y}_1(t) + \beta\mathbf{y}_2(t)$, and vice versa. By hypothesis $\mathbf{q}_1$ satisfies (2.16) for $\mathbf{x} = \mathbf{x}_1$ and $\mathbf{q}_2$ satisfies (2.16) for $\mathbf{x} = \mathbf{x}_2$. Thus

$$\frac{d\mathbf{q}_1}{dt} = \mathbf{A}(t)\mathbf{q}_1 + \mathbf{B}(t)\mathbf{x}_1 \tag{2.26}$$

$$\frac{d\mathbf{q}_2}{dt} = \mathbf{A}(t)\mathbf{q}_2 + \mathbf{B}(t)\mathbf{x}_2 \tag{2.27}$$

Multiplication of (2.26) and (2.27) by α and β, respectively, and addition gives

$$\alpha\frac{d\mathbf{q}_1}{dt} + \beta\frac{d\mathbf{q}_2}{dt} = \frac{d}{dt}[\alpha\mathbf{q}_1 + \beta\mathbf{q}_2] = \mathbf{A}[\alpha\mathbf{q}_1 + \beta\mathbf{q}_2] + \mathbf{B}[\alpha\mathbf{x}_1 + \beta\mathbf{x}_2]$$

† For the conditions under which a system of differential equations possesses a unique solution, see E. A. Coddington and N. Levinson, "Theory of Ordinary Differential Equations," chaps. 1 and 2, McGraw-Hill Book Company, New York, 1955. We shall not be concerned with these conditions in this book since the differential equations which will be our principal concern are known to possess unique solutions.

Hence the state $\mathbf{q} = \alpha\mathbf{q}_1 + \beta\mathbf{q}_2$ satisfies (2.16) for the input $\mathbf{x} = \alpha\mathbf{x}_1 + \beta\mathbf{x}_2$, and the output is

$$\mathbf{y} = \mathbf{C}(\alpha\mathbf{q}_1 + \beta\mathbf{q}_2) + \mathbf{D}(\alpha\mathbf{x}_1 + \beta\mathbf{x}_2)$$

which is evidently the sum of the outputs obtained for each of the individual inputs. This completes the proof.

The principal concern of this book is with systems whose behavior is governed by a system of differential equations of the form (2.16) and (2.17), and more particularly with systems in which the matrices $\mathbf{A}$, $\mathbf{B}$, $\mathbf{C}$, and $\mathbf{D}$ appearing in these equations are independent of time.

2.4 ANALOG SIMULATION

The electronic analog computer is an important tool for the investigation of linear and nonlinear lumped systems; it solves systems of ordinary differential equations. In an analog computer each dependent variable is represented by a voltage which varies with time and whose value at any instant is proportional to that dependent variable, i.e., an unknown in the differential equation. Only one independent variable, time, can be handled.

The objective of simulation by means of an analog computer is to connect a number of basic components in such a manner that the voltages at different points obey a set of differential equations which have the same form as the differential equations governing the physical process under study. Since the time variation of the voltages corresponds to that of quite different physical variables which they represent, the equations and variables of the computer are said to be analogous to those of the physical process which is simulated.

The components of an analog computer are:

1. Summing amplifiers, or summers
2. Integrating amplifiers, or integrators
3. Amplifiers and attenuators
4. Instantaneous nonlinear elements

A summer has several input terminals and one output terminal; the voltage at the output is the sum of the voltages applied to the several input terminals. In an integrator, the output voltage y is the sum of an initial voltage $y(0)$ (which can be adjusted) and the integral of the input voltage x:

$$y(t) = y(0) + \int_0^t x(\lambda)\, d\lambda$$

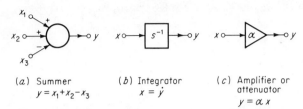

(a) Summer   (b) Integrator   (c) Amplifier or
$y = x_1 + x_2 - x_3$ $x = \dot{y}$ attenuator
                                        $y = \alpha x$

FIG. 2.3   Analog-computer components.

The input voltage is thus the derivative of the output voltage:

$$x(t) = \dot{y}(t)$$

Amplifiers and attenuators are used to multiply voltages by a constant factor.   Nonlinear elements include multipliers whose output is the product of two inputs, and function generators whose output is a specified function $f(x)$ of the input x.   The only dynamic component is the integrator; all the others are instantaneous.   All the devices are somewhat imperfect, but the errors can be kept small by observing certain precautions which are considered in detail in books dealing with the practice of analog computation.†   Although it would often be desirable to have differentiators, there are several practical reasons why differentiators are not generally employed.   The analog-computer components needed for the simulation of linear systems and their input-output relations are shown in Fig. 2.3.

One advantage of having the differential equations of a process in normal form is that this form leads directly to the analog-computer setup. Consider the general linear system

$$\frac{dq_i}{dt} = \sum_{j=1}^{k} a_{ij}q_j + \sum_{j=1}^{n} b_{ij}x_j \qquad i = 1, 2, \ldots, k \qquad (2.28)$$

$$y_i = \sum_{j=1}^{k} c_{ij}q_j + \sum_{j=1}^{n} d_{ij}x_j \qquad i = 1, 2, \ldots, m \qquad (2.29)$$

This system can be simulated by the use of exactly k integrators, where k is the number of components in the state vector.   We *define* the output of the integrator i as q_i.   Then the input to each integrator is the derivative of the output, namely, dq_i/dt.   It is seen from (2.28) that the input to

† See, for example, G. A. Korn and T. M. Korn, "Electronic Analog Computers," 2d ed., McGraw-Hill Book Company, New York, 1956, or A. E. Rogers and T. W. Connolly, "Analog Computation in Engineering Design," McGraw-Hill Book Company, New York, 1960.

each integrator is a sum, a linear combination of the outputs of all the integrators and all the inputs.   According to (2.29) the components y_i of the analog computer are linear combinations of the outputs from the integrators and the inputs.

As an example, Fig. 2.4 shows the interconnections for a second-order system.   In the block diagrams the integrators are represented by rectangles, the summers by circles with signs indicating the polarities of the summed signals, and the amplifiers or attenuators by triangles.   The general, kth-order system follows the same pattern but has k integrators. The operation of differentiation is represented by the symbol s.†   Hence the integrators are labeled with the operational symbol s^{-1}.   The signal-

† The basic reason for the use of the symbol s is that if an exponential e^{st} is applied to a differentiator, the output is se^{st}, or s times the input.   This will be discussed further in Chap. 5.

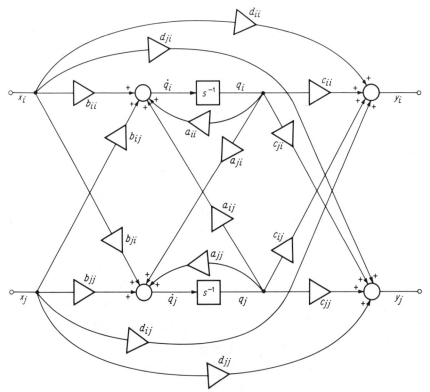

FIG. 2.4   Block diagram of analog-computer connections for simulation of second-order linear system.

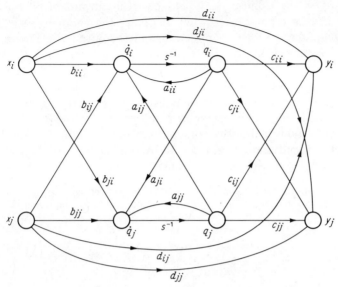

FIG. 2.5   *Signal-flow graph representation of second-order linear system.*

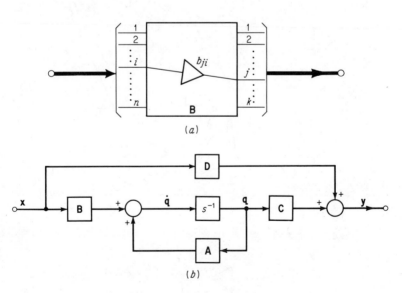

FIG. 2.6   *Analog-computer diagram for linear lumped system. (a) Structure of components in cable diagram; (b) cable diagram.*

flow graph corresponding to this analog-computer diagram is shown in Fig. 2.5.

Since the block diagram for a kth-order system has a large number of lines, it is convenient to represent the connections by a simplified diagram in which all the lines representing similar quantities are grouped into "cables." All amplifiers of the same type (say those with gains b_{ij}) are represented by a single block whose internal structure is shown in Fig. 2.6a. Using this convention, the system of equations in normal form has the structure shown in Fig. 2.6b. It is understood that the box labeled s^{-1} actually consists of k integrators. Note that in this representation a kth-order system has the structure of a first-order system.

Example 2.5   Two-loop network   Equations (2.5) for the two-loop network of Fig. 2.1 may be represented by an analog-computer diagram by letting i_1 and v_2 be the outputs of two integrators. The result is shown in Fig. 2.7.

It is not always necessary to write the differential equations of a system in normal form in order to obtain the analog-computer diagram. It is sometimes simpler to proceed directly from the differential equations in the given form to the analog-computer diagram. In fact, it is often easier to obtain the diagram than the normal form of the equations. When this is the case, the analog-computer diagram may be used to obtain the normal form of the equations by defining the auxiliary state variables q_i as the outputs of the integrators. This process is illustrated by the following examples.

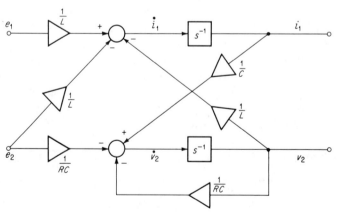

FIG. 2.7   Analog-computer diagram for network of Fig. 2.1.

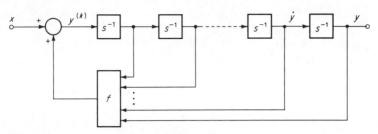

FIG. 2.8   Analog-computer diagram for nonlinear differential equation.

Example 2.6   The analog-computer setup for simulating the nonlinear differential equation (2.14) can be drawn directly if the equation is first solved for the highest derivative as was done in (2.15).   The simulation employs k integrators connected in tandem as shown in Fig. 2.8.   The output of the last integrator is the desired output y, and the outputs of the earlier integrators are its time derivatives, which have been defined as the state variables.   The box labeled f realizes the nonlinear function of (2.15) and has as its inputs the desired output and its derivatives.   It is thus seen that the output of this nonlinear element, when added to the input x, is the input which should be applied to the first integrator, and this is done in Fig. 2.8.

When the differential equation includes the derivatives of the inputs as well as the derivatives of the outputs, the technique of solving for the highest derivative of the output will not directly result in a simulation which does not require differentiators (as in Example 2.3).   One procedure which may be followed is to reduce the differential equation to normal form by the technique described in Example 2.4 and to simulate the resulting differential equations in accordance with the general methods described at the beginning of this section.   An alternative procedure consists of drawing the block diagram, including the differentiators as needed, and then using the signal-flow-graph simplification techniques discussed in Chap. 1 to eliminate the differentiators.   This procedure is illustrated in the following example.

Example 2.7   We consider the system

$$D^2y = -\alpha_1 Dy - \alpha_2 y + \beta_0 D^2x + \beta_1 Dx + \beta_2 x$$

This results in the diagram of Fig. 2.9a.   If the outputs of amplifiers β_0 and β_1 are moved as shown in Fig. 2.9b, in order to avoid successive differentiation and integration, the input to the second integrator remains

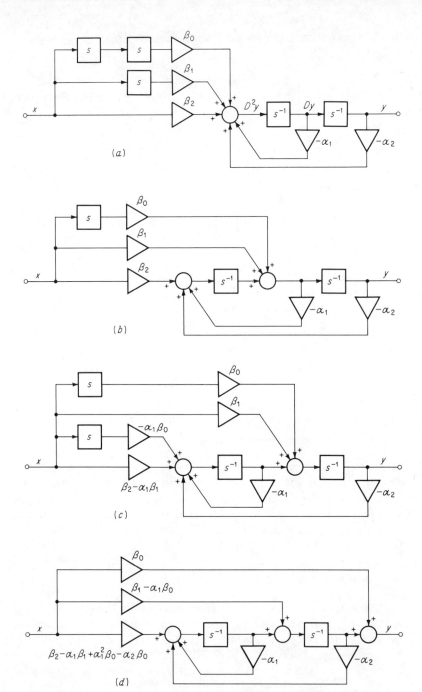

FIG. 2.9 Analog-computer diagram for $(D^2 + \alpha_1 D + \alpha_2)y = (\beta_0 D^2 + \beta_1 D + \beta_2)x$. (a) Block diagram for original equation; (b) first step in simplification; (c) second step in simplification; (d) final block diagram.

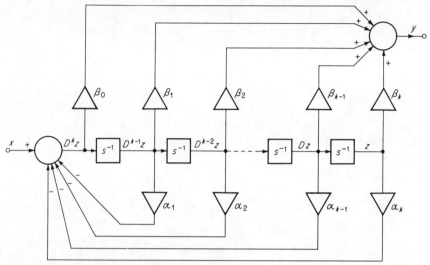

FIG. 2.10   Analog-computer diagram for:

$$(D^k + \alpha_1 D^{k-1} + \cdots + \alpha_{k-1}D + \alpha_k)y(t)$$
$$= (\beta_0 D^k + \beta_1 D^{k-1} + \cdots + \beta_k)x(t)$$

unchanged, but the output of the first integrator is no longer Dy but

$$Dy - \beta_1 x - \beta_0 \, Dx$$

If the output of the first integrator is again fed back after multiplication by $-\alpha_1$ to its input as in Fig. 2.9c, signals $-\alpha_1\beta_1 x$ and $-\alpha_1\beta_0 \, Dx$ must thus be added to the input of this integrator as shown.   The remaining two differentiators are then eliminated in a similar fashion, but signals $\alpha_1{}^2\beta_0 x$ and $-\alpha_2\beta_0 x$ must be added to the first integrator input as shown in Fig. 2.9d.   Note that this is the same diagram which would be obtained by writing the equations in normal form using the algebraic procedure described in Example 2.4.

It should be observed that we have made use of the operational relation $s^{-1}s = ss^{-1} = I$, and also the fact that an amplifier (or attenuator) with *constant* gain and an integrator or differentiator may be interchanged. The procedure described is generally applicable only to time-invariant linear systems, since the interchange of the order of time-varying or non-linear operations on a signal is not permissible.

A third procedure which may be used for (2.19) is to write it as the system of equations

$$(D^k + \alpha_1 D^{k-1} + \cdots + \alpha_k)z(t) = x(t)$$
$$(\beta_0 D^k + \beta_1 D^{k-1} + \cdots + \beta_k)z(t) = y(t)$$

$$(2.30)$$

The correctness of (2.30) may easily be verified by expressing both sides of (2.19) in terms of $z(t)$ and showing that the resulting expressions are identical. The system (2.30) may be most easily derived by using Laplace transforms (Prob. 7.10). The corresponding analog-computer diagram is shown in Fig. 2.10, from which the normal-form equations may easily be written.

2.5 STATE SPACE; EQUILIBRIUM STATES

In the preceding sections we made use of a set of auxiliary dynamic variables q_i, in terms of which the differential equations governing the behavior of the system were formulated. In some problems these variables can be identified with the energy-storing elements of the system, but it is not necessary and often not possible to do so. By the use of the state variables it is possible to represent the behavior of the system in a compact form with the aid of vector notation. The significance of the state variables, or collectively the *state vector*, is deeper than notational convenience. As we shall now show, the state vector at any instant of time summarizes the past history of the process.

Suppose the process is characterized by a system of differential equations

$$\frac{d\mathbf{q}}{dt} = \mathbf{f}[\mathbf{q}(t),\ \mathbf{x}(t),\ t] \quad \text{for all } t \tag{2.31}$$

At any time t_0 the process is in the state $\mathbf{q}(t_0)$ as a result of the application of an input $\mathbf{x}(t)$ during the time $t \leq t_0$. We may, however, regard the state $\mathbf{q}(t_0)$ as the initial state for the same differential equation, which can be solved without any knowledge of how the state $\mathbf{q}(t_0)$ was reached. This property motivates the following definition of the state of a dynamic process.

Definition 2.1 *A state vector $\mathbf{q}(t)$ is any vector whose specification at any time t_0, together with the input $\mathbf{x}(t)$ for $t_0 \leq t \leq t_1$, uniquely determines $\mathbf{q}(t_1)$ for any $t_1 \geq t_0$.*

It is evident that a knowledge of the voltages across the capacitors and the currents in the inductors in an electric network at any time, together with the inputs which are subsequently applied, permits the determination of the subsequent behavior of the network unambiguously; hence the choice of these quantities for the components of the state vector is justified. Similarly, it is clear that a knowledge of the position and momentum of a particle at any time, together with the subsequently

applied forces, is necessary and sufficient for the determination of the motion of the particle; these quantities thus serve to determine the state of the particle.

Geometrically, the state vector may be regarded as a point in k-dimensional space, where k is the number of components of the state vector. The state vector describes a curve in this space in moving from $\mathbf{q}(t_0)$ at time t_0 to a new state $\mathbf{q}(t_1)$. A consequence of the definition of the state is that the curve or trajectory followed by the state vector is unique for a *specified* input applied during the time interval $t_0 \leq t \leq t_1$.

The state vector has the effect of condensing the temporal history of a process for all time prior to t_0 into a set of numbers, the knowledge of which is equivalent to a knowledge of the entire past of the process in so far as its future behavior is concerned. The *minimum* number of quantities required to characterize the state is called the *order* of the system; it is independent of the particular quantities chosen as the components of the state vector.

A state in which the process remains indefinitely in the absence of an input is called an *equilibrium* state. If $\mathbf{q}$ is an equilibrium state, it thus follows that the time derivative of the state vector must be zero when no input is applied. Hence the equilibrium states of a general nonlinear system are given by the vectors $\mathbf{q}$ which satisfy the equation

$$\mathbf{f}(\mathbf{q}, \mathbf{0}, t) = \mathbf{0} \tag{2.32}$$

for all t. In general, (2.32) may have no solutions, one solution, or many solutions. For linear time-invariant systems, (2.32) reduces to

$$\mathbf{A}\mathbf{q} = \mathbf{0} \tag{2.33}$$

From this relation the following facts emerge:

1. The origin $\mathbf{q} = \mathbf{0}$ is an equilibrium state of every time-invariant linear system.
2. If $\mathbf{A}$ is nonsingular, the origin is the only equilibrium state.
3. If $\mathbf{A}$ is singular, the system has infinitely many equilibrium states, all satisfying (2.33).

Example 2.8 Consider the network shown in Fig. 2.11. The differential equations governing the network are

$$\frac{dv_1}{dt} = -\frac{1}{RC_1}(v_1 + v_2)$$
$$\frac{dv_2}{dt} = -\frac{1}{RC_2}(v_1 + v_2)$$

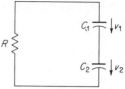

FIG. 2.11   Illustration of equilibrium.

It is evident that the corresponding matrix $\mathbf{A}$ is singular, and thus the origin ($v_1 = 0$, $v_2 = 0$) is not the only equilibrium state.   In fact it is clear, physically as well as from the differential equations, that if the capacitors are charged so that $v_1 + v_2 = 0$, the network will be in equilibrium; i.e., no current will flow.

2.6 LINEARIZATION

In many investigations of nonlinear systems, a solution for a given set of initial conditions and excitation has been determined (either analytically or with the aid of a digital computer) and it is required to determine the behavior of the system in the neighborhood of this solution. This is the case in the so-called small-signal analysis of electronic circuits in the neighborhood of a "quiescent" point—an equilibrium state. For small perturbations from such a solution, the analysis reduces to that of a linear system.

Consider a nonlinear system governed by the usual differential equations

$$\dot{\mathbf{q}} = \mathbf{f}(\mathbf{q}, \mathbf{x}, t)$$

and suppose that one has found a solution to these equations for some initial state $\mathbf{q}(t_0)$ and some input $\mathbf{x}(t)$.   This solution is denoted by $\mathbf{q}(t)$. Suppose now that the initial condition is changed to $\mathbf{q}(t_0) + \mathbf{n}(t_0)$ and the input is changed to $\mathbf{x}(t) + \boldsymbol{\xi}(t)$, where $\mathbf{n}$ and $\boldsymbol{\xi}$ are both small.   It is required to determine the change in the resulting state.   Since the resulting state satisfies the differential equations, we can write

$$\dot{\mathbf{q}} + \dot{\mathbf{n}} = \mathbf{f}(\mathbf{q} + \mathbf{n}, \mathbf{x} + \boldsymbol{\xi}, t) \tag{2.34}$$

If the right-hand side of (2.34) can be expanded about the original input and state using Taylor's theorem in several variables, the result is

$$\dot{\mathbf{q}} + \dot{\mathbf{n}} = \mathbf{f}(\mathbf{q}, \mathbf{x}, t) + \mathbf{A}\mathbf{n} + \mathbf{B}\boldsymbol{\xi} + \text{higher-order terms} \tag{2.35}$$

where the coefficients of the matrices $\mathbf{A}$ and $\mathbf{B}$ are given by

$$a_{ij} = \frac{\partial f_i}{\partial q_j} \qquad b_{ij} = \frac{\partial f_i}{\partial x_j}$$

We know, however, that for the initial condition $\mathbf{q}(t_0)$ and the subsequent input $\mathbf{x}(t)$, the state satisfies $\dot{\mathbf{q}} = \mathbf{f}(\mathbf{q}, \mathbf{x}, t)$. Hence we can cancel these terms from (2.35). We are thus left with

$$\dot{\mathbf{n}} = \mathbf{An} + \mathbf{B\xi} + \text{higher-order terms} \qquad (2.36)$$

as the differential equation for the change in $\mathbf{q}$ which must be solved with the initial condition $\mathbf{n}(t_0)$, the change in the initial state from the original state. If the higher-order terms are small, they may be neglected in obtaining an approximate solution to the problem and the resulting *perturbation equation* is seen to be linear. Note, however, that the coefficients of $\mathbf{A}$ and $\mathbf{B}$ are generally time-varying, since they are evaluated along the original trajectory $\mathbf{q}(t)$.

Example 2.9 Consider the motion of a particle acting under the inverse-square central force as discussed in Example 2.2. It is known that the motion of the particle is along a conic section whose nature is determined by the energy of the particle. We wish to consider the nature of the perturbed motion when the original orbit is circular. For a circular orbit, we know that the radius and angular velocity are constant. Consequently, $\dot{q}_1 = p_1/m = 0$, $\dot{q}_2 = \omega_0 = \text{constant}$, where ω_0 is the angular velocity and $\dot{p}_1 = 0$. In this case all the time derivatives for the original solution are constant, and the perturbation equations turn out to be time-invariant. All the coefficients of the matrix $\mathbf{A}$ are zero, with the following exceptions:

$$a_{13} = \frac{\partial f_1}{\partial p_1} = \frac{1}{m}$$

$$a_{21} = \frac{\partial f_2}{\partial q_1} = -\frac{2p_2}{mq_1{}^3} \qquad a_{24} = \frac{\partial f_2}{\partial p_2} = \frac{1}{mq_1{}^2}$$

$$a_{31} = \frac{\partial f_3}{\partial q_1} = -\frac{3p_2{}^2}{mq_1{}^4} + \frac{2K}{q_1{}^3} \qquad a_{34} = \frac{\partial f_3}{\partial p_2} = \frac{2p_2}{mq_1{}^3}$$

Moreover, from $\dot{p}_1 = 0$ it follows that

$$\frac{p_2{}^2}{mq_1{}^3} = \frac{K}{q_1{}^2} \qquad \text{and} \qquad \omega_0{}^2 = \frac{K}{mr^3}$$

so that the perturbation equations become

$$\dot{\eta}_1 = \frac{1}{m}\eta_3$$

$$\dot{\eta}_2 = -\frac{2\omega_0}{q_1}\eta_1 + \frac{\omega_0}{p_2}\eta_4$$

$$\dot{\eta}_3 = -m\omega_0{}^2\eta_1 + \frac{2\omega_0}{q_1}\eta_4$$

$$\dot{\eta}_4 = 0$$

2.7 DISCRETE-TIME SYSTEMS

A digital computer is one of the most important examples of a discrete-time system.   One is not concerned with the behavior of the computer at every instant of time, but only at those instants which are multiples of a basic interval, usually known as the "clock period."   The logical design of the computer is based on the assumption that the computer is quiescent, except at the ends of these intervals, at which time instantaneous transitions take place.   The circuits used in the computer, in turn, are designed to ensure that this assumption is valid.   If a digital computer is to be used to compute the solution to a differential equation, then this equation must be approximated by a difference equation—a recursion relation—since this is the only type of equation which the computer can handle directly.

Example 2.10 Approximation of differential equation by difference equation   Suppose it is desired to obtain a numerical solution to the differential equation (2.3).   A reasonable technique would be to approximate the derivatives by finite differences, namely,

$$\frac{d\mathbf{q}}{dt} \doteq \frac{\mathbf{q}(t + h) - \mathbf{q}(t)}{h}$$

where h is a suitably chosen small time increment, and to assume that the input $\mathbf{x}(t)$ remains constant in this interval of time.   The differential equation then takes the form

$$\mathbf{q}(t + h) = h\mathbf{f}[\mathbf{q}(t), \mathbf{x}(t), t] + \mathbf{q}(t) \tag{2.37}$$

Starting with the initial state $\mathbf{q}(t_0)$, we calculate $\mathbf{q}(t_0 + h)$, $\mathbf{q}(t_0 + 2h)$, and so forth.   Using the notation adopted in Chap. 1, we write (2.37) as

$$\mathbf{q}(n + 1) = \boldsymbol{\psi}[\mathbf{q}(n), \mathbf{x}(n), n] \tag{2.38}$$

where $\psi(\mathbf{q}, \mathbf{x}, n) = h\mathbf{f}(\mathbf{q}, \mathbf{x}, n) + \mathbf{q}$. This relation states very simply that the next state is a function of the present state and the present input. The relation for the output is similarly expressed by

$$\mathbf{y}(n) = \mathbf{g}[\mathbf{q}(n), \mathbf{x}(n), n] \tag{2.39}$$

For our purposes, we define a discrete-time system as one which can be represented by a set of equations in the form of (2.38) and (2.39). The system is said to be linear if the functions ψ and $\mathbf{g}$ in the defining equations are linear in $\mathbf{q}$ and $\mathbf{x}$. Thus a linear discrete-time system is governed by a system of difference equations of the form

$$\mathbf{q}(n + 1) = \mathbf{A}(n)\mathbf{q}(n) + \mathbf{B}(n)\mathbf{x}(n) \tag{2.40}$$

and the outputs are given by

$$\mathbf{y}(n) = \mathbf{C}(n)\mathbf{q}(n) + \mathbf{D}(n)\mathbf{x}(n) \tag{2.41}$$

where the matrices $\mathbf{A}$, $\mathbf{B}$, $\mathbf{C}$, and $\mathbf{D}$ may depend on the discrete-time variable n. If the matrices are all constant, the system is said to be *time-invariant*.

A continuous-time system may, for appropriate inputs, be treated as a discrete-time system. If a linear time-invariant system is excited by piecewise-constant inputs, in which the transitions take place at multiples of a fundamental period T, the relation between the state $\mathbf{q}(n + 1)$ at time $t = (n + 1)T$ and the state at time $t = nT$ can be expressed by a linear difference equation. We consider a first-order system in the following example, and discuss the more general case in Chap. 4.

Example 2.11 RC network excited by piecewise-constant input
Consider the network illustrated in Fig. 2.12. If the applied voltage $e(t)$ is piecewise-constant in every interval $nT < t \le (n + 1)T$, that is,

$$e(t) = E_n \qquad nT < t \le (n + 1)T$$

the differential equation for the network may be written

$$RC\frac{dv}{dt} + v = E_n \qquad nT < t \le (n + 1)T$$

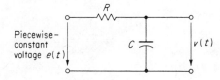

Piecewise-
constant
voltage $e(t)$

$v(t)$

FIG. 2.12   RC network for illustration of first-order difference equation.

The solution which equals $v(nT)$ at $t = nT$ is

$$v(t) = E_n + [v(nT) - E_n]e^{-(t-nT)/RC} \qquad nT < t \leq (n+1)T$$

Evaluating the solution at $t = (n+1)T$, we obtain the difference equation

$$v(nT + T) = E_n + [v(nT) - E_n]e^{-T/RC}$$

or

$$v(n + 1) = e^{-T/RC}\, v(n) + (1 - e^{-T/RC})E_n \qquad (2.42)$$

which is of first order, linear, and time-invariant.

Sometimes the difference equations of a system are not in normal form and it is desired to convert them to normal form. This may be accomplished by the definition of auxiliary state variables, as we have done for continuous-time systems. The technique is illustrated in the following examples.

Example 2.12   Consider the difference equation

$$y(n + k) + \alpha_1 y(n + k - 1) + \cdots + \alpha_k y(n) = x(n) \qquad (2.43)$$

It is convenient to introduce the operator E defined by

$$E^r u(n) = u(n + r) \qquad (2.44)$$

The operator E thus advances the variable by one time interval. The difference equation (2.43) becomes

$$(E^k + \alpha_1 E^{k-1} + \cdots + \alpha_{k-1} E + \alpha_k)y(n) = x(n) \qquad (2.45)$$

For this equation a *reasonable* definition of state variables is

$$q_1(n) = y(n)$$
$$q_2(n) = y(n + 1)$$
$$\cdots \cdots \cdots \cdots$$
$$q_k(n) = y(n + k - 1)$$

From these definitions we obtain

$$q_1(n + 1) = q_2(n)$$
$$q_2(n + 1) = q_3(n)$$
$$\cdots \cdots \cdots \cdots$$
$$q_{k-1}(n + 1) = q_k(n)$$

From the original equation we note that

$$q_k(n + 1) = E^k y(n) = -\alpha_1 q_k(n) - \alpha_2 q_{k-1}(n) - \cdots - \alpha_k q_1(n) + x(n)$$

Hence we obtain the following normal form of the equations:

$$\mathbf{q}(n + 1) = \mathbf{A}\mathbf{q}(n) + \mathbf{B}x(n)$$
$$y(n) = \mathbf{C}\mathbf{q}(n)$$

where

$$\mathbf{A} = \begin{bmatrix} 0 & 1 & 0 & \cdots & 0 \\ 0 & 0 & 1 & \cdots & 0 \\ \cdot & \cdot & \cdot & \cdots & \cdot \\ 0 & 0 & 0 & \cdots & 1 \\ -\alpha_k & -\alpha_{k-1} & -\alpha_{k-2} & \cdots & -\alpha_1 \end{bmatrix} \qquad \mathbf{B} = \begin{bmatrix} 0 \\ 0 \\ \cdot \\ 0 \\ 1 \end{bmatrix}$$

$$\mathbf{C} = \begin{bmatrix} 1 & 0 & 0 & \cdots & 0 \end{bmatrix}$$

Example 2.13   In order to illustrate the parallel between differential equations and difference equations, we next consider the equation

$$(E^k + \alpha_1 E^{k-1} + \cdots + \alpha_k)y(n)$$
$$= (\beta_0 E^k + \beta_1 E^{k-1} + \cdots + \beta_k)x(n) \quad (2.46)$$

which is analogous to (2.19).   By reasoning parallel to that used in Example 2.4, we define the state variables as follows:

$$y(n) = q_1(n) + dx(n)$$
$$q_1(n + 1) = q_2(n) + b_1 x(n)$$
$$\cdot \cdot \cdot \cdot \cdot \cdot \cdot \cdot \cdot \cdot \cdot \cdot \cdot \cdot \cdot$$
$$q_{k-1}(n + 1) = q_k(n) + b_{k-1}x(n)$$
$$q_k(n + 1) = -\alpha_k q_1(n) - \alpha_{k-1}q_2(n) - \cdots$$
$$- \alpha_2 q_{k-1}(n) - \alpha_1 q_k(n) + b_k x(n)$$

where the coefficients $d, b_1, \ldots, b_k$ are to be determined.

As in Example 2.4, we find that these coefficients are given by

$$\begin{bmatrix} 1 & 0 & 0 & \cdots & 0 \\ \alpha_1 & 1 & 0 & \cdots & 0 \\ \alpha_2 & \alpha_1 & 1 & \cdots & 0 \\ \cdot & \cdot & \cdot & \cdots & \cdot \\ \alpha_k & \alpha_{k-1} & \alpha_{k-2} & \cdots & 1 \end{bmatrix} \begin{bmatrix} d \\ b_1 \\ b_2 \\ \cdot \\ b_k \end{bmatrix} = \begin{bmatrix} \beta_0 \\ \beta_1 \\ \beta_2 \\ \cdot \\ \beta_k \end{bmatrix}$$

The matrices $\mathbf{A}$, $\mathbf{B}$, $\mathbf{C}$, and $\mathbf{D}$ are the same as those given in Example 2.4.

Example 2.14   Cascaded two-terminal-pair networks   In the cascade of identical networks characterized by their a, b, c, d coefficients (Fig. 2.13), $V(n)$ and $I(n)$ denote the voltage and current, respectively, at the output of the nth section.   The voltages and currents at the terminals are related by

$$V(n + 1) = aV(n) + bI(n)$$
$$I(n + 1) = cV(n) + dI(n)$$

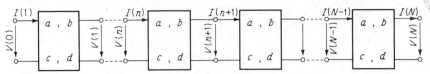

FIG. 2.13   Cascaded two-terminal-pair network.

These equations are in normal form, and the state vector is

$$\mathbf{q}(n) = \begin{bmatrix} V(n) \\ I(n) \end{bmatrix}$$

It should be noted that the independent variable is here one of location (the nth network), and not of time.

2.8 SIMULATION OF DISCRETE-TIME SYSTEMS

While block diagrams representing continuous-time systems are frequently useful as an aid in setting up the simulation of the system on an analog computer, block diagrams representing discrete-time systems are primarily useful for conceptual purposes. The digital computer is the natural tool for simulating discrete-time systems; in fact, the existence of the digital computer is the main reason for studying such systems.

The components of a discrete-time-system diagram are the same as those for a continuous-time system except that the integrator is replaced by a *unit delay*, represented symbolically by E^{-1}. Repeating the arguments for analog simulation, we observe that the structure of the block diagram for the system

$$\mathbf{q}(n+1) = E\mathbf{q}(n) = \mathbf{A}\mathbf{q}(n) + \mathbf{B}\mathbf{x}(n)$$
$$\mathbf{y}(n) = \mathbf{C}\mathbf{q}(n) + \mathbf{D}\mathbf{x}(n)$$

is identical with that of the analog-computer diagram for the system

$$\frac{d\mathbf{q}(t)}{dt} = \dot{\mathbf{q}}(t) = \mathbf{A}\mathbf{q}(t) + \mathbf{B}\mathbf{x}(t)$$
$$\mathbf{y}(t) = \mathbf{C}\mathbf{q}(t) + \mathbf{D}\mathbf{x}(t)$$

provided that the integrators are replaced by unit delays.

Example 2.15 The block diagram for the difference equation (2.42) is given in Fig. 2.14.

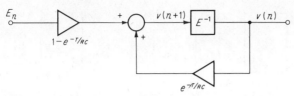

FIG. 2.14   Block diagram for difference equation.

PROBLEMS

2.1   Write the following system of differential equations in normal form, and write down the matrices **A**, **B**.

$$D^2y + 4\,Dy + 3z = x_1 + x_2$$
$$D^2z + 5\,Dz + Dy + y = x_2$$

where x_1 and x_2 are inputs.

2.2   Find a set of matrices **A**, **B**, **C**, and **D** of the normal form for the equation

$$(D^3 + 2D^2 - D + 3)y(t) = x_1(t) + 4x_2(t)$$

where x_1, x_2 are input functions and y is the output.

2.3   Find matrices **A**, **B**, **C**, **D** for the equation

$$(D^3 + 2D^2 - D + 3)y(t) = x(t) + 4\,\frac{dx(t)}{dt}$$

where x and y denote input and output, respectively.

2.4   Draw the analog-computer diagram and find the matrices **A**, **B**, **C**, and **D** for each of the following equations:

(*a*) $(D^3 + 5D^2 + 5D + 1)y = (2D + 1)x.$
(*b*) $(D^2 + 2D + 1)y_1 + (2D + 1)y_2 = x_1$
   $(2D + 1)y_1 + (D^2 + 2D + 2)y_2 = Dx_1 + x_2.$

2.5   A linear system has the following matrices in the normal-form characterization:

$$\mathbf{A} = \begin{bmatrix} 1 & 0 & 0 \\ 1 & 2 & 0 \\ 1 & 2 & 3 \end{bmatrix} \quad \mathbf{B} = \begin{bmatrix} 1 & 0 \\ 0 & 1 \\ 1 & 2 \end{bmatrix} \quad \mathbf{C} = \begin{bmatrix} 1 & 0 & 2 \\ 1 & 1 & 1 \end{bmatrix} \quad \mathbf{D} = \begin{bmatrix} 3 & 1 \\ 2 & 1 \end{bmatrix}$$

(*a*) Write the equations for the system in detail.
(*b*) Draw the analog-computer diagram for the system.

2.6   Write the differential and output equations of each of the networks shown in Fig. P 2.6 in normal form, using matrix notation.

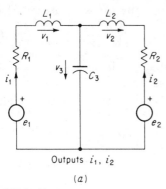
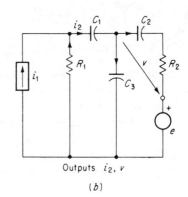

Outputs i_1, i_2

(a)

Outputs i_2, v

(b)

FIG. P 2.6

2.7 Two systems H_1 and H_2 are characterized by the following equations:

$$H_1: \quad \dot{\mathbf{q}} = \mathbf{A}_1\mathbf{q} + \mathbf{B}_1\mathbf{x} \qquad H_2: \quad \dot{\mathbf{r}} = \mathbf{A}_2\mathbf{r} + \mathbf{B}_2\mathbf{y}$$
$$\mathbf{y} = \mathbf{C}_1\mathbf{q} + \mathbf{D}_1\mathbf{x} \qquad\qquad \mathbf{z} = \mathbf{C}_2\mathbf{r} + \mathbf{D}_2\mathbf{y}$$

The number of outputs of H_1 equals the number of inputs of H_2, so that H_2 may be cascaded with H_1 as shown in Fig. P 2.7. Let

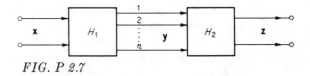

FIG. P 2.7

this number be n. Find the normal-form characterization of the cascade system $H_2H_1 = H_{21}$, using as the state vector of the combined system

$$\mathbf{p} = [r_1 \cdots r_m, q_1 \cdots q_k]'$$

(The prime indicates transposition and permits the column vector to be written as a row vector.) *Hint:* Treat each of the normal forms as scalar equations.

2.8 (a) Show that Eqs. (2.30) are equivalent to (2.19).
(b) Write the normal form of the differential equations in terms of the state variables z, Dz, . . . , $D^{k-1}z$, which are the outputs of the integrators in Fig. 2.10.

2.9 Draw the analog-computer diagram for simulating the system of Example 2.4, with each state variable chosen there as the output of an integrator.

2.10 (a) Reduce (2.19) to normal form by choosing a_{jr} as in Example 2.4, and $b_1 = b_2 = \cdots = b_{k-1} = 0$, $b_k = 1$.

   (b) Draw the corresponding analog-computer diagram.

2.11 Draw the analog-computer diagram for the network of Fig. 2.1 if the desired outputs are the currents i_1 and i_2 by writing the differential equations for these currents. Eliminate the differentiators from the diagram by the method of Sec. 2.4. Compare the numbers of each type of element in the diagram with those of Fig. 2.7.

2.12 Show that a linear system with a single input and arbitrary matrices $\mathbf{A}$ and $\mathbf{B}$ (a column vector) can be transformed to the following form:

$$\dot{\mathbf{p}} = \mathbf{R}\mathbf{p} + \mathbf{S}x$$
$$\mathbf{q} = \mathbf{M}\mathbf{p}$$

where the matrices $\mathbf{R}$, $\mathbf{S}$, and $\mathbf{M}$ are given by

$$\mathbf{R} = \begin{bmatrix} 0 & 0 & \cdots & 0 & r_1 \\ 1 & 0 & \cdots & 0 & r_2 \\ 0 & 1 & \cdots & 0 & r_3 \\ & & \cdots & & \\ 0 & 0 & \cdots & 1 & r_k \end{bmatrix} \qquad \mathbf{S} = \begin{bmatrix} 1 \\ 0 \\ \cdot \\ 0 \\ 0 \end{bmatrix} \qquad \mathbf{M} = \begin{bmatrix} \mathbf{B} & \mathbf{AB} & \cdots & \mathbf{A}^{k-1}\mathbf{B} \end{bmatrix}$$

and $r_1, r_2, \ldots, r_k$ are appropriate constants, provided only that $\mathbf{M}$ is nonsingular. (See Chap. 11 for the significance of a singular $\mathbf{M}$.) *Hint:* Use the fact that $\mathbf{M}\mathbf{M}^{-1} = \mathbf{I}$, the identity matrix.

2.13 Determine the equilibrium points of the motion of a satellite in the gravitational field of the earth and the moon. (These are called *libration points.*) Obtain the perturbation equations for motion in the vicinity of these points.

2.14 Find matrices $\mathbf{A}$, $\mathbf{B}$, $\mathbf{C}$, $\mathbf{D}$ for the system characterized by the difference equation

$$(5\Delta^2 + 4\Delta - 1)y(n) = x(n) + 3\,\Delta x(n)$$

where x and y denote input and output, respectively, and $\Delta y(n) = y(n+1) - y(n)$, $\Delta^2 y(n) = y(n+2) - 2y(n+1) + y(n)$ are, respectively, the *first* and *second forward differences* of $y(n)$.

2.15 Given the simultaneous difference equations

$$y_1(n+1) + 3y_1(n) - 2y_2(n) = x_1(n)$$
$$y_1(n) + y_2(n+2) = x_2(n)$$

   (a) Find a block-diagram representation of this system, using unit delays, amplifiers, and summers.

   (b) Write these equations in the normal form.

2.16 If the integrators of Fig. 2.6 are replaced by unit delays, what is the difference equation of the system?

2.17 (a) The square wave shown in Fig. P 2.17 is applied to the RC circuit of Fig. 2.12. Determine the difference equation for

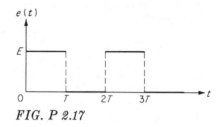

FIG. P 2.17

the voltage $v(2kT)$ across the capacitor at the end of the kth period of the square wave.

(b) Calculate the values of $v(2kT)$ for $k = 1, 2, 3, 4$ if the capacitor is initially uncharged and $T/RC = 0.5$.

(c) What is the steady-state value of $v(2kT)$?

2.18 Write the differential equations in normal form for the network shown in Fig. P 2.18. Use the voltages indicated as state variables.

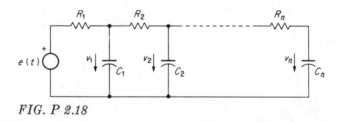

FIG. P 2.18

2.19 In the network of Fig. P 2.19 the switch K is closed at $t = 0$, opened at $t = 1$ sec, closed at $t = 2$ sec, etc. Write a difference equation

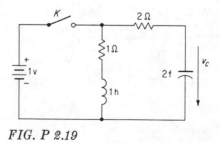

FIG. P 2.19

for the voltage V_c on the capacitor at the end of the nth close-open cycle.

2.20   The diagram shown in Fig. P 2.20 represents a coder which produces a discrete-time signal $y(n)$ from an input $x(n)$; α, β_0, β_1 are constant gains.

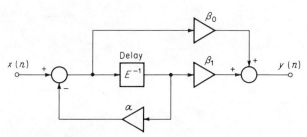

FIG. P 2.20

(a) Determine the output $y(n)$ in terms of the input $x(n)$.

(b) Show that the inverse of this coder [which produces $x(n)$ when $y(n)$ is applied] has the same *structure* and find the gains of the amplifiers in the inverse in terms of α, β_0, β_1.

2.21   The equivalent circuit of a three-stage transistor amplifier is shown in Fig. P 2.21.   Write the differential equations for this amplifier in normal form.

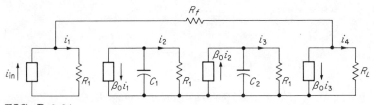

FIG. P 2.21

2.22   Write the differential equations for the coupled circuit of Fig. P 2.22 in normal form, using i_1, i_2, and v as state variables.

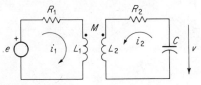

FIG. P 2.22

2.23   Find the equilibrium region of the continuous-time system governed
by

$$\dot{\mathbf{q}}(t) = \mathbf{A}\mathbf{q}(t)$$

where

(a) $\mathbf{A} = \begin{bmatrix} 1 & 1 & 0 \\ 0 & 1 & 0 \\ 2 & 1 & 1 \end{bmatrix}$

(b) $\mathbf{A} = \begin{bmatrix} 0 & 1 & 0 \\ 0 & 0 & 1 \\ 0 & 2 & 3 \end{bmatrix}$

(c) $\mathbf{A} = \begin{bmatrix} 0 & 1 & 1 \\ 0 & 2 & 2 \\ 0 & 0 & 0 \end{bmatrix}$

CHAPTER THREE

PRINCIPLES OF

TIME-DOMAIN ANALYSIS

3.1 INTRODUCTION

This chapter is concerned with the representation and properties of signals in the *time domain* and the time-domain method for determining the response of linear systems to given inputs. We first discuss the resolution of arbitrary continuous- and discrete-time signals into the "elementary functions" of time-domain analysis, and then consider the temporal properties of signals. This is followed by a study of the response of a system to the elementary functions and the combination of these responses to obtain the response to the applied input.

In the time-domain method of analysis the elementary components into which the signals comprising the inputs or outputs of a system under consideration are resolved are *identical in shape*, but occur at different instants of time. (In the frequency-domain method, the elementary components into which the inputs are resolved have *different shapes*, i.e., different

frequencies, but have a common time origin.)   Since the times of occurrence of the elementary components are involved in the time-domain method, the calculations will always entail time as a parameter.

A system generally has a number n of inputs $x_i(t)$ and a (generally different) number m of outputs $y_j(t)$, which, as we have already indicated, may be represented by vectors

$$\mathbf{x}(t) = \begin{bmatrix} x_1(t) \\ x_2(t) \\ \cdot \\ \cdot \\ \cdot \\ x_n(t) \end{bmatrix} \qquad \mathbf{y}(t) = \begin{bmatrix} y_1(t) \\ y_2(t) \\ \cdot \\ \cdot \\ \cdot \\ y_m(t) \end{bmatrix}$$

Although all the results in this chapter may be derived with only slight modification for multidimensional signals by the use of vector-matrix notation, it is expedient first to develop the fundamental concepts in terms of signals with only a single component.

3.2   ELEMENTARY CONTINUOUS-TIME SIGNALS

DEFINITIONS OF ELEMENTARY FUNCTIONS

The elementary functions used in the time-domain analysis of systems with continuous-time signals are defined by the relations

$$\mu_{i+1}(t) = \int_{-\infty}^{t} \mu_i(\lambda) \, d\lambda \qquad i = \ldots, -2, -1, 0, 1, 2, \ldots \quad (3.1)$$

$$\mu_1(t) = \begin{cases} 0 & t < 0 \\ 1 & t \geq 0 \end{cases} \qquad\qquad\qquad (3.2)$$

These elementary functions are also called *singularity functions*.   The functions $\mu_2(t)$, $\mu_1(t)$, $\mu_0(t)$, and $\mu_{-1}(t)$ are shown in Table 3.1 and are generally called the *unit ramp, unit step, unit impulse,* and *unit doublet,* respectively.   The unit impulse and unit step are most frequently employed in time-domain analysis.

THE UNIT IMPULSE

The unit impulse, or delta function, together with the unit step, is basic to the time-domain method of analysis and merits special attention.

Table 3.1 ELEMENTARY FUNCTIONS OF TIME-DOMAIN ANALYSIS

Function	Symbol and definition	Graph
Unit ramp	$\mu_2(t) = \begin{cases} 0 & t < 0 \\ t & t \geq 0 \end{cases}$	
Unit step	$\mu_1(t) = \begin{cases} 0 & t < 0 \\ 1 & t \geq 0 \end{cases}$	
Unit impulse (delta function)	$\mu_0(t) = \delta(t) = 0 \qquad t \neq 0$ and $\int_{-\infty}^{t} \mu_0(\lambda)\, d\lambda = \mu_1(t) \qquad t \neq 0$	
Unit doublet	$\mu_{-1}(t) = 0 \qquad t \neq 0$ and $\int_{-\infty}^{t} \mu_{-1}(\lambda)\, d\lambda = \mu_0(t) \qquad t \neq 0$	

The use of the unit impulse caused considerable controversy among mathematicians until it was given a rigorous treatment in the recent work of Schwartz† on the theory of distributions. This "function" has nevertheless played an important role in the analysis of physical phenomena; since its use by Dirac in his work on quantum mechanics, it has frequently been called the *Dirac delta function*. In a qualitative way, the unit impulse $\delta(t)$ may be regarded as the limit as $\tau \to 0$ of a pulse $p_\tau(t)$ of width τ and height $1/\tau$ as shown in Fig. 3.1a. This pulse may be obtained by differentiating a step with a front of finite slope (Fig. 3.1b). The unit impulse may similarly be regarded as the limit of the derivative of many other approximations to a unit step, such as shown in Fig. 3.2; see also Prob. 3.1. In this book an impulse is indicated by a vertical arrow whose height is proportional to the area, or "strength," of the impulse.

In Table 3.1, a definition of the unit impulse is given which is adequate

† L. Schwartz, "Théorie des distributions," 2 vols., Hermann & Cie., Paris, 1950–1951. For a very brief introduction, see A. Erdélyi, From Delta Functions to Distributions, chap. 1 in E. F. Beckenbach (ed.), "Modern Mathematics for the Engineer," Second Series, McGraw-Hill Book Company, New York, 1961.

for many purposes, but it is not a rigorous definition.   Equation (3.5) may be used as a definition of $\delta(t)$; the unit impulse is then defined by its action on a function.   A heuristic derivation of (3.5), using the limit of the pulse $p_\tau(t)$, is given in Sec. 3.3.

The unit impulse may be approximated in a more precise and general

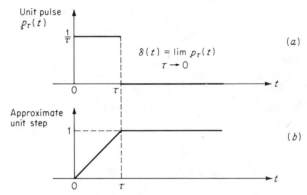

FIG. 3.1   *Unit impulse as limiting form of unit pulse.   (a) Unit pulse; (b) approximation to unit step whose derivative is the unit pulse.*

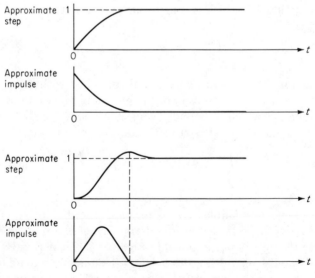

FIG. 3.2   *Approximations to the unit impulse obtained by differentiating approximations to unit step.*

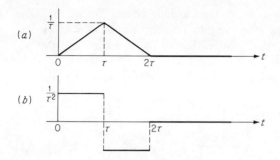

FIG. 3.3 Approximation to unit doublet. (a) Approximation to unit impulse; (b) derivative of (a).

way than the limit of the pulse $p_\tau(t)$ above by using a function which vanishes outside a prescribed interval.† Let $s(t)$ be a function defined for all real t with the following properties:

(1) $s(t) \geq 0$

(2) $s(t) = 0$ if $|t| \geq 1$

(3) $\int_{-\infty}^{\infty} s(t)\, dt = 1$

Then

$$s_n(t) = ns(nt)$$

satisfies the first and third conditions and vanishes for $|t| \geq 1/n$. As $n \to \infty$, $s_n(t)$ may be regarded as approaching the unit impulse. For any function $f(t)$ which is continuous over a finite interval A, it can be shown that

$$\int_{-\infty}^{\infty} s_n(\lambda) f(t - \lambda)\, d\lambda \to f(t) \qquad \text{as } n \to \infty$$

uniformly in t over any interval contained within A. This relation may be used as the definition of the unit impulse [see (3.5)]; it is valid for any function which is bounded and continuous for all t even if property (2) is not satisfied. If $s(t)$ has k continuous derivatives, it also follows that

$$\int_{-\infty}^{\infty} s_n{}^{(k)}(\lambda) f(t - \lambda)\, d\lambda \to f^{(k)}(t) \qquad \text{as } n \to \infty$$

for any t at which $f^{(k)}(t)$ is continuous.

The unit doublet $\delta(t)$ is formally the derivative of the unit impulse. It may be regarded as the derivative of the limit of the approximation to the unit impulse shown in Fig. 3.3. This derivative consists of a positive pulse of width τ and height $1/\tau^2$, immediately followed by a negative pulse of the same shape. As $\tau \to 0$, these pulses approach impulses of

† Erdélyi, *loc. cit.*

infinite area and of infinitesimal separation. The higher-order impulses (unit triplet, unit quadruplet, etc.) may be similarly visualized.

The unit impulse $\delta(t)$ and its derivatives $\dot{\delta}(t)$, $\ddot{\delta}(t)$, . . . can be regarded as generalized functions with rules by which they can be combined. They may be added by adding terms of similar form and multiplied by a constant; i.e., if

$$f(t) = a_1\delta(t) + a_2\dot{\delta}(t) + \cdot\cdot\cdot + a_n\delta^{(n)}(t)$$
$$g(t) = b_1\delta(t) + b_2\dot{\delta}(t) + \cdot\cdot\cdot + b_n\delta^{(n)}(t)$$

then

$$f(t) + g(t) = (a_1 + b_1)\delta(t) + (a_2 + b_2)\dot{\delta}(t) + \cdot\cdot\cdot + (a_n + b_n)\delta^{(n)}(t)$$

The product $f(t)\delta(t)$ is defined as $f(0)\delta(t)$ (provided f is continuous at $t = 0$). This definition is plausible since $\delta(t)$ by definition vanishes for $t \neq 0$. In order to define $f(t)\dot{\delta}(t)$, we use the product rule on $d[f(t)\delta(t)]/dt = f(0)\dot{\delta}(t)$:

$$f(0)\dot{\delta}(t) = d[f(t)\delta(t)]/dt = \dot{f}(t)\delta(t) + f(t)\dot{\delta}(t)$$
$$= \dot{f}(0)\delta(t) + f(t)\dot{\delta}(t)$$

Hence

$$f(t)\dot{\delta}(t) = f(0)\dot{\delta}(t) - \dot{f}(0)\delta(t) \tag{3.3}$$

The product of f and higher derivatives of the unit impulse can be similarly defined.

The integral relation

$$\int_{-\infty}^{\infty} f(t - \lambda)\delta(\lambda)\ d\lambda = f(t)$$

may be "derived" from the definition of the delta function or may be used to define it. From this relation, integrals of products of ordinary functions and derivatives of the delta function may be evaluated. Thus

$$\int_{-\infty}^{\infty} f(t - \lambda)\dot{\delta}(\lambda)\ d\lambda = \int_{-\infty}^{\infty} \dot{f}(t - \lambda)\delta(\lambda)\ d\lambda = \dot{f}(t)$$

by use of (3.3) and

$$\int_{-\infty}^{\infty} \dot{\delta}(\lambda)\ d\lambda = 0$$

By continuing in the same manner, we find

$$\int_{-\infty}^{\infty} f(t - \lambda)\delta^{(k)}(\lambda)\ d\lambda = f^{(k)}(t)$$

provided $f^{(k)}(\lambda)$ is continuous at $\lambda = t$.

3.3   RESOLUTION OF CONTINUOUS-TIME SIGNALS

RESOLUTION INTO UNIT IMPULSES

A signal $f(t)$, as shown in Fig. 3.4, may be approximated in any finite interval $-T \leq t \leq T$ by a finite number of unit pulses of width $\Delta\lambda$, occurring at $t = k\,\Delta\lambda$ ($k = 0, \pm 1, \pm 2, \ldots, \pm N = T/\Delta\lambda$). Since the height of a *unit* pulse is $1/\Delta\lambda$, the pulse occurring at $t = k\,\Delta\lambda$ must be multiplied by $f(k\,\Delta\lambda)\,\Delta\lambda$ to make its amplitude equal to the value of the function approximated. Consequently, the approximation is written

$$f(t) \doteq \sum_{k=-N}^{N} f(k\,\Delta\lambda) p_{\Delta\lambda}(t - k\,\Delta\lambda)\,\Delta\lambda \qquad -T \leq t \leq T \qquad (3.4)$$

Note that a pulse occurring at $t = k\,\Delta\lambda$ is correctly written $p_{\Delta\lambda}(t - k\,\Delta\lambda)$.

As the pulses become narrower and increase in number, the approximation becomes better. Finally, in the limiting case as $\Delta\lambda \to 0$ and $N \to \infty$, so that $N\,\Delta\lambda$ remains constant ($= T$), the values $k\,\Delta\lambda$ of the argument of f in (3.4) can assume all values in the interval $(-T, T)$ and are therefore replaced by the continuous variable λ. Moreover, the pulses become impulses and the summation is replaced by an integral; the approximation becomes exact. Thus, as $\Delta\lambda \to 0$ and $N \to \infty$, (3.4) becomes

$$f(t) = \int_{-T}^{T} f(\lambda)\delta(t - \lambda)\,d\lambda$$

In order to extend this relation to the entire domain of definition of $f(t)$ ($-\infty < t < \infty$), we let $T \to \infty$ and obtain

$$f(t) = \int_{-\infty}^{\infty} f(\lambda)\delta(t - \lambda)\,d\lambda \qquad (3.5)$$

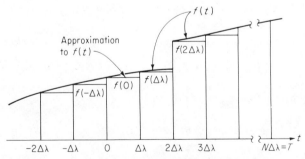

FIG. 3.4   Approximation of $f(t)$ by unit pulses.

As pointed out in Sec. 3.2, (3.5) may be used as the definition of the unit impulse $\delta(t)$. Equation (3.5) is not valid at a point of discontinuity of $f(t)$; it does, however, give the values of $f(t)$ to the left and to the right of the discontinuity.

Equation (3.5) is sometimes referred to as the sifting integral since it selects, or sifts out, the value of $f(\lambda)$ at $\lambda = t$ by means of the operations shown on the right-hand side of (3.5). Note that the resolution (3.5) is in the form given by (1.15).

For multidimensional signals the resolution has the same form. Each component may be resolved by (3.5) into

$$f_i(t) = \int_{-\infty}^{\infty} f_i(\lambda)\delta(t - \lambda)\,d\lambda$$

Thus we obtain

$$\mathbf{f}(t) = \int_{-\infty}^{\infty} \mathbf{f}(\lambda)\delta(t - \lambda)\,d\lambda = \begin{bmatrix} \int_{-\infty}^{\infty} f_1(\lambda)\delta(t - \lambda)\,d\lambda \\ \cdots\cdots\cdots\cdots \\ \int_{-\infty}^{\infty} f_n(\lambda)\delta(t - \lambda)\,d\lambda \end{bmatrix}$$

Equation (3.5) may be obtained directly from the definition of the unit impulse. The derivation is left as an exercise (Prob. 3.3).

RESOLUTION INTO UNIT STEPS

The signal $f(t)$ for $t_0 \leq t \leq t_0 + T$ may also be approximated by a finite number of unit steps (see Fig. 3.5). The approximation is expressed by

$$f(t) \doteq f(t_0)\mu_1(t - t_0) + \sum_{k=1}^{N} \{f[t_0 + k\,\Delta\lambda]$$
$$- f[t_0 + (k - 1)\,\Delta\lambda]\}\mu_1(t - t_0 - k\,\Delta\lambda) \qquad t \geq t_0$$

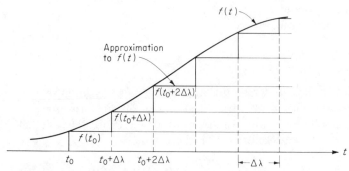

FIG. 3.5   Approximation of $f(t)$ by unit steps.

Multiplying and dividing each term in the summation by $\Delta\lambda$, we obtain
$$f(t) \doteq f(t_0)\mu_1(t - t_0)$$

$$+ \sum_{k=1}^{N} \frac{f[t_0 + k\,\Delta\lambda] - f[t_0 + (k-1)\,\Delta\lambda]}{\Delta\lambda} \mu_1(t - t_0 - k\,\Delta\lambda)\,\Delta\lambda \quad (3.6)$$

As $\Delta\lambda \to 0$ and $N \to \infty$, with $N\,\Delta\lambda = T$, the approximation becomes exact. In the limit, however, the ratio

$$\frac{f[t_0 + k\,\Delta\lambda] - f[t_0 + (k-1)\,\Delta\lambda]}{\Delta\lambda}$$

approaches the derivative of the function $f(t)$ at the point $t = t_0 + \lambda$. Moreover, as $\Delta\lambda \to 0$, the summation in (3.6) becomes an integral. Thus, passing to the limit as $\Delta\lambda \to 0$ in (3.6), we obtain the resolution

$$f(t) = f(t_0)\mu_1(t - t_0) + \int_0^T \dot{f}(t_0 + \lambda)\mu_1(t - t_0 - \lambda)\,d\lambda$$

The change of variable $\xi = t_0 + \lambda$ and extension of the upper limit T to ∞ gives

$$f(t) = f(t_0)\mu_1(t - t_0) + \int_{t_0}^{\infty} \dot{f}(\xi)\mu_1(t - \xi)\,d\xi \qquad t \geq t_0 \quad (3.7)$$

A word of caution is necessary here. The function $f(t)$ was assumed continuous at $t = t_0$, the starting instant of the resolution. In many situations, however, $f(t)$ will be discontinuous at t_0. In such cases the derivative $\dot{f}(t_0)$ of $f(t)$ at t_0 will contain an impulse of strength $[f(t_0^+) - f(t_0^-)]$ occurring at $t = t_0$. If this impulse is included in the integrand of (3.7), the coefficient of $\mu_1(t - t_0)$ preceding the integral must be $f(t_0^-)$. If this impulse is not included, the coefficient must be $f(t_0^+)$. As a practical expedient, the reader is advised always to include impulses resulting at any point from differentiating at a discontinuity and to remember that (3.7) should be written with $f(t_0^-)$. In most cases $t_0 = 0$ and $f(0^-) = 0$; then (3.7) may be written

$$f(t) = \int_0^{\infty} \dot{f}(\xi)\mu_1(t - \xi)\,d\xi \qquad t > 0 \quad (3.8)$$

where it is understood that $\dot{f}(\lambda)$ includes any impulse which may occur at the origin. Note that (3.8) is also of the form given by (1.15). It is possible to obtain (3.7) from (3.5); see Prob. 3.4. For multidimensional signals, the resolution (3.8) becomes

$$\mathbf{f}(t) = \int_0^{\infty} \dot{\mathbf{f}}(\xi)\mu_1(t - \xi)\,d\xi \qquad t > 0$$

If $\lim\limits_{t \to -\infty} f(t) = 0$, we may write, for all t,

$$\mathbf{f}(t) = \int_{-\infty}^{\infty} \dot{\mathbf{f}}(\xi)\mu_1(t - \xi)\, d\xi \tag{3.9}$$

Example 3.1   The resolution of a function into unit steps may be illustrated by the two functions shown in Fig. 3.6.

(a) The ramp function of Fig. 3.6a has a derivative

$$\dot{f}_1(t) = \frac{1}{a}\,\mu_1(t)$$

Hence (3.7) with $t_0 = -\infty$ or (3.9) gives

$$\begin{aligned} f_1(t) &= \frac{1}{a}\int_{-\infty}^{\infty} \mu_1(\xi)\mu_1(t - \xi)\, d\xi \\ &= \frac{1}{a}\int_{0}^{\infty} \mu_1(t - \xi)\, d\xi \end{aligned}$$

This is the resolution of $f_1(t)$ into unit steps and is valid for all t.   As a check, we find

$$\text{For } t < 0: \qquad f_1(t) = \int_{0}^{\infty} 0 \cdot d\xi = 0$$

$$\text{For } t > 0: \qquad f_1(t) = \frac{1}{a}\int_{0}^{t} 1 \cdot d\xi = \frac{1}{a}t$$

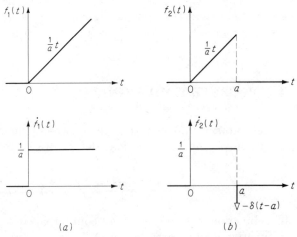

(a)   (b)

FIG. 3.6   Functions to be resolved into unit steps. (a) Ramp function and its derivative; (b) truncated ramp function and its derivative.

(b) The truncated ramp function of Fig. 3.6b has a derivative

$$\dot{f}_2(t) = \frac{1}{a}\mu_1(t) - \frac{1}{a}\mu_1(t - a) - \delta(t - a)$$

The resolution of $f_2(t)$ into unit steps may thus be written, according to (3.7) with $t_0 = -\infty$, or (3.9):

$$f_2(t) = \int_{-\infty}^{\infty}\left[\frac{1}{a}\mu_1(\xi) - \frac{1}{a}\mu_1(\xi - a) - \delta(\xi - a)\right]\mu_1(t - \xi)\,d\xi$$

$$= \int_0^{a^+}\left[\frac{1}{a} - \delta(\xi - a)\right]\mu_1(t - \xi)\,d\xi$$

The upper limit is written a^+ to indicate that the range of integration includes the point $\xi = a$ at which the impulse occurs. To verify the correctness of this resolution, we find

For $t < 0$: $f_2(t) = \int_0^{a^+} 0 \cdot d\xi = 0$

For $0 < t < a$: $f_2(t) = \int_0^t \frac{1}{a} 1 \cdot d\xi = \frac{1}{a}t$

For $t > a$: $f_2(t) = \int_0^{a^+}\left[\frac{1}{a} - \delta(\xi - a)\right] 1 \cdot d\xi = 1 - 1 = 0$

For $t < 0$, the integrand is zero since the unit step is zero throughout the range of integration. For $0 < t < a$, the unit step is zero for $\xi > t$ and the impulse is zero throughout the resulting range of integration. For $t > a$, the unit step is unity throughout the range of integration.

3.4 DISCRETE-TIME SIGNALS

The elementary component used in the time-domain analysis of discrete-time systems is the unit function† defined by

$$\mu_0(n - k) = \delta(n - k) = \begin{cases} 0 & n \neq k \\ 1 & n = k \end{cases} \tag{3.10}$$

This function is the discrete-time counterpart of the unit impulse. The unit function is illustrated in Fig. 3.7.

† In the mathematical literature the unit function is called *Kronecker's delta* and is written δ_{nk}.

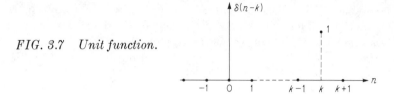

FIG. 3.7   *Unit function.*

The discrete unit step is defined by

$$\mu_1(n - k) = \begin{cases} 0 & n < k \\ 1 & n \geq k \end{cases} \qquad (3.11)$$

but is not frequently employed.

The resolution of an arbitrary discrete-time function $f(n)$ into unit functions is direct and obvious:

$$f(n) = \cdots f(-1)\delta(n + 1) + f(0)\delta(n) + f(1)\delta(n - 1) + \cdots$$

$$= \sum_{k=-\infty}^{\infty} f(k)\delta(n - k) \qquad (3.12)$$

This equation is the discrete-time counterpart of (3.5). Note that (3.12) is exact and is obtained without using a limiting process. For multidimensional signals this resolution becomes

$$\mathbf{f}(n) = \sum_{k=-\infty}^{\infty} \mathbf{f}(k)\delta(n - k)$$

The resolution into discrete unit steps is almost as direct. The derivation is left as an exercise (Prob. 3.8).

3.5 IMPULSE RESPONSE AND STEP RESPONSE IN CONTINUOUS-TIME SYSTEMS

We have seen how continuous-time and discrete-time signals may be resolved into elementary functions. The reason for performing such resolutions was indicated in Sec. 1.5: the problem of determining the response of a linear system to an arbitrary input may be reduced to that of finding the response to the elementary signal. We shall thus consider next some characteristics of the response of linear systems to the elementary functions introduced in Secs. 3.2 and 3.3. The actual determination of the response to a given elementary function may be carried out by

solving a differential or difference equation with the appropriate forcing function. This solution is discussed at the end of this section. We assume for the time being that the systems have one input and one output; the generalization to multiple inputs and outputs is made in Sec. 3.9.

IMPULSE RESPONSE AND ITS PROPERTIES

Since any continuous-time excitation signal can be resolved into a continuum of unit impulses or unit steps, it follows that the response of a linear system to any such excitation can be found if the response of the system to unit impulses or to unit steps applied at every time instant is known. Hence either the (unit) impulse response or the (unit) step response completely characterizes the system.

The impulse response of a linear system is a function of time, which in general depends also on the instant of application of the impulse. Thus we define

$$h(t, \tau) = H\delta(t - \tau) = \text{response of } H \text{ at time } t \text{ to a unit impulse}$$
$$\text{applied at time } \tau \quad (3.13)$$

A causal system cannot respond prior to the instant of application of the input. Hence the impulse response of causal systems is subject to the restriction

$$h(t, \tau) = 0 \qquad \text{for } t < \tau \tag{3.14}$$

If the system is fixed (time-invariant), the response to an impulse applied at τ is identical in shape with that of an impulse applied at the origin of the time scale, but is delayed τ sec. Thus, in a time-invariant system, the impulse response depends only on the elapsed time between the instant τ of application of the impulse and the instant t of observation, so that†

$$h(t, \tau) = H\delta(t - \tau) = h(t - \tau) \tag{3.15}$$

Consequently, a time-invariant system is entirely characterized by the response to a single unit impulse, applied at any instant. Usually this instant is taken as the origin of the time scale, and the system is then characterized by

$$h(t) = H\delta(t) \tag{3.16}$$

† The statement "$h(t, \tau) = h(t - \tau)$" is intended to mean "$h(t, \tau)$ is a function of the difference $t - \tau$." The function h of the two arguments t and τ is clearly not the same as the resulting function of the single argument $t - \tau$, but it is convenient to use the same symbol h for both functions.

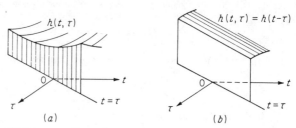

FIG. 3.8 Impulse response of causal systems.
(a) Arbitrary causal system; (b) fixed causal system.

The impulse response may be regarded as defining a surface in the (t, τ) plane. The requirement that $h(t, \tau) = 0$ for $t < \tau$ means that the surface has zero height on one side of the plane $t = \tau$ as shown in Fig. 3.8a. The requirement that $h(t, \tau) = h(t - \tau)$ means that the surface is cylindrical, with its generatrix parallel to the line $t = \tau$ in the (t, τ) plane, as in Fig. 3.8b.

STEP RESPONSE AND ITS PROPERTIES

Any excitation can be resolved into steps as well as impulses. When resolution into steps is employed, the system is appropriately characterized by its responses to unit steps applied at any time τ. Thus we define

$$a(t, \tau) = H\mu_1(t - \tau) = \text{response at time } t \text{ to a unit step applied at}$$
$$\text{time } \tau \quad (3.17)$$

If H is a causal system, then by the same reasoning used for the impulse response,

$$a(t, \tau) = 0 \qquad \text{for } t < \tau \tag{3.18}$$

and if H is a time-invariant system,

$$a(t, \tau) = a(t - \tau) \tag{3.19}$$

RELATION OF STEP RESPONSE TO IMPULSE RESPONSE

The impulse response $h(t, \tau)$ and the step response $a(t, \tau)$ are related in a simple manner. A unit step satisfies the relation

$$\mu_1(t - \tau) = \int_{-\infty}^{t} \delta(\lambda - \tau) \, d\lambda = \int_{-\infty}^{0} \delta(\lambda + t - \tau) \, d\lambda$$

From the definition of the unit-step response, we have

$$a(t, \tau) = H\mu_1(t - \tau) = H \int_{-\infty}^{0} \delta(\lambda + t - \tau) \, d\lambda$$

and in view of the additivity property of H, this becomes

$$a(t, \tau) = \int_{-\infty}^{0} H\delta(\lambda + t - \tau) \, d\lambda = \int_{-\infty}^{0} h(t, \tau - \lambda) \, d\lambda$$

With the change of variable $u = \tau - \lambda$, the step response may be written

$$a(t, \tau) = \int_{\tau}^{\infty} h(t, u) \, du \tag{3.20}$$

This is the desired relation.

For a causal system, the upper limit may be changed to t in view of (3.14), giving

$$a(t, \tau) = \int_{\tau}^{t} h(t, u) \, du \tag{3.21}$$

In the special case of a time-invariant system, (3.20) becomes

$$a(t) = \int_{0}^{\infty} h(t - u) \, du = \int_{-\infty}^{t} h(v) \, dv \tag{3.22}$$

and if H is both causal and time-invariant,

$$a(t) = \int_{0}^{t} h(v) \, dv$$

In order to obtain the impulse response in terms of the step response, we differentiate (3.20) with respect to τ, which gives

$$\frac{\partial a(t, \tau)}{\partial \tau} = -h(t, \tau) \tag{3.23}$$

For a time-invariant system, differentiation of (3.22) with respect to t gives

$$\frac{da(t)}{dt} = h(t) \tag{3.24}$$

Example 3.2 Pulse response of RC circuit In order to illustrate the use of the impulse response and step response in a very simple way, consider the problem of finding the response of the RC network of Fig. 3.9a to the voltage pulse of Fig. 3.9b.

The input pulse is resolved into two steps of height A, $A\mu_1(t)$ occurring at $t = 0$ and $-A\mu_1(t - 1)$ occurring at $t = 1$ (Fig. 3.9c). The response $a(t)$ of the unexcited RC circuit with $RC = 1$ to a unit step (i.e., a suddenly applied unit voltage) is easily found from the solution of the differential equation

$$\frac{da(t)}{dt} + a(t) = \mu_1(t) = 1 \qquad t > 0$$

with the initial condition

$$a(0) = 0$$

The solution is

$$a(t) = H\mu_1(t) = \begin{cases} 0 & t \leq 0 \\ 1 - e^{-t} & t > 0 \end{cases} \tag{3.25}$$

Then the response to the pulse $v_i(t)$ is

$$v_0(t) = Hv_i(t) = H[A\mu_1(t) - A\mu_1(t-1)] = AH\mu_1(t) - AH\mu_1(t-1)$$

by use of the additivity and homogeneity properties.   Thus, from (3.25), the output is

$$v_0(t) = \begin{cases} 0 & t \leq 0 \\ A(1 - e^{-t}) & 0 < t \leq 1 \\ A(1 - e^{-t}) - A(1 - e^{-(t-1)}) = A(1 - e^{-1})e^{-(t-1)} & t > 1 \end{cases}$$

as illustrated in Fig. 3.9d.

(a)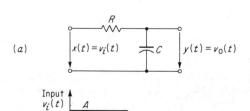

(b)

(c)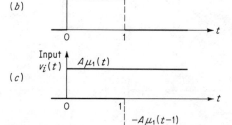

(d)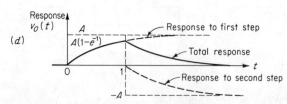

FIG. 3.9   *Pulse response of RC circuit.   (a) RC circuit* $[v_0(0) = 0,\ RC = 1]$; *(b) input; (c) input resolved into two steps; (d) response.*

The appropriate resolution of the input, determination of the system response to each input component, and composition of the responses as illustrated in this example are essentially the techniques underlying the entire time-domain method of analysis.

CALCULATION OF STEP RESPONSE AND IMPULSE RESPONSE

The responses $a(t, \tau)$ to a unit step and $h(t, \tau)$ to a unit impulse may be calculated from the differential equation(s) relating output and input when the input is made $\mu_1(t - \tau)$ (that is, 0 for $t < \tau$ and 1 for $t \geq \tau$) and $\delta(t - \tau)$, respectively. Example 3.2 illustrates the calculation of the step response for the simple case of a fixed first-order system.

The impulse response may be determined from the step response by the use of (3.23). Alternatively, the impulse response may be found directly without the use of impulses in the differential equations in the following manner. According to (2.16), the differential equations with the (single)

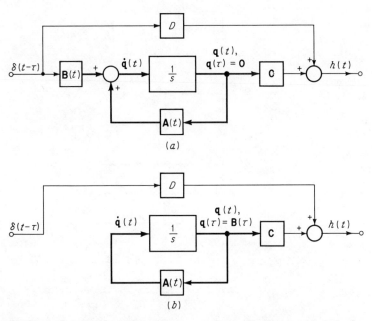

FIG. 3.10 Cable block diagrams for calculation of impulse response. (a) Impulse inputs to integrators, zero initial conditions; (b) no external inputs to integrators, nonzero initial conditions.

input $x(t) = \delta(t - \tau)$ are

$$\dot{\mathbf{q}}(t) = \mathbf{A}(t)\mathbf{q}(t) + \mathbf{B}(t)\delta(t - \tau) \qquad (3.26a)$$

and by definition of impulse response, the initial condition is

$$\mathbf{q}(\tau) = \mathbf{0} \qquad (3.26b)$$

The corresponding cable block diagram introduced in Fig. 2.6 is shown in Fig. 3.10a.   The impulse input may be replaced by zero input if the initial values of the outputs of all integrators are appropriately changed to the values which would have been caused by the impulse input, as shown in Fig. 3.10b.   Thus, for $t > \tau$, (3.26) may be replaced by

$$\dot{\mathbf{q}}(t) = \mathbf{A}(t)\mathbf{q}(t) \qquad (3.27a)$$
$$\mathbf{q}(\tau) = \mathbf{B}(\tau) \qquad (3.27b)$$

The desired impulse response is then computed in either case from

$$y(t) = \mathbf{C}(t)\mathbf{q}(t) + D(t)\delta(t - \tau) \qquad (3.28)$$

The last term in this equation accounts for any direct connections between input and output and must therefore be included regardless of whether (3.26) or (3.27) is used.

Example 3.3   Impulse response of RC circuit   The unit impulse response $h(t)$ of the circuit of Fig. 3.9a may be found by solving the differential equation

$$\frac{dh(t)}{dt} + h(t) = \delta(t) \qquad t > 0 \qquad (3.29)$$

with $h(0) = 0$.   In this case we may let the output $h(t)$ be the state variable $q(t)$ and thus, since $B = 1$, solve

$$\dot{q}(t) + q(t) = 0$$

with $q(0) = 1$.   The solution is

$$q(t) = h(t) = e^{-t} \qquad \text{for } t > 0$$

Since $h(t) = 0$ for $t < 0$, we may write

$$h(t) = e^{-t}\mu_1(t) \qquad \text{for all } t \qquad (3.30)$$

In order to verify that (3.30) satisfies (3.29), we differentiate (3.30) to find

$$\frac{dh(t)}{dt} = e^{-t}\delta(t) - e^{-t}\mu_1(t)$$

Thus

$$\frac{dh(t)}{dt} + h(t) = e^{-t}\delta(t) = \delta(t)$$

since at $t = 0$, when the impulse occurs, $e^{-t} = 1$.

We may also obtain (3.30) by using (3.24) with the step response given by (3.25):

$$a(t) = (1 - e^{-t})\mu_1(t)$$

Then

$$h(t) = \frac{da(t)}{dt} = (1 - e^{-t})\delta(t) + e^{-t}\mu_1(t) = e^{-t}\mu_1(t)$$

which agrees with the earlier result.

It should be noted that if several integrators are connected in cascade, as for example in Fig. 2.10, the input impulse should be replaced by a non-zero initial condition at the output of the first integrator only, since the impulse produces a step only there.   The outputs of the other integrators are initially zero.   (The integral of a step is a ramp with zero value at the time at which the step occurs, and all higher-order integrals of the step are zero at that instant.)

Example 3.4 Impulse response of a variable-mass system   An example of a variable-mass system is a barge used in the chemical treatment of a lake, carrying a load of chemicals.   The chemical is discharged into the lake water at a constant rate of k units of mass per second.   The barge has mass M_0 and speed v_0 at the time $t = 0$ at which the chemical treatment is begun.   Frictional forces may be assumed to be proportional to (α times) the barge speed v.   It is desired to determine the response (speed) of the barge to a unit force impulse applied at time $\tau > 0$.

The barge mass is

$$M(t) = M_0 - kt$$

The differential equation governing the barge motion is

$$\frac{d(Mv)}{dt} + \alpha v = f(t)$$

where $f(t)$ is the applied force.   This equation may be rewritten

$$M(t)\frac{dv}{dt} + \frac{dM(t)}{dt}v + \alpha v = f(t)$$

or

$$(M_0 - kt)\frac{dv}{dt} + (\alpha - k)v = f(t) \tag{3.31}$$

The time-varying coefficient in (3.31) is evidence of the fact that the barge is a time-varying system.

The speed in response to a unit impulse of force may be found by solving (3.31) with $f(t) = \delta(t - \tau)$ and $v(0) = v_0$. Alternatively, it may be obtained by solving

$$(M_0 - kt)\frac{dv}{dt} + (\alpha - k)v = 0 \tag{3.32}$$

with $v(0) = v_0$, evaluating $v(\tau) = v_1$, and then solving the same equation with $v(\tau) = v_1 + 1/M(\tau)$. The term $1/M(\tau)$ is the coefficient of $f(t)$ in (3.31) after the coefficient of dv/dt is made unity; $M(\tau) = M_0 - k\tau$.

The solution of (3.32) is obtained by separating the variables:

$$\frac{dv}{v} = -\frac{\alpha - k}{M_0 - kt} dt$$

We first integrate between $t = 0$, $v = v_0$ and $t = \tau$, $v = v_1$, obtaining

$$\log\frac{v_1}{v_0} = \frac{\alpha - k}{k} \log\frac{M_0 - k\tau}{M_0}$$

or

$$v_1 = v_0\left(\frac{M_0 - k\tau}{M_0}\right)^{(\alpha-k)/k}$$

Next we integrate the same equation between $[t = \tau,\ v = v_1 + 1/M(\tau)]$ and $[t, v]$ to yield

$$v(t) = \left(v_1 + \frac{1}{M(\tau)}\right)\left(\frac{M_0 - kt}{M_0 - k\tau}\right)^{(\alpha-k)/k}$$

or

$$v(t) = v_0\left(\frac{M_0 - kt}{M_0}\right)^{(\alpha-k)/k} + \frac{(M_0 - kt)^{(\alpha-k)/k}}{(M_0 - k\tau)^{\alpha/k}},\ t > \tau \tag{3.33}$$

This is the desired response; the second term is $h(t, \tau)$.

3.6 UNIT RESPONSE IN DISCRETE-TIME SYSTEMS: TRANSMISSION MATRIX

UNIT-FUNCTION RESPONSE

As in the case of continuous-time systems, the unit-function response of a discrete-time system is defined by

$$h(n, k) = H\delta(n - k) = \text{response at } n\text{th instant to a unit function}$$
$$\text{applied at } k\text{th instant} \tag{3.34}$$

For causal systems which cannot respond prior to the instant of application of an input,

$$h(n, k) = 0 \qquad n < k \qquad (3.35)$$

and for time-invariant systems,

$$h(n, k) = h(n - k) \qquad (3.36)$$

The unit response of a causal system may be arranged in an infinite matrix given by

$$\tilde{\mathbf{H}} = [h(n, k)] = \begin{bmatrix} h(0,0) & 0 & 0 & \cdots \\ h(1,0) & h(1,1) & 0 & \cdots \\ h(2,0) & h(2,1) & h(2,2) & \cdots \\ \cdots\cdots\cdots\cdots\cdots\cdots\cdots \end{bmatrix}$$

which we shall call the *transmission matrix* of H. Note that the kth column of $\tilde{\mathbf{H}}$ comprises the sequence of numbers obtained in response to a unit input applied at the kth instant.

If H is time-invariant, the transmission matrix is given by

$$\tilde{\mathbf{H}} = [h(n - k)] = \begin{bmatrix} h(0) & 0 & 0 & \cdots \\ h(1) & h(0) & 0 & \cdots \\ h(2) & h(1) & h(0) & \cdots \\ \cdots\cdots\cdots\cdots\cdots\cdots \end{bmatrix}$$

3.7 COMPOSITION IN CONTINUOUS-TIME SYSTEMS: SUPERPOSITION INTEGRALS

SUPERPOSITION INTEGRALS IN TERMS OF IMPULSE RESPONSE

It was shown in Sec. 3.3 that the resolution of the input $x(t)$ into a continuum of impulses is given by

$$x(t) = \int_{-\infty}^{\infty} x(\lambda)\delta(t - \lambda) \, d\lambda$$

If the output of H is $y(t)$,

$$y(t) = Hx(t) = H \int_{-\infty}^{\infty} x(\lambda)\delta(t - \lambda) \, d\lambda$$

Making use of the additivity property of H (assuming it is valid for integrals), we may write

$$y(t) = \int_{-\infty}^{\infty} H[x(\lambda)\delta(t - \lambda)] \, d\lambda$$

which, in view of the homogeneity property of H, becomes†

$$y(t) = \int_{-\infty}^{\infty} x(\lambda) H\delta(t - \lambda)\, d\lambda$$

Since $H\delta(t - \lambda) = h(t, \lambda)$, we have the following *superposition-integral* expression for the output:

$$y(t) = \int_{-\infty}^{\infty} x(\lambda)h(t, \lambda)\, d\lambda \qquad (3.37)$$

This integral may be thought of as the summation of the responses to impulses occurring at time λ and of strength $x(\lambda)\, d\lambda$ (representing the area of a vertical strip in Fig. 3.4), with λ varying over the entire range $(-\infty, \infty)$. It is assumed that the input $x(t)$ is such that the integral converges.

This superposition integral is frequently written in forms which reflect special properties of the system or input. If H is a causal system, the integration may be terminated at $\lambda = t$, since $h(t, \lambda) = 0$ for $\lambda > t$. Hence

$$y(t) = \int_{-\infty}^{t} x(\lambda)h(t, \lambda)\, d\lambda \qquad (3.38)$$

for causal systems. If the system is time-invariant, $h(t, \lambda) = h(t - \lambda)$ and

$$y(t) = \int_{-\infty}^{\infty} x(\lambda)h(t - \lambda)\, d\lambda \qquad (3.39)$$

With the change of variable $\xi = t - \lambda$, this equation may be written

$$y(t) = \int_{-\infty}^{\infty} x(t - \xi)h(\xi)\, d\xi \qquad (3.40)$$

It is customarily assumed that the input starts at $t = 0$; that is, $x(t) = 0$ for $t < 0$. In this case

$$y(t) = \int_{0}^{\infty} x(\lambda)h(t, \lambda)\, d\lambda \qquad (3.41)$$

For a causal time-invariant system whose input starts at $t = 0$ we have thus, from (3.39) and (3.40),

$$y(t) = \int_{0}^{t} x(\lambda)h(t - \lambda)\, d\lambda = \int_{0}^{t} x(t - \xi)h(\xi)\, d\xi \qquad (3.42)$$

Either of the two integrals in (3.42) is known as the *convolution integral*, or simply the *convolution* (folding, or *Faltung* in German) of $x(t)$ and $h(t)$.

† Note that $x(\lambda)$, the multiplier of $\delta(t - \lambda)$ in the integrand, is not a function of t.

The first integral is conveniently written as

$$\int_0^t x(\lambda)h(t - \lambda)\, d\lambda = x(t) \star h(t) \qquad \text{or} \qquad x \star h \qquad (3.43)$$

The derivation of (3.42) from either (3.39) or (3.40) shows that

$$x(t) \star h(t) = h(t) \star x(t) \qquad (3.44)$$

The integrals in (3.39) and (3.40) are sometimes also considered the convolution of $x(t)$ and $h(t)$; in case of ambiguity, the limits of integration are indicated with the star; for example,

$$\int_{-\infty}^{\infty} x(\lambda)h(t - \lambda)\, d\lambda = x(t) \underset{-\infty}{\overset{\infty}{\star}} h(t) \qquad (3.45)$$

The first expression for the response in (3.42) represents the sum of responses at the observation time t to impulses of strength $x(\lambda)\, d\lambda$ occurring at time λ (so that $t - \lambda$ sec has elapsed at the instant of observation t), with λ varying from the time of application of the input to the observation time t. The equivalent second expression in (3.42), on the other hand, may be thought of as the sum of responses to impulses occurring ξ sec before the observation time and of strength $x(t - \xi)\, d\xi$ (an element of the area under the excitation function at an instant ξ sec before the observation time). Thus, in this form, values of the integrand near $\xi = 0$ represent contributions to the total response due to recent values of the excitation, while its "older" values are included as ξ increases toward t. The change of variable $\xi = t - \lambda$ has essentially made the summation start at the observation instant, working toward the instant at which the impulse was applied.

SUPERPOSITION INTEGRALS IN TERMS OF STEP RESPONSE

The resolution of a signal $x(t)$ into steps is given by (3.7), here repeated:

$$x(t) = x(t_0)\mu_1(t - t_0) + \int_{t_0}^{\infty} \dot{x}(\xi)\mu_1(t - \xi)\, d\xi \qquad t \geq t_0$$

If $x(t)$ is discontinuous at t_0, either t_0^- or t_0^+ must be used consistently in the entire expression. If $x(t) = 0$ for $t < t_0$, the response of H to an input $x(t)$ is given by

$$y(t) = Hx(t) = H[x(t_0)\mu_1(t - t_0) + \int_{t_0}^{\infty} \dot{x}(\xi)\mu_1(t - \xi)\, d\xi]$$

Again making use of the additivity and homogeneity properties of H and recalling that $H\mu_1(t - \tau) = a(t, \tau)$, we obtain the following super-

position equation:

$$y(t) = x(t_0)a(t, t_0) + \int_{t_0}^{\infty} \dot{x}(\xi)a(t, \xi)\, d\xi \qquad t \geq t_0 \tag{3.46}$$

Note that (3.46) is valid only if $x(t) = 0$ for $t < t_0$ and the first term on the right-hand side may be omitted by using t_0^- as the lower limit on the integrals. If $\lim\limits_{t \to -\infty} x(t) = 0$, we may write, for all t,

$$y(t) = \int_{-\infty}^{\infty} \dot{x}(\xi)a(t, \xi)\, d\xi \tag{3.47}$$

It is assumed that (3.46) and (3.47) are used with inputs $x(t)$ which result in converging integrals.

This superposition equation may also be written in forms which reflect special characteristics of H or the input. Thus, for causal systems,

$$y(t) = \int_{-\infty}^{t} \dot{x}(\xi)a(t, \xi)\, d\xi \tag{3.48}$$

If H is time-invariant,

$$y(t) = \int_{-\infty}^{\infty} \dot{x}(\xi)a(t - \xi)\, d\xi \tag{3.49}$$

With the change of variable $\lambda = t - \xi$, this may be written

$$y(t) = \int_{-\infty}^{\infty} \dot{x}(t - \lambda)a(\lambda)\, d\lambda \tag{3.50}$$

Finally, if H is causal and time-invariant and if the input is assumed to begin at $t = 0$, then

$$y(t) = \int_{0}^{t} \dot{x}(\xi)a(t - \xi)\, d\xi = \int_{0}^{t} \dot{x}(t - \lambda)a(\lambda)\, d\lambda \tag{3.51}$$

These results may be interpreted in a manner similar to that discussed after (3.45). Now $\dot{x}(\xi)\, d\xi$ is the increment dx in the excitation at time ξ, and hence the required magnitude of the elementary step contributing to the excitation function at this instant.

Again it is convenient to write the response as the convolution of two functions:

$$y(t) = \dot{x}(t) \star a(t) = a(t) \star \dot{x}(t) \tag{3.52}$$

GRAPHICAL INTERPRETATION OF CONVOLUTION INTEGRALS

The integrals of (3.39), (3.40), and (3.42) and (3.49), (3.50), and (3.51) are examples of convolution integrals. These integrals have the generic

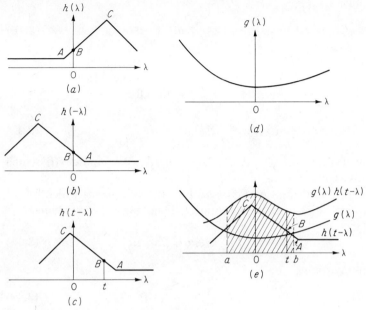

FIG. 3.11   *The convolution process.*

form

$$f(t) = \int_a^b g(\lambda)h(t - \lambda) \, d\lambda$$

and may be interpreted graphically as shown in Fig. 3.11. In part (a) of this figure, $h(\lambda)$ is shown. To obtain $h(-\lambda)$ the curve of (a) is "folded" about the axis, as shown in part (b). The graph of $h(t - \lambda)$ is obtained by shifting $h(-\lambda)$ to the right by an amount t. Then $h(t - \lambda)$ is multiplied by $g(\lambda)$ as shown in part (e). The required integral is the area under the curve $g(\lambda)h(t - \lambda)$ between $\lambda = a$ and $\lambda = b$. This process of folding, shifting, multiplying, and integrating gives $f(t)$ for a single value of t corresponding to the interval by which $h(-\lambda)$ has been shifted. The complete time function $f(t)$ is obtained by shifting $h(-\lambda)$ along the λ axis through the entire range of t and evaluating the integral of the product $h(\lambda)g(t - \lambda)$ for every value of t.

This graphical interpretation is frequently an important aid in the evaluation of the convolution integral, particularly when one or both of the functions in the integrand are discontinuous.

Example 3.5 Consider again the time-invariant linear system (RC network) of Example 3.2. The unit-step response $a(t)$ and input $x(t)$,

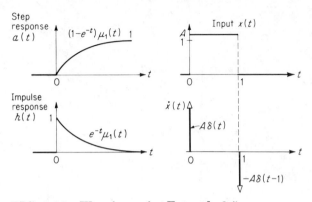

FIG. 3.12   Waveforms for Example 3.5.

together with the derivative $\dot{x}(t)$ of the input and the unit-impulse response $h(t)$ of the network, are shown in Fig. 3.12.

The response is computed by each of the four forms of the superposition integral, namely:

(1) $y(t) = \int_0^t x(\lambda)h(t - \lambda)\, d\lambda$

(2) $y(t) = \int_0^t x(t - \lambda)h(\lambda)\, d\lambda$

(3) $y(t) = \int_0^t \dot{x}(\lambda)a(t - \lambda)\, d\lambda$

(4) $y(t) = \int_0^t \dot{x}(t - \lambda)a(\lambda)\, d\lambda$

The computations are illustrated in Fig. 3.13 for two values of t, $0 < t < 1$ and $t > 1$. The calculation may be done graphically to yield the shaded areas, whose magnitude may then be evaluated by integration. Alternatively, the calculation may be made analytically, as shown in each case below the graphs. It is seen that each of the four computations yields

$$y(t) = \begin{cases} 0 & t \leq 0 \\ A(1 - e^{-t}) & 0 < t \leq 1 \\ A(1 - e^{-1})e^{-(t-1)} & 1 < t \end{cases}$$

The final response is illustrated in Fig. 3.14. The alternative method used in Example 3.2, in which $x(t)$ is written as the sum of two steps, gives the same result.

$(a)\ y(t) = \int_0^t x(\lambda) h(t-\lambda)\,d\lambda$

$h(t_1-\lambda) = [e^{-(t_1-\lambda)}]\mu_1(t_1-\lambda)$

$h(t_2-\lambda) = [e^{-(t_2-\lambda)}]\mu_1(t_2-\lambda)$

$x(\lambda)$ A

Integrand at $\lambda = t_1$
$x(\lambda)h(t_1-\lambda)$

Integrand at $\lambda = t_2$
$x(\lambda)h(t_2-\lambda)$

$t \le 0$ $\quad y(t) = 0$

$0 < t \le 1$ $\quad y(t) =$ shaded area ① $= \int_0^t Ae^{-(t-\lambda)}\,d\lambda$
$\qquad = A(1-e^{-t})$

$1 < t$ $\quad y(t) =$ shaded area ② $= \int_0^1 Ae^{-(t-\lambda)}\,d\lambda$
$\qquad = A(1-e^{-1})e^{-(t-1)}$

$(b)\ y(t) = \int_0^t x(t-\lambda) h(\lambda)\,d\lambda$

$x(t_2-\lambda)$ $x(t_1-\lambda)$ A

$h(\lambda) = e^{-\lambda}\mu_1(\lambda)$

Integrand at $\lambda = t_1$
$x(t_1-\lambda)h(\lambda)$

Integrand at $\lambda = t_2$
$x(t_2-\lambda)h(\lambda)$

$t \le 0$ $\quad y(t) = 0$

$0 < t \le 1$ $\quad y(t) =$ shaded area ① $= \int_0^t Ae^{-\lambda}\,d\lambda$
$\qquad = A(1-e^{-t})$

$1 < t$ $\quad y(t) =$ shaded area ② $= \int_{t-1}^t Ae^{-\lambda}\,d\lambda$
$\qquad = A(1-e^{-1})e^{-(t-1)}$

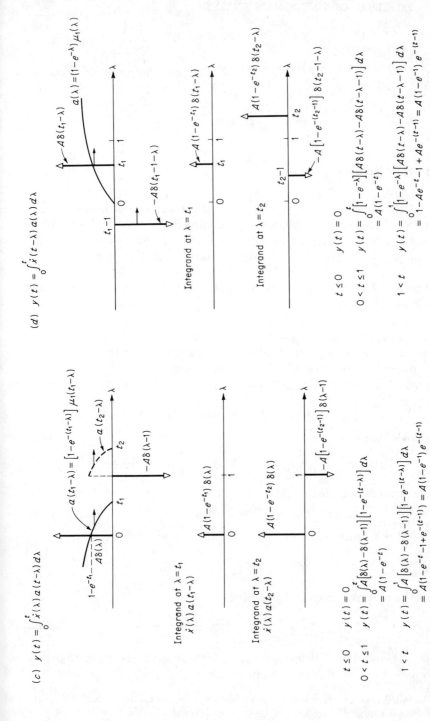

FIG. 3.13 *Computation of response for the four forms of the superposition integral of Example 3.5.*

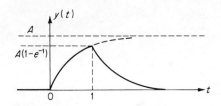

FIG. 3.14   Response in Example 3.5.

3.8 STABILITY

One of the reasons for developing methods of analysis of linear systems is the need to determine whether a system will be stable.   The subject of stability will be treated in detail in Chap. 11, but we may consider one simple and important criterion for stability at this point.

Definition 3.1   *A system is stable if and only if any bounded† input results in a bounded output.*

If the system has several inputs or outputs, the input or output vector is bounded if and only if each of its components is bounded.

In order to determine whether or not a system is stable according to this definition, consider the relation (3.37) between input and output:

$$y(t) = \int_{-\infty}^{\infty} x(\lambda)h(t, \lambda)\, d\lambda$$

It follows that

$$|y(t)| = \left| \int_{-\infty}^{\infty} x(\lambda)h(t, \lambda)\, d\lambda \right| \leq \int_{-\infty}^{\infty} |x(\lambda)|\, |h(t,\lambda)|\, d\lambda$$

If the input is bounded,

$$|x(t)| \leq M$$

where M is a finite constant.   Hence, in this case,

$$|y(t)| \leq M \int_{-\infty}^{\infty} |h(t, \lambda)|\, d\lambda$$

Thus the output is bounded provided

$$\int_{-\infty}^{\infty} |h(t, \lambda)|\, d\lambda < \infty \tag{3.53}$$

This is therefore a sufficient condition for stability.   To show that it is also necessary, we choose as input the function

---

† A bounded time function $u(t)$ is one which never becomes infinite; i.e., there exists a positive constant M such that $|u(t)| \leq M < \infty$ for all t.

$$x(\tau) = \text{sgn } h(t, \tau) = \begin{cases} +1 & \text{if } h(t, \tau) > 0 \\ 0 & \text{if } h(t, \tau) = 0 \\ -1 & \text{if } h(t, \tau) < 0 \end{cases}$$

For this input we have, for any fixed value of t,

$$|y(t)| = \left| \int_{-\infty}^{\infty} |h(t, \lambda)| \, d\lambda \right| = \int_{-\infty}^{\infty} |h(t, \lambda)| \, d\lambda$$

since the integrand is now always nonnegative. Thus the output will be unbounded if (3.53) is not satisfied, which shows that (3.53) is also necessary for stability.

Example 3.6 An integrator is unstable since

$$h(t, \tau) = H\delta(t - \tau) = \int_{-\infty}^{t} \delta(\lambda - \tau) \, d\tau = \mu_1(t - \tau)$$

and (3.53) is thus not satisfied. If the system integrates over a finite interval T preceding the instant of observation, however,

$$h(t, \tau) = \int_{t-T}^{t} \delta(\lambda - \tau) \, d\lambda = \begin{cases} 0 & \text{if } \tau < t - T \\ 1 & \text{if } t - T < \tau < t \\ 0 & \text{if } \tau > t \end{cases}$$

and the system is stable since (3.53) is satisfied.

3.9 COMPOSITION IN DISCRETE-TIME SYSTEMS: SUPERPOSITION SUMMATIONS

If we employ the resolution of the input $x(n)$ into unit functions and make use of additivity and homogeneity, we obtain, as in the case of continuous-time systems,

$$y(n) = Hx(n) = H \sum_{k=-\infty}^{\infty} x(k)\delta(n - k) = \sum_{k=-\infty}^{\infty} x(k)H\delta(n - k)$$

$$= \sum_{k=-\infty}^{\infty} x(k)h(n, k) \qquad (3.54)$$

This relation is the discrete counterpart of the superposition integral (3.37) and will be called the *superposition summation*. If H is a causal

system, the upper limit on (3.54) may be changed from ∞ to n by virtue of (3.35); hence

$$y(n) = \sum_{k=-\infty}^{n} x(k)h(n, k) \tag{3.55}$$

If H is time-invariant,

$$y(n) = \sum_{k=-\infty}^{\infty} x(k)h(n - k) \tag{3.56}$$

The summation index k plays the same role as a variable of integration ("dummy variable"), and we may make a change from k to a new index l by defining $l = n - k$. Then (3.56) becomes

$$y(n) = \sum_{l=-\infty}^{\infty} x(n - l)h(l) \tag{3.57}$$

If the system is both causal and time-invariant and if the input starts at $n = 0$, we may write

$$y(n) = \sum_{k=0}^{n} x(k)h(n - k) = \sum_{l=0}^{n} x(n - l)h(l) \tag{3.58}$$

The form (3.58) is called a *convolution summation*, since it involves the same operations (folding, translating, multiplying, and summing) as used in evaluating a convolution integral. Both forms in (3.58) are written in simplified notation

$$y(n) = x(n) \star h(n) \tag{3.59}$$

Alternatively, the resolution of the input $x(n)$ into steps may be employed. The derivation is left as an exercise (Prob. 3.8).

The input-output relation for a discrete-time system may also be formulated in terms of the transmission matrix $\tilde{H}$ previously defined. We first define input and output *signal vectors*, respectively, by

$$\begin{aligned}\tilde{x} &= \text{col } [x(0), x(1), x(2), \ldots] \\ \tilde{y} &= \text{col } [y(0), y(1), y(2), \ldots]\end{aligned} \tag{3.60}$$

where col [   ] denotes a column vector. Note that the components of a signal vector are values of one signal at specified instants of time, while the components of the input and output vectors of Sec. 1.1 are signals or time functions. If the input is considered to start at $n = 0$, (3.54) becomes

$$y(n) = \sum_{k=0}^{\infty} x(k)h(n, k) \tag{3.61}$$

In terms of the transmission matrix $\tilde{H}$, this may be written

$$\tilde{y} = \tilde{H}\tilde{x} \tag{3.62}$$

3.10   SYSTEMS WITH MULTIPLE INPUTS AND OUTPUTS

When a linear system has multiple inputs and outputs, each output is related to every input through a superposition integral (or summation). Thus the output y_i due to one input x_j is

$$y_i(t) = \int_{-\infty}^{\infty} h_{ij}(t, \lambda)x_j(\lambda) \, d\lambda \qquad i = 1, 2, \ldots, m$$

where $h_{ij}(t, \tau)$ is the response at output i at time t to a unit impulse applied to input j at time τ. By linearity, the total output y_i due to all inputs is

$$y_i(t) = \sum_{j=1}^{n} \int_{-\infty}^{\infty} h_{ij}(t, \lambda)x_j(\lambda) \, d\lambda \qquad i = 1, 2, \ldots, m \qquad (3.63)$$

We may thus characterize a continuous-time system by means of a matrix $\mathbf{H}(t, \tau)$ of impulse responses,

$$\mathbf{H}(t, \tau) = [h_{ij}(t, \tau)] \qquad (3.64)$$

so that

$$\mathbf{y}(t) = \int_{-\infty}^{\infty} \mathbf{H}(t, \lambda)\mathbf{x}(\lambda) \, d\lambda \qquad (3.65)$$

Similarly, a discrete-time system may be characterized by a matrix of unit responses $\mathbf{H}(n, k)$ so that the output may be written

$$\mathbf{y}(n) = \sum_{k=-\infty}^{\infty} \mathbf{H}(n, k)\mathbf{x}(k) \qquad (3.66)$$

In this expression

$$\mathbf{H}(n, k) = [h_{ij}(n, k)] \qquad (3.67)$$

and $h_{ij}(n, k)$ is the response at output i at the nth instant to a unit function applied to input j at the kth instant.

PROBLEMS

3.1   Show that the following functions have $\delta(t)$ as their limit as $a \to \infty$.

(a) $f(t) = \sqrt{\dfrac{a}{\pi}} \, e^{-at^2}$.

(b) $f(t) = \dfrac{a}{2} [\mu_1(at + 1) - \mu_1(at - 1)]$.

(c) $f(t) = \dfrac{1}{\pi} \dfrac{a}{1 + a^2t^2}$.

3.2   Show that the following functions have a unit step $\mu_1(t)$ as their limit as $a \to \infty$.

(a) $\dfrac{1}{2} + \dfrac{1}{\pi} \tan^{-1} at.$

(b) $\dfrac{1}{\sqrt{\pi}} \displaystyle\int_{-at}^{\infty} e^{-u^2}\, du.$

(c) $\dfrac{1}{\pi} \displaystyle\int_{-\infty}^{at} \dfrac{\sin u}{u}\, du.$

(d) $2^{-e^{-at}}$

3.3   Derive the relation

$$f(t) = \int_{-\infty}^{\infty} \delta(t - \lambda) f(\lambda)\, d\lambda$$

from the definition of the unit impulse.

3.4   Derive the relation

$$f(t) = \int_{0}^{\infty} f(\xi)\mu_1(t - \xi)\, d\xi \qquad f(t) = 0 \text{ for } t < 0$$

from (3.5), using integration by parts.

3.5   Write the decomposition into unit steps of the function $f(t)$ shown in Fig. P 3.5. Verify that your answer is correct by evaluating the expression for each time range.

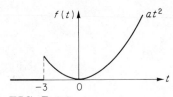

FIG. P 3.5

3.6   For the function shown in Fig. P 3.6:

(a) Find an analytic expression in terms of elementary functions.

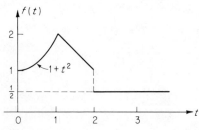

FIG. P 3.6

(b) Sketch the derivative function and find an analytic expression for it.

(c) Sketch the integral function and find an analytic expression for it.

3.7 Show that the resolution of a signal $x(t)$ into exponentials $e^{-t}\mu_1(t)$ is given by

$$x(t) = \int_{-\infty}^{\infty} [x(\lambda) + \dot{x}(\lambda)]e^{-(t-\lambda)}\mu_1(t - \lambda)\, d\lambda$$

Hint: Let $x(t) = \int_{-\infty}^{\infty} g(\lambda)e^{-(t-\lambda)}\mu_1(t - \lambda)\, d\lambda$ and solve the integral equation for $g(\lambda)$.

3.8 Show that the resolution of a discrete-time function into sampled unit steps, defined by (3.11), is given by

$$f(n) = f(n_0)\mu_1(n - n_0) + \sum_{k=n_0+1}^{\infty} \nabla f(k)\mu_1(n - k)$$

for $n \geq n_0$, where $\nabla f(n) = f(n) - f(n - 1)$ is the first backward difference of $f(n)$.

3.9 Find the response of each of the networks of Fig. P 3.9 to a unit ramp, a unit step, and a unit impulse.

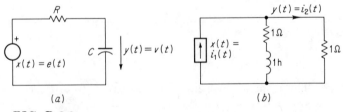

(a)   (b)

FIG. P 3.9

3.10 In practice the impulse response of a system is found by applying a narrow but finite pulse to the system. For the network shown in Fig. P 3.10, let $x(t)$ be a voltage pulse of width τ and height $1/\tau$ occurring at $t = 0$. Sketch the output $y(t)$ for

(a) $\tau = 10RC$.   (b) $\tau = RC$.   (c) $\tau = 0.10RC$.

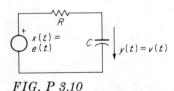

FIG. P 3.10

For which of these cases is the response a good approximation to the impulse response?

3.11   The response of a fixed linear system to a unit impulse is

$$h(t) = \mu_1(t) - \mu_1(t - 1)$$

as shown in Fig. P 3.11.

(a) Determine the response to the input $x(t)$ shown.
(b) Determine the response to the input $z(t)$ shown.

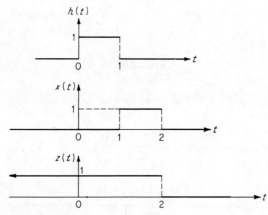

FIG. P 3.11

3.12   The response of a linear fixed system to $\mu_1(t)$, a unit step applied at $t = 0$, is $a(t) = te^{-t}\mu_1(t)$.

(a) Find the response $y(t)$ of this system to the function $x(t)$ shown in Fig. P 3.12.
(b) Find the impulse response $h(t) = H\delta(t)$.

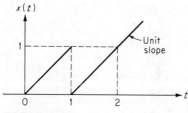

FIG. P 3.12

3.13 A linear fixed system has the response to a unit impulse applied at $t = 0$ given by $h(t) = \mu_1(t - 1) - \mu_1(t - 2)$. Find the response of this system to the input $x(t)$ shown in Fig. P 3.13.

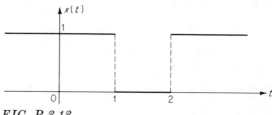

FIG. P 3.13

3.14 The impulse response of a linear fixed system is $te^{-t}\mu_1(t)$. Without using the superposition integral, find the response of the system to the input $x(t) = \mu_1(t) - \mu_1(t - 1)$.

3.15 A system is characterized by the equations

$$\dot{q}_1 = q_2$$
$$\dot{q}_2 = -6q_1 - 5q_2 + x$$
$$y = q_1 + x$$

where x and y are the input and output time functions, respectively, and q_1, q_2 are state variables.

(a) Determine the impulse response of the system.

(b) Determine the step response of the system and use it to verify the answer to part a.

3.16 Determine the step and impulse responses of the system

$$\ddot{y} + 5\dot{y} + y = x(t)$$

3.17 The response of a time-varying system at time t to a unit step applied at time τ is

$$a(t, \tau) = \tau(1 - e^{-t})\mu_1(t - \tau)$$

where μ_1 is the unit-step function. Find the unit-impulse response $h(t, \tau)$.

3.18 A linear time-variable system is described by the differential equation

$$\frac{dy}{dt} + \frac{y}{t} = x(t)$$

(a) Draw a block diagram of the system.

(b) Find the step response of the system.

3.19   The response $a(n)$ of a discrete-time system to a unit step $\mu_1(n)$ is shown in Fig. P 3.19.   Find the response to the input $x(n)$.

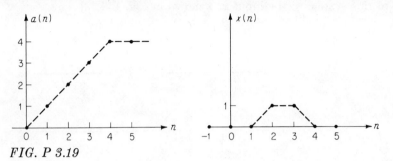

FIG. P 3.19

3.20   The impulse response of a linear fixed system is $\mu_1(t) - \mu_1(t-2)$. Find the response to the input $x(t) = \mu_2(t) - \mu_2(t-1) - \mu_1(t-1)$ by each of the four forms of the superposition integral.

3.21   The impulse response $h(t)$ of a linear fixed system is $e^{-(t-1)}\mu_1(t-1)$. Find the response to $x(t) = e^{-t}\mu_1(t)$ by each of the four forms of the superposition integral.

3.22   The impulse response of a fixed linear system is given by

$$h(t) = (e^{-t} - e^{-2t})\mu_1(t)$$

(*a*) Find the unit-step response of the system.

(*b*) Find the response to an input $x(t) = e^{-t}\mu_1(t)$ by using an appropriate form of the superposition integral.

3.23   The circuit shown in Fig. P 3.23 is approximately analogous to a loudspeaker in which the cone velocity is proportional to the voltage $y(t)$ shown.

(*a*) Find $y(t)$ if the input voltage $x(t)$ is given by

(1) $x(t) = \mu_1(t)$.
(2) $x(t) = \delta(t)$.

(*b*) Using the convolution integral, find $y(t)$ if

(1) $x(t) = \mu_1(t)e^{-t}$.
(2) $x(t) = \mu_1(t)e^{-10t}$.
(3) $x(t) = \mu_1(t)e^{-t}\cos 10t$.

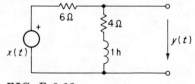

FIG. P 3.23

3.24 Find $y(t)$ for the circuit of Fig. P 3.23 for the following inputs:

(a) $\mu_1(t) \cos 100t$.
(b) $[\mu_1(t-2) - \mu_1(t-3)]e^{-(t-2)}$.
(c) Fig. P 3.24c.

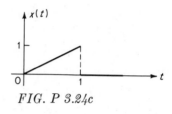

FIG. P 3.24c

3.25 Find the response $y(t)$ of the network shown in Fig. P 3.25, using two forms of the superposition integral.

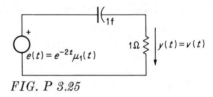

FIG. P 3.25

3.26 A two-dimensional impulse function $\delta(x, y)$ may be defined in a manner analogous to that used for $\delta(t)$:

$$\delta(x, y) = 0 \qquad \text{if } x \neq 0 \text{ or } y \neq 0$$

$$\int_{-\infty}^{\infty} \int_{-\infty}^{\infty} \delta(\xi, \eta) \, d\xi \, d\eta = 1$$

If the response of a two-dimensional system to $\delta(x, y)$ is $h(x, y)$, what is the response to an input $f(x, y)$?

3.27 Two causal networks H_1 and H_2 are connected in cascade. H_1 is fixed and has impulse response $h(t)$. H_2 is instantaneous and has the gain shown in Fig. P 3.27.

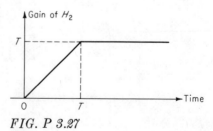

FIG. P 3.27

(a) Find the response of the cascade to a unit impulse applied at time t_0 if H_2 is followed by H_1.

(b) Determine the response of the cascade to an input $x(t)$ if H_1 is followed by H_2.

3.28   Two *fixed* linear systems are connected in cascade, as shown in Fig. P 3.28a. If the two systems are interchanged as in Fig. P 3.28b, show that the response of the overall system to any input is unchanged.

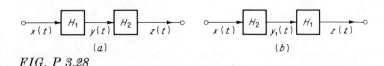

(a)   (b)

FIG. P 3.28

3.29   Given two systems H_1 and H_2, where

$$H_1 x(t) = \int_{-\infty}^{t} x(\lambda)\, d\lambda \qquad \text{and} \qquad H_2 x(t) = t x(t)$$

Find the impulse response $h(t, \lambda)$ of the overall system formed by cascading H_1 and H_2:

(a) With H_1 followed by H_2, as in Fig. P 3.28a.
(b) With H_2 followed by H_1, as in Fig. P 3.28b.

3.30   Consider the system shown in Fig. P 3.30, with zero initial conditions. The time-varying amplifiers have a gain of t.

(a) Calculate the impulse response of this system.
(b) Is the system fixed or time-varying?
(c) Calculate the response of the system to the following input:

$$x(t) = \begin{cases} 1 & 0 < t < 2 \\ 0 & \text{otherwise} \end{cases}$$

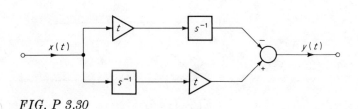

FIG. P 3.30

3.31   Show that the input-output relation for a discrete-time system in terms of the step response is given by

$$y(n) = x(n_0)a(n, n_0) + \sum_{k=n_0+1}^{\infty} a(n, k)\, \nabla x(k)$$

where $a(n, k) = H\mu_1(n, k)$, $\nabla x(k) = x(k) - x(k - 1)$, and

$$x(n) = 0 \text{ for } n < n_0$$

3.32   Obtain the impulse-response matrix $\mathbf{H}(t, \tau)$ of the system shown in Fig. P 3.32.

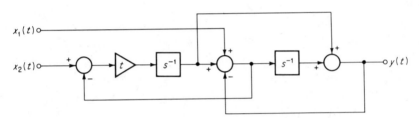

FIG. P 3.32

3.33   Consider the following general integral transform:

$$X(\lambda) = \int_{-\infty}^{\infty} h(\lambda, t)x(t)\, dt$$

and its inverse transform

$$x(t) = \int_{-\infty}^{\infty} k(t, \lambda)X(\lambda)\, d\lambda$$

We may regard $X(\lambda)$ as the response at time λ of a linear system H (possibly time-varying and not causal) to the input $x(t)$ when the impulse response of the system is $h(\lambda, t)$. Then the inverse transform is the response of the inverse linear system K, having an impulse response $k(t, \lambda)$, to $X(\lambda)$.

(a) Use this interpretation to obtain an integral equation relating $h(\lambda, t)$ and $k(t, \lambda)$.

(b) If $h(\lambda, t) = e^{-j\lambda t}$, then the first equation in this problem is the Fourier transform of $x(t)$. Show that the integral equation obtained in part (a) is satisfied in this case.

CHAPTER FOUR

TIME-DOMAIN ANALYSIS

OF LUMPED SYSTEMS

4.1 INTRODUCTION

In the previous chapter it was shown that the response of a linear continuous-time system can be expressed, by use of a superposition integral, as the convolution of the impulse response with the input. (In discrete-time systems, the response is given as a superposition summation.)

This chapter deals with a special class of linear systems: those which can be characterized by ordinary differential or difference equations. Systems of this type are the most commonly encountered in practice, and it is fortunate that a fairly comprehensive theory of such systems has been developed. The principal result of this theory is that the impulse (or unit) response of such systems is directly expressible in terms of the solutions of the unforced (homogeneous) differential or difference equations describing the system. Thus the problem of determining the response to any input is reduced to finding the solution of an unforced system.

For time-invariant systems an explicit expression for the solution of the homogeneous system is readily obtained. In time-varying systems, however, the solution of the homogeneous system is usually difficult to obtain in explicit form.

4.2 SOLUTION OF DIFFERENTIAL EQUATIONS OF CONTINUOUS-TIME SYSTEMS: FUNDAMENTAL MATRIX

FIXED SYSTEMS

The differential equations governing the behavior of a fixed continuous-time system as given in Chap. 2, in vector-matrix form, are

$$\dot{\mathbf{q}}(t) = \mathbf{A}\mathbf{q}(t) + \mathbf{B}\mathbf{x}(t) \tag{4.1}$$
$$\mathbf{y}(t) = \mathbf{C}\mathbf{q}(t) + \mathbf{D}\mathbf{x}(t) \tag{4.2}$$

where $\mathbf{A}$, $\mathbf{B}$, $\mathbf{C}$, and $\mathbf{D}$ are constant matrices. We first consider the unforced (homogeneous) form of (4.1),

$$\dot{\mathbf{q}}(t) = \mathbf{A}\mathbf{q}(t) \tag{4.3}$$

It will be shown that the solution to this system is

$$\mathbf{q}(t) = e^{\mathbf{A}(t-t_0)}\mathbf{q}(t_0) = \mathbf{\Phi}(t - t_0)\mathbf{q}(t_0) \tag{4.4}$$

where $\mathbf{q}(t_0)$ denotes the value of $\mathbf{q}(t)$ at $t = t_0$, and $\mathbf{\Phi}(t) = e^{\mathbf{A}t}$ is a matrix defined by the series

$$e^{\mathbf{A}t} = \mathbf{I} + \mathbf{A}t + \mathbf{A}^2 \frac{t^2}{2!} + \mathbf{A}^3 \frac{t^3}{3!} + \cdots \tag{4.5}$$

and is called the *fundamental matrix*† of the system. This series can be shown to converge for all finite t and any $\mathbf{A}$. To demonstrate that (4.4) satisfies (4.3), we evaluate the time derivative of $e^{\mathbf{A}(t-t_0)}\mathbf{q}(t_0)$. According

† In the mathematical literature any matrix $\mathbf{P}(t)$ which satisfies the matrix differential equation $\dot{\mathbf{P}}(t) = \mathbf{A}\mathbf{P}(t)$ is called a fundamental matrix. The fundamental matrix defined above is the solution to this matrix differential equation with $\mathbf{P}(0) = \mathbf{I}$. See E. A. Coddington and N. Levinson, "Theory of Ordinary Differential Equations," chap. 3, McGraw-Hill Book Company, New York, 1955, or R. Bellman, "Introduction to Matrix Analysis," chaps. 6 and 11, McGraw-Hill Book Company, New York, 1960. In some of the engineering literature $\mathbf{\Phi}(t - t_0)$ is called the *transition* matrix, since it determines the transition from $\mathbf{q}(t_0)$ to $\mathbf{q}(t)$. In earlier literature $\mathbf{\Phi}(t - t_0)$ is often called the *matrizant* or *matricant*.

to (4.5), this is

$$\frac{d}{dt} e^{\mathbf{A}(t-t_0)}\mathbf{q}(t_0) = \frac{d}{d(t-t_0)} e^{\mathbf{A}(t-t_0)}\mathbf{q}(t_0)$$

$$= \left[\mathbf{A} + \mathbf{A}^2(t-t_0) + \mathbf{A}^3\frac{(t-t_0)^2}{2!} + \cdots\right]\mathbf{q}(t_0)$$

$$= \mathbf{A}[e^{\mathbf{A}(t-t_0)}\mathbf{q}(t_0)]$$

Thus (4.4) satisfies the differential equation (4.3) subject to the given initial condition. Note that $\boldsymbol{\Phi}(0) = e^{\mathbf{A}0} = \mathbf{I}$, the $k \times k$ identity matrix.

Note that $\boldsymbol{\Phi}(t - t_0)$ in (4.4) is a matrix which operates on $\mathbf{q}(t_0)$ to give $\mathbf{q}(t)$. It is not necessary that $t > t_0$; the proof given above that $\boldsymbol{\Phi}(t - t_0)$ $\mathbf{q}(t_0)$ satisfies the differential equation (4.3) is valid for $t < t_0$. Thus $\boldsymbol{\Phi}(t - t_0)$ permits calculation of the state vector at time instants before t_0, provided that the system is governed by the differential equation (4.3) during the entire interval defined by t and t_0.

In order to obtain the complete solution to (4.1) we employ the method of *variation of the parameter*. We assume that the solution is

$$\mathbf{q}(t) = e^{\mathbf{A}(t-t_0)}\mathbf{f}(t) \tag{4.6}$$

where $\mathbf{f}(t)$ is to be determined. Then

$$\dot{\mathbf{q}}(t) = \mathbf{A}e^{\mathbf{A}(t-t_0)}\mathbf{f}(t) + e^{\mathbf{A}(t-t_0)}\dot{\mathbf{f}}(t)$$

Substitution of this derivative into (4.1) gives

$$e^{\mathbf{A}(t-t_0)}\dot{\mathbf{f}}(t) = \mathbf{B}\mathbf{x}(t)$$

and premultiplying by $e^{-\mathbf{A}(t-t_0)}$, we obtain

$$\dot{\mathbf{f}}(t) = e^{-\mathbf{A}(t-t_0)}\mathbf{B}\mathbf{x}(t)$$

Integration from $-\infty$ to t (assuming that $\mathbf{f}(-\infty) = \mathbf{0}$) results in

$$\mathbf{f}(t) = \int_{-\infty}^{t} e^{-\mathbf{A}(\lambda-t_0)}\mathbf{B}\mathbf{x}(\lambda)\, d\lambda$$

so that (4.6) gives†

$$\mathbf{q}(t) = e^{\mathbf{A}(t-t_0)}\int_{-\infty}^{t} e^{-\mathbf{A}(\lambda-t_0)}\mathbf{B}\mathbf{x}(\lambda)\, d\lambda$$

$$= e^{\mathbf{A}(t-t_0)}\int_{-\infty}^{t_0} e^{-\mathbf{A}(\lambda-t_0)}\mathbf{B}\mathbf{x}(\lambda)\, d\lambda + \int_{t_0}^{t} e^{\mathbf{A}(t-\lambda)}\mathbf{B}\mathbf{x}(\lambda)\, d\lambda \tag{4.7}$$

Evaluating (4.7) for $t = t_0$, we obtain the initial state in terms of the

† The relation $e^{(u+v)\mathbf{A}} = e^{u\mathbf{A}}e^{v\mathbf{A}}$ is used here; it may be proved directly from the definition (4.5).

input from $-\infty$ to t_0; namely,

$$\mathbf{q}(t_0) = \int_{-\infty}^{t_0} e^{-\mathbf{A}(\lambda - t_0)} \mathbf{B} \mathbf{x}(\lambda) \, d\lambda$$

Hence (4.7) becomes

$$\mathbf{q}(t) = e^{\mathbf{A}(t - t_0)} \mathbf{q}(t_0) + \int_{t_0}^{t} e^{\mathbf{A}(t - \lambda)} \mathbf{B} \mathbf{x}(\lambda) \, d\lambda$$
$$= \mathbf{\Phi}(t - t_0) \mathbf{q}(t_0) + \int_{t_0}^{t} \mathbf{\Phi}(t - \lambda) \mathbf{B} \mathbf{x}(\lambda) \, d\lambda \qquad (4.8)$$

In fixed systems it is usually convenient to take $t_0 = 0$; in this case the fundamental matrix is $\mathbf{\Phi}(t)$.

Example 4.1   Electric network   Consider the network used in Fig. 2.1, which is shown again in Fig. 4.1 for convenience.   The equations for this network in normal form are

$$\begin{bmatrix} \dot{i}_1 \\ \dot{v}_2 \end{bmatrix} = \begin{bmatrix} 0 & -\dfrac{1}{L} \\ \dfrac{1}{C} & -\dfrac{1}{RC} \end{bmatrix} \begin{bmatrix} i_1 \\ v_2 \end{bmatrix} + \begin{bmatrix} \dfrac{1}{L} & -\dfrac{1}{L} \\ 0 & -\dfrac{1}{RC} \end{bmatrix} \begin{bmatrix} e_1 \\ e_2 \end{bmatrix}$$

and

$$\begin{bmatrix} i_1 \\ i_2 \end{bmatrix} = \begin{bmatrix} 1 & 0 \\ 1 & -\dfrac{1}{R} \end{bmatrix} \begin{bmatrix} i_1 \\ v_2 \end{bmatrix} + \begin{bmatrix} 0 & 0 \\ 0 & -\dfrac{1}{R} \end{bmatrix} \begin{bmatrix} e_1 \\ e_2 \end{bmatrix}$$

Substituting the numerical values $R = \frac{1}{3}$, $L = \frac{1}{2}$, $C = 1$, we obtain the

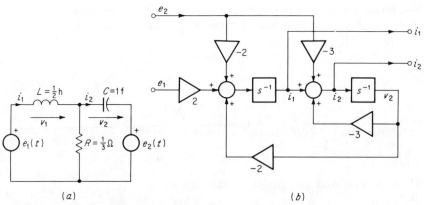

FIG. 4.1   Example 4.1.   (a) Network; (b) analog-computer diagram.

following matrices:

$$\mathbf{A} = \begin{bmatrix} 0 & -2 \\ 1 & -3 \end{bmatrix} \qquad \mathbf{B} = \begin{bmatrix} 2 & -2 \\ 0 & -3 \end{bmatrix}$$

$$\mathbf{C} = \begin{bmatrix} 1 & 0 \\ 1 & -3 \end{bmatrix} \qquad \mathbf{D} = \begin{bmatrix} 0 & 0 \\ 0 & -3 \end{bmatrix}$$

and the analog-computer diagram of Fig. 4.1b.

The fundamental matrix $\mathbf{\Phi}(t) = e^{\mathbf{A}t}$ may be computed by summation of the series

$$e^{\mathbf{A}t} = \mathbf{I} + \mathbf{A}t + \mathbf{A}^2 \frac{t^2}{2!} + \cdots$$

For the matrix $\mathbf{A}$ of this system we find

$$\mathbf{A}^2 = \begin{bmatrix} -2 & 6 \\ -3 & 7 \end{bmatrix} \qquad \mathbf{A}^3 = \begin{bmatrix} 6 & -14 \\ 7 & -15 \end{bmatrix} \qquad \cdots$$

Hence

$$\mathbf{\Phi}(t) = e^{\mathbf{A}t}$$

$$= \begin{bmatrix} 1 + 0t - 2\dfrac{t^2}{2!} + 6\dfrac{t^3}{3!} - \cdots & 0 - 2t + 6\dfrac{t^2}{2!} - 14\dfrac{t^3}{3!} + \cdots \\[2ex] 0 + t - 3\dfrac{t^2}{2!} + 7\dfrac{t^3}{3!} + \cdots & 1 - 3t + 7\dfrac{t^2}{2!} - 15\dfrac{t^3}{3!} + \cdots \end{bmatrix}$$

If the calculation is continued, the series turn out to be the expansions for the sums of two exponentials, and the matrix becomes

$$\mathbf{\Phi}(t) = \begin{bmatrix} -e^{-2t} + 2e^{-t} & 2e^{-2t} - 2e^{-t} \\ -e^{-2t} + e^{-t} & 2e^{-2t} - e^{-t} \end{bmatrix}$$

Alternatively, the fundamental matrix may be calculated by solution of the homogeneous differential equation by classical methods as follows. We start with

$$\dot{\mathbf{q}} = \mathbf{A}\mathbf{q}$$

i.e.,

$$\dot{q}_1 = -2q_2 \tag{4.9}$$
$$\dot{q}_2 = q_1 - 3q_2 \tag{4.10}$$

Combining (4.9) and (4.10) into a single second-order equation, we obtain

$$\ddot{q}_1 + 3\dot{q}_1 + 2q_1 = 0$$

whose general solution, by elementary methods, is

$$q_1(t) = C_1 e^{-2t} + C_2 e^{-t} \tag{4.11}$$

where C_1 and C_2 are arbitrary constants. Using (4.9), we find

$$q_2(t) = C_1 e^{-2t} + \frac{C_2}{2} e^{-t} \tag{4.12}$$

We wish to determine the matrix which multiplies the initial-state vector $\mathbf{q}(0)$ to give $\mathbf{q}(t)$. Hence we must express C_1 and C_2 in terms of the components of $\mathbf{q}(0)$. From (4.11) and (4.12) we obtain

$$C_1 + C_2 = q_1(0)$$
$$C_1 + \frac{C_2}{2} = q_2(0)$$

from which

$$C_1 = -q_1(0) + 2q_2(0) \tag{4.13}$$
$$C_2 = 2q_1(0) - 2q_2(0) \tag{4.14}$$

Substitution of (4.13) and (4.14) into (4.11) and (4.12) gives

$$\begin{bmatrix} q_1(t) \\ q_2(t) \end{bmatrix} = \begin{bmatrix} -e^{-2t} + 2e^{-t} & 2e^{-2t} - 2e^{-t} \\ -e^{-2t} + e^{-t} & 2e^{-2t} - e^{-t} \end{bmatrix} \begin{bmatrix} q_1(0) \\ q_2(0) \end{bmatrix} \tag{4.15}$$

Since $\mathbf{q}(t) = \boldsymbol{\Phi}(t)\mathbf{q}(0)$, the square matrix in (4.15) is $\boldsymbol{\Phi}(t)$. This result agrees with the fundamental matrix computed by summation of the series for the elements of $e^{\mathbf{A}t}$.

Example 4.2   Motion of particle perturbed from circular orbit   In Example 2.9 we determined that the motion of a particle perturbed from a circular orbit in a central inverse-square-law field is governed by the linear differential equations

$$\dot{q}_1 = \frac{1}{m} q_3$$
$$\dot{q}_2 = -\frac{2\omega_0}{r_0} q_1 + \frac{1}{mr_0{}^2} q_4$$
$$\dot{q}_3 = -m\omega_0{}^2 q_1 + \frac{2\omega_0}{r_0} q_4 \tag{4.16}$$
$$\dot{q}_4 = 0$$

where m = mass of particle
ω_0 = angular velocity of circular orbit
r_0 = orbital radius

We use q_1, q_2, q_3, and q_4 to denote small changes in the radius, angle, and radial and angular momenta, respectively. We wish to determine the perturbed state $\mathbf{q}(t)$ at time t, given that the perturbed state at time t_0 is $\mathbf{q}(t_0)$. The result is

$$\mathbf{q}(t) = \boldsymbol{\Phi}(t - t_0)\mathbf{q}(t_0)$$

where $\Phi(t - t_0)$ is the fundamental matrix which must be calculated. No generality is lost by taking $t_0 = 0$ and calculating $\Phi(t)$. The summation of the series is unduly complicated for this fourth-order system, but the equations can be manipulated into a form which will permit an *ad hoc* solution.

First we note that $\dot{q}_4 = 0$ implies directly that $q_4(t) = q_4(0) = $ constant. Hence the third equation of (4.16) can be written

$$\ddot{q}_3 = -m\omega_0^2 \dot{q}_1 = -\omega_0^2 q_3$$

by use of the first equation. Thus q_3 satisfies the homogeneous equation

$$\ddot{q}_3 + \omega_0^2 q_3 = 0$$

This is the differential equation for a harmonic oscillator and has the well-known solution

$$q_3(t) = C_1 \sin \omega_0 t + C_2 \cos \omega_0 t \qquad (4.17)$$

where C_1 and C_2 are constants to be evaluated. Setting $t = 0$ in (4.17), we immediately find that

$$C_2 = q_3(0)$$

Differentiating (4.17), we also obtain

$$\dot{q}_3(t) = C_1 \omega_0 \cos \omega_0 t - q_3(0)\omega_0 \sin \omega_0 t$$
$$= -m\omega_0^2 q_1(t) + \frac{2\omega_0}{r_0} q_4(0)$$

from which

$$q_1(t) = -\frac{C_1}{m\omega_0} \cos \omega_0 t + \frac{q_3(0)}{m\omega_0} \sin \omega_0 t + \frac{2}{mr_0\omega_0} q_4(0) \qquad (4.18)$$

We now determine C_1 by setting $t = 0$ in (4.18). The result is

$$C_1 = -m\omega_0 q_1(0) + \frac{2}{r_0} q_4(0)$$

Substitution of this value of C_1 into (4.18) and (4.17) gives

$$q_1(t) = q_1(0) \cos \omega_0 t + q_3(0) \frac{\sin \omega_0 t}{m\omega_0} + q_4(0) \frac{2(1 - \cos \omega_0 t)}{m\omega_0 r_0}$$
$$q_3(t) = q_1(0)(-m\omega_0 \sin \omega_0 t) + q_3(0) \cos \omega_0 t + q_4(0) \frac{2 \sin \omega_0 t}{r_0} \qquad (4.19)$$

We have thus succeeded in determining the relation between the initial conditions $q_1(0)$, $q_2(0)$, $q_3(0)$, $q_4(0)$ and $q_1(t)$, $q_3(t)$, and $q_4(t)$—the last by recalling that $q_4(t) = q_4(0)$.

It remains only to determine $q_2(t)$; according to the second equation of (4.16), this is given by

$$q_2(t) = q_2(0) + \int_0^t \left(-\frac{2\omega_0}{r_0} q_1(\lambda) + \frac{1}{mr_0{}^2} q_4(\lambda) \right) d\lambda$$

Substitution of $q_1(t)$ from (4.19) and $q_4(t) = q_4(0)$ into the integrand and integration yields the following expression:

$$q_2(t) = q_1(0) \frac{-2 \sin \omega_0 t}{r_0} + q_2(0) + q_3(0) \frac{-2(1 - \cos \omega_0 t)}{m\omega_0 r_0}$$
$$+ q_4(0) \frac{4 \sin \omega_0 t - 3\omega_0 t}{mr_0{}^2\omega_0} \quad (4.20)$$

Arranging (4.19), (4.20), and $q_4(t) = q_4(0)$ in matrix form, we obtain

$$\begin{bmatrix} q_1(t) \\ q_2(t) \\ q_3(t) \\ q_4(t) \end{bmatrix} = \begin{bmatrix} \cos \omega_0 t & 0 & \dfrac{\sin \omega_0 t}{m\omega_0} & \dfrac{2(1 - \cos \omega_0 t)}{m\omega_0 r_0} \\ -\dfrac{2 \sin \omega_0 t}{r_0} & 1 & \dfrac{-2(1 - \cos \omega_0 t)}{m\omega_0 r_0} & \dfrac{4 \sin \omega_0 t - 3\omega_0 t}{mr_0{}^2\omega_0} \\ -m\omega_0 \sin \omega_0 t & 0 & \cos \omega_0 t & \dfrac{2 \sin \omega_0 t}{r_0} \\ 0 & 0 & 0 & 1 \end{bmatrix} \begin{bmatrix} q_1(0) \\ q_2(0) \\ q_3(0) \\ q_4(0) \end{bmatrix}$$

and the square matrix in this expression is the required fundamental matrix $\Phi(t)$.

In the above examples we have illustrated two methods of calculating the fundamental matrix of a fixed system:

1. Term-by-term evaluation of the series for e^{At}
2. Manipulation of the differential equations to obtain a single differential equation of order k or lower; solution of this equation and substitution of the result into the others to evaluate the constants in terms of the initial conditions

The first method is generally unsuited for hand calculation, but is quite feasible for machine calculation of $\Phi(T) = e^{AT}$ with a *fixed T*. (Special caution must sometimes be observed, however, to avoid accumulation of round-off error.) The second method is useful when an inspection of the differential equations indicates exactly the sequence of manipulations to be performed, but is not as systematic as would be desirable. A more systematic method—which in many problems is more cumbersome than method 2—makes use of the Laplace transform and will be described in Chap. 7. This latter method is essentially equivalent to the application

of Sylvester's formula for the evaluation of a function of a matrix, as we shall discuss in Chap. 7.

TIME-VARYING SYSTEMS

If the system is time-varying, the matrices $\mathbf{A}$ and $\mathbf{B}$ appearing in (4.1) are functions of time. The differential equation thus is

$$\dot{\mathbf{q}}(t) = \mathbf{A}(t)\mathbf{q}(t) + \mathbf{B}(t)\mathbf{x}(t) \tag{4.21}$$

Let us assume that the initial condition is $q_i(t_0) = 0$, $i \neq j$; $q_j(t_0) \neq 0$. Let us denote the solution to (4.21) with $\mathbf{x} = \mathbf{0}$ in component form by†

$$q_i(t) = \phi_{ij}(t, t_0)q_j(t_0) \qquad i = 1, 2, \ldots, k \tag{4.22}$$

Then, by superposition of initial conditions, the solution for an arbitrary initial state is

$$q_i(t) = \sum_{j=1}^{k} \phi_{ij}(t, t_0)q_j(t_0) \qquad i = 1, 2, \ldots, k \tag{4.23}$$

or in matrix form

$$\mathbf{q}(t) = \mathbf{\Phi}(t, t_0)\mathbf{q}(t_0) \tag{4.24}$$

where $\mathbf{\Phi}(t, t_0) = [\phi_{ij}(t, t_0)]$. The matrix $\mathbf{\Phi}(t, t_0)$ is called the fundamental matrix of the system.

If the homogeneous form of (4.21) is of first order, i.e.,

$$\frac{dq}{dt} = a(t)q(t)$$

we can write

$$\frac{dq}{q} = a(t) \, dt$$

If we integrate both sides from t_0 to t, we obtain

$$\int_{q(t_0)}^{q(t)} \frac{dq}{q} = \int_{t_0}^{t} a(\lambda) \, d\lambda$$

It follows that

$$\log \frac{q(t)}{q(t_0)} = \int_{t_0}^{t} a(\lambda) \, d\lambda$$

or

$$q(t) = q(t_0)e^{\int_{t_0}^{t} a(\lambda) \, d\lambda}$$

† It is assumed that the solutions exist. Since the system is linear, it follows that the components of the state vector at time t are linearly related to the state at time t_0; hence (4.22) is in the proper form.

Thus we infer that the 1×1 fundamental matrix is

$$\phi(t, t_0) = e^{\int_{t_0}^{t} a(\lambda)\, d\lambda} \tag{4.25}$$

One might be tempted to assert that (4.25) applies also to higher-order systems; i.e.,

$$\mathbf{\Phi}(t, t_0) = e^{\int_{t_0}^{t} \mathbf{A}(\lambda)\, d\lambda}$$

Unfortunately, however, *this relation is not valid unless* $\mathbf{A}(t)$ *and* $\int_{t_0}^{t} \mathbf{A}(\lambda)\, d\lambda$ *commute* (Prob. 4.11).

One case in which the last equation is valid occurs when the matrix $\mathbf{A}(t)$ is the product of a *constant* matrix and a scalar time function $f(t)$, that is, when

$$\mathbf{A}(t) = f(t)\mathbf{K}$$

In this case $\int_{t_0}^{t} \mathbf{A}(\lambda)\, d\lambda = \mathbf{K} \int_{t_0}^{t} f(\lambda)\, d\lambda$, which can readily be shown to commute with $f(t)\mathbf{K}$, and thus

$$\mathbf{\Phi}(t, t_0) = e^{\mathbf{K} \int_{t_0}^{t} f(\lambda)\, d\lambda} \tag{4.26}$$

Although it is generally not possible to obtain an analytic expression for the fundamental matrix, it is nevertheless of conceptual interest to express the solution of the forced equation in terms of this matrix. To find the solution of the forced equation we again use the method of variation of parameters. Assume that

$$\mathbf{q}(t) = \mathbf{\Phi}(t, t_0)\mathbf{f}(t)$$

Then

$$\dot{\mathbf{q}}(t) = \frac{d\mathbf{\Phi}(t, t_0)}{dt}\, \mathbf{f}(t) + \mathbf{\Phi}(t, t_0)\dot{\mathbf{f}}(t) \tag{4.27}$$

Substitution of (4.27) into (4.21) results in

$$\left[\frac{d\mathbf{\Phi}(t, t_0)}{dt} - \mathbf{A}(t)\mathbf{\Phi}(t, t_0)\right]\mathbf{f}(t) + \mathbf{\Phi}(t, t_0)\dot{\mathbf{f}}(t) = \mathbf{B}(t)\mathbf{x}(t) \tag{4.28}$$

Since $\mathbf{\Phi}(t, t_0)$ satisfies the homogeneous equation, the expression in the brackets is identically zero; hence (4.28) becomes

$$\mathbf{\Phi}(t, t_0)\dot{\mathbf{f}}(t) = \mathbf{B}(t)\mathbf{x}(t)$$

Premultiplying by the inverse of $\mathbf{\Phi}(t, t_0)$ and integrating from $-\infty$ to t, we obtain

$$\mathbf{f}(t) = \int_{-\infty}^{t} \mathbf{\Phi}^{-1}(\lambda, t_0)\mathbf{B}(\lambda)\mathbf{x}(\lambda)\, d\lambda$$

Hence the complete solution of (4.21) is

$$\mathbf{q}(t) = \int_{-\infty}^{t} \boldsymbol{\Phi}(t, t_0)\boldsymbol{\Phi}^{-1}(\lambda, t_0)\mathbf{B}(\lambda)\mathbf{x}(\lambda) \, d\lambda$$

$$= \boldsymbol{\Phi}(t, t_0) \int_{-\infty}^{t_0} \boldsymbol{\Phi}^{-1}(\lambda, t_0)\mathbf{B}(\lambda)\mathbf{x}(\lambda) \, d\lambda$$

$$+ \int_{t_0}^{t} \boldsymbol{\Phi}(t, t_0)\boldsymbol{\Phi}^{-1}(\lambda, t_0)\mathbf{B}(\lambda)\mathbf{x}(\lambda) \, d\lambda \quad (4.29)$$

Evaluating $\mathbf{q}(t)$ at $t = t_0$ in (4.29), we find that

$$\mathbf{q}(t_0) = \int_{-\infty}^{t_0} \boldsymbol{\Phi}^{-1}(\lambda, t_0)\mathbf{B}(\lambda)\mathbf{x}(\lambda) \, d\lambda$$

since $\boldsymbol{\Phi}(t_0, t_0) = \mathbf{I}$.   (See Sec. 4.3.)   Hence we may write

$$\mathbf{q}(t) = \boldsymbol{\Phi}(t, t_0)\mathbf{q}(t_0) + \int_{t_0}^{t} \boldsymbol{\Phi}(t, t_0)\boldsymbol{\Phi}^{-1}(\lambda, t_0)\mathbf{B}(\lambda)\mathbf{x}(\lambda) \, d\lambda \quad (4.30)$$

It will be shown in the next section that this may be written

$$\mathbf{q}(t) = \boldsymbol{\Phi}(t, t_0)\mathbf{q}(t_0) + \int_{t_0}^{t} \boldsymbol{\Phi}(t, \lambda)\mathbf{B}(\lambda)\mathbf{x}(\lambda) \, d\lambda \quad (4.31)$$

Example 4.3   A first-order time-varying system is shown in Fig. 4.2. The system is characterized by the following differential equation:

$$\dot{q}(t) = \frac{dq(t)}{dt} = -\frac{1}{t + 1} q(t) + x(t) \qquad t \geq 0$$

By (4.25) the 1×1 fundamental matrix is given by

$$\phi(t, t_0) = \frac{t_0 + 1}{t + 1}$$

This function is shown in Fig. 4.3 for integral values of t_0.

Example 4.4   Network with time-varying elements   Suppose that the capacitance and inductance of the network of Fig. 4.1 vary with time

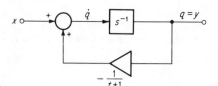

FIG. 4.2   Example of time-varying system.

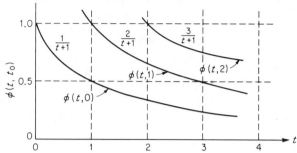

FIG. 4.3   Time-varying fundamental matrix of system of Fig. 4.2.

but that the variations are proportional to the same time function; i.e.,

$$L = \frac{L_0}{f(t)} \quad \text{and} \quad C = \frac{C_0}{f(t)}$$

where L_0 and C_0 are constants.   The differential equations for the network are now more appropriately written in terms of the *inductor flux* $q_1 = Li_1$ and the *capacitor charge* $q_2 = Cv_2$. It is readily established that the unforced differential equations are given by

$$\frac{dq_1}{dt} = -\frac{1}{C} q_2$$

$$\frac{dq_2}{dt} = \frac{1}{L} q_1 - \frac{1}{RC} q_2$$

If $L_0 = \frac{1}{2}$, $C_0 = 1$, and $R = \frac{1}{3}$, these differential equations take the form

$$\begin{bmatrix} \dfrac{dq_1}{dt} \\ \dfrac{dq_2}{dt} \end{bmatrix} = f(t) \begin{bmatrix} 0 & -1 \\ 2 & -3 \end{bmatrix} \begin{bmatrix} q_1 \\ q_2 \end{bmatrix} \tag{4.32}$$

Hence the matrix $\mathbf{A}(t) = f(t)\mathbf{K}$, and it follows that the fundamental matrix is of the form given by (4.26).

Suppose $f(t)$ is fixed at unity.   Then (4.32) is the differential equation for the network considered in Example 4.1, and from the fundamental matrix calculated with the *inductor current* and *capacitor voltage* as state variables [see (4.15)], we have

$$i_1(t) = (-e^{-2t} + 2e^{-t})i_1(0) + (2e^{-2t} - 2e^{-t})v_2(0)$$
$$v_2(t) = (-e^{-2t} + e^{-t})i_1(0) + (2e^{-2t} - e^{-t})v_2(0)$$

Using $i_1 = q_1/L_0 = 2q_1$, $v_2 = q_2/C_0 = q_2$, we obtain

$$\begin{bmatrix} q_1(t) \\ q_2(t) \end{bmatrix} = \begin{bmatrix} -e^{-2t} + 2e^{-t} & e^{-2t} - e^{-t} \\ -2e^{-2t} + 2e^{-t} & 2e^{-2t} - e^{-t} \end{bmatrix} \begin{bmatrix} q_1(0) \\ q_2(0) \end{bmatrix}$$

Hence the matrix in the above relation is the fundamental matrix for (4.32), with $f(t)$ *equal to unity*.

This fundamental matrix could also have been obtained as in Example 4.1 from (4.26) with $f(t) = 1$ and $t_0 = 0$ by summing the series

$$\mathbf{I} + \mathbf{K}t + \frac{\mathbf{K}^2 t^2}{2!} + \cdots$$

The fundamental matrix for an arbitrary $f(t)$ is given by

$$\mathbf{I} + \mathbf{K} \int_{t_0}^t f(\lambda)\, d\lambda + \frac{\mathbf{K}^2}{2!} \left[\int_{t_0}^t f(\lambda)\, d\lambda \right]^2 + \cdots$$

We may thus conclude that the fundamental matrix for (4.32) with *any* $f(t)$ is given by

$$\mathbf{\Phi}(t, t_0) = \begin{bmatrix} -e^{-2\xi} + 2e^{-\xi} & e^{-2\xi} - e^{-\xi} \\ -2e^{-2\xi} + 2e^{-\xi} & 2e^{-2\xi} - e^{-\xi} \end{bmatrix}$$

where

$$\xi = \int_{t_0}^t f(\lambda)\, d\lambda$$

For example, if $f(t) = 1/(1 + t)$, then

$$\xi = \log \frac{1 + t}{1 + t_0}$$

and

$$\mathbf{\Phi}(t, t_0) = \begin{bmatrix} -\left(\dfrac{1 + t_0}{1 + t}\right)^2 + 2\dfrac{1 + t_0}{1 + t} & \left(\dfrac{1 + t_0}{1 + t}\right)^2 - \dfrac{1 + t_0}{1 + t} \\ -2\left(\dfrac{1 + t_0}{1 + t}\right)^2 + 2\dfrac{1 + t_0}{1 + t} & 2\left(\dfrac{1 + t_0}{1 + t}\right)^2 - \dfrac{1 + t_0}{1 + t} \end{bmatrix}$$

4.3 PROPERTIES OF THE FUNDAMENTAL MATRIX

The fundamental matrix $\mathbf{\Phi}(t, t_0)$ (which becomes $\mathbf{\Phi}(t - t_0)$ in fixed systems), relating the solution of an unforced system to the initial conditions, is of considerable interest, since it is this matrix which essentially governs the dynamic behavior of the system. Let us consider the solution $\mathbf{q}(t)$ of an unforced system with the initial condition $\mathbf{q}(t_0)$ at $t = t_0$. This is illustrated in Fig. 4.4 for a first-order system.

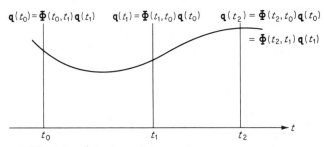

$$\mathbf{q}(t_0) = \mathbf{\Phi}(t_0, t_1)\mathbf{q}(t_1) \qquad \mathbf{q}(t_1) = \mathbf{\Phi}(t_1, t_0)\mathbf{q}(t_0) \qquad \mathbf{q}(t_2) = \mathbf{\Phi}(t_2, t_0)\mathbf{q}(t_0)$$
$$= \mathbf{\Phi}(t_2, t_1)\mathbf{q}(t_1)$$

FIG. 4.4   Solution of first-order system.

We shall now obtain three useful properties of $\mathbf{\Phi}(t, t_0)$ by making use of the uniqueness of the solution of the homogeneous system.   Since $\mathbf{q}(t_0) = \mathbf{\Phi}(t_0, t_0)\mathbf{q}(t_0)$ for any initial state $\mathbf{q}(t_0)$,

(1) $$\mathbf{\Phi}(t_0, t_0) = \mathbf{I} \tag{4.33}$$

For any t_0, t_1, t_2 and any $\mathbf{q}(t_0)$,

$$\mathbf{q}(t_2) = \mathbf{\Phi}(t_2, t_0)\mathbf{q}(t_0) = \mathbf{\Phi}(t_2, t_1)\mathbf{q}(t_1)$$
$$= \mathbf{\Phi}(t_2, t_1)\mathbf{\Phi}(t_1, t_0)\mathbf{q}(t_0)$$

and it follows that

(2) $$\mathbf{\Phi}(t_2, t_0) = \mathbf{\Phi}(t_2, t_1)\mathbf{\Phi}(t_1, t_0) \tag{4.34}$$

which shows how two successive operations may be combined into a single operation.   The third property is established by premultiplying

$$\mathbf{q}(t_2) = \mathbf{\Phi}(t_2, t_1)\mathbf{q}(t_1)$$

by $\mathbf{\Phi}^{-1}(t_2, t_1)$.   This gives

$$\mathbf{\Phi}^{-1}(t_2, t_1)\mathbf{q}(t_2) = \mathbf{q}(t_1) = \mathbf{\Phi}(t_1, t_2)\mathbf{q}(t_2)$$

for any state $\mathbf{q}(t_2)$.   It follows that

(3) $$\mathbf{\Phi}^{-1}(t_2, t_1) = \mathbf{\Phi}(t_1, t_2) \tag{4.35}$$

which relates the fundamental matrix to its inverse.   This relation, together with (4.34), establishes (4.31).   Note that (4.33) to (4.35) are satisfied for $\mathbf{\Phi}(t) = e^{\mathbf{A}t}$.

Example 4.5   For the first-order system of Fig. 4.2 in Example 4.3, we found that

$$\Phi(t, t_0) = \frac{t_0 + 1}{t + 1}$$

The three properties of a fundamental matrix just established may be verified as follows:

(1) $\phi(t_0, t_0) = \dfrac{t_0 + 1}{t_0 + 1} = 1$

(2) $\phi(t_2, t_0) = \dfrac{t_0 + 1}{t_2 + 1} = \dfrac{t_1 + 1}{t_2 + 1} \dfrac{t_0 + 1}{t_1 + 1} = \phi(t_2, t_1)\phi(t_1, t_0)$

(3) $\phi(t_2, t_1) = \dfrac{t_1 + 1}{t_2 + 1} = \left(\dfrac{t_2 + 1}{t_1 + 1}\right)^{-1} = \phi^{-1}(t_1, t_2)$

4.4 RELATION OF THE FUNDAMENTAL MATRIX TO THE IMPULSE RESPONSE

The physical significance of the fundamental matrix

$$\mathbf{\Phi}(t, t_0) = \begin{bmatrix} \phi_{11}(t, t_0) & \cdots & \phi_{1k}(t, t_0) \\ \cdots & \cdots & \cdots \\ \phi_{k1}(t, t_0) & \cdots & \phi_{kk}(t, t_0) \end{bmatrix}$$

was already apparent in (4.23). This relation

$$q_i(t) = \sum_{j=1}^{k} \phi_{ij}(t, t_0)q_j(t_0)$$

shows that $\phi_{ij}(t, t_0) = q_i(t)$ if $q_j(t_0) = 1$, while all other state variables vanish at $t = t_0$; that is, $q_r(t_0) = 0$ for $r \neq j$. Thus, in terms of the analog-computer diagram, $\phi_{ij}(t, t_0)$ is the response observed at the output of the ith integrator resulting from a unit initial condition at $t = t_0$ at the output of the jth integrator when the system is completely connected but the inputs and initial conditions on all other integrators are zero.

The unit initial condition at the output of the jth integrator may be replaced by a unit impulse applied to the input of this integrator. This impulse must, however, be applied *only to this integrator*, and not to any other parts of the system which may be connected to the integrator input, since the impulse serves only to generate the unit initial condition at the integrator output.

In Sec. 3.7 the output of a linear system for any input was written in terms of the response to a unit impulse. In this chapter it was obtained in terms of the fundamental matrix and the matrices **B**, **C**, **D**, according to (4.2) and (4.31). The relation of the fundamental matrix to the impulse response will now be established.

We consider now a causal multiple-input, -output (possibly time-varying) system. As in Sec. 3.10, let $h_{ij}(t, \tau)$ denote the response at time t at the ith output resulting from a unit impulse occurring at time τ at the jth input, or simply the impulse response from x_j to y_i, with no other inputs applied. The corresponding matrix is $\mathbf{H}(t, \tau)$. The output vector $\mathbf{y}$ is given in terms of $\mathbf{H}(t, \tau)$ by (3.65); for a causal system it is

$$\mathbf{y}(t) = \int_{-\infty}^{t} \mathbf{H}(t, \lambda)\mathbf{x}(\lambda)\, d\lambda = \int_{-\infty}^{t_0} \mathbf{H}(t, \lambda)\mathbf{x}(\lambda)\, d\lambda + \int_{t_0}^{t} \mathbf{H}(t, \lambda)\mathbf{x}(\lambda)\, d\lambda$$

$$(4.36)$$

The solution of the differential equations in normal form gives for the output, according to (4.2) and (4.31),

$$\mathbf{y}(t) = \mathbf{C}(t)\mathbf{\Phi}(t, t_0)\mathbf{q}(t_0) + \int_{t_0}^{t} \mathbf{C}(t)\mathbf{\Phi}(t, \lambda)\mathbf{B}(\lambda)\mathbf{x}(\lambda)\, d\lambda + \mathbf{D}(t)\mathbf{x}(t) \quad (4.37)$$

In order to compare this equation with (4.36), the input $\mathbf{x}(t)$ in the last term may be resolved into impulses,

$$\mathbf{x}(t) = \int_{t_0}^{t} \mathbf{x}(\lambda)\delta(t - \lambda)\, d\lambda$$

so that (4.37) becomes

$$\mathbf{y}(t) = \mathbf{C}(t)\mathbf{\Phi}(t, t_0)\mathbf{q}(t_0) + \int_{t_0}^{t} [\mathbf{C}(t)\mathbf{\Phi}(t, \lambda)\mathbf{B}(\lambda) + \mathbf{D}(t)\delta(t - \lambda)]\mathbf{x}(\lambda)\, d\lambda$$

$$(4.38)$$

The first terms in both (4.36) and (4.38) are due to the initial value $\mathbf{y}(t_0)$; the second terms give the contribution to $\mathbf{y}(t)$ due to the point $\mathbf{x}(t)$ from t_0 to the instant of observation t. Since $\mathbf{x}(t)$ is arbitrary, it follows that

$$\mathbf{H}(t, \tau) = \mathbf{C}(t)\mathbf{\Phi}(t, \tau)\mathbf{B}(\tau) + \mathbf{D}(t)\delta(t - \tau) \qquad \tau \leq t \qquad (4.39)$$

Equation (4.39) relates the matrix $\mathbf{H}$ of impulse responses of a causal system to the fundamental matrix $\mathbf{\Phi}$ (which is related to the matrix $\mathbf{A}$) and the matrices $\mathbf{B}, \mathbf{C}, \mathbf{D}$.

Example 4.6 The matrix of impulse responses for the network of Example 4.1 is given by

$$\mathbf{H}(t) = \mathbf{C}\mathbf{\Phi}(t)\mathbf{B} + \mathbf{D}\delta(t)$$

$$= \begin{bmatrix} 1 & 0 \\ 1 & -3 \end{bmatrix} \begin{bmatrix} -e^{-2t} + 2e^{-t} & 2e^{-2t} - 2e^{-t} \\ -e^{-2t} + e^{-t} & 2e^{-2t} - e^{-t} \end{bmatrix} \begin{bmatrix} 2 & -2 \\ 0 & -3 \end{bmatrix}$$

$$+ \begin{bmatrix} 0 & 0 \\ 0 & -3\delta(t) \end{bmatrix}$$

$$= \begin{bmatrix} -2e^{-2t} + 4e^{-t} & -4e^{-2t} + 2e^{-t} \\ 4e^{-2t} - 2e^{-t} & 8e^{-2t} - e^{-t} - 3\delta(t) \end{bmatrix}$$

4.5 SOLUTION OF DIFFERENCE EQUATIONS FOR DISCRETE-TIME SYSTEMS

FIXED SYSTEMS

The vector-matrix form of the difference equations governing the behavior of a fixed linear discrete-time system is given in Chap. 2 as

$$\mathbf{q}(n+1) = \mathbf{A}\mathbf{q}(n) + \mathbf{B}\mathbf{x}(n) \tag{4.40}$$
$$\mathbf{y}(n) = \mathbf{C}\mathbf{q}(n) + \mathbf{D}\mathbf{x}(n) \tag{4.41}$$

The solution of the first of these equations may be found directly by recursion:

$$\mathbf{q}(1) = \mathbf{A}\mathbf{q}(0) + \mathbf{B}\mathbf{x}(0)$$
$$\mathbf{q}(2) = \mathbf{A}\mathbf{q}(1) + \mathbf{B}\mathbf{x}(1) = \mathbf{A}^2\mathbf{q}(0) + \mathbf{A}\mathbf{B}\mathbf{x}(0) + \mathbf{B}\mathbf{x}(1)$$
· ·

$$\mathbf{q}(n) = \mathbf{A}^n\mathbf{q}(0) + \sum_{k=0}^{n-1} \mathbf{A}^{n-k-1}\mathbf{B}\mathbf{x}(k) \tag{4.42}$$

Equation (4.42) shows that the fundamental matrix relating the state vector $\mathbf{q}(n)$ to its initial value is now[†]

$$\mathbf{\Phi}(n) = \mathbf{A}^n \tag{4.43}$$

In terms of the fundamental matrix $\mathbf{\Phi}(n)$, the solution for the state vector is thus

$$\mathbf{q}(n) = \mathbf{\Phi}(n)\mathbf{q}(0) + \sum_{k=0}^{n-1} \mathbf{\Phi}(n-k-1)\mathbf{B}\mathbf{x}(k) \tag{4.44}$$

and the output is given by

$$\mathbf{y}(n) = \mathbf{C}\mathbf{\Phi}(n)\mathbf{q}(0) + \sum_{k=0}^{n-1} \mathbf{C}\mathbf{\Phi}(n-k-1)\mathbf{B}\mathbf{x}(k) + \mathbf{D}\mathbf{x}(n) \tag{4.45}$$

Equations (4.44) and (4.45) are the discrete-time analogs of (4.8) and (4.37) for fixed systems, respectively.

[†] The fundamental matrix for a discrete-time system is denoted by the same symbol as the fundamental matrix for a continuous-time system since the arguments prevent confusion. This is consistent with our use of the symbol h for both the impulse response and the unit-function response.

TIME-VARYING SYSTEMS

For a time-varying linear discrete-time system, the equations in normal form are

$$\mathbf{q}(n + 1) = \mathbf{A}(n)\mathbf{q}(n) + \mathbf{B}(n)\mathbf{x}(n) \tag{4.46}$$
$$\mathbf{y}(n) = \mathbf{C}(n)\mathbf{q}(n) + \mathbf{D}(n)\mathbf{x}(n) \tag{4.47}$$

The solution of the first of these equations may be found by recursion as before:

$$\mathbf{q}(n_0 + 1) = \mathbf{A}(n_0)\mathbf{q}(n_0) + \mathbf{B}(n_0)\mathbf{x}(n_0)$$
$$\mathbf{q}(n_0 + 2) = \mathbf{A}(n_0 + 1)\mathbf{q}(n_0 + 1) + \mathbf{B}(n_0 + 1)\mathbf{x}(n_0 + 1)$$
$$= \mathbf{A}(n_0 + 1)\mathbf{A}(n_0)\mathbf{q}(n_0) + \mathbf{A}(n_0 + 1)\mathbf{B}(n_0)\mathbf{x}(n_0)$$
$$+ \mathbf{B}(n_0 + 1)\mathbf{x}(n_0 + 1)$$

$$\cdot \ \cdot$$

and, by induction,

$$\mathbf{q}(n) = \mathbf{A}(n - 1)\mathbf{A}(n - 2) \ \cdot \ \cdot \ \cdot \ \mathbf{A}(n_0)\mathbf{q}(n_0)$$
$$+ \sum_{k=n_0}^{n-1} \mathbf{A}(n - 1)\mathbf{A}(n - 2) \ \cdot \ \cdot \ \cdot \ \mathbf{A}(k + 1)\mathbf{B}(k)\mathbf{x}(k) \qquad n > n_0 \tag{4.48}$$

where it must be understood that the last term in the summation, for $k = n - 1$, equals $\mathbf{B}(n - 1)\mathbf{x}(n - 1)$.

Thus, for time-varying discrete-time systems, the fundamental matrix is

$$\mathbf{\Phi}(n, n_0) = \mathbf{A}(n - 1)\mathbf{A}(n - 2) \ \cdot \ \cdot \ \cdot \ \mathbf{A}(n_0) \qquad n > n_0 \tag{4.49}$$

We may write for the state

$$\mathbf{q}(n) = \mathbf{\Phi}(n, n_0)\mathbf{q}(n_0) + \sum_{k=n_0}^{n-1} \mathbf{\Phi}(n, k + 1)\mathbf{B}(k)\mathbf{x}(k) \qquad n > n_0 \tag{4.50}$$

and for the output

$$\mathbf{y}(n) = \mathbf{C}(n)\mathbf{\Phi}(n, n_0)\mathbf{q}(n_0) + \sum_{k=n_0}^{n-1} \mathbf{C}(n)\mathbf{\Phi}(n, k + 1)\mathbf{B}(k)\mathbf{x}(k)$$
$$+ \mathbf{D}(n)\mathbf{x}(n) \qquad n > n_0 \tag{4.51}$$

In order to compare this result with the superposition summation used in Sec. 3.9, let $h_{ij}(n, k)$ denote the ith output at the nth instant resulting from a unit function applied to the jth input at the kth instant, or simply the unit-function response from x_j to y_i, with no other inputs applied. Then, by superposition, the component y_i of the output vector of a causal

system is given, according to (3.55), by

$$y_i(n) = \sum_{j=1}^{N} \sum_{k=-\infty}^{n} h_{ij}(n, k)x_j(k) = \sum_{k=-\infty}^{n} \sum_{j=1}^{N} h_{ij}(n, k)x_j(k)$$

$$i = 1, 2, \ldots, M$$

where N and M denote the number of inputs and outputs, respectively. The vector-matrix form of the superposition summation is thus

$$\mathbf{y}(n) = \sum_{k=-\infty}^{n} \mathbf{H}(n, k)\mathbf{x}(k) = \sum_{k=-\infty}^{n_0-1} \mathbf{H}(n, k)\mathbf{x}(k)$$

$$+ \sum_{k=n_0}^{n} \mathbf{H}(n, k)\mathbf{x}(k) \quad (4.52)$$

Comparison of (4.51) and (4.52) shows that the first terms in both equations are due to the initial value $\mathbf{y}(n_0)$, while the remaining terms give the contribution to $\mathbf{y}(n)$ due to the input $\mathbf{x}(n)$ from the n_0th instant to the nth instant. Note that $\mathbf{x}(n_0)$ contributes to the initial value $\mathbf{y}(n_0)$ as well as to later values of $\mathbf{y}(n)$ since it affects later values $\mathbf{q}(n)$ of the state. It is also seen that

$$\mathbf{H}(n, k) = \begin{cases} \mathbf{C}(n)\mathbf{\Phi}(n, k+1)\mathbf{B}(k) & n_0 \le k \le n-1 \\ \mathbf{D}(n) & k = n > n_0 \end{cases} \quad (4.53)$$

Equation (4.53) relates the matrix of unit-function responses for a discrete-time system to the fundamental matrix $\mathbf{\Phi}$ and the matrices $\mathbf{B}, \mathbf{C}, \mathbf{D}$. The relation given in (4.53) is the discrete version of (4.39).

The fundamental matrix $\mathbf{\Phi}$ of a discrete-time system may be given an interpretation similar to that for the matrix $\mathbf{\Phi}$ of a continuous-time system. In the absence of inputs, it follows from (4.50) that

$$q_i(n) = \sum_{j=1}^{k} \phi_{ij}(n, n_0)q_j(n_0) \quad (4.54)$$

where k is the order of the system. It follows that $\phi_{ij}(n, n_0) = q_i(n)$ if $q_j(n_0) = 1$, while all other state variables vanish at $n = n_0$; that is, $q_r(n_0) = 0$ for $r \neq j$. Thus $\phi_{ij}(n, n_0)$ is the response observed at the nth instant at the output of the ith delay element resulting from a unit initial condition applied at the n_0th instant to the output of the jth delay element, when the system is completely connected but the inputs and initial conditions on all other delay elements are zero.

The matrix $\mathbf{\Phi}(n, n_0)$ has properties similar to those of $\mathbf{\Phi}(t, t_0)$. By

recursion it is easily established that

$$\mathbf{\Phi}(n_1, n_2) = \mathbf{A}^{-1}(n_1)\mathbf{A}^{-1}(n_1 + 1) \cdot \cdot \cdot \mathbf{A}^{-1}(n_2 - 1) \qquad n_1 < n_2 \qquad (4.55)$$

from which we immediately find

$$\mathbf{\Phi}(n_0, n_0) = \mathbf{I}$$
$$\mathbf{\Phi}(n_2, n_0) = \mathbf{\Phi}(n_2, n_1)\mathbf{\Phi}(n_1, n_0) \qquad\qquad (4.56)$$
$$\mathbf{\Phi}^{-1}(n_2, n_1) = \mathbf{\Phi}(n_1, n_2)$$

which are analogous to the properties of $\mathbf{\Phi}(t, t_0)$ established in Sec. 4.3.

4.6 CONTINUOUS-TIME SYSTEMS WITH SAMPLED INPUTS

In some systems the input (i.e., every component of the input vector) is a *sampled signal*. This is a signal which is completely specified by its ordinates at sampling instants. Examples of such signals are:

1. Piecewise-constant signals in which the sampling functions are pulses of width T (Fig. 4.5a). In this case $\mathbf{x}(t) = \mathbf{x}(kT)$ for $kT \leq t < kT + T$, or

$$\mathbf{x}(t) = T \sum_{k=0}^{\infty} \mathbf{x}(kT)p_T(t - kT)$$

where $p_T(t)$ is a rectangular pulse of width T and unit area.

2. Impulse-modulated signals in which the sampling functions are unit impulses (Fig. 4.5b), in which case

$$\mathbf{x}(t) = \sum_{k=0}^{\infty} \mathbf{x}(kT)\delta(t - kT)$$

FIG. 4.5 Examples of sampled signals. (a) Piecewise-constant signal; (b) impulse-modulated signal.

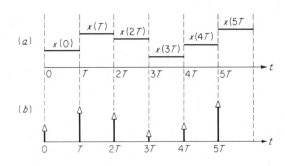

The response of continuous-time systems with sampled inputs may be determined by the methods discussed earlier. It is possible, however, to determine the response at the sampling instants only ($t = 0$, T, $2T$, $3T$, . . . in Fig. 4.5) with considerably less labor than would be required to determine the response for all time, and in many cases the response at the sampling instants is all the information needed. For convenience we shall consider fixed systems, although the results are readily extended to time-varying systems.

Consider the system governed by the differential equation

$$\dot{\mathbf{q}}(t) = \mathbf{A}\mathbf{q}(t) + \mathbf{B}\mathbf{x}(t) \tag{4.57}$$

in which the input signal $\mathbf{x}(t)$ is piecewise-constant and the sampling instants are 0, T, $2T$, ... The solution of this system is

$$\mathbf{q}(t) = e^{\mathbf{A}t}\mathbf{q}(0) + \int_0^t e^{\mathbf{A}(t-\lambda)}\mathbf{B}\mathbf{x}(\lambda)\, d\lambda \tag{4.58}$$

where

$$e^{\mathbf{A}t} = \mathbf{I} + \mathbf{A}t + \mathbf{A}^2 \frac{t^2}{2!} + \mathbf{A}^3 \frac{t^3}{3!} + \cdots$$

We wish to determine the state $\mathbf{q}$ at sampling instants without first finding $\mathbf{q}(t)$ at all times. Therefore we set up a difference equation for $\mathbf{q}(nT)$. At $t = (n + 1)T$, (4.58) becomes

$$\mathbf{q}(nT + T) = e^{\mathbf{A}T(n+1)}\mathbf{q}(0) + \int_0^{nT+T} e^{\mathbf{A}(nT+T-\lambda)}\mathbf{B}\mathbf{x}(\lambda)\, d\lambda$$
$$= e^{\mathbf{A}T}\left[e^{\mathbf{A}Tn}\mathbf{q}(0) + \int_0^{nT} e^{\mathbf{A}(nT-\lambda)}\mathbf{B}\mathbf{x}(\lambda)\, d\lambda \right]$$
$$+ \int_{nT}^{nT+T} e^{\mathbf{A}(nT+T-\lambda)}\mathbf{B}\mathbf{x}(\lambda)\, d\lambda$$

The expression in brackets in the last line is $\mathbf{q}(nT)$ according to (4.58). Hence

$$\mathbf{q}(nT + T) = e^{\mathbf{A}T}\mathbf{q}(nT) + \int_{nT}^{nT+T} e^{\mathbf{A}(nT+T-\lambda)}\mathbf{B}\mathbf{x}(\lambda)\, d\lambda \tag{4.59}$$

If the input $\mathbf{x}(t)$ is constant between sampling instants, i.e.,

$$\mathbf{x}(t) = \mathbf{x}(nT) \qquad \text{for} \qquad nT \leq t < (n + 1)T$$

then (4.59) becomes

$$\mathbf{q}(nT + T) = e^{\mathbf{A}T}\mathbf{q}(nT) + \int_{nT}^{nT+T} e^{\mathbf{A}(nT+T-\lambda)}\mathbf{B}\, d\lambda \cdot \mathbf{x}(nT)$$

With the change of variable $u = nT + T - \lambda$, this equation becomes

$$\mathbf{q}(nT + T) = e^{\mathbf{A}T}\mathbf{q}(nT) + \int_0^T e^{\mathbf{A}u}\mathbf{B}\, du \cdot \mathbf{x}(nT) \tag{4.60}$$

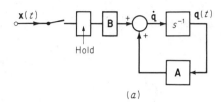

(a)

FIG. 4.6 Equivalent discrete-time system for continuous-time system with sampled input. (a) Continuous-time system with sampled input; (b) discrete-time system.

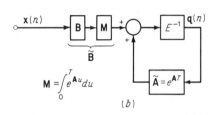

(b)

Writing $\mathbf{q}(nT) = \mathbf{q}(n)$ and $\mathbf{x}(nT) = \mathbf{x}(n)$, we obtain the difference equation

$$\mathbf{q}(n + 1) = \tilde{\mathbf{A}}\mathbf{q}(n) + \tilde{\mathbf{B}}\mathbf{x}(n) \qquad (4.61)$$

where

$$\tilde{\mathbf{A}} = e^{\mathbf{A}T} = \boldsymbol{\Phi}(T) \qquad (4.62)$$

$$\tilde{\mathbf{B}} = \int_0^T e^{\mathbf{A}u}\mathbf{B}\,du = \mathbf{M}\mathbf{B} \qquad (4.63)$$

$$\mathbf{M} = \int_0^T e^{\mathbf{A}u}\,du \qquad (4.64)$$

Thus a system governed by the differential equation (4.57) with piecewise-constant input represented as shown in Fig. 4.6a is equivalent at sampling instants to the system governed by the difference equation (4.61) with the representation of Fig. 4.6b. In Fig. 4.6a the switch following the input components $x_i(t)$ represents the sampling operation at $t = nT$, while the "hold" following the switch represents the operation of maintaining the sampled value over an interval of T sec following the sampling operation.

If the input is not constant between sampling instants, but has the form of a pulse of known shape $f(t - nT)$ and of amplitude $\mathbf{x}(nT)$ for $nT \leq T < nT + T$, the above reasoning results in

$$\mathbf{M} = \int_0^T e^{\mathbf{A}u}f(T - u)\,du \qquad (4.65)$$

The other matrices remain unchanged.

Example 4.7 Suppose the network of Fig. 4.1 is excited by voltage sources which are piecewise-constant, as shown in Fig. 4.5a. Let the sampling interval be $T = 1$ sec.

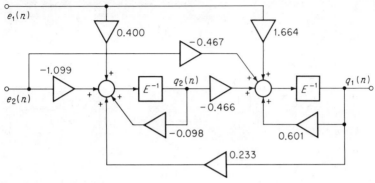

FIG. 4.7   Example 4.7

From the results of Example 4.1 we obtain

$$\tilde{\mathbf{A}} = e^{\mathbf{A}} = \begin{bmatrix} 2e^{-1} - e^{-2} & -2e^{-1} + 2e^{-2} \\ e^{-1} - e^{-2} & -e^{-1} + 2e^{-2} \end{bmatrix} = \begin{bmatrix} 0.600 & -0.465 \\ 0.233 & -0.097 \end{bmatrix}$$

$$\mathbf{M} = \begin{bmatrix} \int_0^1 (-e^{-2u} + 2e^{-u})\, du & \int_0^1 (2e^{-2u} - 2e^{-u})\, du \\ \int_0^1 (-e^{-2u} + e^{-u})\, du & \int_0^1 (2e^{-2u} - e^{-u})\, du \end{bmatrix}$$

$$= \begin{bmatrix} \tfrac{3}{2} - 2e^{-1} + \tfrac{1}{2}e^{-2} & -1 + 2e^{-1} - e^{-2} \\ \tfrac{1}{2} - e^{-1} + \tfrac{1}{2}e^{-2} & e^{-1} - e^{-2} \end{bmatrix}$$

$$= \begin{bmatrix} 0.832 & -0.400 \\ 0.200 & 0.233 \end{bmatrix}$$

Then

$$\tilde{\mathbf{B}} = \mathbf{MB} = \begin{bmatrix} 0.832 & -0.400 \\ 0.200 & 0.233 \end{bmatrix} \begin{bmatrix} 2 & -2 \\ 0 & -3 \end{bmatrix} = \begin{bmatrix} 1.664 & -0.465 \\ 0.400 & -1.097 \end{bmatrix}$$

The block diagram of the equivalent discrete-time system is thus given by Fig. 4.7. If the values of e_1 and e_2 during the 1-sec intervals and an initial value of the output q_1 are given, later values of q_1 at the sampling instants $t = n$ may be computed from (4.61).

PROBLEMS

4.1   If the matrix $\mathbf{A}$ in the normal form of the dynamic equations of a fixed system is

$$\mathbf{A} = \begin{bmatrix} 1 & 0 \\ 2 & -3 \end{bmatrix}$$

what is the fundamental matrix?

4.2 For the network shown (Fig. P 4.2):

(a) Find the matrix **A**.

(b) Find the fundamental matrix by two different methods. Take $RC = 1$.

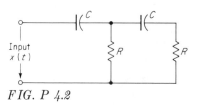

FIG. P 4.2

4.3 For each of the systems shown (Fig. P 4.3):

(a) Find the matrix **A** of the normal form of the differential equations.

(b) Find $\mathbf{\Phi}(t) = e^{\mathbf{A}t}$ by expanding $e^{\mathbf{A}t}$ in a series.

(c) Find $\mathbf{\Phi}(t)$ by finding its components $\phi_{ij}(t)$ as impulse responses.

(d) Find the impulse response $h(t)$ of the system.

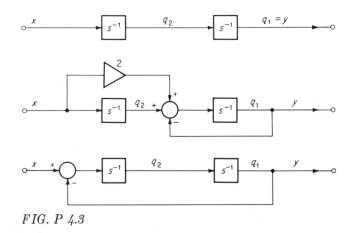

FIG. P 4.3

4.4 For the system shown (Fig. P 4.4):

(a) Define appropriate state variables and write the differential equation in normal form. (Choose $q_1 = y$.)

(b) Find the matrix **A** and the fundamental matrix $\mathbf{\Phi}(t)$ from **A**.

(c) Find the elements $\phi_{ij}(t)$ of the fundamental matrix as the response at the appropriate point to proper initial conditions.

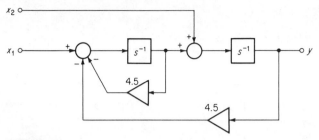

FIG. P 4.4

4.5 Consider a network containing any number of switches operated
in synchronism. All switches are initially either open or closed;
at $t = T_1$ they are reversed, then at $t = T$ the original condition
is restored and the cycle repeated, as shown in Fig. P 4.5. The

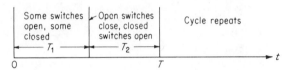

FIG. P 4.5

other network parameters are fixed. Let the state variables be
the capacitor voltages and inductor currents, as explained in
Chap. 2. The system is thus characterized by

(1) $\dot{\mathbf{q}}(t) = \mathbf{A}_1\mathbf{q}(t) + \mathbf{B}_1\mathbf{x}(t)$ $nT \le t < nT + T_1$
(2) $\dot{\mathbf{q}}(t) = \mathbf{A}_2\mathbf{q}(t) + \mathbf{B}_2\mathbf{x}(t)$ $nT + T_1 \le t < (n+1)T$

(a) Show that the solutions to (1) and (2) may be written

(3) $\mathbf{q}(nT + T_1) = e^{\mathbf{A}_1 T_1}\mathbf{q}(nT^+) + \displaystyle\int_0^{T_1} e^{\mathbf{A}_1 \xi}\mathbf{B}_1\mathbf{x}(nT + T_1 - \xi)\,d\xi$

(4) $\mathbf{q}(nT + T^-) = e^{\mathbf{A}_2 T_2}\mathbf{q}(nT + T_1^+)$
$$+ \int_0^{T_2} e^{\mathbf{A}_2 \xi}\mathbf{B}_2\mathbf{x}(nT + T - \xi)\,d\xi$$

(b) If $\mathbf{q}(nT + T_1^-) = \mathbf{q}(nT + T_1^+)$, $\mathbf{q}(nT^-) = \mathbf{q}(nT^+)$ and
$\mathbf{x}(t) = \mathbf{x}(nT)$ for $nT \le t < nT + T$, the difference equation
for the system is given by

(5) $\mathbf{q}(nT + T) = \mathbf{A}\mathbf{q}(nT) + \mathbf{M}\mathbf{x}(nT)$

where $\mathbf{A} = e^{\mathbf{A}_2 T_2}e^{\mathbf{A}_1 T_1}$ and $\mathbf{M} = e^{\mathbf{A}_2 T_2}\displaystyle\int_0^{T_1} e^{\mathbf{A}_1 \xi}\mathbf{B}_1\,d\xi + \int_0^{T_2} e^{\mathbf{A}_2 \xi}\mathbf{B}_2\,d\xi$.

4.6 Solve Prob. 2.19, using the method of Sec. 4.6.
4.7 The systems of Fig. P 4.3 have piecewise-constant inputs, changing

at intervals of 1 sec.   Write the difference equations for each of the systems by the method described in Sec. 4.6.

4.8   Calculate the response of the system in Fig. 4.2 to a unit step applied at $t = \lambda$.

4.9   Consider the discrete-time system shown (Fig. P 4.9).

   (a) Calculate the fundamental matrix and unit response of the system.
   (b) Find the transmission matrix of the system.
   (c) Find the inverse of the system, i.e., the system whose response to the output of the system of Fig. P 4.9 is the input to the system of Fig. P 4.9.

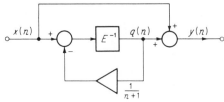

FIG. P 4.9

4.10   Verify (4.33) to (4.35) for the fundamental matrix of Example 4.4.

4.11   Prove that in the time-varying system $\dot{\mathbf{q}}(t) = \mathbf{A}(t)\mathbf{q}(t)$, the fundamental matrix is given by

$$\mathbf{\Phi}(t, t_0) = \exp \int_{t_0}^{t} \mathbf{A}(\lambda) \, d\lambda$$

if and only if $\mathbf{A}(t)$ and $\int_{t_0}^{t} \mathbf{A}(\lambda) \, d\lambda$ commute.

4.12   The amplifiers in the feedback loops of Fig. P 4.12 have constant gain, but the amplifiers preceding the integrators have time-varying gain given by

$$g(t) = \frac{1}{t + 1} \qquad t > 0$$

Calculate the response at time t of the system to a unit impulse applied at time t_0, where $0 \leq t_0 \leq t$.

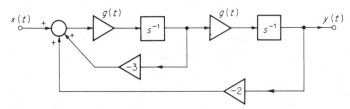

FIG. P 4.12

4.13   Consider the time-varying system of Fig. P 4.13a and b.   The amplifier has a time-varying gain $a(t)$.

   (a) Find the fundamental matrix $\mathbf{\Phi}(t, t_0)$ and demonstrate that $\mathbf{\Phi}^{-1}(t, t_0) = \mathbf{\Phi}(t_0, t)$.
   (b) Let $a(t)$ and $x(t)$ vary periodically as shown in Fig. P 4.13b. Obtain a difference equation relating $y(nT + T)$ and $y(nT)$. Calculate the steady-state value of $y(nT)$.

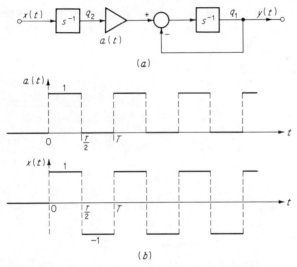

(a)

(b)

FIG. P 4.13

4.14   Show that the perturbed motion of the particle in Example 4.2 is such that the total motion is that of an ellipse with small eccentricity.   Compare the result with an exact calculation.   (See a text in mechanics.)

4.15   Show that $e^{(\mathbf{A}+\mathbf{B})t} = e^{\mathbf{A}t}e^{\mathbf{B}t}$ if and only if $\mathbf{A}$ and $\mathbf{B}$ commute.

4.16   Show that the fundamental matrix $\mathbf{\Phi}(t, \lambda)$ for a time-varying linear system described in terms of the $\mathbf{A}(t)$ matrix must satisfy the equation

$$\frac{\partial \mathbf{\Phi}(t, \lambda)}{\partial \lambda} = -\mathbf{\Phi}(t, \lambda)\mathbf{A}(\lambda)$$

4.17   An "exponential-response matrix" $\mathbf{E}_a(t, \lambda)$ can be defined as the response of a linear system H to the elementary exponential inputs

$$e^{-a(t-\lambda)}\mu_1(t - \lambda)$$

Show how the impulse-response matrix $\mathbf{H}(t, \lambda)$ can be calculated from this matrix $\mathbf{E}_a(t, \lambda)$.

CHAPTER FIVE

FOURIER SERIES

AND TRANSFORMS

5.1 INTRODUCTION

In the previous chapters we based our analysis of the response of linear systems to arbitrary inputs on their response to either unit-step functions or unit-impulse functions. It was seen that a linear system can be characterized by its step response $a(t, \tau)$, or its impulse response $h(t, \tau)$, or a matrix of such responses in case of multiple inputs and outputs. The parameter τ is used to identify the member of the family of step or impulse functions required in the decomposition of the input signal. The response $a(t, \tau)$ to a step $\mu_1(t - \tau)$ has a shape which differs from that of the input step; it is thus a different function of time even in a fixed system. Similarly, $h(t, \tau)$ is a function of t which differs from $\delta(t - \tau)$.

One is tempted to ask whether there is an input signal which will emerge from a fixed linear system without change of shape (i.e., as the same time function with only a change in amplitude). The answer is an exponential

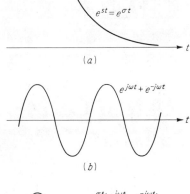

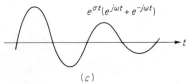

$FIG.\ 5.1\ \ Signals\ of\ the\ form\ e^{st}.$
$(a)\ \ s = \sigma\ (real)\ (\sigma < 0);\ (b)\ \ s = j\omega$
$(imaginary);\ (c)\ \ s = \sigma + j\omega\ (com\text{-}$
$plex)\ (\sigma < 0).$

function e^{st}, where s is a (possibly complex) constant. This function retains its shape under the operations of differentiation and integration:

$$\frac{de^{st}}{dt} = se^{st}$$

$$\int_{-\infty}^{t} e^{st}\, dt = \frac{1}{s} e^{st} \qquad \text{if Re } s > 0$$

Thus, if the input signal is decomposed into elementary signals of form e^{st}, with the parameter s taking on a range of values just as the parameter τ in the unit step $\mu_1(t - \tau)$ takes on a range of values, the responses to the elementary components all have the form e^{st}, but the amplitudes of these components at the output will differ from their respective values at the input.   (The above argument, in mathematical terms, says that exponentials are the *characteristic functions*, sometimes called *normal modes*, of linear differential equations with constant coefficients.)

If the parameter s is the real parameter σ, the elementary functions are the real exponentials $e^{\sigma t}$ (Fig. 5.1a); if s is an imaginary parameter $j\omega$, the elementary functions are sinusoids (Fig. 5.1b); the real sinusoid shown is, of course, obtained only by combining two of the elementary functions. If s is complex, $s = \sigma + j\omega$, the real and imaginary parts of the elementary functions are damped sinusoids (Fig. 5.1c).   Since ω is the angular frequency which determines the number of cycles which the real and imaginary parts of the component functions $e^{st} = e^{\sigma t}e^{j\omega t}$ complete in unit time, the use of the elementary function e^{st} for determining the behavior of

linear systems is referred to as *frequency-domain* analysis; s is sometimes called the *complex frequency.*

We shall now demonstrate formally that in any *fixed* linear system the response to any signal of the form e^{st} (applied at $t = -\infty$) will have the same form. Let H be a fixed linear system, and denote its response to an input e^{st} by $H(s, t)e^{st}$; that is, let

$$He^{st} = H(s, t)e^{st} \tag{5.1}$$

Note that this relation defines $H(s, t)$ as the ratio of (the response of H to e^{st}) to (the input e^{st}). Since it relates the input signal to the output signal, $H(s, t)$ is called the *transfer function* of H. Since H is assumed to be fixed, if the input is translated by an interval τ, the response may be written

$$He^{s(t-\tau)} = H(s, t - \tau)e^{s(t-\tau)} \tag{5.2}$$

By the homogeneity property of H and (5.1),

$$He^{s(t-\tau)} = e^{-s\tau}He^{st} = e^{-s\tau}H(s, t)e^{st} = H(s, t)e^{s(t-\tau)} \tag{5.3}$$

Comparison of (5.2) and (5.3) shows that

$$H(s, t - \tau) = H(s, t)$$

for any value of τ. It follows that in a fixed system the transfer function is independent of t and depends on s only. This is the fundamental reason for the resolution of signals into damped exponentials.

In a time-varying system, the response to a complex exponential is generally not of this form. Two approaches to frequency-domain analysis have been used for time-varying systems. The first, introduced and developed by Zadeh,[†] makes use of time-dependent transfer functions $H(s, t)$ and retains the resolution into complex exponentials. The second, discussed by Aseltine[‡] and Ho and Davis,[§] abandons the resolution into complex exponentials, and instead attempts to find a family of functions[||] $\{\phi(\lambda, t)\}$, called the *characteristic functions* of the system, such that the response of the system to a member of the family remains in the family. If this set of functions is found, the signals may be resolved into members of this family and the techniques developed for fixed systems may be employed.

[†] L. A. Zadeh, Frequency Analysis of Variable Networks, *Proc. IRE,* vol. 38, pp. 291–299, March, 1950.

[‡] J. A. Aseltine, A Transform Method for Linear Time-varying Systems, *J. Appl. Phys.,* vol. 25, pp. 761–764, June, 1954.

[§] E. C. Ho and H. Davis, "Generalized Operational Calculus for Time-varying Networks," University of California, Department of Engineering, Report 54-71, Los Angeles, July, 1954.

[||] The sign { } indicates a set of functions or numbers, obtained by letting a parameter (here λ) assume different values.

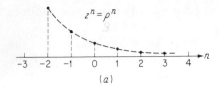

(a)

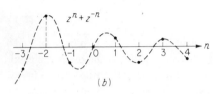

(b)

FIG. 5.2 Signals of the form z^n. (a) $z = \rho$ (real) ($|\rho| < 1$); (b) z complex ($|z| < 1$).

In fixed systems with discrete-time signal inputs, the signals are resolved into a family of components $\{z^n\}$. The reason for this choice is analogous to that used to select e^{st} in continuous-time systems: the difference has the same form as the signal, for

$$\Delta z^n = z^{n+1} - z^n = (z - 1)z^n$$

If z is a real parameter ρ, any member of the family has the appearance shown in Fig. 5.2a. If z is made complex, the real or imaginary part of any member of the family has the appearance shown in Fig. 5.2b.

It can be shown by the method used for continuous-time systems that if H is a fixed discrete-time system, $Hz^n = H(z)z^n$, where $H(z)$ is a function of z, but independent of n. This function is called the *discrete* (or *pulsed*) *transfer function* of H. We shall discuss connections between the continuous-time transfer function and the discrete-time transfer function subsequently.

In this chapter we shall discuss the resolution of continuous-time signals into *undamped* exponentials (sinusoids). This resolution is expressed as Fourier series (for periodic signals) or in terms of Fourier transforms (for nonperiodic signals). We shall discover, however, that the resolution into sinusoids is not possible for many common signals; as a result we must resolve these signals into damped exponentials. The resolution in this case is expressed in terms of Laplace transforms, which is the subject of Chap. 6. The resolution of discrete signals is considered in Chap. 8.

5.2   RESOLUTION OF PERIODIC FUNCTIONS INTO COMPLEX FOURIER SERIES

The reader is probably familiar with the expansion of functions, which are either periodic or of interest only over a finite range of the independent

variable, into a Fourier series.   We shall nevertheless discuss the development and some of the properties of Fourier series for two reasons: first, to show that they represent a decomposition similar to that employed in earlier chapters, and second, to provide a starting point for the representation of nonperiodic functions in terms of Fourier integrals.

A signal $x(t)$ (under a set of rather weak conditions†) may be resolved into a series of complex exponentials over the interval $-T/2 < t < T/2$. This resolution may be written

$$x(t) = \sum_{n=-\infty}^{\infty} X_n e^{jn\omega_0 t} \qquad -T/2 < t < T/2 \qquad (5.4)$$

where $\omega_0 = 2\pi/T$.   The (complex) amplitudes of the exponentials may be found by multiplying both sides of (5.4) by $e^{-jk\omega_0 t}$ and integrating between $-T/2$ and $T/2$.   This gives

$$\int_{-T/2}^{T/2} x(t)e^{-jk\omega_0 t}\, dt = \int_{-T/2}^{T/2} e^{-jk\omega_0 t} \sum_{n=-\infty}^{\infty} X_n e^{jn\omega_0 t}\, dt \qquad (5.5)$$

The series (5.4) is known to be uniformly convergent‡ in the open interval $-T/2 < t < T/2$; hence the order of integration and summation may be interchanged to yield

$$\int_{-T/2}^{T/2} x(t)e^{-jk\omega_0 t}\, dt = \sum_{n=-\infty}^{\infty} X_n \int_{-T/2}^{T/2} e^{jn\omega_0 t}e^{-jk\omega_0 t}\, dt \qquad (5.6)$$

The integral in (5.6) is

$$\int_{-T/2}^{T/2} e^{j(n-k)\omega_0 t}\, dt = \begin{cases} 0 & n \neq k \\ T & n = k \end{cases} \qquad (5.7)$$

The complex functions $e^{jn\omega_0 t}$, $n = 0, \pm 1, \pm 2, \ldots$, are said to form an

---

† These conditions are called the Dirichlet conditions, which require that:

1. $x(t)$ have not more than a finite number of maxima and minima in the interval
2. $x(t)$ have not more than a countable number of finite discontinuities in the interval
3. $x(t)$ have not more than a finite number of infinite discontinuities in the interval and

$$\int_{-T/2}^{T/2} |x(t)|\, dt < \infty$$

See H. S. Carslaw, "Introduction to the Theory of Fourier's Series and Integrals," 3d rev. ed., Dover Publications, Inc., New York, 1930.
‡ Except at points of discontinuity of $x(t)$.   See Carslaw, *op. cit.*, p. 275.

orthogonal set.† As a consequence of the orthogonality property (5.7), the summation in (5.6) reduces to a single term $X_k T$. Hence we obtain

$$X_k = \frac{1}{T} \int_{-T/2}^{T/2} x(t) e^{-jk\omega_0 t} \, dt \tag{5.8}$$

Since each of the complex exponentials in (5.4) is periodic with a period T/n, the sum in (5.4) is also periodic with a period T and does not equal $x(t)$ outside the interval $-T/2 < t < T/2$, unless $x(t)$ is also periodic with a period T. If $x(t)$ is periodic, however,‡

$$x(t) = \sum_{n=-\infty}^{\infty} X_n e^{jn\omega_0 t} \qquad \text{for all } t \tag{5.9}$$

Thus we conclude that if $x(t)$ is periodic with period T, it may be resolved into a countable set of exponentials $\{e^{jn\omega_0 t}\}$, $n = 0, \pm 1, \pm 2, \ldots$, whose components have the (complex) amplitudes X_n. These amplitudes are, by (5.8), the average value over one period of the product $x(t)e^{-jn\omega_0 t}$.

The complex amplitudes X_n may be written

$$X_n = |X_n| e^{j\theta_n} \tag{5.10}$$

The real amplitudes $|X_n|$ and the phases θ_n may be represented by discrete "spectra" as shown in Fig. 5.3. It can easily be shown that, when $x(t)$ is a real signal,

$$X_n = X_{-n}^*$$

where * denotes the complex conjugate (Prob. 5.1). Hence in this case the amplitude spectrum is an even function, while the phase spectrum is an odd function, of n.

It is sometimes convenient to write the resolution of $x(t)$ into sinusoids. If $x(t)$ is a real function of time, we can establish that

$$x(t) = X_0 + \sum_{n=1}^{\infty} 2|X_n| \cos (n\omega_0 t + \theta_n) \tag{5.11}$$

† The set of complex functions $\{\phi_n(t)\}$ is called orthogonal in the interval $a < t < b$ with respect to a weight function $w(t)$ if

$$\int_a^b w(t) \phi_n(t) \phi_m^*(t) \, dt = \begin{cases} 0 & n \neq m \\ \lambda_m & n = m \end{cases}$$

where ϕ_m^* denotes the complex conjugate of ϕ_m.
‡ The series converges to $x(t)$ at a point of continuity, but to $\frac{1}{2}[x(t_0^-) + x(t_0^+)]$ at a point $t = t_0$ of discontinuity.

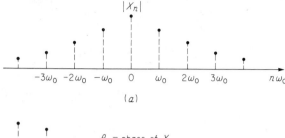

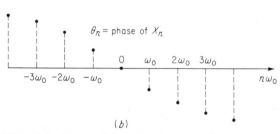

FIG. 5.3   Typical amplitude and phase spectra of a real signal.   (a) Amplitude spectrum; (b) phase spectrum.

with the aid of (5.9) and the property that $X_n = X^*_{-n}$.   The constant

$$X_0 = \frac{1}{T} \int_{-T/2}^{T/2} x(t)\, dt$$

is the average, or d-c, value of the signal.

Example 5.1   Pulse train   Consider the pulse train shown in Fig. 5.4. The amplitudes (coefficients of the Fourier series) are given by

$$X_n = \frac{1}{T} \int_{-\tau/2}^{\tau/2} e^{-jn\omega_0 t}\, dt = \frac{1}{T} \frac{e^{jn\omega_0\tau/2} - e^{-jn\omega_0\tau/2}}{jn\omega_0}$$

$$= \frac{\tau}{T} \frac{\sin (n\omega_0\tau/2)}{n\omega_0\tau/2} \qquad \tau < T \tag{5.12}$$

Hence X_n is real, and a single graph may be used to show both the amplitude and phase spectra.   The "spectrum" is shown in Fig. 5.5; negative values of X_n correspond to values of the phase θ_n of $\pm\pi$ rad.   For $n = 0$,

FIG. 5.4   Pulse train.

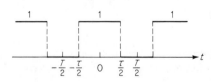

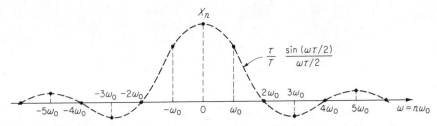

FIG. 5.5   *Spectrum of pulse train;* $\tau = T/2$.

we obtain $X_0 = \tau/T$, which is the average value of the pulse train, as may be verified by inspection of Fig. 5.4.   Note that the envelope is given by

$$\frac{\tau}{T} \frac{\sin (\omega\tau/2)}{\omega\tau/2}$$

While this envelope is a function of the continuous variable ω, the spectrum X_n exists only at the discrete values $\omega = n\omega_0$ and may be considered to be a function of the discrete parameter n, as the subscript n implies.

Example 5.2   Impulse train   If in the previous example the pulse amplitude is made $1/\tau$ (to make the pulse area equal to unity) and then the pulse width is allowed to approach zero, the pulse train becomes an impulse train.   From (5.12), the spectrum becomes

$$X_n = \lim_{\tau\to 0} \frac{1}{T} \frac{\sin (n\omega_0\tau/2)}{n\omega_0\tau/2} = \frac{1}{T}$$

Thus the spectrum is constant for all frequencies, as shown in Fig. 5.6a. Note that this result is also obtained from (5.8) and the definition of a unit impulse:

$$X_n = \frac{1}{T} \int_{-T/2}^{T/2} \delta(t)e^{-jn\omega_0 t}\, dt = \frac{1}{T}$$

The spectrum for a train of impulses phased so that one impulse occurs d sec after the origin $(d \le T/2)$ is given by

$$X_n = \frac{1}{T} \int_{-T/2}^{T/2} \delta(t - d)e^{-jn\omega_0 t}\, dt = \frac{1}{T} e^{-jn\omega_0 d}$$

Thus $|X_n| = 1/T$ and $\theta_n = -n\omega_0 d$.   The amplitude spectrum is the same as in the previous case, but the phase spectrum is linearly decreasing. The envelope has the slope $-d$, as shown in Fig. 5.6b.

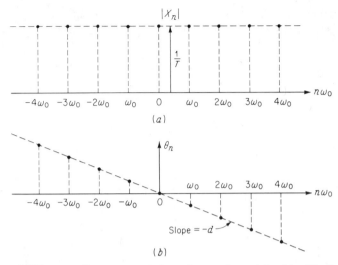

FIG. 5.6   Spectrum of impulse train.   (a) Amplitude spectrum; (b) phase spectrum.

Example 5.3   Triangular wave   A convenient technique for calculating the Fourier series for some types of signals is to differentiate the signal until only impulses appear.   The series for the impulses are known from the previous example.   Term-by-term integration then gives the series for the original signal.   Consider the triangular wave $x(t)$ shown in Fig. 5.7a.   Upon differentiation we obtain the square wave shown in Fig. 5.7b.

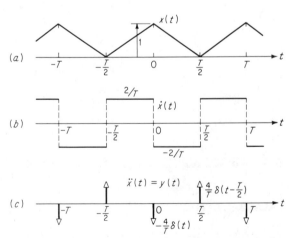

FIG. 5.7   Successive derivatives used for calculation of spectrum for a triangular wave.

Differentiation a second time results in the impulse train $y(t) = \ddot{x}(t)$ shown in Fig. 5.7c.   Using the results of Example 5.2, we find that

$$Y_n = \frac{-4}{T^2}(1 - e^{-jn\omega_0 T/2})$$

Thus

$$\ddot{x}(t) = \sum_{n=-\infty}^{\infty} \frac{-4}{T^2}(1 - e^{-jn\omega_0 T/2})e^{jn\omega_0 t}$$

Integrating, we obtain

$$\dot{x}(t) = \sum_{\substack{n=-\infty \\ n\neq 0}}^{\infty} \frac{-4}{jn\omega_0 T^2}(1 - e^{-jn\omega_0 T/2})e^{jn\omega_0 t} + K$$

where K is a constant of integration.   We note that K is the average value of $\dot{x}(t)$, which is zero (Fig. 5.7b).   Integrating again, we obtain

$$x(t) = \sum_{\substack{n=-\infty \\ n\neq 0}}^{\infty} \frac{-4}{(jn\omega_0 T)^2}(1 - e^{-jn\omega_0 T/2})e^{jn\omega_0 t} + K'$$

where K' is another constant of integration, which must equal the average value of $x(t)$, or $\frac{1}{2}$.   Thus we have

$$X_0 = \tfrac{1}{2}$$

$$X_n = \frac{4}{(n\omega_0 T)^2}(1 - e^{-jn\omega_0 T/2}) \qquad n \neq 0$$

so that

$$X_n = \begin{cases} \dfrac{2}{n^2\pi^2} & n = \text{odd} \\ 0 & n = \text{even} \neq 0 \end{cases}$$

This method is considerably simpler than use of the integral (5.7).

5.3   PROPERTIES OF FOURIER SERIES

PARSEVAL'S THEOREM

If the signal $x(t)$ represents a voltage or current in an electric circuit, then the average power delivered to a resistor is proportional to the mean-

square value of $x(t)$, which is given by†

$$\overline{x^2(t)} = \frac{1}{T} \int_{-T/2}^{T/2} x^2(t) \, dt \tag{5.13}$$

Replacement of $x(t)$ by its Fourier series gives

$$\overline{x^2(t)} = \frac{1}{T} \int_{-T/2}^{T/2} \sum_{k=-\infty}^{\infty} \sum_{l=-\infty}^{\infty} X_k X_l e^{j(k+l)\omega_0 t} \, dt$$

Because of the uniform convergence of the Fourier series, the order of summation and integration may be inverted, so that

$$\overline{x^2(t)} = \sum_{k=-\infty}^{\infty} X_k \sum_{l=-\infty}^{\infty} X_l \frac{1}{T} \int_{-T/2}^{T/2} e^{j(k+l)\omega_0 t} \, dt$$

Making use of the orthogonality property (5.7), we find that only a single term remains in the second summation, and the value of that term is X_{-k}. Hence we conclude that

$$\overline{x^2(t)} = \sum_{k=-\infty}^{\infty} X_k X_{-k} = \sum_{k=-\infty}^{\infty} |X_k|^2 \tag{5.14}$$

for a real signal.‡   This equation states a version of Parseval's theorem and asserts that the mean-square value of a periodic real signal is the sum of the squares of the amplitudes of the harmonics of which it is composed.

LEAST-SQUARES APPROXIMATION

Among the most important properties of Fourier series is their least-squares-approximation property. Suppose a real function $x(t)$ is to be approximated by a *finite* series of exponentials:

$$x_N(t) = \sum_{n=-N}^{N} K_n e^{jn\omega_0 t} \tag{5.15}$$

in which the coefficients K_n are to be chosen to make the mean-square

---

† This assumes that the integral is finite; that is, $x(t)$ is square integrable.
‡ An alternative form of the relation is

$$\overline{x(t)x^*(t)} = \sum_{k=-\infty}^{\infty} X_k X_k{}^*$$

For a real signal, the result is the same as that given by (5.14).

error resulting from approximating $x(t)$ by $x_N(t)$ a minimum.   Let

$$\epsilon(t) = x(t) - x_N(t)$$

$$= \sum_{n=-\infty}^{\infty} X_n e^{jn\omega_0 t} - \sum_{n=-N}^{N} K_n e^{jn\omega_0 t}$$

$$= \sum_{n=-\infty}^{\infty} Y_n e^{jn\omega_0 t} \tag{5.16}$$

where

$$Y_n = \begin{cases} X_n - K_n & -N \le n \le N \\ X_n & |n| > N \end{cases}$$

Thus the error $\epsilon(t)$ is expressed in terms of a Fourier series with coefficients Y_n.   Use of (5.14) then gives

$$\overline{\epsilon^2} = \sum_{n=-N}^{N} |X_n - K_n|^2 + \sum_{|n|>N} |X_n|^2 \tag{5.17}$$

Each term in (5.17) is positive; the mean-square error is thus minimized by setting

$$K_n = X_n \tag{5.18}$$

in which case

$$\overline{\epsilon_{\min}^2} = \sum_{|n|>N} |X_n|^2 \tag{5.19}$$

Thus it is seen that the mean-square error is minimized by making the coefficient K_n in the finite exponential series (5.15) identical with the Fourier coefficient.   The Fourier-series resolution of a function $x(t)$ thus has the property that, if the series is truncated at any given value of n, it approximates $x(t)$ with a smaller mean-square error than any other exponential series which includes the same number of harmonics.   Moreover, it is seen that the error is a sum of positive terms, from which one can conclude that the error is a monotonically decreasing function of the number of harmonics used in the approximation.

Example 5.4   Pulse train   Applying Parseval's theorem, we find that the mean-square value of $x(t)$ in Example 5.1 is

$$\overline{x^2(t)} = \sum_{n=-\infty}^{\infty} \left(\frac{\tau}{T}\right)^2 \left[\frac{\sin (n\omega_0 \tau/2)}{n\omega_0 \tau/2}\right]^2$$

We can also calculate $\overline{x^2(t)}$ directly:

$$\overline{x^2(t)} = \frac{1}{T} \int_{-\tau/2}^{\tau/2} 1 \, dt = \frac{\tau}{T}$$

We now calculate the mean-square error resulting from approximating $x(t)$ by the first N harmonics. We have, from (5.19),

$$\overline{\epsilon_{\min}^2} = \sum_{|n|>N} |X_n|^2 = \sum_{n=-\infty}^{\infty} |X_n|^2 - \sum_{n=-N}^{N} |X_n|^2 = \overline{x^2(t)} - \sum_{n=-N}^{N} |X_n|^2$$

$$= \frac{\tau}{T} \left\{ 1 - \sum_{n=-N}^{N} \frac{\tau}{T} \left[\frac{\sin(n\omega_0\tau/2)}{n\omega_0\tau/2} \right]^2 \right\}$$

and the fractional error is

$$\frac{\overline{\epsilon_{\min}^2}}{\overline{x^2(t)}} = 1 - \sum_{n=-N}^{N} \frac{\tau}{T} \left[\frac{\sin(n\omega_0\tau/2)}{n\omega_0\tau/2} \right]^2 = 1 - \sum_{n=-N}^{N} \frac{\tau}{T} \frac{\sin^2(n\pi\tau/T)}{(n\pi\tau/T)^2}$$

If τ/T is sufficiently small, so that $n\pi\tau/T \ll 1$ for $n \leq N$, each term in the series is approximately equal to τ/T, and we may write

$$\frac{\overline{\epsilon_{\min}^2}}{\overline{x^2(t)}} \doteq 1 - \frac{\tau}{T}(2N + 1)$$

Example 5.5 Impulse train The mean-square value of an impulse train is infinite, and the mean-square error is infinite, regardless of how many harmonics are used in the approximation.

RAPIDITY OF CONVERGENCE

It is often important to have an idea of how rapidly a Fourier series converges, i.e., how rapidly the amplitudes of the harmonics $|X_n|$ approach zero as $n \to \infty$. We shall see that the high-frequency harmonics may be attributed to abrupt changes in the signal, and hence that the smoother a signal is, the more rapidly the harmonics go to zero.

Let us consider a signal resolved into its Fourier series:

$$x(t) = \sum_{n=-\infty}^{\infty} X_n e^{jn\omega_0 t}$$

If this function is differentiated k times, another periodic function results:

$$\frac{d^k x(t)}{dt^k} = \sum_{n=-\infty}^{\infty} (jn\omega_0)^k X_n e^{jn\omega_0 t}$$

Thus the spectrum of the kth derivative is given by

$$(jn\omega_0)^k X_n$$

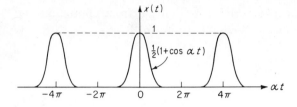

FIG. 5.8 Sinusoidal pulse train.

It is seen that the amplitude of each component of $d^k x(t)/dt^k$ is $(n\omega_0)^k$ times as large as that of the corresponding component of $x(t)$.   Let us now assume that the function and its first k derivatives are continuous. Then it will require $k + 1$ differentiations to produce discontinuities and $k + 2$ differentiations to produce impulses.   As a result of the impulses there will be terms in the spectrum which remain constant with frequency, as we have seen in Example 5.2.   If the function is differentiated fewer than $k + 1$ times, there will be no impulses and the spectrum will approach zero at least as fast as $1/n$.

In general, the spectrum of a signal will approach zero as $1/n^{k+2}$, where $k + 2$ is the number of differentiations required to produce impulses, that is, k is the order of the highest continuous derivative.

Example 5.6   Consider the pulse train shown in Fig. 5.8, in which one pulse is given by

$$x(t) = \begin{cases} \frac{1}{2}(1 + \cos \alpha t) & -\pi \le \alpha t \le \pi \\ 0 & \pi < |\alpha t| < 2\pi \end{cases}$$

Since $x(t)$ and $dx(t)/dt$ are continuous, but $d^2 x(t)/dt^2$ is discontinuous, three differentiations bring impulses and we expect that X_n goes to zero as fast as $1/n^3$.   We calculate

$$X_n = \frac{1}{2T} \int_{-\pi/\alpha}^{\pi/\alpha} (1 + \cos \alpha t) e^{-jn\omega_0 t}\, dt = \frac{\alpha^2}{T} \frac{\sin n\omega_0 \pi/\alpha}{n\omega_0 \alpha^2 - (n\omega_0)^3}$$

where $T = 4\pi$, and see that X_n for large n approaches zero as $1/n^3$.

5.4   RESOLUTION OF NONPERIODIC FUNCTIONS: FOURIER TRANSFORMS

When a function is defined over the infinite time range and is not periodic, the Fourier series representation of Sec. 5.2 is no longer possible.   It is still possible, under certain conditions, to resolve such a nonperiodic func-

tion into complex exponentials of the form $e^{j\omega t}$, where the continuous variable ω takes the place of the discrete variable $n\omega_0$ of Sec. 5.2.

Let us examine the behavior of the Fourier series of the pulse train considered in Example 5.1, when the repetition period T is increased (but the pulse width τ remains unchanged). The original spectrum is shown again in Fig. 5.9a. The spectrum and its envelope are given by

$$X_n = \frac{\tau}{T} \frac{\sin (n\omega_0\tau/2)}{n\omega_0\tau/2} \qquad \text{Envelope} = \frac{\tau}{T} \frac{\sin (\omega\tau/2)}{\omega\tau/2}$$

The period T appears explicitly in the expression for the envelope only in the amplitude factor τ/T. Hence, if the period is doubled, the envelope is halved in amplitude. Since doubling the period also halves the fundamental frequency, the spectrum now has components occurring at multiples of the new fundamental frequency $\omega_1 = \omega_0/2$. The spectrum thus appears as shown in Fig. 5.9b. If the period is again doubled, the amplitude is again halved and the spectrum contains components at multiples of the new fundamental frequency $\omega_2 = \frac{1}{2}\omega_1 = \frac{1}{4}\omega_0$ (see Fig. 5.9c).

If the process is repeated *ad infinitum* it is apparent that the spectrum

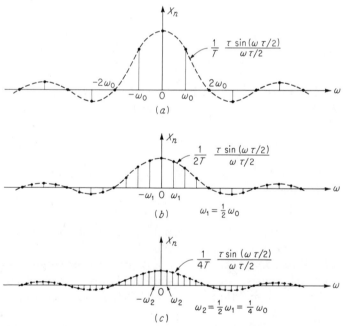

FIG. 5.9   Spectrum of pulse train.   (a) Repetition rate T;
(b) repetition rate $2T$;   (c) repetition rate $4T$.

will have components at *all* frequencies, but that the amplitudes will approach zero.   It should be noted that a given component of the spectrum at a fixed point on the abscissa becomes a higher harmonic of the fundamental as the period is increased.   The spacing $\Delta\omega$ between lines of the spectra equals the fundamental (angular) frequency and decreases as the period is increased.   As the period becomes infinite and the spacing between frequency components becomes the infinitesimal $\Delta\omega$, it is more appropriate to deal with the *frequency density*, defined as

$$\lim_{\Delta\omega\to 0} X(jn\Delta\omega) = \lim_{\Delta\omega\to 0} \frac{X_n}{\Delta\omega/2\pi} = \lim_{T\to\infty} TX_n = \lim_{T\to\infty} \int_{-T/2}^{T/2} x(t)e^{-jn\Delta\omega t}\,dt \tag{5.20}$$

As $T \to \infty$ and $\Delta\omega \to 0$, $n\,\Delta\omega$ approaches the continuous variable ω and (5.20) becomes

$$X(j\omega) = \int_{-\infty}^{\infty} x(t)e^{-j\omega t}\,dt \tag{5.21}$$

This expression is called the Fourier transform of $x(t)$, and may be written symbolically

$$X(j\omega) = \mathfrak{F}[x(t)] \tag{5.22}$$

In order to obtain $x(t)$ from its Fourier transform, we must take into account the contribution to $x(t)$ at *all* frequencies, since $x(t)$ contains all frequencies.   More formally, we make use of (5.9):

$$x(t) = \lim_{\Delta\omega\to 0} \sum_{n=-\infty}^{\infty} X_n e^{jn\Delta\omega t} = \lim_{\Delta\omega\to 0} \frac{1}{2\pi} \sum_{n=-\infty}^{\infty} \frac{X_n}{\Delta\omega/2\pi} e^{jn\Delta\omega t}\,\Delta\omega$$

As $\Delta\omega \to 0$, $n\,\Delta\omega$ approaches the continuous variable ω and the summation becomes an integral over all frequency, so that

$$x(t) = \frac{1}{2\pi} \int_{-\infty}^{\infty} X(j\omega)e^{j\omega t}\,d\omega \tag{5.23}$$

This expression is called the inverse Fourier transform of $X(j\omega)$ and may be written symbolically

$$x(t) = \mathfrak{F}^{-1}[X(j\omega)] \tag{5.24}$$

The derivation of the inverse Fourier transform given above is intended as a heuristic development which shows how the Fourier transform is related to Fourier series, and is not intended to be rigorous.   The rigorous approach consists in postulating the Fourier transform given by (5.21) and then proving that the integral (5.23) converges to $x(t)$ under certain conditions.†

† See, for example, Carslaw, *op. cit.*, pp. 312–314.   Alternatively, see the demonstration of the inversion theorem for the Laplace transform given in Sec. 6.5.

The amplitude and phase spectra of $X(j\omega)$, $|X(j\omega)|$ and $\theta_X(\omega)$, respectively, are now functions of the continuous variable ω. The spectrum is now "dense." Note that, while X_n generally becomes infinitesimal as the period T becomes infinite, the definition of $X(j\omega)$ in (5.20) makes this density finite (or infinite if the signal contains a periodic component).

Example 5.7 Pulse of width τ The Fourier transform of a pulse of unit amplitude and width τ is given by

$$X(j\omega) = \int_{-\tau/2}^{\tau/2} e^{-j\omega t}\, dt = \tau\, \frac{\sin\,(\omega\tau/2)}{\omega\tau/2} \tag{5.25}$$

This spectral density has the shape of the envelope in Fig. 5.9.

Example 5.8 Unit impulse The Fourier transform of a unit impulse is given by

$$X(j\omega) = \int_{-\infty}^{\infty} \delta(t)e^{-j\omega t}\, dt = 1$$

The spectral density is thus constant at all frequencies.

5.5 PROPERTIES OF FOURIER TRANSFORMS

PARSEVAL'S RELATIONS FOR FOURIER TRANSFORMS

It is possible to relate the mean-square value of a nonperiodic signal to its Fourier transform, in a manner analogous to the version of Parseval's theorem given by (5.14) for periodic signals. If we express the conjugate $x^*(t)$ of a (not necessarily real) signal in terms of the Fourier transform of $x(t)$ we may write

$$x(t)x^*(t) = x(t)\frac{1}{2\pi}\int_{-\infty}^{\infty} X^*(j\omega)e^{-j\omega t}\, d\omega$$

Integration of both sides of this equation with respect to t over the infinite time range gives

$$\int_{-\infty}^{\infty} x(t)x^*(t)\, dt = \frac{1}{2\pi}\int_{-\infty}^{\infty} x(t)\int_{-\infty}^{\infty} X^*(j\omega)e^{-j\omega t}\, d\omega\, dt$$

Assuming uniform convergence of the inner integral and inverting the

order of integration, we obtain

$$\int_{-\infty}^{\infty} x(t)x^*(t)\ dt = \frac{1}{2\pi} \int_{-\infty}^{\infty} X^*(j\omega)\ d\omega \int_{-\infty}^{\infty} x(t)e^{-j\omega t}\ dt$$

Now by (5.21), the second integral is the Fourier transform $X(j\omega)$ of $x(t)$; hence

$$\int_{-\infty}^{\infty} x(t)x^*(t)\ dt = \frac{1}{2\pi} \int_{-\infty}^{\infty} X(j\omega)X^*(j\omega)\ d\omega \tag{5.26}$$

which is the desired theorem.†   It may be written

$$\int_{-\infty}^{\infty} |x(t)|^2\ dt = \frac{1}{2\pi} \int_{-\infty}^{\infty} |X(j\omega)|^2\ d\omega \tag{5.27}$$

If $x(t)$ represents the (real) voltage or current in a resistor, the time integral of $x^2(t)$ is proportional to the energy dissipated in the resistor. Thus the total "energy" dissipated by a real signal may be obtained by integrating the square of the magnitude of its Fourier transform over all frequency. We may regard $|X(j\omega)|^2$ as the *energy density spectrum*. Thus we can say that the energy contained in a band of frequencies $\omega_1 \le \omega \le \omega_2$ is given by

$$\frac{1}{2\pi} \int_{\omega_1}^{\omega_2} |X(j\omega)|^2\ d\omega$$

RAPIDITY OF CONVERGENCE

Using an argument similar to that used for Fourier series in Sec. 5.3, it can be shown that the density spectrum $X(j\omega)$ approaches zero as $1/\omega^{k+2}$

† The theorem may be stated for two different time functions $f(t)$ and $g(t)$ with Fourier transforms $F(j\omega)$ and $G(j\omega)$, respectively:

$$\int_{-\infty}^{\infty} f(t)g^*(t)\ dt = \frac{1}{2\pi} \int_{-\infty}^{\infty} F(j\omega)G^*(j\omega)\ d\omega$$

Alternatively, it may be written

$$\int_{-\infty}^{\infty} f(t)g(t)\ dt = \frac{1}{2\pi} \int_{-\infty}^{\infty} F(j\omega)G(-j\omega)\ d\omega$$

since $\mathcal{F}[g^*(t)] = G^*(-j\omega)$ from the definition (5.21). If $f(t) = g(t) = x(t)$, the first form becomes (5.26). A more general form from which these relations may be obtained is the *convolution theorem* (considered later for the Laplace transform)

$$\int_{-\infty}^{\infty} f(\lambda)g(t-\lambda)\ d\lambda = \frac{1}{2\pi} \int_{-\infty}^{\infty} F(j\omega)G(j\omega)e^{j\omega t}\ d\omega$$

if the signal and its first k derivatives are continuous but the $(k + 1)$st derivative is discontinuous.

FOURIER TRANSFORM OF PERIODIC FUNCTIONS

Since the Fourier transform is the spectral density [see (5.20)] of a signal, and since a periodic signal has a discrete amplitude spectrum, the density must be infinite at multiples of the fundamental frequency and zero elsewhere. We thus expect a periodic signal to have a Fourier transform consisting of frequency impulses occurring at multiples of the fundamental frequency. Moreover, we expect that the strength of the impulse occurring at $\omega = n\omega_0$ is given by $2\pi X_n$.

To verify this statement, let us find the inverse Fourier transform of an impulse occurring on the frequency axis at $\omega = \alpha$. We desire

$$x(t) = \mathfrak{F}^{-1}[\delta(\omega - \alpha)] = \frac{1}{2\pi} \int_{-\infty}^{\infty} \delta(\omega - \alpha) e^{j\omega t} \, d\omega \qquad (5.28)$$

From the definition of a unit impulse it is seen that

$$x(t) = \frac{1}{2\pi} e^{j\alpha t}$$

Hence we may conclude that the Fourier transform of $e^{j\alpha t}$ is $2\pi\delta(\omega - \alpha)$, that is,[†]

$$\int_{-\infty}^{\infty} e^{-j(\omega-\alpha)t} \, dt = 2\pi\delta(\omega - \alpha) \qquad (5.29)$$

Now let us resolve a periodic signal $x(t)$ into its Fourier series

$$x(t) = \sum_{n=-\infty}^{\infty} X_n e^{jn\omega_0 t}$$

Then the Fourier transform of the signal is given by

$$X(j\omega) = \mathfrak{F}\left[\sum_{n=-\infty}^{\infty} X_n e^{jn\omega_0 t} \right] = \sum_{n=-\infty}^{\infty} X_n \mathfrak{F}[e^{jn\omega_0 t}] = \sum_{n=-\infty}^{\infty} 2\pi X_n \delta(\omega - n\omega_0)$$

which consists of delta functions of the anticipated magnitude.

[†] It can be seen intuitively that the integral in (5.29) must be zero if $\omega \neq \alpha$, for it represents a sum of two-dimensional vectors whose heads lie on all points of the unit circle. For each increment in t of $2\pi/(\omega - \alpha)$, the vector $e^{j(\omega-\alpha)t}$ describes one revolution around the origin, and the integral must be zero. If $\omega = \alpha$, however, the vector lies on the positive real axis for all values of t, and the integral must be infinite.

5.6 COMPOSITION; INVERSION OF FOURIER TRANSFORM

Up to this point we have been concerned with the resolution of a known signal into its components, which are given by the spectrum.   Suppose, however, that we have the inverse problem: to find the signal whose amplitude and phase spectra are known.   In the case of a discrete spectrum we know that the signal is periodic and is given by

$$x(t) = \sum_{n=-\infty}^{\infty} X_n e^{jn\omega_0 t} = X_0 + \sum_{n=1}^{\infty} 2|X_n|\cos(n\omega_0 t + \theta_n)$$

Although this expression is perfectly valid, it does not enable us to visualize the signal.   It is possible to plot each of the harmonics and add graphically, but if there are more than two harmonics present in appreciable amplitude, this procedure is clearly unsatisfactory.   An alternative technique is to express the spectrum as a sum of several spectra, each of which corresponds to a signal which can be recognized or found from a table.

In the case of nonperiodic functions, whose spectrum is continuous, the graphical method cannot be used.   Fortunately, it is often possible to evaluate the integral in (5.23)

$$x(t) = \frac{1}{2\pi} \int_{-\infty}^{\infty} X(j\omega)e^{j\omega t} \, d\omega$$

which gives $x(t)$ in terms of $X(j\omega)$.   Since $X(j\omega)$ is generally complex even when $x(t)$ is real, this expression is an integral along a line (the real or imaginary axis, depending on the choice of the complex variable) in the complex plane.   The integral may frequently be evaluated by means of the calculus of residues.   Since this technique is essentially the same as that used for the inversion of the Laplace transform, we shall discuss this method in Chap. 6.

Example 5.9   The use of Fourier transforms can be illustrated by a simple example.   In Example 3.3, we found the impulse response of an RC circuit by solving a differential equation.   Let us now determine the response to the time function $e^{-a|t|}$ by using the Fourier transform to decompose this signal.

The Fourier transform of $e^{-a|t|}$ for $a > 0$ is

$$\begin{aligned}
\mathcal{F}[e^{-a|t|}] &= \int_{-\infty}^{\infty} e^{-a|t|}e^{-j\omega t} \, dt \\
&= \int_{-\infty}^{0} e^{+at}e^{-j\omega t} \, dt + \int_{0}^{\infty} e^{-at}e^{-j\omega t} \, dt \\
&= \frac{1}{a - j\omega} + \frac{1}{a + j\omega} = \frac{2a}{a^2 + \omega^2}
\end{aligned} \tag{5.30}$$

Thus the input may be decomposed into exponential elements whose amplitude was just found:

$$e^{-a|t|} = \frac{1}{2\pi} \int_{-\infty}^{\infty} \frac{2a}{a^2 + \omega^2} e^{j\omega t} \, d\omega$$

The response of the RC circuit (Fig. 3.9a) to an input $e^{j\omega t}$ (beginning in the infinite past) is known from steady-state analysis; it is

$$He^{j\omega t} = \frac{1}{1 + j\omega RC} e^{j\omega t}$$

Thus the output voltage across the capacitor in response to an input $e^{-a|t|}$ is the sum of the responses to exponentials of the appropriate amplitude; namely,

$$v(t) = He^{-a|t|} = \frac{1}{2\pi} \int_{-\infty}^{\infty} \frac{2a}{a^2 + \omega^2} \frac{1}{1 + j\omega RC} e^{j\omega t} \, d\omega \qquad (5.31)$$

The integral is best evaluated by the calculus of residues or by recourse to a table of Fourier transform pairs; the result is

$$v(t) = He^{-a|t|} = \begin{cases} \dfrac{1}{1 + aRC} e^{at} & t \leq 0 \\ \dfrac{1}{1 - aRC} e^{-at} - \dfrac{2aRC}{1 - (aRC)^2} e^{-t/RC} & t > 0 \end{cases} \qquad (5.32)$$

The Fourier transform may also be used without explicit knowledge of the response to $e^{j\omega t}$ by starting with the differential equation for $v(t)$,

$$RC \frac{dv}{dt} + v = e^{-a|t|} \qquad (5.33)$$

If the (unknown) Fourier transform of $v(t)$ is $V(j\omega)$, the transform of dv/dt is $j\omega V(j\omega)$ (Prob. 5.12). This property is one of several which give the Fourier transform its great usefulness. By taking the Fourier transform of both sides of (5.33), we obtain

$$(j\omega RC + 1)V(j\omega) = \frac{2a}{a^2 + \omega^2}$$

This is an algebraic equation for $V(j\omega)$; its solution gives

$$V(j\omega) = \frac{1}{1 + j\omega RC} \frac{2a}{a^2 + \omega^2}$$

The inverse Fourier transform now gives $v(t)$ as (5.31) above; the integration has to be performed as before.

We may use (5.32) to find the impulse response.   Note that

$$\mathcal{F}\left[\frac{a}{2}\,e^{-a|t|}\right] = \frac{a^2}{a^2 + \omega^2}$$

and this approaches 1 as $a \to \infty$; it thus becomes the transform of a unit impulse.   If we assume that

$$H\left\{\lim_{a\to\infty}\frac{a}{2}\,e^{-a|t|}\right\} = \lim_{a\to\infty} H\left\{\frac{a}{2}\,e^{-a|t|}\right\}$$

we find the response to a unit impulse from (5.32) to be

$$h(t) = \begin{cases} 0 & t < 0 \\ \dfrac{1}{2RC} & t = 0 \\ \dfrac{1}{RC}\,e^{-t/RC} & t > 0 \end{cases}$$

This agrees with the result of Example 3.3, except that the value of $h(0)$ is specified as the average of $h(0^-)$ and $h(0^+)$.   (See Sec. 6.5 for an explanation of why the inverse Fourier transform gives the average value of the corresponding time function at a point of discontinuity.)

5.7   MEAN FREQUENCY AND BANDWIDTH; SAMPLING THEOREM

BANDWIDTH OF SIGNALS

The space occupied in the frequency spectrum by a signal $x(t)$ is often important in communication engineering.   The distribution in frequency of $x(t)$ is given, as shown in Sec. 5.4, by the Fourier transform $X(j\omega)$. Consider the signal whose Fourier transform has the magnitude shown in Fig. 5.10.   It is apparent that the signal is centered about a mean fre-

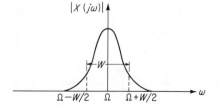

$|X(j\omega)|$

ω

$\Omega-W/2 \quad \Omega \quad \Omega+W/2$

FIG. 5.10   Typical amplitude spectrum.

quency of Ω rad/sec.   (If this signal is to be transmitted on the same channel as other signals, the latter should not infringe upon this portion of the spectrum.)

To formalize the notion of mean frequency and effective bandwidth, the following definitions are useful.† The mean frequency Ω is defined as

$$\Omega = \frac{\int_0^\infty \omega |X(j\omega)|^2 \, d\omega}{\int_0^\infty |X(j\omega)|^2 \, d\omega} \tag{5.34}$$

and the effective bandwidth W is defined as

$$W^2 = \frac{\int_0^\infty (\omega - \Omega)^2 |X(j\omega)|^2 \, d\omega}{\int_0^\infty |X(j\omega)|^2 \, d\omega} = \frac{\int_0^\infty \omega^2 |X(j\omega)|^2 \, d\omega}{\int_0^\infty |X(j\omega)|^2 \, d\omega} - \Omega^2 \tag{5.35}$$

Note that these integrals are defined over positive frequencies only. If the integral in the numerator of (5.34) were taken over positive and negative frequencies, we should find that $\Omega = 0$, since $|X(j\omega)|$ is an even function of ω if $x(t)$ is real (Prob. 5.17).   The use of positive frequencies only in the definitions is justified because the behavior of $X(j\omega)$ at positive frequencies completely determines $x(t)$.   A qualitative relation between the bandwidth of a signal and the shape of the signal may be obtained by observing that (Prob. 5.12)

$$\mathcal{F}\left[\frac{dx}{dt}\right] = j\omega X(j\omega)$$

Hence by (5.27) we obtain

$$\frac{1}{2\pi} \int_{-\infty}^\infty \omega^2 |X(j\omega)|^2 \, d\omega = \int_{-\infty}^\infty \left(\frac{dx}{dt}\right)^2 dt$$

Likewise

$$\frac{1}{2\pi} \int_{-\infty}^\infty |X(j\omega)|^2 \, d\omega = \int_{-\infty}^\infty x^2(t) \, dt$$

so that

$$W^2 = \frac{\int_{-\infty}^\infty \left(\frac{dx}{dt}\right)^2 dt}{\int_{-\infty}^\infty x^2(t) \, dt} - \Omega^2 \tag{5.36}$$

† D. Gabor, Theory of Communication, *Proc. IEE(London)*, vol. 93, pt. III, pp. 429–445, November, 1946. Gabor actually used "analytical" signals in which an imaginary term is added to the real signal $x(t)$. The magnitude $\xi(t)$ of this imaginary term is the Hilbert transform of $x(t)$. The resulting analytical signal $\psi(t) = x(t) + j\xi(t)$ is used in place of $x(t)$. The mean frequency and effective bandwidth are defined with the Fourier transform of $\psi(t)$ in place of $X(j\omega)$ in (5.34) and (5.35).

(since the integrands on the right-hand side of (5.35) are both even functions of ω). Thus the bandwidth of a signal is a measure of its total "roughness." According to the above definition, a signal which is discontinuous has infinite bandwidth, since its derivative has an impulse whose square integral is infinite.

BANDWIDTH OF LINEAR FIXED SYSTEMS

Consider a signal $x(t)$ applied to a linear fixed system H. If $x(t)$ possesses a Fourier transform $X(j\omega)$, that is,

$$x(t) = \frac{1}{2\pi} \int_{-\infty}^{\infty} X(j\omega)e^{j\omega t}\,d\omega$$

the response of H to $e^{j\omega t}$ is, by (5.2) and (5.3),

$$He^{j\omega t} = H(j\omega)e^{j\omega t} \qquad (5.37)$$

where $H(j\omega)$ is the transfer function of H. Hence the output is given by

$$y(t) = Hx(t) = H\left\{\frac{1}{2\pi}\int_{-\infty}^{\infty} X(j\omega)e^{j\omega t}\,d\omega\right\}$$

$$= \frac{1}{2\pi}\int_{-\infty}^{\infty} X(j\omega)H(j\omega)e^{j\omega t}\,d\omega \qquad (5.38)$$

upon use of (5.37) and the linearity of H. Thus the Fourier transform of the output is given by

$$Y(j\omega) = H(j\omega)X(j\omega) \qquad (5.39)$$

If the signal $x(t)$ is to be transmitted by H without distortion, it follows that $H(j\omega)$ should be a constant, say K, for all frequencies. In that case $Y(j\omega) = KX(j\omega)$ and $y(t) = Kx(t)$, a faithful reproduction of $x(t)$, but amplified or attenuated by K. On the other hand, if $H(j\omega)$ is not constant for all frequencies, $y(t)$ will not be a replica of $x(t)$ since all frequencies contained in x will not be transmitted uniformly. From (5.39) it is intuitively evident that if the signal $x(t)$ has a Fourier transform $X(j\omega)$ which is concentrated about a mean frequency Ω with bandwidth W, the fidelity with which the output reproduces $x(t)$ depends on the nature of $H(j\omega)$ in the frequency range $-W/2 < \omega < W/2$. If $H(j\omega)$ is substantially constant in this region, one can expect that $y(t)$ will be a reasonably good reproduction of $x(t)$. Consequently, it is reasonable to define the *mean (resonant) frequency* Ω_H and the *bandwidth* W_H of a linear system.

There are several appropriate definitions of mean frequency and band-

width.   Most frequently the mean frequency Ω_H is defined as that frequency at which $|H(j\omega)|$ is maximum and the bandwidth is defined as the frequency range in which $|H(j\omega)|/|H(j\Omega_H)| \geq 1/\sqrt{2}$.   This is often called the *half-power*, or 3-db, bandwidth.†   These definitions are useful for simple systems or when the quantities are to be determined experimentally.   For analytical work, however, the definitions given by (5.34) and (5.35), with $H(j\omega)$ replacing $X(j\omega)$, are often more convenient.

Example 5.10   N-stage RC-coupled amplifier   The transfer function of a k-stage RC-coupled amplifier is

$$|H(j\omega)| = \frac{K}{(1 + \omega^2\tau^2)^n} \qquad n = k/2$$

where K is a constant and, for convenience, can be set equal to unity. It is evident that the maximum of $|H(j\omega)|$ occurs at $\omega = \Omega_H = 0$ and is unity (with $K = 1$).   The 3-db bandwidth (considering only positive frequencies) is thus given by

$$\frac{1}{(1 + W_H^2\tau^2)^n} = \frac{1}{\sqrt{2}}$$

or

$$W_H^2 = \frac{2^{\frac{1}{2n}} - 1}{\tau^2} \tag{5.40}$$

On the other hand, if the definitions (5.34) and (5.35) are used, we obtain

$$\Omega_H = \frac{\displaystyle\int_0^\infty \frac{\omega\,d\omega}{(1 + \omega^2\tau^2)^n}}{\displaystyle\int_0^\infty \frac{d\omega}{(1 + \omega^2\tau^2)^n}} = \frac{1}{\tau}\frac{\displaystyle\int_0^\infty \frac{x\,dx}{(1 + x^2)^n}}{\displaystyle\int_0^\infty \frac{dx}{(1 + x^2)^n}}$$

and

$$W_H^2 + \Omega_H^2 = \frac{\displaystyle\int_0^\infty \frac{\omega^2\,d\omega}{(1 + \omega^2\tau^2)^n}}{\displaystyle\int_0^\infty \frac{d\omega}{(1 + \omega^2\tau^2)^n}} = \frac{1}{\tau^2}\frac{\displaystyle\int_0^\infty \frac{x^2\,dx}{(1 + x^2)^n}}{\displaystyle\int_0^\infty \frac{dx}{(1 + x^2)^n}}$$

It can be shown that

$$\int_0^\infty \frac{dx}{(1 + x^2)^n} = \frac{(2n - 2)!}{2^{2n-2}[(n - 1)!]^2}\frac{\pi}{2} \qquad n > 0$$

$$\int_0^\infty \frac{x\,dx}{(1 + x^2)^n} = \frac{1}{2(n - 1)} \qquad n > 1$$

$$\int_0^\infty \frac{x^2\,dx}{(1 + x^2)^n} = \frac{1}{2(n - 1)}\frac{(2n - 4)!}{2^{2n-4}[(n - 2)!]^2}\frac{\pi}{2} \qquad n > 1$$

† B. Friedland, O. Wing, and R. Ash, "Principles of Linear Networks," chap. 8, McGraw-Hill Book Company, New York, 1961.

It follows that

$$\Omega_H = \frac{[(n-1)!]^2 2^{2n-2}}{(n-1)(2n-2)!\pi\tau} \tag{5.41}$$

and

$$W_H^2 = \frac{1}{\tau^2}\left[\frac{1}{2n-3} - \frac{[(n-1)!]^4 2^{4n-4}}{(n-1)^2[(2n-2)!]^2\pi^2}\right] \tag{5.42}$$

It is interesting to determine an approximate expression for W_H^2 which can be used for large n. We employ Stirling's asymptotic formula[†] for $n!$,

$$n! \sim \left(\frac{n}{e}\right)^n \sqrt{2n\pi}$$

and find that

$$W_H^2 \sim \frac{1}{2n\tau^2}\left(1 - \frac{2}{\pi}\right)$$

SAMPLING THEOREM

In theoretical investigations of communication systems it is frequently convenient to deal with an ideal, band-limited signal whose Fourier transform is identically zero outside a finite band of frequencies. For positive frequencies, such a signal has an amplitude spectrum of the type illustrated in Fig. 5.11. It is of interest to determine the properties of a signal $x(t)$ which possesses a Fourier transform of this nature. For convenience, we consider the case in which the mean frequency Ω is zero, and thus

$$X(j\omega) \equiv 0 \qquad |\omega| \geq W \tag{5.43}$$

The signal $x(t)$ is given as the inverse Fourier transform of $X(j\omega)$. By virtue of (5.43), the limits of integration on the inversion integral

[†] H. Cramér, "Mathematical Methods of Statistics," pp. 128–131, Princeton University Press, Princeton, N.J., 1947.

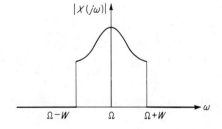

FIG. 5.11   Spectrum of band-limited signal.

(5.23) are $\pm W$. Hence

$$x(t) = \frac{1}{2\pi} \int_{-W}^{W} X(j\omega)e^{j\omega t}\, d\omega \tag{5.44}$$

Now the Fourier transform $X(j\omega)$ can be expanded in a Fourier *series* valid for $|\omega| < W$. The result, using (5.4), is

$$X(j\omega) = \sum_{n=-\infty}^{\infty} C_n e^{jn\omega T} \tag{5.45}$$

where $T = \pi/W$. The coefficients of the Fourier series are given by

$$C_n = \frac{T}{2\pi} \int_{-W}^{W} X(j\omega)e^{-jn\omega T}\, d\omega \tag{5.46}$$

using (5.8). Comparing (5.46) with (5.44), we find that

$$C_n = Tx(-nT)$$

whence (5.45) becomes

$$X(j\omega) = T \sum_{n=-\infty}^{\infty} x(nT)e^{-jn\omega T}$$

Substitution of this relation in (5.44) and inversion of the order of integration and summation (permissible when the sum converges uniformly) results in

$$x(t) = \frac{T}{2\pi} \sum_{n=-\infty}^{\infty} x(nT) \int_{-W}^{W} e^{j\omega(t-nT)}\, d\omega$$

$$= \sum_{n=-\infty}^{\infty} x(nT)\, \frac{\sin\,[W(t-nT)]}{W(t-nT)} \tag{5.47}$$

The result expressed by (5.47) is often called the *sampling theorem*. It may be stated as follows:

If a signal $x(t)$ has a spectrum which vanishes above W rad/sec, it is completely determined by its ordinates at a denumerable set of equally spaced sampling intervals of $T = \pi/W$ sec.†

† In the statement of the sampling theorem, the highest frequency contained in the signal is frequently specified as W cps. Then the sampling interval is $\dfrac{1}{2W}$ sec.

To construct the signal from these ordinates, each ordinate $x(nT)$ is multiplied by the *interpolating function*

$$\phi(t - nT) = \frac{\sin [W(t - nT)]}{W(t - nT)}$$

and the products are summed over all n. Note that $\phi(t - nT)$ is unity for $t = nT$ and is zero for $t = kT \neq nT$, as is required in order that both sides of (5.47) be equal at $t = nT$. Note further that $x(t)$ does not vanish for any finite time, since the interpolating functions extend to $\pm \infty$. (See Fig. 5.5 for a picture of the interpolating function, which has arisen in a different context.)

An important consequence of the sampling theorem is that a discrete-time signal $x(nT)$, such as the output of a digital computer, can be transmitted in the form of (5.47) without loss of "information" in a perfect channel of finite bandwidth proportional to the sampling rate. Conversely, an essentially continuous-time signal (i.e., one which cannot be adequately approximated by a discrete-time signal) cannot be transmitted without loss of information in a channel of finite bandwidth.

5.8 LIMITATIONS OF THE FOURIER TRANSFORM

In the preceding discussion we did not consider the conditions under which it is permissible to resolve a signal into imaginary exponentials, i.e., the conditions on $x(t)$ in order for the integral in the definition (5.21) to exist and for $x(t)$ to be represented by (5.23). It is known that sufficient conditions for such a representation are†

(1) $x(t)$ satisfies the Dirichlet conditions in every finite interval

$$\text{(see footnote p. 137)} \quad (5.48)$$

(2) $$\int_{-\infty}^{\infty} |x(t)|\, dt < \infty \quad (5.49)$$

Although most signals of practical importance satisfy (5.48), there is a broad class of important signals for which (5.49) is not satisfied. Signals like the unit step and the unit ramp do not satisfy (5.49), and hence there are difficulties in using (5.21) to define a Fourier transform for these signals. Since signals of this type occur frequently in practice, it is necessary to have a method of resolution which may also be used conveniently for these. This resolution is given by the Laplace transform, discussed in the next chapter.

† See Carslaw, *op. cit.*, pp. 312–314, or I. N. Sneddon, "Fourier Transforms," sec. 3, McGraw-Hill Book Company, New York, 1951.

PROBLEMS

5.1   Given a periodic function $f(t)$ with period T whose Fourier expansion is

$$f(t) = \sum_{n=-\infty}^{\infty} F_n e^{jn\omega_0 t}$$

Establish the following:

(a) If $f(t)$ is real and even, that is, $f(t) = f(-t)$, then F_n is real.
(b) If $f(t)$ is real and odd, that is, $f(-t) = -f(t)$, then F_n is imaginary.
(c) If $f(t + T/2)$ is equal to $f(t)$, then $F_n = 0$ for odd n.
(d) If $f(t + T/2) = -f(t)$, then $F_n = 0$ for even n.
(e) If $f(t)$ is real, then $F_n = F_{-n}^*$.

5.2   (a) Show that the Fourier series of a periodic function is unique; i.e., if

$$f(t) = \sum_{n=-\infty}^{\infty} c_n e^{jn\omega_0 t}$$

and

$$f(t) = \sum_{n=-\infty}^{\infty} d_n e^{jn\omega_0 t}$$

then $c_n = d_n$ for all n.

5.3   (a) Show that translating a periodic function in time does not change the amplitude spectrum; i.e., if

$$f(t) = \sum_{n=-\infty}^{\infty} c_n e^{jn\omega_0 t}$$

and

$$f(t - a) = \sum_{n=-\infty}^{\infty} d_n e^{jn\omega_0 t}$$

then $|c_n| = |d_n|$.
(b) Show that the nth harmonic is shifted in phase by $n\omega_0 a$ rad.

5.4   Find and sketch the amplitude and phase spectra of the periodic signals for which one cycle is shown in Fig. P 5.4.

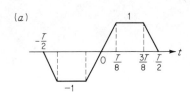

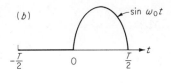

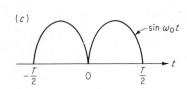

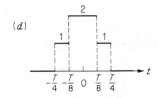

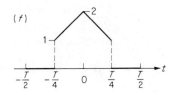

FIG. P 5.4

5.5   Compute the mean-square error resulting from approximating the signals of Fig. P 5.4 by the sum of the first three harmonics present.

5.6   The signals of Fig. P 5.4 are passed through a low-pass filter with the transfer function

$$H(j\omega) = \frac{1}{1 + j\omega T}$$

Sketch the amplitude and phase spectra of the output.

5.7   The signals of Fig. P 5.4 are passed through a high-pass filter with the transfer function

$$H(j\omega) = \frac{j\omega T}{1 + j\omega T}$$

Sketch the amplitude and phase spectra of the output.

5.8   *Poisson's Summation Formula* Let the series $\sum\limits_{n=-\infty}^{\infty} g(2\pi n + t)$ represent a function which can be expanded in a Fourier series, and let this series be uniformly convergent for all t in the interval $0 < t < 2\pi$. By expanding the series $\sum\limits_{n=-\infty}^{\infty} g(2\pi n + t)$ in the

interval $0 < t < 2\pi$, show that

$$\sum_{n=-\infty}^{\infty} g(2\pi n) = \frac{1}{2\pi} \sum_{n=-\infty}^{\infty} \int_{-\infty}^{\infty} g(\lambda)e^{-jn\lambda}\, d\lambda$$

Hint: Note that

$$\sum_{n=-\infty}^{\infty} \int_0^{2\pi} g(2\pi n + \tau)e^{-jm\tau}\, d\tau = \sum_{n=-\infty}^{\infty} \int_{2\pi n}^{2\pi(n+1)} g(\lambda)e^{-jm\lambda}\, d\lambda$$

$$= \int_{-\infty}^{\infty} g(\lambda)e^{-jm\lambda}\, d\lambda$$

5.9   Consider the nonperiodic pulses whose shape is given by one cycle of the signals of Fig. P 5.4. Find and sketch the amplitude and phase spectra of each pulse.

5.10   Find the amplitude and phase spectra of the following signals:

(a) $f(t) = \begin{cases} 1 - \dfrac{|t|}{T} & -T \le t \le T \\ 0 & |t| > T \end{cases}$.

(b) $f(t) = e^{-(t/2T)^2}$.

5.11   Demonstrate the following properties of the Fourier transform:

(a) Linearity: $\mathfrak{F}[af_1(t) + bf_2(t)] = aF_1(j\omega) + bF_2(j\omega)$.
(b) Time translation: $\mathfrak{F}[f(t - a)] = e^{-j\omega a}F(j\omega)$.
(c) Modulation: $\mathfrak{F}[f(t)\cos \omega_0 t] = \frac{1}{2}[F(j\omega - j\omega_0) + F(j\omega + j\omega_0)]$.

5.12   Show that the Fourier transform of the nth derivative of $f(t)$ is $(j\omega)^n$ times the Fourier transform of $f(t)$, provided that the first $n - 1$ derivatives of $f(t)$ vanish as $t \to \pm \infty$.

5.13   Find the Fourier transform of

$$f(t) = \begin{cases} e^{j\omega_0 t} & -T \le t \le T \\ 0 & |t| > T \end{cases}$$

As $T \to \infty$, $f(t)$ becomes periodic in the infinite interval. What does $F(j\omega)$ become in this case? Is this reasonable?

5.14   Find the time functions corresponding to the following Fourier transforms:

(a) $F(j\omega) = \delta(\omega - \omega_0)$.

(b) $F(j\omega) = \begin{cases} 1 & |\omega| \le \omega_0 \\ 0 & |\omega| > \omega_0 \end{cases}$.

Hint: Use the symmetry property of the direct and inverse transforms.

5.15 Discuss the nature of the Fourier transform of the *real* time functions with the following properties:

(a) $f(t) = f(-t)$ even function.
(b) $f(t) = -f(-t)$ odd function.

5.16 Represent the function $f(x)$ defined by

$$f(x) = \begin{cases} 1 & |x| < 1 \\ \frac{1}{2} & |x| = 1 \\ 0 & |x| > 1 \end{cases}$$

in terms of its Fourier integral, and thus show that

$$f(x) = \frac{2}{\pi} \int_0^\infty \frac{\sin u \cos ux}{u} \, du$$

The integral is known as *Dirichlet's discontinuous function.*

5.17 Show that, if $f(t)$ is real, $|F(j\omega)| = |F(-j\omega)|$.

5.18 Let $F(j\omega)$ and $G(j\omega)$ be the Fourier transforms of $f(t)$ and $g(t)$, respectively. Show that

$$\mathfrak{F}[f \star g] = \mathfrak{F} \int_{-\infty}^{\infty} f(\lambda)g(t - \lambda) \, d\lambda = F(j\omega)G(j\omega)$$

Thus the Fourier transform of the convolution of two time functions is the product of their transforms.

5.19 Compare the 3-db bandwidth in Example 5.10 with the bandwidth of (5.42) for large n.

CHAPTER SIX

THE LAPLACE TRANSFORM

6.1 INTRODUCTION: DEFINITION AND INTERPRETATION OF THE LAPLACE TRANSFORM

As indicated in the previous chapter, the Fourier transform (resolution into sinusoids) does not converge in the usual sense for the unit step and the unit ramp because these signals do not go to zero as $t \to \infty$, and hence†

$$\int_{-\infty}^{\infty} |f(t)| \, dt$$

does not exist. Suppose, however, that we multiply $f(t)$ by a damped exponential $e^{-\sigma t}$, where σ is a positive constant. The resulting signal

† Throughout this book, time functions or signals are denoted by lower-case letters and their transforms by the corresponding capital letters. In Chap. 5 we used $x(t)$ and $f(t)$ to denote signals; here and in Chap. 8 we shall use $f(t)$ for signals, since this is widely used in work with Laplace and Z transforms, and reserve $x(t)$ and $y(t)$ for signals which are inputs and outputs, respectively, of systems.

$f(t)e^{-\sigma t}$ has a Fourier transform if

$$\int_{-\infty}^{\infty} |f(t)e^{-\sigma t}| \, dt = \int_{-\infty}^{\infty} |f(t)|e^{-\sigma t} \, dt < \infty \qquad (6.1)$$

But the latter integral exists for such signals as the unit step and the unit ramp (in fact, for any polynomial in t which is zero for $t < 0$) as a result of the convergence factor $e^{-\sigma t}$. The Fourier transform of the modified signal is given by

$$F(\sigma + j\omega) = \int_{-\infty}^{\infty} f(t)e^{-\sigma t}e^{-j\omega t} \, dt = \int_{-\infty}^{\infty} f(t)e^{-(\sigma+j\omega)t} \, dt \qquad (6.2)$$

To obtain $f(t)$ from $F(\sigma + j\omega)$, we observe that

$$f(t)e^{-\sigma t} = \mathfrak{F}^{-1}[F(\sigma + j\omega)] = \frac{1}{2\pi} \int_{-\infty}^{\infty} F(\sigma + j\omega)e^{j\omega t} \, d\omega \qquad (6.3)$$

Hence, multiplying both sides of (6.3) by $e^{\sigma t}$ (with constant σ), we obtain

$$f(t) = \frac{1}{2\pi} \int_{-\infty}^{\infty} F(\sigma + j\omega)e^{(\sigma+j\omega)t} \, d\omega \qquad (6.4)$$

We may express (6.2) and (6.4) more succinctly by the introduction of the complex quantity $s = \sigma + j\omega$. We then have, from (6.2),

$$F(s) = \int_{-\infty}^{\infty} f(t)e^{-st} \, dt \qquad (6.5)$$

In (6.4) we make the change of variable $s = \sigma + j\omega$; then $ds = j \, d\omega$. When $\omega = \pm \infty$, $s = \sigma \pm j\infty$; hence (6.4) becomes

$$f(t) = \frac{1}{2\pi j} \int_{\sigma-j\infty}^{\sigma+j\infty} F(s)e^{st} \, ds \qquad (6.6)$$

The function $F(s)$ obtained by (6.5) is called the two-sided Laplace transform of $f(t)$ and will be written symbolically $\mathcal{L}_{\mathrm{II}}[f(t)]$. A useful alternative notation is

$$f(t) \leftrightarrow F(s)$$

This is read "$f(t)$ transforms into $F(s)$," or "$F(s)$ is the transform of $f(t)$."

The time function $f(t)$ obtained from (6.6) is called the inverse Laplace transform of $F(s)$ and may be indicated by $\mathcal{L}^{-1}[F(s)]$. Note that the integration is performed in the complex-frequency plane along a line $s = \sigma$, where σ is a constant damping factor which ensures the convergence of (6.1); see Fig. 6.1.

We see that the Laplace transform of $f(t)$ is a direct extension of the Fourier transform except that $f(t)$ has been resolved into *damped* exponentials rather than undamped exponentials (sinusoids) and that the

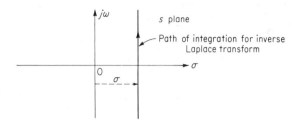

*FIG. 6.1   Path of in-
tegration   for   inverse
Laplace transform.*

damping factor is chosen to ensure the convergence of (6.1).   We note
that the integral (6.1) converges for functions such as the unit step
because of the damping factor.   This damping factor, which results in
convergence for $t > 0$, actually may have the opposite effect for $t < 0$.
For signals which are identically zero for $t < 0$, there is no difficulty; we
may wish to deal with signals, however, which are not zero for $t < 0$.   In
that case we must be certain that the damping factor is chosen properly.

Most problems can be formulated in a manner which permits all signals
to be zero for $t < 0$.†   We can often start with this assumption and work
only with the one-sided Laplace transform

$$\mathcal{L}_I[f(t)] = \int_{0-}^{\infty} f(t)e^{-st} \, dt \tag{6.7}$$

This is identical with the two-sided Laplace transform if and only if
$f(t) = 0$ for $t < 0$.   The necessity of a clear distinction between the
one-sided and two-sided Laplace transform is seen in the following
example.

Example 6.1   We shall first find the two-sided Laplace transform of the
function shown in Fig. 6.2a:

$$f_1(t) = e^{-a|t|} \qquad -\infty < t < \infty, \qquad a > 0$$

From (6.5)

$$F_1(s) = \int_{-\infty}^{0} e^{at}e^{-st} \, dt + \int_{0}^{\infty} e^{-at}e^{-st} \, dt$$

The first integral is

$$\int_{-\infty}^{0} e^{-(s-a)t} \, dt = \left[\frac{e^{-(s-a)t}}{-(s-a)}\right]_{-\infty}^{0} = \left[\frac{e^{-(\sigma-a)t}e^{-j\omega t}}{-(s-a)}\right]_{-\infty}^{0}$$

The numerator remains finite (and goes to zero) as $t \to -\infty$ only if
$\sigma - a < 0$; thus this integral converges to $1/(a - s)$ if $\sigma < a$.   Similarly,

† A notable exception is the class of problems connected with filtering of random or
stochastic signals.   Such signals will be discussed in Chap. 9.

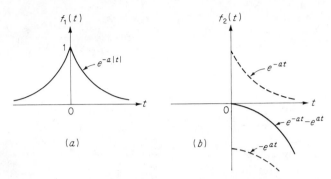

FIG. 6.2   Two signals which appear to have the same Laplace transform.

the second integral converges to $1/(a + s)$ if $\sigma > -a$; hence

$$F_1(s) = \frac{1}{a - s} + \frac{1}{a + s} = \frac{2a}{a^2 - s^2} \qquad -a < \sigma < a$$

Next we shall find the one-sided Laplace transform of $f_2(t) = e^{-at} - e^{at}$ (Fig. 6.2b).   From (6.7)

$$F_2(s) = \int_0^\infty e^{-at} e^{-st}\, dt - \int_0^\infty e^{at} e^{-st}\, dt$$

The first integral converges to $1/(s + a)$ for $\sigma > -a$, and the second integral converges to $1/(s - a)$ for $\sigma > a$.   Thus

$$F_2(s) = \frac{1}{s + a} - \frac{1}{s - a} = \frac{2a}{a^2 - s^2} \qquad \sigma > a$$

We observe that the Laplace transforms of both signals are given by the same expression.   The range of σ (damping factor), however, differs in the two cases.   Since the inversion integral (6.6) must be evaluated for a value of σ for which the Laplace transform exists, the result for each $F(s)$ will be different.   The regions of convergence for $F_1(s)$ and $F_2(s)$ are shown in Fig. 6.3.

It should be noted that the one-sided Laplace transform cannot contain any information about $f(t)$ for negative values of t, while the two-sided transform carries information about $f(t)$ for all t.   In the absence of any remark to the contrary, we shall always assume that the one-sided Laplace transform is intended.†

† For a detailed treatment of the applications of the two-sided Laplace transform, see B. van der Pol and H. Bremmer, "Operational Calculus Based on the Two-sided Laplace Integral," Cambridge University Press, New York, 1950.

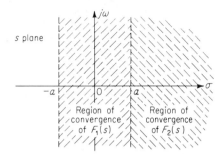

FIG. 6.3   Regions of convergence in Example 6.1.

6.2 LAPLACE TRANSFORMS OF ELEMENTARY FUNCTIONS

The Laplace transform of the exponential e^{-at} is, for any real a,

$$\mathcal{L}[e^{-at}] = \int_0^\infty e^{-at}e^{-st}\,dt = \left[\frac{e^{-(s+a)t}}{-(s+a)}\right]_0^\infty = \left[\frac{e^{-(\sigma+a)t}e^{-j\omega t}}{-(s+a)}\right]_0^\infty$$

The numerator remains finite (and goes to zero) as $t \to \infty$ only if $\sigma + a > 0$; thus

$$\mathcal{L}[e^{-at}] = \frac{1}{s+a} \qquad \sigma > -a \tag{6.8}$$

The restriction on σ is easily explained.   As long as $\sigma > -a$, the product $e^{-at}e^{-\sigma t}$ decreases with increasing t, and the integral in (6.7) converges. For $\sigma \le -a$, the integral diverges.   Note that if a is complex, the restriction becomes $\sigma > -\operatorname{Re} a$.

The Laplace transform of $\cos \alpha t$ may now be easily found by expanding this function into exponentials.   Thus

$$\mathcal{L}[\cos \alpha t] = \int_0^\infty \cos \alpha t\, e^{-st}\,dt = \frac{1}{2}\int_0^\infty (e^{j\alpha t} + e^{-j\alpha t})e^{-st}\,dt$$

$$= \tfrac{1}{2}\mathcal{L}[e^{j\alpha t}] + \tfrac{1}{2}\mathcal{L}[e^{-j\alpha t}] = \frac{1}{2}\left[\frac{1}{s-j\alpha} + \frac{1}{s+j\alpha}\right]$$

For each of the two transforms, we require that $\sigma > -\operatorname{Re}(\mp j\alpha) = 0$. Hence

$$\mathcal{L}[\cos \alpha t] = \frac{s}{s^2 + \alpha^2} \qquad \sigma > 0 \tag{6.9}$$

The elementary functions of time-domain analysis $\mu_k(t)$, which were defined in Chap. 3, have particularly simple Laplace transforms, which

we shall now calculate. By definition,

$$\mathcal{L}[\mu_k(t)] = \int_{0-}^{\infty} \mu_k(t)e^{-st}\,dt \tag{6.10}$$

Integration of (6.10) by parts with $u = e^{-st}$ and $dv/dt = \mu_k(t)$ gives

$$\mathcal{L}[\mu_k(t)] = [\mu_{k+1}(t)e^{-st}]_{0-}^{\infty} + s \int_{0-}^{\infty} \mu_{k+1}(t)e^{-st}\,dt$$

since $\mu_{k+1}(t) = \int_{-\infty}^{t} \mu_k(t)\,dt$. Since $\mu_k(0^-) = 0$ by definition, and since $e^{-st} \to 0$ as $t \to \infty$ only if $\sigma > 0$, this equation becomes

$$\mathcal{L}[\mu_k(t)] = s\mathcal{L}[\mu_{k+1}(t)] \qquad \sigma > 0 \tag{6.11}$$

The Laplace transform of a unit step is

$$\mathcal{L}[\mu_1(t)] = \int_{0}^{\infty} e^{-st}\,dt = \frac{1}{s} \qquad \sigma > 0 \tag{6.12}$$

Hence, from (6.11) and (6.12),

$$\mathcal{L}[\mu_k(t)] = \frac{1}{s^k} \qquad \sigma > 0 \tag{6.13}$$

Table 6.1   ELEMENTARY LAPLACE TRANSFORM
PAIRS

$f(t)$	$F(s)$	$\sigma_a\ (\sigma > \sigma_a)$
(1) $\delta(t)$	1	$-\infty$
(2) $\mu_1(t)$	$\dfrac{1}{s}$	0
(3) $\dfrac{t^{n-1}}{(n-1)!} \qquad n > 0$	$\dfrac{1}{s^n}$	0
(4) e^{-at}	$\dfrac{1}{s+a}$	$-a$
(5) $\cos \alpha t$	$\dfrac{s}{s^2 + \alpha^2}$	0
(6) $\sin \alpha t$	$\dfrac{\alpha}{s^2 + \alpha^2}$	0

If we apply (6.11) to the impulse functions $\{\mu_k(t)\}$, $k = 0, -1, \ldots,$
we find

$$\mathcal{L}[\mu_0(t)] = \mathcal{L}[\delta(t)] = 1 \tag{6.14}$$
$$\mathcal{L}[\mu_{-1}(t)] = s \tag{6.15}$$

and so forth.   Note that (6.14) is consistent with the property of a
unit impulse since†

$$\int_{0-}^{\infty} e^{-st}\delta(t)\, dt = 1$$

Table 6.1 lists the transforms of some of the elementary functions derived
in this section, together with some of the other most frequently occurring
transforms.   By the use of the properties of the Laplace transform
described in Sec. 6.4, it is possible to extend this table to include a large
variety of time functions.

6.3 SOME THEOREMS CONCERNING THE LAPLACE TRANSFORM

The Laplace transform defined by (6.7) is a function of s.   While the
transformation of the function $f(t)$ according to (6.7) was obtained in
a logical manner from the Fourier transform by considering the real part
σ of s to be a constant, the transform is a much more powerful tool if it is
defined by (6.7) as a function of the *complex variable s*.   The steps leading
to the expression for $f(t)$ in terms of $F(s)$ as given in (6.6) are then no
longer valid, since σ may vary along with ω.   Thus the path of integration in Fig. 6.1 is no longer restricted to a straight line parallel to the $j\omega$
axis.   This will be discussed later in this chapter.
   In order to use the Laplace transform in system analysis, we must be
familiar with some of its properties.   We must know when we can be
certain that the transform exists, i.e., that the integral (6.7) converges.
In order to invert the order of integration in the case of a multiple integral,
we have to know the nature of the convergence of the Laplace transform
integral.   It is also important to know when $F(s)$ is an analytic function
of the complex variable s, for then the powerful results of the theory of
functions of a complex variable become available.   Most of the theorems
are merely stated; proofs may be found in the references cited.
   It will be useful first to recall the definitions of absolute convergence
and uniform convergence of an integral.   An improper integral such as

---

† Note that a unit impulse or any of its derivatives occurring at the origin contributes
to the Laplace transform of signals in which these elementary functions appear.

that in (6.7) is defined as

$$\int_0^\infty g(\lambda)\, d\lambda = \lim_{R \to \infty} \int_0^R g(\lambda)\, d\lambda \qquad (6.16)$$

If the limit exists, the integral converges.   The integral converges absolutely if and only if

$$\int_0^\infty |g(\lambda)|\, d\lambda < \infty \qquad (6.17)$$

To define uniform convergence, consider the integral $\int_0^\infty g(\lambda, \omega)\, d\lambda$, where ω is a parameter lying in a specified (possibly infinite) interval. If $\int_0^\infty g(\lambda, \omega)\, d\lambda = F(\omega)$ and for any $\epsilon > 0$ we can choose d large enough so that for any $b > d$ the integral $\int_0^b g(\lambda, \omega)\, d\lambda$ differs from $F(\omega)$ by less than ϵ for any ω in the specified interval, i.e., if

$$\left| \int_0^b g(\lambda, \omega)\, d\lambda - F(\omega) \right| < \epsilon \qquad b > d$$

then the integral $\int_0^\infty g(\lambda, \omega)\, d\lambda$ converges uniformly to $F(\omega)$ for the specified values of ω.   The word "uniform" refers to the fact that the value of b may be used uniformly for any ω in the specified interval; that is, b is independent of ω.

The absolute convergence of the Laplace transform integral is guaranteed by the conditions in the following theorem.

Theorem 6.1   Absolute convergence   *The integral*

$$F(s) = \int_0^\infty f(t)e^{-st}\, dt \qquad (6.18)$$

converges absolutely for all $\sigma(= \operatorname{Re} s) > c$ *if*

$$\int_0^T |f(t)|\, dt \le K < \infty \qquad (6.19)$$

for any finite positive T and some constant K, and

$$|f(t)| \le M e^{ct} \qquad (6.20)$$

for some M and c and $t > T$.

Note that condition (6.20) requires that, beyond some point T, the function $f(t)$ must be "of exponential order"; i.e., it must not increase with t more rapidly than the exponential e^{ct}.   The conditions (6.19) and

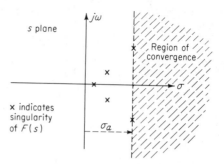

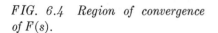

FIG. 6.4   Region of convergence
of $F(s)$.

(6.20) are sufficient, but not always necessary, for the absolute convergence
of the Laplace transform.   Condition (6.19) may be weakened to include
all functions satisfying the Dirichlet conditions in any finite interval
$0 \leq t \leq T$.   For most functions of interest, however, these conditions
may be regarded as also necessary.

It should also be observed that conditions (6.19) and (6.20) permit $f(t)$
to contain a finite number of infinite discontinuities.

In order to prove Theorem 6.1, we consider the integral which, according
to (6.17), must be shown to be finite,

$$\int_0^\infty |f(t)e^{-st}| \, dt = \int_0^\infty |f(t)|e^{-\sigma t} \, dt = \int_0^T |f(t)|e^{-\sigma t} \, dt + \int_T^\infty |f(t)|e^{-\sigma t} \, dt$$

where $\sigma = \operatorname{Re} s$.   Now

$$\int_0^T |f(t)|e^{-\sigma t} \, dt \leq e^{|\sigma|T} \int_0^T |f(t)| \, dt \leq Ke^{|\sigma|T}$$

according to (6.19).   Also, from (6.20), and since $\sigma > c$ by assumption,

$$\int_T^\infty |f(t)|e^{-\sigma t} \, dt \leq M \int_T^\infty e^{-(\sigma-c)t} \, dt = \frac{Me^{-(\sigma-c)T}}{\sigma - c}$$

Hence

$$\int_0^\infty |f(t)e^{-st}| \, dt \leq Ke^{|\sigma|T} + \frac{Me^{-(\sigma-c)T}}{\sigma - c} < \infty \qquad \text{for } \sigma > c$$

and the proof is complete.

The smallest value of σ, say σ_a, such that the Laplace transform $F(s)$
converges absolutely for $\sigma > \sigma_a$, is called the *abscissa of absolute convergence* of $F(s)$.   The *region of absolute convergence* of the Laplace transform is a half plane to the right of (but not including) the line $\sigma = \sigma_a$, as
shown in Fig. 6.4.

Example 6.2

(a) If $f(t) = 0$ for $t > T$ and $\int_0^T |f(t)| \, dt$ exists, $F(s)$ converges abso-
lutely for all $\sigma > -\infty$; hence $\sigma_a = -\infty$.

(b) If $f(t)$ possesses a Fourier transform, $F(s)$ converges absolutely for all $\sigma \geq 0$; hence $\sigma_a < 0$.

(c) If $f(t) = e^{at}$, then $F(s)$ converges to $1/(s - a)$ for $\sigma > a$, but does not converge for $\sigma \leq a$; hence $\sigma_a = a$ (Sec. 6.2).

Example 6.3 The function $f(t) = t^{-\frac{1}{2}}$ is infinite at $t = 0$. However,

$$\int_0^T t^{-\frac{1}{2}} dt = 2T^{\frac{1}{2}} < \infty$$

and $|f(t)| < e^{ct}$ for $t > 1$ and $c \geq 0$; hence the Laplace transform of $f(t)$ exists. In fact, $\mathcal{L}[t^{-\frac{1}{2}}] = (\pi/s)^{\frac{1}{2}}$ for $\sigma > 0$.

A sufficient condition for the uniform convergence of the Laplace transform integral is given by the following theorem.

Theorem 6.2   Uniform convergence†   *If the integral*

$$F(s) = \int_0^\infty f(t)e^{-st} dt$$

converges absolutely for $s = \sigma_0 + j\omega_0$, *it converges uniformly and absolutely in the half plane specified by* $\sigma \geq \sigma_0$.

This theorem guarantees that if the Laplace transform converges absolutely for one value of σ, it will do so for all larger values of σ. Further, it assures uniform convergence whenever the transform converges absolutely.

The Laplace transforms in Table 6.1 are analytic functions of the complex variable s (except at the isolated points where they have singularities). The following theorem establishes that all Laplace transforms are analytic functions of s.

Theorem 6.3   Analyticity‡   *If the Laplace transform integral* (6.7) *converges absolutely for* $\sigma > \sigma_a$, *then* $F(s)$ *is analytic for* $\sigma > \sigma_a$.

A consequence of this theorem is that all singularities of $F(s)$ must lie to the left of the line $\sigma = \sigma_a$ or on that line. At least one singularity of $F(s)$ must lie on the line $\sigma = \sigma_a$; otherwise it would be possible to extend

---

† See D. V. Widder, "The Laplace Transform," p. 46, Princeton University Press, Princeton, N.J., 1941.

‡ *Ibid.*, p. 57; R. V. Churchill, "Operational Mathematics," 2d ed., p. 171, McGraw-Hill Book Company, New York, 1958, or W. Kaplan, "Operational Methods for Linear Systems," p. 316, Addison-Wesley Publishing Company, Inc., Reading, Mass., 1962. Widder proves the theorem under the weaker condition that the integral converges (not necessarily absolutely). Churchill assumes that $f(t)$ is piecewise-continuous in each finite interval and of order $e^{\sigma_a t}$ for $t \geq 0$; these conditions are sufficient for absolute convergence. Kaplan assumes that $f(t)$ is piecewise-continuous and that the integral is absolutely convergent for $\sigma > \sigma_a$.

the region of analyticity of $F(s)$ to the left of the line and thereby extend the region of absolute convergence of the integral.   By the process of analytic continuation, however, it is possible to define $F(s)$ on the entire plane (except, of course, at the singular points).

An important question is whether two different time functions can have the same Laplace transform.   Alternatively, if we are able to find an inverse of a transform $F(s)$, is this the only possible time function whose transform is $F(s)$?   We consider the following uniqueness theorem.

Theorem 6.4   Uniqueness†   *If $f(t)$ and $g(t)$ both have the same Laplace transform, then*

$$f(t) = g(t)$$

almost everywhere.

The phrase "almost everywhere" means that the two functions can differ only at discrete points.‡   For example, two functions which are identical except for the value assigned to them at a point of discontinuity have the same Laplace transform.

6.4   PROPERTIES OF THE LAPLACE TRANSFORM

A number of useful properties of the Laplace transform are given in Table 6.2.   Those properties indicated with an asterisk will be proved below. The others are left as exercises for the reader.

LINEARITY

If $\mathcal{L}[f(t)] = F(s)$ for $\sigma > \sigma_f$ and $\mathcal{L}[g(t)] = G(s)$ for $\sigma > \sigma_g$, and c_1, c_2 are constants,

$$\mathcal{L}[c_1 f(t) + c_2 g(t)] = c_1 F(s) + c_2 G(s) \qquad \sigma > \sigma_f, \sigma > \sigma_g \qquad (6.21)$$

The abscissa of absolute convergence is at most equal to the larger of σ_f, σ_g, but may be smaller.   For example, if $f(t) = e^{at} + e^{-bt}$ with $\sigma_f = a$ and $g(t) = e^{at}$ with $\sigma_g = a$, then $d(t) = f(t) - g(t) = e^{-bt}$ has $\sigma_d = -b$.

The proof of the linearity property (6.21) follows directly from the integral definition of the Laplace transform.   That the restriction on σ is

---

† See Widder, *op. cit.*, pp. 59–63.
‡ To be precise, it means that $f(t) = g(t) + \alpha(t)$, where $\alpha(t)$ is a function of measure zero, i.e., a function which is zero everywhere except at a countable set of points.

Table 6.2 PROPERTIES OF THE LAPLACE TRANSFORM

Property	Time function	Laplace transform
1. Linearity*	$c_1 f(t) + c_2 g(t)$	$c_1 F(s) + c_2 G(s)$
2. Time differentiation*	$f^{(k)}(t) = \dfrac{d^k f(t)}{dt^k}$	$s^k F(s)$ $-s^{k-1}f(0) - \cdots - f^{(k-1)}(0)$
3. Time integration	$f^{(-1)}(t) = \displaystyle\int_{-\infty}^{t} f(\lambda)\, d\lambda$ $\displaystyle\int_0^t f(\lambda)\, d\lambda$	$\dfrac{F(s)}{s} + \dfrac{1}{s} f^{(-1)}(0)$ $\dfrac{F(s)}{s}$
4. Time translation*	$f(t-a)\mu_1(t-a)$ $f(t+a) \quad$ if $f(t) = 0$ for $0 < t < a$	$F(s)e^{-as} \quad a > 0$ $F(s)e^{as} \quad a > 0$
5. Multiplication by exponential	$f(t)e^{-at}$	$F(s+a)$
6. Multiplication by t	$tf(t)$	$\dfrac{-dF(s)}{ds}$
7. Convolution*	$y(t) = \displaystyle\int_0^t h(t-\lambda)x(\lambda)\, d\lambda$	$Y(s) = H(s)X(s)$
8. Product of two time functions*	$f(t)g(t)$	$\dfrac{1}{2\pi j}\displaystyle\int_{c-j\infty}^{c+j\infty} F(s-w)G(w)\, dw$ $\sigma_g < c < \sigma - \sigma_f$
9. Scale change	$f\left(\dfrac{t}{a}\right)$	$aF(as)$
10. Initial value*	$f(0^+) = \lim\limits_{s\to\infty} sF(s)$	
11. Final value*	$\lim\limits_{t\to\infty} f(t) = \lim\limits_{s\to 0} sF(s)$ if $sF(s)$ is analytic for $\sigma \geq 0$	

Properties marked with an asterisk are proved in the text.

sufficient follows if we use

$$|c_1 f + c_2 g| \leq |c_1| \, |f| + |c_2| \, |g|$$

which results in

$$\int_0^\infty |(c_1 f + c_2 g)e^{-st}| \, dt \leq |c_1| \int_0^\infty |f(t)| e^{-\sigma t} \, dt + |c_2| \int_0^\infty |g(t)| e^{-\sigma t} \, dt$$

The first integral on the right-hand side converges for $\sigma > \sigma_f$, the second for $\sigma > \sigma_g$. Thus the integral on the left-hand side exists if σ exceeds the larger of σ_f, σ_g.

DIFFERENTIATION

The transform of the derivative of a time function is important in the solution of differential equations. From the definition the Laplace transform of a derivative is given by

$$\mathcal{L}\left[\frac{df(t)}{dt}\right] = \int_0^\infty \frac{df(\lambda)}{d\lambda} e^{-s\lambda} \, d\lambda$$

We assume that $f(t)$ is piecewise-continuous and that its Laplace transform exists. Integrating by parts with $u = e^{-st}$ and $v = f(t)$, we have

$$\mathcal{L}\left[\frac{df(t)}{dt}\right] = f(\lambda)e^{-s\lambda} \Big|_{\lambda=0}^{\lambda=\infty} - \int_0^\infty -se^{-s\lambda}f(\lambda) \, d\lambda$$

The limit of $f(\lambda)e^{-s\lambda}$ as $\lambda \to \infty$ must be zero; otherwise the transform of $f(t)$ would not exist. Thus

$$\mathcal{L}\left[\frac{df(t)}{dt}\right] = -f(0) + s \int_0^\infty f(\lambda)e^{-s\lambda} \, d\lambda$$

or

$$\mathcal{L}\left[\frac{df(t)}{dt}\right] = sF(s) - f(0) \qquad (6.22)$$

Thus the transform of the derivative of a function is expressed in terms of the transform of the function. Differentiation in the time domain becomes multiplication by s in the frequency domain, except for an additive constant. Higher derivatives may be transformed by induction (Prob. 6.17).

Note that the value of $f(0)$ which is used must be consistent with the definition of the Laplace transform. If $f(t)$ is discontinuous at the origin, $\dot{f}(t)$ will have an impulse equal in strength to the height of the discontinuity. If this impulse is to be included in the Laplace transform of $\dot{f}(t)$,

then 0^- must be used both in (6.22) and in the definition of the Laplace transform. This is illustrated in the following example.

Example 6.4   Determine the transform of

$$g(t) = \frac{d}{dt}[e^{-at}\mu_1(t)]$$

The function $f(t) = e^{-at}\mu_1(t)$ is shown in Fig. 6.5 and has the transform $F(s) = 1/(s + a)$.

(a) If the lower limit for the definition of the Laplace transform is 0^-, then

$$g(t) = \frac{d}{dt}[e^{-at}\mu_1(t)] = e^{-at}\delta(t) - ae^{-at}\mu_1(t) = \delta(t) - ae^{-at}\mu_1(t)$$

The Laplace transform of this function is

$$G^-(s) = \int_{0^-}^{\infty} g(t)e^{-st}\,dt = 1 - \frac{a}{s + a} = \frac{s}{s + a}$$

From the differentiation property (6.22) with $f(0^-) = 0$, we obtain

$$G^-(s) = s\frac{1}{s + a} - 0 = \frac{s}{s + a}$$

which agrees with the direct calculation.

(b) If the lower limit in the definition were taken as 0^+, then

$$g(t) = \frac{d}{dt}[e^{-at}\mu_1(t)] = -ae^{-at}$$

so that

$$G^+(s) = \int_{0^+}^{\infty} g(t)e^{-st}\,dt = \frac{-a}{s + a}$$

From (6.22) with $f(0^+) = 1$, we now find

$$G^+(s) = s\frac{1}{s + a} - 1 = \frac{-a}{s + a}$$

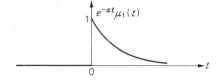

FIG. 6.5 Function to illustrate differentiation property.

which again agrees with the direct calculation.   Thus the transform of $g(t)$ depends on the definition of the Laplace transform chosen, but (6.22) gives results consistent with the definition adopted.

TIME TRANSLATION

It is frequently necessary to express the transform of a function which has been translated along the time axis.   If $f(t)$ is translated to the right by a units of time and if $f(t) = 0$ for $t < 0$, the translated function is $f(t - a)\mu_1(t - a)$.   From the definition, for $a > 0$,

$$\mathcal{L}[f(t - a)\mu_1(t - a)] = \int_0^\infty f(t - a)\mu_1(t - a)e^{-st}\,dt = \int_a^\infty f(t - a)e^{-st}\,dt$$

With the change of variable $\lambda = t - a$, this may be written

$$\mathcal{L}[f(t - a)\mu_1(t - a)] = \int_0^\infty f(\lambda)e^{-s\lambda}e^{-sa}\,d\lambda$$

or

$$\mathcal{L}[f(t - a)\mu_1(t - a)] = F(s)e^{-as} \tag{6.23}$$

Thus translation by a units to the right in the time domain corresponds to multiplication by e^{-as}.   The factor $\mu_1(t - a)$ is necessary since the translation brings into the positive time range values of $f(t)$ for negative arguments which do not contribute to the (one-sided) Laplace transform (Fig. 6.6a).

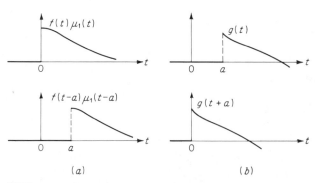

(a)   (b)

FIG. 6.6   Signals for which time-translation property is valid.   (a) Translation to the right; (b) translation to the left.

For a translation to the left, with $a > 0$,

$$\mathcal{L}[f(t + a)] = \int_0^\infty f(t + a)e^{-st}\, dt = \int_a^\infty f(\lambda)e^{-s\lambda}e^{sa}\, d\lambda$$

$$= \int_0^\infty f(\lambda)\mu_1(\lambda - a)e^{-s\lambda}e^{sa}\, d\lambda$$

or

$$\mathcal{L}[f(t + a)] = G(s)e^{as} \qquad (6.24)$$

where

$$G(s) = \mathcal{L}[f(t)\mu_1(t - a)]$$

Thus, in order to express the Laplace transform of a function translated to the left in terms of its Laplace transform before translation, the function must vanish over a positive time range adjacent to the origin ($0 < t < a$) and equal in length to the translation.   This is to be expected since values of the function in this range are moved by the translation into the negative time range where they no longer affect the Laplace transform (Fig. 6.6b).

Example 6.5   The Laplace transform of the unit step $\mu_1(t)$ was shown in Sec. 6.2 to be $1/s$.   Thus the transform of the displaced unit step $\mu_1(t - a)$ with $a > 0$ is e^{-as}/s.

To determine the time function corresponding to

$$F(s) = \frac{se^{-\tau s}}{s^2 + \alpha^2}$$

with $\tau > 0$, we note from Table 6.1 that

$$\mathcal{L}^{-1}\left[\frac{s}{s^2 + \alpha^2}\right] = \cos \alpha t \mu_1(t)$$

Hence

$$\mathcal{L}^{-1}\left[\frac{se^{-\tau s}}{s^2 + \alpha^2}\right] = \cos \alpha(t - \tau)\mu_1(t - \tau)$$

i.e., a cosine wave beginning at $t = \tau$.

INITIAL VALUE

The initial-value property permits calculation of the initial value $f(0)$ of the time function directly from $F(s)$ without the need of inverting the transform.   The derivation is given here since it is important to understand which value of $f(0)$ the limiting process will yield when $f(t)$ has a discontinuity at the origin.

From (6.22) we have

$$\mathcal{L}\left[\frac{df}{dt}\right] = \int_0^\infty \frac{df}{dt} e^{-st}\, dt = sF(s) - f(0)$$

If $f(t)$ is continuous at $t = 0$, df/dt does not include an impulse term at the origin. As $s \to \infty$ with $\sigma > \sigma_a$, the integral vanishes and thus

$$\lim_{s \to \infty} sF(s) = f(0)$$

If $f(t)$ has a discontinuity at the origin, df/dt contains an impulse $[f(0^+) - f(0^-)]\delta(t)$, and if the lower limit on the integral defining the transform is taken as 0^-, we have

$$\lim_{s \to \infty} \int_{0^-}^\infty \frac{df}{dt} e^{-st}\, dt = f(0^+) - f(0^-)$$

Hence

$$f(0^+) - f(0^-) = \lim_{s \to \infty} sF(s) - f(0^-)$$

or

$$\lim_{s \to \infty} sF(s) = f(0^+)$$

If the lower limit on the defining integral were taken as 0^+, we should have

$$\lim_{s \to \infty} \int_{0^+}^\infty \frac{df}{dt} e^{-st}\, dt = 0$$

so that

$$0 = \lim_{s \to \infty} sF(s) - f(0^+)$$

and again

$$\lim_{s \to \infty} sF(s) = f(0^+) \tag{6.25}$$

Thus the limit on the left-hand side, provided it exists, will always give the initial value of the time function as t approaches zero from the positive side, regardless of the definition of the $\mathcal{L}$ transform as an integral with lower limit 0^- or 0^+. The reason for the apparently different behavior here compared with that in the differentiation property is evident. A finite discontinuity in $f(t)$ at the origin gives the same $\mathcal{L}$ transform $F(s)$ regardless of the lower limit used on the integral. The choice of the lower limit does, however, affect the transform of the derivative, which includes an impulse term at the origin if $f(t)$ has a discontinuity there. If $f(t)$ itself contains an impulse term $\delta(t)$, $\lim\limits_{s \to \infty} sF(s)$ does not exist and the initial-value property does not hold.

Example 6.6   The initial value of the time function $f_2(t)$ of Example 6.1 is, from its transform $F_2(s)$,

$$\lim_{s \to \infty} s \frac{2a}{a^2 - s^2} = 0$$

which agrees with Fig. 6.2b.

The initial value of the unit step may be obtained from (6.12) as

$$\lim_{s \to \infty} s \frac{1}{s} = 1$$

which is the correct value of $\mu_1(0^+)$.

The initial value of the time function whose transform is

$$F(s) = \frac{s^2 + 3s + 2}{s^2 + 4}$$

cannot be found since $\lim_{s \to \infty} sF(s)$ does not exist.   The reason is that

$$F(s) = 1 + \frac{3s - 2}{s^2 + 4}$$

and the first term on the right-hand side represents an impulse, according to (6.14).

FINAL VALUE

The value which $f(t)$ approaches as t becomes large may also be found directly from its transform.   Starting again with (6.22), we take the limit as $s \to 0$:

$$\lim_{s \to 0} \int_0^\infty \frac{df}{dt} e^{-st} dt = \lim_{s \to 0} [sF(s) - f(0)] \tag{6.26}$$

For the integral on the left-hand side to exist, the singularities of this transform, hence the singularities of $sF(s)$, must lie in the left half plane (Sec. 6.3).   This condition also ensures the existence of the limit on the right-hand side, and (6.26) may then be written

$$\int_0^\infty \frac{df}{dt} dt = \lim_{s \to 0} sF(s) - f(0)$$

or

$$\lim_{t \to \infty} f(t) - f(0) = \lim_{s \to 0} sF(s) - f(0)$$

Thus the "final value" of $f(t)$ is given by

$$\lim_{t \to \infty} f(t) = \lim_{s \to 0} sF(s) \qquad\qquad (6.27)$$

It may be noted that a simple pole in $F(s)$ at the origin is permitted, but poles on the imaginary axis and in the right half plane and higher-order poles at the origin are excluded. This is illustrated in the following examples.

Example 6.7

$$F(s) = \frac{1}{s + a} \qquad a > 0$$

The singularity of $sF(s)$ is a pole at $s = -a$, which lies in the left half plane. Then

$$\lim_{t \to \infty} f(t) = \lim_{s \to 0} sF(s) = \lim_{s \to 0} \frac{s}{s + a} = 0$$

This is verified by noting that $f(t) = e^{-at}$, which becomes zero as t becomes infinite.

Example 6.8

$$F(s) = \frac{1}{s(s + a)} \qquad a > 0$$

Note that $F(s)$ has singularities on the imaginary axis at $s = 0$, and at $s = -a$, but $sF(s)$ has a singularity only at $s = -a$. Hence

$$\lim_{t \to \infty} f(t) = \lim_{s \to 0} \frac{1}{s + a} = \frac{1}{a}$$

This is verified by noting that

$$F(s) = \frac{1}{s(s + a)} = \frac{1/a}{s} - \frac{1/a}{s + a}$$

so that

$$f(t) = \frac{1}{a}(1 - e^{-at}) \qquad t > 0$$

which approaches $1/a$ as t approaches infinity.

Example 6.9

$$F(s) = \frac{s}{s^2 + a^2}$$

Here $sF(s) = s^2/(s^2 + a^2)$ has singularities at $s = \pm ja$ on the imaginary axis, and the theorem does not apply. Note that $f(t) = \cos at$, which does not approach a limit as $t \to \infty$.

Example 6.10

$$F(s) = \frac{1}{s^2}$$

Here $sF(s) = 1/s$ has a singularity at the origin ($s = 0$) which is part of the imaginary axis, and the theorem does not apply. Note that $f(t) = t$, and its limit as t becomes infinite is not finite, and hence does not exist. The fact that $\lim_{s \to 0} sF(s)$ is also not finite does not mean that the theorem gives the correct result; this limit also does not exist.

CONVOLUTION; TRANSFER FUNCTIONS

The convolution property may be regarded as the cornerstone of frequency-domain analysis since it relates the impulse response of time-domain analysis to the transfer function of frequency-domain analysis. The convolution of the functions $h(t)$ and $x(t)$ was defined by (3.42) as

$$y(t) = \int_0^t h(t - \lambda)x(\lambda)\, d\lambda \tag{6.28}$$

In order to prove the convolution property, we evaluate the Laplace transform of $y(t)$. From the definition

$$Y(s) = \int_0^\infty y(t)e^{-st}\, dt = \int_0^\infty e^{-st}\, dt \int_0^t h(t - \lambda)x(\lambda)\, d\lambda$$

The upper limit on the inner integral may be changed to infinity if $h(t - \lambda) = 0$ for $\lambda > t$ (which is the case for the impulse response in a causal system). The order of integration is then inverted to give

$$Y(s) = \int_0^\infty x(\lambda)\, d\lambda \int_0^\infty h(t - \lambda)e^{-st}\, dt$$

With the change of variable $u = t - \lambda$, this becomes

$$Y(s) = \int_0^\infty x(\lambda)\, d\lambda \int_{-\lambda}^\infty h(u)e^{-su}e^{-s\lambda}\, du$$

The lower limit on the inner integral may be changed from $-\lambda$ to zero again because $h(u) = 0$ for $u < 0$, so that

$$Y(s) = \int_0^\infty x(\lambda)e^{-s\lambda}\, d\lambda \int_0^\infty h(u)e^{-su}\, du = X(s)H(s)$$

or finally,

$$\mathcal{L}[h(t) \star x(t)] = H(s)X(s) \tag{6.29}$$

which proves property 7 of Table 6.2. Thus the Laplace transform of the convolution of two time functions is the product of their respective transforms.†

Since the output $y(t)$ of a fixed causal linear system is the convolution of the input $x(t)$ and the system impulse response $h(t)$, it follows immediately that the Laplace transform of the output is the product of the input transform and the transform of the impulse response,

$$Y(s) = X(s)\mathcal{L}[h(t)] \tag{6.30}$$

We can now show that the transfer function $H(s)$ as defined earlier is identical with the Laplace transform of the impulse response $h(t)$. By definition of the transfer function $H(s)$ in a fixed system,

$$He^{st} = H(s)e^{st} \tag{6.31}$$

If the input $x(t)$ to a linear fixed system H is resolved into complex exponentials, i.e.,

$$x(t) = \frac{1}{2\pi j} \int_{c-j\infty}^{c+j\infty} X(s)e^{st} \, ds$$

then the response is given by

$$y(t) = H \left\{ \frac{1}{2\pi j} \int_{c-j\infty}^{c+j\infty} X(s)e^{st} \, ds \right\} = \frac{1}{2\pi j} \int_{c-j\infty}^{c+j\infty} X(s)He^{st} \, ds$$
$$= \frac{1}{2\pi j} \int_{c-j\infty}^{c+j\infty} X(s)H(s)e^{st} \, ds$$

Since

$$y(t) = \frac{1}{2\pi j} \int_{c-j\infty}^{c+j\infty} Y(s)e^{st} \, ds$$

it follows directly that

$$Y(s) = H(s)X(s)$$

Thus the Laplace transform of the response is the Laplace transform of the input, multiplied by the transfer function. Comparison with (6.30) shows immediately that

$$H(s) = \mathcal{L}[h(t)] \tag{6.32}$$

The fact that the transfer function defined by (6.31) is identical with the

---

† This property of the Laplace transform holds for the convolution with limits of zero and t (or ∞) since the Laplace transform does not carry information about the time function for negative arguments. The Fourier transform has a similar convolution property provided the convolution is defined with infinite limits as in (3.45); see Prob. 5.18.

Laplace transform of the impulse response is the principal reason for the use of the Laplace transform in the theory of linear systems.

MULTIPLICATION OF TIME FUNCTIONS

By definition, the Laplace transform of the product of two time functions $u(t) = f(t)g(t)$ is

$$U(s) = \mathcal{L}[u(t)] = \int_0^\infty f(t)g(t)e^{-st}\,dt \tag{6.33}$$

The inversion integral (6.6) (which will be discussed in the next section) gives, with $\sigma = c$,

$$g(t) = \frac{1}{2\pi j}\int_{c-j\infty}^{c+j\infty} G(w)e^{wt}\,dw \tag{6.34}$$

This integral converges uniformly for $c > \sigma_g$, the abscissa of absolute convergence for $G(w)$. Substitution of (6.34) into (6.33) and inversion of the order of integration, which is permissible because of the uniform convergence of the integrals, gives

$$U(s) = \frac{1}{2\pi j}\int_{c-j\infty}^{c+j\infty} G(w)\,dw \int_0^\infty f(t)e^{(w-s)t}\,dt \qquad c > \sigma_g$$

But

$$\int_0^\infty f(t)e^{(w-s)t}\,dt = F(s - w)$$

which converges for $\mathrm{Re}\,(s - w) > \sigma_f$ or for $c = \mathrm{Re}\,w < \mathrm{Re}\,s - \sigma_f$. Thus

$$U(s) = \frac{1}{2\pi j}\int_{c-j\infty}^{c+j\infty} G(w)F(s - w)\,dw \qquad \sigma_g < c < \mathrm{Re}\,s - \sigma_f \tag{6.35}$$

If $f(t)$ instead of $g(t)$ is replaced by its contour integral expression, we obtain similarly

$$U(s) = \frac{1}{2\pi j}\int_{c-j\infty}^{c+j\infty} F(w)G(s - w)\,dw \qquad \sigma_f < c < \mathrm{Re}\,s - \sigma_g \tag{6.36}$$

Thus the Laplace transform of the product of two time functions is the (complex) convolution of their respective transforms in the frequency domain. This dual of the property that the inverse Laplace transform of a product is the convolution of the respective time functions in the time domain may be expected from the symmetry of the relations for the direct and inverse transforms.

The integrations in the complex convolutions (6.35) and (6.36) are performed in the complex plane, with s as a parameter. Consider two

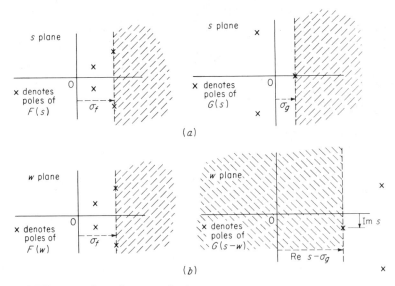

FIG. 6.7   Complex convolution.

(rational) functions $F(s)$ and $G(s)$ having poles located as shown in Fig. 6.7a.   Then $F(w)$ and $G(s - w)$ have the poles shown in Fig. 6.7b.   The integral must be evaluated in a region of the w plane for which $F(w)$ and $G(s - w)$ are both analytic.   From the illustration it is observed that we must make Re s large enough to result in a finite overlap of the individual regions of convergence.   As a consequence we find immediately that Re $s - \sigma_g > \sigma_f$, or

$$\sigma_u = \sigma_f + \sigma_g \tag{6.37}$$

The contour along which the integral is to be evaluated then passes through the strip of overlap.

The complex convolution integral (6.35) or (6.36) is often expeditiously evaluated by means of the calculus of residues.   The line $c - j\infty$ to $c + j\infty$ is made part of a closed contour as shown in Fig. 6.8.   We may use Cauchy's residue theorem,[†] which says that if $f(w)$ is analytic in and upon a closed contour C except at a finite number of poles within C,

$$\frac{1}{2\pi j} \oint_{\substack{\text{closed} \\ \text{path } C}} f(w) \, dw = \text{sum of residues at those poles of } f(w) \text{ enclosed by}$$

contour C.   If $F(s)$ and $G(s)$ both approach zero as $1/s$ when $s \to \infty$,

[†] E. G. Phillips, "Functions of a Complex Variable," pp. 115–116, Interscience Publishers, Inc., New York, 1951.

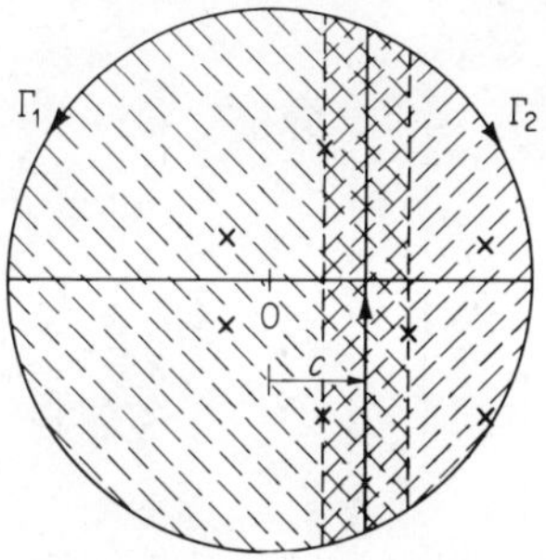

FIG. 6.8 Evaluation of complex-convolution integral.

then $F(w)G(s - w)$ approaches zero as $1/w^2$, and the integral vanishes both along Γ_1 and Γ_2. Hence

$$U(s) = \text{sum of residues of } F(w)G(s - w) \text{ at poles of } F(w) \text{ only} \quad (6.38)$$

or

$$U(s) = -\text{sum of residues of } F(w)G(s - w) \text{ at poles of } G(s - w) \text{ only} \quad (6.39)$$

Note that it is incorrect to use the residues at both sets of poles.

Example 6.11 Consider the functions

$$f(t) = e^{-at}\mu_1(t) \qquad F(s) = \frac{1}{s + a}$$

and

$$g(t) = e^{-bt}\mu_1(t) \qquad G(s) = \frac{1}{s + b}$$

The product $u(t) = f(t)g(t)$ is $e^{-(a+b)t}$, and we know that

$$\sigma_u = -(a + b) = \sigma_f + \sigma_g$$

which agrees with (6.37). Now

$$F(w)G(s - w) = \frac{1}{w + a}\frac{1}{s - w + b} = \frac{1/(s + a + b)}{w + a} + \frac{-1/(s + a + b)}{w - s - b}$$

Hence, using (6.38), we find the residue at $w = -a$ and obtain

$$U(s) = \frac{1}{s + a + b}$$

The same result is obtained by using (6.39) and evaluating the residue at $w = s + b$. The answer is seen to be correct since it is the Laplace transform of $u(t)$.

6.5 LAPLACE TRANSFORM INVERSION THEOREM

We have previously deduced that the inverse Laplace transform of $F(s)$ is given by

$$f(t) = \frac{1}{2\pi j} \int_{\sigma - j\infty}^{\sigma + j\infty} F(s) e^{ts} \, ds$$

where the path of integration is a line $s = \sigma$, a constant damping factor which ensures convergence of $F(s)$. The argument used was an intuitive extension derived from the inversion integral for Fourier transforms, which in turn was an intuitive extension obtained from the Fourier series relations. A completely rigorous proof of the Laplace transform inversion theorem is beyond the scope of this book. The demonstration given below can be regarded as an outline of a rigorous proof, the details of which may be found in a more mathematical treatment.† From now on, the variable s is a *complex variable* whose real part σ may vary, along with its imaginary part ω.

Theorem 6.5   Inversion of Laplace transform   *Consider the integral*

$$I = \frac{1}{2\pi j} \int_{c - jY}^{c + jY} e^{ts} F(s) \, ds \tag{6.40}$$

where $F(s)$ is the Laplace transform of $f(t)$, t is real, and $c > \sigma_a$, the abscissa of absolute convergence for $F(s)$. Then (if $f(t)$ is of bounded variation‡ in the neighborhood of t)

$$\lim_{Y \to \infty} I = \begin{cases} 0 & t < 0 \\ \dfrac{f(t^+) + f(t^-)}{2} & t > 0 \\ \dfrac{f(0^+)}{2} & t = 0 \end{cases} \tag{6.41}$$

† Widder, *op. cit.*, pp. 63–70, or G. Doetsch, "Theory and Application of the Laplace Transform" (in German), pp. 104–108, Dover Publications, Inc., New York, 1943.

‡ **Definition of variation of a function**   *Consider the function $f(t)$ in the interval $a \leq t \leq b$. Consider an arbitrary number of points $t_0, t_1, t_2, \ldots, t_n$ with $a = t_0 < t_1 < \cdots < t_n = b$ and form the sum*

$$v = \sum_{i=1}^{n} |f(t_i) - f(t_{i-1})|$$

The variation of $f(t)$ in the interval is the least upper bound of all such sums, using any possible method of subdivision. If this least upper bound is finite, $f(t)$ is said to be of bounded variation in the interval.

See H. S. Carslaw, "Introduction to the Theory of Fourier's Series and Integrals," 3d rev. ed., pp. 80–81, Dover Publications, Inc., New York, 1930.

An outline of a proof may be given as follows.   By definition

$$F(s) = \int_0^\infty f(x)e^{-sx}\,dx$$

Hence (6.41) becomes

$$I = \frac{1}{2\pi j} \int_{c-jY}^{c+jY} e^{ts}\,ds \int_0^\infty f(x)e^{-sx}\,dx \tag{6.42}$$

Since the Laplace transform converges uniformly for Re $s > \sigma_a$, and c is restricted to be greater than σ_a, the order of integration in (6.42) may be inverted, so that

$$I = \frac{1}{2\pi j} \int_0^\infty f(x)\,dx \int_{c-jY}^{c+jY} e^{s(t-x)}\,ds \qquad c > \sigma_a \tag{6.43}$$

Evaluation of the inner integral in (6.43) gives

$$\int_{c-jY}^{c+jY} e^{s(t-x)}\,ds = \frac{e^{(c+jY)(t-x)} - e^{(c-jY)(t-x)}}{t-x}$$
$$= 2j\,\frac{e^{c(t-x)}\sin Y(t-x)}{t-x}$$

Hence (6.43) becomes

$$I = \frac{1}{\pi} \int_0^\infty f(x)e^{c(t-x)}\frac{\sin Y(t-x)}{t-x}\,dx \qquad c > \sigma_a \tag{6.44}$$

With the change of variable

$$\lambda = Y(t-x)$$

(6.44) becomes

$$I = \frac{1}{\pi} \int_{-\infty}^{Yt} f\left(t - \frac{\lambda}{Y}\right) e^{c(\lambda/Y)}\frac{\sin \lambda}{\lambda}\,d\lambda \tag{6.45}$$

We now consider the following cases: (1) $t < 0$, (2) $t = 0$, (3) $t > 0$.

Case 1   For $t < 0$, (6.45) yields

$$\lim_{Y\to\infty} I = \frac{1}{\pi} \lim_{Y\to\infty} \int_{-\infty}^{Yt} f\left(t - \frac{\lambda}{Y}\right) e^{c(\lambda/Y)}\frac{\sin \lambda}{\lambda}\,d\lambda$$

The integral vanishes in the limit since, with negative t, the upper limit approaches the lower limit.

For cases 2 and 3, (6.45) is written

$$I = \frac{1}{\pi} \int_{-\infty}^0 f\left(t - \frac{\lambda}{Y}\right) e^{c(\lambda/Y)}\frac{\sin \lambda}{\lambda}\,d\lambda + \frac{1}{\pi} \int_0^{Yt} f\left(t - \frac{\lambda}{Y}\right) e^{c(\lambda/Y)}\frac{\sin \lambda}{\lambda}\,d\lambda \tag{6.46}$$

With the change of variable in the first integral

$$\xi = -\lambda$$

(6.46) becomes

$$I = \frac{1}{\pi} \int_0^\infty f\left(t + \frac{\xi}{Y}\right) e^{-c\xi/Y} \frac{\sin \xi}{\xi}\, d\xi + \frac{1}{\pi} \int_0^{Yt} f\left(t - \frac{\lambda}{Y}\right) e^{c(\lambda/Y)} \frac{\sin \lambda}{\lambda}\, d\lambda$$

$$(6.47)$$

Case 2   For $t = 0$, only the first integral in (6.47) remains.   Hence

$$\lim_{Y \to \infty} I = \lim_{Y \to \infty} \frac{1}{\pi} \int_0^\infty f\left(0 + \frac{\xi}{Y}\right) e^{-c\xi/Y} \frac{\sin \xi}{\xi}\, d\xi$$

To this point we have proceeded with complete rigor.   To carry the demonstration further, it is necessary to invert the order of taking the limit and integrating.   The justification of this operation, which requires the fact that $f(t)$ be of bounded variation, is the step we omit here.   Thus

$$\lim_{Y \to \infty} I = \frac{1}{\pi} \int_0^\infty \lim_{Y \to \infty} f\left(0 + \frac{\xi}{Y}\right) e^{-c\xi/Y} \frac{\sin \xi}{\xi}\, d\xi$$

$$= f(0^+) \cdot \frac{1}{\pi} \int_0^\infty \frac{\sin \xi}{\xi}\, d\xi \qquad (6.48)$$

Since

$$\int_0^\infty \frac{\sin \xi}{\xi}\, d\xi = \frac{\pi}{2} \qquad (6.49)$$

we obtain for $t = 0$

$$\lim_{Y \to \infty} I = \frac{f(0^+)}{2}$$

Case 3   For $t > 0$, the order of taking the limit and integrating is inverted in (6.47) to yield

$$\lim_{Y \to \infty} I = \frac{1}{\pi} \int_0^\infty \lim_{Y \to \infty} f\left(t + \frac{\xi}{Y}\right) e^{-c\xi/Y} \frac{\sin \xi}{\xi}\, d\xi$$

$$+ \frac{1}{\pi} \int_0^\infty \lim_{Y \to \infty} f\left(t - \frac{\lambda}{Y}\right) e^{c\lambda/Y} \frac{\sin \lambda}{\lambda}\, d\lambda$$

$$= \frac{f(t^+) + f(t^-)}{\pi} \int_0^\infty \frac{\sin \lambda}{\lambda}\, d\lambda$$

By use of (6.49), this becomes

$$\lim_{Y \to \infty} I = \frac{f(t^+) + f(t^-)}{2} \qquad t > 0$$

which completes the demonstration.

We have gone through this lengthy demonstration to show that the inversion integral converges to $f(t)$ at a point of continuity and to the *average value of $f(t)$ at a point of discontinuity.* Moreover, the inversion integral yields at $t = 0$ one-half the value of $f(0^+)$, even if the lower limit in the defining integral is 0^-

We may thus write

$$f(t) = \frac{1}{2\pi j} \int_{c-j\infty}^{c+j\infty} F(s)e^{ts}\, ds \qquad (6.50)$$

where it must be understood that $c \pm j\infty$ is to be interpreted as $\lim_{Y \to \infty} c \pm jY$, that is, that the path of integration is an open contour and does not include the point at infinity. The values of $f(t)$ at points of discontinuity are given by (6.41).

Examples of the inversion of Laplace transforms by use of the contour integral (6.50) are given in the next section.

6.6 TECHNIQUES FOR INVERSION OF THE LAPLACE TRANSFORM

The most general method of obtaining the inverse Laplace transform is the evaluation of the inversion integral, usually by means of the calculus of residues. In a majority of cases of interest, however, it is not necessary to evaluate this integral, since the function to be inverted can be expressed as a sum of functions, each of which can be associated with the corresponding time function with the aid of a short table of transforms. There are also several extensive published tables† of Laplace transform pairs which will be found useful when the techniques described below prove inadequate. For the sake of completeness, the application of the calculus of residues will also be described and illustrated.

RATIONAL FUNCTIONS

The inverse Laplace transform of a rational function $F(s) = N(s)/D(s)$ (i.e., a ratio of two polynomials) is most readily obtained by expanding $F(s)$ into partial fractions. If $F(s)$ is a proper rational function (i.e., the degree of $D(s)$ is greater than that of $N(s)$), the poles of $F(s)$ are

---

† M. F. Gardner and J. L. Barnes, "Transients in Linear Systems," vol. 1, pp. 338–354, John Wiley & Sons, Inc., New York, 1942; R. V. Churchill, "Operational Mathematics," pp. 324–331; B. J. Starkey, "Laplace Transforms for Electrical Engineers," pp. 263–275, Philosophical Library, Inc., New York, 1954.

located at $s = \alpha_1, \alpha_2, \ldots, \alpha_n$, and the order of the pole at $s = \alpha_j$ is m_j, this expansion takes the form

$$F(s) = \sum_{j=1}^{n} \sum_{i=1}^{m_j} A_{ij} \frac{1}{(s - \alpha_j)^i} \qquad (6.51)$$

This results from the fact that each nonrepeated factor $s - \alpha_r$ in the denominator $D(s)$ gives rise to a term

$$\frac{A_{1r}}{s - \alpha_r}$$

but a repeated factor $(s - \alpha_j)^{m_i}$ gives rise to m_j terms

$$\frac{A_{m_j j}}{(s - \alpha_j)^{m_j}} + \frac{A_{m_j-1,j}}{(s - \alpha_j)^{m_j-1}} + \cdots + \frac{A_{1j}}{s - \alpha_j}$$

The coefficients A_{ij} may be evaluated† as follows.   For a simple (first-order) pole at $s = \alpha_r$,

$$A_{1r} = \frac{N(s)}{D(s)/(s - \alpha_r)} \bigg|_{s=\alpha_r} \qquad (6.52)$$

or

$$A_{1r} = \frac{N(\alpha_r)}{D'(\alpha_r)} \qquad (6.53)$$

where $D'(\alpha_r)$ indicates the derivative‡ of $D(s)$ evaluated at $s = \alpha_r$. Either (6.52) or (6.53) may be used to evaluate A_{1r}, but the second form is particularly useful when the denominator $D(s)$ is not easily factored (its zeros must, of course, be known).   Note that, since the pole at $s = \alpha_r$ is simple, $m_r = 1$ and there are no other coefficients arising from this pole.   For a pole of order m_j at $s = \alpha_j$,

$$A_{ij} = \frac{1}{(m_j - i)!} \frac{d^{m_j-i}}{ds^{m_j-i}} \left[\frac{N(s)}{D(s)/(s - \alpha_j)^{m_j}} \right]\bigg|_{s=\alpha_j} \qquad i = 1, 2, \ldots, m_j$$

If $m_j = 1$, this reduces to (6.52).

The inverse transform of (6.51) may be obtained by using pair 3 in Table 6.1 and property 5 of Table 6.2 to give

$$f(t) = \sum_{j=1}^{n} e^{\alpha_j t} \sum_{i=1}^{m_j} A_{ij} \frac{t^{i-1}}{(i - 1)!} \qquad (6.54)$$

† See, for example, C. R. Wylie, Jr., "Advanced Engineering Mathematics," 2d ed., pp. 317–323, McGraw-Hill Book Company, New York, 1960.
‡ In using (6.53), only that part of the denominator of $F(s)$ causing the pole at α_r needs to be differentiated; all other factors may be considered part of $N(s)$.

Example 6.12   The inverse Laplace transform of

$$F(s) = \frac{4s^4 + 11s^3 + 6s^2 - 12s - 8}{s^2(s + 1)(s + 2)^2} = \frac{1}{s} - \frac{2}{s^2} + \frac{3}{s + 1} - \frac{4}{(s + 2)^2}$$

is

$$f(t) = 1 - 2t + 3e^{-t} - 4te^{-2t} \text{ for } t > 0$$

MEROMORPHIC FUNCTIONS

A function $F(s)$ whose only singularities in the finite plane are poles is called a *meromorphic* function.   If the number of poles is finite, $F(s)$ is rational; there are many situations, however, in which $F(s)$ has infinitely many poles and cannot be expanded into partial fractions in the manner described above.   Instead, a more general expansion, based on the Mittag-Leffler theorem, can be employed.   The expansion formula† is

$$F(s) = F(0) + \sum_{n=1}^{\infty} A_n \left(\frac{1}{s - s_n} + \frac{1}{s_n} \right) \tag{6.55}$$

if $F(s)$ has only simple poles at $s = s_n$ with corresponding residues A_n, $0 < |s_1| \leq |s_2| \leq \cdots$, and provided there exist closed contours C_n, $n = 1, 2, 3, \ldots$, such that:

1. C_n encloses the poles at $s_1, s_2, \ldots, s_n$, but no others.
2. The minimum distance R_n from C_n to the origin approaches infinity with n.
3. The length of C_n is of order R_n.
4. $\left| \dfrac{F(s)}{R_n} \right| \to 0$ on C_n as $n \to \infty$.

The use of this expansion is illustrated in the following example.

Example 6.13   Find the inverse Laplace transform of

$$F(s) = \frac{1}{\sinh s}$$

Since $F(s)$ has a pole at the origin, precluding the use of (6.55), we deal with $G(s) = sF(s) = s/\sinh s$, which is analytic at the origin with $G(0) = 1$.   The poles of $F(s)$ occur when $\sinh s = 0$, i.e., when $s = jn\pi$, $n = 0, \pm1, \pm2, \ldots$, and are simple since $(s - jn\pi)/\sinh s$ is analytic at $s = jn\pi$.   It is not too difficult to establish that the conditions under

† Phillips, *op. cit.*, pp. 131–132.

which (6.55) holds obtain in the present example. We obtain the residues at the poles by use of (6.53):

$$A_n = \lim_{s \to jn\pi} \frac{s - jn\pi}{\sinh s}\, jn\pi = \frac{jn\pi}{\cosh jn\pi} = \frac{jn\pi}{\cos n\pi} = (-1)^n jn\pi$$

Hence

$$G(s) = 1 + \sum_{n=1}^{\infty} (-1)^n \left[jn\pi \left(\frac{1}{s - jn\pi} + \frac{1}{jn\pi} \right) - jn\pi \left(\frac{1}{s + jn\pi} + \frac{1}{-jn\pi} \right) \right]$$

$$= 1 + \sum_{n=1}^{\infty} (-1)^n \left(\frac{s}{s - jn\pi} + \frac{s}{s + jn\pi} \right)$$

and

$$F(s) = \frac{1}{s} + \sum_{n=1}^{\infty} (-1)^n \frac{1}{s + jn\pi} + \sum_{n=1}^{\infty} (-1)^n \frac{1}{s - jn\pi}$$

$$= \sum_{n=-\infty}^{\infty} (-1)^n \frac{1}{s - jn\pi}$$

Hence

$$f(t) = \sum_{n=-\infty}^{\infty} (-1)^n e^{jn\pi t} \qquad t > 0$$

This indicates that $f(t)$ is periodic for $t > 0$. If we extend $f(t)$ periodically for negative t, we obtain a completely periodic function of fundamental frequency $\omega_0 = \pi$, that is, with a period of 2 sec, and a Fourier spectrum given by

$$F_n = (-1)^n = e^{-jn\pi} = e^{-jn\omega_0}$$

This frequency spectrum corresponds to a time function which is the impulse train shown in Fig. 6.9. The Laplace transform of this function is

$$F(s) = 2(e^{-s} + e^{-3s} + e^{-5s} + \cdots) = \frac{2e^{-s}}{1 - e^{-2s}} = \frac{1}{\sinh s}$$

with which we started.

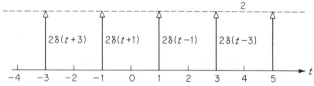

FIG. 6.9 The periodic function corresponding to $(\sinh s)^{-1}$.

This example suggests a method of finding the spectrum of a periodic function (Prob. 6.11).

EVALUATION OF THE INVERSION INTEGRAL BY CALCULUS OF RESIDUES

Direct evaluation of the inversion integral (6.50) may be used to determine the time function $f(t)$ from its Laplace transform $F(s)$ regardless of the nature of the singularities of $F(s)$, although for meromorphic functions the methods discussed earlier are usually simpler.

To begin with, we note that the inversion integral (6.50) is an open integral, i.e., an integral along an open contour in the complex-frequency plane. The point at infinity is not included in the contour, and cannot be so included, since the integrand has an essential singularity at $s = \infty$ because of the presence of the factor e^{st}. If the calculus of residues is to be employed, the point at infinity must be avoided by appropriately chosen detours. Detours around the point at infinity appear in the s plane as circular arcs of infinite radius centered at the origin, as shown in Fig. 6.10.

The detour, either Γ_1 or Γ_2, is chosen to result in a closed contour when added to the contour parallel to the $j\omega$ axis. The value of the integral of $F(s)e^{ts}$ along the detour must be zero, however, in order that the integral along the closed contour be equal to the integral along the original open contour.

We can show that

$$\int_{\Gamma_l} F(s)e^{ts}\,ds \to 0 \text{ as } R \to \infty \qquad \text{for } t > 0 \qquad (6.56)$$

where Γ_l is a semicircle in the left half plane centered at the origin and

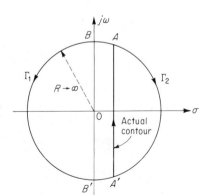

FIG. 6.10   Contours for evaluation of inverse Laplace transform.

of radius R if

(1) $F(s)$ is meromorphic in left half plane
(2) $F(s) \to 0$ uniformly with respect to phase of s as   (6.57)
$$|s| \to \infty \text{ with } \sigma \leq 0$$

This result is known as *Jordan's lemma*;[†] a proof follows. By condition
(2) of (6.57) we have for sufficiently large R, for all points on Γ_l, $|F(s)| < \epsilon$.
Further, with $s = Re^{j\theta}$,

$$|e^{ts}| = |e^{tR(\cos \theta + j \sin \theta)}| = e^{tR \cos \theta}$$

(where the exponent is negative on Γ_l, since $\cos \theta$ is nonpositive in the
left half plane and on the imaginary axis). Hence

$$\left| \int_{\Gamma_l} F(s) e^{ts} \, ds \right| = \left| \int_{\pi/2}^{3\pi/2} F(Re^{j\theta}) e^{tRe^{j\theta}} Re^{j\theta} j \, d\theta \right| < \epsilon R \int_{\pi/2}^{3\pi/2} e^{tR \cos \theta} \, d\theta$$

$$= 2\epsilon R \int_{\pi/2}^{\pi} e^{tR \cos \theta} \, d\theta$$

It is apparent from Fig. 6.11 that, for $\pi/2 \leq \theta \leq \pi$,

$$\cos \theta \leq -\frac{2}{\pi}\left(\theta - \frac{\pi}{2}\right)$$

Hence

$$\left| \int_{\Gamma_l} F(s) e^{ts} \, ds \right| < 2\epsilon R \int_{\pi/2}^{\pi} e^{-\frac{2}{\pi}\left(\theta - \frac{\pi}{2}\right)tR} \, d\theta = 2\epsilon R \int_0^{\pi/2} e^{-\frac{2}{\pi}\left(\theta - \frac{\pi}{2}\right)tR} \, d\left(\theta - \frac{\pi}{2}\right)$$

$$= 2\epsilon R \frac{\pi}{2tR}(1 - e^{-tR}) < \frac{\pi \epsilon}{t} \to 0 \text{ as } R \to \infty$$

which proves (6.56) under the conditions (6.57).

If the contour $A'A$ of Fig. 6.10 lies in the right half plane because of
singularities on or to the right of the imaginary axis, we can either show
that the integrals of $F(s)e^{ts}$ from A to B and from B' to A' together con-

[†] E. T. Whittaker and G. N. Watson, "A Course of Modern Analysis," p. 115, Cambridge University Press, New York, 1954.

FIG. 6.11 Inequality used in Jordan's lemma.

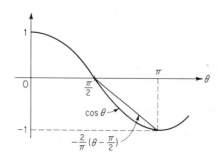

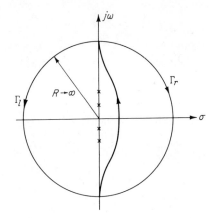

FIG. 6.12 Deformed contour for evaluation of inverse Laplace transform.

tribute nothing or we can deform the contour (when the number of such singularities is finite) so that it coincides with the imaginary axis for large positive and negative values of ω (Fig. 6.12).

If the conditions (6.57) apply to $F(s)$ in the right half plane with $\sigma \geq 0$, then

$$\int_{\Gamma_r} F(s)e^{ts}\, ds \to 0 \text{ as } R \to \infty \qquad \text{for } t < 0 \qquad (6.58)$$

where Γ_r is now a semicircle in the right half plane of radius R centered at the origin.

If $F(s)$ meets the requirements of (6.57), we can write

$$f(t) = \frac{1}{2\pi j}\int_{c-j\infty}^{c+j\infty} F(s)e^{ts}\, ds + \frac{1}{2\pi j}\int_{\Gamma_l} F(s)e^{ts}\, ds \qquad t > 0$$

or

$$f(t) = \text{sum of residues of } F(s)e^{ts} \text{ at poles of } F(s) \qquad t > 0 \quad (6.59)$$

since e^{ts} is an integral function and all poles [the only singularities permitted by condition (1) of (6.57)] of $F(s)$ occur for $\sigma \leq \sigma_a < c$. Likewise,

$$f(t) = \frac{1}{2\pi j}\int_{c-j\infty}^{c+j\infty} F(s)e^{ts}\, ds + \frac{1}{2\pi j}\int_{\Gamma_r} F(s)e^{ts}\, ds = 0 \qquad t < 0 \quad (6.60)$$

since $F(s)$ is analytic to the right of $\sigma = c$. This result agrees with the inversion theorem.

The requirement that $F(s) \to 0$ as $|s| \to \infty$ on Γ_l is easily understood. Suppose $F(s)$ does not approach zero; then we can write, as a consequence of Laurent's theorem,

$$F(s) = G(s) + a_0 + a_1 s + a_2 s^2 + \cdots$$

where $G(s) \to 0$ as $|s| \to \infty$. Then

$$f(t) = g(t) + a_0\delta(t) + a_1\mu_{-1}(t) + a_2\mu_{-2}(t) + \cdots$$

which is seen to contain impulsive terms of unbounded variation. We should not expect the inversion theorem to be useful for the Laplace transforms of such signals. To employ the inversion theorem, it is necessary first to remove those terms in $F(s)$ which are the Laplace transforms of impulsive signals and deal separately with them.

It is also noted that (6.59) is not always applicable for $t = 0$ even if $F(s) \to 0$ for $|s| \to \infty$.

Example 6.14   Find the inverse Laplace transform of $F(s) = 1/(s + a)$, $a > 0$. Using (6.59), we obtain

$$f(t) = \text{residue of } \frac{e^{st}}{s + a} \qquad \text{at } s = -a$$

$$= e^{-at} \qquad\qquad t > 0$$

Using (6.60), we find that $f(t) = 0$ for $t < 0$. For $t = 0$ we evaluate the integral

$$I = \lim_{Y \to \infty} \frac{1}{2\pi j} \int_{c-jY}^{c+jY} \frac{ds}{s + a} = \lim_{Y \to \infty} \frac{1}{2\pi j} \ln\,(s + a) \Big|_{c-jY}^{c+jY}$$

$$= \frac{1}{2\pi j} \lim_{Y \to \infty} \ln \frac{c + a + jY}{c + a - jY} = \frac{1}{2\pi j} \lim_{\theta \to \pi/2} \ln e^{j2\theta}$$

where $\theta = \tan^{-1}\,[Y/(c + a)]$. Hence $I = \frac{1}{2} = f(0^+)/2$ as given by (6.41).

If $F(s)$ possesses branch points or essential singularities in the finite part of the s plane, (6.59) cannot be used directly, since (6.57) is not valid. When the singularities are branch points, a single-valued function may be constructed by the use of branch cuts. The open contour from $c - j\infty$ to $c + j\infty$ is closed by selecting a path which remains on a single branch of $F(s)$. A typical closed contour is shown in Fig. 6.13.

We choose a contour Λ in addition to Γ_1 such that the function $F(s)$ is always single-valued on the closed contour. Then we have

$$f(t) = \frac{1}{2\pi j} \int_{c-j\infty}^{c+j\infty} F(s)e^{ts}\,ds$$

$$= \text{sum of residues at poles of } F(s) \text{ inside contour}$$

$$- \frac{1}{2\pi j} \int_{\Gamma_1} F(s)e^{ts}\,ds - \frac{1}{2\pi j} \int_{\Lambda} F(s)e^{ts}\,ds \qquad (6.61)$$

If $F(s)$ is meromorphic on the branch chosen (i.e., if the only other enclosed singularities are poles) and if $F(s) \to 0$ as $s \to \infty$ in the left

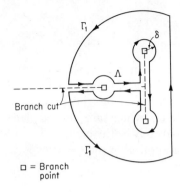

FIG. 6.13   Typical contour for evaluating $f(t)$ when $F(s)$ contains branch points.

half plane, then the integral on Γ_1 vanishes.   On the other hand, the integral around Λ will not vanish, since the integrals along opposite sides of the branch cut will not cancel each other.   The integral along the circular arcs around the branch points may or may not vanish, depending on the nature of $F(s)$ in the neighborhood of the branch points.

Example 6.15   We shall evaluate the inverse Laplace transform of

$$F(s) = \frac{1}{\sqrt{s}}$$

It is seen that $F(s)$ possesses a branch point at $s = 0$ as its only singularity. $F(s)$ satisfies the conditions of (6.57), so that (6.61) gives

$$f(t) = -\frac{1}{2\pi j} \int_\Lambda \frac{e^{ts}}{\sqrt{s}} \, ds$$

where Λ in this case is the contour shown in Fig. 6.14, comprising Λ_1, Λ_2, and Λ_3.

On Λ_3, $s = \delta e^{j\theta}$, and the contribution to $f(t)$ along this path is

$$-\frac{1}{2\pi j} \int_\pi^{-\pi} \frac{e^{t\delta e^{j\theta}}}{\delta^{\frac{1}{2}} e^{j\theta/2}} \, j\delta e^{j\theta} \, d\theta = \frac{\delta^{\frac{1}{2}}}{2\pi} \int_{-\pi}^{\pi} e^{j\theta/2} e^{t\delta e^{j\theta}} \, d\theta$$

Since the integral on the right is finite, the factor $\delta^{\frac{1}{2}}$ outside the integral causes the entire contribution to vanish as $\delta \to 0$.

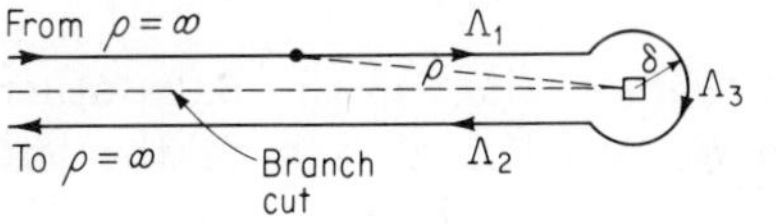

FIG. 6.14   Additional contour for branch point at origin.

On Λ_1, $s = \rho e^{j\pi}$, $\sqrt{s} = \sqrt{\rho}\, e^{j\pi/2} = j\sqrt{\rho}$, and the contribution from Λ_1 is thus

$$-\frac{1}{2\pi j}\int_\infty^\delta \frac{e^{-\rho t}(-d\rho)}{\rho^{\frac{1}{2}}e^{j\pi/2}} = \frac{1}{2\pi}\int_\delta^\infty \frac{e^{-\rho t}\,d\rho}{\rho^{\frac{1}{2}}}$$

On Λ_2, $s = \rho e^{-j\pi}$, $\sqrt{s} = \sqrt{\rho}\, e^{-j\pi/2} = -j\sqrt{\rho}$, and the contribution from Λ_2 is

$$-\frac{1}{2\pi j}\int_\delta^\infty \frac{e^{-\rho t}(-d\rho)}{\rho^{\frac{1}{2}}e^{-j\pi/2}} = \frac{1}{2\pi}\int_\delta^\infty \frac{e^{-\rho t}\,d\rho}{\rho^{\frac{1}{2}}}$$

It is important to note that the contributions from Λ_1 and Λ_2 do not cancel, because $\sqrt{\rho e^{j\pi}} \neq \sqrt{\rho e^{-j\pi}}$ on the same branch of $F(s)$.

Adding the contributions from Λ_1 and Λ_2, we have

$$f(t) = \lim_{\delta\to 0}\frac{1}{\pi}\int_\delta^\infty \frac{e^{-\rho t}\,d\rho}{\rho^{\frac{1}{2}}} = \frac{2}{\pi}\int_0^\infty e^{-tx^2}\,dx$$

by the change of variable $\rho = x^2$. The second integral is tabulated and is known to equal $\sqrt{\pi/4t}$. Hence

$$f(t) = \frac{1}{\sqrt{\pi t}} \qquad t > 0$$

An illustration of the care with which the contributions from the various parts of the contour must be evaluated is given in the next example, in which the integral around the circular arc surrounding the branch point does not vanish.

Example 6.16 Evaluation of inverse Laplace transform of $1/s^{\frac{3}{2}}$
Again the only singularity is a branch point at $s = 0$, and the contour of Fig. 6.14 is again appropriate, with

$$f(t) = -\frac{1}{2\pi j}\int_\Lambda \frac{e^{ts}}{s^{\frac{3}{2}}}\,ds$$

On Λ_3, the contribution is now, with $s = \delta e^{j\theta}$,

$$I_3 = -\frac{1}{2\pi j}\int_\pi^{-\pi} \frac{e^{t\delta e^{j\theta}}}{\delta^{\frac{3}{2}}e^{j3\theta/2}}\,\delta e^{j\theta} j\,d\theta = \frac{1}{2\pi\sqrt{\delta}}\int_{-\pi}^\pi e^{-j\theta/2}e^{t\delta e^{j\theta}}\,d\theta \quad (6.62)$$

This expression does not vanish as $\delta \to 0$, but will be shown to be canceled by the other contributions.

On Λ_1 and Λ_2, with s and $\sqrt{s}$ given by the same expressions as in

Example 6.15, the contribution is

$$I_1 + I_2 = -\frac{1}{2\pi j} \int_\infty^\delta \frac{1}{-j\rho^{\frac{3}{2}}} e^{-\rho t}(-d\rho) - \frac{1}{2\pi j} \int_\delta^\infty \frac{1}{j\rho^{\frac{3}{2}}} e^{-\rho t}(-d\rho)$$

$$= -\frac{1}{\pi} \int_\delta^\infty \frac{1}{\rho^{\frac{3}{2}}} e^{-\rho t}\, d\rho \qquad (6.63)$$

the integral (6.63) may be integrated by parts and gives

$$I_1 + I_2 = -\frac{2}{\pi} \frac{e^{-\delta t}}{\sqrt{\delta}} + \frac{2t}{\pi} \int_\delta^\infty \frac{e^{-\rho t}}{\rho^{\frac{1}{2}}}\, d\rho$$

$$= -\frac{2}{\pi \sqrt{\delta}} + O(\sqrt{\delta}) + \frac{2t}{\pi} \int_\delta^\infty \frac{e^{-\rho t}}{\rho^{\frac{1}{2}}}\, d\rho \qquad (6.64)$$

after expansion of $e^{-\delta t}$. The integral (6.62) becomes by expansion of $e^{t\delta e^{i\theta}}$

$$I_3 = \frac{1}{2\pi \sqrt{\delta}} \int_{-\pi}^\pi e^{-j\theta/2}\, d\theta + O(\sqrt{\delta}) = \frac{2}{\pi \sqrt{\delta}} + O(\sqrt{\delta}) \qquad (6.65)$$

Adding the contributions given by (6.64) and (6.65), we finally obtain†

$$f(t) = \lim_{\delta \to 0} \left[\frac{2t}{\pi} \int_\delta^\infty \frac{e^{-\rho t}}{\rho^{\frac{1}{2}}}\, d\rho + O(\sqrt{\delta}) \right] = 2\sqrt{\frac{t}{\pi}}$$

The result may be verified by using the integration theorem (property 3 of Table 6.2) with the result of Example 6.15 to give

$$\mathcal{L}^{-1}\left[\frac{1}{s\sqrt{s}} \right] = \int_0^t \frac{1}{\sqrt{\pi\lambda}}\, d\lambda = 2\sqrt{\frac{t}{\pi}}$$

PROBLEMS

6.1   Derive the Laplace transforms of the following functions and tabulate results.

    (a) $f(t) = t \sin \omega_0 t$.   (b) $f(t) = e^{-at} \sin \omega_0 t$.

    (c) $f(t) = t^n e^{-at}$.   (d) $f(t) = \dfrac{\sin \omega_0 t}{\omega_0 t}$.

This table will be useful for subsequent calculations.

6.2   Consider the pulses whose shapes are given by one cycle of the signals in Fig. P 5.4. Find the one- and two-sided Laplace transforms of these pulses.

† B. O. Peirce, "A Short Table of Integrals," No. 497, Ginn and Company, Boston, 1929.

6.3   Consider a function $f(t)$ which is periodic (for $t > 0$) as shown in Fig. P 6.3.   Let

$$f_T(t) = \begin{cases} f(t) & 0 < t \leq T \\ 0 & t > T \end{cases}$$

and let $\mathcal{L}[f_T(t)] = F_T(s)$.   Find the Laplace transform of $f(t)$ in terms of $F_T(s)$.

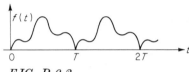

FIG. P 6.3

6.4   Use the result of Prob. 6.3 to find the Laplace transforms of:

(a) A half-wave rectified sinusoid, original frequency $= \omega_0$.
(b) A full-wave rectified sinusoid, original frequency $= \omega_0$.
(c) A train of impulses occurring every T sec.

6.5   Let $F(s) = \mathcal{L}[f(t)]$ be a rational function; i.e.,

$$F(s) = \frac{N(s)}{D(s)} = \sum_{j=1}^{n} \sum_{i=1}^{m_j} \frac{A_{ij}}{(s - \alpha_j)^i}$$

where α_j are the poles of $F(s)$ of order m_j.   Show by use of the calculus of residues that $f(t)$ is given by

$$f(t) = \sum_{j=1}^{n} e^{\alpha_j t} \sum_{i=1}^{m_j} A_{ij} \frac{t^{i-1}}{(i-1)!}$$

6.6   Find the inverse Laplace transforms of the following rational functions:

(a) $F(s) = \dfrac{4s + 6}{(s + 1)(s + 2)(s + 3)}$

(b) $F(s) = \dfrac{2s^2 + 7s + 26}{(s + 2)(s^2 + 2s + 10)}$

(c) $F(s) = \dfrac{3s^2 + 2s + 1}{s^2(s + 1)}$

(d) $F(s) = \dfrac{s^2 + 10s + 19}{s^2 + 5s + 6}$

(e) $F(s) = \dfrac{2s}{s(s^2 + 4)}$

6.7 Find the inverse Laplace transforms of the following meromorphic functions:

$$(a)\ F(s) = \frac{1}{s \cosh s} \qquad\qquad (b)\ F(s) = \frac{1}{\cosh \sqrt{s}}$$

6.8 Evaluate the inverse Laplace transforms of the following functions:

$$(a)\ F(s) = \frac{e^{k/s}}{\sqrt{s}} \quad (b)\ F(s) = e^{-k\sqrt{s}}(k > 0) \quad (c)\ F(s) = \frac{\sqrt{s+1}}{s}$$

6.9 Derive the following properties of the Laplace transform:

$$(a)\ \mathcal{L}\left[\int_{-\infty}^{t} f(\lambda)\,d\lambda\right] = \frac{F(s)}{s} + \frac{1}{s}\int_{-\infty}^{0} f(\lambda)\,d\lambda$$

$$(b)\ \mathcal{L}\left[f\left(\frac{t}{a}\right)\right] = aF(as)$$

$$(c)\ \mathcal{L}[e^{-at}f(t)] = F(a + s)$$

$$(d)\ \mathcal{L}[tf(t)] = -\frac{dF(s)}{ds}$$

6.10 Find the Laplace transforms of each of the functions illustrated (Fig. P 6.10) by applying appropriate properties of the Laplace transform.

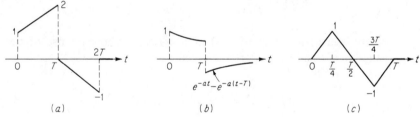

(a)   (b)   (c)

FIG. P 6.10

6.11 The (one-sided) Laplace transform of a periodic signal $x(t)$ is given by

$$X(s) = \frac{1 - e^{-s}}{s^2(1 + e^{-s})}$$

Find the spectrum of the signal by (a) calculating $x(t)$ and determining the coefficients of its Fourier series, and (b) the method of Example 6.13.

6.12 Show that the Laplace transform of a periodic function has a pole at the origin if and only if the average value of the periodic time function is not zero.

6.13 Find the Laplace transform of the periodic function expressed in one period $(0 < t \leq T)$ by

$$f(t) = t - \frac{T}{2}$$

Show that there is no pole at $s = 0$ by finding the residue at $s = 0$.

6.14 (a) Show that the Laplace transform of the square wave of Fig. P 6.14a is $(1/s) \tanh (sT/4)$.

(b) Show that the Laplace transform of the triangular wave of Fig. P 6.14b is $(1/s^2) \tanh (sT/4)$.

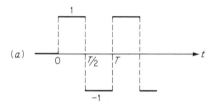

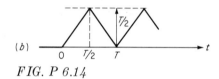

FIG. P 6.14

6.15 Prove that, if the function $f(t)$ is bounded for all $t \geq 0$, the Laplace transform of $f(t)$ converges absolutely for Re $s > 0$. In what way does this theorem differ from Theorem 6.1?

6.16 Show that if $f(t)$ is an even function of time having the (one-sided) Laplace transform $F(s)$, the Fourier transform of $f(t)$ is $F(j\omega) + F(-j\omega)$.

6.17 Verify the expression given in Table 6.2 for the Laplace transform of $d^k f(t)/dt^k$.

6.18 *Delay and Duration of Signals* Consider a signal $h(t)$. Its *effective delay* d and *duration* τ can be defined, respectively, by

$$d = \frac{\int_0^\infty t h(t)\, dt}{\int_0^\infty h(t)\, dt} \tag{6.66}$$

$$\tau^2 = \frac{\int_0^\infty (t - d)^2 h(t)\, dt}{\int_0^\infty h(t)\, dt} \tag{6.67}$$

(a) If $H(s)$ is the Laplace transform of $h(t)$, show that

$$d = \frac{-H'(0)}{H(0)} \qquad (6.68)$$

$$\tau^2 = \frac{H''(0)}{H(0)} - \left(\frac{H'(0)}{H(0)}\right)^2 \qquad (6.69)$$

where $H'(s) = dH/ds$, $H''(s) = d^2H/ds^2$.

(b) Suppose that $g(t) = g_1(t) \star g_2(t)$; that is, $G(s) = G_1(s)G_2(s)$. Let d, d_1, d_2 and τ, τ_1, τ_2 be the delay and duration times of $g(t)$, $g_1(t)$, and $g_2(t)$, respectively. Show that

$$d = d_1 + d_2 \qquad (6.70)$$
$$\tau^2 = \tau_1^2 + \tau_2^2 \qquad (6.71)$$

6.19   For the signal shown in Fig. P 6.19, show that

$$d = \delta + \frac{T}{2} \qquad \tau = \frac{T}{\sqrt{12}}$$

(a) by using the integral definitions (6.66) and (6.67); (b) by using (6.68) and (6.69).

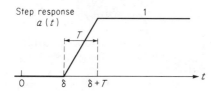

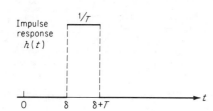

FIG. P 6.19

6.20   The impulse response of an n-stage RC-coupled amplifier has the Laplace transform (transfer function)

$$H(s) = (1 + Ts)^{-n}$$

Show that

$$d = nT \qquad \tau = \sqrt{n}\, T$$

(a) by using (6.68) and (6.69); (b) by using (6.70) and (6.71) extended to the convolution of n signals.

CHAPTER SEVEN

LUMPED-PARAMETER

CONTINUOUS-TIME SYSTEMS

IN THE FREQUENCY DOMAIN

7.1 INTRODUCTION

The principal advantage of the Laplace transform in linear fixed systems
is that the differential equations by which such systems are characterized
are transformed to algebraic equations, which can usually be manipulated
much more easily than the differential equations. Consider, for example,
a system governed by the differential equation

$$(D^k + \alpha_1 D^{k-1} + \cdots + \alpha_{k-1}D + \alpha_k)y(t) = (\beta_1 D + \beta_2)x(t) \quad (7.1)$$

which is considered earlier, in Example 2.3. The Laplace transforms of
the two sides are equal since the $\mathcal{L}$ transform of a time function is unique.
Further, the linearity property (6.21) permits taking the transform of
(7.1) term by term. From (6.22) we find

$$\mathcal{L}\left[\frac{d^2y}{dt^2}\right] = s^2Y(s) - sy(0) - \dot{y}(0)$$

and

$$\mathcal{L}\left[\frac{d^n y}{dt^n}\right] = s^n Y(s) - s^{n-1}y(0) - s^{n-2}\dot{y}(0) - \cdots - y^{(n-1)}(0)$$

Hence Laplace transformation of (7.1) gives

$$\begin{aligned}(s^k + \alpha_1 s^{k-1} + \cdots + \alpha_{k-1}s + \alpha_k)Y(s) = {} &(\beta_1 s + \beta_2)X(s) - \beta_1 x(0) \\ &+ (s^{k-1} + \alpha_1 s^{k-2} + \cdots + \alpha_{k-1})y(0) \\ &+ (s^{k-2} + \alpha_1 s^{k-3} + \cdots + \alpha_{k-2})\dot{y}(0) + \cdots \\ &+ (s + \alpha_1)y^{(k-2)}(0) + y^{(k-1)}(0) \end{aligned} \qquad (7.2)$$

In writing (7.2), we have assumed that $y(t)$ has a Laplace transform $Y(s)$. Since $y(t)$ is not known yet, this assumption cannot be verified until a solution has been found, but this uncertainty is no problem in the linear equations in which we are interested. Note that (7.2) is now an algebraic equation in the unknown transform $Y(s)$, which may be solved to yield

$$Y(s) = \frac{\beta_1 s + \beta_2}{s^k + \alpha_1 s^{k-1} + \cdots + \alpha_{k-1}s + \alpha_k} X(s) + E(s) \qquad (7.3)$$

where $E(s)$ is a proper rational function involving the initial values of $y(t)$ and its first $k-1$ derivatives. If these are known and if the function $x(t)$ and its transform $X(s)$ are given, the solution $y(t)$ of (7.1) may be found as the inverse Laplace transform of (7.3).

The initial conditions represented by $E(s)$ can be regarded as having arisen in the system as a result of an excitation between $t = -\infty$ and $t = 0$. If the only excitation is that which starts at $t = 0$, i.e., if all initial conditions are zero, then $E(s) = 0$, and the ratio of $Y(s)$ to $X(s)$ is, according to the definition of Chap. 6, the transfer function of the system. Thus

$$H(s) = \frac{Y(s)}{X(s)} = \frac{\beta_1 s + \beta_2}{s^k + \alpha_1 s^{k-1} + \cdots + \alpha_{k-1}s + \alpha_k}$$

The impulse response $h(t)$ of the system can then be calculated by finding the inverse Laplace transform of the transfer function $H(s)$.

Example 7.1   Consider the system governed by

$$(D^2 + 3D + 2)y(t) = (2D + 1)x(t)$$

with initial conditions $y(0) = 1$, $\dot{y}(0) = -3$.

(a) Find the transfer function and impulse response of the system. The transfer function is

$$H(s) = \frac{2s + 1}{s^2 + 3s + 2}$$

To find the impulse response, the inverse Laplace transform must be calculated. Using a partial fraction expansion,

$$H(s) = \frac{3}{s+2} + \frac{-1}{s+1}$$

Thus, by taking the inverse Laplace transform, we find

$$h(t) = 3e^{-2t} - e^{-t} \qquad t > 0$$

(b) Find the response of the system to the input $x(t) = 1 - e^{-t}$, so that $x(0) = 0$. For this purpose we use (7.3), which for this problem is

$$Y(s) = \frac{2s+1}{s^2+3s+2} X(s) + E(s)$$

where

$$X(s) = \mathcal{L}[1 - e^{-t}] = \frac{1}{s} - \frac{1}{s+1} = \frac{1}{s(s+1)}$$

and from (7.2),

$$E(s) = \frac{(s+3)y(0) + \dot{y}(0) - 2x(0)}{s^2+3s+2} = \frac{s}{s^2+3s+2}$$

Thus

$$Y(s) = \frac{2s+1}{(s+1)(s+2)} \frac{1}{s(s+1)} + \frac{s}{(s+1)(s+2)} = \frac{s^3+s^2+2s+1}{s(s+1)^2(s+2)}$$

$$= \frac{\frac{1}{2}}{s} + \frac{1}{(s+1)^2} + \frac{-3}{s+1} + \frac{\frac{7}{2}}{s+2}$$

Hence

$$y(t) = \tfrac{1}{2} + te^{-t} - 3e^{-t} + \tfrac{7}{2}e^{-2t} \qquad t > 0$$

Note that $y(\infty) = \tfrac{1}{2}$, which could be obtained by use of the final-value theorem

$$y(\infty) = \lim_{s \to 0} sY(s) = \lim_{s \to 0} \left[\frac{2s+1}{(s+1)(s^2+3s+2)} + \frac{s^2}{s^2+3s+2} \right] = \tfrac{1}{2}$$

This illustrates the utility of the Laplace transform in calculating certain properties of the solution without first calculating the entire solution.

When the system under investigation is characterized by a single linear differential equation, the use of the Laplace transform is often more cumbersome than direct solution of the differential equation by classical methods. The full advantage of the transform method is generally realized only when the system is characterized by a number of differential equations with interrelated inputs and outputs.

Example 7.2 Consider the system illustrated by Fig. 7.1, comprising a mass M to which a tube is connected and a small mass m moving in the

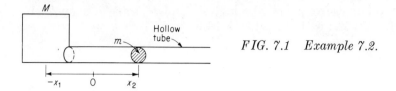

FIG. 7.1   Example 7.2.

tube with viscous friction.   The system is at rest prior to $t = 0$, when an impulsive force is applied to accelerate m with respect to M.   Determine the motion of the two masses.   (The tube may be assumed to be infinitely long.)

Let x_1 and x_2 denote the displacements of M and m, respectively, in relation to some reference chosen such that $x_1(0) = x_2(0) = 0$.   The equations of motion are

$$M\ddot{x}_1 + K(\dot{x}_1 - \dot{x}_2) = -P\delta(t)$$
$$m\ddot{x}_2 - K(\dot{x}_1 - \dot{x}_2) = P\delta(t)$$

where P is the strength of the impulse, and $K(\dot{x}_1 - \dot{x}_2)$ is the viscous force.   (Notice that no net force acts on the combined system.)   Since the initial conditions are all zero, transformation of the equations of motion results in

$$(Ms^2 + Ks)X_1(s) - KsX_2(s) = -P$$
$$-KsX_1(s) + (ms^2 + Ks)X_2(s) = P$$

from which

$$X_1(s) = \frac{-mP}{s[mMs + K(m + M)]}$$

$$= -\frac{Pm}{K(m + M)}\left[\frac{1}{s} - \frac{1}{s + K(m + M)/mM}\right]$$

$$X_2(s) = \frac{MP}{s[mMs + K(m + M)]}$$

$$= \frac{PM}{K(m + M)}\left[\frac{1}{s} - \frac{1}{s + K(m + M)/mM}\right]$$

Thus the displacements are

$$x_1(t) = -\frac{Pm}{K(m + M)}(1 - e^{-\alpha t})$$

$$x_2(t) = \frac{PM}{K(m + M)}(1 - e^{-\alpha t})$$

where $\alpha = K(m + M)/mM$.

Example 7.3   Operational amplifier and its application   An amplifier with a very large negative gain and used for such operations as chang-

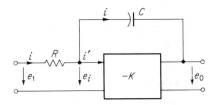

*FIG.   7.2   Operational   amplifier
used as integrator.*

ing sign, adding, integrating, or differentiating is called an operational
amplifier.† It has important applications in analog computers. The
typical use of an operational amplifier is illustrated in Fig. 7.2. The
operational amplifier is represented by the box labeled $-K$ and has an
input-output relation

$$e_0 = -Ke_i$$

where K is a large positive number. In the ideal case the input impedance
of the amplifier is infinite and thus $i' = 0$. Then, with a capacitor and
resistor connected as shown, we obtain

$$\frac{e_1 - e_i}{R} = i = C\frac{d}{dt}(e_i - e_0)$$

Taking Laplace transforms with zero initial conditions, we obtain

$$E_0(s) = -KE_i(s)$$

and

$$\frac{E_1(s) - E_i(s)}{R} = Cs[E_i(s) - E_0(s)]$$

Thus the transfer function is

$$H(s) = \frac{E_0(s)}{E_1(s)} = -\frac{K}{(1 + K)RCs + 1}$$

which, for large K and $|s| > 1/RC$, becomes

$$H(s) \doteq -\frac{1}{RCs}$$

Thus the transfer function is that of an integrator, except for the factor
RC. A circuit of this type is generally used for simulating an integrator
in an electronic analog computer.

† See, for example, J. Millman, "Vacuum Tube and Semiconductor Electronics,"
sec. 17-10, McGraw-Hill Book Company, New York, 1958.

7.2 GENERAL RELATIONS FOR TRANSFER FUNCTIONS AND FUNDAMENTAL MATRIX

The Laplace transform is a convenient method of calculating the fundamental matrix of a system whose differential equations are in normal form.   Thus consider the equations

$$\frac{d\mathbf{q}(t)}{dt} = \mathbf{A}\mathbf{q}(t) + \mathbf{B}\mathbf{x}(t)$$
$$\mathbf{y}(t) = \mathbf{C}\mathbf{q}(t) + \mathbf{D}\mathbf{x}(t) \tag{7.4}$$

where $\mathbf{A}$, $\mathbf{B}$, $\mathbf{C}$, and $\mathbf{D}$ are constant matrices.   Taking the Laplace transform of both sides of (7.4), we obtain

$$s\mathbf{Q}(s) - \mathbf{q}(0) = \mathbf{A}\mathbf{Q}(s) + \mathbf{B}\mathbf{X}(s) \tag{7.5}$$
$$\mathbf{Y}(s) = \mathbf{C}\mathbf{Q}(s) + \mathbf{D}\mathbf{X}(s) \tag{7.6}$$

where

$$\mathbf{Q}(s) = \begin{bmatrix} Q_1(s) \\ Q_2(s) \\ \cdot \\ \cdot \\ \cdot \\ Q_k(s) \end{bmatrix} = \begin{bmatrix} \mathfrak{L}[q_1(t)] \\ \mathfrak{L}[q_2(t)] \\ \cdot \\ \cdot \\ \cdot \\ \mathfrak{L}[q_k(t)] \end{bmatrix}$$

The definitions of $\mathbf{X}(s)$ and $\mathbf{Y}(s)$ are similar, and $\mathbf{Q}(s)$, $\mathbf{X}(s)$, and $\mathbf{Y}(s)$ are thus the Laplace transforms of $\mathbf{q}(t)$, $\mathbf{x}(t)$, and $\mathbf{y}(t)$, respectively.
    From (7.5)

$$(s\mathbf{I} - \mathbf{A})\mathbf{Q}(s) = \mathbf{q}(0) + \mathbf{B}\mathbf{X}(s)$$

where $\mathbf{I}$ is the $k \times k$ unit matrix.   Hence

$$\mathbf{Q}(s) = (s\mathbf{I} - \mathbf{A})^{-1}\mathbf{q}(0) + (s\mathbf{I} - \mathbf{A})^{-1}\mathbf{B}\mathbf{X}(s) \tag{7.7}$$

Substitution of (7.7) into (7.6) results in

$$\mathbf{Y}(s) = \mathbf{C}(s\mathbf{I} - \mathbf{A})^{-1}\mathbf{q}(0) + [\mathbf{C}(s\mathbf{I} - \mathbf{A})^{-1}\mathbf{B} + \mathbf{D}]\mathbf{X}(s) \tag{7.8}$$

With zero initial conditions this becomes

$$\mathbf{Y}(s) = [\mathbf{C}(s\mathbf{I} - \mathbf{A})^{-1}\mathbf{B} + \mathbf{D}]\mathbf{X}(s) = \mathbf{H}(s)\mathbf{X}(s) \tag{7.9}$$

where

$$\mathbf{H}(s) = \mathbf{C}(s\mathbf{I} - \mathbf{A})^{-1}\mathbf{B} + \mathbf{D} = \begin{bmatrix} H_{11}(s) & H_{12}(s) & \cdots & H_{1n}(s) \\ H_{21}(s) & H_{22}(s) & \cdots & H_{2n}(s) \\ \cdots\cdots\cdots\cdots\cdots\cdots\cdots \\ H_{m1}(s) & H_{m2}(s) & \cdots & H_{mn}(s) \end{bmatrix} \tag{7.10}$$

Thus the ith component $Y_i(s)$ of the transform $\mathbf{Y}(s)$ of the output vector

may be written

$$Y_i(s) = H_{i1}X_1(s) + H_{i2}X_2(s) + \cdots + H_{in}X_n(s) \qquad (7.11)$$

Hence it is apparent that $H_{ij}(s)$, which is the ijth element of

$$\mathbf{H}(s) = \mathbf{C}(s\mathbf{I} - \mathbf{A})^{-1}\mathbf{B} + \mathbf{D}$$

is the transfer function between $x_j(t)$ and $y_i(t)$.   From (6.32),

$$H_{ij}(s) = \mathcal{L}[h_{ij}(t)]$$

where $h_{ij}(t)$ is the response at the ith output terminal to a unit impulse at the jth input terminal.

We have thus found a general expression for the transfer functions of an arbitrary lumped fixed system in terms of the matrices appearing in the normal-form characterization.   We shall call the matrix $\mathbf{H}(s) = [H_{ij}(s)]$ the *transfer matrix* of the system.

The general time-domain solution of a fixed system was previously [Eq. (4.8)] shown to be

$$\mathbf{q}(t) = \mathbf{\Phi}(t)\mathbf{q}(0) + \int_0^t \mathbf{\Phi}(t - \lambda)\mathbf{B}\mathbf{x}(\lambda)\, d\lambda \qquad (7.12)$$

where we have taken $t_0 = 0$ for convenience.   Laplace transformation of (7.12) results, by use of the theorem for the Laplace transform of a convolution, in

$$\mathbf{Q}(s) = \mathbf{\hat{\Phi}}(s)\mathbf{q}(0) + \mathbf{\hat{\Phi}}(s)\mathbf{B}\mathbf{X}(s) \qquad (7.13)$$

In this expression

$$\mathbf{\hat{\Phi}}(s) = \mathcal{L}[\mathbf{\Phi}(t)]$$

where $\mathbf{\Phi}(t)$ is the fundamental matrix of the system.   Comparing (7.13) with (7.7), we obtain the following relation for the fundamental matrix:

$$\mathbf{\hat{\Phi}}(s) = (s\mathbf{I} - \mathbf{A})^{-1} \qquad (7.14)$$

or

$$e^{\mathbf{A}t} = \mathbf{\Phi}(t) = \mathcal{L}^{-1}[(s\mathbf{I} - \mathbf{A})^{-1}] \qquad (7.15)$$

Thus the fundamental matrix is the inverse Laplace transform of the matrix $\mathbf{\hat{\Phi}}(s) = (s\mathbf{I} - \mathbf{A})^{-1}$, which we shall call the *characteristic frequency matrix* of the system.

Note that in a first-order system, $\phi(t) = e^{at}$, whose Laplace transform is $\cdot\Phi(s) = (s - a)^{-1}$.   This fact can serve as a mnemonic for (7.15).

Example 7.4   The network considered in Example 4.1, repeated in Fig. 7.3, was shown to have matrices

$$\mathbf{A} = \begin{bmatrix} 0 & -2 \\ 1 & -3 \end{bmatrix} \quad \mathbf{B} = \begin{bmatrix} 2 & -2 \\ 0 & -3 \end{bmatrix}$$

$$\mathbf{C} = \begin{bmatrix} 1 & 0 \\ 1 & -3 \end{bmatrix} \quad \mathbf{D} = \begin{bmatrix} 0 & 0 \\ 0 & -3 \end{bmatrix}$$

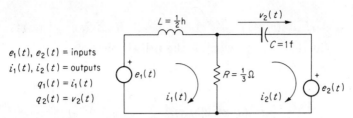

FIG. 7.3   Network for Example 7.4.

The Laplace transform of the fundamental matrix is

$$\hat{\mathbf{\Phi}}(s) = (s\mathbf{I} - \mathbf{A})^{-1} = \begin{bmatrix} s & 2 \\ -1 & s+3 \end{bmatrix}^{-1}$$

$$= \frac{\begin{bmatrix} s+3 & -2 \\ 1 & s \end{bmatrix}}{s^2 + 3s + 2} = \begin{bmatrix} \dfrac{s+3}{(s+2)(s+1)} & \dfrac{-2}{(s+2)(s+1)} \\ \dfrac{1}{(s+2)(s+1)} & \dfrac{s}{(s+2)(s+1)} \end{bmatrix}$$

$$= \begin{bmatrix} \dfrac{-1}{s+2} + \dfrac{2}{s+1} & \dfrac{2}{s+2} + \dfrac{-2}{s+1} \\ \dfrac{-1}{s+2} + \dfrac{1}{s+1} & \dfrac{2}{s+2} + \dfrac{-1}{s+1} \end{bmatrix}$$

The inverse Laplace transform of $\hat{\mathbf{\Phi}}(s)$ yields the fundamental matrix

$$\mathbf{\Phi}(t) = e^{\mathbf{A}t} = \begin{bmatrix} -e^{-2t} + 2e^{-t} & 2e^{-2t} - 2e^{-t} \\ -e^{-2t} + e^{-t} & 2e^{-2t} - e^{-t} \end{bmatrix}$$

which is the same result obtained by calculating $e^{\mathbf{A}t}$ by the methods of Chap. 4.

The transfer matrix is given by

$$\mathbf{H}(s) = \mathbf{C}(s\mathbf{I} - \mathbf{A})^{-1}\mathbf{B} + \mathbf{D}$$

$$= \frac{1}{s^2 + 3s + 2}\begin{bmatrix} 1 & 0 \\ 1 & -3 \end{bmatrix}\begin{bmatrix} s+3 & -2 \\ 1 & s \end{bmatrix}\begin{bmatrix} 2 & -2 \\ 0 & -3 \end{bmatrix} + \begin{bmatrix} 0 & 0 \\ 0 & -3 \end{bmatrix}$$

$$= \begin{bmatrix} \dfrac{2(s+3)}{s^2 + 3s + 2} & -\dfrac{2s}{s^2 + 3s + 2} \\ \dfrac{2s}{s^2 + 3s + 2} & -\dfrac{3s^2 + 2s}{s^2 + 3s + 2} \end{bmatrix}$$

Thus the response i_2 to the input $e_1(t) = \delta(t)$ is the inverse transform of $H_{21}(s)$, giving

$$h_{21}(t) = 4e^{-2t} - 2e^{-t}$$

which agrees with the result of a direct calculation.   It may also be noted that only $H_{22}(s)$ has a numerator of second degree, so that only $h_{22}(t)$

involves an impulsive term. This is exactly what we expect, since $e_2(t) = \delta(t)$ will result in an impulse of current through C.

7.3 PROPERTIES OF THE FUNDAMENTAL MATRIX AND ITS TRANSFORM

The general form of the characteristic frequency matrix $\hat{\Phi}(s) = (s\mathbf{I} - \mathbf{A})^{-1}$ makes evident a number of important properties of this matrix and of the fundamental matrix $\Phi(t)$ of which $\hat{\Phi}(s)$ is the Laplace transform.

We observe first that

$$\hat{\Phi}(s) = \frac{\text{adj } (s\mathbf{I} - \mathbf{A})}{|s\mathbf{I} - \mathbf{A}|} \tag{7.16}$$

where adj $(s\mathbf{I} - \mathbf{A}) = $ adjoint matrix of $s\mathbf{I} - \mathbf{A} = [|s\mathbf{I} - \mathbf{A}|^{ji}]$

$$|s\mathbf{I} - \mathbf{A}|^{ji} = \text{cofactor of } ji\text{th element of } s\mathbf{I} - \mathbf{A}$$
$$|s\mathbf{I} - \mathbf{A}| = \text{determinant of } s\mathbf{I} - \mathbf{A}$$

From (7.16) it is clear that the denominator of each element of $\hat{\Phi}(s)$ is either $|s\mathbf{I} - \mathbf{A}|$ or a factor thereof. The latter is the case when a cofactor of $|s\mathbf{I} - \mathbf{A}|$ has a zero in common with $|s\mathbf{I} - \mathbf{A}|$ itself (as, for example, in the (2, 2) and (3, 1) elements of $\hat{\Phi}(s)$ in Example 7.5).

In a system of kth order, $\mathbf{A}$ is a $k \times k$ matrix; hence the determinant $|s\mathbf{I} - \mathbf{A}|$ is a kth-degree polynomial, which may be written†

$$|s\mathbf{I} - \mathbf{A}| = s^k + a_1 s^{k-1} + \cdots + a_{k-1}s + a_k$$
$$= (s - \alpha_1)^{m_1}(s - \alpha_2)^{m_2} \cdots (s - \alpha_{k'})^{m_{k'}} \tag{7.17}$$

This polynomial, which is the denominator of each element of $\hat{\Phi}(s)$, is called the *characteristic polynomial* of the system. The zeros of this polynomial $\alpha_1, \alpha_2, \ldots, \alpha_{k'}$ (that is, those values of s for which $|s\mathbf{I} - \mathbf{A}| = 0$) are called the *eigenvalues*, or *characteristic roots*, of the system. The equation

$$|s\mathbf{I} - \mathbf{A}| = 0 \tag{7.18}$$

for the eigenvalues is called the *characteristic equation*.

The theory of determinants gives the following expression‡ for the coefficients of the characteristic polynomial,

$$a_i = (-1)^i \text{tr}_i \mathbf{A} \qquad i = 1, 2, \ldots, k = \text{order of system} \tag{7.19}$$

---

† The symbol k' is used since the number k' of distinct roots is less than k if at least one root is repeated.

‡ A. C. Aitken, "Theory of Matrices," 9th ed., p. 88, Interscience Publishers, Inc., New York, 1958.

where $\mathrm{tr}_i\,\mathbf{A}$ denotes the sum of the principal minors of order i of the characteristic matrix $\mathbf{A}$. In particular, $\mathrm{tr}_1\,\mathbf{A} = \mathrm{trace}\,\mathbf{A} = \mathrm{sum}$ of diagonal elements of $\mathbf{A}$ and $\mathrm{tr}_k\,\mathbf{A} = |\mathbf{A}|$. Since $s = 0$ is a root of (7.18) if and only if $a_k = 0$, it follows as a consequence of (7.19) that the system has a characteristic frequency at $s = 0$ if and only if $\mathbf{A}$ is singular, i.e., if $|\mathbf{A}| = 0$.

Each element of the adjoint matrix in the numerator of (7.16) is a polynomial of degree $k - 1$; consequently we can write

$$\hat{\mathbf{\Phi}}(s) = \frac{\mathrm{adj}\,(s\mathbf{I} - \mathbf{A})}{|s\mathbf{I} - \mathbf{A}|} = \frac{\mathbf{B}_1 s^{k-1} + \mathbf{B}_2 s^{k-2} + \cdots + \mathbf{B}_k}{s^k + a_1 s^{k-1} + \cdots + a_k} \tag{7.20}$$

where $\mathbf{B}_1, \mathbf{B}_2, \ldots, \mathbf{B}_k$ are $k \times k$ matrices. By inspection of the matrix $(s\mathbf{I} - \mathbf{A})$ for any typical $\mathbf{A}$, it is evident that

$$\mathbf{B}_1 = \mathbf{I}$$

The task of computing the cofactors of $(s\mathbf{I} - \mathbf{A})$ is quite laborious when $k > 3$; it may be avoided by computing instead the matrices $\mathbf{B}_n$ of the numerator and the coefficients a_n of the denominator of $\hat{\mathbf{\Phi}}(s)$ by means of the following algorithm:[†]

$$a_n = -\frac{1}{n}\,\mathrm{trace}\,(\mathbf{A}\mathbf{B}_n) \qquad n = 1, 2, \ldots, k \tag{7.21}$$

$$\mathbf{B}_{n+1} = \mathbf{A}\mathbf{B}_n + a_n\mathbf{I} \qquad n = 1, 2, \ldots, k - 1 \tag{7.22}$$

The last relation with $n = k$ may be used as a check and should result in $\mathbf{B}_{k+1} = \mathbf{0}$.

Example 7.5   Motion of particle perturbed from circular orbit

The equations for the motion of a particle perturbed from a circular orbit in a central inverse-square-law field were derived in Example 2.9, and the fundamental matrix was obtained in Example 4.2. We now calculate the fundamental matrix by obtaining the characteristic frequency matrix. Equations (4.16) give the matrix $\mathbf{A}$ as

$$\mathbf{A} = \begin{bmatrix} 0 & 0 & \dfrac{1}{m} & 0 \\[2mm] \dfrac{-2\omega_0}{r_0} & 0 & 0 & \dfrac{1}{mr_0^2} \\[2mm] -m\omega_0^2 & 0 & 0 & \dfrac{2\omega_0}{r_0} \\[2mm] 0 & 0 & 0 & 0 \end{bmatrix}$$

[†] J-M. Souriau, Une méthode pour la décomposition spectrale a l'inversion des matrices, *Compt. rend.*, vol. 227, pp. 1010–1011, 1948. For a proof, see also J. S. Frame, Matrix Functions and Applications, part IV, *IEEE Spectrum*, vol. 1, pp. 123–131, June, 1964, or V. N. Faddeeva, "Computational Methods of Linear Algebra," Dover Publications, Inc., New York, 1959.

In order to find $\hat{\mathbf{\Phi}}(s)$ in the form (7.20), we employ the algorithm (7.21) and (7.22) and obtain

$$\mathbf{B}_1 = \mathbf{I}$$
$$a_1 = -\text{trace } (\mathbf{AB}_1) = -\text{trace } \mathbf{A} = 0$$
$$\mathbf{B}_2 = \mathbf{AB}_1 + a_1\mathbf{I} = \mathbf{A}$$
$$a_2 = -\tfrac{1}{2} \text{trace } (\mathbf{AB}_2) = -\tfrac{1}{2}(-2\omega_0^2) = \omega_0^2$$
$$\mathbf{B}_3 = \mathbf{AB}_2 + a_2\mathbf{I} = \mathbf{A}^2 + \omega_0^2\mathbf{I}$$
$$a_3 = -\tfrac{1}{3} \text{trace } (\mathbf{AB}_3) = -\tfrac{1}{3} \text{trace } \mathbf{A}^3 = 0$$
$$\mathbf{B}_4 = \mathbf{AB}_3 + a_3\mathbf{I} = \mathbf{A}^3 + \omega_0^2\mathbf{A}$$
$$a_4 = -\tfrac{1}{4} \text{trace } (\mathbf{AB}_4) = -\tfrac{1}{4} \text{trace } (\mathbf{A}^4 + \omega_0^2\mathbf{A}^2)$$
$$= -\tfrac{1}{4}(2\omega_0^4 - 2\omega_0^4) = 0$$

The characteristic polynomial in the denominator of (7.20) is thus

$$|s\mathbf{I} - \mathbf{A}| = s^4 + \omega_0^2 s^2 = s^2(s^2 + \omega_0^2)$$

The same result may, of course, be obtained by evaluating the determinant $|s\mathbf{I} - \mathbf{A}|$ by some other method. Use of (7.20) now yields

$$\hat{\mathbf{\Phi}}(s) = \frac{\mathbf{I}s^3 + \mathbf{A}s^2 + (\mathbf{A}^2 + \omega_0^2\mathbf{I})s + (\mathbf{A}^3 + \omega_0^2\mathbf{A})}{s^2(s^2 + \omega_0^2)}$$

After computing $\mathbf{A}^2$ and $\mathbf{A}^3$, we find

$$\hat{\mathbf{\Phi}}(s) = (s\mathbf{I} - \mathbf{A})^{-1}$$

$$= \frac{1}{s^2(s^2 + \omega_0^2)} \begin{bmatrix} s^3 & 0 & \dfrac{s^2}{m} & \dfrac{2\omega_0}{mr_0}s \\[2mm] -\dfrac{2\omega_0}{r_0}s^2 & s(s^2 + \omega_0^2) & -\dfrac{2\omega_0}{mr_0}s & \dfrac{s^2 + \omega_0^2 - 4\omega_0^2}{mr_0^2} \\[2mm] -m\omega_0^2 s^2 & 0 & s^3 & \dfrac{2\omega_0}{r_0}s^2 \\[2mm] 0 & 0 & 0 & s(s^2 + \omega_0^2) \end{bmatrix}$$

or

$$\hat{\mathbf{\Phi}}(s) = \begin{bmatrix} \dfrac{s}{s^2 + \omega_0^2} & 0 & \dfrac{1}{m(s^2 + \omega_0^2)} & \dfrac{2\omega_0}{mr_0 s(s^2 + \omega_0^2)} \\[2mm] -\dfrac{2\omega_0}{r_0(s^2 + \omega_0^2)} & \dfrac{1}{s} & \dfrac{-2\omega_0}{mr_0 s(s^2 + \omega_0^2)} & \dfrac{1}{mr_0^2 s^2}\left(1 - \dfrac{4\omega_0^2}{s^2 + \omega_0^2}\right) \\[2mm] -\dfrac{m\omega_0^2}{s^2 + \omega_0^2} & 0 & \dfrac{s}{s^2 + \omega_0^2} & \dfrac{2\omega_0}{r_0(s^2 + \omega_0^2)} \\[2mm] 0 & 0 & 0 & \dfrac{1}{s} \end{bmatrix}$$

The inverse transform of this matrix gives the fundamental matrix

$$\Phi(t) = \begin{bmatrix} \cos \omega_0 t & 0 & \dfrac{1}{m\omega_0} \sin \omega_0 t & \dfrac{2}{m\omega_0 r_0} (1 - \cos \omega_0 t) \\[2ex] -\dfrac{2}{r_0} \sin \omega_0 t & 1 & -\dfrac{2}{m\omega_0 r_0} (1 - \cos \omega_0 t) & \dfrac{-3\omega_0 t + 4 \sin \omega_0 t}{m r_0{}^2 \omega_0} \\[2ex] -m\omega_0 \sin \omega_0 t & 0 & \cos \omega_0 t & \dfrac{2}{r_0} \sin \omega_0 t \\[2ex] 0 & 0 & 0 & 1 \end{bmatrix}$$

which agrees with the result obtained in Example 4.2.

The fundamental matrix $\Phi(t) = e^{At}$ is the inverse Laplace transform of $\hat{\Phi}(s) = (sI - A)^{-1}$. In order to find the general form of $\Phi(t)$, we expand $\hat{\Phi}(s)$ in partial fractions and obtain

$$\hat{\Phi}(s) = (sI - A)^{-1} = \sum_{p=1}^{k'} \sum_{r=1}^{m_p} A_{rp} \frac{1}{(s - \alpha_p)^r} \qquad (7.23)$$

where the α_p $(p = 1, 2, \ldots, k' \le k)$ are the roots of the characteristic equation (7.18), and m_p are their respective multiplicities. After $\hat{\Phi}(s)$ has been found by (7.16) or (7.20), the matrices A_{rp} may be found by the technique outlined in Sec. 6.6 for scalar coefficients. The inverse Laplace transform of (7.23) gives the required fundamental matrix,

$$\Phi(t) = e^{At} = \sum_{p=1}^{k'} e^{\alpha_p t} \sum_{r=1}^{m_p} A_{rp} \frac{t^{r-1}}{(r - 1)!} \qquad (7.24)$$

It is thus seen that each term in the fundamental matrix of a fixed system generally consists of a sum of products of exponentials (with exponential coefficients which are the roots of the characteristic equation) and polynomials in t (of degrees one less than the multiplicity of the corresponding characteristic roots). It can happen, however, that

$$A_{qp} = A_{q+1,p} = \cdots = A_{m_p p} = 0 \qquad q \ge 1$$

for one or more characteristic roots α_p. In this case, the fundamental matrix will appear to be that of a lower-order system, i.e., one having a lower-order characteristic equation. This situation arises when the *minimum polynomial*† is of lower degree than the characteristic poly-

---

† The minimum polynomial $f(s) = b_l + b_{l-1}s + \cdots + s^l$ ($l \le k$, the degree of the characteristic polynomial) is the polynomial of lowest degree for which the matrix equation $f(A) = b_l I + b_{l-1} A + \cdots + A^l = 0$ holds. For further details and the significance of a reducible system, i.e., one in which the minimum polynomial is not of degree k, see L. A. Zadeh and C. A. Desoer, "Linear System Theory," McGraw-Hill Book Company, pp. 300–310, New York, 1963.

nomial; the degree of the minimum polynomial is the apparent order of the system. When the minimum polynomial and the characteristic polynomial are identical, the system is said to be *irreducible*.

The case of distinct characteristic roots is of special interest since it occurs most frequently. In this case, the characteristic polynomial is irreducible and (7.23) becomes

$$\hat{\mathbf{\Phi}}(s) = \sum_{p=1}^{k} \frac{\mathbf{A}_p}{s - \alpha_p}$$

The matrices $\mathbf{A}_p$ are given by

$$\mathbf{A}_p = \lim_{s \to \alpha_p} \frac{\text{adj } (s\mathbf{I} - \mathbf{A})}{|s\mathbf{I} - \mathbf{A}|} (s - \alpha_p) = \frac{\text{adj } (\alpha_p\mathbf{I} - \mathbf{A})}{\displaystyle\prod_{\substack{i=1 \\ i \neq p}}^{k} (\alpha_p - \alpha_i)}$$

and (7.24) then gives

$$\mathbf{\Phi}(t) = \sum_{p=1}^{k} e^{\alpha_p t} \frac{\text{adj } (\alpha_p\mathbf{I} - \mathbf{A})}{\displaystyle\prod_{\substack{i=1 \\ i \neq p}}^{k} (\alpha_p - \alpha_i)} \tag{7.25}$$

It is interesting to note that a slightly different form of this expression for the fundamental matrix is furnished directly by *Sylvester's formula*[†] for analytic functions $f(\mathbf{A})$ of a diagonable[‡] matrix $\mathbf{A}$ with distinct characteristic roots. The formula is

$$f(\mathbf{A}) = \sum_{p=1}^{k} f(\alpha_p) \prod_{\substack{i=1 \\ i \neq p}}^{k} \frac{\mathbf{A} - \alpha_i\mathbf{I}}{\alpha_p - \alpha_i} \tag{7.26}$$

A similar expansion is possible for any square matrix.[§]

The foregoing discussion of the properties of the fundamental matrix permits us now to deduce a few useful facts in connection with *stability*, which will receive more complete attention in Chaps. 11 and 12.

The solution of the unforced system is given by

$$\mathbf{q}(t) = \mathbf{\Phi}(t)\mathbf{q}(0)$$

[†] See F. B. Hildebrand, "Methods of Applied Mathematics," Prentice-Hall, Inc., Englewood Cliffs, N.J., 1952, or J. S. Frame, *op. cit.*, Part II, pp. 102–108, April, 1964.
[‡] A *diagonable* matrix $\mathbf{A}$ is one which can be reduced to diagonal form by the transformation $\mathbf{S}^{-1}\mathbf{A}\mathbf{S}$.
[§] See J. S. Frame, *op. cit.*, Part IV, or F. R. Gantmacher, "Theory of Matrices," vol. 1, Chelsea Publishing Company, New York, 1959.

Hence the components of the state vector are given by

$$q_i(t) = \sum_{j=1}^{k} \phi_{ij}(t)q_j(0) \qquad i = 1, 2, \ldots, k$$

It thus follows from (7.24) that:

1. If every eigenvalue has a negative real part (that is, Re $\alpha_p < 0$ for all p),

$$\mathbf{q}(t) \rightarrow 0 \text{ as } t \rightarrow \infty$$

2. If any eigenvalue has a positive real part (that is, Re $\alpha_p > 0$ for some p), at least one component of $\mathbf{q}(t) \rightarrow \infty$ as $t \rightarrow \infty$; hence†

$$\mathbf{q}(t) \rightarrow \infty \text{ as } t \rightarrow \infty$$

(A vector is said to be infinite if any component is infinite.)

3. If every eigenvalue has a nonpositive real part (that is, Re $\alpha_p \leq 0$ for all p) and

   (a) all eigenvalues having zero real parts are simple (i.e., in (7.24) $m_p = 1$ for all p), each element of $\mathbf{q}(t)$ remains bounded but $\mathbf{q}(t)$ does not approach zero as $t \rightarrow \infty$ (unless it happens that the initial values $q_j(0)$ corresponding to each constant ϕ_{ij} are zero);

   (b) if any eigenvalue with zero real part is multiple, then

$$\mathbf{q}(t) \rightarrow \infty \text{ as } t \rightarrow \infty$$

(unless again the appropriate initial values $q_j(0)$ are zero).

These cases are depicted in Fig. 7.4.

† By $\mathbf{q}(t) \rightarrow \infty$ we mean that $\lim_{t \to \infty} \mathbf{q}(t)$ is not finite.   This notation includes possible unbounded oscillations.

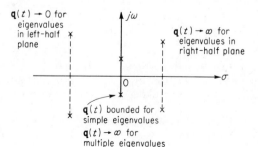

FIG. 7.4 *Behavior of unforced system for various eigenvalue locations.*

Systems falling into category 1 are called *asymptotically stable*. Those falling into category 2 or 3b are called *unstable*, while those corresponding to category 3a are for the present called *weakly stable*. These definitions will be made more precise in Chap. 11.

It should be noted that, since the degree of the numerator is strictly less than the degree of the denominator in each element of $\hat{\mathbf{\Phi}}(s)$, there are no impulsive terms in $\mathbf{\Phi}(t)$. The impulse-response matrix, which is

$$\mathbf{H}(t) = \mathbf{C}\mathbf{\Phi}(t)\mathbf{B} + \mathbf{D}\delta(t)$$

contains impulses if and only if $\mathbf{D}$ is not identically zero, since the only manner in which an impulse can be transmitted through the system is by the direct connections represented in $\mathbf{D}$.

A system governed by the transfer matrix

$$\mathbf{H}(s) = \mathbf{C}\hat{\mathbf{\Phi}}(s)\mathbf{B} + \mathbf{D}$$

is called *high-pass* if $\mathbf{H}(s)$ does not go to zero as $s \to \infty$, that is, if $\mathbf{D}$ is nonzero. If $\mathbf{H}(s) \to 0$ as $s \to \infty$, that is, if $\mathbf{D}$ is identically zero, the system is called *low-pass*. A high-pass system is thus one which transmits impulses (without distortion), and a low-pass system is one which does not.

7.4   SIMULTANEOUS EQUATIONS AND NETWORK ANALYSIS

The normal form of the differential equations is particularly useful in the discussion of the properties common to all lumped-parameter systems. In many physical systems, however, it is more convenient to write the differential equations in a different form. Although the equations can be converted into normal form by the introduction of appropriate additional variables, it is generally not necessary to do this to obtain the properties of the system.

Frequently a system is described by a set of simultaneous integro-differential equations of the form

$$L_{11}(D)y_1(t) + \cdots + L_{1m}(D)y_m(t) = K_{11}(D)x_1(t) + \cdots$$
$$+ K_{1n}(D)x_n(t)$$
$$L_{21}(D)y_1(t) + \cdots + L_{2m}(D)y_m(t) = K_{21}(D)x_1(t) + \cdots$$
$$+ K_{2n}(D)x_n(t) \quad (7.27)$$
$$\cdots \cdots \cdots \cdots \cdots \cdots \cdots \cdots \cdots \cdots \cdots \cdots \cdots \cdots \cdots$$
$$L_{m1}(D)y_1(t) + \cdots + L_{mm}(D)y_m(t) = K_{m1}(D)x_1(t) + \cdots$$
$$+ K_{mn}(D)x_n(t)$$

where the $L_{ij}(D)$ and $K_{ij}(D)$ are linear fixed differential operators of the form

$$L_{ij}(D) = l_{ij}^{-1}D^{-1} + l_{ij}^0 + l_{ij}^1 D + \cdots + l_{ij}^p D^p$$

$$D^k = \frac{d^k}{dt^k} \quad k \geq 1$$

$$D^{-1} = \int_{-\infty}^t d\lambda$$

and l_{ij}^k, $k = -1, 0, 1, \ldots, p$, are constants. In matrix form these equations may be written

$$\mathbf{L}(D)\mathbf{y}(t) = \mathbf{K}(D)\mathbf{x}(t)$$

where $\mathbf{L}(D)$ and $\mathbf{K}(D)$ are matrices with components $L_{ij}(D)$ and $K_{ij}(D)$, respectively. The Laplace transform of this set of equations is given by the set of algebraic equations

$$L_{11}(s)Y_1(s) + \cdots + L_{1m}(s)Y_m(s) = K_{11}(s)X_1(s) + \cdots$$
$$+ K_{1n}(s)X_n(s) + J_1(s)$$
$$L_{21}(s)Y_1(s) + \cdots + L_{2m}(s)Y_m(s) = K_{21}(s)X_1(s) + \cdots$$
$$+ K_{2n}(s)X_n(s) + J_2(s) \quad (7.28)$$
$$\cdots \cdots \cdots \cdots \cdots \cdots \cdots \cdots \cdots \cdots \cdots$$
$$L_{m1}(s)Y_1(s) + \cdots + L_{mm}(s)Y_m(s) = K_{m1}(s)X_1(s) + \cdots$$
$$+ K_{mn}(s)X_n(s) + J_m(s)$$

In (7.28)

$$L_{ij}(s) = l_{ij}^{-1}s^{-1} + l_{ij}^0 + l_{ij}^1 s + \cdots + l_{ij}^p s^p$$

i.e., each D in the differential operator $L_{ij}(D)$ is replaced by the complex frequency s in $L_{ij}(s)$. The terms $J_1(s)$, $J_2(s)$, $\ldots$, $J_m(s)$ are polynomials in s due to the initial conditions on the $x_i(t)$ and $y_j(t)$.

In matrix form (7.28) may be written

$$\mathbf{L}(s)\mathbf{Y}(s) = \mathbf{K}(s)\mathbf{X}(s) + \mathbf{J}(s) \quad (7.29)$$

The solution of this system of simultaneous algebraic equations is given by

$$\mathbf{Y}(s) = \mathbf{L}^{-1}(s)\mathbf{K}(s)\mathbf{X}(s) + \mathbf{L}^{-1}(s)\mathbf{J}(s) \quad (7.30)$$

The expressions for the polynomials representing the initial conditions may be readily calculated as in (7.2).

Since the transfer functions are defined for zero initial conditions, we set $\mathbf{J}(s) = 0$ in (7.30) and obtain

$$\mathbf{Y}(s) = \mathbf{L}^{-1}(s)\mathbf{K}(s)\mathbf{X}(s)$$

Hence the transfer matrix is

$$\mathbf{H}(s) = \mathbf{L}^{-1}(s)\mathbf{K}(s) \quad (7.31)$$

in terms of the differential operators in the simultaneous equations

governing the behavior of the system. Therefore the characteristic equation of the system is given by

$$|\mathbf{L}(s)| = 0 \tag{7.32}$$

This equation is equivalent to (7.18).

The nodal and loop equations governing a linear electric network have the form of (7.27). In particular, the nodal equations are†

$$Y_{11}(D)v_1(t) + \cdots + Y_{1n}(D)v_n(t) = i_1(t)$$

$$\cdots\cdots\cdots\cdots\cdots\cdots\cdots\cdots\cdots\cdots \tag{7.33}$$

$$Y_{n1}(D)v_1(t) + \cdots + Y_{nn}(D)v_n(t) = i_n(t)$$

or in matrix form,

$$\mathbf{Y}(D)\mathbf{v}(t) = \mathbf{i}(t)$$

where $i_j(t)$ is the total source current entering node j. The elements of the matrix $Y(D)$ are given by

$$Y_{ii}(D) = C_{ii}D + \frac{1}{R_{ii}} + \frac{1}{L_{ii}}\frac{1}{D}$$

where

C_{ii} = total parallel capacitance between node i and all other nodes
R_{ii} = total parallel resistance between node i and all other nodes
L_{ii} = total parallel inductance between node i and all other nodes

and for $i \neq j$

$$Y_{ij}(D) = -C_{ij}D - \frac{1}{R_{ij}} - \frac{1}{L_{ij}}\frac{1}{D}$$

where

C_{ij} = total parallel capacitance between nodes i and j
R_{ij} = total parallel resistance between nodes i and j
L_{ij} = total parallel inductance between nodes i and j

After taking the Laplace transform of (7.33), we obtain in matrix form

$$\mathbf{Y}(s)\mathbf{V}(s) = \mathbf{I}(s) + \mathbf{J}(s) \tag{7.34}$$

where the components of the initial condition vector $\mathbf{J}(s)$ are given by

$$\mathbf{J}(s) = \begin{bmatrix} +C_{11}v_1(0) - \cdots - C_{1n}v_n(0) \\ \quad + \frac{1}{s}\left[\frac{-1}{L_{11}}\int_{-\infty}^{0} v_1(\lambda)\,d\lambda + \cdots + \frac{1}{L_{1n}}\int_{-\infty}^{0} v_n(\lambda)\,d\lambda\right] \\ \cdots\cdots\cdots\cdots\cdots\cdots\cdots\cdots\cdots\cdots\cdots \\ -C_{n1}v_1(0) - \cdots + C_{nn}v_n(0) \\ \quad + \frac{1}{s}\left[\frac{1}{L_{n1}}\int_{-\infty}^{0} v_1(\lambda)\,d\lambda + \cdots - \frac{1}{L_{nn}}\int_{-\infty}^{0} v_n(\lambda)\,d\lambda\right] \end{bmatrix}$$

† B. Friedland, O. Wing, and R. Ash, "Principles of Linear Networks," chap. 5, McGraw-Hill Book Company, New York, 1961.

The following features of (7.34) are significant:

1. In the absence of initial conditions [$\mathbf{J}(s) = 0$], the equations are formally identical with the sinusoidal-steady-state equations of elementary network theory, when the frequency variable $j\omega$ is replaced by the complex frequency s.
2. The initial conditions appear as additional excitations. Each of these in the time domain consists of an impulsive term,

$$[C_{ii}v_i(0) - \sum_{j \neq i} C_{ij}v_j(0)]\delta(t)$$

whose Laplace transform is a constant, and a step of height

$$- \frac{1}{L_{ii}} \int_{-\infty}^{0} v_i(\lambda)\, d\lambda + \sum_{j \neq i} \frac{1}{L_{ij}} \int_{-\infty}^{0} v_j(\lambda)\, d\lambda$$

These results make it possible to employ the various methods developed for sinusoidal-steady-state analysis for solving dynamic network problems. As a preliminary to the use of these techniques it is necessary to represent initial conditions by equivalent excitations. This consists of replacing charged capacitors by uncharged capacitors in series with constant voltage sources or in parallel with impulsive current sources and of replacing fluxed inductors by unfluxed inductors in parallel with constant current sources or in series with impulsive voltage sources. These equivalents are illustrated in Fig. 7.5.

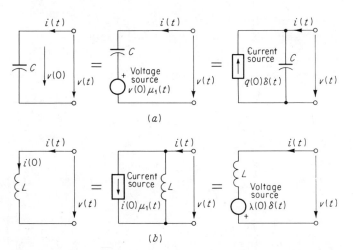

FIG. 7.5   Equivalent circuits of excited electrical elements.
(a) Charged capacitor; (b) fluxed inductor.

The validity of the equivalents may be demonstrated by showing that the terminal relations for arbitrary terminal voltages and currents are identical.   For example, in Fig. 7.5 the terminal relation for the charged capacitor is

$$v(t) = \frac{1}{C} \int_{-\infty}^{t} i(\lambda) \, d\lambda \qquad t > 0$$

Taking the Laplace transform, we obtain

$$V(s) = \frac{1}{Cs} I(s) + \frac{1}{Cs} \int_{-\infty}^{0} i(\lambda) \, d\lambda = \frac{1}{Cs} I(s) + \frac{1}{s} v(0) \qquad (7.35)$$

since

$$v(0) = \frac{1}{C} \int_{-\infty}^{0} i(\lambda) \, d\lambda$$

It is seen that (7.35) is also the terminal relation for the series equivalent. The parallel equivalent is obtained by the use of Norton's theorem or by direct analysis.

If all charged capacitors and all fluxed inductors in a network are replaced by their parallel equivalents and the nodal equations are written for the resulting circuit by the use of the techniques developed for sinusoidal-steady-state analysis, the nodal equations of (7.34) result.

Similarly, if the charged capacitors and fluxed inductors in a network are replaced by their series equivalents and the loop equations are written by sinusoidal-steady-state methods, the resulting equations are the Laplace transforms of the loop integrodifferential equations of the network.

All the methods of sinusoidal-steady-state analysis such as combination of parallel and series impedance and the various network theorems may be employed, as well as analysis by nodal and loop equations.

Example 7.6   We shall obtain the fundamental matrix and the other transfer functions of the network of Fig. 7.3.   To find the fundamental matrix we require the response to initial conditions, without external excitation.   The equivalent circuit with voltage and current sources representing initial conditions is shown in Fig. 7.6.

FIG. 7.6   Calculation of $\hat{\Phi}(s)$.

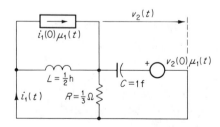

The calculation is performed by use of the principle of superposition. With the current source set equal to zero, we find

$$I_1(s) = -\frac{\frac{1}{3}}{\frac{1}{3} + \frac{1}{2}s}\left(\frac{1}{\frac{1}{s} + \frac{(\frac{1}{3})(\frac{1}{2}s)}{\frac{1}{3} + \frac{1}{2}s}}\right)\frac{v_2(0)}{s} = -\frac{2}{s^2 + 3s + 2}v_2(0)$$

and

$$V_2(s) = \frac{v_2(0)}{s} - \left(\frac{\frac{1}{s}}{\frac{1}{s} + \frac{(\frac{1}{3})(\frac{1}{2}s)}{\frac{1}{3} + \frac{1}{2}s}}\right)\frac{v_2(0)}{s} = \frac{s}{s^2 + 3s + 2}v_2(0)$$

With the voltage source set equal to zero,

$$I_1(s) = \frac{\frac{1}{2}s}{\frac{1}{2}s + \frac{\frac{1}{3}\left(\frac{1}{s}\right)}{\frac{1}{3} + \frac{1}{s}}}\frac{i_1(0)}{s} = \frac{s + 3}{s^2 + 3s + 2}i_1(0)$$

and

$$V_2(s) = \frac{1}{3 + \frac{2}{s} + s}\frac{i_1(0)}{s} = \frac{1}{s^2 + 3s + 2}i_1(0)$$

Adding these results and arranging in matrix form, we obtain

$$\begin{bmatrix} I_1(s) \\ V_2(s) \end{bmatrix} = \begin{bmatrix} \dfrac{s + 3}{s^2 + 3s + 2} & -\dfrac{2}{s^2 + 3s + 2} \\ \dfrac{1}{s^2 + 3s + 2} & \dfrac{s}{s^2 + 3s + 2} \end{bmatrix} \begin{bmatrix} i_1(0) \\ v_2(0) \end{bmatrix} \qquad (7.36)$$

The fundamental matrix relates the state vector to its initial value by

$$\mathbf{q}(t) = \mathbf{\Phi}(t)\mathbf{q}(0)$$

or, taking the Laplace transform, by

$$\mathbf{Q}(s) = \hat{\mathbf{\Phi}}(s)\mathbf{q}(0)$$

Hence the square matrix in (7.36) is $\hat{\mathbf{\Phi}}(s)$. This result is identical with that previously computed.

The specified outputs are the mesh currents $i_1(t)$ and $i_2(t)$, and the excitations are the mesh voltages. The mesh equations for the network are

$$\begin{bmatrix} \dfrac{1}{2}s + \dfrac{1}{3} & -\dfrac{1}{3} \\[2ex] -\dfrac{1}{3} & \dfrac{1}{s} + \dfrac{1}{3} \end{bmatrix} \begin{bmatrix} I_1(s) \\[1ex] I_2(s) \end{bmatrix} = \begin{bmatrix} E_1(s) \\[1ex] -E_2(s) \end{bmatrix}$$

Inverting the matrix which operates on the output vector, we obtain

$$\begin{bmatrix} I_1(s) \\[1ex] I_2(s) \end{bmatrix} = \dfrac{1}{\left(\dfrac{1}{2}s + \dfrac{1}{3}\right)\left(\dfrac{1}{s} + \dfrac{1}{3}\right) - \dfrac{1}{9}} \begin{bmatrix} \dfrac{1}{s} + \dfrac{1}{3} & \dfrac{1}{3} \\[2ex] \dfrac{1}{3} & \dfrac{1}{2}s + \dfrac{1}{3} \end{bmatrix} \begin{bmatrix} E_1(s) \\[1ex] -E_2(s) \end{bmatrix}$$

$$= \begin{bmatrix} \dfrac{2(s + 3)}{s^2 + 3s + 2} & \dfrac{-2s}{s^2 + 3s + 2} \\[2ex] \dfrac{2s}{s^2 + 3s + 2} & \dfrac{-(3s^2 + 2s)}{s^2 + 3s + 2} \end{bmatrix} \begin{bmatrix} E_1(s) \\[1ex] E_2(s) \end{bmatrix}$$

Since

$$\mathbf{I}(s) = \mathbf{H}(s)\mathbf{E}(s)$$

the expression for $\mathbf{H}(s)$ found here is identical with that obtained in Sec. 7.2.

7.5 ANALYSIS BY SIMPLIFICATION OF ANALOG-COMPUTER DIAGRAM

In the frequency domain the analog-computer diagram is a graphical representation of *algebraic* relations existing between the Laplace transforms of the variables of concern. Since the dynamic (or operator) relations of the time domain have been replaced by algebraic relations in the frequency domain, which are in turn represented by means of the analog-computer diagram, simplification of the latter is the equivalent of solving algebraic equations. Thus the operational algebra of Chap. 1 reduces to ordinary matrix algebra.

In the analog-computer diagram developed in Chap. 2, all transfer functions start out as either integrators, with a transfer function $1/s$, or as amplifiers, with transfer functions which are constants. The operator relations of Fig. 1.16 and Prob. 1.13, for example, remain valid if $\mathbf{x}$, $\mathbf{y}$, and $\mathbf{z}$ are replaced by the transform vectors $\mathbf{X}(s)$, $\mathbf{Y}(s)$, $\mathbf{Z}(s)$ and if the operator H is replaced by the transfer function matrix $\mathbf{H}(s)$. The operator I becomes the unit matrix $\mathbf{I}$.

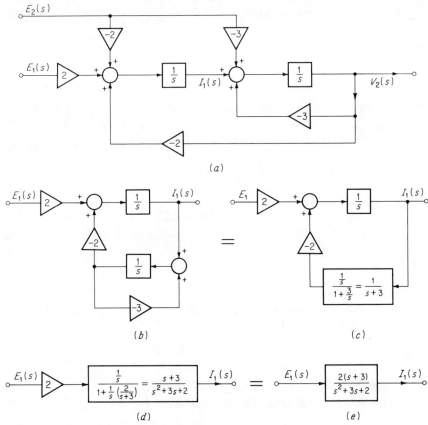

FIG. 7.7   *Example of block-diagram simplification.*

Example 7.7   The transfer functions from the inputs to the outputs of the network of Example 7.4 will be found by means of block-diagram simplification.   The analog-computer diagram which was originally found in Fig. 2.7 is reproduced, with the numerical values of Fig. 7.3, in Fig. 7.7a.   In order to compute $H_{11}(s) = I_1(s)/E_1(s)$, we may assume $E_2(s) = 0$, i.e., that connections from $E_2(s)$ are absent.   This results in the block diagram of Fig. 7.7b.   Two feedback-loop simplifications using the result of Prob. 1.13 are shown in Fig. 7.7c and d; a simple combination shown in Fig. 7.7e results in the required transfer function

$$H_{11}(s) = \frac{2(s+3)}{s^2 + 3s + 2}$$

which agrees with the corresponding element of $\mathbf{H}(s)$ previously calculated. In a similar manner the other transfer functions may be obtained.

PROBLEMS

7.1   Calculate the transfer matrix for the network of Fig. P 7.1, taking as inputs the two voltages and as outputs the three currents:

(a) By use of sinusoidal-steady-state network analysis methods.
(b) By writing the differential equations of the network in normal form.

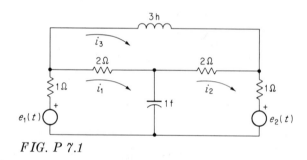

FIG. P 7.1

7.2   (a) Find the transfer function of the RC circuit of Fig. P 7.2 by writing the loop-voltage equations.
(b) Find the transfer function by circuit simplification, using the voltage-source–current-source transformations of Fig. 7.5.
(c) Determine the impulse response, and check its value at $t = 0$ by inspection of the circuit.
(d) Find $i_2(t)$ with the initial capacitor voltages shown.

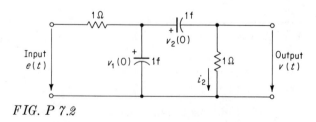

FIG. P 7.2

7.3   Calculate the fundamental matrix of the network of Fig. P 7.1.

7.4   Calculate $\mathbf{H}(s)$, $\mathbf{\Phi}(s)$, $h(t)$, and $\mathbf{\Phi}(t)$ for each of the systems of Fig. P 7.4, which were previously studied in Prob. 4.3, by use of the technique of Sec. 7.2.

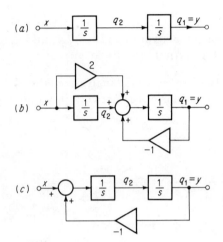

FIG. P 7.4

7.5   By considering the nature of the characteristic matrix $\mathbf{A}$, show that:

(a) The eigenvalues of a network containing only resistance and inductance (or capacitance) are all negative real.

(b) The eigenvalues of a network containing only inductance and capacitance (no resistance) are all imaginary.

7.6   For the network of Fig. P 7.6, choose an appropriate set of state variables and determine the characteristic frequency matrix.

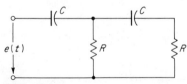

FIG. P 7.6

7.7   For the system shown in Fig. P 7.7:

(a) Find the transfer function.

(b) Find the impulse response.

(c) Find the fundamental matrix and discuss the significance of this result.

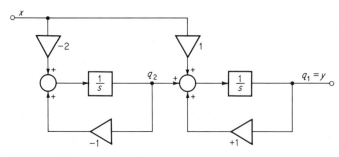

FIG. P 7.7

7.8 Find the transfer-function matrices $\mathbf{H}(s)$ of Prob. 7.4, using block-diagram simplifications.

7.9 A three-stage feedback amplifier is shown in Fig. P 7.9. The transfer function of each stage is given by

$$\frac{E_2(s)}{E_1(s)} = \frac{E_3(s)}{E_2(s)} = \frac{E_4(s)}{E_3(s)} = -\frac{\mu}{s+\alpha}$$

Assume that the input impedance of each amplifier is infinite ($i' = 0$).

(a) Calculate the transfer function $E_4(s)/E_0(s)$ with $R_2 = \infty$ and with R_2 finite.

(b) Compare the steady-state response to a unit-step input when $R_2 = \infty$ with that when R_2 is finite.

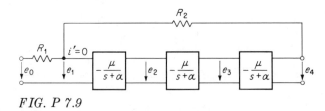

FIG. P 7.9

7.10 Show that the differential equation (2.19) may be written as the system (2.30) by writing

$$\frac{Y(s)}{X(s)} = \frac{B(s)}{A(s)} = \frac{B(s)Z(s)}{A(s)Z(s)}$$

7.11   Consider the transfer function

$$H(s) = \frac{b_1 s^{n-1} + \cdots + b_n}{s^n + a_1 s^{n-1} + \cdots + a_n}$$

Assume that the poles of $H(s)$ are *real* and distinct.   Show that the structures shown in Fig. P 7.11 are realizations of this transfer function by developing an algorithm for calculating the coefficients α_i

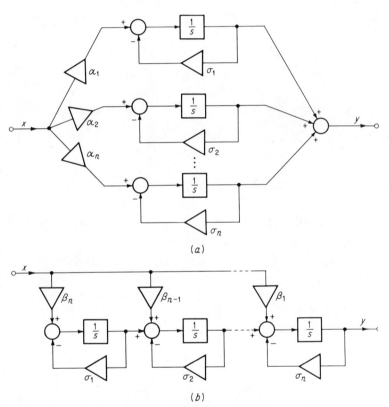

FIG. P 7.11   (a) Disjoint form; (b) cascade form.

and β_i.   (Note that the $-\sigma_i$ are the roots of the characteristic equation.   Why?)   Is the requirement that the roots be distinct necessary?   Explain.

7.12   Demonstrate that it is always possible to simulate the transfer function of Prob. 7.11 by the use of the ladder structure shown in Fig. P 7.12.

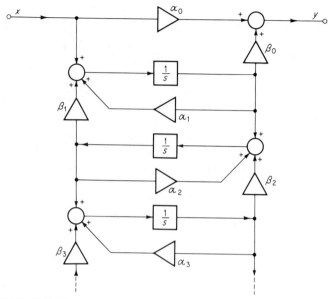

FIG. P 7.12

7.13 Draw the block diagrams of Figs. P 7.11a and b and P 7.12 for the transfer function

$$H(s) = \frac{(s+1)(s+3)}{s(s+2)(s+4)}$$

7.14 Determine the transfer function $E_2(s)/E_1(s)$ of the vacuum-tube equivalent circuit shown in Fig. P 7.14.

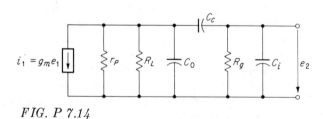

FIG. P 7.14

CHAPTER EIGHT

THE Z TRANSFORM

AND ITS USE

IN DISCRETE-TIME SYSTEMS

8.1 INTRODUCTION

What is now known as the Z transform was already used by deMoivre and Laplace in connection with their research in the theory of probability. For the reason which will shortly become evident, these "transforms" were called "generating functions," a name which has been retained in the mathematical literature of the theory of probability† and of the calculus of finite differences.‡

The engineering problems which resulted in the rediscovery of the Z transform arose in the analysis of sampled-data control systems and first occurred during World War II when such systems came into prominence.

† W. Feller, "An Introduction to Probability Theory and Its Applications," vol. 1, 2d ed., chap. 11, John Wiley & Sons, Inc., New York, 1957.

‡ See, for example, C. Jordan, "Calculus of Finite Differences," 2d ed., Chelsea Publishing Company, New York, 1952, or L. M. Milne-Thomson, "The Calculus of Finite Differences," St. Martin's Press, New York, 1933; reprinted 1951.

Sampled-data systems operate with discrete-time (or sampled) functions for one or two reasons. It may be that the data are available only at discrete instants (as in a scanning radar). It is possible, on the other hand, that the use of sampled data permits design of a system with better dynamical performance than could be obtained using the continuous-time data. Since the Laplace transform was the principal tool for the study of continuous-time control systems, its extension to sampled-data systems was entirely natural. It appears more reasonable now, however, to develop the Z transform as a tool for the study of discrete-time systems independently of the Laplace transform. We reserve a discussion of the connection between the two methods until this development is completed.

The introduction of the Z transform into the analysis of discrete-time systems is motivated by the same considerations which make the Laplace transform useful for the study of continuous-time systems: by using the Z transform, the difference equations which govern the behavior of the system are transformed to linear algebraic equations which are often simpler to solve than the original difference equations and which may give more insight into the behavior of the system.

In the analysis of discrete-time systems by means of the Z transform, the same steps are employed as in the analysis of continuous-time systems by means of the Laplace transform. The discrete-time signals of the system are replaced by their respective transforms; the system itself is represented by means of a "discrete-time transfer function"† which, like the transfer function of a continuous-time system, can be obtained by algebraic combination of the discrete-time transfer functions of its components. The Z transform of the discrete-time response is found to be equal to the product of the transfer function of the system and the Z transform of the input signal. As a last step, the actual response in the (discrete-) time domain is obtained by inversion of the Z transform of the output.

The principal distinctions between the Laplace transform and the Z transform are that the elementary function into which signals are resolved to obtain the Z transform is z^n (where z is a complex variable), instead of e^{st} as in the case of the Laplace transform, and that the Z transform is defined as a sum rather than as an integral.

8.2 DEFINITION OF Z TRANSFORM; REGIONS OF CONVERGENCE

The Z transform of a discrete-time signal $f(n)$ is defined as a power series in z^{-1} whose coefficients are the amplitudes of the discrete-time signal.

† In the literature of sampled-data control systems, discrete-time transfer functions are often called "pulse transfer functions," or "pulsed transfer functions."

As in the case of the Laplace transform, we can define a one-sided Z transform and a two-sided Z transform. These definitions are, respectively,

$$Z_I[f(n)] = F_I(z) = \sum_{n=0}^{\infty} f(n)z^{-n} \tag{8.1}$$

$$Z_{II}[f(n)] = F_{II}(z) = \sum_{n=-\infty}^{\infty} f(n)z^{-n} \tag{8.2}$$

To be useful in the analysis of discrete-time systems, it is desirable for these series to be expressible in closed form for the signals under consideration. Since the coefficient of z^{-n} in the series expansion is $f(n)$, it follows that the expansion of the closed form into a power series in z^{-n} will "generate" the signal. Hence the Z transform can be described as the "generating function" for the discrete-time signal to which it corresponds. The negative powers z^{-n} rather than positive powers z^n are used in the definition because this conforms with the most frequent engineering usage. In the mathematical literature dealing with generating functions and in some literature on sampled-data control systems, the coefficients of positive powers of z (or whatever other complex variable is used) often correspond to the values of $f(n)$ at positive values of n.

If $f(n) = 0$ for $n < 0$, the one-sided and the two-sided transforms are identical; however, if $f(n) \neq 0$ for all $n < 0$, the two definitions yield different expressions. The two-sided Z transform clearly incorporates information concerning the values of the signal $f(n)$ at all discrete instants at which it is defined. The one-sided Z transform carries information on values of $f(n)$ for nonnegative n only.

The one-sided Z transform

$$F_I(z) = f(0) + f(1)z^{-1} + f(2)z^{-2} + \cdots$$

is seen to be the principal part of a Laurent series about the point $z = 0$, plus an added constant $f(0)$. Thus the one-sided Z transform converges outside a circle centered at the origin as shown in Fig. 8.1a. The two-

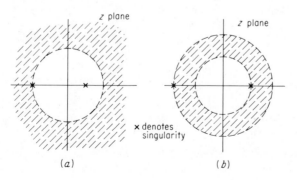

FIG. 8.1 Region of convergence of Z transform. (a) Region of convergence of one-sided Z transform; (b) region of convergence of two-sided Z transform.

$\times$ denotes singularity

(a) (b)

sided Z transform

$$F_{II}(z) = \cdots f(-2)z^2 + f(-1)z + f(0) + f(1)z^{-1} + \cdots$$

also defines a Laurent series about $z = 0$, but in this case the positive powers of z are also present; hence the two-sided Z transform converges in an *annulus* centered at the origin,† as shown in Fig. 8.1b. Thus, to determine the discrete-time signal $f(n)$ to which a given Z transform $F(z)$ corresponds, it is necessary to know whether $F(z)$ is a one-sided or a two-sided Z transform, as the following example illustrates.

Example 8.1   Consider the function

$$F(z) = \frac{z^2 - 4z + 1}{z^2 - \frac{5}{2}z + 1} = 1 - \frac{2}{z - 2} + \frac{\frac{1}{2}}{z - \frac{1}{2}}$$

The expansion of $F(z)$ into a Laurent series in the annulus $\frac{1}{2} < |z| < 2$ gives

$$F(z) = \cdots + (\tfrac{1}{2})^2 z^2 + \tfrac{1}{2}z + 2 + \tfrac{1}{2}z^{-1} + (\tfrac{1}{2})^2 z^{-2} + \cdots$$

Evidently $f(n)$, the coefficient of z^{-n}, is

$$f(n) = \begin{cases} (\tfrac{1}{2})^{|n|} & n \neq 0 \\ 2 & n = 0 \end{cases}$$

On the other hand, the expansion of $F(z)$ into a Taylor series about $z = \infty$ ($z^{-1} = 0$), valid for $|z| > 2$ ($|z^{-1}| < \frac{1}{2}$), gives

$$F(z) = 1 + \tfrac{1}{2}z^{-1} + (\tfrac{1}{2})^2 z^{-2} + \cdots - 2z^{-1} - 2^2 z^{-2} - \cdots$$

and the coefficient of z^{-n} is

$$f(n) = \begin{cases} (\tfrac{1}{2})^n - 2^n & n > 0 \\ 1 & n = 0 \end{cases}$$

We thus see that the two expressions for $f(n)$ are quite different.

The two-sided Z transform is useful primarily for problems involving stationary random processes, in which it cannot be assumed that $f(n) = 0$ for $n < 0$. In most other cases the one-sided Z transform may be used since the values of $f(n)$ for $n < 0$ are of no interest. Therefore, unless otherwise stated, we shall always use the one-sided Z transform and shall not use the subscript I.

The following theorems establish some fundamental properties of the Z transform.

---

† By way of analogy we note that a one-sided Laplace transform converges in a half plane to the right of the line $\sigma = \sigma_a$, while a two-sided Laplace transform converges in a vertical strip of the s plane.

Theorem 8.1 Convergence *If $f(n)$ has the properties*

(1) *$|f(n)| < \infty$ for all finite n,*
(2) *there exist positive constants N, r, and K such that*

$$|f(n)| \le Kr^n \qquad \text{for } n \ge N$$

then the one-sided Z transform

$$F(z) = \sum_{n=0}^{\infty} f(n)z^{-n}$$

converges absolutely for $\rho = |z| > r$.

Proof   We write the Z transform of $f(n)$ as

$$F(z) = \sum_{n=0}^{N-1} f(n)z^{-n} + \sum_{n=N}^{\infty} f(n)z^{-n}$$

Hence

$$|F(z)| \le \sum_{n=0}^{N-1} |f(n)|\rho^{-n} + \sum_{n=N}^{\infty} |f(n)|\rho^{-n}$$

By property (1), there exists a number M (which may depend on N) such that

$$\sum_{n=0}^{N-1} |f(n)|\rho^{-n} \le M \sum_{n=0}^{N-1} \rho^{-n}$$

By property (2),

$$\sum_{n=N}^{\infty} |f(n)|\rho^{-n} \le K \sum_{n=N}^{\infty} (r/\rho)^n$$

It follows that

$$|F(z)| \le M \frac{1 - \rho^{-N}}{1 - \rho^{-1}} + K \sum_{n=N}^{\infty} \left(\frac{r}{\rho}\right)^n$$

The first sum is finite for all ρ and $N < \infty$, and the second sum, which is a geometric series, is finite for all $\rho > r$. Thus the theorem is proved.

The smallest value of r such that $F(z)$ converges absolutely for $\rho = |z| > r$ is called the *radius of absolute convergence* of $F(z)$ and is denoted by ρ_a. The radius of absolute convergence is analogous to the abscissa of absolute convergence of the Laplace transform.

Theorem 8.2   *If $F(z)$ converges absolutely for $|z| > \rho_a$, then $F(z)$ converges uniformly for $|z| > \rho_a$, and $F(z)$ is analytic in the region $\rho > \rho_a$.*

This theorem is a direct consequence of the definition of the Z transform as a power series in z^{-1}. As a result of the second part of this theorem

Table 8.1   TRANSFORMS OF COMMON
FUNCTIONS

Function $f(n)$	Z transform $F(z)$	Radius of convergence ρ_a
$\delta(n - k)$	z^{-k}	0
$\mu_1(n)$	$\dfrac{1}{1 - z^{-1}}$	1
a^n	$\dfrac{1}{1 - az^{-1}}$	a
n	$\dfrac{z^{-1}}{(1 - z^{-1})^2}$	1

it is seen that the singularities of $F(z)$ must lie within or on a circle of radius ρ_a centered at the origin.   In general, the circle passes through the singularity of $F(z)$ which is at the greatest distance from the origin.

Theorem 8.3   Linearity   *If* $F(z) = \mathbb{Z}[f(n)]$ *and* $G(z) = \mathbb{Z}[g(n)]$, *then*

$$\mathbb{Z}[af(n) + bg(n)] = aF(z) + bG(z)$$

for any $f(n)$ *and* $g(n)$ *which possess Z transforms and for any constants a and b.*

The theorem follows directly from the definition (8.1) or (8.2) of the Z transform.

The calculation of the Z transform of a signal $f(n)$ necessitates the summation of the infinite series defined by (8.1) (or (8.2) in the case of two-sided Z transforms).   The Z transforms of a few functions, obtained by summing the defining series, are tabulated in Table 8.1.   By the use of the appropriate properties of the Z transform, to be developed subsequently, Table 8.1 can be extended considerably.   Another technique for calculating the Z transform of $f(n)$ consists in the use of the Laplace transform as described in Sec. 8.9.

8.3   INVERSION OF THE Z TRANSFORM

To determine the signal $f(n)$ corresponding to a given $F(z)$, that is, to generate $f(n)$, it is necessary to expand $F(z)$ into a power series in z^{-1}.

Since in any region of convergence the power series expansion of $F(z)$ is unique, the method employed for obtaining the expansion is a matter of convenience.

Obviously, the simplest method is to look up the discrete-time function corresponding to the transform to be inverted in an appropriate table.† By use of a short table and the technique of partial fraction expansion discussed in Sec. 6.6, where necessary, it is possible to invert most Z transforms which arise in engineering problems.

A more elegant and general technique is to use the inversion formula

$$f(n) = \frac{1}{2\pi j} \oint_C F(z) z^{n-1} \, dz \qquad (8.3)$$

where C is a circle of radius $r > \rho_a$, that is, a circle enclosing all the singularities of $F(z)z^{n-1}$.

The inversion formula follows directly from the fact that $F(z)$ is a Laurent series with only a principal part and a constant term; (8.3) is precisely the formula for the coefficients of the Laurent series. It may be noted that, if $F(z)$ is expanded as in (8.1), the coefficient of z^{-1} in (8.3) is $f(n)$, and $f(n)z^{-1}$ is the only term whose integral does not vanish.

The actual evaluation of (8.3) is most effectively carried out by means of the calculus of residues. Specifically, (8.3) may be written as

$f(n)$ = sum of residues of product $F(z)z^{n-1}$
    'at its poles *within* circle of convergence of $F(z)$

Note that, when $n = 0$, $F(z)z^{n-1}$ may have a pole at the origin even when $F(z)$ has no pole at the origin, and the residue of $F(z)z^{-1}$ must be evaluated there.

A third method which can be applied when $F(z)$ is rational is to express the numerator and denominator of $F(z)$ in polynomials in z^{-1} and then, using algebraic "long division," to divide the numerator by the denominator, thereby obtaining a series in powers of z^{-1}. This method, which has no counterpart in the Laplace transform, is particularly effective when tables of Z transforms or the inversion formula cannot be used because knowledge of the locations of the poles of $F(z)$ is lacking. Only the numerical values of the coefficients $f(n)$, however, and not a general expression, are obtained by this method.

Example 8.2   Evaluate the inverse Z transform of

$$F(z) = \frac{2z^2 - 0.5z}{z^2 - 0.5z - 0.5}$$

---

† See J. R. Ragazzini and G. F. Franklin, "Sampled-data Control Systems," McGraw-Hill Book Company, New York, 1958, or E. I. Jury, "Sampled-Data Control Systems," John Wiley & Sons, Inc., New York, 1958.

Partial Fractions.   We may write

$$F(z) = \frac{z}{z-1} + \frac{z}{z+0.5} = \frac{1}{1-z^{-1}} + \frac{1}{1+0.5z^{-1}}$$

Hence, from Table 8.1,

$$f(n) = 1 + (-0.5)^n$$

Inversion Formula.   The poles of $F(z)z^{n-1}$ are at $z = 1$ and $z = -\frac{1}{2}$. There is no pole at the origin even for $n = 0$.   Hence

$$f(n) = \text{residue of } \frac{2z^2 - 0.5z}{(z-1)(z+0.5)} z^{n-1} \qquad \text{at } z = 1$$

$$+ \text{ residue of } \frac{2z^2 - 0.5z}{(z-1)(z+0.5)} z^{n-1} \qquad \text{at } z = -\frac{1}{2}$$

$$= \frac{2-0.5}{1+0.5} (1)^n + \frac{2(-0.5)-0.5}{-0.5-1} (-0.5)^n = 1 + (-0.5)^n$$

Long Division.   Division of $F(z)$ by z^2 gives

$$F(z) = \frac{2 - 0.5z^{-1}}{1 - 0.5z^{-1} - 0.5z^{-2}}$$

The long division is then performed as follows:

$$
\begin{array}{r}
2 + 0.5z^{-1} + 1.25z^{-2} + 0.875z^{-3} + \cdots \\
1.0 - 0.5z^{-1} - 0.5z^{-2} \overline{)2 - 0.5z^{-1}} \\
2 - 1.0z^{-1} - 1.00z^{-2} \\
\hline
0.5z^{-1} + 1.00z^{-2} \\
0.5z^{-1} - 0.25z^{-2} - 0.250z^{-3} \\
\hline
1.25z^{-2} + 0.250z^{-3} \\
1.25z^{-2} - 0.625z^{-3} - \cdots \\
\hline
0.875z^{-3} + \cdots
\end{array}
$$

whence $f(0) = 2.0 \quad = 1 + (-0.5)^0$

$f(1) = 0.5 \quad = 1 + (-0.5)^1$

$f(2) = 1.25 \quad = 1 + (-0.5)^2$

$f(3) = 0.875 = 1 + (-0.5)^3$

$\cdots\cdots\cdots\cdots\cdots\cdots\cdots\cdots$

8.4   PROPERTIES OF THE Z TRANSFORM

Some of the important properties of the Z transform are given in Table 8.2.   Those properties marked with an asterisk will be proved here; the

Table 8.2 PROPERTIES OF Z TRANSFORM

Property	Time function	Z transform
1. *Linearity**	$af(n) + bg(n)$	$aF(z) + bG(z)$
2. *Differences* a. *Forward**	$\Delta^k f(n)$	$(z - 1)^k F(z)$ $- z \displaystyle\sum_{j=0}^{k-1} (z - 1)^{k-i-1}\Delta^i f(0)$
b. *Backward*	$\nabla^k f(n)$	$(1 - z^{-1})^k F(z)$ $- \displaystyle\sum_{j=0}^{k-1} (1 - z^{-1})^{k-i-1}\nabla^i f(-1)$
3. *Sums*	$\displaystyle\sum_{k=-\infty}^{n} f(k)$	$\dfrac{1}{1 - z^{-1}} F(z)$ $+ \dfrac{1}{1 - z^{-1}} \displaystyle\sum_{k=-\infty}^{-1} f(k)$
4. *Translation**	$f(n + k) \qquad k > 0$	$z^k F(z) - z^k \displaystyle\sum_{j=0}^{k-1} f(j)z^{-i}$
5. *Multiplication by a^n*	$a^n f(n)$	$F(a^{-1}z)$
6. *Multiplication by n^k*	$n^k f(n)$	$\left(z^{-1} \dfrac{d}{dz^{-1}} \right)^k F(z) \qquad$ (see *Note*)
7. *Convolution**	$y(n) = \displaystyle\sum_{k=0}^{n} h(n - k)x(k)$	$Y(z) = H(z)X(z)$
8. *Product of two functions**	$f(n)g(n)$	$\dfrac{1}{2\pi j} \displaystyle\oint_C \dfrac{F(w)G(zw^{-1})}{w} \, dw$
9. *Initial value*	$f(0) = \displaystyle\lim_{z \to \infty} F(z)$	
10. *Final value*	$f(\infty) = \displaystyle\lim_{z \to 1} (1 - z^{-1})F(z)$ if $(1 - z^{-1})F(z)$ is analytic for $\lvert z \rvert \geq 1$	

Properties marked with an asterisk are proved in the text.

Note: $\left(z^{-1} \dfrac{d}{dz^{-1}} \right)^k F(z)$ means "apply the operation k times in succession, first taking the derivative with respect to z^{-1} and then multiplying by z^{-1}."

others may be proved by steps similar to those used for proving the corresponding property of the Laplace transform, but using sums instead of integrals and differences† instead of derivatives.

A careful comparison of Table 8.2 with Table 6.2 in which corresponding properties of the Laplace transform are tabulated will be found worthwhile. In particular, the similarity of the role of $1 - z^{-1}$ in the Z transform to s in the Laplace transform should be noted.

DIFFERENCES

The Z transform of the first forward difference is

$$Z[\Delta f(n)] = Z[f(n + 1)] - Z[f(n)]$$

Since

$$Z[f(n)] = F(z) = \sum_{n=0}^{\infty} f(n)z^{-n} = f(0) + f(1)z^{-1} + f(2)z^{-2} + \cdots$$

it follows that

$$Z[f(n + 1)] = f(1) + f(2)z^{-1} + f(3)z^{-2} + \cdots = z[F(z) - f(0)]$$

Hence

$$Z[\Delta f(n)] = z[F(z) - f(0)] - F(z) = (z - 1)F(z) - zf(0)$$

The Z transform of the second forward difference is thus

$$Z[\Delta^2 f(n)] = Z\{\Delta[\Delta f(n)]\} = (z - 1)Z[\Delta f(n)] - z\,\Delta f(0)$$
$$= (z - 1)^2 F(z) - z(z - 1)f(0) - z\,\Delta f(0)$$

which is the expression in Table 8.2 for $k = 2$.

The relation for the Z transform of the kth forward difference in Table 8.2 may be established by induction.

† The first differences of discrete-time signals are defined as

$$\begin{aligned} \Delta f(n) &= f(n + 1) - f(n) && \text{forward difference} \\ \nabla f(n) &= f(n) - f(n - 1) && \text{backward difference} \end{aligned}$$

The second forward difference is $\Delta^2 f(n) = \Delta[\Delta f(n)]$; higher-order forward and backward differences are defined similarly.

The following relations, analogous to the formula for integration by parts, will be useful in deriving many of the properties of Table 8.2:

$$\sum_{n=A}^{B} u(n)\,\Delta v(n) = u(n)v(n)\Big|_A^{B+1} - \sum_{n=A}^{B} v(n + 1)\,\Delta u(n)$$

$$\sum_{n=A}^{B} u(n)\,\nabla v(n) = u(n)v(n)\Big|_{A-1}^{B} - \sum_{n=A}^{B} v(n - 1)\,\nabla u(n)$$

TRANSLATION

By definition

$$Z[f(n + k)] = \sum_{n=0}^{\infty} f(n + k)z^{-n}$$

Then

$$Z[f(n + k)] = \sum_{j=k}^{\infty} f(j)z^{-j+k} = z^k \sum_{j=k}^{\infty} f(j)z^{-j}$$

$$= z^k \Big[\sum_{j=0}^{\infty} f(j)z^{-j} - \sum_{j=0}^{k-1} f(j)z^{-j} \Big] = z^k[F(z) - \sum_{j=0}^{k-1} f(j)z^{-j}]$$

The result for $k = 1$ is particularly useful. We have

$$Z[f(n + 1)] = zF(z) - zf(0)$$

CONVOLUTION

The discrete convolution property is the cornerstone of Z-transform analysis, as is the analogous theorem for Laplace-transform analysis of continuous-time systems. In order to prove this property, we begin with the convolution summation (3.58), corresponding to the output of a time-invariant causal system with input $x(n)$ starting at $n = 0$ and with unit-function response $h(n)$:

$$y(n) = \sum_{k=0}^{n} x(k)h(n - k) \qquad (8.4)$$

Taking the Z transform of both sides, we obtain

$$Z[y(n)] = Y(z) = \sum_{n=0}^{\infty} z^{-n} \sum_{k=0}^{n} h(n - k)x(k) = \sum_{n=0}^{\infty} z^{-n} \sum_{k=0}^{\infty} h(n - k)x(k)$$

Inversion of the order of summation gives

$$Y(z) = \sum_{k=0}^{\infty} x(k) \sum_{n=0}^{\infty} h(n - k)z^{-n} = \sum_{k=0}^{\infty} x(k)z^{-k} \sum_{l=-k}^{\infty} h(l)z^{-l}$$

$$= \sum_{k=0}^{\infty} x(k)z^{-k} \sum_{l=0}^{\infty} h(l)z^{-l} \qquad (8.5)$$

since by assumption $h(l) = 0$ for $l < 0$.

Thus the Z transform of the convolution summation (8.4) is the product of the Z transforms of the two functions. It may be noted that if the two-sided Z transform were used, $h(n)$ need not correspond to a causal system, and $x(n)$ need not start at $n = 0$ (Prob. 8.4).

PRODUCT OF TWO FUNCTIONS

By definition, the Z transform of a product is

$$Z[f(n)g(n)] = \sum_{n=0}^{\infty} f(n)g(n)z^{-n} \qquad (8.6)$$

Now by the inversion integral (8.3)

$$f(n) = \frac{1}{2\pi j} \oint_C \frac{F(w)}{w} w^n \, dw \qquad (8.7)$$

where C is a contour enclosing the singularities of the integrand. Use of (8.7) in the definition (8.6) of the Z transform gives

$$Z[f(n)g(n)] = \frac{1}{2\pi j} \sum_{n=0}^{\infty} g(n)z^{-n} \oint_C \frac{F(w)}{w} w^n \, dw \qquad (8.8)$$

The conditions already imposed on $f(n)$ and $g(n)$ in Theorem 8.1 are sufficient to permit interchange of the order of integration and summation. Hence we may write

$$Z[f(n)g(n)] = \frac{1}{2\pi j} \oint_C \frac{F(w)}{w} \sum_{n=0}^{\infty} g(n)(zw^{-1})^{-n} \, dw \qquad (8.9)$$

The summation in (8.9) is recognized as $G(zw^{-1})$ and converges (uniformly) for $|zw^{-1}| > \rho_g$, where ρ_g is the radius of absolute convergence of $G(zw^{-1})$. Hence $G(zw^{-1})$ converges for $|w| < |z|/\rho_g$. Since $F(w)$ converges for $|w| > \rho_f$, where ρ_f is the radius of convergence of $F(w)$, the region of convergence of the integral (8.9) is an annulus which separates the singularities of $F(w)/w$ and those of $G(zw^{-1})$. Hence

$$Z[f(n)g(n)] = \frac{1}{2\pi j} \oint_C \frac{F(w)G(zw^{-1})}{w} \, dw \qquad (8.10)$$

where C lies in the annulus; i.e., for points on C for which

$$\rho_f < |w| < \frac{|z|}{\rho_g}$$

The following examples illustrate the use of the properties of Table 8.2 to extend the Z transform pairs of Table 8.1.

Example 8.3   Calculate the Z transform of $x(n) = na^n$.   Let

$$f(n) = n \qquad g(n) = a^n$$

Then, from Table 8.1,

$$F(z) = \frac{z^{-1}}{(1 - z^{-1})^2} \qquad G(z) = \frac{1}{1 - az^{-1}}$$

Thus, from property 8 of Table 8.2,

$$
\begin{aligned}
X(z) &= \frac{1}{2\pi j} \oint_C \frac{w^{-1}}{(1 - w^{-1})^2} \frac{1}{1 - awz^{-1}} \frac{dw}{w} \\
&= \text{residue of } \frac{1}{(w - 1)^2} \frac{1}{1 - awz^{-1}} \qquad \text{at } w = 1 \\
&= \frac{d}{dw} \left[\frac{1}{1 - awz^{-1}} \right]_{w=1} = \frac{az^{-1}}{(1 - az^{-1})^2}
\end{aligned}
$$

Alternatively, property 6 of Table 8.2 may be used with $k = 1$:

$$X(z) = \mathbb{Z}[na^n] = \left(z^{-1} \frac{d}{dz^{-1}} \right) \frac{1}{1 - az^{-1}} = \frac{az^{-1}}{(1 - az^{-1})^2}$$

Example 8.4   Calculate the Z transform of $f(n) = n^k$.   Since the Z transform of $f(n) = 1$ is $1/(1 - z^{-1})$, it follows from property 6 of Table 8.2 that

$$\mathbb{Z}[n^k] = \left(z^{-1} \frac{d}{dz^{-1}} \right)^k \left(\frac{1}{1 - z^{-1}} \right)$$

Hence, for $k = 1$,

$$\mathbb{Z}[n] = \left(z^{-1} \frac{d}{dz^{-1}} \right) \frac{1}{1 - z^{-1}} = \frac{z^{-1}}{(1 - z^{-1})^2}$$

and for $k = 2$,

$$\mathbb{Z}[n^2] = \left(z^{-1} \frac{d}{dz^{-1}} \right) \frac{z^{-1}}{(1 - z^{-1})^2} = \frac{z^{-1} + z^{-2}}{(1 - z^{-1})^3}$$

8.5   THE DISCRETE-TIME TRANSFER FUNCTION

Like the transfer function of a continuous-time system, the discrete-time transfer function is defined for a fixed discrete-time system as the Z trans-

form of the unit response $h(n)$.   Thus

$$H(z) = \mathcal{Z}[h(n)] \tag{8.11}$$

For a multiple-input multiple-output system, we may define a discrete-time transfer matrix $\mathbf{H}(z)$, each of whose elements $H_{ij}(z)$ is the Z transform of the corresponding unit response $h_{ij}(n)$.

As a consequence of the convolution property 7 of Table 8.2, the time-domain input-output relation

$$y(n) = \sum_{k=0}^{n} h(n - k)x(k)$$

as given by (3.58), is converted to the algebraic relation

$$Y(z) = H(z)X(z) \tag{8.12}$$

in the "Z domain."   This property considerably simplifies the analysis of fixed discrete-time systems; it permits such systems to be analyzed by calculating the transfer functions of each of the constituent components and combining these in accordance with the algebraic rules for combining transfer functions.   The response of the system to a given input is then obtained by inverting the product of the transfer function and the transform of the input.   The technique parallels that for continuous-time systems.

In many cases it is not necessary to carry out this last step; many useful properties of the response of the system can often be obtained directly from the discrete-time transfer function.   Among such properties are the stability of the system and the initial and final values of the response.

It is shown in Sec. 5.1 that the transfer function of a continuous-time system can be interpreted as the ratio of the response to a complex exponential e^{st} to this fictitious input e^{st}.   A similar interpretation is possible for the Z transform.   Consider a system H to which the input sequence $\{\cdots z^{-2}, z^{-1}, 1, z, z^2, \ldots\}$ is applied, starting at $n = -\infty$.   According to (3.57), the response is

$$y(n) = \sum_{k=-\infty}^{n} h(n - k)z^k \tag{8.13}$$

With the change of index $m = n - k$, (8.13) becomes

$$y(n) = \sum_{m=0}^{\infty} h(m)z^{n-m} = z^n H(z)$$

Hence it follows that

$$H(z) = \frac{\text{response to } z^n}{z^n} \tag{8.14}$$

8.6 DISCRETE-TIME TRANSFER FUNCTIONS FOR SYSTEMS CHARACTERIZED BY DIFFERENCE EQUATIONS IN NORMAL FORM

Having defined the discrete-time transfer function of a general system, we now turn to the calculation of the transfer functions of fixed discrete-time systems whose difference equations are known. As in continuous-time systems, we start with the characterization in normal form; namely,

$$\mathbf{q}(n+1) = \mathbf{A}\mathbf{q}(n) + \mathbf{B}\mathbf{x}(n) \tag{8.15}$$
$$\mathbf{y}(n) = \mathbf{C}\mathbf{q}(n) + \mathbf{D}\mathbf{x}(n) \tag{8.16}$$

where $\mathbf{A}$, $\mathbf{B}$, $\mathbf{C}$, $\mathbf{D}$ are constant matrices. $\mathbf{A}$ is a $k \times k$ square matrix, where k is the order of the system. Taking the Z transform of both sides of (8.15) and (8.16) and using the property that

$$Z[q(n+1)] = zQ(z) - zq(0)$$

we obtain

$$z\mathbf{Q}(z) - z\mathbf{q}(0) = \mathbf{A}\mathbf{Q}(z) + \mathbf{B}\mathbf{X}(z) \tag{8.17}$$
$$\mathbf{Y}(z) = \mathbf{C}\mathbf{Q}(z) + \mathbf{D}\mathbf{X}(z) \tag{8.18}$$

where

$$\mathbf{Q}(z) = Z[\mathbf{q}(n)]$$
$$\mathbf{X}(z) = Z[\mathbf{x}(n)]$$
$$\mathbf{Y}(z) = Z[\mathbf{y}(n)]$$

Solving (8.17) for $\mathbf{Q}(z)$, we obtain

$$\mathbf{Q}(z) = (z\mathbf{I} - \mathbf{A})^{-1}z\mathbf{q}(0) + (z\mathbf{I} - \mathbf{A})^{-1}\mathbf{B}\mathbf{X}(z) \tag{8.19}$$

and

$$\mathbf{Y}(z) = \mathbf{C}(z\mathbf{I} - \mathbf{A})^{-1}z\mathbf{q}(0) + [\mathbf{C}(z\mathbf{I} - \mathbf{A})^{-1}\mathbf{B} + \mathbf{D}]\mathbf{X}(z) \tag{8.20}$$

where $\mathbf{I}$ is a $k \times k$ unit matrix.

This result may also be obtained from the time-domain expression for the response of the system. It was shown in Chap. 4 that the recursive solution of (8.15) and (8.16) is given by [see (4.42)]

$$\mathbf{y}(n) = \mathbf{C}\mathbf{A}^n\mathbf{q}(0) + \sum_{k=0}^{n-1} \mathbf{C}\mathbf{A}^{n-k-1}\mathbf{B}\mathbf{x}(k) + \mathbf{D}\mathbf{x}(n) \tag{8.21}$$

We take the Z transform of (8.21), using the relation

$$Z\left[\sum_{k=0}^{n} a(n-k)b(k)\right] = A(z)B(z)$$

which is valid also when $a(n)$ and $b(n)$ are matrices (Prob. 8.5). The

result is

$$\mathbf{Y}(z) = \mathbf{C}(z\mathbf{I} - \mathbf{A})^{-1}z\mathbf{q}(0) + [\mathbf{C}(z\mathbf{I} - \mathbf{A})^{-1}\mathbf{B} + \mathbf{D}]\mathbf{X}(z)$$

which is identical with (8.20).

The fundamental matrix of the discrete-time system has previously been defined as

$$\mathbf{\Phi}(n) = \mathbf{A}^n$$

In terms of the fundamental matrix we write (8.21) as

$$\mathbf{y}(n) = \mathbf{C}\mathbf{\Phi}(n)\mathbf{q}(0) + \sum_{k=0}^{n-1} \mathbf{C}\mathbf{\Phi}(n - k - 1)\mathbf{B}\mathbf{x}(k) + \mathbf{D}\mathbf{x}(n) \quad (8.22)$$

If we denote the Z transform of $\mathbf{\Phi}(n)$ by $\hat{\mathbf{\Phi}}(z)$,

$$\hat{\mathbf{\Phi}}(z) = Z[\mathbf{\Phi}(n)] = Z[\mathbf{A}^n]$$

the Z transform of (8.22) becomes

$$\mathbf{Y}(z) = \mathbf{C}\hat{\mathbf{\Phi}}(z)\mathbf{q}(0) + [\mathbf{C}\hat{\mathbf{\Phi}}(z)z^{-1}\mathbf{B} + \mathbf{D}]\mathbf{X}(z)$$

Comparing this with (8.20), we find that

$$\hat{\mathbf{\Phi}}(z) = Z[\mathbf{\Phi}(n)] = Z[\mathbf{A}^n] = (z\mathbf{I} - \mathbf{A})^{-1}z \quad (8.23)$$

This result can be deduced from (8.19) directly, since $\hat{\mathbf{\Phi}}(z)$ is the matrix operating on $\mathbf{q}(0)$ to produce $\mathbf{Q}(z)$ when $\mathbf{x}(n) = \mathbf{X}(z) \equiv \mathbf{0}$. We can also obtain this result directly from the definition of the Z transform:

$$Z[\mathbf{A}^n] = \sum_{n=0}^{\infty} \mathbf{A}^n z^{-n}$$

This expression is a geometric series in $\mathbf{A}z^{-1}$ which converges uniformly to the matrix $(\mathbf{I} - \mathbf{A}z^{-1})^{-1} = (z\mathbf{I} - \mathbf{A})^{-1}z$ for all values of z satisfying $|z_i z^{-1}| < 1$ ($i = 1, 2, \ldots, k$), where z_i are the characteristic roots of $\mathbf{A}$ (Prob. 8.7). Note that (8.23) is the matrix equivalent of

$$Z[a^n] = (1 - az^{-1})^{-1}$$

For zero initial conditions, (8.20) has the form

$$\mathbf{Y}(z) = [\mathbf{C}(z\mathbf{I} - \mathbf{A})^{-1}\mathbf{B} + \mathbf{D}]\mathbf{X}(z)$$
$$= [\mathbf{C}\hat{\mathbf{\Phi}}(z)z^{-1}\mathbf{B} + \mathbf{D}]\mathbf{X}(z)$$

Hence the transfer-function matrix is given by

$$\mathbf{H}(z) = \mathbf{C}(z\mathbf{I} - \mathbf{A})^{-1}\mathbf{B} + \mathbf{D} \quad (8.24)$$

Table 8.3 displays the analogy between these results and those obtained in Chap. 6 for continuous-time systems.

Note that the discrete case has a few complications not present in the continuous case. The Z transform of the fundamental matrix for dis-

Table 8.3   ANALOGOUS QUANTITIES IN FIXED CONTINUOUS-TIME AND
DISCRETE-TIME SYSTEMS

Quantity	Continuous-time system	Discrete-time system
Fundamental matrix	$\Phi(t) = e^{\mathbf{A}t}$	$\Phi(n) = \mathbf{A}^n$
Transform of fundamental matrix	$\hat{\Phi}(s) = (s\mathbf{I} - \mathbf{A})^{-1}$	$\hat{\Phi}(z) = (z\mathbf{I} - \mathbf{A})^{-1}z = (\mathbf{I} - \mathbf{A}z^{-1})^{-1}$
Impulse- or unit-response matrix	$\mathbf{H}(t) = \mathbf{C}\Phi(t)\mathbf{B} + \mathbf{D}\delta(t)$	$\begin{aligned}\mathbf{H}(n) &= \mathbf{C}\Phi(n-1)\mathbf{B} \quad n \geq 1 \\ &= \mathbf{D} \qquad\qquad\quad n = 0\end{aligned}$
Transfer-function matrix	$\mathbf{H}(s) = \mathbf{C}\hat{\Phi}(s)\mathbf{B} + \mathbf{D}$	$\mathbf{H}(z) = \mathbf{C}\hat{\Phi}(z)z^{-1}\mathbf{B} + \mathbf{D}$

crete-time systems has a factor z which is not present in continuous-time systems, but this factor z disappears in the matrix of transfer functions, since the unit-response matrix $\mathbf{H}(n)$ is given in terms of $\Phi(n-1)$. The complications destroy the perfect analogy between discrete-time and continuous-time systems, but are of little practical importance.

The differences could be avoided by defining the state variables of the discrete-time system as the *inputs* to the delays instead of the outputs. If this were done, however, the block diagram for the discrete-time system would no longer be analogous to the block diagram for the continuous-time system.

Example 8.5   (Continuation of Example 4.7)   We found in Chap. 4 that the network of Fig. 4.1, when excited with piecewise-constant voltages with a sampling interval of 1 sec, is characterized by the difference equations

$$\begin{bmatrix} i_1(n+1) \\ v_2(n+1) \end{bmatrix} = \begin{bmatrix} 0.600 & -0.465 \\ 0.233 & -0.097 \end{bmatrix} \begin{bmatrix} i_1(n) \\ v_2(n) \end{bmatrix} + \begin{bmatrix} 1.664 & -0.465 \\ 0.400 & -1.097 \end{bmatrix} \begin{bmatrix} e_1(n) \\ e_2(n) \end{bmatrix}$$

$$\begin{bmatrix} i_1(n) \\ i_2(n) \end{bmatrix} = \begin{bmatrix} 1 & 0 \\ 1 & -3 \end{bmatrix} \begin{bmatrix} i_1(n) \\ v_2(n) \end{bmatrix} + \begin{bmatrix} 0 & 0 \\ 0 & -3 \end{bmatrix} \begin{bmatrix} e_1(n) \\ e_2(n) \end{bmatrix}$$

The Z transform of the fundamental matrix is given by

$$\hat{\Phi}(z) = (z\mathbf{I} - \tilde{\mathbf{A}})^{-1}z = \begin{bmatrix} z - 0.600 & 0.465 \\ -0.233 & z + 0.097 \end{bmatrix}^{-1} z$$

$$= \frac{\begin{bmatrix} z + 0.097 & -0.465 \\ 0.233 & z - 0.600 \end{bmatrix} z}{z^2 - 0.503z + 0.0498}$$

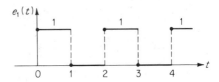

FIG. 8.2   Input signal for Example
8.5.

Note that the denominator in the last expression is $|z\mathbf{I} - \mathbf{A}|$. The transfer matrix is, from (8.24) with $\mathbf{A} = \tilde{\mathbf{A}}$ and $\mathbf{B} = \tilde{\mathbf{B}}$,

$$
\mathbf{H}(z) = \frac{\begin{bmatrix} 1 & 0 \\ 1 & -3 \end{bmatrix} \begin{bmatrix} z + 0.097 & -0.465 \\ 0.233 & z - 0.600 \end{bmatrix} \begin{bmatrix} 1.664 & -0.465 \\ 0.400 & -1.097 \end{bmatrix}}{z^2 - 0.503z + 0.0498}
$$

$$
+ \begin{bmatrix} 0 & 0 \\ 0 & -3 \end{bmatrix}
$$

$$
= \frac{\begin{bmatrix} 1.664z - 0.024 & -0.465z + 0.465 \\ 0.465z - 0.465 & -3z^2 + 4.335z - 1.334 \end{bmatrix}}{z^2 - 0.503z + 0.0498}
$$

Now suppose it is required to find the current i_1 at sampling instants when $e_2 = 0$ and $e_1(t)$ is a square wave as shown in Fig. 8.2 and the circuit is initially unexcited.   We have

$$
I_1(z) = H_{11}(z)E_1(z)
$$

where $H_{11}(z)$ is the $(1, 1)$ element of $\mathbf{H}(z)$ calculated above; i.e.,

$$
H_{11}(z) = \frac{1.664z - 0.024}{z^2 - 0.503z + 0.0498} = \frac{1.664z^{-1} - 0.024z^{-2}}{1 - 0.503z^{-1} + 0.0498z^{-2}}
$$

and $E_1(z)$ is the Z transform of $e_1(n) = e_1(nT)$; that is,

$$
E_1(z) = 1 + 0z^{-1} + z^{-2} + 0z^{-3} + \cdots = \frac{1}{1 - z^{-2}}
$$

Hence various expressions for the Z transform of $i_1(n)$ are

$$
I_1(z) = \frac{1.664z^{-1} - 0.024z^{-2}}{(1 - 0.503z^{-1} + 0.0498z^{-2})(1 - z^{-2})}
$$

$$
= \frac{1.664z^{-1} - 0.024z^{-2}}{(1 - 0.368z^{-1})(1 - 0.135z^{-1})(1 - z^{-1})(1 + z^{-1})}
$$

$$
= \frac{1.664z^{-1} - 0.024z^{-2}}{1 - 0.503z^{-1} - 0.950z^{-2} + 0.503z^{-3} - 0.0497z^{-4}}
$$

$$
= -\frac{1.07}{1 - 0.368z^{-1}} + \frac{0.119}{1 - 0.135z^{-1}} + \frac{1.50}{1 - z^{-1}} - \frac{0.543}{1 + z^{-1}}
$$

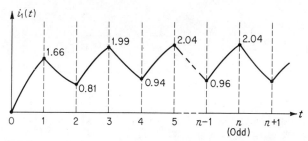

FIG. 8.3   Response of network to square wave.

where $z = 0.368$ and $z = 0.135$ are the roots of $|z\mathbf{I} - \mathbf{A}| = 0$.   Hence

$$i_1(n) = -1.07(0.368)^n + 0.119(0.135)^n + 1.50 - 0.543(-1)^n$$

The solution is shown in Fig. 8.3.   Note that the steady-state maximum and minimum amplitudes may be calculated by observing that only the constant term 1.50 and the term $-0.543(-1)^n$ remain as $n \to \infty$.

Alternatively, the long-division inversion of $I_1(z)$ is given by the following tabulation, which yields the same result as the partial fraction expansion.

```
                              1.664    0.814    1.990    0.937    2.036
1  -0.503  -0.950  +0.503  -0.0497)1.664  -0.023
                              1.664  -0.837  -1.581  +0.837  -0.083
                                     +0.814  +1.581  -0.837  +0.083
                                     +0.814  -0.409  -0.773  +0.409  -0.040
                                             1.990  -0.064  -0.326  +0.040
                                             1.990  -1.001  -1.891  +1.001  -0.099
                                                     +0.937  +1.565  -0.960  +0.099
                                                     +0.937  -0.471  -0.890  +0.471  - · · ·
                                                             +2.036  - · · ·
```

8.7   PROPERTIES OF THE FUNDAMENTAL MATRIX AND ITS TRANSFORM

By use of reasoning similar to that employed in Sec. 7.3, it is found that

$$\hat{\boldsymbol{\Phi}}(z) = (\mathbf{I} - \mathbf{A}z^{-1})^{-1} = z(z\mathbf{I} - \mathbf{A})^{-1} = \frac{z \, \text{adj} \, (z\mathbf{I} - \mathbf{A})}{|z\mathbf{I} - \mathbf{A}|} \qquad (8.25)$$

where adj $(z\mathbf{I} - \mathbf{A})$ is the adjoint matrix of $z\mathbf{I} - \mathbf{A}$, which can be expressed as a matrix polynomial in z.   Thus, as in Sec. 7.3,

$$\hat{\boldsymbol{\Phi}}(z) = \frac{z(\mathbf{B}_1 z^{k-1} + \mathbf{B}_2 z^{k-2} + \cdots + \mathbf{B}_k)}{z^k + a_1 z^{k-1} + \cdots + a_k}$$

$$= \frac{\mathbf{B}_1 + \mathbf{B}_2 z^{-1} + \cdots + \mathbf{B}_k z^{-k+1}}{1 + a_1 z^{-1} + \cdots + a_k z^{-k}} \qquad (8.26)$$

where

$$\mathbf{B}_1 = \mathbf{I}$$

and a_n and $\mathbf{B}_n$ can be computed by the algorithm

$$a_n = -\frac{1}{n} \text{ trace } (\mathbf{AB}_n)$$
$$\mathbf{B}_{n+1} = \mathbf{AB}_n + a_n\mathbf{I}$$

(See footnote reference p. 216.)

If we denote the distinct roots of the characteristic equation

$$|z\mathbf{I} - \mathbf{A}| = 0$$

by z_r $(r = 1, 2, \ldots, k' \le k)$, we can write (8.26) as

$$\hat{\boldsymbol{\Phi}}(z) = \sum_{r=1}^{k'} \sum_{p=1}^{m_r} \mathbf{P}_{rp} \frac{z}{(z - z_r)^p} = \sum_{r=1}^{k'} \sum_{p=1}^{m_r} \mathbf{P}_{rp} \frac{z^{-p+1}}{(1 - z_r z^{-1})^p} \qquad (8.27)$$

where m_r is the multiplicity of the root z_r, and $\mathbf{P}_{rp}$ is a constant matrix obtained in the partial fraction expansion of (8.26). On taking the inverse Z transform of (8.27), we obtain

$$\boldsymbol{\Phi}(n) = \sum_{r=1}^{k'} \sum_{p=1}^{m_r} \mathbf{Q}_{rp} n^{p-1} z_r{}^n \qquad (8.28)$$

where $\mathbf{Q}_{rp}$ are constant matrices. Unfortunately, $\mathbf{Q}_{rp} \ne \mathbf{P}_{rp}$ unless $m_r = 1$, since $Z^{-1}[z^{-p+1}/(1 - z_r z^{-1})^p]$ is the product of a polynomial of degree $p - 1$ in n and $z_r{}^n$ (Prob. 8.13).

If the roots z_i $(i = 1, 2, \ldots, k)$ of $|z\mathbf{I} - \mathbf{A}| = 0$ are nonrepeated,

$$\hat{\boldsymbol{\Phi}}(z) = \sum_{r=1}^{k} \frac{1}{1 - z_r z^{-1}} \frac{\text{adj } (z_r\mathbf{I} - \mathbf{A})}{\displaystyle\prod_{\substack{i=1 \\ i \ne r}}^{k} (z_r - z_i)}$$

or, upon use of Sylvester's formula (7.26),

$$\hat{\boldsymbol{\Phi}}(z) = \sum_{r=1}^{k} \frac{1}{1 - z_r z^{-1}} \prod_{\substack{i=1 \\ i \ne r}}^{k} \frac{\mathbf{A} - z_i\mathbf{I}}{z_r - z_i}$$

After inversion, we obtain

$$\boldsymbol{\Phi}(n) = \sum_{r=1}^{k} \mathbf{Q}_r z_r{}^n$$

where

$$\mathbf{Q}_r = \frac{\text{adj } (z_r\mathbf{I} - \mathbf{A})}{\prod\limits_{\substack{i=1 \\ i \neq r}}^{k} (z_r - z_i)} = \prod\limits_{\substack{i=1 \\ i \neq r}}^{k} \frac{\mathbf{A} - z_i\mathbf{I}}{z_r - z_i}$$

By (8.28) every term in the fundamental matrix consists of k' terms corresponding to the distinct roots of the characteristic equation. The term corresponding to a root $z = z_r$ is a polynomial in n, of one degree less than the multiplicity m_r, multiplied by the root to the nth power. Thus we observe that every term of $\mathbf{\Phi}(n)$ approaches zero as $n \rightarrow \infty$ if and only if all the roots z_r are smaller in magnitude than unity. If, on the contrary, there is a root of magnitude exceeding unity, at least one element of $\mathbf{\Phi}(n)$ approaches infinity as $n \rightarrow \infty$. If no root exceeds unity in magnitude but one or more roots have magnitude equal to unity, either every $|\phi_{ij}(n)| \leq C_{ij} = $ constant as $n \rightarrow \infty$ or some $|\phi_{ij}(n)| \rightarrow \infty$ with n, depending on whether the root is simple or multiple. The roots of the characteristic equation $|z\mathbf{I} - \mathbf{A}| = 0$ thus determine the nature of the fundamental matrix.

8.8   SIMULTANEOUS DIFFERENCE EQUATIONS

If a system is governed by a set of simultaneous difference equations which are not in normal form, it is not necessary to put them into normal form before proceeding with a solution by means of the Z transform. By using the Z transform of higher-order differences (forward or backward) or of $f(n + k)$, the given equations can be transformed directly. Consider the system of equations

$$L_{11}(\Delta)y_1(n) + \cdots + L_{1r}(\Delta)y_r(n) = M_{11}(\Delta)x_1(n) + \cdots + M_{1s}(\Delta)x_s(n)$$
$$\cdot \cdot \cdot \cdot \cdot \cdot \cdot \cdot \cdot \cdot \cdot \cdot \cdot \cdot \cdot \cdot \cdot \cdot \cdot \cdot \cdot \cdot \cdot \cdot \cdot \cdot \cdot \cdot \cdot \cdot \cdot \cdot \cdot \cdot \cdot \cdot \cdot \cdot$$
$$L_{r1}(\Delta)y_1(n) + \cdots + L_{rr}(\Delta)y_r(n) = M_{r1}(\Delta)x_1(n) + \cdots + M_{rs}(\Delta)x_s(n)$$

or in matrix form,

$$\mathbf{L}(\Delta)\mathbf{y}(n) = \mathbf{M}(\Delta)\mathbf{x}(n) \tag{8.29}$$

where $L_{ij}(\Delta)$ and $M_{ij}(\Delta)$ are polynomials in the forward difference operator; i.e.,

$$L_{ij}(\Delta) = a_0 + a_1\Delta + a_2\Delta^2 + \cdots + a_p\Delta^p$$

and $\Delta u(n) = u(n + 1) - u(n)$. By use of property 2 of Table 8.2,

$$Z[\Delta^k u(k)] = (z - 1)^k U(z) - z \sum_{j=0}^{k-1} (z - 1)^{k-j-1} \Delta^j u(0)$$

the matrix equation (8.29) becomes

$$\mathbf{L}(z - 1)\mathbf{Y}(z) = \mathbf{M}(z - 1)\mathbf{X}(z) + \mathbf{J}(z) \qquad (8.30)$$

where $\mathbf{J}(z)$ is a vector of transformed initial conditions. The solution of this system is

$$\mathbf{Y}(z) = \mathbf{L}^{-1}(z - 1)\mathbf{M}(z - 1)\mathbf{X}(z) + \mathbf{L}^{-1}(z - 1)\mathbf{J}(z) \qquad (8.31)$$

Hence the transfer matrix of the system is given by

$$\mathbf{H}(z) = \mathbf{L}^{-1}(z - 1)\mathbf{M}(z - 1) \qquad (8.32)$$

and the characteristic equation is

$$|\mathbf{L}(z - 1)| = 0$$

If the equations are formulated in terms of backward differences, then instead of (8.29), we have

$$\mathbf{L}_1(\nabla)\mathbf{y}(n) = \mathbf{M}_1(\nabla)\mathbf{x}(n) \qquad (8.33)$$

and we obtain as the solution

$$\mathbf{Y}(z) = \mathbf{L}_1^{-1}(1 - z^{-1})\mathbf{M}_1(1 - z^{-1})\mathbf{X}(z) + \mathbf{L}_1^{-1}(1 - z^{-1})\mathbf{J}_1(z) \qquad (8.34)$$

where $\mathbf{J}_1(z)$ is a vector of transformed initial conditions. In this case the transfer matrix is

$$\mathbf{H}(z) = \mathbf{L}_1^{-1}(1 - z^{-1})\mathbf{M}_1(1 - z^{-1}) \qquad (8.35)$$

and the characteristic equation is

$$|\mathbf{L}_1(1 - z^{-1})| = 0 \qquad (8.36)$$

Finally, if the equations are formulated in terms of the translation operator E $[Eu(n) = u(n + 1)]$, we have

$$\mathbf{L}_2(E)\mathbf{y}(n) = \mathbf{M}_2(E)\mathbf{x}(n) \qquad (8.37)$$

Then we obtain

$$\mathbf{Y}(z) = \mathbf{L}_2^{-1}(z)\mathbf{M}_2(z)\mathbf{X}(z) + \mathbf{L}_2^{-1}(z)\mathbf{J}_2(z) \qquad (8.38)$$

whence

$$\mathbf{H}(z) = \mathbf{L}_2^{-1}(z)\mathbf{M}_2(z) \qquad (8.39)$$

and the characteristic equation is

$$|\mathbf{L}_2(z)| = 0 \qquad (8.40)$$

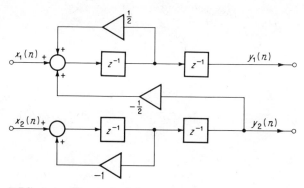

FIG. 8.4   Example 8.6.

Example 8.6   Consider the fourth-order system of Fig. 8.4.   From the diagram the difference equations governing the system are

$$y_1(n + 2) = x_1(n) + \tfrac{1}{2}y_1(n + 1) - \tfrac{1}{2}y_2(n)$$
$$y_2(n + 2) = x_2(n) - y_2(n + 1)$$

Arrangement of these in the form of (8.37) gives

$$y_1(n + 2) - \tfrac{1}{2}y_1(n + 1) + \tfrac{1}{2}y_2(n) = x_1(n)$$
$$y_2(n + 2) + y_2(n + 1) = x_2(n)$$

(8.41)

or

$$\begin{bmatrix} E^2 - \tfrac{1}{2}E & \tfrac{1}{2} \\ 0 & E^2 + E \end{bmatrix} \begin{bmatrix} y_1(n) \\ y_2(n) \end{bmatrix} = \begin{bmatrix} x_1(n) \\ x_2(n) \end{bmatrix}$$

Thus the transfer matrix is

$$\mathbf{H}(z) = \begin{bmatrix} z^2 - \tfrac{1}{2}z & \tfrac{1}{2} \\ 0 & z^2 + z \end{bmatrix}^{-1} = \frac{\begin{bmatrix} z^2 + z & -\tfrac{1}{2} \\ 0 & z^2 - \tfrac{1}{2}z \end{bmatrix}}{(z^2 - \tfrac{1}{2}z)(z^2 + z)}$$

$$= \begin{bmatrix} \dfrac{z^{-2}}{1 - \tfrac{1}{2}z^{-1}} & \dfrac{-z^{-4}/2}{(1 - \tfrac{1}{2}z^{-1})(1 + z^{-1})} \\ 0 & \dfrac{z^{-2}}{1 + z^{-1}} \end{bmatrix}$$

In terms of forward differences (8.41) becomes

$$\begin{bmatrix} \Delta^2 + \tfrac{3}{2}\Delta + \tfrac{1}{2} & \tfrac{1}{2} \\ 0 & \Delta^2 + 3\Delta + 2 \end{bmatrix} \begin{bmatrix} y_1(n) \\ y_2(n) \end{bmatrix} = \begin{bmatrix} x_1(n) \\ x_2(n) \end{bmatrix}$$

and it follows from (8.32) that the transfer matrix is

$$\mathbf{H}(z) = \begin{bmatrix} (z-1)^2 + \frac{3}{2}(z-1) + \frac{1}{2} & \frac{1}{2} \\ 0 & (z-1)^2 + 3(z-1) + 2 \end{bmatrix}^{-1}$$

$$= \begin{bmatrix} z^2 - \frac{1}{2}z & \frac{1}{2} \\ 0 & z^2 + z \end{bmatrix}^{-1}$$

as before.

8.9 SAMPLED-DATA SYSTEMS AND THE Z TRANSFORM

As was mentioned in the introduction to this chapter, the Z transform entered the engineering literature as a tool for studying the behavior of sampled-data systems and was developed through modification of the Laplace transform.   To follow this method of development, it is appropriate to visualize a sampled-data system as a number of continuous-time components, each of which is separated from its neighbors by a "sampler." A typical sampled-data system thus might have the appearance illustrated schematically in Fig. 8.5.   The diamond-shaped blocks represent samplers whose function it is to convert a continuous-time input signal into a train of identically shaped pulses whose amplitudes are proportional to the input at the corresponding sampling instant.   If a typical input signal is $x(t)$, the output $x_s(t)$ of the corresponding sampler is thus expressed by

$$x_s(t) = \sum_{k=0}^{\infty} x(kT)p(t - kT)$$

where $p(t)$ is the waveform or shape of a single sampling pulse.   The outputs of three different types of samplers are illustrated in Fig. 8.6.   In Fig. 8.6a the output is a train of impulses modulated by the input; in Fig. 8.6b the output is piecewise-constant; in Fig. 8.6c the output consists of triangular segments of height equal to the input at the sampling instants.

It is further convenient to represent every sampler as a cascade com-

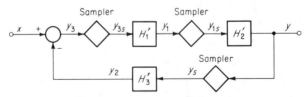

FIG. 8.5   A typical sampled-data feedback system.

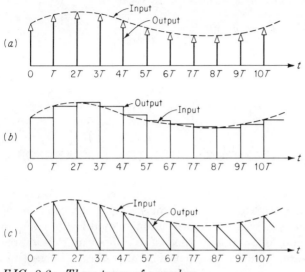

FIG. 8.6   Three types of samplers.

bination of an *impulse modulator* (represented by a switch) followed by a *pulse shaper*. The impulse modulator converts a continuous-time input signal $x(t)$ into an impulse train $x^*(t)$. The pulse shaper has an impulse response which generates the output pulse shape and thus transforms $x^*(t)$ into $x_s(t)$ (Fig. 8.7). The sampled-data system of Fig. 8.5 can thus be represented as shown in Fig. 8.8a. Finally, the pulse shapers can be merged with the components they precede to yield a schematic diagram such as that of Fig. 8.8b, in which every component is separated from its neighbors by an impulse modulator.

By this artifice it is possible to represent a system with various types of sampling (provided that the sampling interval T is everywhere the same) as if all the sampling operations were accomplished by impulse modulators acting in synchronism. It is important to note, however, that true impulse modulation is rarely realized in a physical system and that the appropriate pulse shaper must be included to obtain a valid representation. Erroneous results can often be attributed to failure to include such pulse shapers.

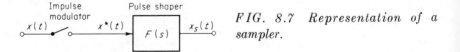

FIG. 8.7   Representation of a sampler.

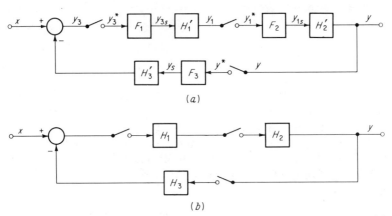

FIG. 8.8   Reduction of sampling to impulse modulation.   (a) Samplers replaced by impulse modulators and pulse shapers; (b) pulse shapers merged with components they precede.

The input-output relation for an impulse modulator can be expressed as

$$x^*(t) = \sum_{k=0}^{\infty} x(kT)\delta(t - kT) \qquad (8.42)$$

If this impulse-modulated signal is applied to a fixed continuous-time linear component H, it produces an output $y(t)$ which, by direct application of the superposition principle, is

$$y(t) = \sum_{k=0}^{\infty} H[x(kT)\delta(t - kT)] = \sum_{k=0}^{\infty} x(kT)h(t - kT)$$

where $h(t)$ is the impulse response of H.   If $y(t)$ is now impulse-modulated at the input to the next component, it is evident that the strength of the impulse occurring at $t = nT$ in $y^*(t)$ is given by

$$y(nT) = \sum_{k=0}^{\infty} h(nT - kT)x(kT) \qquad (8.43)$$

It is seen that (8.43) is the input-output relation for a discrete-time component with an input† $x(nT)$, an output $y(nT)$, and a unit response $h(nT)$. Thus a continuous-time component H preceded and followed by impulse

---

† To be precise, $x(nT)$, $y(nT)$, $h(nT)$ are the numerical values of the continuous-time signals $x(t)$, $y(t)$, $h(t)$ at $t = nT$, from which the discrete-time signals $\bar{x}(n) = x(nT)$, $\bar{y}(n) = y(nT)$, $\bar{h}(n) = h(nT)$ can be formed.   To avoid notational complexity, we use $x(nT)$ in place of $\bar{x}(n)$, etc.

modulators can be represented as a discrete-time component having a unit response $h(nT)$ and a discrete-time transfer function

$$H(z) = \sum_{n=0}^{\infty} h(nT)z^{-n} \tag{8.44}$$

Calculation of $H(z)$ by means of (8.44) entails, first, calculation of the continuous-time impulse response $h(t)$, then replacement of t by nT, and finally the evaluation of (8.44) in closed form.

An alternative and frequently more convenient method for calculating the discrete-time transfer function results from the observation that $h(nT)$ is the amplitude of the nth impulse in the impulse-modulated version $h^*(t)$; that is,

$$h^*(t) = \sum_{n=0}^{\infty} h(nT)\delta(t - nT)$$

If the Laplace transform of $h^*(t)$ is calculated, it is found that

$$H^*(s) = \mathcal{L}[h^*(t)] = \sum_{n=0}^{\infty} h(nT)\mathcal{L}[\delta(t - nT)] = \sum_{n=0}^{\infty} h(nT)e^{-nTs} \tag{8.45}$$

By comparison of (8.45) and (8.44) it is seen that the required discrete-time transfer function $H(z)$ is the function obtained by replacing e^{-Ts} by z^{-1} in the Laplace transform of $h^*(t)$ (which is always a function of e^{-Ts}).

Now observe that $h^*(t)$ may be written as the product of $h(t)$ and a train of unit impulses spaced at intervals of T sec:

$$h^*(t) = h(t)\delta_T(t)$$

where

$$\delta_T(t) = \sum_{n=0}^{\infty} \delta(t - nT)$$

From the relation for the Laplace transform of a product (property 8 of Table 6.2) we find that

$$H^*(s) = \frac{1}{2\pi j} \int_{c-j\infty}^{c+j\infty} H(w)\Delta_T(s - w)\, dw \tag{8.46}$$

where

$$\Delta_T(s) = \mathcal{L}[\delta_T(t)] = 1 + e^{-Ts} + e^{-2Ts} + \cdots = \frac{1}{1 - e^{-Ts}},$$
$$|e^{-Ts}| < 1 \tag{8.47}$$

Substituting (8.47) into (8.46) and writing z^{-1} for e^{-Ts}, we find

$$H(z) = \frac{1}{2\pi j} \int_{c-j\infty}^{c+j\infty} \frac{H(w)\, dw}{1 - z^{-1}e^{Tw}} \tag{8.48}$$

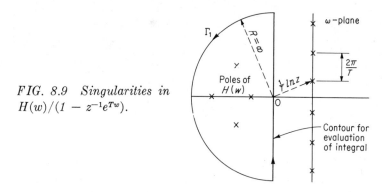

FIG. 8.9 Singularities in $H(w)/(1 - z^{-1}e^{Tw})$.

It is customary to write this as

$$H(z) = Z[H(s)] \tag{8.49}$$

which is a shorthand notation for the function obtained by replacing e^{-Ts} by z^{-1} in the Laplace transform of $h^*(t)$.

The contour in (8.48) is a line parallel to the imaginary axis in the w plane which separates the singularities of $H(w)$ from those of $1/(1 - z^{-1}e^{Tw})$. The latter occur for

$$w = \frac{1}{T}(\ln z \pm j2\pi k) \qquad k = 0, \pm 1, \pm 2, \ldots$$

If $H(w)$ is rational, the singularities of the integrand are typically distributed as shown in Fig. 8.9. If the integral along the semi-infinite arc Γ_1 vanishes,† we can write, using the residue theorem,

$$H(z) = \text{sum of residues of } \frac{H(w)}{1 - z^{-1}e^{Tw}} \qquad \text{at poles of } H(w) \quad (8.50)$$

Example 8.7 Let $h(n) = e^{-aTn}$. The continuous-time signal corresponding to $h(n)$ is $h(t) = e^{-at}$, whose Laplace transform is $H(s) = 1/(s + a)$. Hence, evaluating (8.48) by the method of residues, we find that

$$H(z) = \text{residue of } \frac{1}{(w + a)(1 - z^{-1}e^{Tw})}$$

at $w = -a$, less the contribution of the integral along Γ_1, or

$$H(z) = \frac{1}{1 - e^{-aT}z^{-1}} - \frac{1}{2\pi j}\int_{\Gamma_1} \frac{dw}{(w + a)(1 - e^{Tw}z^{-1})} \tag{8.51}$$

† *Warning:* The integral along Γ_1 does not always vanish. When it does not, its value divided by $2\pi j$ must be subtracted from the right-hand side of (8.50). See Examples 8.7 and 8.8.

With the change of variable $w + a = Re^{j\theta}$,

$$\frac{1}{2\pi j} \int_{\Gamma_1} \frac{dw}{(w + a)(1 - e^{Tw}z^{-1})} = \lim_{R \to \infty} \frac{1}{2\pi j} \int_{\pi/2}^{3\pi/2} \frac{jRe^{j\theta}\, d\theta}{Re^{j\theta}(1 - e^{TRe^{j\theta}}e^{-Ta}z^{-1})} = \frac{1}{2}$$

Thus

$$H(z) = \frac{1}{1 - e^{-aT}z^{-1}} - \frac{1}{2}$$

This is the Z transform of the sequence $(\frac{1}{2}, e^{-aT}, e^{-2aT}, \ldots)$, obtained by sampling the inverse Laplace transform of $H(s)$, as evaluated by use of the inversion integral which gives $h(0) = \frac{1}{2}$. To avoid this difficulty and still retain rigor, we can take the Z transform of

$$h'(t) = h(t + \epsilon) = e^{-a(t+\epsilon)}\mu_1(t + \epsilon)$$

with $\epsilon > 0$. The (two-sided!) Laplace transform of $h(t + \epsilon)$ is $e^{\epsilon s}/(s + a)$. In this case the integral along Γ_1 vanishes because of the presence of the factor $e^{\epsilon w}$ in the numerator of the integrand. Hence

$$H'(z) = \text{residue of } \frac{e^{\epsilon w}}{(w + a)(1 - z^{-1}e^{Tw})} \quad \text{at } w = -a$$

$$= \frac{e^{-\epsilon a}}{1 - e^{-aT}z^{-1}}$$

Then, as $\epsilon \to 0$,

$$H'(z) \to H(z) = \frac{1}{1 - e^{-aT}z^{-1}}$$

as before.

Example 8.8 Consider the system characterized by the first-order equation

$$\frac{dq}{dt} = -q + x$$

$$y = q$$

If the input is piecewise-constant,

$$x(t) = x(n) \qquad nT < t \le nT + T$$

Then, from (4.60), we have the difference equation

$$q(n + 1) = e^{-T}q(n) + \int_0^T e^{-\lambda}\, d\lambda\, x(n) = e^{-T}q(n) + (1 - e^{-T})x(n)$$

Hence, from (8.24), the discrete-time transfer function is

$$H(z) = 1(z - e^{-T})^{-1}(1 - e^{-T}) + 0 = \frac{(1 - e^{-T})z^{-1}}{1 - e^{-T}z^{-1}} \qquad (8.52)$$

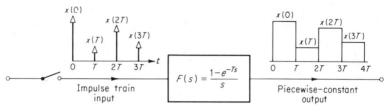

FIG. 8.10   Boxcar hold circuit.

In order to calculate the transfer function by the method described in this section, we first calculate the transfer function of the continuous-time system. This is

$$H'(s) = \frac{1}{s + 1}$$

We also note that the piecewise-constant input can be obtained from an impulse train by the use of a shaping circuit having the impulse response

$$f(t) = \mu_1(t) - \mu_1(t - T)$$

as shown in Fig. 8.10. Because of the shape of this impulse response, the circuit is often called a "boxcar" circuit; it has the transfer function

$$F(s) = \frac{1 - e^{-Ts}}{s}$$

The calculation of $H(z)$ by (8.50) is facilitated by breaking $F(s)$ into two transfer functions:

$$F(s) = (1 - e^{-Ts}) \frac{1}{s}$$

The effect of the term $1 - e^{-Ts}$ is to transmit each impulse and then its negative with a delay of one sampling instant. Thus the effect of this component is accounted for by a discrete-time component preceding the impulse modulator having the transfer function $1 - z^{-1}$. Hence, since the integral along Γ_1 can be shown to vanish in this case,

$$
\begin{aligned}
H(z) &= (1 - z^{-1})\mathbb{Z}\left[\frac{1}{s(s + 1)}\right] \\
&= (1 - z^{-1})\frac{1}{2\pi j}\int_{c-j\infty}^{c+j\infty} \frac{dw}{w(w + 1)(1 - e^{Tw}z^{-1})} \\
&= (1 - z^{-1})\left[\frac{1}{1 - z^{-1}} + \frac{1}{-1(1 - e^{-T}z^{-1})}\right] = \frac{(1 - e^{-T})z^{-1}}{1 - e^{-T}z^{-1}} \quad (8.53)
\end{aligned}
$$

which is the expression obtained in (8.52). However, if (8.50) is applied to

$$H(s) = \frac{1 - e^{-sT}}{s(s + 1)}$$

we find that

$$\frac{H(w)}{1 - e^{Tw}z^{-1}} = \frac{1 - e^{-wT}}{w(w + 1)(1 - e^{Tw}z^{-1})}$$

is analytic at $w = 0$. The residue of this expression at $w = -1$ is given by

$$-\frac{1 - e^{T}}{1 - e^{-T}z^{-1}} \tag{8.54}$$

which is not the correct expression for $H(z)$. The integral along Γ_1 in this case does not vanish and, if evaluated, would contribute just the difference between (8.53) and (8.54).

Example 8.9 (Continuation of Example 8.5) The problem of finding the input current of the network of Fig. 4.1 subject to a square-wave input voltage may be solved by use of the sampled-data-system technique developed in this section. First, the transfer function of the continuous network is calculated. We have

$$H_{11}(s) = \frac{I_1(s)}{E_1(s)} = Y_{11}(s) = \cfrac{1}{\cfrac{3}{s} + \cfrac{3s}{\cfrac{1}{3} + \cfrac{1}{s}}}$$

$$= \frac{2s + 6}{(s + 1)(s + 2)}$$

The square-wave (piecewise-constant) input $e_1(t)$ can be generated by passing an appropriate impulse train through a boxcar circuit. Consequently, we find the discrete-time transfer function by the technique of Example 8.8 to be

$$H_{11}(z) = (1 - z^{-1})Z\left(\frac{2s + 6}{s(s + 1)(s + 2)}\right)$$

$$= (1 - z^{-1})\left(\frac{3}{1 - z^{-1}} - \frac{4}{1 - e^{-T}z^{-1}} + \frac{1}{1 - e^{-2T}z^{-1}}\right)$$

The half period T of the square wave is 1 sec. Hence

$$H_{11}(z) = (1 - z^{-1})\left(\frac{3}{1 - z^{-1}} - \frac{4}{1 - 0.368z^{-1}} + \frac{1}{1 - 0.135z^{-1}}\right)$$

$$= \frac{1.664z^{-1} - 0.023z^{-2}}{(1 - 0.368z^{-1})(1 - 0.135z^{-1})}$$

which is the same result as that obtained in Example 8.5 with a considerable saving in labor.

PROBLEMS

8.1 Find the inverse Z transforms of the following functions by (1) inversion formula; (2) power series expansion, using long division.

(a) $F(z) = \dfrac{1}{(1 - z^{-1})(1 - 0.5z^{-1})}$

(b) $F(z) = \dfrac{z^{-1}}{(1 - 0.5z^{-1})^2}$

(c) $F(z) = \dfrac{z^{-1} + z^{-2}}{(1 - z^{-1})^2}$

8.2 Derive the following properties of the Z transform:

(a) $Z[\Delta^k f(n)] = (z^{-1})^k F(z) - z \sum\limits_{j=0}^{k-1} (z - 1)^{k-j-1} \Delta^j f(0)$

(b) $Z[\nabla^k f(n)] = (1 - z^{-1})^k F(z) - \sum\limits_{j=0}^{k-1} (1 - z^{-1})^{k-j-1} \nabla^j f(-1)$

(c) $Z\left[\sum\limits_{k=-\infty}^{n} f(k) \right] = \dfrac{1}{1 - z^{-1}} F(z) + \dfrac{1}{1 - z^{-1}} \sum\limits_{k=-\infty}^{-1} f(k)$

(d) $Z[a^n f(n)] = F(a^{-1}z)$

(e) $Z[n^k f(n)] = \left(z^{-1} \dfrac{d}{dz^{-1}} \right)^k F(z)$

8.3 Prove the initial- and final-value theorems:

(a) $f(0) = \lim\limits_{z \to \infty} F(z)$

(b) $f(\infty) = \lim\limits_{z \to 1} (1 - z^{-1})F(z)$ if $(1 - z^{-1})F(z)$ is analytic for $|z| \geq 1$

8.4 Show that the two-sided Z transform of the output of a fixed linear (not necessarily causal) system is the product of the two-sided Z transforms of the input and the unit-function response.

8.5 Show that the relation

$$Z\left[\sum\limits_{k=0}^{n} a(n - k)b(k) \right] = A(z)B(z)$$

is valid if $a(n)$ and $b(n)$ are matrices.

8.6 Show, in a manner similar to that used for $H(s, t)$ in Chap. 5, that the discrete-time transfer function $H(z, n)$ of a linear *fixed* system is independent of n.

8.7   Prove that

$$Z[A^n] = \sum_{n=0}^{\infty} A^n z^{-n}$$

converges to $(I - Az^{-1})^{-1}$ for all z such that $|z_i z^{-1}| < 1$ ($i = 1$, $2, \ldots, k$), where the z_i are the roots of $|zI - A| = 0$.

8.8   Consider the system governed by the following difference equations:

$$q_1(n + 1) = -\tfrac{5}{2}q_1(n) - q_2(n)$$
$$q_2(n + 1) = 3q_1(n) + q_2(n) + x(n)$$
$$y(n) = q_1(n) + q_2(n) + x(n)$$

(a) It is desired to characterize the system by a difference equation of the following form:

$$y(n + 2) + \alpha_1 y(n + 1) + \alpha_0 y(n)$$
$$= \beta_2 x(n + 2) + \beta_1 x(n + 1) + \beta_0 x(n)$$

Show that this is possible by evaluating the α's and β's.

(b) The following input is applied to the system:

$$x(n) = \begin{cases} 1 & n = 0 \\ 1 & n = 1 \\ 0 & n = 2, 3, 4, \ldots \end{cases}$$

Calculate the output $y(n)$ by use of the Z transform.

8.9   Consider the feedback system shown in Fig. P 8.9. The sampler converts the continuous-time signal $e(t)$ into the piecewise-constant signal $e_s(t)$ as shown in Fig. 8.6b.

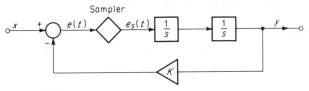

FIG. P 8.9

(a) Calculate the discrete-time transfer function by the following methods:

(1) By obtaining the difference equation for the system in the manner described in Chap. 4 and then calculating the transfer function using (8.24).

(2) By performing an analysis as described in Sec. 8.9.

(b) With $K = 1$ and $T = 1$, calculate the response $y(nT)$ for the input signals whose Z transforms are given in Prob. 8.1. Is the system stable?

8.10 In the feedback system shown in Fig. P 8.10, the switch S in the feedback path is operated as follows:

$t = 0$, S closed

$t = \frac{1}{2}$, S opened

$t = 1$, S closed

$t = \frac{3}{2}$, S opened, etc.

The input $x(t)$ is a unit step.   Calculate $y(t)$ for integral values of t ($t = 0, 1, \ldots$).   *Hint:* Use an analog-computer diagram for H and the technique described in Prob. 4.5.

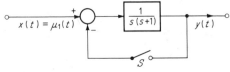

FIG. P 8.10

8.11 By expressing the sampled function $f^*(t)$, obtained by sampling the continuous-time function $f(t)$, in terms of a train of unit impulses and representing this periodic function as a Fourier series, show that

$$F^*(s) = \frac{1}{T} \sum_{n=-\infty}^{\infty} F\left(s + jn\frac{2\pi}{T}\right)$$

This relation gives the Laplace transform of the sampled function in terms of the Laplace transform of the continuous-time function.

8.12 Derive the discrete-time transfer function of the sampled-data system shown in Fig. P 8.12.   The sampler has the characteristic of Fig. 8.6b with a sampling period of $T = 1$ sec.

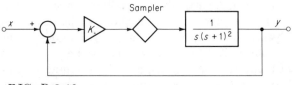

FIG. P 8.12

8.13 Obtain an expression for the inverse Z transform of

$$F(z) = \frac{z^{-p+1}}{(1 + az^{-1})^p}$$

CHAPTER NINE

RANDOM SIGNALS

9.1 RANDOM PROCESSES

The signals in many physical systems are not known functions of time and can be given only a statistical description. Among the countless examples of such signals are the positions of the molecules in a gas, the velocity of winds at the earth's surface, the current in a vacuum tube, the number of circuits engaged in a telephone exchange. A statistical description of physical phenomena is, in fact, the only description consistent with modern physics. Many phenomena can be described by the average behavior of many random signals, and these averages can be described by known (*deterministic*) time functions. In many situations, however, the average behavior is of relatively slight interest, and the principal concern is with other statistical properties. Such situations arise in the design of communications systems, control systems, and in many other areas of technology. A study of random signals and systems in which they occur is an important aspect of system theory.

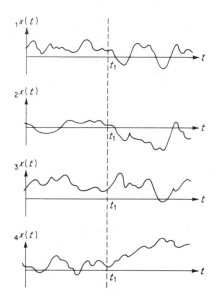

FIG. 9.1 Sample functions of a random process.

In this chapter we shall discuss the statistical description of random signals. In the next, the response of linear systems to random signals will be considered. The reader is assumed to have some familiarity with elementary probability theory, including the notions of discrete and continuous random variables, probability density and distribution functions for one random variable, joint density and distribution functions for two or more random variables, statistical independence, and measures of distributions such as the mean, the variance, and other moments.† The extension of these concepts to random time functions will be discussed in this chapter.

The notion of a random process may be illustrated by an example. Suppose that a large number of radio receivers of one model are tested simultaneously under identical conditions, and the noise output voltage of each receiver is recorded when the receivers are tuned to a frequency at which no station is operating. The noise at the output arises from atmospheric disturbances received by the antenna, in the receiver itself due to the electronic phenomena in the vacuum tubes used as amplifiers or the hole-conduction phenomena in the semiconductors, and as thermal noise due to the dissipative circuit elements. The records of these noise output voltages might appear as shown in Fig. 9.1. The set of all possible output signals which might be produced by all such radio receivers is called

† A brief introduction to probability theory may be found in C. Derman and M. Klein, "Probability and Statistical Inference for Engineers," Oxford University Press, Fair Lawn, N.J., 1959. For an excellent detailed treatment, see E. Parzen, "Modern Probability Theory and Its Applications," John Wiley & Sons, Inc., New York, 1960.

the *ensemble* of signals; any of these signals is a *sample function* of the ensemble. The ensemble of signals is the physical embodiment of a *random process;* the statistical information necessary to describe the ensemble completely defines the random process mathematically. If a sample function is denoted by $x(t)$, the ensemble is denoted by $\{x(t)\}$. In Fig. 9.1, different prescripts are used to identify different sample functions.

Consider a specific instant t_1. The amplitudes of the sample functions of the random process at this instant constitute a random variable $X_1 = X(t_1)$ whose possible values are denoted by $x_1 = x(t_1)$. The statistical behavior of the random variable is described by a (first-order) probability distribution function

$$P_{X_1}(x_1, t_1) = \text{Probability } [X(t_1) \leq x_1] \tag{9.1}$$

and the corresponding (first-order) probability density function

$$p_{X_1}(x_1, t_1) = \frac{\partial P_{X_1}(x_1, t_1)}{\partial x_1} \tag{9.2}$$

The subscript X_1 on p indicates the random variable whose probability density function is described, x_1 is the function variable,† and t_1 is a parameter indicating the time instant for which the statistical description holds. Thus the probability that the random variable X_1 lies in the small range between x_1 and $x_1 + dx_1$ is given by the probability element $p_{X_1}(x_1, t_1)\, dx_1$. It follows that

$$\text{Prob } [a < X(t_1) \leq b] = \int_a^b p_{X_1}(x_1, t_1)\, dx_1 \tag{9.3}$$

and

$$\int_{-\infty}^{\infty} p_{X_1}(x_1, t_1)\, dx_1 = 1 \tag{9.4}$$

At other time instants t_2, t_3, . . . , the random variables $X(t_2) = X_2$, $X(t_3) = X_3$, . . . are described by density functions $p_{X_2}(x_2, t_2)$, $p_{X_3}(x_3, t_3)$, ... The probability distribution function $P(x, t)$ may not be a continuous function of x, and hence $p(x, t)$ may contain impulses.

The pair of random variables X_1 and X_2 is described by the second-order joint probability distribution function

$$P_{X_1, X_2}(x_1, t_1; x_2, t_2) = \text{Prob } [X(t_1) \leq x_1; X(t_2) \leq x_2] \tag{9.5}$$

or the corresponding second-order joint probability density function

$$p_{X_1, X_2}(x_1, t_1; x_2, t_2) = \frac{\partial^2 P_{X_1, X_2}(x_1, t_1; x_2, t_2)}{\partial x_1\, \partial x_2} \tag{9.6}$$

† It should be noted that any symbol could be used for the argument x_1, which is thus a "dummy variable." The use of the particular argument x_1 is a convenient convention which reminds us that p corresponds to the random variable X_1, and thus sometimes eliminates the need for the cumbersome subscripts.

Thus the probability that the random process $\{x(t)\}$ has values at t_1 between x_1 and $x_1 + dx_1$ and at t_2 between x_2 and $x_2 + dx_2$ is given by $p_{X_1,X_2}(x_1, t_1; x_2, t_2)\, dx_1\, dx_2$. Since the subscript notation is cumbersome, the subscripts on the density function are frequently omitted, and we write $p(x_1, t_1; x_2, t_2)$ for the joint probability density function. Sometimes a single subscript is used, indicating the order, here second order, of the density function.

The first-order probability density function may be obtained from the second-order probability density function by using the fact that

$$\text{Prob}\ [X(t_1) \leq x_1] = \text{Prob}\ [X(t_1) \leq x_1; X(t_2) \leq \infty]$$

Hence

$$P_{X_1}(x_1, t_1) = P_{X_1,X_2}(x_1, t_1; \infty, t_2)$$

and thus

$$p_{X_1}(x_1, t_1) = \int_{-\infty}^{\infty} p_{X_1,X_2}(x_1, t_1; x_2, t_2)\, dx_2 \tag{9.7}$$

Distribution and density functions of third and higher orders describe the joint statistical behavior of three and more random variables derived from a random process. Thus the joint statistical behavior of $X(t_1)$, $X(t_2)$, . . . , $X(t_n)$ is described by

$$p_{X_1, X_2, \dots, X_n}\ (x_1, t_1; x_2, t_2; \ \dots\ ; \ x_n, t_n)$$

or, with simpler notation when no ambiguity exists,

$$p_n(x_1, t_1; x_2, t_2; \ \dots\ ; \ x_n, t_n)$$

A random process is completely characterized by the specification of its infinitely many joint probability distribution functions $P_1, P_2, P_3, \ \dots$ or density functions $p_1, p_2, p_3, \ \dots$, where each P_i or p_i is a function of $2i$ arguments. Such higher-order functions, however, will not be needed in our discussion of linear systems.

Example 9.1 Consider the random process $\{x(t)\}$, with sample functions

$$x(t) = \cos{(\omega_0 t + \theta)}$$

where θ denotes possible values of a random variable Θ, and ω_0 is a constant. If the distribution of Θ is given, the behavior of the random process $\{x(t)\}$ is completely described. The ensemble of waveforms consists of sinusoids with random initial phase; to each sample signal $x(t)$ corresponds some phase angle θ. Suppose Θ is distributed uniformly in the range 0 to 2π so that

$$p_\Theta(\theta) = \begin{cases} \dfrac{1}{2\pi} & 0 \leq \theta \leq 2\pi \\[2mm] 0 & \text{otherwise} \end{cases} \tag{9.8}$$

The first-order probability density function $p_X(x, t)$ may be obtained as follows.   For fixed values of t such that $0 \leq \omega_0 t + \theta \leq \pi$,

$$p_\Theta(\theta)|d\theta| = p_X(x, t)|dx|$$

or

$$p_X(x, t) = \frac{p_\Theta(\theta)}{|dx/d\theta|}$$

Since $|dx/d\theta| = \sin(\omega_0 t + \theta) = \sqrt{1 - x^2}$, we obtain

$$p_X(x, t) = \frac{1}{2\pi \sqrt{1 - x^2}} \qquad 0 \leq \omega_0 t + \theta \leq \pi$$

with $|x| \leq 1$.   Since for values of θ for which $\pi \leq \omega_0 t + \theta \leq 2\pi$, the x-versus-θ curve is symmetrical with its other half, the probability density of X is doubled, giving

$$p_X(x, t) = \begin{cases} \dfrac{1}{\pi \sqrt{1 - x^2}} & |x| \leq 1 \\ 0 & |x| > 1 \end{cases} \tag{9.9}$$

This result may be obtained in another manner which is advantageous when the distribution of Θ is less simple than in this case.   We first determine the distribution function for X by expressing it in terms of Θ.   For an arbitrary instant t, and for values of x in the range $[-1, 1]$,

$$\begin{aligned} P_X(x, t) &= \text{Prob}\,[X(t) \leq x] = \text{Prob}\,[\cos(\omega_0 t + \Theta) \leq x] \\ &= \text{Prob}\,[\cos^{-1} x \leq \omega_0 t + \Theta \leq 2\pi - \cos^{-1} x] \end{aligned}$$

if we limit the values of $\cos^{-1} x$ to the interval $[0, 2\pi]$.   Hence, because of symmetry and the uniform distribution of Θ,

$$\begin{aligned} P_X(x, t) &= 2\,\text{Prob}\,[\cos^{-1} x \leq \omega_0 t + \Theta \leq \pi] \\ &= 2\,\text{Prob}\,[\cos^{-1} x - \omega_0 t \leq \Theta \leq \pi - \omega_0 t] \\ &= 2 \int_{\cos^{-1} x - \omega_0 t}^{\pi - \omega_0 t} \frac{1}{2\pi}\, d\theta \\ &= \frac{1}{\pi}\,(\pi - \omega_0 t - \cos^{-1} x + \omega_0 t) \\ &= 1 - \frac{1}{\pi} \cos^{-1} x \qquad |x| \leq 1 \end{aligned}$$

Hence the first probability density function is

$$p_X(x, t) = \frac{\partial P_X(x, t)}{\partial x} = \begin{cases} \dfrac{1}{\pi \sqrt{1 - x^2}} & |x| \leq 1 \\ 0 & \text{otherwise} \end{cases}$$

as before.   This density function is independent of t.

If the random phase Θ is distributed uniformly only over the range $[0, \pi]$, however, we have

$$p_\Theta(\theta) = \begin{cases} \dfrac{1}{\pi} & 0 \leq \theta \leq \pi \\ 0 & \text{otherwise} \end{cases} \tag{9.10}$$

In this case

$$P_X(x, t) = \text{Prob } [\cos^{-1} x \leq \dot{\omega}_0 t + \Theta \leq 2\pi - \cos^{-1} x]$$

as before.   For a fixed value of $\omega_0 t$, the density function for $U = \Theta + \omega_0 t$ is

$$P_U(\theta) = \begin{cases} \dfrac{1}{\pi} & \omega_0 t \leq \theta \leq \pi + \omega_0 t \\ 0 & \text{otherwise} \end{cases}$$

Hence

$$P_X(x, t) = \int_{\cos^{-1} x}^{2\pi - \cos^{-1} x} p_U(\theta)\, d\theta$$

If we first consider values of $\omega_0 t$ in the interval $[0, \pi/2]$, we have (see Fig. 9.2, which shows the range of integration for different values of x)

$$P_X(x, t) = \begin{cases} \dfrac{1}{\pi}(2\pi - 2\cos^{-1} x) & \pi - \omega_0 t < \cos^{-1} x \leq \pi \\ & \text{or } -1 \leq x < -\cos \omega_0 t \\[4pt] \dfrac{1}{\pi}(\pi + \omega_0 t - \cos^{-1} x) & \omega_0 t < \cos^{-1} x \leq \pi - \omega_0 t \\ & \text{or } -\cos \omega_0 t \leq x < \cos \omega_0 t \\[4pt] \dfrac{1}{\pi}\pi & 0 \leq \cos^{-1} x \leq \omega_0 t \\ & \text{or } \cos \omega_0 t \leq x \leq 1 \end{cases}$$

The distribution function is similarly evaluated for other values of $\omega_0 t$. Differentiation then yields, for $0 \leq \omega_0 t \leq \pi$,

$$p_X(x, t) = \begin{cases} \dfrac{2}{\pi \sqrt{1 - x^2}} & -1 \leq x < -|\cos \omega_0 t| \\[4pt] \dfrac{1}{\pi \sqrt{1 - x^2}} & -|\cos \omega_0 t| \leq x < |\cos \omega_0 t| \\[4pt] 0 & |\cos \omega_0 t| \leq x \leq 1 \\[4pt] 0 & |x| > 1 \end{cases} \tag{9.11}$$

and for $\pi < \omega_0 t \le 2\pi$,

$$p_X(x, t) = \begin{cases} 0 & -1 \le x < -|\cos \omega_0 t| \\ \dfrac{1}{\pi \sqrt{1 - x^2}} & -|\cos \omega_0 t| \le x < |\cos \omega_0 t| \\ \dfrac{2}{\pi \sqrt{1 - x^2}} & |\cos \omega_0 t| \le x \le 1 \\ 0 & |x| > 1 \end{cases} \tag{9.12}$$

The density function now clearly depends on t.

This result is shown graphically in Fig. 9.3, together with the result for the uniform distribution of the initial phase over $[0, 2\pi]$. The result may be verified qualitatively by considering the possible sample functions as shown in Fig. 9.4. For very nearly all values of t, there are certain amplitude ranges which can occur only with zero probability; hence the density function is zero for such amplitudes.

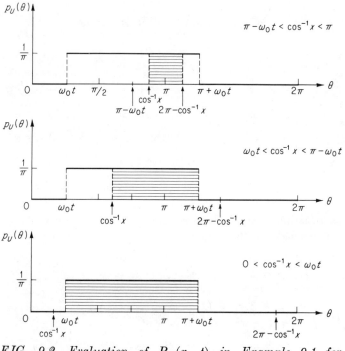

FIG. 9.2 Evaluation of $P_X(x, t)$ in Example 9.1 for $0 < \omega_0 t \le \pi/2$.

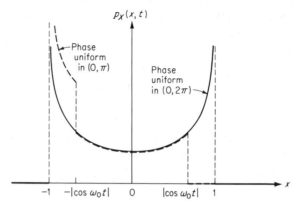

FIG. 9.3   *Probability density function for sinusoid with random phase,* $0 < \omega_0 t \leq \pi$.

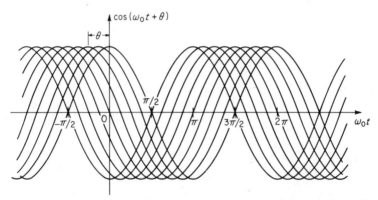

FIG. 9.4   *Sample functions of random process* $\{\cos (\omega_0 t + \theta)\}$.

DISCRETE-TIME AND QUANTIZED SIGNALS

Measured data of noise or of noisy signals frequently are obtained only at discrete instants of time, so that we then have to deal with discrete-time signals.   When such signals are obtained from sample functions of a random process, they are often referred to as *time series.*

In the case of discrete-time signals, the probability density functions are defined only at the sampling instants.   In other respects the statistical description of random processes as described above applies to discrete-time random processes.

Since quantized signals can take only discrete amplitude values, probability distributions are often more convenient than density functions. Probability density functions may still be defined, but comprise only impulse functions. If $Pr_X(x_i, t)$ denotes the probability that $X = x_i$ at time t, the density function is

$$p_X(x, t) = \sum_i Pr_X(x_i, t)\delta(x - x_i)$$

Example 9.2 A binary circuit produces random output voltages V of $+1$ and -1 volt with probability of 0.6 and 0.4, respectively. The probability distribution and density functions are shown in Fig. 9.5. The time parameter is left out since the given probabilities do not depend on time.

The (first-order) density function may be expressed by

$$p_V(v) = 0.4\delta(v + 1) + 0.6\delta(v - 1)$$

We may, however, equally well specify the probability that $V = 1$ and that $V = -1$ by

$$\text{Prob } [V = v] = 0.4\delta_{v,-1} + 0.6\delta_{v,+1}$$

where δ_{nk} is the unit function or Kronecker delta defined in Sec. 3.4. It should be noted that Prob $[V = v_i]$ equals the height of the discontinuity in the distribution function $P_V(v, t)$ at $v = v_i$.

If a second binary circuit *independently* produces similar random output voltages with the same respective probabilities, the second-order joint density function is

$$\begin{aligned} p_{V_1,V_2}(v_1, v_2) = {} & 0.16\delta(v_1 + 1)\delta(v_2 + 1) + 0.24\delta(v_1 + 1)\delta(v_2 - 1) \\ & + 0.24\delta(v_1 - 1)\delta(v_2 + 1) + 0.36\delta(v_1 - 1)\delta(v_2 - 1) \end{aligned}$$

because the joint density of two *independent* random variables is the product of their first-order densities.

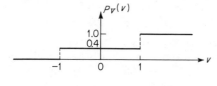

FIG. 9.5 Distribution and density functions for a quantized random variable.

9.2 AVERAGES, CHARACTERISTIC FUNCTION, AND CORRELATION FUNCTION

AVERAGES

We may define ensemble averages for a random process in a manner analogous to that used for a random variable, since for any fixed value of t the random process defines a random variable. Thus

$$\text{Mean value of } X(t) = E[X(t)] = \overline{X(t)} = \int_{-\infty}^{\infty} x p_X(x, t)\, dx \quad (9.13)$$

for continuous-amplitude signals, or

$$\overline{X(t)} = \sum_i x_i Pr_X(x_i, t) \quad (9.14)$$

for quantized signals.   Note that (9.14) is a special case of (9.13).   Here the operator E or a bar over the random variable denotes the expectation, or mean.   The averaging is carried out at one instant t over all members of the ensemble of functions constituting the random process.   Hence the averages are called *ensemble averages*.

For any single-valued function $g[X(t)]$—which also defines a random process and, for fixed t, a random variable—we have

$$\text{Mean value of } g[X(t)] = \int_{-\infty}^{\infty} g(x) p_X(x, t)\, dx \quad \text{or} \quad \sum_i g(x_i) Pr_X(x_i, t)$$

$$(9.15)$$

In particular, the kth moment of a continuous-amplitude process is

$$\alpha_k(t) = E[X^k(t)] = \overline{X^k(t)} = \int_{-\infty}^{\infty} x^k p_X(x, t)\, dx \quad (9.16)$$

Example 9.3   We may determine the mean-square value of the random process of Example 9.1 by using the density function (9.9).   Thus

$$\overline{X^2(t)} = \int_{-\infty}^{\infty} x^2 p_X(x, t)\, dx = \int_{-1}^{1} x^2 \frac{1}{\pi \sqrt{1 - x^2}}\, dx$$

$$= 2 \int_0^1 x^2 \frac{1}{\pi \sqrt{1 - x^2}}\, dx$$

$$= \frac{2}{\pi} \left[-\frac{x}{2} \sqrt{1 - x^2} + \tfrac{1}{2} \sin^{-1} x \right]_0^1$$

$$= \frac{2}{\pi} \left[\frac{\pi}{4} \right] = \frac{1}{2}$$

Alternatively, we may regard $X(t)$ as a function of the random variable Θ and use the density function for Θ [Eq. (9.8)]:

$$\overline{X^2(t)} = \int_{-\infty}^{\infty} x^2(\theta)p_\Theta(\theta)\,d\theta = \int_0^{2\pi} \cos^2(\omega_0 t + \theta)\,\frac{1}{2\pi}\,d\theta$$

$$= \frac{1}{4\pi} \int_0^{2\pi} [1 + \cos 2(\omega_0 t + \theta)]\,d\theta$$

$$= \frac{1}{4\pi}\,2\pi = \tfrac{1}{2} \qquad \text{as before}$$

We also find

$$\overline{X(t)} = \int_0^{2\pi} \cos(\omega_0 t + \theta)\,\frac{1}{2\pi}\,d\theta = 0$$

If the random phase is distributed according to (9.10), we find

$$\overline{X^2(t)} = \int_0^{\pi} \cos^2(\omega_0 t + \theta)\,\frac{1}{\pi}\,d\theta$$

$$= \frac{1}{2\pi} \int_0^{\pi} [1 + \cos 2(\omega_0 t + \theta)]\,d\theta$$

$$= \frac{1}{2\pi}\,\pi = \tfrac{1}{2}$$

It is noted that the mean-square value is independent of t, although the density function is time-dependent in this case. The mean value, however, is

$$\overline{X(t)} = \int_0^{\pi} \cos(\omega_0 t + \theta)\,\frac{1}{\pi}\,d\theta$$

$$= \frac{1}{\pi} [\sin(\omega_0 t + \theta)]\,\Big|_0^{\pi}$$

$$= \frac{1}{\pi}(-2\sin\omega_0 t) = -\frac{2}{\pi}\sin\omega_0 t$$

It is also clear from an inspection of Fig. 9.4 that the mean value in this case depends on t.

Example 9.4 The kth moment of the random variable V of Example 9.2 is

$$\overline{V^k} = \int_{-\infty}^{\infty} v^k p_V(v)\,dv = \sum_i v_i^k Pr_V(v_i)$$

$$= (-1)^k 0.4 + (1)^k 0.6 = \begin{cases} 1 & k = \text{even} \\ 0.2 & k = \text{odd} \end{cases}$$

THE CHARACTERISTIC FUNCTION

An important average of a function of a random variable or a random process is the *characteristic function*. For a random process $\{x(t)\}$ it is defined as

$$M_X(u; t) = E[e^{juX(t)}] = \int_{-\infty}^{\infty} e^{jux} p_X(x, t) \, dx \qquad (9.17)$$

It is seen that the characteristic function is the Fourier transform of the probability density function.   (The positive sign in the exponent simply means that the negative sign must be used in obtaining the inverse.) Hence the density function may be obtained from the characteristic function as the inverse Fourier transform:

$$p_X(x, t) = \frac{1}{2\pi} \int_{-\infty}^{\infty} M_X(u; t) e^{-jux} \, du \qquad (9.18)$$

The moments of the random process or variable may be obtained from a series expansion of the characteristic function.†   Expanding the exponential, we obtain

$$M_X(u; t) = \int_{-\infty}^{\infty} \sum_{k=0}^{\infty} \frac{(jux)^k}{k!} p_X(x, t) \, dx = \sum_{k=0}^{\infty} \frac{(ju)^k}{k!} \int_{-\infty}^{\infty} x^k p_X(x, t) \, dx$$

$$= \sum_{k=0}^{\infty} \alpha_k(t) \frac{(ju)^k}{k!} \qquad (9.19)$$

Thus the moments are the coefficients of $(ju)^k/k!$ in the Maclaurin series expansion of the characteristic function.   Using the well-known formula for the coefficients of a Maclaurin series, we obtain the moments $\alpha_k(t)$ by differentiating the characteristic function and setting $u = 0$:

$$\alpha_k(t) = (-j)^k \frac{\partial^k M_X(u; t)}{\partial u^k} \bigg]_{u=0} \qquad (9.20)$$

For a quantized process or variable, the characteristic function may be written

$$M_X(u; t) = \sum_i e^{jux_i} Pr_X(x_i, t) \qquad (9.21)$$

If $M_X(u; t)$ is given for a quantized process $\{x(t)\}$, the probability distribution $Pr_X(x_i, t)$ may be obtained by determining the coefficient of e^{jux_i} in the series (9.21) or by using (9.18).   The moments are still given by (9.20).

† If a real variable v is used in place of ju, the characteristic function is, in fact, called the moment generating function.

Example 9.5   The characteristic function of the random process of Example 9.1 with phase uniformly distributed in the interval $[0, 2\pi]$ is

$$
\begin{aligned}
M_X(u; t) &= \int_{-\infty}^{\infty} e^{jux} p_X(x, t) \, dx \\
&= \int_{-\infty}^{\infty} e^{jux(\theta)} p_\theta(\theta) \, d\theta \\
&= \int_0^{2\pi} e^{ju \cos (\omega_0 t + \theta)} \frac{1}{2\pi} \, d\theta \\
&= J_0(u)
\end{aligned}
$$

where $J_0(u)$ is the Bessel function of the first kind of order zero.   Expanding the Bessel function, we find

$$
\begin{aligned}
M_X(u) &= J_0(u) = 1 - \left(\frac{u}{2}\right)^2 + \frac{1}{2!2!} \left(\frac{u}{2}\right)^4 - \cdots \\
&= 1 + \frac{1}{2} \frac{(ju)^2}{2!} + \frac{3}{8} \frac{(ju)^4}{4!} + \cdots
\end{aligned}
$$

Thus $\alpha_1 = \alpha_3 = \cdots = 0$, $\alpha_2 = \frac{1}{2}$, as obtained earlier, and $\alpha_4 = \frac{3}{8}$.   The leading term is $M_X(0)$ and must be unity in view of the definition of characteristic function and (9.4).

For the random process of Example 9.1 with phase distributed uniformly in the interval $[0, \pi]$, we have

$$
\begin{aligned}
M_X(u; t) &= \int_0^{\pi} e^{ju \cos (\omega_0 t + \theta)} \frac{1}{\pi} \, d\theta = \frac{1}{\pi} \int_{\omega_0 t}^{\omega_0 t + \pi} e^{ju \cos \beta} \, d\beta \\
&= \frac{1}{\pi} \int_{\omega_0 t}^{\omega_0 t + \pi} \left[1 + ju \cos \beta + \frac{(ju)^2}{2!} \cos^2 \beta + \cdots \right] d\beta \\
&= 1 - \frac{2}{\pi} \sin \omega_0 t (ju) + \frac{1}{2} \frac{(ju)^2}{2!} + \cdots
\end{aligned}
$$

Thus the mean value $\alpha_1 = -(2/\pi) \sin \omega_0 t$, and $\alpha_2 = \frac{1}{2}$, as obtained earlier.

An important and useful property of the characteristic function relates to the sum of independent random variables.   Let $X_1, X_2, \ldots, X_n$ denote n independent random variables and let Y be their sum:

$$
Y = \sum_{i=1}^{n} X_i
$$

The characteristic function of Y is

$$
M_Y(u) = E[e^{juY}] = E\left[\exp ju \sum_{i=1}^{n} X_i \right] = \prod_{i=1}^{n} E[e^{juX_i}]
$$

since the X_i are independent. Since the expectation in each factor of this product is the characteristic function of one of the random variables X_i, we find

$$M_Y(u) = \prod_{i=1}^{n} M_{X_i}(u) \tag{9.22}$$

Thus the characteristic function of the sum of independent random variables is the product of their characteristic functions.

For a number of random variables $X_1, X_2, \ldots, X_n$ (which may all be derived from a single random process $\{x(t)\}$ at the instants $t_1, t_2, \ldots, t_n$, respectively), the *joint characteristic function* is

$$M_{X_1, \ldots, X_n}(u_1, \ldots, u_n; t_1, \ldots, t_n) = E\left[\exp j \sum_{i=1}^{n} u_i X_i\right]$$

$$= \int_{-\infty}^{\infty} \cdots \int_{-\infty}^{\infty} \exp\left(j \sum_{i=1}^{n} u_i x_i\right) p_{X_1, \ldots, X_n}(x_1, t_1; \ldots; x_n, t_n) \, dx_1 \cdots dx_n \tag{9.23}$$

which is the n-dimensional Fourier transform of the joint probability density function $p_{X_1, \ldots, X_n}(x_1, t_1; \ldots; x_n, t_n)$. The inverse Fourier transform of $M_{X_1, \ldots, X_n}(u_1, \ldots, u_n; t_1, \ldots, t_n)$ thus gives the probability density function

$$p_{X_1, \ldots, X_n}(x_1, t_1; \ldots; x_n, t_n)$$

$$= \frac{1}{(2\pi)^n} \int_{-\infty}^{\infty} \cdots \int_{-\infty}^{\infty} M_{X_1, \ldots, X_n}(u_1, \ldots, u_n; t_1, \ldots, t_n) \exp\left(-j \sum_{i=1}^{n} u_i x_i\right) du_1 \ldots du_n \tag{9.24}$$

Some useful properties of such joint characteristic functions are discussed in Sec. 9.7.

THE CORRELATION FUNCTION

Averages may involve more than one random variable and may thus necessitate the use of joint density functions for their evaluation. Thus the second-order joint moments of the random process $\{x(t)\}$ at the pair of instants t_1, t_2 are

$$\alpha_{ij}(t_1, t_2) = E[X^i(t_1) X^j(t_2)] = \int_{-\infty}^{\infty} \int_{-\infty}^{\infty} x_1^i x_2^j p_{X_1, X_2}(x_1, t_1; x_2, t_2) \, dx_1 \, dx_2$$

Of particular importance is the moment α_{11}, which is called the *autocorrela-*

tion function, or correlation function, and is given a special symbol r_x:†

$$r_x(t_1, t_2) = E[X(t_1)X(t_2)]$$

$$= \int_{-\infty}^{\infty} \int_{-\infty}^{\infty} x_1 x_2 p_{X_1, X_2}(x_1, t_1; x_2, t_2) \, dx_1 \, dx_2 \quad (9.25)$$

It is evident that, if $t_2 = t_1 = t$,

$$r_x(t, t) = E[X^2(t)]$$

gives the mean-square value of $X(t)$. If the values of $X(t)$ at instants t_1 and t_2 are independent,‡

$$r_x(t_1, t_2) = \overline{X(t_1)X(t_2)} = \overline{X(t_1)} \; \overline{X(t_2)}$$

By definition, the correlation function is the ensemble average of the product of values of $X(t)$ at two time instants. Intuitively, one would expect that if $X(t)$ changes very slowly, the average of the product cannot deviate very much from the mean-square value $\overline{X^2(t)}$, while if $X(t)$ can change rapidly (compared with the interval $t_2 - t_1$), the average of the product will be nearly the product of the means $\overline{X(t_1)} \; \overline{X(t_2)}$. This relation of the correlation function to the frequency content of the random process will be formulated more precisely later on.

Instead of the correlation function, statisticians frequently use the covariance, which is

$$\begin{aligned} \text{cov}_x(t_1, t_2) &= E[X(t_1) - \overline{X(t_1)}][X(t_2) - \overline{X(t_2)}] \\ &= \overline{X(t_1)X(t_2)} - \overline{X(t_1)} \; \overline{X(t_2)} \\ &= r_x(t_1, t_2) - \overline{X(t_1)} \; \overline{X(t_2)} \end{aligned} \quad (9.26)$$

The correlation coefficient is the normalized covariance and is given by

$$\rho_x(t_1, t_2) = \frac{\text{cov}_x(t_1, t_2)}{\sigma_{X_1} \sigma_{X_2}} \quad (9.27)$$

where σ_{X_1} and σ_{X_2} are the standard deviations of $X(t_1)$ and $X(t_2)$, respectively.

Example 9.6   The correlation function of the random process of Example 9.1 with phase distributed uniformly in $[0, 2\pi]$ may be obtained by

† In general, the correlation function is defined as $E[X(t_1)X^*(t_2)]$, where * denotes the complex conjugate. Since we deal only with real processes, however, the definition given is adequate.
‡ It may often be assumed that $x(t_1)$ and $x(t_2)$ are independent when $t_2 - t_1$ is very large.

again considering each sample function as a function of θ:

$$r_x(t_1, t_2) = \overline{X(t_1)X(t_2)} = \int_{-\infty}^{\infty} x(t_1, \theta)x(t_2, \theta)p_\theta(\theta)\, d\theta$$

$$= \int_0^{2\pi} \cos(\omega_0 t_1 + \theta) \cos(\omega_0 t_2 + \theta) \frac{1}{2\pi}\, d\theta$$

$$= \frac{1}{4\pi} \int_0^{2\pi} [\cos \omega_0(t_2 - t_1) + \cos(\omega_0 t_1 + \omega_0 t_2 + 2\theta)]\, d\theta$$

$$= \frac{1}{2} \cos \omega_0(t_2 - t_1)$$

The correlation function depends only on the difference $t_2 - t_1$, not on t_1 itself. This, like the independence of time of the mean and the mean-square value, is evidence of the fact that we are dealing with a stationary process. This will be discussed in the next section.

For the random process with phase distributed uniformly in $[0, \pi]$, we find

$$r_x(t_1, t_2) = \int_0^{\pi} \cos(\omega_0 t_1 + \theta) \cos(\omega_0 t_2 + \theta) \frac{1}{\pi}\, d\theta$$

$$= \frac{1}{2\pi} \int_0^{\pi} [\cos \omega_0(t_2 - t_1) + \cos(\omega_0 t_1 + \omega_0 t_2 + 2\theta)]\, d\theta$$

Since the second term completes one period in the integration range, we have again

$$r_x(t_1, t_2) = \tfrac{1}{2} \cos \omega_0(t_2 - t_1)$$

Example 9.7 A quantized process which occurs frequently has sample functions which consist of sequences of pulses of unit width (Fig. 9.6a). The pulse amplitudes can take the values $+1$ and -1 with equal probability; successive amplitudes are independent. The pulse sequences have random, uniformly distributed phase; i.e., the starting time B of any pulse is uniformly distributed over a unit interval. We shall find the correlation function of this process.

Let $P(i, j)$ be the probability that $X(t_1) = i$ and $X(t_2) = j$. Then, according to (9.25), the correlation function is

$$r_x(t_1, t_2) = E[X(t_1)X(t_2)]$$
$$= (1)(1)P(1, 1) + (1)(-1)P(1, -1) + (-1)(1)P(-1, 1)$$
$$+ (-1)(-1)P(-1, -1)$$
$$= P(1, 1) - P(1, -1) - P(-1, 1) + P(-1, -1)$$

Now

$$P(1, 1) = \text{Prob } [X(t_2) = 1 | X(t_1) = 1] \cdot \text{Prob } [X(t_1) = 1]$$

where Prob $[A|C]$ denotes the conditional probability of event A given that event C has occurred.

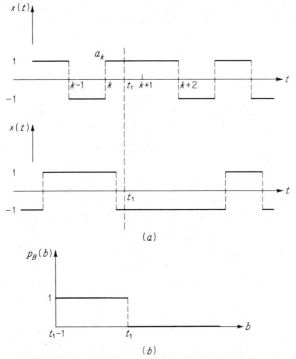

FIG. 9.6   Example 9.7.   (a) Sample functions
of random process; (b) probability density function
of start time of pulse containing t_1.

Consider a sample function of the ensemble. Let B be the starting
time of the pulse in which t_1 occurs. Then B is uniformly distributed
over the interval $(t_1 - 1, t_1)$ as shown in Fig. 9.6b. Since t_2 occurs either
during the same pulse as $t_1 < t_2$ or during another pulse, we may write

Prob $[X(t_2) = 1 | X(t_1) = 1]$ = Prob $(t_2 < B + 1) + \frac{1}{2}$ Prob $(t_2 > B + 1)$
Prob $[X(t_1) = 1] = \frac{1}{2}$

Thus, by use of symmetry,

$$P(1, 1) = P(-1, -1) = \frac{1}{2}[\text{Prob } (t_2 < B + 1) + \frac{1}{2} \text{Prob } (t_2 > B + 1)]$$
$$= \frac{1}{2}[\text{Prob } (B > t_2 - 1) + \frac{1}{2} \text{Prob } (B < t_2 - 1)]$$
$$= \begin{cases} \frac{1}{2}[1 - (t_2 - t_1) + \frac{1}{2}(t_2 - t_1)] & t_2 - t_1 \le 1 \\ \frac{1}{2}[0 + \frac{1}{2}] & t_2 - t_1 > 1 \end{cases}$$

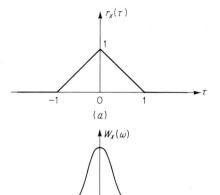

FIG. 9.7   *Examples 9.7 and 9.11.*
(a) Correlation function; (b) power
spectral density.

Similarly, we find

$$P(1, -1) = P(-1, 1) = \begin{cases} \frac{1}{4}(t_2 - t_1) & t_2 - t_1 \leq 1 \\ \frac{1}{4} & t_2 - t_1 > 1 \end{cases}$$

Thus, with $t_2 - t_1 = \tau$ and (9.33),

$$r_x(\tau) = \begin{cases} 1 - |\tau| & |\tau| \leq 1 \\ 0 & |\tau| > 1 \end{cases} \tag{9.28}$$

The correlation function is shown on Fig. 9.7a.

In the case of a discrete-time random process, the correlation function is defined only for pairs of instants (t_1, t_2) for which the signals are defined. The values of the correlation function may then be arranged in the correlation matrix

$$\mathbf{R}_x = \begin{bmatrix} r_x(t_1, t_1) & r_x(t_1, t_2) & r_x(t_1, t_3) & \cdots \\ r_x(t_2, t_1) & r_x(t_2, t_2) & r_x(t_2, t_3) & \cdots \\ r_x(t_3, t_1) & r_x(t_3, t_2) & r_x(t_3, t_3) & \cdots \\ \cdots \cdots \cdots \cdots \cdots \cdots \cdots \cdots \end{bmatrix} \tag{9.29}$$

9.3 STATIONARY PROCESSES

In general, the statistical properties of a random process depend upon time. Thus the probability density function $p_X(x, t)$ in general depends on the instant t as in the random process of Example 9.1 with uniform phase in $[0, \pi]$. The joint density function $p_X(x_1, t_1; x_2, t_2)$ in general depends on both t_1 and t_2. In many important processes, however, the

statistical properties do not vary with time. If the joint density functions of all orders are invariant under a translation of the time origin, the process is called *stationary in the strict sense.* Such a process thus requires

$$p_1(x, t) = p_1(x, t + \tau)$$
$$p_2(x_1, t_1; x_2, t_2) = p_2(x_1, t_1 + \tau; x_2, t_2 + \tau)$$
$$\cdots \cdots \cdots \cdots \cdots \cdots \cdots \cdots$$

or simply

$$p_n(x_1, t_1; x_2, t_2; \cdots ; x_n, t_n) = p_n(x_1, t_1 + \tau; x_2, t_2 + \tau; \cdots ; x_n, t_n + \tau)$$

for all sets $t_1, \ldots, t_n$, any τ, and all n. For a process to be stationary, it is clearly necessary that all sample functions begin at $t = -\infty$. In practice, the process may be treated as if it were stationary if the statistics do not change over the time range of interest.

Since in linear systems we frequently deal only with the mean and the correlation function, it is often sufficient to know whether these two quantities are invariant under a translation of the time origin. If they are, the process is called *stationary in the wide sense,*† which thus means, for real processes $\{x(t)\}$,

$$E[X(t)] = \bar{X} \qquad \text{independent of } t \tag{9.30}$$
$$r_x(t_1, t_2) = r_x(t_2 - t_1) \qquad \text{a function of difference } t_2 - t_1 \text{ only} \tag{9.31}$$

Wide-sense stationarity also requires that the mean-square value of the process be finite:

$$E[X^2(t)] < \infty \tag{9.32}$$

Any strictly stationary process is clearly also stationary in the wide sense. The random process of Example 9.1 is wide-sense stationary if the phase is uniformly distributed in $[0, 2\pi]$, for all conditions are satisfied as shown in Examples 9.3 and 9.6. (The process is, in fact, also stationary in the strict sense.) If the phase is uniformly distributed in $[0, \pi]$, however, the mean is time-dependent (Examples 9.3 and 9.5), so that this process is not stationary in either sense.

Since the correlation function of a wide-sense-stationary process is a function only of the difference $t_2 - t_1 = \tau$, certain useful properties of the correlation function follow immediately.

1. Since, from the definition of the correlation function of a *real* random process, $r_x(t_1, t_2) = r_x(t_2, t_1)$, it follows that

$$r_x(\tau) = r_x(-\tau) \tag{9.33}$$

---

† See J. L. Doob, "Stochastic Processes," chap. 2, sec. 8, John Wiley & Sons, Inc., New York, 1953.

Thus the correlation function of a real stationary process is an even function of its argument.

2. Since $\overline{[X(t_1) \pm X(t_2)]^2} \geq 0$, or
$$\overline{X^2(t_1)} + \overline{X^2(t_2)} \pm \overline{2X(t_1)X(t_2)} \geq 0$$

it follows that
$$|r_x(t_1, t_2)| = |\overline{X(t_1)X(t_2)}| \leq \frac{\overline{X^2(t_1)} + \overline{X^2(t_2)}}{2}$$

Hence for a wide-sense stationary process, in which $\overline{X^2(t_1)} = \overline{X^2(t_2)} = \overline{X^2}$,
$$|r_x(\tau)| \leq r_x(0) = \overline{X^2} \tag{9.34}$$

Thus the magnitude of the correlation function never exceeds its value at the origin, or the mean-square value of the process.

3. If the random process contains periodic components, the correlation function contains components with the same periods (Example 9.6). A nonzero average ("d-c") value is a special case of a periodic component, i.e., one in which the frequency of the periodic component is zero. Its appearance in the correlation function can be made evident by defining the sample functions of the random process $\{y(t)\}$ as
$$y(t) = x(t) - \tilde{X}$$

so that $\{y(t)\}$ has zero mean. Then
$$r_y(\tau) = E[X(t) - \tilde{X}][X(t + \tau) - \tilde{X}]$$
$$= r_x(\tau) - \tilde{X}^2 \tag{9.35}$$
or
$$r_x(\tau) = r_y(\tau) + \tilde{X}^2$$

4. If the random process contains no periodic components and the values of $x(t_2)$ become independent of the values $x(t_1)$ as the difference $t_2 - t_1 = \tau$ becomes sufficiently large, then
$$r_x(\tau) = \overline{X(t)X(t + \tau)} \to \overline{X(t)}\ \overline{X(t + \tau)} = 0$$

If the process $\{x(t)\}$ has a mean value $\tilde{X}$ but no other periodic components, the result of property 3 above shows that
$$\lim_{\tau \to \infty} r_x(\tau) = \tilde{X}^2 \tag{9.36}$$

5. For a discrete-time real stationary process whose sample functions are defined at equal intervals differing by T sec, the correlation

matrix (9.29) becomes

$$\mathbf{R}_x = \begin{bmatrix} r_x(0) & r_x(T) & r_x(2T) & \cdots \\ r_x(T) & r_x(0) & r_x(T) & \cdots \\ r_x(2T) & r_x(T) & r_x(0) & \cdots \\ \cdot\cdot\cdot\cdot\cdot\cdot\cdot\cdot\cdot\cdot\cdot\cdot\cdot\cdot\cdot\cdot \end{bmatrix} \tag{9.37}$$

ERGODIC PROCESSES

Any practical application of statistical methods necessitates a knowledge of the relevant statistical properties of the random processes of concern. These properties are inferred from empirical measurements. Since the properties relate to an ensemble of signals, it would, in principle, be necessary to have a large number of members of the ensemble available upon which to perform the required measurements; the accumulation of this data would often be a handicap to the application of statistical methods.

Consider, for example, the problem of determining the statistics of the ensemble $\{x(t)\}$ whose members are the number of circuits (as a function of time) engaged in a certain telephone exchange. To obtain these statistics one would require a large number of identical exchanges, each serving a statistically equivalent population of subscribers. It is possible to conceive of this ideal arrangement, but it is clearly not practical. How can the required data be obtained? It would seem reasonable, if the population remains statistically constant, to observe the record of behavior at a single exchange for a very long time and then cut the record (say a tape) into a large number of pieces and regard each piece as a record of a different member of the ensemble. Thus a single member of the ensemble (the original record) is assumed to represent the entire ensemble. When this assumption is permitted, the ensemble is said to be *ergodic*. Mathematically, an ensemble is said to be ergodic if and only if the following conditions are satisfied:[†]

1. The ensemble is stationary.
2. No *proper subensemble* (i.e., set of members of probability other than zero or one) is stationary.

An ergodic process clearly must be stationary, for otherwise the ensemble average at two different instants could differ, and at least one of the ensemble averages would differ from the time average. A stationary process is, however, not necessarily ergodic. This may be demonstrated

[†] D. Middleton, "An Introduction to Statistical Communication Theory," p. 56, McGraw-Hill Book Company, New York, 1960. For a rigorous discussion of ergodic theorems, see M. Loève, "Probability Theory," D. Van Nostrand Company, Inc., Princeton, N.J., 1955.

by means of an example due to Bennett.† Consider an ensemble of amplifiers some of which contain noisy tubes only, while others contain quiet tubes only. The noise voltage at the amplifier outputs will, under suitable conditions, be a stationary process. Ensemble averages (e.g., of the squared noise voltage) will thus be the same at any time instant. The time average will, however, depend on whether the sample output voltage chosen corresponds to a quiet or a noisy amplifier and will be either smaller or larger than the ensemble average. The process is thus not ergodic. In this case the subensemble of noisy amplifiers is stationary and the second condition is not satisfied. Ergodic processes are thus a subclass of stationary processes.

Except in contrived situations such as that above, it is very difficult to establish whether a process is ergodic; often a process is assumed to be ergodic when ergodicity is a useful property to have and when it is intuitively reasonable.

The principal analytical advantage in dealing with ergodic processes, which can be shown to follow from the requirements for ergodicity, is that ensemble averages and time averages are equal.‡ Specifically,

$$E(X) = \lim_{T \to \infty} \frac{1}{2T} \int_{-T}^{T} x(\lambda) \, d\lambda$$

$$E(X^2) = \lim_{T \to \infty} \frac{1}{2T} \int_{-T}^{T} x^2(\lambda) \, d\lambda$$

$$r_x(\tau) = E[X(t)X(t + \tau)] = \lim_{T \to \infty} \frac{1}{2T} \int_{-T}^{T} x(\lambda)x(\lambda + \tau) \, d\lambda$$

and so forth. The averages are, of course, independent of time.

Example 9.8 The correlation function of a process whose sample functions are sine waves with random phase was found as an ensemble average in Example 9.6. Let us now calculate the time-average correlation function, which is

$$\lim_{T \to \infty} \frac{1}{2T} \int_{-T}^{T} x(\lambda)x(\lambda + \tau) \, d\lambda$$

$$= \lim_{T \to \infty} \frac{1}{2T} \int_{-T}^{T} \cos(\omega_0\lambda + \theta) \cos(\omega_0\lambda + \omega_0\tau + \theta) \, d\lambda$$

$$= \lim_{T \to \infty} \frac{1}{2T} \int_{-T}^{T} [\tfrac{1}{2} \cos(2\omega_0\lambda + \omega_0\tau + 2\theta) + \tfrac{1}{2} \cos \omega_0\tau] \, d\lambda$$

$$= \lim_{T \to \infty} \frac{1}{2T} \left[\frac{1}{4\omega_0} \sin(2\omega_0T + \omega_0\tau + 2\theta) \right.$$

$$\left. + \frac{1}{4\omega_0} \sin(2\omega_0T - \omega_0\tau - 2\theta) + T \cos \omega_0\tau \right]$$

$$= \tfrac{1}{2} \cos \omega_0\tau$$

† W. R. Bennett, Methods of Solving Noise Problems, *Proc. IRE*, vol. 44, pp. 609–638, May, 1956.
‡ Middleton, *loc. cit.*

This is the same expression as that obtained in Example 9.6, and is evidence of the ergodic nature of the process when the initial phase is uniformly distributed in $[0, 2\pi]$. It is not difficult to show that this process is indeed ergodic.

9.4 POWER SPECTRAL DENSITY

The basic method used for system analysis in the earlier chapters in both the time and the frequency domain consists in the decomposition of signals into simple elementary components. In particular, in the frequency-domain method this leads to the use of Fourier series coefficients for signals defined over a finite interval (or periodic signals) and the Fourier and Laplace transforms for nonperiodic signals defined over an infinite interval. While such signal decompositions are theoretically possible for random signals,† they involve many difficulties (the appropriate elementary functions are in general not exponentials and are difficult to find) and will not be used here. It is possible and very useful, however, to consider such a decomposition for the *signal power*.

We have already seen in Sec. 5.5 that, for a real signal $x(t)$ with Fourier transform‡ $X(\omega)$, we may regard $|X(\omega)|^2$ as the energy density spectrum, since (except for a constant of proportionality)

$$\text{Energy of } x(t) = \int_{-\infty}^{\infty} x^2(t)\, dt = \int_{-\infty}^{\infty} |X(\omega)|^2\, \frac{d\omega}{2\pi} \qquad (9.38)$$

The quantity $x^2(t)$ is the instantaneous power associated with $x(t)$. The average power of $x(t)$ is

$$\text{Average power} = \lim_{T \to \infty} \frac{1}{2T} \int_{-T}^{T} x^2(t)\, dt \qquad (9.39)$$

It is possible that the total energy of $x(t)$ is infinite, but that the average power is finite. This is the case, for example, with a steady or a sinusoidal current. The question arises whether we can define a spectral density

† See, for example, W. B. Davenport, Jr., and W. L. Root, "An Introduction to the Theory of Random Signals and Noise," McGraw-Hill Book Company, New York, 1958.

‡ The Fourier transform may be regarded as a function of $j\omega = j2\pi f$ or as a function of ω. In connection with random signals, the frequency f is frequently used as the variable, but we shall continue to use ω as the variable as in Chap. 5. Note also that $X(\omega)$ is here used to denote the Fourier transform of a signal which may be one of the sample functions of a random process, while $X(t)$ was also used to denote the random variable obtained from the random process $\{x(t)\}$ at time t. Since in the following treatment the Fourier transforms of truncated sample functions are denoted by $X_T(\omega)$, no confusion should arise.

for the power so that the integral of this spectral density over all values of frequency will equal the average power.

Since $x(t)$ may not have a Fourier transform if its energy is not finite, it is convenient to define the *truncated* signal corresponding to $x(t)$ as

$$x_T(t) = \begin{cases} x(t) & |t| \le T \\ 0 & |t| > T \end{cases} \tag{9.40}$$

with its corresponding Fourier transform

$$X_T(\omega) = \int_{-\infty}^{\infty} x_T(t)e^{-j\omega t}\, dt = \int_{-T}^{T} x(t)e^{-j\omega t}\, dt \tag{9.41}$$

It is clear that as $T \to \infty$, the truncated signal approaches $x(t)$. The average power of $x(t)$ over the interval $(-T, T)$ may now be written

$$\frac{1}{2T} \int_{-T}^{T} x^2(t)\, dt = \int_{-\infty}^{\infty} \frac{x_T{}^2(t)}{2T}\, dt = \int_{-\infty}^{\infty} \frac{|X_T(\omega)|^2}{2T}\, \frac{d\omega}{2\pi}$$

in view of (9.38). It is thus reasonable to consider the quantity $|X_T(\omega)|^2/2T$ as the *power spectral density* of the signal $x(t)$ in the interval $(-T, T)$.

If we are dealing with a random process, we may associate with each sample function $x(t)$ a truncated sample function $x_T(t)$, its Fourier transform $X_T(\omega)$, and its power spectral density. The power spectral density $W_x(\omega)$ of the random process is defined as the limit of the ensemble average of the power spectral densities of its truncated sample functions:†

$$W_x(\omega) = \lim_{T \to \infty} \frac{1}{2T} \overline{|X_T(\omega)|^2} = \lim_{T \to \infty} \frac{1}{2T} \overline{X_T(\omega)X_T^*(\omega)} \tag{9.42}$$

where $X_T^*(\omega)$ is the complex conjugate of $X_T(\omega)$. Here, and subsequently when ensemble averages are taken, $X_T(\omega)$ denotes a random variable.

Example 9.9 To illustrate the computation of the power spectral density of a random process by means of (9.42), consider again the random process of Example 9.7.

Any sample function of the process may be represented in the interval $[-N, N]$ by

$$x(t) = \sum_{k=-N}^{N} a_k p_1(t - k + r)$$

where a_k = amplitude in interval $[k, k + 1)$
$\quad p_1(t)$ = unit-pulse function of Fig. 3.1
$\quad\quad r$ = value of a random variable which is uniformly distributed in interval $[0, 1]$

† In the definition of power spectral density, the unit of frequency is cps. If the unit of frequency is rad/sec, a factor $1/(2\pi)$ is required on the right-hand side of (9.42).

Note that $2N + 1$ pulses are included, so that $x(t)$ is defined in $[-N, N]$ regardless of the value of r. The Fourier transform of the truncated sample function is

$$
X_N(\omega) = \int_{-N}^{N} \sum_{k=-N}^{N} a_k p_1(t - k + r)e^{-j\omega t}\, dt
$$

$$
= \sum_{k=-N+1}^{N-1} a_k \int_{k-r}^{k+1-r} e^{-j\omega t}\, dt + a_{-N} \int_{-N}^{-N-r+1} e^{-j\omega t}\, dt
$$

$$
+ a_N \int_{N-r}^{N} e^{-j\omega t}\, dt
$$

The last two terms are due to the first and last pulses in the interval $[-N, N]$. It can readily be shown (Prob. 9.20) that they do not contribute to the power spectral density, and they will therefore be neglected. Then

$$
X_N(\omega) = \frac{\sin (\omega/2)}{\omega/2} \sum_{k=-N+1}^{N-1} a_k e^{-j\omega(k-r+\frac{1}{2})}
$$

Multiplying $X_N(\omega)$ by its complex conjugate and dividing by the interval length $2N$, we obtain

$$
\frac{X_N(\omega)X_N^*(\omega)}{2N} = \frac{1}{2N} \frac{\sin^2 (\omega/2)}{\omega^2/4} \sum_{k=-N+1}^{N-1} \sum_{m=-N+1}^{N-1} a_k a_m e^{-j\omega(k-m)}
$$

In order to take the ensemble average, we note that

$$
\overline{a_k a_m} = \begin{cases} 0 & k \neq m \ (\text{since } \overline{a_k} = 0) \\ 1 & k = m \end{cases}
$$

Therefore the ensemble average of the double sum reduces to $2N - 1$, and

$$
\frac{\overline{X_N(\omega)X_N^*(\omega)}}{2N} = \frac{2N - 1}{2N} \frac{\sin^2(\omega/2)}{(\omega/2)^2}
$$

The limit as $N \to \infty$ gives the power spectral density as

$$
W_x(\omega) = \frac{\sin^2(\omega/2)}{(\omega/2)^2}
$$

In the next section, we shall find another, frequently simpler, method for the calculation of the power spectral density.

Example 9.10 We now compute the power spectral density for the random process whose sample functions are cosine waves with random

initial phase, as in Example 9.1.   We find for a sample function

$$X_T(\omega) = \int_{-T}^{T} \cos(\omega_0 t + \theta) e^{-j\omega t} \, dt$$

$$= \frac{\sin(\omega_0 - \omega)T}{\omega_0 - \omega} e^{j\theta} + \frac{\sin(\omega_0 + \omega)T}{\omega_0 + \omega} e^{-j\theta}$$

Hence

$$|X_T(\omega)|^2 = X_T(\omega) X_T^*(\omega)$$

$$= \frac{\sin^2(\omega_0 - \omega)T}{(\omega_0 - \omega)^2} + \frac{\sin^2(\omega_0 + \omega)T}{(\omega_0 + \omega)^2}$$

$$+ \frac{\sin(\omega_0 - \omega)T \sin(\omega_0 + \omega)T}{(\omega_0 - \omega)(\omega_0 + \omega)} 2 \cos 2\theta$$

The ensemble average of the last term vanishes if the random variable is distributed uniformly in the interval $[0, 2\pi]$ or the interval $[0, \pi]$.   Thus

$$W_x(\omega) = \lim_{T \to \infty} \frac{1}{2T} \overline{|X_T(\omega)|^2}$$

$$= \lim_{T \to \infty} \frac{1}{2T} \left[\frac{\sin^2(\omega_0 - \omega)T}{(\omega_0 - \omega)^2} + \frac{\sin^2(\omega_0 + \omega)T}{(\omega_0 + \omega)^2} \right]$$

For $\omega \neq \omega_0$, the quantity in the brackets is bounded and in the limit $W_x(\omega) \to 0$.   If $\omega = \pm \omega_0$, one of the terms in the brackets is of order T^2, so that the limit does not exist.   Integrating either term over all frequencies, however, we find

$$\int_{-\infty}^{\infty} \frac{1}{2T} \frac{\sin^2(\omega_0 \pm \omega)T}{(\omega_0 \pm \omega)^2} \, d\omega = \frac{1}{2} \int_{-\infty}^{\infty} \frac{\sin^2 u}{u^2} \, du$$

$$= \tfrac{1}{2}\pi$$

Thus each of the two terms, whose sum in the limit is $W_x(\omega)$, satisfies the definition of an impulse function of strength $\pi/2$, and

$$W_x(\omega) = \frac{\pi}{2} [\delta(\omega - \omega_0) + \delta(\omega + \omega_0)] = \tfrac{1}{4}[\delta(f - f_0) + \delta(f + f_0)]$$

This result is entirely reasonable since the sample functions are single-frequency sine waves.   No contribution is made to the average power by angular frequencies different from $\pm \omega_0$.   The total average power is

$$\int_{-\infty}^{\infty} \frac{W_x(\omega) \, d\omega}{2\pi} = \tfrac{1}{4} + \tfrac{1}{4} = \tfrac{1}{2}$$

It is usually not convenient to calculate the power spectral density from the definition (9.42).   We shall now show that, for a stationary

process, $W_x(\omega)$ is the Fourier transform of the correlation function. Replacing $X_T(\omega)$ in (9.42) by its definition (9.41), we have

$$
\begin{aligned}
W_x(\omega) &= \lim_{T \to \infty} \frac{1}{2T} \overline{X_T(\omega) X_T^*(\omega)} \\
&= \lim_{T \to \infty} \frac{1}{2T} E\left[\int_{-T}^{T} X(t) e^{-j\omega t} \, dt \int_{-T}^{T} X(t) e^{j\omega t} \, dt \right] \\
&= \lim_{T \to \infty} \frac{1}{2T} E\left[\int_{-T}^{T} dt_1 \int_{-T}^{T} dt_2 \, X(t_1) X(t_2) e^{-j\omega(t_1 - t_2)} \right] \quad (9.43)
\end{aligned}
$$

If we first carry out the indicated ensemble averaging, we note that

$$
E[X(t_1) X(t_2)] = r_x(t_1, t_2)
$$

If we now assume that the random process $\{x(t)\}$ is wide-sense stationary,

$$
W_x(\omega) = \lim_{T \to \infty} \frac{1}{2T} \int_{-T}^{T} dt_1 \int_{-T}^{T} dt_2 \, r_x(t_1 - t_2) e^{-j\omega(t_1 - t_2)}
$$

The integrand is now a function of $t_1 - t_2$ only, and the double integral may be written as a single integral by the changes of variable,

$$
u = t_1 - t_2 \qquad v = t_1 + t_2
$$

which correspond to a rotation of the axes of 45° and a scale change of $\sqrt{2}$. Since the Jacobian is

$$
J = \left| \frac{\partial(u, v)}{\partial(t_1, t_2)} \right| = \begin{vmatrix} 1 & -1 \\ 1 & 1 \end{vmatrix} = 2
$$

we have

$$
\begin{aligned}
\int_{-T}^{T} dt_1 \int_{-T}^{T} dt_2 \, g(t_1 - t_2) &= \frac{1}{2} \int_{-2T}^{2T} du \int_{-2T+|u|}^{2T-|u|} g(u) \, dv \\
&= \int_{-2T}^{2T} (2T - |u|) g(u) \, du \quad (9.44)
\end{aligned}
$$

Using this result in the expression for $W_x(\omega)$, we obtain

$$
\begin{aligned}
W_x(\omega) &= \lim_{T \to \infty} \frac{1}{2T} \int_{-2T}^{2T} (2T - |u|) r_x(u) e^{-j\omega u} \, du \\
&= \lim_{T \to \infty} \int_{-2T}^{2T} \left(1 - \frac{|u|}{2T} \right) r_x(u) e^{-j\omega u} \, du \\
&= \int_{-\infty}^{\infty} r_x(u) e^{-j\omega u} \, du \quad (9.45)
\end{aligned}
$$

Thus, for a stationary process, the power spectral density is the Fourier transform of the correlation function.† This relation may be used as

† Although for Fourier transforms we use capital letters which correspond to the letter used for the time function, the symbol W is chosen here because it is widely employed for the power spectral density.

the definition of $W_x(\omega)$.   Such a definition avoids mathematical difficulties which arise with the definition of (9.42) for many random processes, but it does not have the same intuitive appeal.

From (9.45), we immediately obtain $r_x(\tau)$ as the inverse Fourier transform of $W_x(\omega)$:

$$r_x(\tau) = \frac{1}{2\pi} \int_{-\infty}^{\infty} W_x(\omega) e^{j\omega\tau} \, d\omega \qquad (9.46)$$

The relationships between the power spectral density and the correlation function given in (9.45) and (9.46) are known as the *Wiener-Khintchine theorem*.

It follows from the definition (9.42) that $W_x(\omega)$ is an even function of frequency for a real random process; we already know that in this case $r_x(\tau)$ is an even function of its argument.   The pair of Fourier transforms (9.45) and (9.46) may be written in slightly different form by expanding the exponential and making use of the symmetry in $W_x(\omega)$ and $r_x(\tau)$.   Thus

$$W_x(\omega) = \int_{-\infty}^{\infty} r_x(\tau) \cos \omega\tau \, d\tau + j \int_{-\infty}^{\infty} r_x(\tau) \sin \omega\tau \, d\tau$$

The second integral vanishes since the integrand is an odd function of τ. Thus

$$W_x(\omega) = 2 \int_{0}^{\infty} r_x(\tau) \cos \omega\tau \, d\tau \qquad (9.47)$$

Similarly, we find

$$r_x(\tau) = \frac{1}{\pi} \int_{0}^{\infty} W_x(\omega) \cos \omega\tau \, d\omega \qquad (9.48)$$

Example 9.11   The power spectral density of the process described in Example 9.7 may be obtained from the correlation function (9.28). Use of (9.47) gives

$$W_x(\omega) = 2 \int_{0}^{1} (1 - \tau) \cos \omega\tau \, d\tau$$

$$= \frac{2}{\omega^2} (1 - \cos \omega)$$

$$= \left(\frac{\sin (\omega/2)}{\omega/2} \right)^2$$

This agrees with the result of Example 9.9.   The correlation function and power spectral density are shown in Fig. 9.7.

Example 9.12   The correlation function of the random process of Example 9.1 in Example 9.6 was found to be

$$r_x(\tau) = \tfrac{1}{2} \cos \omega_0\tau$$

Hence

$$W_x(\omega) = \mathfrak{F}\,[r_x(\tau)]$$

$$= \frac{1}{2} \int_{-\infty}^{\infty} \cos \omega_0 \tau\, e^{-j\omega \tau}\, d\tau$$

$$= \frac{1}{4} \int_{-\infty}^{\infty} [e^{-j(\omega - \omega_0)\tau} + e^{-j(\omega + \omega_0)\tau}]\, d\tau$$

Since the integrals are the Fourier integral representations of impulse functions, we may write

$$W_x(\omega) = \frac{\pi}{2}\,[\delta(\omega - \omega_0) + \delta(\omega + \omega_0)]$$

as found in Example 9.10.

Several useful relations may be obtained from the Wiener-Khintchine theorem. If we set $\omega = 0$ in (9.45), we obtain

$$W_x(0) = \int_{-\infty}^{\infty} r_x(\tau)\, d\tau \tag{9.49}$$

Thus the total area under the correlation function equals the power spectral density at zero frequency. If the random process includes a steady component $\bar{X}$ but no other periodic components, the correlation function was seen to approach $\bar{X}^2$ as $\tau \to \infty$; the spectral density then has an impulse component of strength $\bar{X}^2$ at $\omega = 0$. If we set $\tau = 0$ in (9.46), we find

$$r_x(0) = \int_{-\infty}^{\infty} W_x(\omega)\, \frac{d\omega}{2\pi} \tag{9.50}$$

Since $r_x(0) = E[X^2(t)]$, the left-hand side represents the average power in $X(t)$. Thus it is apparent that $W_x(\omega)$ is the power spectral density [even if it had been defined not by (9.42) but by (9.45)].

9.5 SOME COMMON RANDOM PROCESSES

WHITE NOISE

A random process whose power spectral density is constant at all frequencies is called a *white-noise process*. An ideal white-noise process thus implies infinite average power [(9.50)] and is physically impossible. It is frequently convenient, however, to use a white-noise approximation to an actual process whose spectral density is nearly flat over a frequency band which is large compared with that of the system through which

it passes, since the error in the spectral density is then of no consequence. White noise is thus characterized by a power spectral density

$$W(\omega) = W_0$$

and a correlation function

$$r(\tau) = W_0 \delta(\tau)$$

where W_0 is the average power per cycle per second.

White noise which is passed through a lumped-parameter network produces a process with a rational power spectral density (Chap. 10). Conversely, it is frequently convenient to think of a random process as generated by passing white noise through an appropriate filter.

The thermal noise generated in a resistor due to the random motion of free electrons has a nearly flat power spectral density and is thus usually considered to be white noise. Another example is the shot noise due to the random emission of electrons from the cathode in a temperature-limited diode. This noise process is also approximately white provided that the frequency of operation is small compared with the reciprocal of the electron transit time of the diode.

GAUSSIAN RANDOM PROCESS

A random process $\{x(t)\}$ is a *Gaussian* (or *normal*) *random process* if the variables $X_1 = X(t_1)$, $X_2 = X(t_2)$, . . . , $X_n = X(t_n)$ have a jointly (n-dimensional) Gaussian probability distribution for any set of values $t_1, t_2, \ldots, t_n$ and any value of n. If we write $\bar{X}_i = m_i$ for the means, the n-dimensional density function is given by

$$p_n(x_1, t_1; x_2, t_2; \cdots; x_n, t_n)$$
$$= \frac{1}{(2\pi)^{n/2} \sqrt{|\mathbf{\Lambda}|}} \exp -\tfrac{1}{2}(\mathbf{x} - \mathbf{m})' \mathbf{\Lambda}^{-1} (\mathbf{x} - \mathbf{m}) \quad (9.51)$$

where $\mathbf{x} = \text{col} [x_1, x_2, \ldots, x_n]$, $\mathbf{m} = \text{col} [m_1, m_2, \ldots, m_n]$ and $|\mathbf{\Lambda}|$ is the determinant of the covariance matrix

$$\mathbf{\Lambda} = \begin{bmatrix} \lambda_{11} & \lambda_{12} & \cdots & \lambda_{1n} \\ \lambda_{21} & \lambda_{22} & \cdots & \lambda_{2n} \\ \cdots & \cdots & \cdots & \cdots \\ \lambda_{n1} & \lambda_{n2} & \cdots & \lambda_{nn} \end{bmatrix}$$

whose elements are the covariances

$$\lambda_{ij} = E[(X_i - m_i)(X_j - m_j)] = \sigma_i \sigma_j \rho_{ij} = r_x(t_i, t_j) - m_i m_j$$

[see (9.26) and (9.27)]. For a wide-sense stationary process,

$$m_i = m_j = m \qquad \sigma_i = \sigma_j = \sigma$$

and $r_x(t_i, t_j)$ depends only on $t_i - t_j$; (9.51) shows that in this case the process is also stationary in the strict sense.

If the set of values $t_1, \ldots, t_n$ is so chosen that the variables $X_1, \ldots, X_n$ are uncorrelated, i.e., that

$$\lambda_{ij} = \begin{cases} 0 & \text{for } i \neq j \\ \sigma_i{}^2 & \text{for } i = j \end{cases}$$

then $\boldsymbol{\Lambda}$ is a diagonal matrix with diagonal elements $\sigma_i{}^2$, and $\boldsymbol{\Lambda}^{-1}$ is diagonal with diagonal elements $1/\sigma_i{}^2$. It follows that the exponent in (9.51) is

$$-\tfrac{1}{2}(\mathbf{x} - \mathbf{m})'\boldsymbol{\Lambda}^{-1}(\mathbf{x} - \mathbf{m}) = -\frac{1}{2} \sum_{i=1}^{n} \frac{1}{\sigma_i{}^2} (x_i - m_i)^2$$

The joint density function then is a product of n first-order density functions, which shows that the random variables $X_1, \ldots, X_n$ are independent. The fact that zero correlation implies independence is true only for random variables with a jointly Gaussian distribution, for only in this case is the complete joint statistical behavior specified by second-order moments. In the special case of stationary white Gaussian noise, the random variables $X_1, \ldots, X_n$ are uncorrelated and hence independent regardless of the choice of $t_1, \ldots, t_n$.

The joint characteristic function [see (9.23)] of the jointly Gaussian variables $X_1, \ldots, X_n$ is

$$M_n(u_1, \ldots, u_n; t_1, \ldots, t_n) = \exp\left(j\mathbf{m}'\mathbf{u} - \tfrac{1}{2}\mathbf{u}'\boldsymbol{\Lambda}\mathbf{u}\right) \quad (9.52)$$

where $\mathbf{u}$ is the column vector with components $u_1, \ldots, u_n$. The use of this characteristic function is illustrated in Example 9.15.

For a single variable $X = X(t)$, the (first-order) Gaussian probability density is

$$p(x) = \frac{1}{\sqrt{2\pi}\,\sigma} e^{-\frac{(x-m)^2}{2\sigma^2}} \quad (9.53)$$

where m and σ^2 denote the mean and variance, respectively. For the two random variables $X_1 = X(t_1)$ and $X_2 = X(t_2)$, the two-dimensional Gaussian density function is

$$p(x_1, x_2) = \frac{1}{2\pi\sigma_1\sigma_2\sqrt{1-\rho^2}} \exp\left\{-\frac{1}{1-\rho^2}\left[\frac{(x_1-m_1)^2}{2\sigma_1{}^2}\right.\right.$$
$$\left.\left. - \rho\,\frac{(x_1-m_1)(x_2-m_2)}{\sigma_1\sigma_2} + \frac{(x_2-m_2)^2}{2\sigma_2{}^2}\right]\right\} \quad (9.54)$$

where ρ is the correlation coefficient given by (9.27).

Random processes are often approximately Gaussian if the sample functions are made up of many superposed effects, so that the central-limit theorem[†] is applicable. Thus the thermal noise voltage in a resistor is due to the sum of a large number of pulses, and the resulting noise voltage is very nearly a Gaussian process.

In addition to its frequent occurrence, the Gaussian process is important since its density functions of all orders are determined by the covariances of all pairs of variables; no higher-order moments are needed. Further, a linear transformation of a set of jointly Gaussian random variables results in a new set of jointly Gaussian random variables. As a consequence, a Gaussian process passing through a linear system again emerges as a Gaussian process.

MARKOV PROCESSES

Markov processes characterize physical phenomena with a special kind of memory. A random process $\{x(t)\}$ is a Markov process if the value of $X_n = X(t_n)$ depends on the values of X at a set of earlier instants only through the last available value X_{n-1}. We require that, for any n and any choice of $(t_1, t_2, \ldots, t_n)$, the conditional density function for X_n satisfy the relation

$$p_n(x_n, t_n | x_1, t_1; \ldots ; x_{n-1}, t_{n-1}) = p_n(x_n, t_n | x_{n-1}, t_{n-1}) \qquad (9.55)$$

It follows that the joint probability density function may be written

$$
\begin{aligned}
p(x_1, t_1; \ldots ; x_n, t_n) &= p_1(x_1)p_2(x_2|x_1)p_3(x_3|x_1, x_2) \cdots \\
&= p_1(x_1)p_2(x_2|x_1)p_3(x_3|x_2) \cdots \\
&= p_1(x_1) \prod_{i=2}^{n} p_i(x_i|x_{i-1})
\end{aligned}
$$

where the parameters $t_1, \ldots, t_n$ have been omitted for convenience. A Markov process is thus defined by the conditional density functions $p_i(x_i|x_{i-1})$ for any i and the density function $p_1(x_1)$.

It can be shown[‡] that a stationary Gaussian process can be a Markov process only if the autocorrelation function is

$$r(\tau) = e^{-a|\tau|}$$

[†] See, for example, Parzen, *op. cit.*, sec. 8.5.
[‡] J. L. Doob, The Brownian Movement and Stochastic Equations, *Ann. Math.*, vol. 43, pp. 351–369, April, 1942, reprinted in N. Wax (ed.), "Selected Papers on Noise and Stochastic Processes," Dover Publications, Inc., New York, 1954. See also J. S. Bendat, "Principles and Applications of Random Noise Theory," pp. 215–217, John Wiley & Sons, Inc., New York, 1958.

where a is a positive constant.   The corresponding power spectral density is

$$W(\omega) = \frac{2a}{\omega^2 + a^2}$$

The correlation over a time interval τ thus decreases exponentially, and this is very nearly the case in many noise processes.

If the time variable is discrete, (9.55) describes a discrete-time Markov process.   If the random variable also assumes discrete values $1, 2, \ldots, k$, the sequence of values taken by X is called a *Markov chain*, and the k possible values of X are the states of the system.   The Markov chain thus specifies the time sequence of states of the system in which the conditional probability of reaching a particular state at a time n depends only on the state which occurred at time $n - 1$.   The probability that the system at time n is in state j, given that at time $n - 1$ it was in state i, may be denoted by $P(j|i)$, called the *transition probability*.   If the total number of states is k, the transition probabilities form a matrix

$$\mathbf{P} = \begin{bmatrix} P(1|1) & P(2|1) & \cdots & P(k|1) \\ P(1|2) & P(2|2) & \cdots & P(k|2) \\ \multicolumn{4}{c}{\dotfill} \\ P(1|k) & P(2|k) & \cdots & P(k|k) \end{bmatrix} \tag{9.56}$$

It is assumed here that the transition probabilities are independent of n; the Markov chain is then called *homogeneous* (and is analogous to a stationary random process).

The r-step transition probability $P_r(j|i)$ is defined as the conditional probability that the system is in state j at time n, given that it was in state i at time $n - r$.   Since state j is reached with probability $P(j|m)$ if the state at $n - 1$ was m, it is seen that

$$P_r(j|i) = \sum_{m=1}^{k} P_{r-1}(m|i)P(j|m) \tag{9.57}$$

or

$$\mathbf{P}_r = \mathbf{P}_{r-1}\mathbf{P} \qquad r > 1 \tag{9.58}$$

where $\mathbf{P}_r$ is the matrix of r-step transition probabilities similar to (9.56) for the one-step transition probabilities.

Example 9.13   A digital communication system transmits a sequence of two binary digits.   The probability of an error in a digit (a change from 0 to 1 or from 1 to 0) is $\frac{1}{3}$; the errors in successive digits are independent.

The transition probability matrix for the four states (00, 01, 10, 11) is thus

$$\mathbf{P} = \frac{1}{9} \begin{bmatrix} 4 & 2 & 2 & 1 \\ 2 & 4 & 1 & 2 \\ 2 & 1 & 4 & 2 \\ 1 & 2 & 2 & 4 \end{bmatrix}$$

If the digits pass through two such systems (e.g., to an active communication satellite and back), the two-step transition probability matrix is

$$\mathbf{P}_2 = \mathbf{PP} = \frac{1}{81} \begin{bmatrix} 25 & 20 & 20 & 16 \\ 20 & 25 & 16 & 20 \\ 20 & 16 & 25 & 20 \\ 16 & 20 & 20 & 25 \end{bmatrix}$$

The probability of receiving (00) when (00) is sent is thus $\frac{25}{81}$. This may be verified as follows. The probability of no error in each of the two steps is $(\frac{2}{3})^2 = \frac{4}{9}$, and the probability of obtaining (00) as output as the result of no errors is thus $(\frac{4}{9})^2 = \frac{16}{81}$. In addition, (00) may be received as the result of multiple canceling errors. The transmission may give the sequences $(00, 01, 00)$ and $(00, 10, 00)$ with probability $(\frac{2}{9})^2 = \frac{4}{81}$ each, and $(00, 11, 00)$ with probability $(\frac{1}{9})^2 = \frac{1}{81}$. The total probability of receiving (00) when (00) is sent is thus $(16 + 4 + 4 + 1)/81 = \frac{25}{81}$, as shown in the matrix $\mathbf{P}_2$.

9.6 POWER SPECTRAL DENSITY OF DISCRETE-TIME PROCESSES

In many practical situations the noisy data are obtained at discrete equally spaced instants, and we must deal with discrete-time random processes. Examples of such data are the returns from a scanning radar and the output of a digital computer. In this section, the correlation function and power spectral density of stationary discrete-time processes and their relation to the corresponding quantities for continuous-time processes are discussed.

The correlation function of a stationary discrete-time process is defined, as was noted in Sec. 9.2, only at discrete time intervals. If the sample functions are defined at intervals of T sec, the correlation function of a process $\{x(kT)\}$ is defined by

$$r_x(nT) = E[X(kT)X(kT + nT)] \qquad n = 0, \pm 1, \pm 2, \ldots \qquad (9.59)$$

In order to define the power spectral density of a stationary discrete-time process, we may proceed in two ways. We may use a definition analogous to (9.45) by applying the Z transform, or we may use the sampling theorem and deal with any continuous-time process whose values at the instants $t = kT$ equal those of the given discrete-time process. We shall consider both approaches in turn.

Since the sample functions of a stationary random process must necessarily extend into the past, the two-sided Z transform defined by (8.2) must be used. Thus we can define the power spectral density of the process $\{x(kT)\}$ as[†]

$$W'_x(z) = T\mathsf{Z}_{II}[r_x(nT)] = T \sum_{n=-\infty}^{\infty} r_x(nT)z^{-n} \qquad (9.60)$$

The factor T is used in order to make the dimensions of $W'_x(z)$ identical with those of $W_x(\omega)$ defined by (9.42) or (9.45). The correlation function may be obtained, when $W'_x(z)$ is known, by any of the Z-transform inversion methods discussed in Sec. 8.3.

If we set $n = 0$ in the inversion formula (8.3), we obtain

$$r_x(0) = \frac{1}{2\pi jT} \oint W'_x(z)z^{-1}\,dz$$

The contour of integration is the unit circle, since, by virtue of the symmetry of $r_x(nT)$, each pole at z_i outside the unit circle corresponds to one at $1/z_i$ inside the unit circle. With $z = e^{j\omega T}$ as in Sec. 8.9,[‡] we find

$$r_x(0) = \int_0^{2\pi/T} W'_x(e^{j\omega T}) \frac{d\omega}{2\pi} \qquad (9.61)$$

Thus $W'_x(z)$ is seen again to represent a power spectral density which corresponds to the average power in $\{x(nT)\}$ when integrated over a frequency range of $2\pi/T$ rad/sec.

While the discrete data may be all that is available, we may construct a continuous-time sample function $y(t)$ whose values at the sampling instants $t = kT$ equal the actual sampled values $x(kT)$. The sampling theorem (Sec. 5.7§) permits us to construct a band-limited signal $y(t)$

[†] The prime on $W'_x(z)$ is used to avoid confusion with the different function $W_x(\omega)$.

[‡] Note that replacement of z by $e^{j\omega T}$ can be interpreted as the representation of the discrete-time signal $x(kT)$ by a train of impulses of strength $x(kT)$.

§ See also J. M. Whittaker, "Interpolatory Function Theory," Cambridge Tracts in Mathematics and Mathematical Physics, no. 33, Cambridge University Press, New York, 1935, and C. E. Shannon, Communication in the Presence of Noise, *Proc. IRE*, vol. 37, pp. 10–21, January, 1949.

which contains no frequencies greater than $F = 1/2T$.   The signal is

$$y(t) = \sum_{k=-\infty}^{\infty} x(kT) \frac{\sin \pi(t/T - k)}{\pi(t/T - k)} \tag{9.62}$$

It should be noted that the signal $x(t)$ from which $x(kT)$ is obtained by sampling may not be band-limited, but if it is sampled at intervals of $1/T$ sec, we have no information about its frequency content at frequencies greater than $F = 1/2T$ cps.   The signal $y(t)$, on the other hand, is band-limited by construction.   It is, in fact, the signal which appears at the output of an ideal low-pass filter if the input consists of a sequence of impulses of strength $x(kT)$.   Thus no conclusion about $x(t)$ requiring knowledge of frequencies outside the band can be drawn from any properties of $x(kT)$.   If we set $t = nT$ in (9.62), we find that

$$y(nT) = x(nT) \tag{9.63}$$

Thus the sampled values of $y(t)$ actually equal the given data values.

The ensemble of sample functions $x(t)$ has a correlation function $r_x(\tau)$ and a power spectral density $W_x(\omega)$ which, according to (9.46), are related by

$$r_x(\tau) = \frac{1}{2\pi} \int_{-\infty}^{\infty} W_x(\omega)e^{j\omega\tau}\, d\omega \tag{9.64}$$

Note that, at $\tau = nT$, this correlation function equals that of the discrete-time process, justifying use of the same function r_x as in (9.59).   We can now establish a relation between the spectral density $W_x(\omega)$ of the continuous-time process $\{x(t)\}$ and the spectral density $W'_x(z)$ of the discrete-time process $\{x(kT)\}$.   At $\tau = nT$, (9.64) gives

$$r_x(nT) = \frac{1}{2\pi} \int_{-\infty}^{\infty} W_x(\omega)e^{j\omega nT}\, d\omega$$

If we use this in (9.60) and replace z by $e^{j\omega T}$ as in Sec. 8.9, the result is

$$W'_x(e^{j\omega T}) = \frac{T}{2\pi} \sum_{n=-\infty}^{\infty} e^{-j\omega nT} \int_{-\infty}^{\infty} W_x(\omega')e^{j\omega' nT}\, d\omega'$$

This expression can readily be simplified with the aid of Poisson's summation formula (Prob. 5.8)

$$\frac{1}{2\pi} \sum_{n=-\infty}^{\infty} \int_{-\infty}^{\infty} g(\lambda)e^{jn\lambda}\, d\lambda = \sum_{n=-\infty}^{\infty} g(2\pi n) \tag{9.65}$$

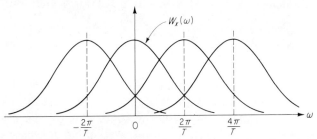

FIG. 9.8   Components of power spectral density of a discrete-time process.

We obtain, with $\lambda = (\omega' - \omega)T$,

$$W'_x(e^{j\omega T}) = \sum_{n=-\infty}^{\infty} W_x\left(\omega + \frac{2\pi n}{T}\right) \tag{9.66}$$

Thus the power spectral density of the discrete-time process is obtained by superposing the spectral density of the continuous-time process and replicas shifted by multiples of $2\pi/T$ rad/sec, the angular frequency at which the continuous-time process may be considered sampled to give the discrete-time process. As a result, the spectral density of the discrete-time process is made up of contributions from $W_x(\omega)$ around zero frequency and around all harmonics of the angular sampling frequency (Fig. 9.8). This effect is known as "sideband overlap" in telephony, or as "aliasing." It must be remembered, however, that in order to obtain this interpretation of $W'_x(z)$, we have implicitly replaced the discrete-time signal $x(kT)$ by a train of impulses of strength $x(kT)$, since this leads to the equivalence of z and $e^{j\omega T}$.

The use of (9.66) gives a good qualitative insight into the behavior of $W'_x(z)$, but is not well suited for calculation. If the power spectral density $W_x(\omega)$ is a known rational function of ω, the discrete-time power spectral density may be calculated by use of (8.48).

Since $r_x(\tau)$ is an even function, we may write (Prob. 6.16)

$$W_x(\omega) = R_x(\omega) + R_x(-\omega) \tag{9.67}$$

where $R_x(\omega)$ is the (one-sided) Laplace transform of $r_x(\tau)$ with $s = j\omega$ and has poles in the left-half s plane or upper-half ω plane only, while $R_x(-\omega)$ has poles in the right-half s plane or lower-half ω plane only. We may rewrite (9.60) as

$$W'_x(z) = T\left[\sum_{n=0}^{\infty} r_x(nT)z^{-n} + \sum_{n=0}^{\infty} r_x(nT)z^n - r_x(0) \right]$$

$$= T[R_x(z) + R_x(z^{-1}) - r_x(0)]$$

where $R_x(z)$ is the one-sided z transform of $r_x(nT)$. Using (8.48) for $R_x(z)$ with $w = j\omega$ and writing

$$r_x(0) = \frac{2}{2\pi} \int_{-\infty}^{\infty} R_x(\omega)\, d\omega$$

we obtain

$$W'_x(z) = T\frac{1}{2\pi} \int_{-\infty}^{\infty} R_x(\omega) \left(\frac{1}{1 - z^{-1}e^{j\omega T}} + \frac{1}{1 - ze^{j\omega T}} - 2 \right) d\omega$$

$$= \frac{T}{2\pi} \int_{-\infty}^{\infty} R_x(\omega) \frac{(z - 2e^{j\omega T} + z^{-1})e^{j\omega T}}{(1 - z^{-1}e^{j\omega T})(1 - ze^{j\omega T})}\, d\omega \qquad (9.68)$$

In order to determine the sampled power spectral density, it is thus necessary only to break up $W_x(\omega)$ as in (9.67) and to evaluate the integral in (9.68) by means of the calculus of residues.

It is also possible to express the power spectral density $W_y(\omega)$ of the band-limited process $\{y(t)\}$ in terms of $W_x(\omega)$ of the continuous-time process $\{x(t)\}$ from which the samples $x(kT)$ are drawn. The details will not be given here.† The correlation function of $y(t)$ is computed using (9.62); the result is

$$r_y(\tau) = \sum_{k=-\infty}^{\infty} r_x(kT) \frac{\sin \pi(\tau/T + k)}{\pi(\tau/T + k)} \qquad (9.69)$$

From this, the power spectral density of $\{y(t)\}$ is obtained by (9.45) and subsequent integration as

$$W_y(\omega) = \begin{cases} T \displaystyle\sum_{k=-\infty}^{\infty} r_x(kT)e^{jk\omega T} & |\omega| < \dfrac{\pi}{T} \\ 0 & |\omega| > \dfrac{\pi}{T} \end{cases} \qquad (9.70)$$

If we substitute for $r_x(kT)$ its expression (9.46) in terms of $W_x(\omega)$ and use Poisson's summation formula, the result is

$$W_y(\omega) = \begin{cases} \displaystyle\sum_{n=-\infty}^{\infty} W_x\left(\omega + \frac{2\pi n}{T}\right) & |\omega| < \dfrac{\pi}{T} \\ 0 & |\omega| > \dfrac{\pi}{T} \end{cases} \qquad (9.71)$$

Thus the power spectral density of the band-limited process is identical with that of the discrete-time (impulse-modulated) process for frequencies below one-half the sampling frequency $1/T$ cps, and of course vanishes at higher frequencies. It is clear that the sideband-overlap, or aliasing,

† See W. R. Bennett, Methods of Solving Noise Problems, *Proc. IRE*, vol. 44, pp. 609–638, May, 1956.

effect must occur if we remember that, while the band-limited sample functions do not contain frequencies outside the band $|\omega| < \pi/T$, the sample values $x(kT)$ from which the functions $y(t)$ are constructed are affected by the higher-frequency components.

Example 9.14   Let us consider again the quantized random process of Examples 9.7 and 9.9 and determine the power spectral density of the discrete-time process obtained by sampling the given process.

If the process is sampled at intervals of $T = 1$ sec, we find from (9.28)

$$r_x(nT) = \begin{cases} 1 & n = 0 \\ 0 & n \neq 0 \end{cases}$$

Hence (9.60) gives

$$W'_x(z) = 1$$

The sampled process thus has a constant power spectral density. This is to be expected since the amplitudes at 1-sec intervals are independent, and with this low sampling rate the process is indistinguishable from a white-noise process.

If we increase the sampling rate by setting $T = \frac{1}{2}$ sec (since Fig. 9.7b shows that the spectral density is very small for $|\omega| > 2\pi$), we obtain from (9.28) and (9.60)

$$W'_x(z) = \tfrac{1}{2}(\tfrac{1}{2}z + 1 + \tfrac{1}{2}z^{-1}) \tag{9.72}$$

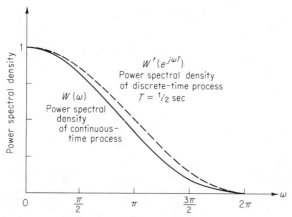

FIG. 9.9   Power spectral densities of continuous- and discrete-time processes of Examples 9.7 and 9.9.

or, with $z = e^{j\omega T} = e^{j\omega/2}$,

$$W(\omega) = W'_x(e^{j\omega/2}) = \frac{1}{2}\left(1 + \cos\frac{\omega}{2}\right) \tag{9.73}$$

For the band-limited process $\{y(t)\}$ obtained by using the $\frac{1}{2}$-sec samples, we thus have

$$W_y(\omega) = \begin{cases} \frac{1}{2}\left(1 + \cos\dfrac{\omega}{2}\right) & |\omega| < 2\pi \\ 0 & |\omega| > 2\pi \end{cases} \tag{9.74}$$

Graphs of the power spectral density obtained in Example 9.9 and of (9.73) are shown in Fig. 9.9. The graphs confirm that a $\frac{1}{2}$-sec sampling interval is a reasonable choice for the purpose of estimating the power spectral density of the process.

9.7 MULTIPLE RANDOM PROCESSES

We have until now been concerned with a single random process. Since even a simple system may have associated with it more than one random process, we are led to extend the definitions of Secs. 9.2 to 9.4 to two random processes. We may, for example, be interested in how the random processes at the input and the output of a linear system are related. Second-order statistics will be sufficient for our purposes in the analysis of linear systems. The use of second-order statistics will be illustrated in the discussion of filtering with linear systems in Chap. 10.

The joint characteristic function for several random variables was defined in (9.23); this definition may also be used for random variables arising from two or more random processes. Thus the joint characteristic function of the random variables $X(t_1)$ and $Y(t_2)$ derived from two random processes $\{x(t)\}$ and $\{y(t)\}$ is

$$\begin{aligned} M_{X,Y}(u, v; t_1, t_2) &= E[e^{juX(t)+jvY(t)}] \\ &= \int_{-\infty}^{\infty} \int_{-\infty}^{\infty} e^{jux+jvy}\, p_{X,Y}\,(x, t_1; y, t_2)\, dx\, dy \end{aligned} \tag{9.75}$$

which is the two-dimensional Fourier transform of the joint probability density function $p_{X,Y}(x, t_1; y, t_2)$. The inverse Fourier transform of $M_{X,Y}(u, v; t_1, t_2)$ thus gives the probability density function:

$$p_{X,Y}(x, t_1; y, t_2) = \frac{1}{(2\pi)^2} \int_{-\infty}^{\infty} \int_{-\infty}^{\infty} M_{X,Y}(u, v; t_1, t_2)e^{-jux-jvy}\, du\, dv \tag{9.76}$$

The subscripts X and Y will be omitted when there is no ambiguity.

It may readily be verified (Prob. 9.29) that

$$M_{X,Y}(u, 0; t_1, t_2) = M_X(u; t_1) \tag{9.77}$$

so that the joint characteristic function contains the one-dimensional characteristic functions. The joint moments may be obtained by differentiation of the joint characteristic function (Prob. 9.30):

$$E[X^k(t_1) Y^m(t_2)] = (-j)^{k+m} \frac{\partial^{k+m} M_{X,Y}(u, v; t_1, t_2)}{\partial u^k \partial v^m}\bigg]_{u,v=0} \tag{9.78}$$

Example 9.15 A narrowband signal (i.e., a signal whose frequency components are confined to a small band of frequencies), such as an amplitude-modulated carrier wave, may be represented by

$$g(t) = x(t) \cos \omega_0 t + y(t) \sin \omega_0 t$$

where ω_0 is the angular carrier frequency (or center frequency of the band), and $x(t)$, $y(t)$ are slowly varying signals. If $g(t)$ is a sample function of a stationary Gaussian process with zero mean, $x(t)$ and $y(t)$ are also sample functions of stationary Gaussian processes with zero mean. If the variance of $\{g(t)\}$ is σ^2, it can be shown† that

$$E[X^2(t)] = E[Y^2(t)] = \sigma^2$$
$$E[X(t)X(t + \tau)] = E[Y(t)Y(t + \tau)]$$
$$= \frac{1}{2\pi} \int_{-\infty}^{\infty} W_g(\omega) \cos (\omega\tau - \omega_0\tau) \, d\omega = \sigma^2\rho(\tau)$$
$$E[X(t)Y(t + \tau)] = 0$$

where $W_g(\omega)$ is the power spectral density of $\{g(t)\}$ and is symmetrical about $\omega = \omega_0$. Let us define the four random variables

$$X_1 = X(t) \qquad X_2 = X(t + \tau)$$
$$X_3 = Y(t) \qquad X_4 = Y(t + \tau)$$

The covariance matrix $\mathbf{\Lambda}$ of these four random variables is

$$\mathbf{\Lambda} = \sigma^2 \begin{bmatrix} 1 & \rho(\tau) & 0 & 0 \\ \rho(\tau) & 1 & 0 & 0 \\ 0 & 0 & 1 & \rho(\tau) \\ 0 & 0 & \rho(\tau) & 1 \end{bmatrix}$$

The determinant is

$$|\mathbf{\Lambda}| = \sigma^8(1 - \rho^2)^2$$

† S. O. Rice, Mathematical Analysis of Random Noise, *Bell System Tech. J.*, vol. 24, pp. 46–156 (Sec. 3.7), January, 1945, reprinted in Wax, *op. cit.* See also Davenport and Root, *op. cit.*, sec. 8-5.

The four-dimensional joint characteristic function is completely determined by the moment matrix according to (9.52):

$$M(u_1, u_2, u_3, u_4; \tau)$$
$$= \exp - \tfrac{1}{2}\mathbf{u}'\Lambda\mathbf{u}$$
$$= \exp - \tfrac{1}{2}\sigma^2[u_1{}^2 + u_2{}^2 + u_3{}^2 + u_4{}^2 + 2\rho(u_1 u_2 + u_3 u_4)]$$

If the sample functions $g(t)$ are applied to a square-law detector (i.e., a square-law device producing $g^2(t)$, followed by a low-pass filter), the output is proportional to

$$z(t) = x^2(t) + y^2(t)$$

We now want to determine the correlation function of $\{z(t)\}$. We find

$$r_z(\tau) = E[Z(t)Z(t + \tau)] = E[(X_1{}^2 + X_3{}^2)(X_2{}^2 + X_4{}^2)]$$
$$= E(X_1{}^2 X_2{}^2) + E(X_3{}^2 X_4{}^2) + E(X_1{}^2 X_4{}^2) + E(X_2{}^2 X_3{}^2)$$

These moments may be computed conveniently from the characteristic function. Use of (9.78) gives

$$E(X_1{}^2 X_2{}^2) = E(X_3{}^2 X_4{}^2) = \sigma^4(1 + 2\rho^2)$$

and

$$E(X_1{}^2 X_4{}^2) = E(X_2{}^2 X_3{}^2) = \sigma^4$$

Hence

$$r_z(\tau) = 4\sigma^4[1 + \rho^2(\tau)]$$

which is the desired result.

If the random processes $\{x(t)\}$ and $\{y(t)\}$ are independent (so that the random variables $X(t_1)$ and $Y(t_2)$ are independent for any t_1 and t_2), it follows from (9.75) that

$$M_{X,Y}(u, v; t_1, t_2) = M_X(u; t_1)M_Y(v; t_2)$$

i.e., that the joint characteristic function is the product of the individual characteristic functions. This important result may readily be extended to any number of random variables which are independent.

Corresponding to the autocorrelation function defined by (9.25), we define the *cross-correlation function* by

$$r_{xy}(t_1, t_2) = E[X(t_1)Y(t_2)] = \int_{-\infty}^{\infty}\int_{-\infty}^{\infty} xy p_{X,Y}(x, t_1; y, t_2)\, dx\, dy \quad (9.79)$$

If $\{x(t)\}$ and $\{y(t)\}$ are jointly stationary processes, the cross-correlation function depends only on $\tau = t_2 - t_1$, as does the autocorrelation function. Instead of (9.33), we find, however,

$$r_{xy}(-\tau) = E[X(t)Y(t - \tau)] = E[X(t + \tau)Y(t)] = E[Y(t)X(t + \tau)]$$

or

$$r_{xy}(-\tau) = r_{yx}(\tau) \quad (9.80)$$

so that the cross-correlation function is not in general symmetrical with respect to the origin $\tau = 0$.

In a manner similar to that used to establish (9.34), it may be shown (Prob. 9.32) that for two stationary processes

$$|r_{xy}(\tau)| \leq \sqrt{r_x(0)}\, \sqrt{r_y(0)} \tag{9.81}$$

Just as the autocorrelation function contains the same periodic components present in the process, so the cross-correlation function contains those periodic components which are present in both random processes. The detection of such common periodic components is one of the uses of the cross-correlation function.

It is interesting to consider the cross-correlation between $\{x(t)\}$ and the derivative process $\{\dot{y}(t)\}$. The cross-correlation function is

$$
\begin{aligned}
r_{x\dot{y}}(t_1, t_2) &= E[X(t_1)\dot{Y}(t_2)] \\
&= E\left[X(t_1) \lim_{\Delta \to 0} \frac{Y(t_2 + \Delta) - Y(t_2)}{\Delta} \right] \\
&= \lim_{\Delta \to 0} E\left[\frac{X(t_1)Y(t_2 + \Delta) - X(t_1)Y(t_2)}{\Delta} \right] \\
&= \lim_{\Delta \to 0} \frac{r_{xy}(t_1, t_2 + \Delta) - r_{xy}(t_1, t_2)}{\Delta}
\end{aligned}
$$

so that

$$r_{x\dot{y}}(t_1, t_2) = \frac{\partial r_{xy}(t_1, t_2)}{\partial t_2} \tag{9.82}$$

Similarly, we find

$$r_{\dot{x}\dot{y}}(t_1, t_2) = \frac{\partial^2 r_{xy}(t_1, t_2)}{\partial t_1\, \partial t_2} \tag{9.83}$$

If $\{x(t)\}$ and $\{y(t)\}$ are stationary processes, these relations become

$$r_{x\dot{y}}(\tau) = \frac{dr_{xy}(\tau)}{d\tau} \qquad r_{\dot{x}y}(\tau) = -\frac{dr_{xy}(\tau)}{d\tau} \tag{9.84}$$

$$r_{\dot{x}\dot{y}}(\tau) = -\frac{d^2 r_{xy}(\tau)}{d\tau^2} \tag{9.85}$$

The cross-power spectral density is defined, in a manner similar to (9.42), as

$$W_{xy}(\omega) = \lim_{T \to \infty} \frac{1}{2T}\, \overline{X_T^*(\omega)Y_T(\omega)} \tag{9.86}$$

It follows from this definition that

$$W_{xy}(\omega) = W_{yx}^*(\omega) \tag{9.87}$$

Note that $W_{xy}(\omega)$ is generally complex even for a real random process.

Proceeding exactly as in the case of one random process, we can show that, for jointly stationary processes, the cross-power spectral density is the Fourier transform of the cross-correlation function,

$$W_{xy}(\omega) = \int_{-\infty}^{\infty} r_{xy}(\tau) e^{-j\omega\tau} \, d\tau \tag{9.88}$$

The inverse thus gives

$$r_{xy}(\tau) = \frac{1}{2\pi} \int_{-\infty}^{\infty} W_{xy}(\omega) e^{j\omega\tau} \, d\omega \tag{9.89}$$

Example 9.16 Consider two jointly stationary processes $\{x(t)\}$ and $\{y(t)\}$ and let their sum be $\{z(t)\}$ with sample functions

$$z(t) = x(t) + y(t)$$

The correlation function of this random process is

$$
\begin{aligned}
r_z(\tau) &= E[Z(t)Z(t+\tau)] = E\{[X(t) + Y(t)][X(t+\tau) + Y(t+\tau)]\} \\
&= E[X(t)X(t+\tau) + X(t)Y(t+\tau) + X(t+\tau)Y(t) + Y(t)Y(t+\tau)]
\end{aligned}
$$

so that

$$r_z(\tau) = r_x(\tau) + r_{xy}(\tau) + r_{yx}(\tau) + r_y(\tau) \tag{9.90}$$

From (9.88), we immediately find

$$W_z(\omega) = W_x(\omega) + W_{xy}(\omega) + W_{yx}(\omega) + W_y(\omega) \tag{9.91}$$

In view of (9.87), this may be written

$$W_z(\omega) = W_x(\omega) + W_y(\omega) + 2 \operatorname{Re} W_{xy}(\omega) \tag{9.92}$$

Thus we may interpret twice the real part of the cross spectral density as the quantity which must be added to the sum of the separate spectral densities of the two processes to give the spectral density of the sum. Only if $\{x(t)\}$ and $\{y(t)\}$ are uncorrelated, so that the cross-correlation functions and cross spectral densities are zero, is

$$W_z(\omega) = W_x(\omega) + W_y(\omega)$$

It is seen from (9.86) and (9.87) that the real part of $W_{xy}(\omega)$ is an even function of frequency; the imaginary part is an odd function of frequency.

From the definition (9.86) of $W_{xy}(\omega)$ and the differentiation property of Fourier transforms (Prob. 5.12), we can readily determine the cross-power spectral density of $\{x(t)\}$ and the derivative process $\{\dot{y}(t)\}$. We find

$$W_{x\dot{y}}(\omega) = -W_{\dot{x}y}(\omega) = j\omega W_{xy}(\omega) \tag{9.93}$$
$$W_{\dot{x}\dot{y}} = \omega^2 W_{xy}(\omega) \tag{9.94}$$

As a special case of these relations, we note that

$$W_{x\dot{x}}(\omega) = j\omega W_x(\omega) \tag{9.95}$$

and

$$|W_{x\dot{x}}|^2 = \omega^2 W_x{}^2(\omega) = W_x(\omega)W_{\dot{x}}(\omega) \tag{9.96}$$

In view of (9.96), the process $\{x(t)\}$ and its derivative are said to be *fully correlated* (or coherent to second order). Since the cross-power spectral density (9.95) is purely imaginary, the two processes are further said to be in quadrature.

It will be seen in the next chapter that the factor ω^2 in (9.94) is a special case of $|H(j\omega)|^2$, the square of the magnitude of the transfer function, which in this case is that of a differentiator. Similarly, the factor $j\omega$ in (9.93) is the transfer function of the differentiator through which the process $\{x(t)\}$ must be passed in order to obtain $\{\dot{x}(t)\}$.

PROBLEMS

9.1   Find the characteristic function for the normal density function with mean m and standard deviation σ.

9.2   Two independent continuous random variables X and Y are distributed uniformly in the interval $[-a, a]$. If $Z = X + Y$, find:

(a) The characteristic function of Z.
(b) The probability density function of Z.
(c) The mean-square value of Z.

9.3   The n random variables $X_1, X_2, \ldots, X_n$ are independent, and each is uniformly distributed in the interval $[-a, a]$. Find the characteristic function of the sum

$$Y = \sum_{i=1}^{n} X_i$$

9.4   A continuous random variable X has the distribution function

$$P_X(x) = \begin{cases} 0 & x \le 0 \\ 1 - (1 + \lambda x)e^{-\lambda x} & x > 0 \end{cases}$$

where λ is a constant. Find:

(a) The characteristic function.
(b) The mean value.
(c) The mean-square value.
(d) The standard deviation.

9.5 Use the characteristic-function method to show that sums of independent random variables having the following density functions will have the same density functions as the variables themselves. Determine the new mean and standard deviation in each case.

(a) $p(x) = \sum_{i=0}^{\infty} \frac{\mu^i e^{-\mu}}{i!} \delta(x - i)$ $x \geq 0$ (Poisson distribution)

(b) $p(x) = \frac{1}{\sqrt{2\pi}\,\sigma} e^{-\frac{(x-m)^2}{2\sigma^2}}$ (normal distribution)

9.6 A random process consists of sample functions which are unit-step functions starting at $t = t_0$, where t_0 is the value of a random variable T_0 with probability density function

$$f(t_0) = \begin{cases} \dfrac{1}{T} & 0 \leq t_0 \leq T \\ 0 & \text{otherwise} \end{cases}$$

Find the characteristic function of this process.

9.7 The sample functions of a random process consist of sine waves

$$x(t) = a \cos(\omega_0 t + \theta)$$

where a and θ are values of independent random variables A and Θ. A has moments α_k, and Θ is distributed uniformly in the range $[0, \pi/2]$ and takes values outside this interval with zero probability. Find:

(a) The mean of the process $\{x(t)\}$.
(b) The correlation function of the process.
(c) The cross-correlation function between this process and a process with sample functions

$$y(t) = b \cos(\omega_0 t + \psi)$$

where B is distributed like A, ψ is distributed uniformly in $[0, 2\pi]$, and B, ψ are independent of each other and of A, Θ.

9.8 A sequence of numbers is generated in the form

$$y_n = A y_{n-2} + B x_n$$

where A and B are constants. The numbers x_n are values of a random variable with mean zero and variance σ^2; successive values $x_1, x_2, \ldots$ are uncorrelated. Determine the correlation function $E[y_n y_{n-k}]$ as a function of k.

9.9 (a) The values 0 and 1 occur independently and with probabilities p and q, respectively, in the form of a sequence. Find an expression for the autocorrelation function of this sequence.

  (b) Consider the more general case in which the occurrences of 0 and 1 depend on the previous symbol. Determine the autocorrelation function if the joint probabilities for symbol pairs are given by

$$P(0,0) = \tfrac{1}{3} \qquad P(0,1) = \tfrac{1}{6}$$
$$P(1,0) = \tfrac{1}{6} \qquad P(1,1) = \tfrac{1}{3}$$

9.10 The sample functions of a random process are given by

$$y(t) = \cos (\omega_0 t + \theta) + \sin (2\omega_0 t + \theta)$$

where θ is a value of a random variable distributed uniformly over the range $[0, 2\pi]$.

  (a) Determine the probability density function $p(y; t)$.
  (b) Find the mean-square value of the process.
  (c) Is the process wide-sense stationary? Justify your answer.

9.11 The sample functions of a random process are pulse trains of repetition frequency f, comprising pulses of duration T and random amplitudes x (Fig. P 9.11). All sample functions are in phase;

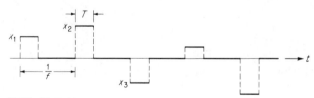

FIG. P 9.11

i.e., pulses occur in each sample function during the same time interval. The pulse amplitudes are independent and distributed according to

$$p(x) = \frac{a}{2} e^{-a|x|}$$

Find and sketch the autocorrelation function (a) By time averaging and (b) By ensemble averaging, and thus show that the process is not stationary. Show that the time average of the result of (b) is identical with the answer to (a).

9.12 If all sample functions in Example 9.9 are in phase (that is, $r = 0$ for all sample functions), the process is not stationary.

(a) Show that the result for the power spectral density obtained in Example 9.9 is still valid.

(b) Find the correlation function for the process for values of t corresponding to the beginning and middle of the pulses.

(c) Explain why the power spectral density remains unchanged.

9.13 A message $m(t)$ consists of a signal $s(t)$ and added noise $n(t)$:

$$m(t) = s(t) + n(t)$$

The signal and noise are independent stationary processes with first-order probability density functions $p_S(s)$ and $p_N(n)$, respectively. Find the conditional distribution function $F(s|m)$; that is, the distribution of the signal when the message is given.

9.14 Find the correlation function and power spectral density function for each of the processes whose sample functions are given below.

(a) $x(t) = a \cos(\omega_1 t + \theta_1) + b \cos(\omega_2 t + \theta_2)$, where a and b are constants, θ_1 and θ_2 are values of independent random variables which are uniformly distributed in $[0, 2\pi]$.

(b) $x(t)$ is a series of narrow pulses of width w and height h, with repetition period T. The starting time of the sample functions is random and uniformly distributed in $[0, T]$.

(c) $x(t)$ is a series of narrow pulses of width w and random independent heights y. The starting time of the sample functions is random and uniformly distributed in $[0, T]$ as in (b).

9.15 For the random process of Example 9.7, determine:

(a) The first-order probability density function $p_1(x, t)$.

(b) The second-order probability density function $p_2(x_1, t_1; x_2, t_2)$.

9.16 The power spectral density $W(\omega)$ of the random current flowing through a resistor of resistance R ohms is shown in Fig. P 9.16. What is the average power dissipated in R?

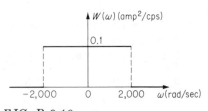

FIG. P 9.16

9.17   The power spectral density of a stationary random process $\{x(t)\}$ is shown in Fig. P 9.17.

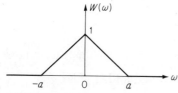

FIG. P 9.17

(a) What is the mean-square value of the process?

(b) What are the frequencies of the periodic components in the process?

(c) Sample functions from this process are used to modulate sine waves of random phase, giving sample functions

$$y(t) = x(t) \cos (\omega_0 t + \theta)$$

where the initial phase θ is uniformly distributed in $[0, 2\pi]$ and θ is independent of $\{x(t)\}$. What is the power spectral density of $\{y(t)\}$? Take $\omega_0 = 2a$. Sketch $W(\omega)$.

9.18   Sample functions from a random process $\{x(t)\}$ are delayed by T sec and added to the original sample functions to give the sample functions of a new process $\{y(t)\}$. Find the power spectral density of $\{y(t)\}$ in terms of that of $\{x(t)\}$.

9.19   The two-dimensional normal (Gaussian) density function of two random variables X_1 and X_2 is given by (9.54).

(a) Show that the symbols $\overline{X_1}$ and $\overline{X_2}$ are justified.

(b) Show that ρ is the correlation coefficient.

(c) Show that in this case $\rho = 0$ (X_1 and X_2 uncorrelated) implies that X_1 and X_2 are independent.

(d) Find the probability density for X_1.

(e) If $\overline{X_1} = \overline{X_2} = 0$, what are the loci of constant probability density? What are the loci if $\rho = 0$? What are they if, in addition, $\sigma_1 = \sigma_2$?

(f) In order to see what happens as $\rho \to 1$, let $\rho = 1 - \epsilon^2/2$ (and take $\overline{X_1} = \overline{X_2} = 0$). What happens in the limit as $\epsilon \to 0$? Find the limiting form of the density function.

9.20   Show that the two terms in $X_N(\omega)$ of Example 9.9 due to the first and last pulses in the interval $[-N, N]$ do not contribute to the power spectral density.

9.21   Demonstrate that the process of Example 9.1 is ergodic, i.e., that it satisfies the conditions on page 288.

9.22   Find the characteristic function for a normally distributed random variable whose probability density function is given by (9.53). It is convenient to find the characteristic function first for $\bar{X} = 0$ and $\sigma = 1$, and then to obtain it for arbitrary mean and variance through appropriate changes of variable.

9.23   Show that, if $\{n(t)\}$ is a stationary Gaussian process with correlation function $r(\tau)$,

$$E[n^2(t)n^2(t + \tau)] = 2r^2(\tau) + r^2(0)$$

9.24   The sample functions of a random process are given by

$$x(t) = s(t) + n(t)$$

where

$$s(t) = A \cos (\omega_0 t + \theta)$$

The amplitude A is constant, and θ is the value of a random variable with uniform density function in $[0, 2\pi]$. The independent normal noise process $\{n(t)\}$ has the correlation function

$$r_n(\tau) = Be^{-a|\tau|}$$

where B is a constant, and its second-order normal joint density function is given by (9.54). If the sample functions $x(t)$ are passed through a squaring device, find the power spectral density at the output. Use the result of Prob. 9.23.

9.25   (a) Determine the correlation function of "band-limited white noise," i.e., noise with a power spectral density

$$W(\omega) = \begin{cases} W_0 & \omega_1 < |\omega| < \omega_2 \\ 0 & |\omega| < \omega_1 \text{ and } |\omega| > \omega_2 \end{cases}$$

(b) Repeat for "low-pass white noise" with

$$W(\omega) = \begin{cases} W_0 & |\omega| < \omega_c \\ 0 & |\omega| > \omega_c \end{cases}$$

9.26   A digital data-transmission system transmits sequences of binary digits. The probability of changing a 0 to a 1 is $\frac{1}{4}$; that of changing a 1 to a 0 is $\frac{1}{6}$.

(a) Determine the transition probability matrix $\mathbf{P}$ for the possible states produced by sequences of two digits.

(b) Determine the two-step transition probability matrix $\mathbf{P}_2$.

(c) Find the matrix $\mathbf{P}$ for the possible states produced by sequences of three digits.

9.27   Let the correlation function of a stationary discrete-time random process $\{x(t)\}$ be represented by

$$r_x(\tau) = \sum_{n=-\infty}^{\infty} r_y(\tau)\delta(\tau - nT)$$

where $r_y(\tau)$ is the correlation function of a continuous-time random process. Derive (9.66) by expressing the train of delta functions as a Fourier series.

9.28   Consider a low-pass white-noise process as in Prob. 9.25b.

(a) Determine the power spectral density $W'(z)$ of the discrete-time process obtained by sampling with

(1) $T = \dfrac{1}{2f_c}$ and (2) $T = \dfrac{3}{4f_c}$, where $f_c = \omega_c/2\pi$.

(b) Determine the power spectral density $W_y(\omega)$ of the band-limited continuous-time process constructed from the samples obtained for both sampling intervals in (a).

9.29   Show that
$$M_{X,Y}(u, 0; t_1, t_2) = M_X(u; t_1)$$
and
$$M_{X,Y}(0, v; t_1, t_2) = M_Y(v; t_2)$$

where M denotes the characteristic function.

9.30   Prove (9.78).

9.31   The random process $\{x(t)\}$ has the normal second-order probability density of (9.54), is stationary, and has zero mean value and power spectral density $W(\omega)$. Find the joint probability density function of the two random variables defined at time t by $\{x(t)\}$ and the second-derivative process $\{\ddot{x}(t)\}$.

9.32   Prove (9.81).

9.33   If a process $\{x(t)\}$ has a power spectral density which is zero for frequencies greater than some value ω_c, any sample function may be represented in the form of (9.62) by its values at time instants separated by an interval π/ω_c; that is,

$$x(t) = \sum_{k=-\infty}^{\infty} x\left(\frac{k\pi}{\omega_c}\right) \frac{\sin \omega_c(t - k\pi/\omega_c)}{\omega_c(t - k\pi/\omega_c)}$$

If the power spectral density is constant for $|\omega| < \omega_c$ (that is, $\{x(t)\}$ is a low-pass white-noise process), show that the coefficients $x(k\pi/\omega_c)$ are values of *uncorrelated* random variables.

9.34 Let $\{x(t)\}$ be a stationary process with the normal second-order probability density of (9.54), spectral density $W_x(\omega)$, zero mean value, and variance σ^2. A new random process is defined by the sample functions

$$y(t) = \int_t^{t+T} x(\lambda)\, d\lambda$$

Determine the mean and variance of the random process $\{y(t)\}$ in terms of $W_x(\omega)$.

9.35 Show that for a Markov process

$$p(x_n|x_{n-2}) = \int_{-\infty}^{\infty} p_1(x_n|\lambda) p_2(\lambda|x_{n-2})\, d\lambda$$

This relation is known as the *Chapman-Kolmogorov equation.*

9.36 Let $i = 1, 2, \ldots, k$ be the (distinct) roots of the characteristic equation

$$|\lambda\mathbf{I} - \mathbf{P}| = 0$$

where $\mathbf{P}$ is the transition probability matrix (9.56). Let $\mathbf{a}_i$ and $\mathbf{b}_i'$ be column and row vectors, respectively, defined by

$$\mathbf{Pa}_i = \lambda_i \mathbf{a}_i \quad \text{and} \quad \mathbf{b}_i'\mathbf{P} = \lambda_i\mathbf{b},$$

(Note that $\mathbf{a}_i$ and $\mathbf{b}_i'$ are the vectors whose direction is unchanged when $\mathbf{P}$ operates on them as prefactor or postfactor, respectively.) Since the magnitudes of $\mathbf{a}_i$ and $\mathbf{b}_i'$ are arbitrary, let $\mathbf{b}_i'\mathbf{a}_i = 1$.

(a) Show that the matrices $\mathbf{A}_i = \mathbf{a}_i\mathbf{b}_i'$ have the properties

$$\mathbf{A}_i\mathbf{A}_j = \begin{cases} \mathbf{0} & i \neq j \\ \mathbf{A}_i & i = j \end{cases}$$

and

$$\sum_{i=1}^{k} \mathbf{A}_i = \mathbf{I}$$

(b) Show that $\mathbf{P}^n = \sum_{i=1}^{k} \lambda_i{}^n \mathbf{A}_i$.

9.37 In a binary channel the symbols 0 and 1 are transmitted with probability of error of $\frac{1}{3}$.

(a) Find the characteristic roots of the transition probability matrix $\mathbf{P}$.

(b) Determine the vectors $\mathbf{a}_i$, $\mathbf{b}_i'$ (Prob. 9.36) and show that the matrices $\mathbf{A}_i$ satisfy the properties of Prob. 9.36a.

(c) Write the expansion for $\mathbf{P}^n$ in the form of Prob. 9.36b.

CHAPTER TEN

RANDOM SIGNALS
IN LINEAR SYSTEMS

10.1 INTRODUCTION

Random signals occur in many kinds of communication and control systems. Frequently the information-bearing signals are contaminated by noise, and the system must be designed to operate properly in spite of the interfering noise. In other cases, such as radar detection systems, the system is designed to determine whether or not a signal is present. In another class of problems, the system must operate with a variety of input signals which can only be described statistically. In all these cases, it is essential to determine some of the statistical properties of the random process at the output in terms of the known statistical properties of the input process and suitable descriptions of the system.

It turns out that determination of the first-order and higher-order output probability density function is, in general, a very difficult problem which has been solved only for special cases. The correlation function

and power spectral density of the output and the cross-correlation function between output and input may, however, be determined quite easily, as will be seen in this chapter. Fortunately, these quantities are often sufficient for system analysis and design. In particular, they are sufficient for the determination of the optimum linear system for filtering a signal from a combination of signal and noise (smoothing) and for predicting future values of a signal (extrapolation), provided that the "optimum" system is defined as that which minimizes the mean-square error between the actual and desired outputs. This application is discussed in this chapter, along with the matched filter for maximizing the signal-to-noise ratio at one instant.

10.2 INPUT-OUTPUT RELATIONS

A convenient model to determine both the output correlation function and the output-input cross-correlation function resulting from the passage of a stationary random process through a linear system is shown in Fig. 10.1. Sample functions from the random process $\{x(t)\}$ are applied to two fixed systems characterized by unit-impulse responses $h_1(t)$ and $h_2(t)$, respectively. For any input function $x(t)$, the output $y_1(t)$ is, by (3.40),

$$y_1(t) = \int_{-\infty}^{\infty} h_1(u)x(t - u)\, du$$

and similarly for $y_2(t)$. It is assumed that all sample functions $x(t)$ are bounded† and that the system is stable in the sense of Sec. 3.8, so that all output sample functions are bounded.

The cross-correlation function of the two outputs is‡

$$r_{12}(\tau) = E[y_1(t)y_2(t + \tau)]$$
$$= E\left[\int_{-\infty}^{\infty} dv \int_{-\infty}^{\infty} du\, h_1(u)h_2(v)x(t - u)x(t + \tau - v) \right]$$

In view of the assumptions made, the order of integration and averaging

† It is sufficient to assume that the random process $\{x(t)\}$ is bounded, which means that all sample functions are bounded, with the possible exception of a set of probability zero.

‡ In this chapter it is convenient to denote both the sample functions of a random process and the random variables derived from it by the same lower-case letters. Only when an ensemble average is indicated are the averaged quantities random variables. We will thus be able to reserve capital letters for the Fourier transforms of sample functions. This practice is widely used in the literature.

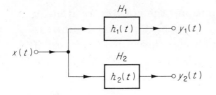

FIG. 10.1   *Model for determination of statistical characteristics of system response to continuous-time random inputs.*

may be reversed, giving

$$r_{12}(\tau) = \int_{-\infty}^{\infty} dv \int_{-\infty}^{\infty} du\, h_1(u)h_2(v)E[x(t - u)x(t + \tau - v)]$$

or

$$r_{12}(\tau) = \int_{-\infty}^{\infty} dv \int_{-\infty}^{\infty} du\, h_1(u)h_2(v)r_x(u - v + \tau) \tag{10.1}$$

The autocorrelation function of the output of H_1 is obtained by setting $h_2 = h_1$; the cross-correlation function between the output of H_1 and its input, by setting $h_2(t) = \delta(t)$. Although (10.1) may be used to compute these correlation functions, it is simpler to introduce first the filter correlation function of Lampard.†

If we let $v - u = \lambda$ in (10.1), the output correlation function may be written

$$r_{12}(\tau) = \int_{-\infty}^{\infty} d\lambda \int_{-\infty}^{\infty} du\, h_1(u)h_2(u + \lambda)r_x(\tau - \lambda) \tag{10.2}$$

It is now convenient to define the *filter cross-correlation function*

$$g_{12}(\tau) = \int_{-\infty}^{\infty} h_1(u)h_2(u + \tau)\, du \tag{10.3}$$

which depends only on the characteristics of the two systems or filters H_1 and H_2 and resembles a (time) cross-correlation function. For negative argument, it is readily shown (Prob. 10.1) that

$$g_{12}(-\tau) = g_{21}(\tau) \tag{10.4}$$

It is frequently convenient to use (10.3) for positive τ only and to calculate the filter correlation function for negative arguments from (10.4). For a causal system, the filter cross-correlation function becomes

$$g_{12}(\tau) = \int_0^{\infty} h_1(u)h_2(u + \tau)\, du$$

Equation (10.4) may still be used to determine $g_{12}(\tau)$ for negative τ.

The expression for $r_{12}(\tau)$ in (10.2) thus becomes

$$r_{12}(\tau) = \int_{-\infty}^{\infty} g_{12}(\lambda)r_x(\tau - \lambda)\, d\lambda = g_{12} \star r_x \tag{10.5}$$

† D. G. Lampard, The Response of Linear Networks to Suddenly Applied Stationary Random Noise, *IRE Trans. Circuit Theory*, vol. CT-2, pp. 49–57, March, 1955.

which is the convolution of $r_x(\tau)$ and $g_{12}(\tau)$.   Thus the output cross-correlation function is obtained from the input correlation function and the filter correlation function in exactly the same manner used to find the output time function in terms of the input time function and the impulse response.

We may now easily obtain results for special cases.   The autocorrelation function $r_y(\tau)$ at the output of a linear system with impulse response $h(t)$ is found by setting $h_1(t) = h_2(t) = h(t)$:

$$r_y(\tau) = \int_{-\infty}^{\infty} g(\lambda) r_x(\tau - \lambda)\, d\lambda = g \star r_x \qquad (10.6)$$

where

$$g(\tau) = \int_{-\infty}^{\infty} h(u) h(u + \tau)\, du \qquad (10.7)$$

is the filter autocorrelation function.

The cross-correlation function $r_{xy}(\tau)$ between input and output is found by letting $h_1(t) = \delta(t)$ (direct connection), $h_2(t) = h(t)$ in (10.3).   The filter cross-correlation function now is

$$g_{xy}(\tau) = \int_{-\infty}^{\infty} \delta(u) h(u + \tau)\, du$$
$$= h(\tau) \qquad (10.8)$$

Hence

$$r_{xy}(\tau) = \int_{-\infty}^{\infty} h(\lambda) r_x(\tau - \lambda)\, d\lambda = h \star r_x \qquad (10.9)$$

or

$$r_{xy}(\tau) = \int_{0}^{\infty} h(\lambda) r_x(\tau - \lambda)\, d\lambda \qquad (10.10)$$

if the system H is causal.

Example 10.1   Filter cross-correlation function   Consider two RC networks as shown in Fig. 10.2.   The unit-impulse response is given by

$$h_i(t) = \frac{1}{\alpha_i} e^{-t/\alpha_i} \qquad t \geq 0$$

where $\alpha_i = R_i C_i$ is the time constant, and $i = 1, 2$.

The filter cross-correlation function is, according to (10.3),

$$g_{12}(\tau) = \int_0^\infty \frac{1}{\alpha_1} e^{-u/\alpha_1} \frac{1}{\alpha_2} e^{-(u+\tau)/\alpha_2}\, du \qquad \tau \geq 0$$
$$= \frac{1}{\alpha_1 + \alpha_2} e^{-\tau/\alpha_2} \qquad \tau \geq 0$$

For $\tau < 0$, we have thus, from (10.4),

$$g_{12}(\tau) = g_{21}(-\tau) = \frac{1}{\alpha_1 + \alpha_2} e^{\tau/\alpha_1} \qquad \tau < 0$$

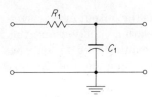

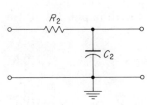

FIG. 10.2   Two RC networks.

It is apparent that the filter cross-correlation function is not an even function of its argument unless $\alpha_1 = \alpha_2$. A graph of $g_{12}(\tau)$ for this example is shown in Fig. 10.3.

To find the filter autocorrelation function for one RC network, we set $\alpha_1 = \alpha_2 = \alpha$ and obtain

$$g(\tau) = \frac{1}{2\alpha} e^{-|\tau|/\alpha}$$

Example 10.2   We shall find the correlation function at the output of an RC filter when the input noise has a known correlation function. If the input noise is white, with correlation function

$$r_x(\tau) = W_0 \, \delta(\tau)$$

the output autocorrelation function is, from (10.6),

$$r_y(\tau) = \int_{-\infty}^{\infty} \frac{1}{2\alpha} e^{-|\lambda|/\alpha} W_0 \, \delta(\tau - \lambda) \, d\lambda$$

$$= \frac{W_0}{2\alpha} e^{-|\tau|/\alpha}$$

An RC filter may thus be used to obtain exponentially correlated noise from white noise.

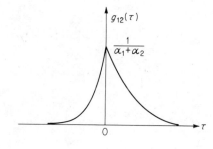

FIG. 10.3   Filter correlation function for Example 10.1.

The cross-correlation function between the outputs of two RC networks with time constants α_1 and α_2 is, from (10.5) and Example 10.1,

$$r_{12}(\tau) = \int_{-\infty}^{\infty} g_{12}(\lambda) r_x(\tau - \lambda)\, d\lambda$$

$$= \int_{-\infty}^{0} \frac{W_0}{\alpha_1 + \alpha_2} e^{\lambda/\alpha_1}\, \delta(\tau - \lambda)\, d\lambda + \int_{0}^{\infty} \frac{W_0}{\alpha_1 + \alpha_2} e^{-\lambda/\alpha_2}\, \delta(\tau - \lambda)\, d\lambda$$

$$= \begin{cases} \dfrac{W_0}{\alpha_1 + \alpha_2} e^{\tau/\alpha_1} & \tau < 0 \\[2ex] \dfrac{W_0}{\alpha_1 + \alpha_2} e^{-\tau/\alpha_2} & \tau \geq 0 \end{cases}$$

If the correlation function at the input is that of the sine-wave process with random phase (Example 9.6), we have

$$r_x(\tau) = \tfrac{1}{2} \cos \omega_0 \tau$$

Thus the correlation function at the output of the RC filter is

$$r_y(\tau) = \int_{-\infty}^{\infty} \frac{1}{2\alpha} e^{-|\lambda|/\alpha} \tfrac{1}{2} \cos \omega_0(\tau - \lambda)\, d\lambda$$

$$= \frac{\cos \omega_0 \tau}{2\,(1 + \alpha^2 \omega_0^2)}$$

The correlation function at the output is also periodic, as might be expected.

10.3 POWER SPECTRAL DENSITIES

The power spectral density at the output of a linear system may be determined from the output correlation function, or it may be found directly by using frequency-domain descriptions of the system and the input. Taking the Fourier transform of (10.5), we obtain the cross-power spectral density $W_{12}(\omega)$ of the outputs as

$$W_{12}(\omega) = \mathcal{F}[r_{12}(\tau)] = \mathcal{F}[g_{12} \star r_x]$$

From the convolution property of Fourier transforms (Prob. 5.18), we obtain

$$W_{12}(\omega) = G_{12}(\omega) W_x(\omega) \tag{10.11}$$

where $W_x(\omega)$ is the input power spectral density, and the symbol $G_{12}(\omega)$ is used to denote the Fourier transform of the filter correlation function:

$$G_{12}(\omega) = \int_{-\infty}^{\infty} g_{12}(\lambda) e^{-j\omega\lambda}\, d\lambda \tag{10.12}$$

This quantity may be called the *filter cross-power spectral density*. It is equal to the cross-power spectral density of the outputs if white noise of constant spectral density is applied to the input.

Special cases of (10.11) are of interest. The output power spectral density $W_y(\omega)$ of a linear system is given by

$$W_y(\omega) = G(\omega)W_x(\omega) \tag{10.13}$$

where $G(\omega)$ is the Fourier transform of the filter correlation function $g(\tau)$ given by (10.7).

The cross-power spectral density $W_{xy}(\omega)$ between output and input is obtained as the Fourier transform of (10.9),

$$W_{xy}(\omega) = H(\omega)W_x(\omega) \tag{10.14}$$

where $H(\omega)$ is the transfer function of the fixed system defined by

$$H(\omega) = \mathcal{F}[h(t)] \tag{10.15}$$

Since the system H is causal, this Fourier transform is identical with the Laplace transform of the impulse response, with s replaced by $j\omega$.

The filter power spectral density $G(\omega)$ can be related explicitly to the transfer function. Use of the expression (10.3) for $g_{12}(\tau)$ in the definition (10.12) of the filter power spectral density gives

$$G_{12}(\omega) = \int_{-\infty}^{\infty} d\lambda \, e^{-j\omega\lambda} \int_{-\infty}^{\infty} h_1(u)h_2(u + \lambda) \, du$$

Changing the order of integration and setting $v = \lambda + u$, we have

$$G_{12}(\omega) = \int_{-\infty}^{\infty} du \, h_1(u)e^{j\omega u} \int_{-\infty}^{\infty} dv \, h_2(v)e^{-j\omega v}$$

or

$$G_{12}(\omega) = H_1^*(\omega)H_2(\omega) \tag{10.16}$$

where $H_1(\omega)$ and $H_2(\omega)$ are the Fourier transforms of the impulse responses $h_1(t)$ and $h_2(t)$, respectively.

For a single system, we thus have

$$G(\omega) = |H(\omega)|^2 \tag{10.17}$$

so that (10.13) becomes

$$W_y(\omega) = |H(\omega)|^2 W_x(\omega) \tag{10.18}$$

This relation is not unexpected, since power is defined in terms of the square of the time function and average power is independent of the phase of the time-function components. The cross-power spectral density of (10.14), however, does depend on the phase variation of the transfer function since it involves only the first power of the output time function $y(t)$. Equation (10.14) may also be verified by noting that if H_1 is a direct connection, $G_{12}(\omega) = H_2(\omega)$, and by using this fact in (10.11).

The average output power, or the mean-square value of the output $\{y(t)\}$, of a system H with random inputs may be expressed in different ways. From (10.1) with $\tau = 0$ and $h_1(t) = h_2(t) = h(t)$,

$$\overline{y^2} = \int_{-\infty}^{\infty} dv \int_{-\infty}^{\infty} du \, h(u)h(v)r_x(u - v) \tag{10.19}$$

From (10.6) with $\tau = 0$,

$$\overline{y^2} = \int_{-\infty}^{\infty} g(\lambda)r_x(\lambda) \, d\lambda \tag{10.20}$$

since $r_x(\tau)$ is an even function for real $x(t)$. From (9.50)

$$\overline{y^2} = \int_{-\infty}^{\infty} W_y(\omega) \frac{d\omega}{2\pi} \tag{10.21}$$

or, using (10.13) and (10.18), respectively,

$$\overline{y^2} = \int_{-\infty}^{\infty} G(\omega)W_x(\omega) \frac{d\omega}{2\pi} \tag{10.22}$$

or

$$\overline{y^2} = \int_{-\infty}^{\infty} |H(\omega)|^2 W_x(\omega) \frac{d\omega}{2\pi} \tag{10.23}$$

The most important relations of this and the preceding sections are summarized in Table 10.1 on p. 334.

Example 10.3   Filter power spectral density   For the RC filters of Example 10.1, we found

$$g_{12}(\tau) = \begin{cases} \dfrac{1}{\alpha_1 + \alpha_2} e^{-\tau/\alpha_2} & \tau \geq 0 \\[2mm] \dfrac{1}{\alpha_1 + \alpha_2} e^{\tau/\alpha_1} & \tau < 0 \end{cases}$$

Thus the filter (cross-) power spectral density is

$$\begin{aligned} G_{12}(\omega) &= \int_{-\infty}^{\infty} g_{12}(\lambda)e^{-j\omega\lambda} \, d\lambda \\ &= \int_{-\infty}^{0} \frac{1}{\alpha_1 + \alpha_2} e^{\left(\frac{1}{\alpha_1} - j\omega\right)\lambda} \, d\lambda + \int_{0}^{\infty} \frac{1}{\alpha_1 + \alpha_2} e^{-\left(\frac{1}{\alpha_2} + j\omega\right)\lambda} \, d\lambda \\ &= \frac{1}{(1 - j\omega\alpha_1)(1 + j\omega\alpha_2)} \end{aligned}$$

For one filter, the filter power spectral density is

$$G(\omega) = \frac{1}{1 + \omega^2\alpha^2}$$

The transfer function of one RC filter is

$$H(\omega) = \frac{1}{1 + j\omega RC} = \frac{1}{1 + j\omega\alpha}$$

which, together with the expressions obtained for $G_{12}(\omega)$ and $G(\omega)$, illustrates (10.16) and (10.17).

Example 10.4   Signal plus noise in linear system   Let the input sample functions applied to an RC filter as in Example 10.1 consist of a signal $s(t)$ and added stationary noise $n(t)$,

$$x(t) = s(t) + n(t)$$

where $s(t)$ is a sine wave with random initial phase,

$$s(t) = A \cos (\omega_0 t + \theta) \qquad \text{volts}$$

with the random variable Θ distributed uniformly in $[0, 2\pi]$. Let the noise be white, with zero mean and constant power spectral density

$$W_n(\omega) = W_0 \qquad \text{watts/cps}$$

The signal and noise are assumed to be uncorrelated; i.e.,

$$r_{sn}(\tau) = \overline{s(t)n(t + \tau)} = 0$$

As shown in Examples 9.16 and 9.10, the input power spectral density

$$\begin{aligned}
W_x(\omega) &= W_s(\omega) + W_n(\omega) \\
&= \frac{A^2\pi}{2} [\delta(\omega - \omega_0) + \delta(\omega + \omega_0)] + W_0
\end{aligned}$$

The average output power is

$$\begin{aligned}
\overline{y^2} &= \frac{1}{2\pi} \int_{-\infty}^{\infty} |H(\omega)|^2 W_x(\omega) \, d\omega \\
&= \frac{1}{2\pi} \int_{-\infty}^{\infty} |H(\omega)|^2 [W_s(\omega) + W_n(\omega)] \, d\omega
\end{aligned}$$

The output power due to the signal is thus

$$\begin{aligned}
\overline{y_s^2} &= \frac{1}{2\pi} \int_{-\infty}^{\infty} |H(\omega)|^2 W_s(\omega) \, d\omega \\
&= \int_{-\infty}^{\infty} \frac{1}{1 + \omega^2\alpha^2} \frac{A^2}{4} [\delta(\omega - \omega_0) + \delta(\omega + \omega_0)] \, d\omega \\
&= \frac{A^2}{2} \frac{1}{1 + \omega_0^2\alpha^2} \qquad \text{watts}
\end{aligned}$$

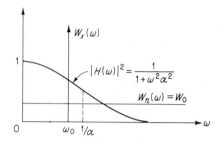

FIG. 10.4 *Effect of RC filter on signal plus noise input.*

The output noise power is

$$\overline{y_n{}^2} = \frac{1}{2\pi} \int_{-\infty}^{\infty} |H(\omega)|^2 W_n(\omega)\, d\omega$$

$$= \frac{1}{2\pi} \int_{-\infty}^{\infty} \frac{1}{1 + \omega^2 \alpha^2}\, W_0\, d\omega$$

$$= \frac{1}{2\alpha}\, W_0 \qquad \text{watts}$$

The signal-to-noise power ratio at the output is thus

$$\frac{\overline{y_s{}^2}}{\overline{y_n{}^2}} = \frac{A^2}{W_0} \frac{\alpha}{1 + \omega_0{}^2 \alpha^2}$$

For fixed ω_0, the maximum signal-to-noise power ratio is obtained when $\alpha = RC = 1/\omega_0$, that is, when the half-power point of the filter equals the frequency of the applied signal (Fig. 10.4). If $1/\alpha$ is increased, the "gain" for the signal is increased, but the noise frequency components are also transmitted with higher gain and the total output noise power increases more than the output signal power. If $1/\alpha$ is decreased below ω_0, the output signal power decreases more than the output noise power, again resulting in a smaller signal-to-noise power ratio. It is clear that a tuned filter with large gain at ω_0 and small gain at all other frequencies would be much more effective in suppressing white noise than the RC filter used here (Prob. 10.9).

10.4 DISCRETE-TIME SYSTEMS

For fixed systems whose inputs and outputs are sample functions of discrete-time stationary random processes (and possibly discrete-time signals as well), we may proceed in a manner completely analogous to that used in Secs. 10.2 and 10.3. The model of Fig. 10.5 corresponds to that of Fig.

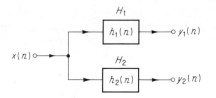

10.1 for continuous-time signals.   A few of the relations are first formulated for time-varying systems with nonstationary input processes since these relations are needed in Sec. 10.6.

If sample functions $x(n)$ of a discrete-time random process are applied to the two systems H_1 and H_2 characterized by their unit-function responses $h_1(n, k)$ and $h_2(n, k)$, respectively, the output $y_1(n)$ is, by (3.54),

$$y_1(n) = \sum_{j=-\infty}^{\infty} h_1(n, j)x(j)$$

with a similar expression for $y_2(n)$.   The cross-correlation function of the two outputs is thus

$$
\begin{aligned}
r_{12}(n, l) &= E[y_1(n)y_2(l)] \\
&= E\left[\sum_{i=-\infty}^{\infty} \sum_{j=-\infty}^{\infty} h_1(n, j)h_2(l, i)x(j)x(i) \right] \\
&= \sum_{i=-\infty}^{\infty} \sum_{j=-\infty}^{\infty} h_1(n, j)h_2(l, i)r_x(j, i) \qquad (10.24)
\end{aligned}
$$

For fixed systems, $h_1(n, j) = h_1(n - j)$ and $h_2(l, i) = h_2(l - i)$; for stationary inputs, $r_x(j, i) = r_x(i - j)$.   Thus, with both of these conditions, we may set $n-j = s$, $l-i = s+m$, $l-n = k$, to obtain

$$r_{12}(k) = \sum_{m=-\infty}^{\infty} \sum_{s=-\infty}^{\infty} h_1(s)h_2(s + m)r_x(k - m) \qquad (10.25)$$

The _discrete-filter cross-correlation function_ $g_{12}(m)$ may now be defined as

$$g_{12}(m) = \sum_{s=-\infty}^{\infty} h_1(s)h_2(s + m) \qquad (10.26)$$

which depends only on the unit-function responses of the two linear systems H_1 and H_2.   It follows readily that

$$g_{12}(-m) = g_{21}(m) \qquad (10.27)$$

For causal systems, the lower limit in the summation of (10.26) may be made zero.

The output cross-correlation function given by (10.25) may now be expressed in terms of the discrete-filter cross-correlation function by

$$r_{12}(k) = \sum_{m=-\infty}^{\infty} g_{12}(m)r_x(k-m) = g_{12} \star r_x \qquad (10.28)$$

This convolution summation, like the convolution integral (10.5) for continuous-time systems, permits the determination of the output correlation function in terms of the input correlation function and the discrete-filter correlation function in precisely the manner in which the output time function is found from the input time function and the unit-function response.

The autocorrelation function of the output $y(n)$ of a system with unit-function response $h(n)$ now becomes

$$r_y(k) = \sum_{m=-\infty}^{\infty} g(m)r_x(k-m) = g \star r_x \qquad (10.29)$$

where

$$g(m) = \sum_{j=-\infty}^{\infty} h(j)h(j+m) \qquad (10.30)$$

In order to obtain the cross-correlation function $r_{xy}(k)$ between input and output, we set $h_1(n) = \delta(n)$, $h_2(n) = h(n)$ in (10.26) so that

$$g_{xy}(m) = h(m)$$

and (10.28) yields

$$r_{xy}(k) = \sum_{m=-\infty}^{\infty} h(m)r_x(k-m) = h \star r_x \qquad (10.31)$$

The frequency-domain relations between the discrete-time output processes $\{y_1(n)\}$ and $\{y_2(n)\}$ and the input process $\{x(n)\}$ may be obtained by applying the two-sided Z transform to the time-domain relation (10.28). Thus the cross-power spectral density of the two outputs is

$$W'_{12}(z) = T\mathsf{Z}_{11}[r_{12}(k)] = T \sum_{k=-\infty}^{\infty} r_{12}(k)z^{-k}$$

$$= T \sum_{k=-\infty}^{\infty} \sum_{m=-\infty}^{\infty} g_{12}(m)r_x(k-m)z^{-k} \qquad (10.32)$$

We set $j = k - m$, invert the order of summation, and obtain

$$W'_{12}(z) = T \sum_{m=-\infty}^{\infty} g_{12}(m)z^{-m} \sum_{j=-\infty}^{\infty} r_x(j)z^{-j}$$

or

$$W'_{12}(z) = G_{12}(z)W'_x(z) \qquad (10.33)$$

In this expression,

$$G_{12}(z) = Z_{II}[g_{12}(m)] = \sum_{m=-\infty}^{\infty} g_{12}(m)z^{-m} \qquad (10.34)$$

is the discrete-filter cross-power spectral density. It is the discrete analog of the quantity defined by (10.12) for a continuous-time system.

It may be noted that the two-sided Z transform of the convolution summation (10.28) is the product of the Z transforms of the convolved functions $g_{12}(m)$ and $r_x(m)$, a property already noted in Prob. 8.4 and for the one-sided Z transform in (8.5), although there a special requirement (corresponding to a causal system) had to be imposed on one of the functions.

Use of (10.33) when $H_1 = H_2$ now gives the discrete-time power spectral density of the output of a discrete-time system as

$$W'_y(z) = G(z)W'_x(z) \qquad (10.35)$$

where $G(z)$ is the two-sided Z transform of the discrete-filter correlation function $g(m)$ of (10.30). The cross-power spectral density between the input and output discrete-time processes may be obtained as the two-sided Z transform of (10.31), giving

$$W'_{xy}(z) = H(z)W'_x(z) \qquad (10.36)$$

where

$$H(z) = Z_{II}[h(k)] \qquad (10.37)$$

or

$$H(z) = Z_I[h(k)] \qquad \text{for causal systems} \qquad (10.38)$$

This discrete-time transfer function is related to the transfer function $H(\omega)$ by (8.48).

An explicit relation between the discrete-filter power spectral density $G_{12}(z)$ and the discrete-time transfer functions analogous to (10.16) may be formulated from the definition of $G_{12}(z)$ in (10.34) by substituting in this relation the definition of $g_{12}(m)$ provided by (10.26). Thus

$$G_{12}(z) = \sum_{m=-\infty}^{\infty} \sum_{j=-\infty}^{\infty} h_1(j)h_2(j+m)z^{-m}$$

which becomes, with $i = j + m$,

$$G_{12}(z) = \sum_{j=-\infty}^{\infty} h_1(j)z^j \sum_{i=-\infty}^{\infty} h_2(i)z^{-i}$$

or

$$G_{12}(z) = H_1(z^{-1})H_2(z) \qquad (10.39)$$

Thus the discrete-filter cross-power spectral density is the product of the two discrete-time transfer functions if the argument z in the transfer function corresponding to the first subscript is replaced by z^{-1}. It may be noted that, if we equate z with e^{Ts} as in Sec. 8.9 and let $s = j\omega$, the replacement of z by z^{-1} is equivalent to replacing $H_1(\omega)$ by its conjugate as required in (10.16) for continuous-time systems.

For a single discrete-time system with discrete-time transfer function $H(z)$, (10.39) gives

$$G(z) = H(z^{-1})H(z) \tag{10.40}$$

On the other hand, by setting $H_1(z) = 1$ and $H_2(z) = H(z)$ in (10.39), we obtain

$$G_{xy}(z) = H(z)$$

which may be used to obtain (10.36) from (10.33).

The mean-square value of the output $\{y(t)\}$ of a system with transfer function $H(z)$ to which a discrete-time random process is applied may be expressed in several ways by use of the results obtained above. From (10.25) with $k = 0$,

$$\overline{y^2(n)} = \overline{y^2} = \sum_{j=-\infty}^{\infty} \sum_{i=-\infty}^{\infty} h(j)h(i)r_x(j-i) \tag{10.41}$$

Equation (10.28) gives

$$\overline{y^2(n)} = \sum_{m=-\infty}^{\infty} g(m)r_x(m) \tag{10.42}$$

where the symmetry of $r_x(m)$ for real $\{x(n)\}$ has been used. The inversion formula (8.3) with $n = 0$ gives, in terms of the discrete-time output spectral density,

$$\overline{y^2(n)} = \frac{1}{2\pi jT} \oint_C W_y'(z)z^{-1}\,dz \tag{10.43}$$

Using (10.35) and (10.40), we may write this

$$\overline{y^2(n)} = \frac{1}{2\pi j} \oint_C G(z)W_x'(z)z^{-1}\,dz \tag{10.44}$$

or

$$\overline{y^2(n)} = \frac{1}{2\pi j} \oint_C H(z^{-1})H(z)W_x'(z)z^{-1}\,dz \tag{10.45}$$

The most important relations of this section are summarized in Table 10.1, together with the relations for continuous-time systems.

Table 10.1   SUMMARY OF RELATIONS FOR LINEAR SYSTEMS WITH RANDOM INPUTS

	Continuous-time systems	Discrete-time systems
Filter cross-correlation function	$g_{12}(\tau) =$ $$\int_{-\infty}^{\infty} h_1(u)h_2(u+\tau)\,du$$	$g_{12}(n) =$ $$\sum_{j=-\infty}^{\infty} h_1(j)h_2(j+n)$$
Output cross-correlation function	$r_{12}(\tau) = g_{12}(\tau) \star r_x(\tau)$	$r_{12}(n) = g_{12}(n) \star r_x(n)$
Input-output correlation function	$r_{xy}(\tau) = h(\tau) \star r_x(\tau)$	$r_{xy}(n) = h(n) \star r_x(n)$
Filter cross-power spectral density	$G_{12}(\omega) = \mathfrak{F}[g_{12}(\tau)]$ $= H_1^*(\omega)H_2(\omega)$	$G_{12}(z) = \mathsf{Z}[g_{12}(n)]$ $= H_1(z^{-1})H_2(z)$
Output cross-power spectral density	$W_{12}(\omega) = G_{12}(\omega)W_x(\omega)$	$W_{12}'(z) = G_{12}(z)W_x'(z)$
Input-output power spectral density	$W_{xy}(\omega) = H(\omega)W_x(\omega)$	$W_{xy}'(z) = H(z)W_x'(z)$
Output power spectral density	$W_y(\omega) = \|H(\omega)\|^2 W_x(\omega)$	$W_y'(z) = H(z^{-1})H(z)W_x'(z)$
Average output power	$\overline{y^2} = \int_{-\infty}^{\infty} g(\lambda)r_x(\lambda)\,d\lambda$ $= \dfrac{1}{2\pi}\int_{-\infty}^{\infty} W_y(\omega)\,d\omega$	$\overline{y^2} = \displaystyle\sum_{j=-\infty}^{\infty} g(j)r_x(j)$ $= \dfrac{1}{2\pi jT}\displaystyle\oint_C W_y'(z)z^{-1}\,dz$

Subscripts: x = input; y = output; $1, 2$ = outputs.

10.5   LINEAR LEAST-SQUARES FILTERING OF CONTINUOUS-TIME SIGNALS

The use of the input-output relations in linear systems with random inputs can be illustrated in the important problem of smoothing and prediction. We shall consider here the problem of filtering a random process whose sample functions may consist of an additive mixture of a signal $s(t)$ and noise $n(t)$. The purpose of filtering may be either to extract the signal with as little noise as possible (*smoothing*) or to predict the value of the signal as accurately as possible at a future time (*prediction*). The prediction may be attempted without any noise present (*pure prediction*) or

may be made in the presence of noise, so that the prediction problem in general is a combination of smoothing and pure prediction. This problem arises in the design of communication systems such as radar, in control systems, in chemical processes, and even in economics, where it occurs in the prediction of product demand or of stock prices.

The smoothing-and-prediction problem was first treated by Wiener[†] and nearly simultaneously by Kolmogorov.[‡] In order to make the filtering problem analytically tractable, Wiener assumed (1) that the system to be used for processing the data is restricted to be fixed and linear; (2) that it is desired to minimize the mean-square error between the actual output and the desired output, i.e., that the mean-square error criterion is used; (3) that the inputs are sample functions of an ergodic process. Various extensions of the theory have subsequently been made to nonstationary processes.[§]

It should be noted that the error criterion is adapted to random inputs since it is phrased in terms of the mean or expectation of the squared error over the entire ensemble. The "optimum" system determined by the Wiener theory may not perform as well as some other linear systems for a given sample function, but it should on the average be the best linear system—subject to the constraints imposed—when all possible sample functions of the input process are considered. The *squared* error is used since it is the simplest function of the error which is never negative and thus does not have the disadvantage of having positive-error contributions canceled by negative-error contributions. The absolute value of the error or the fourth power of the error could also be used, but these are harder to handle analytically. These error measures, as well as the squared error, may be unrealistic in some systems. For example, in some weapons systems, errors in hitting a target may be tolerable so long as they do not exceed a limiting error beyond which the target is not damaged; larger errors are equally undesirable and should be weighted equally.

† N. Wiener, "The Extrapolation, Interpolation and Smoothing of Stationary Time Series," John Wiley & Sons, Inc., New York, 1949 (first published in report form in 1942).

‡ *Ibid.*, p. 59, note.

§ R. C. Booton, Jr., An Optimization Theory for Time-varying Linear Systems with Nonstationary Statistical Inputs, *Proc. IRE*, vol. 40, pp. 977–981, August, 1952; R. C. Davis, On the Theory of Prediction of Nonstationary Stochastic Processes, *J. Appl. Phys.*, vol. 23, pp. 1047–1053, September, 1952; B. Friedland, Least Squares Filtering and Prediction of Nonstationary Sampled Data, *Information and Control*, vol. 1, pp. 297–313, December, 1958; R. E. Kalman, A New Approach to Linear Filtering and Prediction Problems, *Trans. ASME*, ser. D (*J. Basic Eng.*), vol. 82, pp. 35–45, March, 1960; R. E. Kalman and R. S. Bucy, New Results in Linear Filtering and Prediction Theory, *Trans. ASME*, ser. D (*J. Basic Eng.*), vol. 83, pp. 95–108, March, 1961.

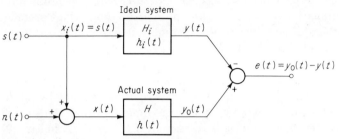

FIG. 10.6   Model for Wiener filtering theory.

The system model for the Wiener theory is shown in Fig. 10.6.   The input to the ideal system H_i is the signal $s(t)$ without noise; the output of the ideal system is the desired quantity $y(t)$.   This may, for example, be the signal $s(t)$, future values $s(t + \alpha)$ of the signal, or functions of the signal.   The actual system operates on the additive mixture of signal and noise and represents, in general, an approximation to the ideal system, embodying various constraints.   Its transfer function $H(\omega)$ or impulse response $h(t)$ is to be determined.

A simple derivation of some of Wiener's results was given by Bode and Shannon,† and their method will be used in this section.   We assume that the input signal and noise processes are stationary and uncorrelated and that they have power spectral densities $W_s(\omega)$ and $W_n(\omega)$, respectively. The desired output is taken to be the future value $s(t + \alpha)$ of the signal, where α is the prediction time and the transfer function to be determined is $H(\omega)$.

The error signal (for any input signal and noise sample functions) is

$$e(t) = y_0(t) - y(t) \tag{10.46}$$

Its Fourier transform, since $H_i(\omega) = e^{j\omega\alpha}$, is thus

$$
\begin{aligned}
E(\omega) &= Y_0(\omega) - Y(\omega) \\
&= [S(\omega) + N(\omega)]H(\omega) - S(\omega)e^{j\omega\alpha} \\
&= [H(\omega) - e^{j\omega\alpha}]S(\omega) + H(\omega)N(\omega)
\end{aligned}
$$

where $S(\omega)$ and $N(\omega)$ are the Fourier transforms of the signal and noise sample functions, respectively.   It follows that the power spectral density of the error is, in accordance with (10.18),

$$W_e(\omega) = |H(\omega) - e^{j\omega\alpha}|^2 W_s(\omega) + |H(\omega)|^2 W_n(\omega)$$

† H. W. Bode and C. E. Shannon, A Simplified Derivation of Linear Least Square Smoothing and Prediction Theory, *Proc. IRE*, vol. 38, pp. 417–425, April, 1950. For an approach to the optimum linear filtering problem using differential equations, see Kalman, *loc. cit.*

Therefore the mean-square value of the error is, by use of (10.21),

$$\overline{e^2(t)} = \frac{1}{2\pi} \int_{-\infty}^{\infty} \{|H(\omega) - e^{j\omega\alpha}|^2 W_s(\omega) + |H(\omega)|^2 W_n(\omega)\} \, d\omega \quad (10.47)$$

and this is to be minimized by proper choice of $H(\omega)$.

It should be noted that, because of the choice of the mean-square-error criterion, determination of the optimum filter depends only on the power spectral densities of the input signal and noise.   Phase information about the input is not needed or, if known, is not and cannot be used.   More complete statistical information, such as third- or higher-order density functions, cannot be used either; it is useful only if a different error criterion or a nonlinear filter is employed.

FILTERING WITH A NONCAUSAL SYSTEM

Much of the difficulty in the Wiener theory stems from the condition that the system H be causal.   Therefore we shall first ignore this condition and permit H to be noncausal and let it operate on the future as well as on the past of its input functions.

If $H(\omega) = C(\omega)e^{j\theta(\omega)}$, then (10.47) becomes, after expansion of the exponentials into cosines and sines,

$$\overline{e^2(t)} = \frac{1}{2\pi} \int_{-\infty}^{\infty} \{C^2 W_n + [C^2 + 1 - 2C \cos(\theta - \omega\alpha)]W_s\} \, d\omega \quad (10.48)$$

Since C, W_s, and W_n are nonnegative, this expression is minimized when $\cos(\theta - \omega\alpha)$ reaches its largest value; i.e., when $\theta(\omega) = \omega\alpha$.   The mean-square error thus becomes

$$\overline{e^2(t)} = \frac{1}{2\pi} \int_{-\infty}^{\infty} [C^2(W_n + W_s) - 2C W_s + W_s] \, d\omega$$

In order to find what $C(\omega)$ minimizes this expression, we complete the square in C, obtaining

$$\overline{e^2(t)} = \frac{1}{2\pi} \int_{-\infty}^{\infty} \left[\left(C\sqrt{W_n + W_s} - \frac{W_s}{\sqrt{W_n + W_s}} \right)^2 + \frac{W_s W_n}{W_s + W_n} \right] d\omega$$

$$(10.49)$$

Since the squared quantity is nonnegative, this expression is minimized by setting

$$C(\omega) = \frac{W_s(\omega)}{W_s(\omega) + W_n(\omega)} \quad (10.50)$$

so that

$$H(\omega) = \frac{W_s(\omega)}{W_s(\omega) + W_n(\omega)} e^{j\omega\alpha} \qquad (10.51)$$

This transfer function now makes the mean-square error of (10.49)

$$\overline{e^2(t)} = \frac{1}{2\pi} \int_{-\infty}^{\infty} \frac{W_s(\omega)W_n(\omega)}{W_s(\omega) + W_n(\omega)} d\omega \qquad (10.52)$$

The impulse response is, from (10.51),

$$h(t) = \frac{1}{2\pi} \int_{-\infty}^{\infty} \frac{W_s(\omega)}{W_s(\omega) + W_n(\omega)} e^{j\omega(t+\alpha)} d\omega \qquad (10.53)$$

which will, in general, not vanish for $t < 0$.

The impulse response of (10.53) is thus generally not physically realizable. Values of $h(t)$ for negative argument multiply (or weight) future values of the input, as shown by (3.40). Thus, if we can wait until all the input (signal plus noise) is available, the required impulse response can be realized. In other words, if we permit a sufficiently long delay, values of the input $s(t + \tau) + n(t + \tau)$ are available for positive τ, and are weighted by $h(-\tau)$ without requiring a noncausal filter. The delay has to be sufficiently large so that $h(-\tau)$ for values of τ exceeding this delay is very small, i.e., that the effect of future input values is negligible. With a delay which makes $h(t)$ or $H(\omega)$ physically realizable, the filter thus does not predict and is a pure smoothing filter. It is also called the *infinite-lag smoothing filter*.

The transfer function (10.51) shows that, for best smoothing, frequencies for which the ratio of signal spectral density to noise spectral density is largest should be transmitted with least attenuation, while frequencies at which the noise spectral density is relatively high should be attenuated.

PURE PREDICTION WITH A CAUSAL FILTER

We next ask which filter gives the best estimate of the value of the signal α sec ahead in the absence of noise when the signal $s(t)$ is known over the infinite past up to the present.

Bode and Shannon solve this problem by first changing the actual signal power spectral density to that of white noise and then operating on this white-noise signal. It turns out that this required operation is easily determined. In order to obtain the appropriate filter which changes the signal process to white noise, we first note that the power spectral density $W_s(\omega)$ of the signal may be obtained by passing white noise (of unit power spectral density) through a filter with transfer-function

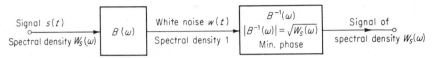

FIG. 10.7   Shaping filters.

magnitude $\sqrt{W_s(\omega)}$. The inverse of this filter will change the signal process to white noise (Fig. 10.7). Thus we have to determine a transfer function $B^{-1}(\omega)$ which satisfies

$$W_s(\omega) = B^{-1}(\omega)[B^{-1}(\omega)]^* = |B^{-1}(\omega)|^2 \qquad (10.54)$$

and which has a causal inverse $B(\omega)$. This inverse is called a *whitening filter*, since it produces white noise. Both B and its inverse are sometimes called *shaping filters*, since their function is to shape the spectral density of their output processes. The factor of $W_s(\omega)$ in (10.54) to be selected as the filter must be such that its singularities and those of its inverse (reciprocal) all lie in the upper half ω plane (or left half $j\omega$ plane). This will ensure that the impulse response of the filter and its inverse will be zero for negative time (see Sec. 6.5).

If $W_s(\omega)$ is a rational function of frequency, the transfer function of the filter which will generate $W_s(\omega)$ from white noise may be obtained more easily. If we write

$$W_s(\omega) = \frac{A(\omega)}{D(\omega)} \qquad (10.55)$$

then in the polynomial $D(\omega)$ there are (1) no real zeros, since this would make the integral of $W_s(\omega)$ infinite, giving infinite mean-square value of the signal; (2) any pure imaginary zeros occur in pairs $j\beta$ and $-j\beta$, since $W_s(\omega)$ is an even function; (3) any complex zeros occur in sets of four $(\omega_k, \omega_k^*, -\omega_k, -\omega_k^*)$, since $W_s(\omega)$ is even and real for real ω. Properties (2) and (3) are also true of $A(\omega)$. Further, since $W_s(\omega)$ is nonnegative and $A(\omega)$ thus cannot change sign, any real zeros of $A(\omega)$ are multiple and of even order. Hence $W_s(\omega)$ may be written in the form of (10.54), where $B^{-1}(\omega)$ has poles and zeros only in the upper half ω plane (and possibly zeros on the real axis). The poles and zeros in the upper half ω plane become poles and zeros in the left half $j\omega$ or s plane, and thus $B^{-1}(\omega)$ and its reciprocal $B(\omega)$ have zeros and poles only in the left half s plane† and are therefore transfer functions of causal filters.

† Such transfer functions are called *minimum-phase transfer functions*. A minimum-phase transfer function need not be a rational function, and if $W_s(\omega)$ is not a rational function, $B^{-1}(\omega)$ in (10.54) is a nonrational minimum-phase transfer function. This case is of little interest here, since $W_s(\omega)$ can nearly always be approximated by a rational function. See H. W. Bode, "Network Analysis and Feedback Amplifier Design," chap. 14, D. Van Nostrand Company Inc., Princeton, N.J., 1945.

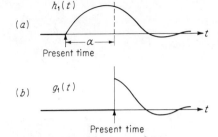

FIG. 10.8 (a) Impulse response $h_1(t)$ of B^{-1}; (b) impulse response $g_1(t)$ of predicting filter G_1.

The best operation on the white noise, in order to obtain a best estimate of $s(t + \alpha)$, may now be determined by thinking of the white-noise signal as a sequence of uncorrelated impulses. Any impulses which have occurred before the present time (called $t = 0$ for convenience) at which we want to predict the signal are known, and the future responses of a given filter to any of these impulses may be found. The total contribution of all these impulses to the value of the signal α sec ahead is the predictable part of $s(t + \alpha)$; the contribution of those impulses occurring between $t = 0$ and $t = \alpha$ is not predictable since the impulses are uncorrelated with those which have already occurred. The mean of this unpredictable contribution is, however, zero, since the impulses themselves have zero mean.

If the response $h_1(t)$ of B^{-1} to a unit impulse is the signal shown in Fig. 10.8a, the impulse response $g_1(t)$ of the predicting filter G_1 should be that of part (b) of this figure, since this corresponds to a causal filter whose response to an impulse at the present time is the desired value of the impulse response of B^{-1} at an instant α sec in the future. It is apparent that the impulse response $g_1(t)$ may be found as

$$g_1(t) = \begin{cases} 0 & t < 0 \\ h_1(t + \alpha) & t \geq 0 \end{cases} \tag{10.56}$$

Since the mean of $s(t + \alpha)$ is thus given by the response of G_1, we may immediately conclude that the mean-square error is minimized for this value of the predicted signal, because this is a property of any distribution. This conclusion may be verified, and an expression for the mean-square error obtained, by evaluating the mean-square error when an arbitrary causal filter H' is used. The future value of the signal is obtained by (3.38) and (3.39) from the white-noise input $\{w(t)\}$ of Fig. 10.7 as

$$s(t + \alpha) = \int_{-\infty}^{t+\alpha} h_1(t + \alpha - \lambda)w(\lambda)\, d\lambda \tag{10.57}$$

If this is written in two parts,

$$s(t + \alpha) = \int_{-\infty}^{t} h_1(t + \alpha - \lambda)w(\lambda)\, d\lambda + \int_{t}^{t+\alpha} h_1(t + \alpha - \lambda)w(\lambda)\, d\lambda$$
$$= s_p + s_f \tag{10.58}$$

the first integral s_p is seen to involve impulses which have already occurred and thus to correspond to the predictable part of $s(t + \alpha)$. The second integral s_f is the unpredictable part. The alternative filter H' with impulse response $h'(t)$ would give a prediction

$$s'_p = \int_{-\infty}^{t} h'(t - \lambda)w(\lambda) \, d\lambda \qquad (10.59)$$

The predictable part s_p and the unpredictable part s_f are uncorrelated, as will be shown. The cross-correlation of s_p and s_f is

$$\overline{s_p s_f} = \int_{-\infty}^{t} d\lambda_1 \int_{t}^{t+\alpha} d\lambda_2 \, h_1(t + \alpha - \lambda_1)h_1(t + \alpha - \lambda_2)\overline{w(\lambda_1)w(\lambda_2)}$$

Since $w(t)$ is a sample function of white noise, the correlation function in the integrand is an impulse function, giving

$$\overline{s_p s_f} = \int_{-\infty}^{t} d\lambda_1 \int_{t}^{t+\alpha} d\lambda_2 \, h_1(t + \alpha - \lambda_1)h_1(t + \alpha - \lambda_2)\delta(\lambda_1 - \lambda_2)$$

This vanishes since the ranges of λ_1 and λ_2 do not overlap, and the delta-function argument is thus never zero. The argument is equally valid if s'_p is used instead of s_p, so that

$$\overline{s_p s_f} = \overline{s'_p s_f} = 0 \qquad (10.60)$$

The mean-square error in the prediction when H' is used is, by (10.58) and (10.60),

$$\begin{aligned} \overline{e^2} &= E[\{s(t + \alpha) - s'_p\}^2] = E[(s_p + s_f - s'_p)^2] \\ &= E[(s_p - s'_p)^2] + 2E[(s_p - s'_p)s_f] + E[s_f^2] \\ &= E[(s_p - s'_p)^2] + E[s_f^2] \end{aligned}$$

This expression is clearly a minimum if

$$s'_p = s_p = \int_{-\infty}^{t} h_1(t + \alpha - \lambda)w(\lambda) \, d\lambda \qquad (10.61)$$

and this is the best prediction in the least-squares sense if the predictor is restricted to a linear causal device.

The minimum mean-square error is thus

$$\overline{e^2_{\min}} = E[s_f^2] = E\left\{ \int_{t}^{t+\alpha} h_1(t + \alpha - \lambda)w(\lambda) \, d\lambda \right\}^2$$

which may be written, by the change of variable $u = t + \alpha - \lambda$,

$$\overline{e^2_{\min}} = E\left\{ \int_{0}^{\alpha} h_1(u)w(t + \alpha - u) \, du \right\}^2 \qquad (10.62)$$

This expression shows that the error is due to the values of the white-noise input $w(t)$ in the interval from t to $t + \alpha$ or to the nonzero values of

the impulse response $h_1(u)$ between $u = 0$ and $u = \alpha$.   The mean-square error may be written

$$\overline{e_{\min}^2} = E\left\{ \int_0^\alpha h_1(u)w(t + \alpha - u)\, du \int_0^\alpha h_1(v)w(t + \alpha - v)\, dv \right\}$$

$$= \int_0^\alpha \int_0^\alpha h_1(u)h_1(v)E[w(t + \alpha - u)w(t + \alpha - v)]\, du\, dv$$

$$= \int_0^\alpha \int_0^\alpha h_1(u)h_1(v)\delta(u - v)\, du\, dv$$

or

$$\overline{e_{\min}^2} = \int_0^\alpha h_1{}^2(u)\, du \qquad (10.63)$$

In a similar manner it follows from (10.57) that the mean-square value of $s(t + \alpha)$ is

$$\overline{s^2(t + \alpha)} = \int_0^\infty h_1{}^2(u)\, du \qquad (10.64)$$

so that the fractional root-mean-square prediction error is

$$\frac{\text{rms of prediction error}}{\text{rms of future signal}} = \sqrt{\frac{\int_0^\alpha h_1{}^2(u)\, du}{\int_0^\infty h_1{}^2(u)\, du}} \qquad (10.65)$$

Thus, the smaller the area under the curve of $h_1{}^2(t)$ between $t = 0$ and $t = \alpha$, compared with its total area, the better the prediction.   The error increases monotonically with the prediction interval α.

In summary, the predicting filter which minimizes the mean-square error is obtained as follows:

1. For a signal with rational power spectral density $W_s(\omega)$, find the minimum-phase filter which has a transfer function of magnitude $\sqrt{W_s(\omega)}$ by factoring $W_s(\omega)$ in accordance with (10.54).   The complex transfer function is $B^{-1}(\omega)$, and the corresponding impulse response is $h_1(t)$.   The transfer function of the inverse of this network is $B(\omega)$.
2. Construct a filter with impulse response

$$g_1(t) = \begin{cases} 0 & t < 0 \\ h_1(t + \alpha) & t \geq 0 \end{cases}$$

The corresponding transfer function is $G_1(\omega)$.
3. The best least-squares predicting filter has the transfer function

$$G_1(\omega)B(\omega)$$

SMOOTHING AND PREDICTION WITH A CAUSAL FILTER

The problem of determining a best linear causal least-squares filter for prediction in the presence of noise may be solved in a manner very similar to that used above for pure prediction. The minimum-phase filter which produces a power spectral density equal to that of the signal plus noise from a white-noise input must have a transfer function of magnitude $\sqrt{W_s(\omega) + W_n(\omega)}$ and associated minimum phase. Let the complex transfer function be denoted by $B^{-1}(\omega)$. Since (10.51) gives the best noncausal operation on the *input* signal plus noise, the best noncausal operation (if $\alpha = 0$) on the *white noise* requires a transfer function

$$H_2(\omega) = \frac{W_s(\omega)}{W_s(\omega) + W_n(\omega)} B^{-1}(\omega) \qquad (10.66)$$

This is again a noncausal transfer function. The corresponding impulse response is denoted by $h_2(t)$. By an argument similar to that used for the pure-prediction filter, we next construct a causal filter with impulse response

$$g_2(t) = \begin{cases} 0 & t < 0 \\ h_2(t + \alpha) & t \geq 0 \end{cases} \qquad (10.67)$$

This filter, with transfer function $G_2(\omega)$, will perform the best operation on *past* values of the white-noise sample functions. Finally, the desired filter for operation on the signal-plus-noise inputs has a transfer function

$$H_0(\omega) = G_2(\omega)B(\omega) \qquad (10.68)$$

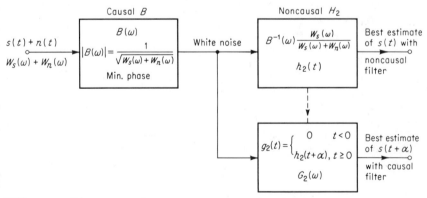

FIG. 10.9   *Linear causal least-squares filter for prediction in the presence of noise.*

The process by which this transfer function for the linear causal least-squares filter for prediction in the presence of noise is obtained is summarized in Fig. 10.9.

Example 10.5   It is desired to find the optimum smoothing and predicting filter when the signal has a power spectral density

$$W_s(\omega) = \frac{1}{1 + \omega^2}$$

and the (uncorrelated) noise is white, with $W_n(\omega) = 1$.

The input power spectral density is

$$W_x(\omega) = W_s(\omega) + W_n(\omega) = \frac{1}{1 + \omega^2} + 1 = \frac{2 + \omega^2}{1 + \omega^2}$$

This may be factored into

$$W_x(\omega) = \frac{(\sqrt{2} + j\omega)(\sqrt{2} - j\omega)}{(1 + j\omega)(1 - j\omega)}$$

Thus the transfer function required to produce this spectrum from white noise is, from (10.54),

$$B^{-1}(\omega) = \frac{\sqrt{2} + j\omega}{1 + j\omega}$$

The inverse of this transfer function will produce white noise from the signal-plus-noise input.

The best noncausal operation on the input (for $\alpha = 0$) is obtained by (10.51) with a transfer function

$$H(\omega) = \frac{W_s(\omega)}{W_s(\omega) + W_n(\omega)} = \frac{1}{2 + \omega^2}$$

The best noncausal transfer function with white-noise input is therefore, from (10.66),

$$H_2(\omega) = H(\omega)B^{-1}(\omega) = \frac{1}{2 + \omega^2} \frac{\sqrt{2} + j\omega}{1 + j\omega}$$

$$= \frac{1}{(\sqrt{2} - j\omega)(1 + j\omega)}$$

$$= \frac{1}{2.414}\left(\frac{1}{\sqrt{2} - j\omega} + \frac{1}{1 + j\omega}\right)$$

The corresponding impulse response is

$$h_2(t) = \begin{cases} \dfrac{1}{2.414} e^{\sqrt{2}t} & t < 0 \\[2mm] \dfrac{1}{2.414} e^{-t} & t \geq 0 \end{cases}$$

The first term in $H_2(\omega)$, due to its pole in the right half $j\omega$ plane (or lower half ω plane), results in a noncausal impulse response which does not have to be evaluated since it does not contribute to the required physical impulse response.

The best causal impulse response is now

$$g_2(t) = \begin{cases} 0 & t < 0 \\ \dfrac{1}{2.414}\, e^{-(t+\alpha)} & t \geq 0 \end{cases}$$

The corresponding transfer function is

$$G_2(\omega) = \frac{1}{2.414} \frac{1}{1 + j\omega}\, e^{-\alpha}$$

Finally, the required transfer function of the smoothing and predicting filter is, by (10.68),

$$H_0(\omega) = G_2(\omega)B(\omega)$$
$$= \frac{1}{2.414} \frac{1}{\sqrt{2} + j\omega}\, e^{-\alpha}$$

Example 10.6 Bates, Bock, and Powell† give the design for a predictor for certain low-frequency random processes such as airplane oscillations, ship motion, or ocean swells. From a magnetic-tape record, the power

† M. R. Bates, D. H. Bock, and F. D. Powell, Analog Computer Applications in Predictor Design, *IRE Trans. Electron. Computers*, vol. EC-6, pp. 143–153, September, 1957.

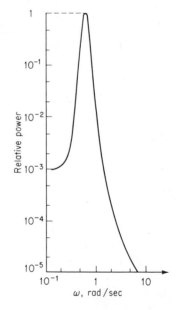

FIG. 10.10 Analytic approximation to power spectral density of low-frequency random process of Example 10.6. (From M. R. Bates, D. H. Bock, and F. D. Powell, Analog Computer Applications in Predictor Design, IRE Trans. Electron. Computers, vol. EC-6, pp. 143–153, September, 1957.)

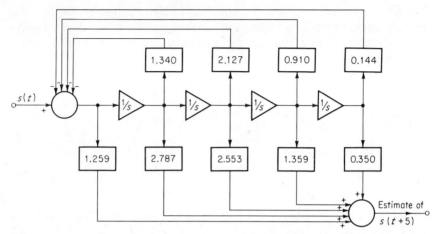

FIG. 10.11   *Predictor block diagram for Example 10.6.   (From M. R. Bates, D. H. Bock, and F. D. Powell, Analog Computer Applications in Predictor Design, IRE Trans. Electron. Computers, vol. EC-6, pp. 143–153, September, 1957.)*

spectral density is estimated to be

$$W(\omega) = \frac{(0.197\omega)^4}{(\omega^2 - 0.379)^4 + (0.197\omega)^4} + \frac{0.00379}{\omega^2 + 0.379}$$

This spectral density is shown in Fig. 10.10.

Factorization of the spectrum according to (10.54) gives

$$B^{-1}(\omega) = \frac{0.0195(-\omega^2 + 0.820j\omega + 1.611)(-\omega^2 + 0.520j\omega + 0.089)}{(j\omega + 0.616)(-\omega^2 + 0.123j\omega + 0.302)(-\omega^2 + 0.155j\omega + 0.476)}$$

For 5-sec prediction ($\alpha = 5$), the transfer function of the optimum filter is found to be

$$G_1(\omega)B(\omega) = \frac{1.259(j\omega)^4 + 2.787(j\omega)^3 + 2.553(j\omega)^2 + 1.395j\omega + 0.350}{(j\omega)^4 + 1.340(j\omega)^3 + 2.127(j\omega)^2 + 0.910j\omega + 0.144}$$

The analog-computer network for this transfer function is shown in Fig. 10.11.   The mean-square error, computed from (10.63) as a function of the prediction interval α, is shown in Fig. 10.12.

FIG. 10.12   *Prediction error in Example 10.6.   (From M. R. Bates, D. H. Bock, and F. D. Powell, Analog Computer Applications in Predictor Design, IRE Trans. Electron. Computers, vol. EC-6, pp. 143–153, September, 1957.)*

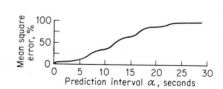

10.6 FILTERING OF DISCRETE-TIME SIGNALS

In the preceding section, we considered the filtering of stationary continuous-time signals using the Bode-Shannon approach in the frequency domain.   In this section we shall continue the discussion of linear least-squares filtering by studying the filtering of possibly nonstationary discrete-time signals in the time domain, with some indication of how the same methods may be used for continuous-time signals.

If the inputs are nonstationary, the filter minimizing the mean-square error is generally a time-varying system.   We must therefore determine a unit response $h(n, k)$..   In order to make the problem meaningful, we again require that the filter be causal, i.e., that it operate only on past data.   This means that the impulse response $h(n, k) = 0$ for $n < k$.

The model of Fig. 10.6 is still applicable, except that all signals are now discrete-time signals.   If we express the output $y(n)$ by the superposition summation (3.55), the difference between the output of the optimum causal filter and the desired (ideal) signal is the error

$$e(n) = y_0(n) - y(n) = \sum_{k=-\infty}^{n} h(n, k)x(k) - y(n) \qquad (10.69)$$

The square of the error at the instant n is thus

$$e^2(n) = \sum_{j=-\infty}^{n} \sum_{k=-\infty}^{n} h(n, j)h(n, k)x(j)x(k)$$
$$- 2 \sum_{k=-\infty}^{n} h(n, k)x(k)y(n) + y^2(n) \qquad (10.70)$$

We now take the mean or expected value of (10.70) and use the fact that the expected value of a sum equals the sum of the expected values.   Thus

$$\overline{e^2(n)} = \sum_{j=-\infty}^{n} \sum_{k=-\infty}^{n} h(n, j)h(n, k)r_x(j, k)$$
$$- 2 \sum_{k=-\infty}^{n} h(n, k)r_{xy}(k, n) + \overline{y^2(n)} \qquad (10.71)$$

where

$$r_x(j, k) = E[x(j)x(k)]$$
$$r_{xy}(k, n) = E[x(k)y(n)]$$

as defined in (9.25) and (9.79), respectively.

Our objective is the determination of the coefficients of the unit response $h(n, k)$, for $k = n, n - 1, n - 2, \ldots$, which minimizes $\overline{e^2(n)}$

for all n. We proceed in the usual manner by setting

$$\frac{\partial \overline{e^2(n)}}{\partial h(n, k)} = 0 \qquad \text{for } k = n, n - 1, n - 2, \ldots$$

The differentiation of (10.71) is carried out for a fixed value of n and results in

$$r_{xy}(k, n) = \sum_{j=-\infty}^{n} h(n, j)r_x(j, k) \qquad k = n, n - 1, n - 2, \ldots \qquad (10.72)$$

If the input $x(n)$ is not applied until a finite time which can be conveniently taken as $n = 0$, the lower limits in the summations of (10.69) to (10.72) become 0, and (10.72) becomes

$$r_{xy}(k, n) = \sum_{j=0}^{n} h(n, j)r_x(j, k) \qquad k = 0, 1, 2, \ldots, n \qquad (10.73)$$

In detail, (10.73) may be written

$n = 0$: $r_{xy}(0, 0) = h(0, 0)r_x(0, 0)$

$n = 1$: $r_{xy}(0, 1) = h(1, 0)r_x(0, 0) + h(1, 1)r_x(1, 0)$
$\qquad\;\; r_{xy}(1, 1) = h(1, 0)r_x(0, 1) + h(1, 1)r_x(1, 1)$

$n = 2$: $r_{xy}(0, 2) = h(2, 0)r_x(0, 0) + h(2, 1)r_x(1, 0) + h(2, 2)r_x(2, 0)$
$\qquad\;\; r_{xy}(1, 2) = h(2, 0)r_x(0, 1) + h(2, 1)r_x(1, 1) + h(2, 2)r_x(2, 1)$
$\qquad\;\; r_{xy}(2, 2) = h(2, 0)r_x(0, 2) + h(2, 1)r_x(1, 2) + h(2, 2)r_x(2, 2)$

and so on. Thus it is seen that the nth row of the transmission matrix (Sec. 3.6)

$$\tilde{\mathbf{H}} = \begin{bmatrix} h(0, 0) & 0 & 0 & \cdots \\ h(1, 0) & h(1, 1) & 0 & \cdots \\ h(2, 0) & h(2, 1) & h(2, 2) & \cdots \\ \cdots\cdots\cdots\cdots\cdots\cdots\cdots \end{bmatrix} \qquad (10.74)$$

of the optimum filter is obtained as the solution to a system of simultaneous equations.

Example 10.7 Filtering of step from uncorrelated noise†

As an illustration of the use of (10.73) for the design of an optimum filter, consider the problem of separating a step signal from additive white noise which is statistically independent of the signal.

The correlation function of an ensemble of steps of zero mean is

$$r_s(n, k) = \begin{cases} S & n, k \geq 0 \\ 0 & n, k < 0 \end{cases}$$

† Friedland, *loc. cit.*

where S is the mean-square amplitude of the ensemble, and the correlation function of the noise is

$$r_\nu(n, k) = \begin{cases} N\delta(n, k) & n, k \geq 0 \\ 0 & n, k < 0 \end{cases}$$

where N is the mean-square amplitude of the noise ensemble. The correlation function of signal plus noise equals the sum of the respective correlation functions, since the signal and noise are uncorrelated [see (9.90)]. Normalizing with respect to S and letting the noise-to-signal ratio $N/S = r$, we obtain for the required correlation functions

$$r_x(n, k) = \frac{1}{S}[r_s(n, k) + r_\nu(n, k)]$$

$$= \begin{cases} 1 + r\delta(n, k) & n, k \geq 0 \\ 0 & n, k < 0 \end{cases}$$

and

$$r_{xy}(k, n) = \frac{1}{S}[r_s(n, k)] = \begin{cases} 1 & n, k \geq 0 \\ 0 & n, k < 0 \end{cases}$$

Substituting these into (10.73) gives the following set of equations for the nth row of $\tilde{\mathbf{H}}$:

$$\begin{aligned} 1 &= (1 + r)h(n, 0) + & h(n, 1) + \cdots + & h(n, n) \\ 1 &= h(n, 0) + (1 + r)h(n, 1) + \cdots + & h(n, n) \\ & \cdots \cdots \cdots \cdots \cdots \cdots \cdots \cdots \cdots \cdots \cdots \\ 1 &= h(n, 0) + & h(n, 1) + \cdots + (1 + r)h(n, n) \end{aligned}$$

Subtracting each equation in this set from the one above it, we find

$$h(n, 0) = h(n, 1) = \cdots = h(n, n)$$

and adding the entire set of equations, we obtain

$$n + 1 = (n + 1 + r)[h(n, 0) + h(n, 1) + \cdots + h(n, n)]$$
$$= (n + 1 + r)(n + 1)h(n, 0)$$

Thus

$$h(n, 0) = h(n, 1) = \cdots = h(n, n) = \frac{1}{n + 1 + r}$$

and the transmission matrix of the optimum filter is

$$\tilde{\mathbf{H}} = \begin{bmatrix} (1 + r)^{-1} & 0 & 0 & \cdots \\ (2 + r)^{-1} & (2 + r)^{-1} & 0 & \cdots \\ (3 + r)^{-1} & (3 + r)^{-1} & (3 + r)^{-1} & \cdots \\ \cdots \cdots \cdots \cdots \cdots \cdots \cdots \cdots \cdots \end{bmatrix}$$

which can be written

$$
\tilde{\mathbf{H}} = \begin{bmatrix} (1+r)^{-1} & 0 & 0 & \cdots \\ 0 & (2+r)^{-1} & 0 & \cdots \\ 0 & 0 & (3+r)^{-1} & \cdots \\ \cdot\cdot\cdot\cdot\cdot\cdot\cdot\cdot\cdot\cdot\cdot\cdot\cdot\cdot\cdot\cdot\cdot \end{bmatrix} \begin{bmatrix} 1 & 0 & 0 & \cdots \\ 1 & 1 & 0 & \cdots \\ 1 & 1 & 1 & \cdots \\ \cdot\cdot\cdot\cdot\cdot\cdot\cdot\cdot \end{bmatrix} \quad (10.75)
$$

The first matrix on the right-hand side of (10.75) is the transmission matrix of an amplifier with a time-varying gain $a(n) = 1/(n + r + 1)$, and the second is recognized as the transmission matrix of a discrete-time integrator with the discrete-time transfer function $1/(1 - z^{-1})$. Since the amplifier gain approaches 0 as $n \to \infty$, there is no steady-state filter. The best estimate of the input signal in the steady state is zero because the ensemble of input steps was assumed to have zero mean.

The special form in which (10.73) appears in the above example is fortuitous. In general, one cannot expect to obtain an analytic solution for the optimum filter, and the computation required for the evaluation of $h(n, k)$ by solving the simultaneous equations obtained from (10.73) is formidable, even with the use of a digital computer. A whitening filter as used in Sec. 10.5 avoids this problem and will be discussed later.

It is of interest to compute the mean-square error when the filter which satisfies (10.73) is employed. Use of (10.72) in (10.71) gives

$$
[\overline{e^2(n)}]_{\min} = \overline{y^2(n)} - \sum_{k=-\infty}^{n} h(n, k) r_{xy}(k, n) \quad (10.76)
$$

If a different filter, say H', is used, it can readily be shown (Prob. 10.19) that

$$
[\overline{e^2(n)}]_{H'} = [\overline{e^2(n)}]_{\min} + \sum_{j=-\infty}^{n} \sum_{k=-\infty}^{n} a(n, j) a(n, k) r_x(j, k) \quad (10.77)
$$

where $a(n, k) = h'(n, k) - h(n, k)$. Since the correlation matrix $\mathbf{R}_x$ is positive-definite,[†] the quadratic form on the right-hand side of (10.77) is positive-definite. Thus the mean-square error due to the use of any filter H' different from H always exceeds that due to H. Thus H is the optimum filter in the least-squares sense.

Suppose that the input process is stationary. If H is a fixed filter, the output process $\{y(n)\}$ is then also stationary. In order to find the optimum filter H, we use (10.72) and set $r_{xy}(k, n) = r_{xy}(n - k)$,

---

[†] H. Cramér, "Mathematical Methods of Statistics." p. 295, Princeton University Press, Princeton, N.J., 1947.

$h(n, j) = h(n - j)$, and $r_x(j, k) = r_x(k - j)$, giving

$$r_{xy}(n - k) = \sum_{j=-\infty}^{n} h(n - j)r_x(k - j)$$

$$k = n, n - 1, n - 2, \ldots \quad (10.78)$$

This represents an infinite set of equations which cannot generally be solved explicitly. If we let $n - k = l$, $n - j = m$, (10.78) becomes

$$r_{xy}(l) = \sum_{m=0}^{\infty} h(m)r_x(m - l) \qquad (10.79)$$

which must be solved for $h(0), h(1), \ldots$, the values of the unit-function response of the system. Note that (10.79) is identical with (10.31) since r_x is an even function of its argument.

THE USE OF SHAPING FILTERS

The problem of solving (10.73) or (10.79) for discrete-time filters can be approached by the use of shaping filters as discussed in Sec. 10.5. The whitening filter B in the discrete-time case must convert the input process $\{x(n)\}$ into white noise $\{w(t)\}$ with correlation function

$$r_w(k, n) = \delta(n - k) = \begin{cases} 1 & n = k \\ 0 & n \neq k \end{cases} \qquad (10.80)$$

The second unit G must be optimum for white noise; both B and G must be causal and linear, so that the tandem combination will also be causal and linear.

In order to find the whitening filter B in discrete-time systems, we employ (10.24) with $h_1(n, k) = h_2(n, k) = b(n, k)$, the unit-function response of the causal whitening filter. The upper limits in the summations become n since B must be causal; the lower limits become 0 if the input $x(j)$ is first applied at a finite time $j = 0$. Hence

$$r_w(n, k) = \sum_{j=0}^{n} \sum_{i=0}^{n} b(n, j)b(k, i)r_x(j, i) \qquad (10.81)$$

In matrix form (10.81) becomes

$$\mathbf{R}_w = \mathbf{B}\mathbf{R}_x\mathbf{B}'$$

where $\mathbf{B}$ = transmission matrix of B

$\mathbf{R}_w, \mathbf{R}_x$ = correlation matrices of $\{w\}$ and $\{x\}$, respectively

$\mathbf{B}'$ = transpose of $\mathbf{B}$

In view of (10.80), however, we require that

$$\mathbf{R}_w = \begin{bmatrix} 1 & 0 & 0 & 0 & \cdots \\ 0 & 1 & 0 & 0 & \cdots \\ 0 & 0 & 1 & 0 & \cdots \\ 0 & 0 & 0 & 1 & \cdots \\ \cdots & \cdots & \cdots & \cdots & \cdots \end{bmatrix} = \mathbf{I}$$

Thus it is required to find the matrix $\mathbf{B}$ with only zero elements above the principal diagonal which satisfies

$$\mathbf{I} = \mathbf{B}\mathbf{R}_x\mathbf{B}' \tag{10.82}$$

Since $\mathbf{R}_x$ is a positive-definite symmetric matrix, it can always be factored as

$$\mathbf{R}_x = \mathbf{CC}'$$

where $\mathbf{C}$ is a lower triangular matrix, and $\mathbf{C}'$ is its transpose. Specifically, the elements of $\mathbf{C}$ are

$$c_{00} = \sqrt{r_x(0, 0)}$$
$$c_{10} = \frac{r_x(1, 0)}{c_{00}}$$
$$c_{20} = \frac{r_x(2, 0)}{c_{00}}$$

$$c_{01} = 0$$
$$c_{11} = \sqrt{r_x(1, 1) - c_{10}^2}$$
$$c_{21} = \frac{r_x(2, 1) - c_{10}c_{20}}{c_{11}}$$

$$c_{02} = 0$$
$$c_{12} = 0$$
$$c_{22} = \sqrt{r_x(2, 2) - c_{20}^2 - c_{21}^2}$$
$$\cdots \cdots \cdots \cdots \cdots \cdots \cdots \cdots \cdots$$

The required matrix is therefore

$$\mathbf{B} = \mathbf{C}^{-1} \tag{10.83}$$

It should be noted that the problem of factoring $\mathbf{R}_x$ in order to obtain the filter C which converts white noise to $\{x\}$ is analogous to that of factoring the power spectral density as in (10.54). The problem is much more difficult, however, in the nonstationary case treated here.

When we are dealing with stationary processes, the difficulty of finding the filter C may be avoided by operating in the frequency domain as in Sec. 10.5. We seek a transfer function which will convert a signal of spectral density $W_x(\omega)$ to white noise. In the discrete-time case, using

(10.35) and (10.40), we require

$$1 = B(z)B(z^{-1})W'_x(z) \tag{10.84}$$

Since $B(z)$ is causal, the Z transform is

$$B(z) = \sum_{n=0}^{\infty} b(n)z^{-n}$$

If $b(n)$ satisfies the conditions of Theorem 8.1, $B(z)$ is analytic, by Theorem 8.2, for sufficiently large values of $|z|$. Likewise, $B(z^{-1})$ must then be analytic for sufficiently small values of $|z|$. If now $W'_x(z)$ can be factored into a product,

$$W'_x(z) = \bar{W}_x(z)\bar{W}_x(z^{-1}) \tag{10.85}$$

where $\bar{W}_x(z)$ is analytic for large $|z|$, and $\bar{W}_x(z^{-1})$ is analytic for small $|z|$, it follows that

$$B(z) = \frac{1}{\bar{W}_x(z)} \tag{10.86}$$

This result corresponds to that obtained in Sec. 10.5 for continuous-time filters and rational spectral densities $W_x(\omega)$.

The filter which is optimum for a white-noise input may now easily be found since (10.72) with $r_x(j, k) = \delta(j, k)$ reduces to

$$r_{wy}(k, n) = g(n, k) \qquad n > k \tag{10.87}$$

for a system G with unit response $g(n, k)$. For $n < k$ we require
$$r_{wy}(k, n) = 0$$

in order to ensure that the filter will be causal. Thus the optimum filter for operation on white noise has unit-response coefficients which numerically equal the cross-correlation between $\{w\}$ and $\{y\}$. In matrix notation, if

$$\mathbf{R}_{wy} = \begin{bmatrix} r_{wy}(0, 0) & r_{wy}(0, 1) & r_{wy}(0, 2) & \cdots \\ r_{wy}(1, 0) & r_{wy}(1, 1) & r_{wy}(1, 2) & \cdots \\ r_{wy}(2, 0) & r_{wy}(2, 1) & r_{wy}(2, 2) & \cdots \\ \cdots & \cdots & \cdots & \cdots \end{bmatrix}$$

then

$$\mathbf{G} = \begin{bmatrix} r_{wy}(0, 0) & 0 & 0 & \cdots \\ r_{wy}(0, 1) & r_{wy}(1, 1) & 0 & \cdots \\ r_{wy}(0, 2) & r_{wy}(1, 2) & r_{wy}(2, 2) & \cdots \\ \cdots & \cdots & \cdots & \cdots \end{bmatrix} \tag{10.88}$$

This may be written symbolically as

$$\mathbf{G} = [\mathbf{R}'_{wy}]_c = [(\mathbf{BR}_{xy})']_c \tag{10.89}$$

where the symbol [ ]$_c$ stands for "the causal part of," and the prime indicates transposition.† It is easily shown (Prob. 10.15) that $\mathbf{R}_{wy} = \mathbf{BR}_{xy}$. Note that the appearance of the 0 elements in (10.88) corresponds to the truncation of the impulse response in (10.56).

For stationary processes, the result in (10.89) can again be expressed in the frequency domain. With $n - k = m$, (10.87) becomes

$$r_{wy}(m) = g(m) \qquad m > 0$$

Taking the one-sided Z transform of both sides, we obtain

$$G(z) = \sum_{m=0}^{\infty} r_{wy}(m)z^{-m} = \mathcal{Z}_I[r_{wy}(m)] \tag{10.90}$$

This is the expression for the discrete-time transfer function of G. The right-hand side is *not* equal to $W'_{wy}(z)/T$ since this is defined in (9.60) as the two-sided Z transform of $r_{wy}(m)$. Thus the required $G(z)$ is obtained by taking that part of $W'_{wy}(z)/T$ which corresponds to the sum in (10.90), i.e., the nonnegative values of the index. The result may be written

$$G(z) = \left[\frac{W'_{wy}(z)}{T} \right]_c$$

By writing $W'_{wy}(z)$ as the Z transform of $r_{wy}(k)$, using the definition of $r_{wy}(k)$ and expressing $w(n)$ by (3.57) in terms of $b(k)$, it is readily established that

$$W'_{wy}(z) = W'_{xy}(z)B(z^{-1})$$

so that

$$G(z) = \left[\frac{W'_{xy}(z)B(z^{-1})}{T} \right]_c \tag{10.91}$$

The optimum least-squares filter is thus given by

$$H(z) = \left[\frac{W'_{xy}(z)B(z^{-1})}{T} \right]_c B(z) \tag{10.92}$$

Example 10.8   Let us find the optimum discrete-time smoothing-and-predicting filter for a signal and additive uncorrelated noise similar to

† The transposition is required because the indices n, k appear in different order on the two sides of (10.87); this, in turn, is due to our conventions for the ordering of the arguments in the definitions (3.34) for the unit response and (9.79) for the cross-correlation function.

those in Example 10.5.   The signal and noise correlation functions are, respectively,

$$r_s(kT) = e^{-|k|T}$$

and

$$r_n(kT) = r\delta(k)$$

where r is the noise-to-signal ratio.   It is desired to predict the signal α sampling intervals (αT sec) ahead, where α is an integer.

We find for the sampled power spectral density of the signal

$$W_s'(z) = T\mathcal{Z}_{\mathrm{II}}[r_s(kT)] = T\frac{1 - \epsilon^2}{(1 - \epsilon z^{-1})(1 - \epsilon z)}$$

where $\epsilon = e^{-T}$.   For the noise

$$W_n'(z) = Tr$$

and thus, for the signal-plus-noise input,

$$W_x'(z) = W_s'(z) + W_n'(z)$$
$$= T\frac{1 + r - \epsilon^2(1 - r) - r\epsilon z^{-1} - r\epsilon z}{(1 - \epsilon z^{-1})(1 - \epsilon z)}$$

In order to factor $W_x'(z)$ in the form of (10.85), it is written

$$W_x'(z) = T\frac{\epsilon r}{b}\frac{(1 - bz^{-1})(1 - bz)}{(1 - \epsilon z^{-1})(1 - \epsilon z)}$$

where b is a solution of

$$b^2 - b\left[\frac{1 + r - \epsilon^2(1 - r)}{r\epsilon}\right] + 1 = 0$$

or

$$b = \frac{1 + r - \epsilon^2(1 - r) - \sqrt{(1 - \epsilon^2)[(1 + r)^2 - \epsilon^2(1 - r)^2]}}{2\epsilon r} \qquad (10.93)$$

Hence, from (10.85) and (10.86), we find

$$B(z) = \sqrt{\frac{b}{\epsilon rT}}\frac{1 - \epsilon z^{-1}}{1 - bz^{-1}}$$

for the discrete-time transfer function which converts $\{x\}$ to white noise.

The optimum filter for operating on the white noise is given by (10.91). In order to find $W_{xy}'(z)$, we first determine $r_{xy}(k)$, which, by definition, is

$$r_{xy}(k) = E[x(m)y(m + k)]$$

where $x(n) = s(m) + n(m)$ and $y(m) = s(m + \alpha)$.   Since the noise and

signal are uncorrelated, we find

$$r_{xy}(k) = E[s(m)s(m + k + \alpha)] = r_s(k + \alpha)$$
$$= re^{-|k+\alpha|T}$$

Hence

$$W'_{xy}(z) = T \sum_{k=-\infty}^{\infty} e^{-|k+\alpha|T} z^{-k}$$

$$= T \sum_{m=-\infty}^{-1} e^{mT} z^{-m+\alpha} + T \sum_{m=0}^{\infty} e^{-mT} z^{-m+\alpha}$$

$$= z^{\alpha} W'_s(z)$$

Thus the optimum filter operating on the white noise is, according to (10.91),

$$G(z) = \frac{1}{T} [W'_{xy}(z)B(z^{-1})]_c$$

$$= \left[\frac{(1 - \epsilon^2)z^{\alpha}}{(1 - \epsilon z^{-1})(1 - \epsilon z)} \sqrt{\frac{b}{erT}} \frac{1 - \epsilon z}{1 - bz} \right]_c$$

Using the result of Prob. 10.21, we find

$$G(z) = \sqrt{\frac{b}{erT}} \frac{(1 - \epsilon^2)\epsilon^{\alpha}}{1 - b\epsilon} \frac{1}{1 - \epsilon z^{-1}}$$

The discrete-time transfer function of the optimum smoothing-and-predicting filter is therefore

$$H_0(z) = G(z)B(z) = \frac{b}{Ter} \frac{(1 - \epsilon^2)\epsilon^{\alpha}}{1 - b\epsilon} \frac{1}{1 - bz^{-1}}$$

where b is given by (10.93) and $\epsilon = e^{-T}$. It is seen that the prediction time α enters into the optimum transfer function in the same way as it did in Example 10.5.

10.7   THE MATCHED FILTER

When a radar system is used to detect targets such as aircraft or missiles, the form of the signal may be completely known.   The pulses sent by the radar are reflected by the target and are returned to a receiver.   They are now imbedded in noise, and the problem at the receiver is to determine whether a signal (i.e., a reflected radar pulse) is present in the received waveform or whether this consists of noise only.   In order to make this determination with the least error, one approach consists of using a filter

which maximizes the ratio of the signal power to the noise power at one instant.

We assume that the signal $s(t)$ is known and has a Fourier transform $S(\omega)$ and that the added noise process has an expected value of zero and is stationary, with power spectral density $W_n(\omega)$. If the signal and noise are passed through a linear filter with transfer function $H(\omega)$, the value of the output component $y_s(t)$ due to the signal at $t = t_1$ is

$$y_s(t_1) = \frac{1}{2\pi} \int_{-\infty}^{\infty} H(\omega)S(\omega)e^{j\omega t_1}\, d\omega \qquad (10.94)$$

The output noise power is, according to (10.18) and (10.21),

$$\overline{y_n{}^2} = \frac{1}{2\pi} \int_{-\infty}^{\infty} |H(\omega)|^2 W_n(\omega)\, d\omega \qquad (10.95)$$

The ratio ρ of signal power to noise power which is to be maximized is thus

$$\rho = \frac{\left[\int_{-\infty}^{\infty} H(\omega)S(\omega)e^{j\omega t_1}\, d\omega \right]^2}{2\pi \int_{-\infty}^{\infty} |H(\omega)|^2 W_n(\omega)\, d\omega} \qquad (10.96)$$

In the Schwarz inequality†

$$|\textstyle\int f(\omega)g(\omega)\, d\omega|^2 \le \int |f(\omega)|^2\, d\omega \int |g(\omega)|^2\, d\omega \qquad (10.97)$$

we may set

$$f(\omega) = H(\omega)\sqrt{W_n(\omega)} \quad \text{and} \quad g(\omega) = \frac{S(\omega)}{\sqrt{W_n(\omega)}}\, e^{j\omega t_1}$$

since $s(t_1)$, and hence the numerator in ρ, are real. It follows that

$$\rho \le \frac{1}{2\pi} \int_{-\infty}^{\infty} \frac{|S(\omega)|^2}{W_n(\omega)}\, d\omega \qquad (10.98)$$

Since the equality in (10.97) holds if $f(\omega) = kg^*(\omega)$, where k is any constant, it is seen that ρ reaches its maximum value in (10.98) if

$$H(\omega) = k\, \frac{S^*(\omega)}{W_n(\omega)}\, e^{-j\omega t_1} \qquad (10.99)$$

Equation (10.99) gives the best linear filter in the sense of maximizing the signal-to-noise power ratio at $t = t_1$. The physical meaning of (10.99) is apparent: the filter should pass those frequencies for which the amplitude spectrum of the signal is large compared with the power spectrum of the noise.

† See, for example, W. Kaplan, "Advanced Calculus," Addison-Wesley Publishing Company, Inc., Reading, Mass., 1952.

The case in which the noise process is white is of particular interest. With $W_n(\omega) = W_0$, (10.99) gives

$$H(\omega) = \frac{k}{W_0} S^*(\omega) e^{-j\omega t_1} \tag{10.100}$$

The factor k/W_0 corresponds to a simple gain and may be made unity for convenience. Since the filter is matched to a particular signal waveform, it is usually called a *matched filter*. Since the transfer function of the best filter is the conjugate of the signal amplitude spectrum (except for the factor $e^{-j\omega t_1}$), the term *conjugate filter* is sometimes used. The impulse response corresponding to (10.100) is, with $k/W_0 = 1$,

$$h(t) = \frac{1}{2\pi} \int_{-\infty}^{\infty} S^*(\omega) e^{-j\omega t_1} e^{j\omega t}\, d\omega$$

Since $s(t)$ is real, $S^*(\omega) = S(-\omega)$, and with $\lambda = -\omega$ we obtain

$$h(t) = \frac{1}{2\pi} \int_{-\infty}^{\infty} S(\lambda) e^{j\lambda(t_1 - t)}\, d\lambda$$

or

$$h(t) = s(t_1 - t) \tag{10.101}$$

Thus the impulse response of the best filter in the white-noise case is the mirror image of the signal, delayed by t_1 sec.

The response $y_s(t)$ of the matched filter of (10.101) to the signal $s(t)$ is, according to (3.39),

$$y_s(t) = s(t) \star h(t) = s(t) \star s(t_1 - t)$$
$$= \int_{-\infty}^{\infty} s(\lambda) s(t - t_1 + \lambda)\, d\lambda \tag{10.102}$$

At $t = t_1$, the response to $s(t)$ is therefore

$$y_s(t_1) = \int_{-\infty}^{\infty} s^2(\lambda)\, d\lambda = E_s \tag{10.103}$$

which is the total signal energy. The integral in (10.102) is proportional to the time-average correlation function which was defined in Example 9.8. It may readily be shown that (9.34) also applies to the time-average correlation function, and therefore (10.103) is the maximum value which $y_s(t)$ can assume. Thus the maximum value of the output signal of the matched filter equals the energy of the input signal. The maximum signal-to-noise power ratio of (10.98) for the white-noise case becomes, in

view of (5.27) and (10.103),

$$\rho_{\max} = \frac{E_s}{W_0} \tag{10.104}$$

It follows that the only way in which this ratio may be increased and the signal detection in the presence of white noise may be improved is by increasing the total energy of the signal.   If the noise is not white, (10.98) shows that change of the signal waveform, and hence of the energy spectral density $|S(\omega)|^2$, can increase ρ.

Example 10.9   The tapped delay line† of Fig. 10.13 generates an impulse response whose Fourier transform is

$$S(\omega) = \begin{cases} T \sum_{k=0}^{n} s(kT)e^{-j\omega kT} & |\omega| < \frac{\pi}{T} \\ 0 & |\omega| > \frac{\pi}{T} \end{cases}$$

The signal at the output of the generator is therefore, by use of (5.23) or (5.47)

$$s(t) = \sum_{k=0}^{n} s(kT) \frac{\sin \pi(t/T - k)}{\pi(t/T - k)}$$

This is a band-limited low-pass signal as in (9.62) whose sample values $s(kT)$ are zero for $k < 0$ and $k > n$.

† Adapted from G. Turin, An Introduction to Matched Filters, *IRE Trans. Information Theory*, vol. IT-6, pp. 311–329, June, 1960.

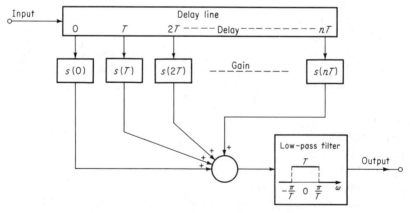

FIG. 10.13   *Tapped-delay-line signal generator.*

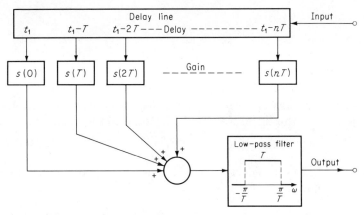

FIG. 10.14   Tapped-delay-line matched filter for signal produced by generator of Fig. 10.13.

The transfer function of the filter matched to this signal in the case of white noise is, by (10.100),

$$H(\omega) = \begin{cases} T \sum_{k=0}^{n} s(kT)e^{-j\omega(t_1-kT)} & |\omega| < \dfrac{\pi}{T} \\ 0 & |\omega| > \dfrac{\pi}{T} \end{cases}$$

A tapped-delay-line embodiment of this transfer function is shown in Fig. 10.14.   The structure of this filter is identical with that of the signal generator of Fig. 10.13, except that the delay line is reversed relative to the set of amplifiers whose gain equals the sampled values $s(kT)$ of the signal.

It has been assumed in the equations for $S(\omega)$ and $H(\omega)$ and in the corresponding Figs. 10.13 and 10.14 that the low-pass filter has the perfect amplitude characteristic shown and has no associated phase shift (or at least a phase shift increasing linearly with frequency over the transmission band).   It is known that such a filter cannot be realized, so that the generator and filter of Figs. 10.13 and 10.14 cannot be realized as shown.

PROBLEMS

10.1   Show that $g_{12}(-\tau) = g_{21}(\tau)$.

10.2   White noise of power spectral density $W(\omega) = W_0$ is applied to the RLC circuit shown in Fig. P 10.2.   Determine the output correlation function:

(a) By first finding the output power spectral density.

(b) By using the impulse response and the filter correlation function.

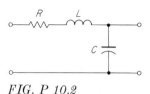

FIG. P 10.2

10.3   A random process characterized by a continuous random variable X having a uniform probability density in the interval $(-x_0 \leq X \leq x_0)$ is passed through a nonlinear device with the amplitude characteristic shown in Fig. P 10.3. Determine and sketch the

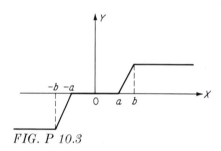

FIG. P 10.3

probability density function and the distribution function for each of the following cases:

(a) $x_0 < a$.   (b) $a < x_0 < b$.   (c) $x_0 > b$.

10.4   A stationary white-noise voltage process $\{x(t)\}$ of power spectral density W_0 and zero mean is applied to the RL circuit shown in Fig. P 10.4a. The output voltage process is $\{y(t)\}$. (Alternatively, the input sample functions may be the force functions acting on the mass-friction system shown in Fig. P 10.4b; the output sample functions are then the frictional force functions.) Determine:

(a) The mean of $\{y(t)\}$.

(b) The average power dissipated in the resistor R (or in friction).

(c) The correlation function $r_y(\tau)$.

(d) The power spectral density $W_y(\omega)$. Obtain $W_y(\omega)$ both by working in the frequency domain and from $r_y(\tau)$.

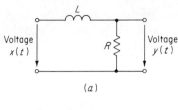

(a)

FIG. P 10.4 (a) Electric circuit;
(b) dual mechanical system.

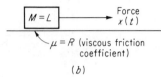

(b)

10.5   The differential equation for an RC filter (integrating circuit) whose input is $e(t)$ and whose output is the voltage $v(t)$ across the capacitor is

$$RC \frac{dv(t)}{dt} + v(t) = e(t)$$

If $e(t)$, and hence $v(t)$, are sample functions of stationary random processes:

(a) Express the correlation function of $\{e(t)\}$ in terms of that of $\{v(t)\}$ and its derivatives.

(b) By Fourier-transforming the differential equation for $r_v(\tau)$ obtained in (a), determine the power spectral density of the output process in terms of that of the input process.

(c) Check your answer to (b) by using the transfer function of the filter.

10.6   A fixed linear system has the impulse response $h(t)$ shown in Fig. P 10.6. A sine wave of frequency f_0 and added stationary white noise are passed through this system.

(a) For which of the three frequencies $f_0 = \dfrac{1}{2T}, f_0 = \dfrac{1}{T}, f_0 = \dfrac{3}{2T}$ is the system most effective as a filter of the noise from the signal?

(b) What is the filter correlation function of this system?

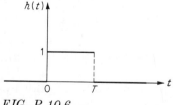

FIG. P 10.6

10.7   White noise with Gaussian probability density is passed through the filter shown in Fig. P 10.7a into the limiter shown in Fig. P 10.7b. The output power is measured by a square-law detector.

(a) Find the fractional reduction in power due to limiting in the amplifier, i.e., the ratio (power with limiting)/(power without limiting).

(b) Consider the symmetrical case $V_1 = V_2$ and find how much larger the saturation level must be than the rms value of the voltage for 0.5 percent accuracy.

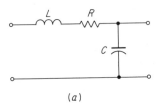

(a)

FIG. P 10.7   (a) Filter; (b) limiter.

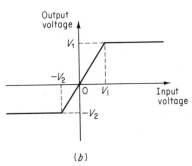

(b)

10.8   A fixed linear system H has an impulse response

$$h(t) = e^{-\alpha t}\mu_1(t)$$

Sample functions from a stationary noise process of correlation function

$$r(\tau) = e^{-\beta|\tau|}$$

are suddenly applied to this system at $t = 0$; before this instant the input is zero. Determine the mean-square value of the output as a function of time.

10.9   The filter shown in Fig. P 10.9 with $R = \frac{1}{2}\sqrt{L/C}$ is used to suppress stationary white noise of power spectral density W_0 added to a random-signal process whose sample functions are

$$s(t) = A \cos(\omega_0 t + \theta)$$

where A and ω_0 are constants, and θ is a value of a random variable distributed uniformly in $[0, 2\pi]$. The signal and noise are uncorrelated.

(a) Determine the output signal-to-noise power ratio.

(b) What happens to the signal-to-noise power ratio if LC is made large? What happens if $\omega_0 = 1/\sqrt{LC}$ and LC is made large? Are these results reasonable?

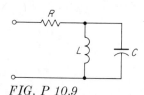

FIG. P 10.9

10.10 In the filter of Prob. 10.9, $R = (b/2) \sqrt{L/C}$, with $b < 1$. Determine the signal-to-noise power ratio, and note how it varies as LC is increased.

10.11 A velocity estimator is used to obtain the speed of a moving target by differentiating the input position data. The impulse response of such a velocity estimator is

$$h(t) = \begin{cases} A + Bt + Ct^2 & 0 \le t \le T \\ 0 & \text{otherwise} \end{cases}$$

where A, B, C are constants.

(a) If white noise of power spectral density W_0 is applied to the input of this estimator, find the mean-square value of the output.

(b) If the input signal represents a position measurement given by

$$x(t) = a_0 + a_1 t + \cdots + a_n t^n$$

what is the highest possible degree n of this polynomial for which the velocity estimate in the absence of noise can be made perfect through appropriate choice of the constants A, B, C?

10.12 A simple proportional feedback control system is shown in Fig. P 10.12. The input consists of sample functions $s(t)$ of a stationary random-signal process with correlation function

$$r(\tau) = A e^{-a|\tau|}$$

and superposed white noise $\{n(t)\}$ of spectral density W_0 which is

independent of the signal.   Determine the mean-square error by
which the system output fails to follow the input.

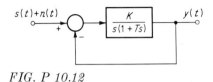

$$s(t)+n(t) \qquad \boxed{\dfrac{K}{s(1+Ts)}} \qquad y(t)$$

FIG. P 10.12

10.13   Show that the correlation function $r_y(\tau)$ of the output of a fixed
linear system with impulse response $h(t)$ may be written

$$r_y(\tau) = h(-\tau) \star r_x(\tau) \star h(\tau)$$

where $r_x(\tau)$ is the input correlation function.

10.14   Express the correlation matrix $\mathbf{R}_{12}$ whose elements are given by
(10.24) in terms of the transmission matrices $\tilde{\mathbf{H}}_1$ and $\tilde{\mathbf{H}}_2$ and the
input correlation matrix $\mathbf{R}_x$.

10.15   A discrete-time random process $\{x\}$ passes through a time-varying
discrete-time system with transmission matrix $\tilde{\mathbf{H}}$; the output
process is denoted by $\{z\}$.   Show that, if $\{y\}$ is any other process,
the correlation matrix $\mathbf{R}_{zy}$ is given by

$$\mathbf{R}_{zy} = \tilde{\mathbf{H}}\mathbf{R}_{xy}$$

10.16   Derive an expression for the power spectral density $W_e(\omega)$ of the
error which may be used for minimizing the mean-square error as
in (10.47) if the signal and noise processes are correlated.   The
cross-power spectral densities are $W_{sn}(\omega)$ and $W_{ns}(\omega)$.

10.17   It is desired to predict a signal whose power spectral density is

$$W(\omega) = \frac{1}{\omega^2 + 4}$$

The desired prediction time is α sec.

(a) Determine the transfer function of the optimum linear least-
squares predictor if the predictor does not have to be physically realizable.

(b) What is the transfer function of the optimum linear least-
squares *causal* predictor?

10.18   Determine the best predictor for a signal whose power spectral
density is

$$W_s(\omega) = \frac{W_0}{(1 + \omega^2)^2}$$

10.19   Verify (10.77) for the mean-square error resulting from the use of a discrete-time filter H'.

10.20   Show that the optimum (least-squares-error) filter for a random process $\{x\}$ and a desired process $\{y\}$ may be written

$$H = [R'_{xy}B^*]_c B$$

where B is given by

$$R_x = (B^{-1})(B^{-1})^*$$

with the following interpretations:

(a) In the time domain, $*$ means transposition and R'_{xy} is the transpose of the correlation matrix $\mathbf{R}_{xy}$.

(b) In the frequency domain for discrete-time systems,

$$B^* = B(z^{-1})$$

and $R'_{xy} = W'_{xy}(z)/T$.

(c) In the frequency domain for continuous-time systems, $B^* = B^*(\omega) = $ complex conjugate of $B(\omega)$ and $R'_{xy} = W_{xy}(\omega)$.

10.21   (a) Show that

$$\left[\frac{1}{(1 - az^{-1})(1 - bz)}\right]_c = \frac{1}{(1 - ab)(1 - az^{-1})}$$

where subscript c denotes the causal part of the quantity in the brackets.

(b) Show that

$$\left[\frac{z^m}{(1 - az^{-1})(1 - bz)}\right]_c = \frac{a^m}{1 - ab}\frac{1}{1 - az^{-1}}$$

10.22   A filter with impulse response $e^{-\alpha t}\mu_1(t)$ is to maximize the square of the signal-to-noise ratio of a signal in the presence of white noise at one instant. If the signal is a rectangular pulse of duration T sec, determine the best value of α.

CHAPTER ELEVEN

STABILITY

11.1 INTRODUCTION

The advent of high-speed digital computers has largely eliminated the problem of obtaining a numerical solution of the differential equations relating the response of a system to its excitation. There are many situations, however, in which numerical solutions are not needed and where such solutions, even if available, either do not provide the information required or make this information difficult to extract. As a representative example, consider the problem of evaluating the dynamic behavior of an aircraft. From the known physical laws of aerodynamics, fluid mechanics, elasticity, and so forth, one could write a system of differential equations which govern the dynamic behavior of the vehicle and determine, with reasonable confidence, the exact dynamic behavior for a given set of excitations—as represented by control surface settings, winds, and other excitations which affect the performance. A numerical solution of the

differential equations in this case is almost useless, however, since the questions which must be answered are essentially qualitative: How well does the aircraft fly? Will the failure of an engine be catastrophic? An attempt to answer these questions by solving the differential equations for the variety of excitations which are possible, even with the fastest available computers, is inconceivable. If this were the only approach, the successful design of aircraft would have been impossible. Moreover, the physical laws upon which the differential equations are based, in aerodynamics as well as in many other branches of technology, are not known with the precision required for an exact numerical solution of the differential equations.

Clearly, what one often desires are qualitative measures of the behavior of a system which, on the one hand, do not require solution of the differential equations and, on the other, cannot readily be obtained from such solutions. This chapter and the following are concerned with such qualitative properties.

The property of most frequent concern is that of *stability*. Loosely, a system may be said to be stable if its response to *any* "reasonable" excitation does not get out of hand. (Note that if the set of "reasonable" excitations is infinite—as it usually is—the question of stability cannot be definitely settled by obtaining the numerical solution of the governing differential equation with any finite number of excitations.) Unfortunately, it is difficult to give a single precise definition of stability that is universally satisfactory, simply because behavior which under some circumstances would be regarded as stable would be considered unstable under others. As a case in point, consider an electric motor. If the motor were used to position an antenna, for example, a continuously increasing angular position would be regarded as unstable (undesirable), but if the motor were used to drive a rotating machine, such behavior would be regarded as stable (desirable).

The absence of a universally acceptable definition of stability has led to the evolution of a number of definitions, each reasonable in a limited context. These definitions may be put into two classes: those concerning the stability of an equilibrium state in the absence of excitation and those concerning the stability of the response to a limited class of excitations with the system initially unexcited. The former class has received by far the greater attention and, when nonlinear systems are considered, actually subsumes the latter.

In considering the stability of a system, attention is properly focused on the *state* of the system, rather than upon the output, since it is possible that the state of a system could grow without bound without similar behavior of the output. This is illustrated by the following example.

Example 11.1 Consider the system shown in Fig. 11.1. The characteristic matrix of the system is

$$A = \begin{bmatrix} 0 & 1 \\ 2 & -1 \end{bmatrix}$$

whence the fundamental matrix is

$$\boldsymbol{\Phi}(t) = \mathcal{L}^{-1}[(s\mathbf{I} - \mathbf{A})^{-1}] = \frac{1}{3} \begin{bmatrix} 2e^t + e^{-2t} & e^t - e^{-2t} \\ 2e^t - 2e^{-t} & e^t + 2e^{-2t} \end{bmatrix}$$

It is evident that $\mathbf{q}(t) = \boldsymbol{\Phi}(t - t_0)\mathbf{q}(t_0)$ will grow without bound as a result of the term e^t with any initial condition; thus the system is unstable. Yet the output is

$$
\begin{aligned}
y(t) &= c_1 q_1(t) + c_2 q_2(t) \\
&= \tfrac{1}{3}[(2c_1 + 2c_2)q_1(0) + (c_1 + c_2)q_2(0)]e^t \\
&\qquad + \tfrac{1}{3}[(c_1 - 2c_2)q_1(0) + (-c_1 + 2c_2)q_2(0)]e^{-2t}
\end{aligned}
$$

and if $c_1 = -c_2$, the output $y(t)$ will not contain the e^t term and will not grow without bound, irrespective of the initial conditions.   (In Sec. 11.6, we shall consider the conditions under which this situation could arise.)

If any component of the state vector should grow without bound, it would be reasonable to regard the system as unstable, even if all the other components remained finite. Accordingly, we deal with the *norms* of vectors, which may be defined by

$$\|\mathbf{q}\| = \max_i |q_i| \qquad i = 1, 2, \ldots, k \tag{11.1}$$

and classify the stability of the system in accordance with the behavior of the norm of the state vector.

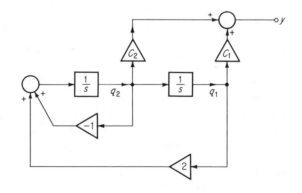

FIG. 11.1 *Example of a system in which unstable mode does not appear in output.*

More generally, any scalar function of the state having the following properties may be used to define a norm:

$$\|\mathbf{q}\| = 0 \qquad \text{if and only if } \mathbf{q} = 0 \tag{11.2a}$$
$$\|\mathbf{q}_1 + \mathbf{q}_2\| \leq \|\mathbf{q}_1\| + \|\mathbf{q}_2\| \tag{11.2b}$$
$$\|\alpha\mathbf{q}\| = |\alpha|\,\|\mathbf{q}\| \tag{11.2c}$$

The norm (11.1) clearly possesses all three properties. The second property is called the *triangle inequality*. A bit of reflection reveals that the properties (11.2) are those normally associated with *length*, and one can thus regard the norm of a vector as a generalized length. Some other useful norms are the Euclidean norm

$$\|\mathbf{q}\| = \left(\sum_i q_i^2\right)^{\frac{1}{2}}$$

and, more generally,

$$\|\mathbf{q}\| = \left(\sum_i q_i^p\right)^{1/p} \qquad p \geq 1$$

At several points in the sequel we shall employ the obvious fact that *the norm of a vector is finite if and only if every one of its components is finite* (Prob. 11.1).

We shall also have occasion to use the norm of a matrix $\mathbf{M}$ defined by

$$\|\mathbf{M}\| = \sup_{\mathbf{x}\neq 0} \frac{\|\mathbf{M}\mathbf{x}\|}{\|\mathbf{x}\|} \tag{11.3}$$

which, in words, is the least upper bound (supremum) of the ratio of the norm of the vector $\mathbf{y} = \mathbf{M}\mathbf{x}$ to the norm of $\mathbf{x}$, the ratio being evaluated for all possible (nonzero) vectors. Although the ratio, for any specific $\mathbf{x}$, may depend on $\mathbf{x}$, its least upper bound, of course, does not. It can be demonstrated that the norm of a matrix satisfies the three requirements (11.2). It can also be shown† by the use of the homogeneity property (11.2c) that the following formulas are equivalent to (11.3):

$$\|\mathbf{M}\| = \sup_{\|\mathbf{x}\|\leq 1} \|\mathbf{M}\mathbf{x}\| \tag{11.4}$$
$$= \sup_{\|\mathbf{x}\|=1} \|\mathbf{M}\mathbf{x}\| \tag{11.5}$$

The use of (11.4) narrows the search for the least upper bound of the ratio to those vectors of norm equal to or less than unity, and (11.5) narrows the search still further to those vectors of exactly unit norm.

† See P. Halmos, "Finite-dimensional Vector Spaces," 2d ed., p. 178, D. Van Nostrand Company, Inc., Princeton, N.J., 1958.

From the definition of the norm (11.3) it follows that

$$\|\mathbf{Mx}\| \leq \|\mathbf{M}\| \, \|\mathbf{x}\| \tag{11.6}$$

for any $\mathbf{x}$.   This is another relation we use frequently in the remainder of this chapter.   We also use the fact that, like the norm of a vector, *the norm of a matrix is finite if and only if every component of the matrix is finite*† (Prob. 11.2).

We shall concentrate our attention on continuous-time systems since, with obvious modifications, the results can be extended to discrete-time systems.   Where the extension is not obvious, however, both cases will be considered.

11.2 DEFINITIONS OF STABILITY FOR UNFORCED SYSTEMS

An equilibrium state, it will be recalled from Chap. 2, is any state in which the system remains at rest, i.e., any state for which $\dot{\mathbf{q}} \equiv \mathbf{0}$.   In linear systems, as we have seen, the set of all equilibrium states is a linear manifold—a hyperplane which includes the origin of the state space.   (In nonlinear systems, the set of equilibrium states may be finite—even empty—and may not include the origin.)

If the system is initially in an equilibrium state, it will remain in that state indefinitely.   However, suppose that the system is displaced even an infinitesimal amount from an equilibrium state.   Then one of the following mutually exclusive events can occur: (1) either the state will ultimately return to the neighborhood of the equilibrium point; or (2) the state will not return to the neighborhood of the equilibrium point, but its distance from the equilibrium point will remain finite; or (3) the state vector will grow without bound.   In the first case the equilibrium state is said to be *stable;* in the second, it is *bounded but unstable;* and in the third case it is neither bounded nor stable.

Greater precision in the definitions is achieved through the introduction of the concept of a *neighborhood N* of the equilibrium state $\mathbf{q}_e$.   For our purposes a neighborhood is the set of *all* points which lie less than a fixed distance ϵ from $\mathbf{q}_e$, distance being measured by the *norm*.   Thus a neighborhood of $\mathbf{q}_e$ is the set of all points $\mathbf{q}$ for which $\|\mathbf{q} - \mathbf{q}_e\| < \epsilon$.   It is important to note that a subset of a neighborhood, that is, a set of some, but not all, points for which $\|\mathbf{q} - \mathbf{q}_e\| < \epsilon$ is not a neighborhood.   It is

---

† For simplicity, we shall speak of a "finite matrix" when we mean that its norm is finite.

sometimes desirable to identify the "size" ϵ of the neighborhood and its "center" q_e, and this is done by means of the notation $N(q_e, \epsilon)$.

Definition 11.1   Boundedness† *An equilibrium state q_e is said to be bounded if and only if there exists a neighborhood $N(q_e, \delta)$ such that, if the initial state $q(t_0)$ lies within N, then $\|q(t) - q_e\| < \infty$ for all $t > t_0$. If such a neighborhood does not exist, the equilibrium state is said to be unbounded.*

Definition 11.2   Stability (in the sense of Lyapunov) *An equilibrium state q_e is said to be stable if and only if to any neighborhood $N(q_e, \epsilon)$ there corresponds a neighborhood $N(q_e, \delta)$ such that, if $q(t_0)$ lies in $N(q_e, \delta)$, then $q(t)$ lies in $N(q_e, \epsilon)$ for all $t > t_0$.*

Although it may at first appear that boundedness and stability are equivalent properties, this is generally not the case.   For an equilibrium state to be bounded, it is necessary only that for sufficiently small displacements the state remain a finite distance from the equilibrium state. The possibility that the state vector moves to a different equilibrium point or to a trajectory which traces out a closed curve (limit cycle) in the space is thus allowed.   (Motion to a new equilibrium point is characteristic of a bistable multivibrator, and motion toward a limit cycle is characteristic of an oscillator.)

In the definition of stability, on the other hand, one *starts* by specifying a neighborhood—which may be arbitrarily small—within which the state vector must be located for all time, and one must be able to find a corresponding neighborhood such that any initial state lying therein always remains inside the first neighborhood.   On this basis an *ideal* multivibrator must be classified as *unstable*, since, if it is displaced infinitesimally from one equilibrium state, it goes to the other, which, being a finite distance away, is outside an arbitrarily small neighborhood of the original equilibrium state.   An ideal nonlinear oscillator is also unstable: although there may be an equilibrium state at which all motion ceases, once the system is displaced from equilibrium, it goes into an oscillation of finite amplitude and the state vector is always more than an arbitrarily small distance from the origin.

The situation is different in a conservative system in which the amplitude of oscillation is proportional to the initial displacement from equilibrium, since in this case it is possible to limit the size of the oscillation—and thereby keep the state vector as close as desired to the equilibrium

† The term "bounded" is not standard; the definitions of stability and asymptotic stability given below, however, are generally used in the standard literature on differential equations.   See, for example, S. Lefschetz, "Differential Equations: Geometric Theory," Interscience Publishers, Inc., New York, 1957.

state—simply by limiting the initial displacement.   Hence such a system would be classified as *stable*.

It is sometimes desired to have a definition of stability which rules out even infinitesimal oscillations.   The following definition serves this purpose.

Definition 11.3 Asymptotic stability   *An equilibrium state is said to be asymptotically stable* (1) *if it is stable, and* (2) *if* $\|\mathbf{q}(t) - \mathbf{q}_e\| \to 0$ *as* $t \to \infty$, *for any initial condition lying in the neighborhood* $N(\mathbf{q}_e, \delta)$ *for which it is stable.*

Although it would seem that the condition $\|\mathbf{q}(t) - \mathbf{q}_e\| \to 0$ as $t \to \infty$ alone implies stability, this is not the case, although the situations where this is not so† are contrived and not likely to arise in physical situations.

The previous definitions are local in character, the region of stability being an unspecified neighborhood $N(\mathbf{q}_e, \delta)$ of the equilibrium state.   If this neighborhood can be the entire state space, the state $\mathbf{q}_e$ is said to be *globally* stable, or stable *in the large*.   Otherwise, the largest $N(\mathbf{q}_e, \delta)$ is said to be the region of stability of the state $\mathbf{q}_e$.   One can readily imagine that if the initial displacement from the equilibrium state is too great, the motion might be unstable, although for small displacements the motion could well be stable.   A familiar example is a nonideal multivibrator, which requires a "trigger" displacement to exceed a given level before it "flips" from one equilibrium point to another.   If the trigger is too small, the circuit returns to the first equilibrium state.   Hence each equilibrium state is locally asymptotically stable, but not asymptotically stable in the large.   The qualification "global" or "in the large" is used to indicate that with *every* initial displacement of the equilibrium state, not merely any one within a small neighborhood, the requirements of stability are satisfied.

The above definitions are further qualified for time-varying systems by the term "uniform."   Boundedness or stability (simple or asymptotic) is said to be *uniform* if the neighborhood in which the initial state must lie can be *independent of the starting time*.

The foregoing definitions are applicable to linear and nonlinear systems, but as we shall subsequently see, several turn out to be equivalent in the case of linear systems.

Although formulated using continuous-time variables, the definitions are obviously applicable to discrete-time systems with the use of n and n_0, respectively, in place of t and t_0.

† See R. E. Kalman and J. E. Bertram, Control System Analysis and Design via the "Second Method" of Lyapunov, *Trans. ASME*, ser. D (*J. Basic Eng.*), vol. 82, pp. 371–393, June, 1960.

11.3   CONDITIONS FOR STABILITY OF UNFORCED LINEAR SYSTEMS

We now turn our attention to linear continuous-time systems, governed by ordinary differential equations of the form

$$\dot{\mathbf{q}}(t) = \mathbf{A}(t)\mathbf{q}(t) + \mathbf{B}(t)\mathbf{x}(t)$$

As discussed in Chap. 4, the unforced system $(\mathbf{x}(t) = \mathbf{0}, t \geq t_0)$ has the solution

$$\mathbf{q}(t) = \mathbf{\Phi}(t, t_0)\mathbf{q}(t_0) \qquad (11.7)$$

Because it is possible to represent the state at a time subsequent to t_0 as a linear transformation—by the fundamental matrix $\mathbf{\Phi}(t, t_0)$—of the initial state $\mathbf{q}(t_0)$, it is possible to determine conditions for the stability of linear systems which depend only on the fundamental matrix. Here we assume that the equilibrium state in question is the *origin* $\mathbf{q} = \mathbf{0}$, which, as already observed, is an equilibrium state of any linear system. These conditions are embodied in the theorems which follow.

Theorem 11.1 *The origin of a linear system is bounded if and only if the fundamental matrix $\mathbf{\Phi}(t, t_0)$ is finite for all $t > t_0$.*

To prove this theorem we apply (11.6) to (11.7) and thereby obtain

$$\|\mathbf{q}(t)\| \leq \|\mathbf{\Phi}(t, t_0)\| \, \|\mathbf{q}(t_0)\|$$

If $\mathbf{\Phi}(t, t_0)$ is finite, there is a constant K such that $\|\mathbf{\Phi}(t, t_0)\| \leq K$. Hence $\|\mathbf{q}(t)\| \leq K\|\mathbf{q}(t_0)\|$. Then, if $\|\mathbf{q}(t_0)\| \leq \delta < \infty$, we have

$$\|\mathbf{q}(t)\| \leq K\delta$$

which shows that if the fundamental matrix is finite, the origin is bounded. Moreover, for any t_0 and t, there is some $\mathbf{q}(t_0) = \mathbf{q}_0$ with unit norm (hence finite) such that

$$\|\mathbf{q}(t)\| = \|\mathbf{\Phi}(t, t_0)\| \, \|\mathbf{q}_0\|$$

It thus follows that if, for some combination of t_0 and $t > t_0$, $\mathbf{\Phi}(t, t_0)$ is not finite, then, with $\mathbf{q}(t_0) = \mathbf{q}_0$, $\|\mathbf{q}(t)\|$ is not finite. This shows that if the fundamental matrix is not finite, the origin is not bounded, and completes the proof of the theorem.

Theorem 11.2 *Boundedness and stability (of the origin) are equivalent in linear systems.*

To prove this theorem we must show that for any constant $\epsilon > 0$ it is possible to find another constant $\delta(\epsilon)$ such that, if $\|\mathbf{q}(t_0)\| < \delta(\epsilon)$, then $\|\mathbf{q}(t)\| < \epsilon$ for $t \geq t_0$. If the origin is bounded, $\|\mathbf{\Phi}(t, t_0)\| \leq K$. Hence, for the given ϵ, select $\delta(\epsilon) = \epsilon/K$. Then

$$\|\mathbf{q}(t)\| \leq K\|\mathbf{q}(t_0)\| < \frac{K\epsilon}{K} = \epsilon$$

which shows that boundedness implies stability. It is obvious that stability implies boundedness; and hence the two are equivalent.

If the constant K which bounds the fundamental matrix is independent of the starting time t_0, it is evident that the stability is uniform. If the constant K depends on t_0, however, the stability is not uniform.

Theorem 11.3 *The origin of a linear system is asymptotically stable if and only if $\mathbf{\Phi}(t, t_0)$ is bounded for all t_0 and $t > t_0$, and $\mathbf{\Phi}(t, t_0) \to \mathbf{0}$ for $t \to \infty$.*

The proof of Theorem 11.3 is similar to those of the previous theorems and is left as an exercise for the reader (Prob. 11.7).

Since the conditions for stability of linear systems depend only on the fundamental matrix and are independent of the initial state, it follows that if the origin is locally asymptotically stable, it is also asymptotically stable in the large.

The manner in which these theorems were proved shows that they hold for discrete-time systems when $\mathbf{\Phi}(t, t_0)$ is replaced by its discrete analog $\mathbf{\Phi}(n, n_0)$.

11.4 STABILITY CRITERIA FOR UNFORCED FIXED LINEAR SYSTEMS

The conditions for the stability of fixed linear systems depend on the norm of the fundamental matrix, which is usually difficult to calculate in time-varying systems. In fixed systems, however, the form of the fundamental matrix is entirely governed by the characteristic roots of the system—or eigenvalues, or natural frequencies, as they are sometimes called—namely, the roots of the characteristic equation

$$|s\mathbf{I} - \mathbf{A}| = 0$$

for the unforced system governed by $\dot{\mathbf{q}} = \mathbf{A}\mathbf{q}$. Let us denote the distinct characteristic roots by $s_1 = \sigma_1 + j\omega_1$, $s_2 = \sigma_2 + j\omega_2$, . . . , $s_r = \sigma_r + j\omega_r$ $(r \leq k = \text{order of system})$ with $\sigma_1 \geq \sigma_2 \geq \cdots \geq \sigma_r$. We then can

write the fundamental matrix in the following manner (Sec. 7.3):

$$\mathbf{\Phi}(t) = \sum_{i=1}^{r} \mathbf{A}_i(t) e^{s_i t} \tag{11.8}$$

where $\mathbf{A}_i(t)$ $(i = 1, 2, \ldots, r)$ is a polynomial in t (with matrix coefficients) of degree one less than the multiplicity of the corresponding characteristic root s_i. It is evident that $\mathbf{\Phi}(t)$, as given by (11.8), is finite for every *finite* t; hence only the behavior of $\mathbf{\Phi}(t)$ as $t \to \infty$ is of concern. Suppose that there are p characteristic roots which have the same largest real part σ_1. Then we can write

$$\mathbf{\Phi}(t) = e^{\sigma_1 t} \left(\sum_{i=1}^{p} \mathbf{A}_i e^{j\omega_i t} + \sum_{i=p+1}^{r} \mathbf{A}_i e^{-(\sigma_1 - \sigma_i) t} e^{j\omega_i t} \right) \tag{11.9}$$

Since $\sigma_1 - \sigma_i > 0$ for $i = p + 1, \ldots, r$, only the first term on the right side of (11.9) remains as $t \to \infty$. We write

$$\mathbf{\Phi}(t) \sim e^{\sigma_1 t} \sum_{i=1}^{p} \mathbf{A}_i e^{j\omega_i t}$$

It is evident that $\mathbf{\Phi}(t) \to 0$ if σ_1 is negative, and then the origin is asymptotically stable; $\mathbf{\Phi}(t) \to \infty$ if σ_1 is positive, and the origin is unstable. The only remaining condition to be investigated is $\sigma_1 = 0$. In this case

$$\mathbf{\Phi}(t) \sim \sum_{i=1}^{p} \mathbf{A}_i e^{j\omega_i t}$$

It is evident that $\mathbf{\Phi}(t)$ does not approach zero, and hence that the origin is *not asymptotically* stable. Is it stable at all? If every characteristic root whose largest real part is zero is *simple*, every $\mathbf{A}_i$ is a constant matrix and $\mathbf{\Phi}(t)$ remains bounded; in fact,

$$\|\mathbf{\Phi}(t)\| \leq \sum_{i=1}^{p} \|\mathbf{A}_i\| \text{ as } t \to \infty$$

and the answer is yes. However, if there is at least one multiple characteristic root, say s_q, whose largest real part is zero, there is in general a corresponding matrix

$$\mathbf{A}_q = \mathbf{A}_{q1} + \mathbf{A}_{q2} t + \cdots + \mathbf{A}_{qm} t^{m-1}$$

in (11.8), where m is the multiplicity of the root; this matrix approaches ∞ with t. It is clear that $\mathbf{\Phi}(t) \to \infty$ and that the origin is unstable. An exception to this situation may arise when the minimum equation (Chap. 7, p. 218) is of lower degree than the characteristic equation, and

then only when all the roots of the minimum equation are nonrepeated. These results can be summarized in the following theorem.

Theorem 11.4   *The stability of a continuous-time linear fixed system is determined by the characteristic root, or roots, with the largest real part σ_1.*

1. *The origin is asymptotically stable if and only if $\sigma_1 < 0$.*
2. *The origin is stable if and only if $\sigma_1 \leq 0$ and all roots of the minimum equation with zero real parts are simple.*

This theorem has thus reduced the problem of determining whether a fixed system is stable to that of determining the location and multiplicity of the characteristic root (or roots) of the largest real part.   There are, of course, many methods for solving for the roots of an algebraic equation, but all are relatively tedious when the order of the system is higher than 2. Fortunately, it is not necessary to determine the *exact* location of the roots, but only the half plane in which they lie.   Several algorithms for performing this calculation are derived in the next chapter.

For discrete-time systems governed by $\mathbf{x}(n + 1) = \mathbf{A}\mathbf{x}(n)$, an analogous derivation is used.   We employ the expansion

$$\boldsymbol{\Phi}(n) = \sum_{i=1}^{r} \mathbf{A}_i(n)z_i^{n}$$

where z_i are the roots of the characteristic equation $|z\mathbf{I} - \mathbf{A}| = 0$.   Reasoning as for continuous-time systems, we arrive at Theorem 11.5.

Theorem 11.5   *The stability of a discrete-time linear fixed system is determined by the characteristic root, or roots, of largest magnitude $|z_1|$.*

1. *The origin is asymptotically stable if and only if $|z_1| < 1$.*
2. *The origin is stable if and only if $|z_1| \leq 1$ and all roots of the minimum equation with unit magnitudes are simple.*

11.5   STABILITY OF FORCED SYSTEMS

We now examine linear systems which are unexcited—"at rest" or quiescent—at the starting time t_0, but in which an excitation is present thereafter.   Under these conditions the state is given by

$$\mathbf{q}(t) = \int_{t_0}^{t} \mathbf{R}(t, \lambda)\mathbf{x}(\lambda) \, d\lambda \tag{11.10}$$

where $\mathbf{R}(t, \lambda)$ is the matrix of impulse responses from the input vector $\mathbf{x}$ to the state vector $\mathbf{q}$; that is, $r_{ij}(t, \lambda) = q_i(t)$ when $x_j(t) = \delta(t - \lambda)$ and $x_i(t) = 0$ for $i \neq j$ (Chap. 4). We define stability for such a forced system as follows:

Definition 11.4   Stability of a forced system   *A forced system is stable with respect to a set of inputs $\mathfrak{X} = \{x(t)\}$ if and only if the state is bounded (i.e., there exists a constant Q such that $\|\mathbf{q}(t)\| \leq Q < \infty$) for all $\mathbf{x}(t)$ in the set $\mathfrak{X}$ for all $t \geq t_0$.*

By this definition the stability of a forced system depends on the nature of the set of inputs, and it is to be expected that a system which is stable for one set $\mathfrak{X}$ need not be stable for another set $\mathfrak{Y}$ unless $\mathfrak{Y}$ is a subset of $\mathfrak{X}$. This is reasonable, since one would not wish to call a system unstable if the only inputs which could cause the state to become unbounded could not physically occur.

Definition 11.4 applies to any system which can be characterized by a matrix of impulse responses and is not limited to systems which can be represented only by ordinary differential equations. It applies, for example, to distributed systems characterized by partial differential equations (Chap. 13).

Moreover, the definition is entirely different from those for the stability of unexcited systems. It is thus entirely reasonable that a system which is stable when unexcited (in accordance with the earlier definitions) is unstable with respect to a given set of inputs, and vice versa.[†]

Most frequently, the set $\mathfrak{X}$ is the set of all bounded inputs, namely, those inputs for which $\|\mathbf{x}(t)\| \leq M < \infty$ for all t. In this case the system will be said to be stable without any further qualification.

Note that under this definition a differentiator is unstable, since the response to a unit step is an impulse which is unbounded. If it is desired to regard systems like differentiators as stable, one can restrict the set $\mathfrak{X}$ to all *continuous* inputs. Since all physical inputs are continuous, this seems like a reasonable restriction. However, physical inputs will often change very rapidly, if not discontinuously. In such cases, if $\mathfrak{X}$ is the set of all continuous inputs, the outputs may be extremely large even if finite, and such behavior might be so undesirable as to make the system practically unstable. A further difficulty is mathematical: it is more

---

[†] The connection between unforced stability and forced stability, particularly in time-varying systems, has been the subject of much discussion. See T. F. Bridgland, Jr., and R. E. Kalman, Some Remarks on the Stability of Linear Systems, *IEEE Trans. Circuit Theory*, vol. CT-10, pp. 539–542, December, 1963, and R. E. Kalman, On the Stability of Linear Time-varying Systems, *IRE Trans. Circuit Theory*, vol. CT-9, pp. 420–423, December, 1962.

difficult to find conditions for which a system is stable with respect to the set of continuous bounded inputs than it is to find them with respect to the bounded inputs which are not necessarily continuous.   This will become clear in the proof of Theorem 11.6, which is the basic stability theorem for forced systems.

Theorem 11.6   *A forced system is stable (with respect to the set of bounded inputs) if and only if*

$$\int_{t_0}^{t} |r_{ij}(t, \lambda)| \, d\lambda \leq K_{ij} < \infty$$

$$i = 1, 2, \ldots, k; \quad j = 1, 2, \ldots, m \quad (11.11)$$

for every t_0 and all $t > t_0$.

To prove that (11.11) is a sufficient condition for stability we apply (11.6) and (11.2b) to (11.10) and obtain thereby

$$\|\mathbf{q}(t)\| \leq \int_{t_0}^{t} \|\mathbf{R}(t, \lambda)\| \; \|\mathbf{x}(\lambda)\| \, d\lambda \qquad (11.12)$$

We now employ the fact (Prob. 11.2) that

$$\|\mathbf{R}\| \leq \sum_{i=1}^{k} \sum_{j=1}^{m} |r_{ij}|$$

from which (11.12) becomes

$$\|\mathbf{q}(t)\| \leq \sum_{i=1}^{k} \sum_{j=1}^{m} \int_{t_0}^{t} |r_{ij}(t, \lambda)| \; \|\mathbf{x}(\lambda)\| \, d\lambda \qquad (11.13)$$

Now if $\mathbf{x}(t)$ is bounded, $\|\mathbf{x}(t)\| \leq M < \infty$ for $t \geq t_0$, and thus (11.13) becomes

$$\|\mathbf{q}(t)\| \leq M \sum_{i=1}^{k} \sum_{j=1}^{m} \int_{t_0}^{t} |r_{ij}(t, \lambda)| \, d\lambda$$

which, by virtue of (11.11), becomes

$$\|\mathbf{q}(t)\| \leq M \sum_{i=1}^{k} \sum_{j=1}^{m} K_{ij}$$

which is thus finite.   To prove that (11.11) is also necessary, we assume that, for some t_0 and $t_1 > t_0$ and some i and j, say $i = \mu$, $j = \nu$, (11.11) does not hold.   Then we select the following *bounded* input $x(t)$:

$$x_k(t) = \begin{cases} 0 & k \neq \nu \\ \text{sgn } r_{\mu\nu} \, (t_1, t) & k = \nu \end{cases}$$

where

$$\text{sgn } x = \begin{cases} 0 & x = 0 \\ 1 & x > 0 \\ -1 & x < 0 \end{cases}$$

With this input,

$$q_\mu(t_1) = \int_{t_0}^{t_1} r_{\mu\nu}(t_1, \lambda) \text{ sgn } r_{\mu\nu}(t_1, \lambda) \, d\lambda = \int_{t_0}^{t_1} |r_{\mu\nu}(t_1, \lambda)| \, d\lambda = \infty$$

and the state vector is unbounded.

Note that if $r_{\mu\nu}(t_1, t)$ changes sign in the interval $t_0 \leq t \leq t_1$, the input which produced the unbounded state is discontinuous; hence the proof of the theorem would have been impossible had $\mathbf{x}(t)$ been required to be continuous.

Note also that the stability criterion is expressed in terms of the impulse responses, which themselves are responses to unbounded inputs.

By the manner of proof it is evident that Theorem 11.6 holds for discrete-time systems if the integral of (11.11) is replaced by a sum and if $r_{ij}(t, t_0)$ is replaced by $r_{ij}(n, n_0)$, the unit response from x_j to q_i.

If the system being considered is governed by the differential equation

$$\dot{\mathbf{q}}(t) = \mathbf{A}(t)\mathbf{q}(t) + \mathbf{B}(t)\mathbf{x}(t)$$

then, as shown in Chap. 4, the forced response is given by

$$\mathbf{q}(t) = \int_{t_0}^{t} \mathbf{\Phi}(t, \lambda)\mathbf{B}(\lambda)\mathbf{x}(\lambda) \, d\lambda$$

and thus

$$\mathbf{R}(t, \lambda) = \mathbf{\Phi}(t, \lambda)\mathbf{B}(\lambda)$$

where $\mathbf{\Phi}(t, \lambda)$ is the fundamental matrix, and

$$r_{ij}(t, \lambda) = \sum_{l=1}^{k} \phi_{il}(t, \lambda)b_{lj}(\lambda)$$

Thus, if $\mathbf{B}(\lambda)$ is finite for all $t > t_0$, (11.11) means that the forced system is stable if

$$\int_{t_0}^{t} |\phi_{ij}(t,\lambda)| \, d\lambda \leq K_{ij} < \infty$$

However, even if for some $i = \mu$, $j = \nu$, $\phi_{\mu\nu}$ is unbounded, it does not necessarily follow that the forced system is unstable, since the terms which result in instability may not be excited by the input. This is illustrated by the system of the following example.

Example 11.2   Consider the system shown in Fig. 11.2.   The relevant matrices of the system are

$$A = \begin{bmatrix} 1 & 1 \\ 0 & -1 \end{bmatrix} \qquad B = \begin{bmatrix} 1 \\ -2 \end{bmatrix}$$

whence

$$\hat{\Phi}(s) = (s\mathbf{I} - \mathbf{A})^{-1} = \begin{bmatrix} \dfrac{1}{s-1} & \dfrac{1}{(s-1)(s+1)} \\ 0 & \dfrac{1}{s+1} \end{bmatrix}$$

and the fundamental matrix is

$$\Phi(t) = \mathcal{L}^{-1}[\hat{\Phi}(s)] = \begin{bmatrix} e^t & \tfrac{1}{2}e^t - \tfrac{1}{2}e^{-t} \\ 0 & e^{-t} \end{bmatrix} \qquad t > 0$$

Because of the presence of the term e^t in $\phi_{11}(t)$ and $\phi_{12}(t)$,

$$\int_{t_0}^{\infty} |\phi_{11}(t)|\, dt \to \infty \qquad \int_{t_0}^{\infty} |\phi_{12}(t)|\, dt \to \infty$$

Nevertheless, from (4.39) the impulse response is

$$\mathbf{R}(t) = \Phi(t)\mathbf{B} = \begin{bmatrix} e^{-t} \\ -2e^{-t} \end{bmatrix}$$

and the integrals

$$\int_{t_0}^{\infty} |r_1(t)|\, dt \qquad \text{and} \qquad \int_{t_0}^{\infty} |r_2(t)|\, dt$$

are both finite.

The foregoing example has thus illustrated a very important fact: although the unforced system is unstable, it is entirely possible for the forced system to be stable in accordance with the definition. This apparent paradox results from the fact that the input is connected in such a way that it does not excite all the natural modes of the system, one of which is unstable.   The conditions for which this behavior is

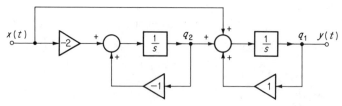

FIG. 11.2   Example of a system in which input does not excite unstable mode.

possible are similar to the conditions for which all the natural modes do not appear in the output, and will be discussed in Sec. 11.7.

One may also inquire whether stability of the unforced system implies stability of the forced system. Although, as we shall see subsequently, the implication does hold for fixed systems, it does not hold for time-varying systems, as the following example clearly shows.

Example 11.3   Consider the system governed by

$$\dot{q}(t) + \frac{1}{t+1} q(t) = x(t) \qquad t > 0$$

As shown in Example 4.3, the 1×1 fundamental matrix is

$$\phi(t, t_0) = \frac{t_0 + 1}{t + 1} \qquad t > t_0$$

and $\phi(t, t_0) \rightarrow 0$ as $t \rightarrow \infty$ for every t_0 and $t > t_0$. Thus the origin is asymptotically stable, by Definition 11.3. However, the response to a unit step applied at $t = 0$ is

$$q(t) = \int_0^t \frac{1 + \lambda}{1 + t} \, d\lambda = t \left(\frac{1 + \frac{1}{2}t}{1 + t} \right) \rightarrow \infty$$

as $t \rightarrow \infty$, and the forced system is unstable.

11.6   CRITERIA FOR THE STABILITY OF FORCED FIXED SYSTEMS

The conditions for stability with respect to the set of bounded inputs in the preceding section are expressed in terms of time-domain quantities, namely, impulse responses from the inputs to the state variables. These quantities are often not easy to determine, and it is desirable to obtain stability criteria in terms of the more readily calculable transfer functions.

For fixed systems, the relation between the input and state is expressed by

$$\mathbf{q}(t) = \int_0^t \mathbf{R}(t - \lambda)\mathbf{x}(\lambda) \, d\lambda \qquad (11.14)$$

and the frequency-domain equivalent, obtained by taking the Laplace transform of (11.14), is

$$\mathbf{Q}(s) = \hat{\mathbf{R}}(s)\mathbf{X}(s)$$

where $\mathbf{Q}(s)$, $\hat{\mathbf{R}}(s)$, and $\mathbf{X}(s)$ are the Laplace transforms of $\mathbf{q}(t)$, $\mathbf{R}(t)$, and $\mathbf{x}(t)$, respectively; $\hat{\mathbf{R}}(s)$ is the matrix of transfer functions from the inputs to the state variables.' The basic stability criterion is expressed by the following theorem.

Theorem 11.7 *A necessary condition for the stability of a forced fixed continuous-time system is that every transfer function $R_{ij}(s)$ be finite for* Re $s \geq 0$.

To prove this theorem, we write

$$R_{ij}(s) = \int_0^\infty r_{ij}(t)e^{-st}\, dt$$

It then follows that

$$|R_{ij}(s)| \leq \int_0^\infty |r_{ij}(t)|e^{-\sigma t}\, dt \qquad (11.15)$$

where $\sigma =$ Re s.   But for $\sigma =$ Re $s \geq 0$, $e^{-\sigma t} \leq 1$; hence (11.15) becomes

$$|R_{ij}(s)| \leq \int_0^\infty |r_{ij}(t)|\, dt \qquad \text{Re } s \geq 0 \qquad (11.16)$$

Now, if the system is stable, the right-hand side of (11.16) is finite; this establishes that $|R_{ij}(s)|$ is finite.

In an analogous manner, the following theorem is readily proved.

Theorem 11.8 *A necessary condition for the stability of a forced discrete-time system is that every discrete-time transfer function $R_{ij}(z)$ be finite for* Re $z \geq 1$.

Since we have not made use of the lumped nature of the system in the proof of Theorem 11.7, it follows that they apply even to systems which are not lumped—in fact, they apply to any fixed system for which the impulse response can be meaningfully defined.

Note also that the theorem requires only that the transfer functions be finite for Re $s \geq 0$ if the system is stable.   It does not require them to be analytic there, nor does it state that boundedness of the transfer functions in the right half plane is sufficient to ensure stability.

When the system is lumped, however, the situation is clearer, since the transfer functions are all *rational functions* of s.   More specifically, if the system is governed by

$$\dot{\mathbf{q}} = \mathbf{Aq} + \mathbf{Bx}$$

the matrix of transfer functions is given by

$$\hat{\mathbf{R}}(s) = (s\mathbf{I} - \mathbf{A})^{-1}\mathbf{B} = \frac{\text{adj } (s\mathbf{I} - \mathbf{A})\mathbf{B}}{|s\mathbf{I} - \mathbf{A}|}$$

Thus

$$r_{ij}(t) = \sum_l a_{ij}{}^l(t)e^{s_l t}$$

where s_l are the poles of $\hat{\mathbf{R}}(s)$, that is, the roots of $|s\mathbf{I} - \mathbf{A}| = 0$. It is thus evident that if all the poles—the only kind of singularities which can be present in a lumped system—are in the left half plane, the system is stable, since every $r_{ij}(t)$ is a sum of decreasing exponentials (with coefficients which can increase at most as fast as t raised to some finite power), and thus integrable over the semi-infinite interval $t \geq 0$. Consequently, we have the following theorem.

Theorem 11.9 *A lumped fixed continuous-time system is stable if and only if every transfer function $R_{ij}(s)$ is analytic in the right half plane and on the imaginary axis.*

In an analogous manner, we can establish the following theorem.

Theorem 11.10 *A lumped fixed discrete-time system is stable if and only if every transfer function $R_{ij}(z)$ is analytic outside and on the unit circle.*

11.7 CONDITIONS FOR EXCITATION AND OBSERVATION OF ALL NATURAL MODES

In most cases the input to a fixed linear system will excite all the natural frequencies;[†] i.e., every zero of the characteristic equation will appear in the denominator of at least one element of the matrix $\hat{\mathbf{R}}(s)$. In these cases, stability of the forced system with respect to bounded inputs is equivalent to asymptotic stability of the unforced system. There are situations, however, in which the input is incapable of exciting all the natural modes or frequencies. If this is true, it is possible that a characteristic root with positive real part might be absent in every element of $\hat{\mathbf{R}}(s)$; the forced system could thus be stable although the unforced system is unstable.

To determine the conditions under which such a situation could arise,

[†] In control theory such a system is said to be *controllable*. See R. E. Kalman, Y.-C. Ho, and K. S. Narendra, Controllability of Linear Dynamical Systems, *Contrib. Differential Equations*, vol. 1, pp. 189–213, 1961.

we consider first the case in which the system has a single input $x(t)$ and distinct eigenvalues. The differential equation for this system may be written

$$\dot{\mathbf{q}} = \mathbf{Aq} + \mathbf{b}x \tag{11.17}$$

(Since there is only a single input, the matrix $\mathbf{B}$ becomes the column matrix or vector $\mathbf{b}$.) Since the characteristic roots are distinct, there is a nonsingular matrix $\mathbf{T}$ which transforms $\mathbf{A}$ into diagonal form; i.e.,

$$\mathbf{TAT}^{-1} = \mathbf{\Lambda} = \text{diag.}\,[s_1, s_2, \ldots, s_k]$$

where s_i $(i = 1, 2, \ldots, k)$ are the eigenvalues of $\mathbf{A}$, or natural frequencies, i.e., the roots of the characteristic equation $|s\mathbf{I} - \mathbf{A}| = 0$. We let

$$\mathbf{q} = \mathbf{T}^{-1}\boldsymbol{\xi}$$

Substituting into (11.17) and premultiplying by $\mathbf{T}$, we obtain

$$\dot{\boldsymbol{\xi}} = \mathbf{TAT}^{-1}\boldsymbol{\xi} + \mathbf{Tb}x = \mathbf{\Lambda}\boldsymbol{\xi} + \boldsymbol{\beta}x \tag{11.18}$$

where $\boldsymbol{\beta} = \mathbf{Tb}$. In scalar form (11.18) is

$$\dot{\xi}_i = s_i\xi_i + \beta_i x \qquad i = 1, 2, \ldots, k$$

We conclude that each natural frequency occurs in $\boldsymbol{\xi}$ and hence in $\mathbf{q}$ (since $\mathbf{q} = \mathbf{T}^{-1}\boldsymbol{\xi}$ and $\mathbf{T}^{-1}$ is nonsingular) if and only if

$$\beta_i \neq 0 \qquad i = 1, 2, \ldots, k$$

We define the matrix

$$\mathbf{M} = [\boldsymbol{\beta} \quad \mathbf{\Lambda}\boldsymbol{\beta} \quad \cdots \quad \mathbf{\Lambda}^{k-1}\boldsymbol{\beta}] = \begin{bmatrix} \beta_1 & s_1\beta_1 & \cdots & s_1{}^{k-1}\beta_1 \\ \cdot & \cdot & \cdots & \cdot \\ \beta_k & s_k\beta_k & \cdots & s_k{}^{k-1}\beta_k \end{bmatrix}$$

Since the eigenvalues of $\mathbf{\Lambda}$ are assumed to be distinct, the matrix $\mathbf{M}$ is nonsingular if and only if $\beta_i \neq 0$ $(i = 1, 2, \ldots, k)$, that is, if and only if all the natural frequencies are excited. (The nullity of $\mathbf{M}$, in fact, is precisely equal to the number of unexcited natural frequencies.) Now

$$\boldsymbol{\beta} = \mathbf{Tb}$$
$$\mathbf{\Lambda}\boldsymbol{\beta} = \mathbf{TAT}^{-1}\mathbf{Tb} = \mathbf{TAb}$$
$$\cdot\ \cdot\ \cdot\ \cdot\ \cdot\ \cdot\ \cdot\ \cdot\ \cdot\ \cdot\ \cdot\ \cdot\ \cdot$$
$$\mathbf{\Lambda}^{k-1}\boldsymbol{\beta} = \mathbf{TA}^{k-1}\mathbf{b}$$

so that

$$\mathbf{M} = \mathbf{T}[\mathbf{b} \quad \mathbf{Ab} \quad \cdots \quad \mathbf{A}^{k-1}\mathbf{b}]$$

Consequently, since $\mathbf{T}$ is nonsingular, the rank of $\mathbf{M}$ is equal to the rank of

$$\mathbf{P} = [\mathbf{b} \quad \mathbf{Ab} \quad \cdots \quad \mathbf{A}^{k-1}\mathbf{b}]$$

We thus have the following theorem.

Theorem 11.11 *The necessary and sufficient condition for an input* $x(t) \neq 0$ *to excite all the natural frequencies of a linear fixed system (with distinct eigenvalues) is that the matrix*

$$\mathbf{P} = [\mathbf{b} \quad \mathbf{Ab} \quad \cdots \quad \mathbf{A}^{k-1}\mathbf{b}]$$

be nonsingular.

The restriction to distinct eigenvalues is not necessary. The proof of the more general case is similar to that above, except that the matrix **A** is transformed to the Jordan canonical form (Prob. 11.12). Note that the natural frequencies corresponding to an eigenvalue s_i repeated m_i times are to be interpreted as $e^{s_i t}, te^{s_i t}, \ldots, t^{m_i-1}e^{s_i t}$.

If the system has n inputs, i.e.,

$$\dot{\mathbf{q}} = \mathbf{Aq} + \mathbf{Bx} = \mathbf{Aq} + \mathbf{b}_1 x_1 + \mathbf{b}_2 x_2 + \cdots + \mathbf{b}_n x_n$$

where $\mathbf{b}_i$ is the ith column of the matrix **B**, Theorem 11.11 may be generalized as follows.

Theorem 11.12 *The necessary and sufficient condition for all the natural frequencies of a linear fixed system to be excited by any input* $x_i(t)$ $(i = 1, 2, \ldots, n)$ *is that every matrix*

$$\mathbf{P}_i = [\mathbf{b}_i \quad \mathbf{Ab}_i \quad \cdots \quad \mathbf{A}^{k-1}\mathbf{b}_i] \qquad i = 1, 2, \ldots, n$$

be nonsingular; the necessary and sufficient condition for all the natural frequencies to be excited by some input is that the rank of the matrix

$$\mathbf{P} = [\mathbf{B} \quad \mathbf{AB} \quad \ldots \quad \mathbf{A}^{k-1}\mathbf{B}]$$

be k (= *order of the system*).

Example 11.4 The system of Example 11.2, in Fig. 11.2, does not have all the natural frequencies excited by the input. Thus, although the forced system is stable, the unforced system is unstable, because of the presence of the eigenvalue $s_i = 1$. The matrix

$$\mathbf{P} = [\mathbf{b} \quad \mathbf{Ab}] = \begin{bmatrix} 1 & -1 \\ -2 & 2 \end{bmatrix}$$

is singular as expected. If the gain b_2 were changed from -2 to any other value, all natural frequencies would be excited.

Example 11.5 In electric circuits the most common occurrence of the inability of the input to excite all natural modes is in balanced bridges. Consider, for example, the circuit shown in Fig. 11.3. By elementary

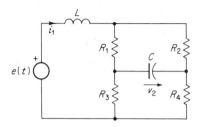

FIG. 11.3 *Bridge circuit illustrating condition that input does not excite all modes.*

methods of circuit analysis, it is readily established that the differential equations governing the behavior of the circuit are

$$\frac{di_1}{dt} = -\frac{i_1}{L}\left(\frac{R_1 R_2}{R_1 + R_2} + \frac{R_3 R_4}{R_3 + R_4}\right) + \frac{v_2}{L}\left(\frac{R_1}{R_1 + R_2} - \frac{R_3}{R_3 + R_4}\right) + \frac{e}{L}$$

$$\frac{dv_2}{dt} = -\frac{i_1}{C}\left(\frac{R_1}{R_1 + R_2} - \frac{R_3}{R_3 + R_4}\right) - \frac{v_2}{C}\left(\frac{1}{R_3 + R_4} + \frac{1}{R_1 + R_2}\right)$$

Then if the state is defined by

$$\mathbf{q} = \begin{bmatrix} i_1 \\ v_2 \end{bmatrix}$$

the corresponding matrices are

$$\mathbf{A} = \begin{bmatrix} -\dfrac{1}{L}\left(\dfrac{R_1 R_2}{R_1 + R_2} + \dfrac{R_3 R_4}{R_3 + R_4}\right) & \dfrac{1}{L}\left(\dfrac{R_1}{R_1 + R_2} - \dfrac{R_3}{R_3 + R_4}\right) \\ -\dfrac{1}{C}\left(\dfrac{R_1}{R_1 + R_2} - \dfrac{R_3}{R_3 + R_4}\right) & -\dfrac{1}{C}\left(\dfrac{1}{R_3 + R_4} + \dfrac{1}{R_1 + R_2}\right) \end{bmatrix}$$

$$\mathbf{B} = \begin{bmatrix} \dfrac{1}{L} \\ 0 \end{bmatrix}$$

The system is obviously of second order, and there are thus two natural modes. However,

$$\mathbf{P} = [\mathbf{B} \quad \mathbf{AB}] = \begin{bmatrix} \dfrac{1}{L} & -\dfrac{1}{L^2}\left(\dfrac{R_1 R_2}{R_1 + R_2} + \dfrac{R_3 R_4}{R_3 + R_4}\right) \\ 0 & -\dfrac{1}{LC}\left(\dfrac{R_1}{R_1 + R_2} - \dfrac{R_3}{R_3 + R_4}\right) \end{bmatrix}$$

It is evident that $\mathbf{P}$ is singular if and only if

$$\frac{R_1}{R_1 + R_2} = \frac{R_3}{R_3 + R_4}$$

or

$$R_1 R_4 = R_2 R_3$$

which is precisely the condition for the bridge to be balanced. In this case it is evident that the differential equation for i_1 is uncoupled from the one for v_2, which behaves as if there were a short circuit from the top of R_1 to the bottom of R_3. If the capacitance and the resistances are all positive, the "vanishing" mode is stable and will not cause any difficulty; however, if the capacitance should be negative (as could happen in some electronic circuits), the circuit would be unstable.

Other situations in electric circuits where the input may not excite all the natural modes can occur in networks which use redundant elements. Many of the well-known methods of network synthesis result in a circuit which has more energy-storing elements than the order of the network (transfer) function to be realized. What happens is that the synthesis is accomplished by locating zeros of the numerator at the undesirable poles— or characteristic frequencies. No complications arise as long as the elements used in the synthesis are passive, since the modes which have been made to disappear are stable. However, extreme caution should be employed when active elements are to be used, since there may be unstable modes which the analysis may not reveal.

Closely related to the ability of the input to excite all the natural frequencies is the possibility of all the natural frequencies to be observed in the output.† Suppose that the system has a single output which is related to the state by

$$y = \mathbf{c}'\mathbf{q}$$

where $\mathbf{c}'$ is a row matrix. Again assuming that the eigenvalues—characteristic frequencies—are distinct, we can again write

$$\mathbf{q} = \mathbf{T}^{-1}\boldsymbol{\xi}$$

Then we can express the output as

$$y = \boldsymbol{\gamma}'\boldsymbol{\xi} = \sum_{i=1}^{k} \gamma_i \xi_i$$

where $\boldsymbol{\gamma}' = \mathbf{c}'\mathbf{T}^{-1}$ or $\boldsymbol{\gamma} = \mathbf{T}'^{-1}\mathbf{c}$. Evidently, each of the natural modes will appear in the output y if and only if each γ_i ($i = 1, 2, \ldots, k$) is nonzero.

---

† In control theory such a system is termed *observable*. See *ibid.;* also R. E. Kalman, On the General Theory of Control Systems, in Automatic and Remote Control, *Proc. First Intern. Congr. IFAC, Moscow,* 1960, pp. 481–492 [Butterworth & Co., Ltd. (Publishers), London, 1961].

We define the matrix

$$N' = \begin{bmatrix} \gamma' \\ \gamma'\Lambda \\ \cdot \\ \cdot \\ \cdot \\ \gamma'\Lambda^{k-1} \end{bmatrix}$$

or

$$N = [\gamma \quad \Lambda\gamma \quad \cdots \quad \Lambda^{k-1}\gamma] = \begin{bmatrix} \gamma_1 & s_1\gamma_1 & \cdots & s_1{}^{k-1}\gamma_1 \\ \cdot & \cdot & \cdots & \cdot \\ \gamma_k & s_k\gamma_k & \cdots & s_k{}^{k-1}\gamma_k \end{bmatrix}$$

Hence N is nonsingular if and only if none of the γ_i $(i = 1, 2, \ldots, k)$ is zero, i.e., if and only if all the natural modes appear in the output.   Now

$$\gamma = T'^{-1}c$$
$$\Lambda\gamma = \Lambda'\gamma = T'^{-1}A'T'T'^{-1}c = T'^{-1}A'c$$
$$\cdots\cdots\cdots\cdots\cdots\cdots\cdots\cdots\cdots$$
$$\Lambda^{k-1}\gamma = \Lambda'^{k-1}\gamma = T'^{-1}A'^{k-1}c$$

whence

$$N = T'^{-1}[c \quad A'c \quad \cdots \quad A'^{k-1}c]$$

Since T is nonsingular, the rank of N is equal to the rank of

$$Q = [c \quad A'c \quad \cdots \quad A'^{k-1}c]$$

Thus we see that all the natural modes appear in the output if and only if the rank of Q is k.   More generally, if there are m outputs and

$$y = Cq$$

where C is an $m \times k$ matrix, we have the following theorem.

Theorem 11.13   *The necessary and sufficient condition for all the natural frequencies of a linear fixed system to be observed in every output is that every matrix*

$$Q_i = [c_i \quad A'c_i \quad \cdots \quad A'^{k-1}c_i] \qquad i = 1, 2, \ldots, m$$

be of rank k, where c_i is the transpose of the ith row of C; the necessary and sufficient condition for all the natural frequencies to be observed in some output is that the matrix

$$Q = [C' \quad A'C' \quad \cdots \quad A'^{k-1}C']$$

be of rank k.

Example 11.6 The system used for Example 11.1, illustrated in Fig. 11.1, has the matrices

$$\mathbf{A} = \begin{bmatrix} 0 & 1 \\ 2 & -1 \end{bmatrix} \qquad \mathbf{C} = [c_1 \quad c_2]$$

Hence

$$\mathbf{Q} = [\mathbf{C}' \quad \mathbf{A}'\mathbf{C}'] = \begin{bmatrix} c_1 & 2c_2 \\ c_2 & c_1 - c_2 \end{bmatrix}$$

and

$$|\mathbf{Q}| = c_1{}^2 - c_1 c_2 - 2c_2{}^2 = (c_1 + c_2)(c_1 - 2c_2)$$

Hence, if $c_1 = -c_2$ or $c_1 = 2c_2$, one of the natural modes is not observed in the output. This is substantiated by the response as calculated in Example 11.1.

The manner in which Theorems 11.12 and 11.13 are proved makes it evident that the results apply also to discrete-time systems.

11.8 LYAPUNOV'S SECOND METHOD

A great deal of information about the fundamental matrix is needed in order to test the stability conditions of Sec. 11.3. As we have already shown, when the system is fixed, the required information is embodied in the characteristic equation. In time-varying systems, however, the form of the fundamental matrix generally cannot be obtained by any simple method and the theorems cannot be applied. The stability problem is even more difficult in nonlinear systems in which the form of the solution depends on the initial conditions.

The need for a stability criterion which does not require extensive knowledge of the form of the solution of the differential equations was apparently recognized by Lyapunov,[†] whose work was done near the beginning of the twentieth century, but largely ignored until the 1950's, when interest in this method was revived by Russian investigators in the field of automatic control.[‡] The method proposed by Lyapunov, which

[†] M. A. Lyapunov, "Le problème général de la stabilité du mouvement," *Ann. Fac. Sci. Toulouse*, vol. 9, pp. 203–474, 1907 (originally published in Russian in 1892; reprinted as Annals of Math. Studies, no. 17, Princeton University Press, Princeton, N.J., 1947).

[‡] The principal expository Russian works are by A. M. Letov, "Stability in Nonlinear Control Systems" (English transl. by J. G. Adashko), Princeton University Press, Princeton, N.J., 1961, and A. I. Lur'e, "Some Nonlinear Problems in the Theory of Automatic Control" (English transl.), H. M. Stationery Office, London, 1957. A comprehensive survey of the method, with a number of examples, is given by Kalman

is now referred to as his "second," or "direct," method, derives from the concept of energy.   It is a well-known physical principle that in a stable system the total energy always *decreases* or, in the case of a conservative system, *remains constant.*

In systems where the state variables have no evident physical interpretation, it may be a difficult matter to determine the energy.   The remarkable result of Lyapunov is that any scalar positive-definite function of the state variables can take the role of energy.   If one can find any energylike function which never increases, the origin is a stable equilibrium point.

More precisely, the results of Lyapunov are embodied in Theorem 11.14, which employs positive- and negative-definite functions defined as follows.

Definition 11.5   *A scalar function $V(\mathbf{q})$ is said to be positive-definite if and only if*

(1) $V(\mathbf{0}) \equiv 0$
(2) $V(\mathbf{q}) > 0$ *whenever* $\mathbf{q}(t) \neq \mathbf{0}$

Likewise, a function is negative-definite if condition (1) holds and condition (2) holds with the inequality reversed.

A time-dependent scalar function $V(\mathbf{q}, t)$ is said to be positive-definite if it is bounded from below by a time-independent positive-definite function, i.e., if there exists a scalar function $W(\mathbf{q})$ such that

$$V(\mathbf{q}, t) > W(\mathbf{q}) \qquad \text{for all } t > t_0$$

Likewise, $V(\mathbf{q}, t)$ is negative-definite if there exists a positive-definite time-independent function such that

$$V(\mathbf{q}, t) < -W(\mathbf{q}) \qquad t > t_0$$

The results of Lyapunov's work can be stated in the following theorem.

Theorem 11.14   Lyapunov stability theorem†   *Let $V(\mathbf{q}(t), t)$ be any positive-definite function of the state and (possibly) time, which is differentiable with respect to all its arguments.   Then*
  1. If

$$\dot{V}(\mathbf{q}(t), t) = \frac{dV}{dt} = \frac{\partial V}{\partial t} + \sum_{i=1}^{k} \frac{\partial V}{\partial q_i} \frac{dq_i}{dt} \leq 0 \qquad (11.19)$$

the origin is stable.

---

and Bertram, Control System Analysis and Design via the "Second Method" of Lyapunov, *loc. cit.*   A detailed mathematical account of the method is given by J. P. LaSalle and S. Lefschetz, "Stability by Lyapunov's Second Method with Applications," Academic Press, Inc., New York, 1961.

† For a more precise statement of this theorem, see Kalman and Bertram, *op. cit.*

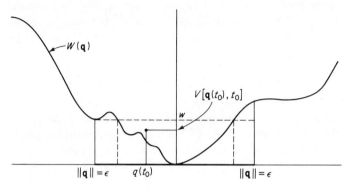

FIG. 11.4   Interpretation of Lyapunov's theorem.

2. *If dV/dt ≤ 0 and is nonzero along any trajectory, the origin is asymptotically stable.*

A geometric interpretation of the theorem and an aid in understanding its proof are given in Fig. 11.4.

To prove part 1 of Theorem 11.14, observe that

$$V(\mathbf{q}(t), t) = \int_{t_0}^{t} \dot{V}(\mathbf{q}(\lambda), \lambda) \, d\lambda + V(\mathbf{q}(t_0), t_0)$$

Thus, since $dV/dt \leq 0$, it follows that $V(\mathbf{q}(t), t) \leq V(\mathbf{q}(t_0), t_0)$, and moreover, by the definition of a time-dependent positive-definite function, $V(\mathbf{q}(t), t) > W(\mathbf{q}(t))$. Thus—since $V(\mathbf{q}(t), t)$ is positive-definite within the (possibly dented) bowl-shaped region $W(\mathbf{q})$ for any state $\mathbf{q}(t)$—if the region $\|\mathbf{q}\| = \epsilon$ is projected upward, it intersects the bowl in a curve (two points in Fig. 11.4), some point w of which is nearest to the $\mathbf{q}$ plane. If the initial state is chosen such that $V(\mathbf{q}(t_0), t_0)$ is smaller than w (this can always be done because of the continuity of V), then $V(\mathbf{q}(t), t)$ will remain smaller than w for all subsequent time, and the state will not be able to wander outside the projection of the region $W(\mathbf{q}) = w$ on the $\mathbf{q}$ plane (shown by the heavier portion of the axis in Fig. 11.4). Note that if $W(\mathbf{q})$ dips down and touches the $\mathbf{q}$ plane at a point, say $\bar{\mathbf{q}}$, other than the origin, it is possible that the state will move toward $\bar{\mathbf{q}}$ rather than toward the origin. If the origin is the only point, however, at which $W(\mathbf{q})$ touches the $\mathbf{q}$ plane, then the state must tend to the origin if V is always decreasing with time; but if V can remain constant along some trajectory, it is also possible that $\mathbf{q}(t)$ will not move toward the origin although it remains a fixed distance from it.

Part 2 of Theorem 11.14 is established by *reductio ad absurdum*. Sup-

pose that $dV/dt \leq 0$ but nonzero along some trajectory and that the origin is not asymptotically stable, i.e., that $\|\mathbf{q}(t)\|$ does not approach zero as $t \to \infty$. Then there is a positive constant η such that $\|\mathbf{q}(t)\| \geq \eta$ for $t \geq T$, where T is a sufficiently large time; moreover, since $dV/dt \leq 0$ and nonzero along some trajectory, there must be another constant $\xi = \xi(\eta)$ such that $dV/dt \leq -\xi$ for $t \geq T$.

Hence we can write

$$\begin{aligned} V(\mathbf{q}(t), t) &= V(\mathbf{q}(T), T) + \int_T^t \dot{V}\, d\lambda \\ &\leq V(\mathbf{q}(T), T) - (t - T)\xi \end{aligned} \tag{11.20}$$

Thus ultimately, as $t \to \infty$, $V(\mathbf{q}(t), t)$ will become negative and contradicts the hypothesis that it is positive-definite. This establishes the second part of the theorem.

It is essential to bear in mind that the theorem supplies only a sufficient condition for stability; if one is fortunate to find† a positive-definite function which turns out to be nonincreasing, the origin is thereby proved to be stable. However, if some arbitrarily selected positive-definite function turns out not to be nonincreasing for every motion of the state vector, no conclusion can be drawn. The function selected may be inappropriate for the particular system under investigation. This fact is illustrated by the following example.

Example 11.7 Suppose we select

$$V = \sum_{i=1}^k q_i^2 = \mathbf{q}'\mathbf{q}$$

where $\mathbf{q}'$ denotes the transpose of the vector $\mathbf{q}$.

Evidently, V is positive-definite, and its derivative is given by

$$\dot{V} = \sum_{i=1}^k 2q_i\dot{q}_i = 2\mathbf{q}'\dot{\mathbf{q}}$$

Now suppose the system is governed by the linear (unforced) differential equation $\dot{\mathbf{q}} = \mathbf{A}\mathbf{q}$. Then $\dot{V} = 2\mathbf{q}'\mathbf{A}\mathbf{q}$, which is negative-definite if and only if the quadratic form $\mathbf{q}'\mathbf{A}\mathbf{q}$ is negative-definite, i.e., only when the eigenvalues of $\mathbf{A}$ are all real and negative. We know, however, from Theorem 11.4 that the origin is asymptotically stable even if $\mathbf{A}$ has complex eigenvalues, provided the *real parts* of all eigenvalues are negative. Thus, when the eigenvalues of $\mathbf{A}$ are complex, the use of the function $V = \mathbf{q}'\mathbf{q}$ gives no indication of the stability of the origin. For a numer-

† "Find" is meant literally, for there is in general no systematic way of determining such a function.

ical example consider the matrix

$$A = \begin{bmatrix} 0 & 1 \\ -2 & -2 \end{bmatrix}$$

whose eigenvalues are $s_1 = -1 + j$ and $s_2 = -1 - j$. The origin is therefore asymptotically stable. However,

$$\dot{V} = 2q'Aq$$
$$= 2[q_1 \quad q_2] \begin{bmatrix} 0 & 1 \\ -2 & -2 \end{bmatrix} \begin{bmatrix} q_1 \\ q_2 \end{bmatrix} = -2(q_1 q_2 + 2q_2{}^2)$$

which may be positive.

A modicum of encouragement for someone seeking a positive-definite function with a negative-definite derivative—or a Lyapunov function as it has come to be known—comes from a theorem of Massera,[†] which asserts that if the origin is asymptotically stable, a Lyapunov function exists.

To apply Lyapunov's theorem for the determination of the stability of a fixed linear system, we can employ the following theorem, also due to Lyapunov.

Theorem 11.15 *The origin of a linear fixed system $\dot{q} = Aq$ is asymptotically stable if and only if, for any symmetric positive-definite matrix Q, there exists a positive-definite matrix M which satisfies the matrix equation*

$$A'M + MA = -Q \tag{11.21}$$

To prove that the condition is sufficient to ensure stability, we choose as the Lyapunov function

$$V = q'Mq \tag{11.22}$$

Then, using (11.21) and $\dot{q} = Aq$, we find

$$\dot{V} = \dot{q}'Mq + q'M\dot{q} = q'(A'M + MA)q = -q'Qq$$

which is negative-definite when Q is positive-definite. If a positive-definite matrix M can be found which satisfies (11.21), V is positive-definite and, by Theorem 11.14, the origin is stable.

To prove that the condition is necessary, suppose the origin is asymptotically stable. Then the characteristic roots of A all have negative real parts. There is an algebraic theorem[‡] which asserts that (11.21)

---

† J. L. Massera, Contributions to Stability Theory, *Ann. Math.*, vol. 64, pp. 182–206, 1956.

‡ F. R. Gantmacher, "Theory of Matrices," vol. 2, pp. 186–187, Chelsea Publishing Company, New York, 1959. The theorem states that there is a unique solution M to (11.21) if and only if A has no characteristic roots which are zero or equal in magnitude and opposite in sign.

possesses a unique solution $\mathbf{M}$. Suppose that this solution is not positive-definite. Then the quadratic form $V = \mathbf{q}'\mathbf{Mq}$ is negative or zero for some $\mathbf{q} \neq \mathbf{0}$. But, for an asymptotically stable system,

$$V[x(t)] = \int_t^\infty \mathbf{q}'(\lambda)\mathbf{Qq}(\lambda)\,d\lambda = \mathbf{q}'\mathbf{Mq}$$

If $\mathbf{Q}$ is positive-definite, however, the integrand is always positive and hence the integral must be positive for $\mathbf{q} \neq \mathbf{0}$. This contradicts the previous assertion that $\mathbf{q}'\mathbf{Mq}$ is zero for some $\mathbf{q} \neq \mathbf{0}$ and establishes the necessity of the condition.

To employ the theorem one can select any convenient positive-definite matrix for $\mathbf{Q}$; in particular, we can take $\mathbf{Q} = \mathbf{I}$, the unit matrix.

Example 11.8   Consider the general second-order system

$$\dot{\mathbf{q}} = \mathbf{Aq}$$

with

$$\mathbf{A} = \begin{bmatrix} a_{11} & a_{12} \\ a_{21} & a_{22} \end{bmatrix}$$

Let

$$\mathbf{Q} = \begin{bmatrix} 1 & 0 \\ 0 & 1 \end{bmatrix}$$

Equation (11.21) reads

$$\begin{bmatrix} a_{11} & a_{21} \\ a_{12} & a_{22} \end{bmatrix}\begin{bmatrix} m_{11} & m_{12} \\ m_{12} & m_{22} \end{bmatrix} + \begin{bmatrix} m_{11} & m_{12} \\ m_{12} & m_{22} \end{bmatrix}\begin{bmatrix} a_{11} & a_{12} \\ a_{21} & a_{22} \end{bmatrix} = \begin{bmatrix} -1 & 0 \\ 0 & -1 \end{bmatrix}$$

which yields the following three simultaneous equations:

$$2(a_{11}m_{11} + a_{21}m_{12}) = -1$$
$$a_{11}m_{12} + a_{21}m_{22} + a_{12}m_{11} + a_{22}m_{12} = 0 \qquad (11.23)$$
$$2(a_{12}m_{12} + a_{22}m_{22}) = -1$$

Simultaneous solution of (11.23) gives the following expression for $\mathbf{M}$:

$$\mathbf{M} = \frac{1}{2(a_{11} + a_{22})|\mathbf{A}|}\begin{bmatrix} -(|\mathbf{A}| + a_{21}{}^2 + a_{22}{}^2) & a_{12}a_{22} + a_{21}a_{11} \\ a_{12}a_{22} + a_{21}a_{11} & -(|\mathbf{A}| + a_{11}{}^2 + a_{12}{}^2) \end{bmatrix}$$

and $\mathbf{M}$ is positive-definite if and only if

$$m_{11} = -\frac{|\mathbf{A}| + a_{21}{}^2 + a_{22}{}^2}{2(a_{11} + a_{22})|\mathbf{A}|} > 0$$

$$|\mathbf{M}| = \frac{(a_{11} + a_{22})^2 + (a_{12} - a_{21})^2}{4(a_{11} + a_{22})^2|\mathbf{A}|} > 0$$

The second equation requires that $|\mathbf{A}| > 0$, and this fact, together with the first equation, requires that $a_{11} + a_{22} < 0$, in order that the origin be asymptotically stable. To verify this result we note that the charac-

teristic equation is given by

$$|s\mathbf{I} - \mathbf{A}| = \begin{vmatrix} s - a_{11} & -a_{12} \\ -a_{21} & s - a_{22} \end{vmatrix} = s^2 - (a_{11} + a_{22})s + |\mathbf{A}| = 0$$

which has roots with negative-real parts if and only if

$$|\mathbf{A}| > 0 \qquad a_{11} + a_{22} < 0$$

In the next chapter we shall make use of the following slightly more general form of Theorem 11.15.

Theorem 11.15A   *The origin of the linear fixed system $\dot{\mathbf{q}} = \mathbf{A}\mathbf{q}$ is asymptotically stable if and only if, for any symmetric positive-semidefinite matrix $\mathbf{Q}$, there exists a positive-definite matrix $\mathbf{M}$ which satisfies (11.21) and $dV/dt = -\mathbf{q}'\mathbf{Q}\mathbf{q}$ is not identically zero along any trajectory.*

This theorem differs from Theorem 11.15 in that $\mathbf{Q}$ is permitted to be *semidefinite*.   The proof is similar to that of Theorem 11.15.

For a system of nth order, the calculation of the elements of the matrix $\mathbf{M}$ necessitates the solution of $n(n - 1)/2$ simultaneous equations.   After $\mathbf{M}$ has been calculated, one must then evaluate its determinant and its principal minors of all orders to determine whether the system is asymptotically stable.   The first step makes this algorithm practically inapplicable for hand calculation in systems of order higher than 2.   As we shall see in the following chapter, the Routh-Hurwitz algorithms accomplish the same result with much less calculation.

For discrete-time systems the analogs of Theorems 11.14 and 11.15 are the following.

Theorem 11.16   *Let $V(\mathbf{q}(n), n)$ be any continuous (in q), positive-definite scalar function of the state and the sampling instant n.   Then*
   1. If
$$V(\mathbf{q}(n + 1), n + 1) \leq V(\mathbf{q}(n), n)$$
the origin is stable.
   2. If
$$V(\mathbf{q}(n + 1), n + 1) < V(\mathbf{q}(n), n) \qquad \mathbf{q}(n) \neq 0$$
the origin is asymptotically stable.

Theorem 11.17   *The origin of the linear fixed system $\mathbf{q}(n + 1) = \mathbf{A}\mathbf{q}(n)$ is asymptotically stable if and only if there exists a (unique symmetric) matrix $\mathbf{M}$ satisfying*
$$\mathbf{A}'\mathbf{M}\mathbf{A} - \mathbf{M} = -\mathbf{Q} \qquad (11.24)$$
for any positive-definite symmetric matrix $\mathbf{Q}$.

The proofs of these theorems follow the lines of those of Theorems 11.14 and 11.15 and are left as exercises (Probs. 11.13 and 11.14).

PROBLEMS

11.1 Prove that $\|\mathbf{x}\|$ is finite if and only if each component x_i of $\mathbf{x}$ is finite.

11.2 (a) Prove that $\|\mathbf{M}\|$ defined by (11.3) has all the properties of a norm, namely,

(1) $\|\mathbf{M}\| = 0$ if and only if $\mathbf{M} = \mathbf{0}$.
(2) $\|\mathbf{M}_1 + \mathbf{M}_2\| \leq \|\mathbf{M}_1\| + \|\mathbf{M}_2\|$.
(3) $\|\alpha\mathbf{M}\| = |\alpha|\,\|\mathbf{M}\|$.

(b) Prove that $\|\mathbf{M}\|$ is finite if and only if every element m_{ij} of $\mathbf{M}$ is finite.

(c) Show that $\|\mathbf{M}\| \leq \sum\limits_{i=1}^{k} \sum\limits_{j=1}^{l} |m_{ij}|$.

11.3 Show that the following norms of $\mathbf{x}$ have the requisite properties:

(a) $\|\mathbf{x}\| = \left(\sum\limits_{i} x_i^2\right)^{\frac{1}{2}}$ (b) $\|\mathbf{x}\| = \max\limits_{i} |x_i|$

11.4 Show that the following definitions of the norm of a matrix are equivalent:

$$\|\mathbf{A}\| = \sup_{\mathbf{x} \neq 0} \frac{\|\mathbf{A}\mathbf{x}\|}{\|\mathbf{x}\|} = \sup_{\|\mathbf{x}\|=1} \|\mathbf{A}\mathbf{x}\| = \sup_{\|\mathbf{x}\| \leq 1} \|\mathbf{A}\mathbf{x}\|$$

11.5 Calculate the norm of the following matrix:

$$\mathbf{A} = \begin{bmatrix} 1 & 2 \\ -2 & 1 \end{bmatrix}$$

when

(a) $\|\mathbf{x}\| = \max\limits_{i} |x_i|$.

(b) $\|\mathbf{x}\| = (x_1^2 + x_2^2)^{\frac{1}{2}}$.
(c) $\|\mathbf{x}\| = |x_1| + |x_2|$.

11.6 Show that

$$\|\mathbf{M}\| = \max_{i} \sum_{j} |m_{ij}|$$

when

$$\|\mathbf{x}\| = \max_{i} |x_i|$$

11.7   Prove Theorem 11.3.

11.8   Prove that a discrete-time fixed system (a) is asymptotically stable if and only if the magnitudes of all eigenvalues are smaller than unity, and (b) is stable if and only if the magnitude of no eigenvalue is greater than unity and all eigenvalues with unity magnitude are simple (Theorem 11.5).

11.9   (a) Determine the equilibrium states of the system

$$\dot{x}_1 = x_2$$
$$\dot{x}_2 = -x_1 - x_2 + a^2 x_1{}^3$$

(b) Determine the nature of each equilibrium state—unstable, stable, asymptotically stable.

11.10   Prove that in a stable forced discrete-time system governed by $\mathbf{Q}(z) = \mathbf{R}(z)\mathbf{X}(z)$, every element of $\mathbf{R}(z)$ is finite for $|z| \geq 1$.

11.11   Show that the input $x(t)$ can excite all the natural modes of the system shown (Fig. P 11.11) if and only if $c \neq 0$:

(a) By calculating the transfer functions from x to q_1 and q_2.
(b) By using the test of Theorem 11.11.

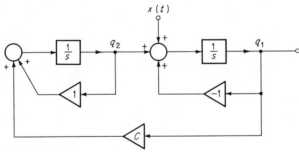

FIG. P 11.11

11.12   Prove Theorem 11.11 without the restriction that $\mathbf{A}$ have distinct eigenvalues.

11.13   Prove Theorem 11.16.

11.14   Prove Theorem 11.17.

11.15   Discuss the stability of the time-varying systems

(a) $\dfrac{dy}{dt} = ty + x,$

(b) $\dfrac{dy}{dt} = -ty + x,$

where y is the output and state and $x = x(t)$ is the input.

CHAPTER TWELVE

STABILITY CRITERIA

FOR FIXED SYSTEMS

12.1 INTRODUCTION

The theorems of the preceding chapter are generally not immediately useful for evaluating the stability of practical systems. In many cases no prescription can be given for using these theorems. When the system in question is linear and time-invariant, however, the situation is much more favorable. It will be recalled (Theorem 11.4) that the necessary and sufficient condition for the asymptotic stability of fixed continuous-time systems is that the zeros of the minimum polynomial

$$D(s) = |s\mathbf{I} - \mathbf{A}| = s^k + a_1 s^{k-1} + \cdots + a_{k-1} s + a_k$$

have negative real parts. This condition is also sufficient to ensure the stability (with respect to the class of bounded inputs) of forced systems. Moreover, when all the natural frequencies are excited by the input and observed in the output (Theorems 11.12 and 11.13), this condition is

also necessary. Hence we may state the following *practically* equivalent stability criteria for continuous-time systems:

(1) *A fixed continuous-time system is stable if and only if the zeros of the minimum polynomial $D(s)$ have negative real parts.*

$$(12.1)$$

(2) *A fixed continuous-time system is stable if the poles of every (input-output) transfer function in the system have negative real parts.*

By the same reasoning, analogous criteria can be stated for discrete-time systems:

(1) *A fixed discrete-time system is stable if and only if the zeros of the minimum polynomial*

$$D(z) = |z\mathbf{I} - \mathbf{A}|$$

lie within the unit circle centered at the origin of the z plane.

$$(12.2)$$

(2) *A fixed discrete-time system is stable if and only if the poles of every (input-output) transfer function in the system lie within the unit circle.*

If the minimum polynomial $D(s)$ is of degree greater than 3, an attempt to calculate the location of its zeros is generally not feasible. The problem of determining whether the zeros of a polynomial all have negative real parts without actually computing their location is thus seen to be a major problem in the dynamics of linear systems.   Its significance was recognized by many investigators during the late nineteenth and early twentieth centuries.   The first solution appears to have been given by Routh† in 1874, although partial solutions were found earlier.‡ In 1895 Hurwitz§ gave an independent but equivalent solution of the problem.   The various algorithms for determining whether the zeros of a given polynomial all have negative real parts are here collectively referred to as *Routh-Hurwitz algorithms.*

The analogous problem in discrete-time systems—that of determining whether the zeros of a polynomial lie within the unit circle of the complex plane—was the subject of investigations by Marden‖ and was adapted as a practical stability criterion in a series of papers by Jury.¶

† E. J. Routh, "A Treatise on the Stability of a Given State of Motion," Macmillan & Co., Ltd., London, 1877 (presented orally, 1874).
‡ For an account of the various investigations, see F. R. Gantmacher, "Theory of Matrices," vol. 2, pp. 172–173, Chelsea Publishing Company, New York, 1959.
§ A. Hurwitz, Über die Bedingungen, unter welchen eine Gleichung nur Wurzeln mit negativen reellen Teilen besitzt, *Math. Ann.*, vol. 146, pp. 273–284, 1895.
‖ M. Marden, "The Geometry of the Zeros of a Polynomial in a Complex Variable," *Math. Surveys*, no. 3, American Mathematical Society, New York, 1949.
¶ E. I. Jury, A Simplified Stability Criterion for Linear Discrete Systems, *Proc. IRE*, vol. 50, pp. 1493–1500, June, 1962.

The investigations by Routh and Hurwitz and by Marden were based on purely algebraic and analytic reasoning totally unrelated to the source of the problem in stability theory.   Although Lyapunov's second method seemed to be naturally suited to the problem, this method was not used to derive the earlier Hurwitz algorithm until 1962, when Parks[†] presented such a derivation.

In the treatment which follows, the Routh-Hurwitz algorithms are first derived in Sec. 12.2 by means of techniques similar to those used by the earlier investigators, and then Lyapunov's second method is used in the manner of Parks, in Sec. 12.3.

For discrete-time systems, a method of employing the Routh-Hurwitz algorithms is given first, and the algorithm developed by Jury is then stated without proof.

The chapter concludes with a brief discussion of graphical methods, which in many instances are more convenient than the algebraic techniques and often yield additional insight into the performance of a system.

12.2 ROUTH-HURWITZ ALGORITHMS

A polynomial whose zeros all have negative real parts is called a *Hurwitz polynomial*.   The problem is thus to develop algorithms for determining when a polynomial

$$D(s) = s^k + a_1 s^{k-1} + \cdots + a_{k-1} s + a_k$$

with real coefficients is a Hurwitz polynomial.   Since a Hurwitz polynomial is a product of factors of the form $s + \alpha$ or $s^2 + \beta s + \gamma$ with all α's, β's, and γ's *strictly* positive, it follows that all the coefficients of $D(s)$ must be *strictly positive*.   (This means that no coefficient may be absent.)   Unfortunately, this condition is insufficient to ensure that $D(s)$ will be a Hurwitz polynomial.

We shall develop the required Routh-Hurwitz algorithms by way of several subsidiary lemmas.   In these lemmas, we shall need the functions

$$W(s) = \frac{D(s)}{D(-s)} \tag{12.3}$$

and

$$F(s) = \frac{W(s) + 1}{W(s) - 1} = \frac{D(s) + D(-s)}{D(s) - D(-s)} \tag{12.4}$$

[†] P. C. Parks, A New Proof of the Routh-Hurwitz Stability Criterion Using the Second Method of Lyapunov, *Proc. Cambridge Phil. Soc.*, vol. 58, pt. 4, pp. 694–702, 1962.

From (12.4) we find

$$F(s) = \frac{a_1 s^{k-1} + a_3 s^{k-3} + \cdots + a_k}{s^k + a_2 s^{k-2} + \cdots + a_{k-1}s} \qquad k \text{ odd}$$

$$F(s) = \frac{s^k + a_2 s^{k-2} + \cdots + a_k}{a_1 s^{k-1} + a_3 s^{k-3} + \cdots + a_{k-1}s} \qquad k \text{ even} \tag{12.5}$$

Thus $F(s)$ is the ratio of an even polynomial in s to an odd polynomial in s, and for $s = 0 + j\omega$,

$$F(s) = F(j\omega) = \frac{a_k - \omega^2 a_{k-2} + \omega^4 a_{k-4} + \cdots}{j\omega(a_{k-1} - \omega^2 a_{k-3} + \omega^4 a_{k-5} + \cdots)} \tag{12.6}$$

Hence $F(j\omega)$ is a *purely imaginary odd function* of ω. Also note that $F(s)$ has a simple pole at the origin and either a simple pole or a simple zero at $s = \infty$.

Lemma 12.1 $D(s)$ *is a Hurwitz polynomial if and only if*

$$|W(s)| \begin{cases} >1 & \text{Re } s > 0 \\ =1 & \text{Re } s = 0 \\ <1 & \text{Re } s < 0 \end{cases} \tag{12.7}$$

   Proof Let $s + s_i$ $(i = 1, 2, \ldots, k)$ be the factors of $D(s)$. Then, in factored form,

$$W(s) = W_1(s)W_2(s) \cdots W_k(s)$$

where

$$W_i(s) = \frac{s + s_i}{-s + s_i^*} \qquad i = 1, 2, \ldots, k$$

Now with $s = \sigma + j\omega$, $s_i = \sigma_i + j\omega_i$,

$$|W_i(s)|^2 = \frac{|s + s_i|^2}{|-s + s_i^*|^2} = \frac{(\sigma + \sigma_i)^2 + (\omega + \omega_i)^2}{(\sigma - \sigma_i)^2 + (\omega + \omega_i)^2}$$

If $D(s)$ is a Hurwitz polynomial, $\sigma_i > 0$ $(i = 1, 2, \ldots, k)$, and consequently

$$|W_i(s)|^2 \begin{cases} >1 & \sigma = \text{Re } s > 0 \\ =1 & \sigma = \text{Re } s = 0 \\ <1 & \sigma = \text{Re } s < 0 \end{cases}$$

for each factor W_i. Hence (12.7) is satisfied. If $D(s)$ is not a Hurwitz polynomial, $D(-s)$ has a zero for some s with Re $s \leq 0$. This means that $W(s)$ has a pole for this value of s and does not satisfy (12.7). The lemma is thus proved.

Lemma 12.2 $D(s)$ *is a Hurwitz polynomial if and only if the poles of $F(s)$ are imaginary and simple and have positive residues.*

Proof   The transformation

$$F = \frac{W + 1}{W - 1}$$

transforms the interior of the unit circle of the W plane into the left half of the F plane.   Using this property and (12.7), we can establish the following corresponding regions, if and only if $D(s)$ is a Hurwitz polynomial:

$$\begin{aligned}
\operatorname{Re} F(s) &> 0 \leftrightarrow \operatorname{Re} s > 0 \\
\operatorname{Re} F(s) &= 0 \leftrightarrow \operatorname{Re} s = 0 \\
\operatorname{Re} F(s) &< 0 \leftrightarrow \operatorname{Re} s < 0
\end{aligned} \qquad (12.8)$$

whenever $F(s)$ is analytic.   Suppose now that $F(s)$ has a pole of order k at a point $s = s_p$.   Then, by expanding $F(s)$ into a Laurent series, with $s - s_p = \rho e^{j\theta}$ ($\rho > 0$), we obtain

$$F(s) = \frac{1}{\rho^k} \frac{re^{j\alpha}}{e^{jk\theta}} + Q(\rho) \qquad (12.9)$$

where $Q(\rho) \to 0$ uniformly with ρ, and $re^{j\alpha}$ is the coefficient of $(s - s_p)^{-k}$ in the Laurent series expansion of $F(s)$.   Hence

$$\operatorname{Re} F(s) = \frac{r}{\rho^k} \cos(k\theta - \alpha) + \operatorname{Re} Q(\rho)$$

Since $Q(\rho)$ can be made as small as desired, it is obvious that $\operatorname{Re} F(s)$ takes on both negative and positive values in the neighborhood of $s = s_p$. But since (12.8) requires $\operatorname{Re} F(s)$ to have a constant sign in each half plane, $F(s)$ cannot have a pole anywhere but on the imaginary axis. Even on the imaginary axis, (12.8) can be satisfied only if $k = 1$ and $\alpha = 0$, which implies that the pole must be simple and have a positive residue.   Necessity of the conditions in the lemma is thus established.

To establish sufficiency, we consider the partial fraction expansion of $F(s)$ having only simple imaginary poles with positive residues.   Noting that the residues at $s = \pm j\omega_i$ are equal, we have

$$F(s) = \sum_i a_i \left(\frac{1}{s + j\omega_i} + \frac{1}{s - j\omega_i} \right) \qquad a_i > 0$$

from which we find

$$\operatorname{Re} F(s) = \sigma \sum_i a_i \left[\frac{1}{\sigma^2 + (\omega + \omega_i)^2} + \frac{1}{\sigma^2 + (\omega - \omega_i)^2} \right]$$

The terms in brackets are always positive, as is a_i.   Moreover, the bracketed expression is finite, except at the poles of $F(s)$.   Hence the sign of $\operatorname{Re} F(s)$ is the same as the sign of $\sigma = \operatorname{Re} s$ and $\operatorname{Re} F(s) = 0$ when $\sigma = 0$ (except, of course, at the poles).   This is consistent with (12.8) and hence establishes sufficiency.

Example 12.1   Consider

$$D(s) = s^5 + s^4 + 3s^3 + 13s^2 + 2s + 36$$

Then

$$F(s) = \frac{D(s) + D(-s)}{D(s) - D(-s)} = \frac{s^4 + 13s^2 + 36}{s^5 + 3s^3 + 2s} = \frac{(s^2 + 4)(s^2 + 9)}{s(s^2 + 1)(s^2 + 2)}$$

We observe that the poles of $F(s)$ and $1/F(s)$ lie on the imaginary axis. The poles of $F(s)$ occur at $s = 0$, $\pm j$, $\pm j\sqrt{2}$, with the residues given by

$$\begin{aligned} R(0) &= 18 \\ R(-j) = R(j) &= -12 \\ R(-j\sqrt{2}) = R(j\sqrt{2}) &= \tfrac{7}{2} \end{aligned}$$

Since the residue at $s = j$ is nonpositive, $D(s)$ is not a Hurwitz polynomial.

Lemma 12.3 $D(s)$ is a Hurwitz polynomial if and only if the poles of $1/F(s)$ are imaginary and simple and have positive residues.

Proof

$$F^{-1}(s) = \frac{1}{F(s)} = \frac{1}{\text{Re } F(s) + j \text{ Im } F(s)} = \frac{\text{Re } F(s) - j \text{ Im } F(s)}{|F(s)|^2}$$

Hence, from (12.8),

$$\begin{aligned} \text{Re } F^{-1}(s) > 0 &\leftrightarrow \text{Re } s > 0 \\ \text{Re } F^{-1}(s) = 0 &\leftrightarrow \text{Re } s = 0 \\ \text{Re } F^{-1}(s) < 0 &\leftrightarrow \text{Re } s < 0 \end{aligned} \qquad (12.10)$$

Therefore $\text{Re } F^{-1}(s)$ must have the same properties as $\text{Re } F(s)$.

As a consequence of this lemma it is possible to investigate the poles of $F^{-1}(s)$ instead of those of $F(s)$. This lemma also indicates that the zeros of $F(s)$ must be imaginary and simple.

CONTINUED FRACTION ALGORITHM

Direct use of Lemma 12.2 (or 12.3) as a stability test necessitates the determination of the poles of $F(s)$ [or $F^{-1}(s)$], which requires an inconvenient calculation. The algorithm which we shall now develop does not require knowledge of the location of the poles of $F(s)$ [or $F^{-1}(s)$].

Let

$$G(s) = \begin{cases} F(s) & k \text{ even} \\ \dfrac{1}{F(s)} & k \text{ odd} \end{cases} \qquad (12.11)$$

We observe that $G(s)$ is an improper rational function of s; that is, the numerator of $G(s)$ is of higher degree than the denominator. In particular, from the definition of $F(s)$ given by (12.5), the degree of the numerator exceeds that of the denominator by unity. As a result we can write

$$G(s) = \alpha_1 s + G_1(s)$$

Since α_1 is the residue of the pole of $G(s)$ at $s = \infty$, it must be positive if $D(s)$ is a Hurwitz polynomial. Moreover $G_1(s)$ has the following properties. The remainder $G_1(s)$ is now a proper rational function whose poles are the same as the (finite) poles of $G(s)$ and have the same residues as those of $G(s)$. Thus $G_1(s)$ satisfies the conditions of Lemma 12.2 if $D(s)$ is a Hurwitz polynomial. By Lemma 12.3, $G_1^{-1}(s)$ also satisfies the conditions of Lemma 12.2. It is further clear that the degree of the numerator of $G_1^{-1}(s)$ exceeds that of the denominator by unity. Hence we can write

$$\frac{1}{G_1(s)} = \alpha_2 s + G_2(s)$$

where α_2 *must be finite and positive* if $D(s)$ is a Hurwitz polynomial. Proceeding in this fashion, we obtain

$$\frac{1}{G_2(s)} = \alpha_3 s + G_3(s) \qquad 0 < \alpha_3 < \infty \text{ if } D(s) \text{ is a Hurwitz polynomial}$$

$$\frac{1}{G_3(s)} = \alpha_4 s + G_4(s) \qquad 0 < \alpha_4 < \infty \text{ if } D(s) \text{ is a Hurwitz polynomial}$$

. . . .

$$\frac{1}{G_{k-2}} = \alpha_{k-1} s + G_{k-1}(s) \qquad 0 < \alpha_{k-1} < \infty \text{ if } D(s) \text{ is a Hurwitz polynomial}$$

$$\frac{1}{G_{k-1}(s)} = \alpha_k s \qquad 0 < \alpha_k < \infty \text{ if } D(s) \text{ is a Hurwitz polynomial}$$

These results lead to the following *Stieltjes continued fraction expansion* for $G(s)$:

$$G(s) = \alpha_1 s + \cfrac{1}{\alpha_2 s + \cfrac{1}{\alpha_3 s + {}}}$$

(12.12)

$$\cfrac{1}{\alpha_{k-1} s + \cfrac{1}{\alpha_k s}}$$

We thus have the following algorithm.

Theorem 12.1 $D(s)$ *is a Hurwitz polynomial if and only if every* α_i $(i = 1, 2, \ldots, k)$ *in the continued fraction expansion* (12.12) *is positive.*

Example 12.2   In Example 12.1

$$F(s) = \frac{s^4 + 13s^2 + 36}{s^5 + 3s^3 + 2s}$$

We perform the continued fraction expansion as follows:

$$
\begin{array}{r}
s \\ \hline
s^4 + 13s^2 + 36 \,\overline{)\,s^5 + 3s^3 + 2s} \\
s^5 + 13s^3 + 36s \\ \hline
-10s^3 - 34s
\end{array}
\qquad \alpha_1 = 1
$$

$$
\begin{array}{r}
-\tfrac{1}{10}s \\ \hline
-10s^3 - 34s \,\overline{)\,s^4 + 13s^2 + 36} \\
s^4 + \tfrac{34}{10}s^2 \\ \hline
\tfrac{96}{10}s^2 + 36
\end{array}
\qquad \alpha_2 = -\tfrac{1}{10}
$$

$$
\begin{array}{r}
-\tfrac{100}{96}s \\ \hline
\tfrac{96}{10}s^2 + 36 \,\overline{)\,-10s^3 - 34s} \\
-10s^3 - \tfrac{75}{2}s \\ \hline
\tfrac{7}{2}s
\end{array}
\qquad \alpha_3 = -\tfrac{100}{96}
$$

$$
\begin{array}{r}
\tfrac{96}{35}s \\ \hline
\tfrac{7}{2}s \,\overline{)\,\tfrac{96}{10}s^2 + 36} \\
\tfrac{96}{10}s^2 \\ \hline
36
\end{array}
\qquad \alpha_4 = \tfrac{96}{35}
$$

$$
\begin{array}{r}
\tfrac{7}{72}s \\ \hline
36 \,\overline{)\,\tfrac{7}{2}s}
\end{array}
\qquad \alpha_5 = \tfrac{7}{72}
$$

We see that α_2 and α_3 are nonpositive; hence $D(s)$ is not a Hurwitz polynomial.   Note that a single nonpositive coefficient establishes that the polynomial under investigation is not a Hurwitz polynomial and the subsequent divisions are unnecessary.   It is also evident that the leading coefficient of the remainder in each subtraction must be positive.

ROUTH'S ALGORITHM

Much of the writing in the continued fraction algorithm may be eliminated by use of the tabular algorithm originally developed by Routh. The first long division required in the continued fraction expansion is

given by

$$a_1 s^{k-1} + a_3 s^{k-3} + \cdots \overline{\big)\, s^k \;+\; a_2 s^{k-2} \;+\; a_4 s^{k-4} + \cdots}$$

$$\frac{\dfrac{1}{a_1} s}{\;}$$

$$\alpha_1 = \frac{1}{a_1}$$

$$\underline{s^k + \alpha_1 a_3 s^{k-2} + \alpha_1 a_5 s^{k-4} + \cdots}$$
$$b_1 s^{k-2} + b_2 s^{k-4} + \cdots$$

where $b_1 = a_2 - \alpha_1 a_3$, $b_2 = a_4 - \alpha_1 a_5$, ...
   The second division is given by

$$\frac{a_1}{b_1} s \qquad\qquad \alpha_2 = \frac{a_1}{b_1}$$

$$b_1 s^{k-2} + b_2 s^{k-4} + \cdots \overline{\big)\, a_1 s^{k-1} + \; a_3 s^{k-3} + \; a_5 s^{k-5} + \cdots}$$
$$\underline{a_1 s^{k-1} + \alpha_2 b_2 s^{k-3} + \alpha_2 b_3 s^{k-5} + \cdots}$$
$$c_1 s^{k-3} + \; c_2 s^{k-5} + \cdots$$

where $c_1 = a_3 - \alpha_2 b_2$, $c_2 = a_5 - \alpha_2 b_3$, ...
   The third division is given by

$$\frac{b_1}{c_1} s \qquad\qquad \alpha_3 = \frac{b_1}{c_1}$$

$$c_1 s^{k-3} + c_2 s^{k-5} + \cdots \overline{\big)\, b_1 s^{k-2} + \; b_2 s^{k-4} + \cdots}$$
$$\underline{b_1 s^{k-2} + \alpha_3 c_2 s^{k-4} + \cdots}$$
$$d_1 s^{k-4} + d_2 s^{k-6}$$

where $d_1 = b_2 - \alpha_3 c_2$, $d_2 = b_3 - \alpha_3 c_3$, ...
   The calculations required by these divisions can be carried out in tabular form as shown in Table 12.1, which is the algorithm originally given by Routh.
   It is observed that each element in the rth row of the table is calculated by subtracting α_r times the element in the $(r - 1)$st row and next column

Table 12.1 ROUTH TABLE

	1	a_2	a_4	$a_6 \cdots$
	a_1	a_3	a_5	$a_7 \cdots$
$\alpha_1 = \dfrac{1}{a_1}$	$b_1 = a_2 - \alpha_1 a_3$	$b_2 = a_4 - \alpha_1 a_5$	$b_3 = a_6 - \alpha_1 a_7$	$\cdots\cdots$
$\alpha_2 = \dfrac{a_1}{b_1}$	$c_1 = a_3 - \alpha_2 b_2$	$c_2 = a_5 - \alpha_2 b_3$	$\cdots\cdots\cdots$	
$\alpha_3 = \dfrac{b_1}{c_1}$	$d_1 = b_2 - \alpha_3 c_2$	$\cdots\cdots\cdots$		
$\alpha_4 = \dfrac{c_1}{d_1}$	$\cdots\cdots\cdots$			

from the element above it.   The leading elements of each row are the
leading coefficients of the remainders in the successive long divisions.
Hence we have the following algorithm.

Theorem 12.2 $D(s)$ *is a Hurwitz polynomial if and only if the elements*
$a_1, b_1, c_1, d_1, \ldots$ *in the Routh table are positive.*

Example 12.3   The Routh table for the polynomial of Example 12.2
has the following appearance:

	1	3	2
	1	13	36
$\alpha_1 = 1$	-10	-34	0
$\alpha_2 = -\frac{1}{10}$	$\frac{96}{10}$	36	0
$\alpha_3 = -\frac{100}{96}$	$\frac{7}{2}$	0	0
$\alpha_4 = \frac{96}{35}$	36	0	0
$\alpha_5 = \frac{7}{72}$	0	0	0

HURWITZ ALGORITHM

The Hurwitz stability algorithm is based on the so-called Hurwitz matrix
$\mathbf{H}$, which is a square $k \times k$ matrix for a polynomial of degree k.   The
matrix $\mathbf{H}$ has the following form:†

$$\mathbf{H} = \begin{bmatrix} a_1 & a_3 & a_5 & \cdots & a_{2k-1} \\ 1 & a_2 & a_4 & \cdots & a_{2k-2} \\ 0 & a_1 & a_3 & \cdots & a_{2k-3} \\ 0 & 1 & a_2 & \cdots & a_{2k-4} \\ & & \cdots & \\ 0 & 0 & \cdot & \cdots & 0 \\ 0 & 0 & \cdot & \cdots & a_k \end{bmatrix} \tag{12.13}$$

where $a_\nu = 0$ for $\nu > k$.   The first two rows of the matrix are formed by
placing unity in the 2, 1 position, a_1 in the 1, 1 position, a_2 in the 2, 2 position, and so forth, until all the coefficients of $D(s)$ are used up, and filling
the remaining positions with zero.   The next two rows are obtained by

---

† If the coefficient of s^k in the polynomial is $a_0 \neq 1$, the following results are still
valid when this value of a_0 is used in place of 1 in the 2, 1 position of $\mathbf{H}$.

shifting the first two rows to the right by one position and placing zeros in the first positions.   This procedure is followed until the required $k \times k$ matrix is completed.

The Hurwitz matrix for $k = 6$ thus appears as follows:

$$\mathbf{H} = \begin{bmatrix} a_1 & a_3 & a_5 & 0 & 0 & 0 \\ 1 & a_2 & a_4 & a_6 & 0 & 0 \\ 0 & a_1 & a_3 & a_5 & 0 & 0 \\ 0 & 1 & a_2 & a_4 & a_6 & 0 \\ 0 & 0 & a_1 & a_3 & a_5 & 0 \\ 0 & 0 & 1 & a_2 & a_4 & a_6 \end{bmatrix}$$

and for $k = 7$,

$$\mathbf{H} = \begin{bmatrix} a_1 & a_3 & a_5 & a_7 & 0 & 0 & 0 \\ 1 & a_2 & a_4 & a_6 & 0 & 0 & 0 \\ 0 & a_1 & a_3 & a_5 & a_7 & 0 & 0 \\ 0 & 1 & a_2 & a_4 & a_6 & 0 & 0 \\ 0 & 0 & a_1 & a_3 & a_5 & a_7 & 0 \\ 0 & 0 & 1 & a_2 & a_4 & a_6 & 0 \\ 0 & 0 & 0 & a_1 & a_3 & a_5 & a_7 \end{bmatrix}$$

The stability criterion of Hurwitz can now be stated as the following theorem.

Theorem 12.3   *The necessary and sufficient conditions for*

$$D(s) = s^k + a_1 s^{k-1} + \cdots + a_{k-1}s + a_k$$

to be a Hurwitz polynomial is that the principal minors of $\mathbf{H}$, *namely,*

$$D_1 = a_1$$

$$D_2 = \begin{vmatrix} a_1 & a_3 \\ 1 & a_2 \end{vmatrix}$$

$$D_3 = \begin{vmatrix} a_1 & a_3 & a_5 \\ 1 & a_2 & a_4 \\ 0 & a_1 & a_3 \end{vmatrix}$$

. . . .

$$D_k = |\mathbf{H}|$$

all be positive.

The theorem is proved by converting $\mathbf{H}$ into a new matrix $\mathbf{H}_k$ by a series of operations which do not alter the values of the principal minors, and

then showing that the principal minors of $\mathbf{H}_k$ are all positive if and only if all the elements in the first column of the Routh Table 12.1 are positive. We transform $\mathbf{H}$ into a new matrix $\mathbf{H}_2$ by the following operations:

1. Every *odd* row of $\mathbf{H}_2$ is the same as the corresponding *odd* row of $\mathbf{H}$.
2. Every *even* row of $\mathbf{H}_2$ is obtained by multiplying the preceding *odd* row of $\mathbf{H}$ by $\alpha_1 = 1/a_1$ and subtracting the products from the corresponding *even* row of $\mathbf{H}$.

This results in the following matrix for $\mathbf{H}_2$ if $m = k - 2$ for even k and $m = k - 1$ for odd k:

$$\mathbf{H}_2 = \begin{bmatrix} a_1 & a_3 & \cdots & & a_{m+1} & 0 & \cdots & 0 \\ 0 & a_2 - \alpha_1 a_3 & \cdots & & a_m - \alpha_1 a_{m+1} & \cdot & \cdots & 0 \\ 0 & a_1 & \cdots & & a_{m-1} & \cdot & \cdots & 0 \\ 0 & 0 & \cdots & a_{m-2} - \alpha_1 a_{m-1} & & \cdot & \cdots & 0 \\ 0 & 0 & \cdots & \cdots & & \cdot & \cdots & 0 \\ \cdots & \cdots & \cdots & \cdots & & \cdot & \cdots & \cdot \end{bmatrix}$$

We observe the following facts:

1. Each even row of $\mathbf{H}_2$ is the "b row" of the Routh table shifted to the right and augmented by an appropriate number of zeros, i.e., for (say) $k = 6$:

$$\mathbf{H}_2 = \begin{bmatrix} a_1 & a_3 & a_5 & 0 & 0 & 0 \\ 0 & b_1 & b_2 & b_3 & 0 & 0 \\ 0 & a_1 & a_3 & a_5 & 0 & 0 \\ 0 & 0 & b_1 & b_2 & b_3 & 0 \\ 0 & 0 & a_1 & a_3 & a_5 & 0 \\ 0 & 0 & 0 & b_1 & b_2 & b_3 \end{bmatrix}$$

2. The minors of order p in the first p rows of $\mathbf{H}_2$ are equal to the corresponding minors of $\mathbf{H}$ for all $p \leq k$. This statement is true because the minors of order p in the first p rows of a matrix are unchanged if every row is replaced by the difference of that row and any multiple of any preceding row.

We transform $\mathbf{H}_2$ into $\mathbf{H}_3$ by the following operations:

1. The first two rows of $\mathbf{H}_3$ are identical with the first two rows of $\mathbf{H}_2$.
2. The remaining *even* rows of $\mathbf{H}_3$ are identical with the corresponding even rows of $\mathbf{H}_2$.
3. The remaining *odd* rows of $\mathbf{H}_3$ are obtained by multiplying the pre-

ceding *even* row of $\mathbf{H}_2$ by α_2 and subtracting from the corresponding *odd* row of $\mathbf{H}_2$.

From the manner in which $\mathbf{H}_3$ is formed, we observe that:

1. The third row of $\mathbf{H}_3$ is the "c row" of the Routh table. In particular (for $k = 6$), we have

$$
\mathbf{H}_3 = \begin{bmatrix}
a_1 & a_3 & a_5 & 0 & 0 & 0 \\
0 & b_1 & b_2 & b_3 & 0 & 0 \\
0 & 0 & c_1 & c_2 & 0 & 0 \\
0 & 0 & b_1 & b_2 & b_3 & 0 \\
0 & 0 & 0 & c_1 & c_2 & 0 \\
0 & 0 & 0 & b_1 & b_2 & b_3
\end{bmatrix}
$$

Again the minors of order p in the first p rows of $\mathbf{H}_3$ are equal to the corresponding minors of $\mathbf{H}_1 = \mathbf{H}$ for all $p \leq k$.

By forming $\mathbf{H}_4$, $\mathbf{H}_5$, . . . in the manner used to form $\mathbf{H}_2$ and $\mathbf{H}_3$, we ultimately arrive at a matrix $\mathbf{H}_k$, which has as its rows the rows of the Routh table shifted to the right so that the first elements of that table appear on the principal diagonal. In particular (for $k = 6$), we have

$$
\mathbf{H}_4 = \begin{bmatrix}
a_1 & a_3 & a_5 & 0 & 0 & 0 \\
0 & b_1 & b_2 & b_3 & 0 & 0 \\
0 & 0 & c_1 & c_2 & 0 & 0 \\
0 & 0 & 0 & d_1 & d_2 & 0 \\
0 & 0 & 0 & c_1 & c_2 & 0 \\
0 & 0 & 0 & 0 & d_1 & d_2
\end{bmatrix}
$$

$$
\mathbf{H}_5 = \begin{bmatrix}
a_1 & a_3 & a_5 & 0 & 0 & 0 \\
0 & b_1 & b_2 & b_3 & 0 & 0 \\
0 & 0 & c_1 & c_2 & 0 & 0 \\
0 & 0 & 0 & d_1 & d_2 & 0 \\
0 & 0 & 0 & 0 & e_1 & 0 \\
0 & 0 & 0 & 0 & d_1 & d_2
\end{bmatrix}
$$

$$
\mathbf{H}_6 = \begin{bmatrix}
a_1 & a_3 & a_5 & 0 & 0 & 0 \\
0 & b_1 & b_2 & b_3 & 0 & 0 \\
0 & 0 & c_1 & c_2 & 0 & 0 \\
0 & 0 & 0 & d_1 & d_2 & 0 \\
0 & 0 & 0 & 0 & e_1 & 0 \\
0 & 0 & 0 & 0 & 0 & f_1
\end{bmatrix}
$$

2. The minors of order p in the first p rows of $\mathbf{H}_k$ are identical with the corresponding minors of $\mathbf{H}$.   Thus we have established that

$$D_1 = a_1$$
$$D_2 = a_1b_1$$
$$D_3 = a_1b_1c_1$$
$$\cdot \cdot \cdot \cdot \cdot \cdot$$
$$D_k = a_1b_1c_1 \cdot \cdot \cdot$$

Thus $D_1 > 0$, $D_2 > 0$, . . . , $D_n > 0$ if and only if $a_1 > 0$, $b_1 > 0$, $c_1 > 0$, ...   The latter holds, by Theorem 12.2, if and only if $D(s)$ is a Hurwitz polynomial.   This establishes the theorem.

Example 12.4   Find the range of K for which the system shown in Fig. 12.1 is stable.   The criterion to be used is that of a bounded input producing a bounded output since the states are unspecified.   The overall transfer function is given by

$$H(s) = \frac{Y(s)}{X(s)} = \frac{K \dfrac{1}{s(s+2)^2}}{1 + K \dfrac{1}{s(s+2)^2}} = \frac{K}{s^3 + 4s^2 + 4s + K}$$

We wish to establish the range of K for which the denominator

$$D(s) = s^3 + 4s^2 + 4s + K$$

is a Hurwitz polynomial.   We form the Hurwitz matrix

$$\mathbf{H} = \begin{bmatrix} 4 & K & 0 \\ 1 & 4 & 0 \\ 0 & 4 & K \end{bmatrix}$$

Then Theorem 12.3 requires that

$$D_1 = 4 > 0 \qquad D_2 = \begin{vmatrix} 4 & K \\ 1 & 4 \end{vmatrix} = 16 - K > 0 \qquad D_3 = KD_2 > 0$$

Hence the system is stable for $0 < K < 16$.

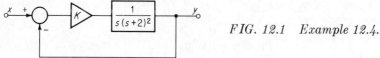

FIG. 12.1   Example 12.4.

REMARKS ON ROUTH-HURWITZ ALGORITHMS

The Routh algorithm is simply a skeleton form of the computations required in the continued fraction algorithm. Since it is easy to forget the exact manner in which the Routh table is completed, however, it is recommended that the occasional user employ the continued fraction algorithm as a mnemonic device.

The Hurwitz algorithm is fairly simple to remember, but has the disadvantage that much more calculation is required when the problem is to determine whether a polynomial with known coefficients is a Hurwitz polynomial. On the other hand, when the problem is to determine the range of a parameter for which a polynomial is a Hurwitz polynomial, the Hurwitz algorithm is usually superior to the other two.

It has been demonstrated[†] that the minors D_p of the Hurwitz matrix **H** are not independent. As a result, the Hurwitz algorithm has been simplified and requires the evaluation of only the even-order (or odd-order) minors. The simplification is given by the following theorem.

Theorem 12.4 *The necessary and sufficient conditions for a polynomial*

$$D(s) = s^k + a_1 s^{k-1} + \cdots + a_{k-1}s + a_k$$

to be a Hurwitz polynomial are either

$$a_1 > 0, a_3 > 0, a_5 > 0, \ldots$$
$$D_2 > 0, D_4 > 0, D_6 > 0, \ldots$$

or

$$a_2 > 0, \quad a_4 > 0, \quad a_6 > 0, \ldots$$
$$D_1 > 0, D_3 > 0, D_5 > 0, \ldots$$

12.3 DEVELOPMENT OF ROUTH-HURWITZ ALGORITHMS BY LYAPUNOV'S SECOND METHOD

A purely algebraic proof of the Routh-Hurwitz algorithms utilizing Lyapunov's theorem (Theorem 11.15A) can be given. The proof we give below follows that of Parks.[‡] It is convenient to start with the structure shown in Fig. 12.2, in which the α_i are exactly those numbers obtained in

---

† Liénard and Chipart, Sur le signe de la partie réelle des racines d'une équation algébrique, *J. Math. Pures Appl.*, 6th ser., vol. 10, pp. 291–346, 1914. See also Gantmacher, *op. cit.*, vol. 2, p. 221.

‡ *Op. cit.*

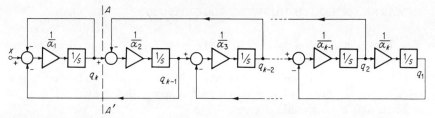

FIG. 12.2   Structure for demonstration of Routh-Hurwitz algorithms.

the Routh table.   The α_i are assumed to be nonzero.   First we calculate the transfer function

$$H(s) = \frac{Q_k(s)}{X(s)}$$

Using the methods of Chap. 7, we find

$$H(s) = \frac{\dfrac{1}{\alpha_1 s}}{1 + \dfrac{1 + H_2}{\alpha_1 s}} = \frac{1}{1 + \alpha_1 s + H_2} \tag{12.14}$$

where H_2 is the transfer function $Q_{k-1}(s)/Q_k(s)$ to the right of the dashed line AA'.   This transfer function is calculated to be

$$H_2(s) = \frac{Q_{k-1}(s)}{Q_k(s)} = \frac{1}{\alpha_2 s + H_3}$$

where $H_3(s) = Q_{k-2}(s)/Q_{k-1}(s)$.   Thus, from (12.14),

$$H(s) = \frac{1}{1 + \alpha_1 s + \dfrac{1}{\alpha_2 s + H_3}}$$

Proceeding in this fashion we find that

$$H(s) = \cfrac{1}{1 + \alpha_1 s + \cfrac{1}{\alpha_2 s + \cfrac{1}{\alpha_3 s + \cdot}}}$$

$$\cfrac{1}{\alpha_{k-1} s + \cfrac{1}{\alpha_k s}}$$

Comparing this expression with (12.12), we note that

$$H(s) = \frac{1}{1 + G(s)}$$

where, by (12.4), $G(s) = [D(s) \pm D(-s)]/[D(s) \mp D(-s)]$. Consequently

$$H(s) = \frac{\frac{1}{2}[D(s) \mp D(-s)]}{D(s)}$$

The denominator of $H(s)$ is thus identical with the characteristic polynomial $D(s)$ under investigation, and the characteristic equation for the system of Fig. 12.2 is identical with the equation $D(s) = 0$. Hence the conditions for stability of this system are equivalent to the conditions that $D(s)$ be a Hurwitz polynomial. We shall determine the conditions for the stability of the system by the use of Theorem 11.15A.

In vector-matrix form the unforced differential equations for the system can be written

$$\dot{\mathbf{q}} = \mathbf{A}\mathbf{q} \tag{12.15}$$

where

$$\mathbf{A} = \begin{bmatrix} 0 & \dfrac{1}{\alpha_k} & 0 & \cdots & 0 & 0 & 0 \\ -\dfrac{1}{\alpha_{k-1}} & 0 & \dfrac{1}{\alpha_{k-1}} & \cdots & 0 & 0 & 0 \\ 0 & -\dfrac{1}{\alpha_{k-2}} & 0 & \cdots & 0 & 0 & 0 \\ \cdots & \cdots & \cdots & & \cdots & \cdots & \cdots \\ 0 & 0 & 0 & \cdots & -\dfrac{1}{\alpha_2} & 0 & \dfrac{1}{\alpha_2} \\ 0 & 0 & 0 & \cdots & 0 & -\dfrac{1}{\alpha_1} & -\dfrac{1}{\alpha_1} \end{bmatrix} \tag{12.16}$$

Consider the quadratic form

$$V = \mathbf{q}'\mathbf{P}\mathbf{q} \tag{12.17}$$

where

$$\mathbf{P} = \begin{bmatrix} \alpha_k & 0 & \cdots & 0 & 0 \\ 0 & \alpha_{k-1} & \cdots & 0 & 0 \\ \cdots & \cdots & \cdots & \cdots & \cdots \\ 0 & 0 & \cdots & \alpha_2 & 0 \\ 0 & 0 & \cdots & 0 & \alpha_1 \end{bmatrix}$$

Then

$$\mathbf{PA} = \begin{bmatrix} 0 & 1 & 0 & \cdots & 0 & 0 \\ -1 & 0 & 1 & \cdots & 0 & 0 \\ 0 & -1 & 0 & \cdots & 0 & 0 \\ \cdots & \cdots & \cdots & & \cdots & \cdots \\ 0 & 0 & 0 & \cdots & 0 & 1 \\ 0 & 0 & 0 & \cdots & -1 & -1 \end{bmatrix}$$

that is, **PA** is skew-symmetric except for -1 in the lower right-hand corner. Thus we find that

$$\frac{dV}{dt} = \mathbf{q}'(\mathbf{A'P} + \mathbf{PA})\mathbf{q} = -2q_k{}^2 \qquad (12.18)$$

If the α_i are all positive, V given by (12.17) is a positive-definite quadratic form and dV/dt is negative-semidefinite. Moreover, $\dot{V}$ cannot be zero along a trajectory unless $q_k \equiv 0$; that is, $\dot{q}_k \equiv 0$. Examining (12.15) in detail, we find that this cannot happen unless $\mathbf{q} \equiv \mathbf{0}$. Thus the conditions of Theorem 11.15A are satisfied, and we conclude that, if all the α_i are positive, the origin is asymptotically stable. However, if one or more α_i are negative, the origin is not asymptotically stable. If any of the α_i are zero, the matrix **A** cannot be constructed as described and this derivation does not hold.

12.4 CRITERIA FOR STABILITY OF FIXED DISCRETE-TIME SYSTEMS

In discrete-time systems the unit circle of the z plane plays the same role as the imaginary axis of the s plane in continuous-time systems. The problem in discrete-time systems is thus to determine whether the zeros of a given polynomial

$$D(z) = z^k + a_1 z^{k-1} + \cdots + a_{k-1}z + a_k$$

lie inside the unit circle without actually calculating these zeros. We note that if the zeros of $D(z)$ lie within the unit circle, we may write

$$D(z) = \prod_i (z - z_i)$$

where $|z_i| < 1$. It follows for a kth-degree polynomial that

$$|a_1| = |z_1 + z_2 + \cdots + z_k| \leq |z_1| + |z_2| + \cdots + |z_k| < k$$

$$|a_2| = |\underbrace{z_1 z_2 + z_2 z_3 + \cdots}_{k(k-1)/2 \text{ terms}}| \leq |z_1 z_2| + |z_2 z_3| + \cdots < \frac{k(k-1)}{2!}$$

. . . .

$$|a_{k-1}| = |\underbrace{z_1 z_2 \cdots z_{k-1} + z_2 z_3 \cdots z_{k-2}z_k + \cdots}_{k \text{ terms}}| < k$$

$$|a_k| = |z_1 z_2 \cdots z_k| < 1$$

Hence necessary conditions for $D(z)$ to have its zeros inside the unit circle are

$$|a_i| < \binom{k}{i} = \frac{k!}{i!(k-i)!} \qquad i = 1, 2, \ldots, k \qquad (12.19)$$

These conditions, however, are not sufficient to ensure that $D(z)$ has its zeros inside the unit circle.

Thus, while the tests in (12.19) should be performed as a preliminary, it is usually necessary to perform an additional calculation to establish whether the zeros of a given $D(z)$ lie within the unit circle.

MODIFICATION OF ROUTH-HURWITZ ALGORITHMS

By a modification of the Routh-Hurwitz algorithms, we may determine conclusively whether $D(z)$ has any zeros outside the unit circle. Consider the bilinear transformation

$$s = \frac{z+1}{z-1} \qquad z = \frac{s+1}{s-1} \qquad (12.20)$$

This transformation transforms the interior of the unit circle into the left half plane and the exterior of the unit circle into the right half plane. Hence the zeros of

$$D\left(\frac{s+1}{s-1}\right) = \left(\frac{s+1}{s-1}\right)^k + a_1\left(\frac{s+1}{s-1}\right)^{k-1} + \cdots + a_{k-1}\left(\frac{s+1}{s-1}\right) + a_k$$

$$= \frac{(s+1)^k + a_1(s+1)^{k-1}(s-1) + \cdots}{+ a_{k-1}(s+1)(s-1)^{k-1} + a_k(s-1)^k} \qquad (12.21)$$

in the right half s plane correspond to zeros of $D(z)$ outside the unit circle in the z plane. The zeros of (12.21) are the zeros of its numerator $P(s)$:

$$P(s) = (s+1)^k + a_1(s+1)^{k-1}(s-1) + \cdots$$
$$+ a_{k-1}(s+1)(s-1)^{k-1} + a_k(s-1)^k$$
$$= b_0 s^k + b_1 s^{k-1} + \cdots + b_{k-1}s + b_k \qquad (12.22)$$

Hence failure of one of the Routh-Hurwitz tests when applied to $P(s)$ indicates that $D(z)$ has one or more zeros on or outside the unit circle.

The coefficients b_i of $P(s)$ are linear combinations of the coefficients a_i of the original $D(z)$.   Thus we can write

$$
\begin{bmatrix} b_0 \\ b_1 \\ \cdot \\ \cdot \\ \cdot \\ b_{k-1} \\ b_k \end{bmatrix} = \mathbf{M}_k \begin{bmatrix} 1 \\ a_1 \\ \cdot \\ \cdot \\ \cdot \\ a_{k-1} \\ a_k \end{bmatrix}
\tag{12.23}
$$

The matrices $\mathbf{M}_k$ for the first few values of k are tabulated as follows:

$$
\mathbf{M}_2 = \begin{bmatrix} 1 & 1 & 1 \\ 2 & 0 & -2 \\ 1 & -1 & 1 \end{bmatrix}
$$

$$
\mathbf{M}_3 = \begin{bmatrix} 1 & 1 & 1 & 1 \\ 3 & 1 & -1 & -3 \\ 3 & -1 & -1 & 3 \\ 1 & -1 & 1 & -1 \end{bmatrix}
$$

$$
\mathbf{M}_4 = \begin{bmatrix} 1 & 1 & 1 & 1 & 1 \\ 4 & 2 & 0 & -2 & -4 \\ 6 & 0 & -2 & 0 & 6 \\ 4 & -2 & 0 & 2 & -4 \\ 1 & -1 & 1 & -1 & 1 \end{bmatrix}
$$

Example 12.5 $D(z) = z^3 - 1.3z^2 - 1.3z - 0.2$.   Since $D(z)$ satisfies (12.19), it might have its zeros inside the unit circle.   We form

$$
\begin{bmatrix} b_0 \\ b_1 \\ b_2 \\ b_3 \end{bmatrix} = \begin{bmatrix} 1 & 1 & 1 & 1 \\ 3 & 1 & -1 & -3 \\ 3 & -1 & -1 & 3 \\ 1 & -1 & 1 & -1 \end{bmatrix} \begin{bmatrix} 1 \\ -1.3 \\ -1.3 \\ -0.2 \end{bmatrix} = \begin{bmatrix} -1.8 \\ 3.6 \\ 5.0 \\ 1.2 \end{bmatrix}
$$

Since the first coefficient is negative and the rest are positive, $P(s)$ has a zero in the right half plane, and hence $D(z)$ has a zero outside the unit circle.

Example 12.6   Sampled-data feedback system   The continuous feedback system of Example 12.4 (Fig. 12.1) is modified by the addition of a sampler as shown in Fig. 12.3.   The operation of the sampler is indicated in Fig. 8.6b with $T = 1$ sec.   By use of techniques described in

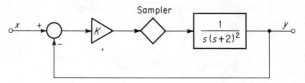

FIG. 12.3   Example 12.6, sampled-data feedback system.

Secs. 4.6 and 8.9, it is found that the overall transfer function of the equivalent discrete-time system is given by

$$H(z) = \frac{Y(z)}{X(z)} = \frac{K'F(z)}{1 + K'F(z)}$$

where

$$F(z) = \frac{z^2 + 1.627z + 0.135}{(z - 1)(z - 0.135)^2} = \frac{(z + 1.539)(z + 0.088)}{(z - 1)(z - 0.135)^2}$$

and $K' = 0.0677K$.

The characteristic equation of the system is

$$D(z) = (z - 1)(z - 0.135)^2 + K'(z^2 + 1.627z + 0.135)$$
$$= z^3 + a_1 z^2 + a_2 z + a_3$$

where $a_1 = K' - 1.270$

$a_2 = 1.627K' + 0.288$

$a_3 = 0.135K' - 0.0182$

Using the modified Routh-Hurwitz method, we first form $P(s)$.   From (12.23), with $k = 3$, we find

$$b_0 = 2.762K'$$
$$b_1 = -1.032K' + 1.497$$
$$b_2 = -2.222K' + 3.927$$
$$b_3 = 0.492K' + 2.576$$

Thus the Hurwitz matrix is

$$\mathbf{H} = \begin{bmatrix} -1.032K' + 1.497 & 0.492K' + 2.576 & 0 \\ 2.762K' & -2.222K' + 3.927 & 0 \\ 0 & -1.032K' + 1.497 & 0.492K' + 2.576 \end{bmatrix}$$

The requirement that b_0, b_1, b_2, b_3 must be positive establishes that

$$K' > 0$$
$$K' < 1.497/1.032 = 1.45$$
$$K' < 3.927/2.222 = 1.77$$
$$K' > -2.576/0.492 = -5.23$$

Simultaneous satisfaction of the above requires that

$$0 < K' < 1.45$$

In addition, we must satisfy

$$D_2 = \begin{vmatrix} -1.032K' + 1.497 & 0.492K' + 2.576 \\ 2.762K' & -2.222K' + 3.927 \end{vmatrix}$$

$$= 0.934K'^2 - 14.49K' + 5.88 > 0$$

The roots of $D_2 = 0$ and $K' = 15.1$ and $K' = 0.423$; hence $D_2 > 0$ for $K' < 0.423$ and $K' > 15.1$. The region of stability is thus given by

$$0 < K' < 0.423$$

or

$$0 < K < 6.24$$

Note that the system with sampling has a smaller maximum allowable loop gain than the system without sampling.

DIRECT ALGORITHM

The algorithm just described is easy to remember and usually not too difficult to apply. It is less convenient than the original Routh-Hurwitz algorithm, however, in that a subsidiary calculation of **b** in terms of **a** is required. This calculation is particularly inconvenient when the coefficients involve a parameter (whose range for stability of the system is to be determined). In this case the multiplication of **a** by **M** may turn out to be tedious.

To avoid this inconvenience, Jury[†] has developed an algorithm, based on results of Marden,[‡] which permits operating directly upon the coefficients of a_i of $D(z)$. This algorithm is tabular and resembles the Routh table in form and in the nature of its entries. For a polynomial

$$D(z) = a_0 z^k + a_1 z^{k-1} + \cdots + a_k \qquad (a_0 > 0)$$

the procedure is indicated in Table 12.2.

† E. I. Jury and J. Blanchard, A Stability Test for Linear Discrete Systems in Table Form, *Proc. IRE*, vol. 49, pp. 1947–1948, December, 1961; E. I. Jury, On the Roots of a Real Polynomial Inside the Unit Circle and a Stability Criterion for Linear Discrete Systems, in *Proc. Second Intern. Congr. IFAC*, Basle, 1963, paper no. 413 [Butterworth & Co., Ltd.—Oldenbourg (Publishers), London-Munich, Preprint 1963].
‡ *Op. cit.*

Table 12.2 STABILITY TABLE FOR DISCRETE-TIME SYSTEMS

Row							
1	a_0	a_1	a_2	$\cdots$	a_{k-2}	a_{k-1}	a_k
2	a_k	a_{k-1}	a_{k-2}	$\cdots$	a_2	a_1	a_0
3	b_0	b_1	b_2	$\cdots$	b_{k-2}	b_{k-1}	—
4	b_{k-1}	b_{k-2}	b_{k-3}	$\cdots$	b_1	b_0	—
5	c_0	c_1	c_2	$\cdots$	c_{k-2}	—	
6	c_{k-2}	c_{k-3}	c_{k-4}	$\cdots$	c_0	—	
$\cdots\cdots$	$\cdots\cdots\cdots$						
$2k-3$	s_0	s_1	s_2				

The rows of the table are computed in pairs: in the first the coefficients are entered in the order in which they appear in $D(z)$; in the second they are entered in reverse order. The third row is filled by computing

$$b_0 = \begin{vmatrix} a_0 & a_k \\ a_k & a_0 \end{vmatrix} \qquad b_1 = \begin{vmatrix} a_0 & a_{k-1} \\ a_k & a_1 \end{vmatrix} \qquad \cdots \qquad b_{k-1} = \begin{vmatrix} a_0 & a_1 \\ a_k & a_{k-1} \end{vmatrix}$$

These determinants are seen to consist of pairs of columns of the first two rows of the table. The fourth row is the reverse of the third. The fifth row is

$$c_0 = \begin{vmatrix} b_0 & b_{k-1} \\ b_{k-1} & b_0 \end{vmatrix} \qquad c_1 = \begin{vmatrix} b_0 & b_{k-2} \\ b_{k-1} & b_1 \end{vmatrix} \qquad \cdots \qquad c_{k-2} = \begin{vmatrix} b_0 & b_1 \\ b_{k-1} & b_{k-2} \end{vmatrix}$$

and so forth, until only three elements appear.

The following theorem is used to determine whether all the zeros of $D(z)$ lie within the unit circle.

Theorem 12.5 *The necessary and sufficient conditions for $D(z)$ to have all its zeros within the unit circle of the z plane are, with $a_0 > 0$,*

$$D(1) > 0 \qquad (-1)^k D(-1) > 0$$
$$a_0 > |a_k|$$
$$|b_0| > |b_{k-1}|$$
$$|c_0| > |c_{k-2}|$$
$$\cdots\cdots\cdots$$
$$|s_0| > |s_2|$$

Example 12.7   For the polynomial $D(z) = z^3 - 1.3z^2 - 1.3z - 0.2$, we find that $D(1) = -1.8 < 0$ and $(-1)^3 D(-1) = 1.2 > 0$.

The stability table is

$$
\begin{array}{cccc}
1.0 & -1.3 & -1.3 & -0.2 \\
-0.2 & -1.3 & -1.3 & 1.0 \\
\hline
0.96 & -1.56 & -1.56 &
\end{array}
$$

Thus

$$
\begin{array}{lllll}
a_0 = 1.0 & a_3 = -0.2 & \text{or} & a_0 > |a_3| \\
b_0 \equiv s_0 = 0.96 & b_2 \equiv s_2 = -1.56 & \text{or} & |s_0| < |s_2|
\end{array}
$$

Since two of the required conditions fail to be met, we conclude that $D(z)$ has zeros outside the unit circle.   Upon discovering the first failure, we need not have proceeded further; the above calculation was completed only to illustrate its full extent for a third-degree polynomial.

The algorithm described in this section should suffice for most users. The reader who has frequent need to perform the calculations is referred to the literature cited for techniques by which the direct algorithm given above can be further simplified.

12.5   GRAPHICAL METHODS

In the design of a linear system the usual problem is to determine the range of a parameter for which the system is stable rather than to test whether a given system is stable.   Although the Hurwitz algorithm is better suited for this problem than the Routh algorithms, even the former often entails a great deal of laborious calculation.   The result of this calculation tells whether or not a system is stable or, when performed with one or more literal coefficients or parameters, gives the range of these parameters for which the system is stable.   In many engineering problems more information is desired, such as an indication of how to stabilize a system which is found to be unstable, or how to estimate its dynamic behavior.   In order to obtain information of this nature, several graphical methods for studying the stability of linear control systems have been developed.

The application of these techniques to the design of control systems is beyond the scope of this book.†   The objective in this section is to

† See, for example, J. G. Truxal, "Automatic Feedback Control System Synthesis," pp. 223–250, McGraw-Hill Book Company, New York, 1955.

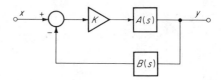

FIG. 12.4   Typical feedback system.

provide an introduction to these techniques in order to round out the discussion of methods of evaluating system stability.   Unlike the algebraic algorithms, the graphical techniques have a further advantage of not being restricted to lumped systems.

The graphical techniques to be described are designed to investigate the behavior of a linear system with a single adjustable parameter K. They are motivated by the observation that the transfer function of a linear system can usually be written in the form

$$H(s) = \frac{F(s)}{1 + KT(s)} \tag{12.24}$$

where $F(s)$ and $T(s)$ are rational (or in the case of distributed systems,† irrational) functions of s; $F(s)$ may depend on K, but $T(s)$ is independent of K.

In the feedback system of Fig. 12.4, for example, $F(s) = KA(s)$, $T(s) = A(s)B(s)$.   The systems of Prob. 12.2 are additional examples of systems in which the transfer functions can be written in the form of (12.24).

It is evident that the poles of the overall transfer function (i.e., the eigenvalues excited by the input and appearing in the output) are located at the poles of $F(s)$ and at the zeros of $1 + KT(s)$, unless one or more poles of the former are fortuitously canceled by poles of the latter.   (There are good reasons for assuming that this cannot happen in practical systems.)   One customarily knows the location of the poles of $F(s)$, and thus the problem is to locate the zeros of $1 + KT(s)$.

NYQUIST CRITERION‡

The Nyquist criterion is a graphical method of determining whether $1 + KT(s)$ is equal to zero for any value of s in the right half plane or on the imaginary axis, i.e., whether $T(s) = -1/K$ for any s in the right half plane or on the imaginary axis.   If we map the right half of the s plane

† See Chap. 13.
‡ H. Nyquist, Regeneration Theory, *Bell System Tech. J.*, vol. 11, pp. 126–147, January, 1932.

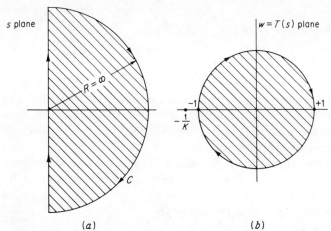

FIG. 12.5   Nyquist diagram for $1 + K[(s - 1)/(s + 1)]$.

onto the plane $w = T(s)$ and the resulting map covers the point $-1/K$, we know that $1 + KT(s)$ has a zero in the right half plane.   Conversely, if the map does not cover the point $-1/K$, then $1 + KT(s)$ has no zeros in the right half plane.   If the map of the imaginary axis passes through the point $-1/K$, then $1 + KT(s)$ has a zero on the imaginary axis. This situation is illustrated in Fig. 12.5 for $T(s) = (s - 1)/(s + 1)$. The shaded portion of the s plane corresponds to the shaded portion of the $w = T(s)$ plane.   We observe that the range of K for stability is given by $|1/K| > 1$ or $-1 < K < 1$.   This result is obviously correct, since the corresponding polynomial is $D(s) = (1 + K)s + (1 - K)$.   This example is intended to illustrate the underlying principle involved in the Nyquist criterion.   The problems to which the Nyquist criterion is applied in practice involve a loop transmission function $T(s)$ which has a denominator (and sometimes a numerator) of fairly high degree.   In such cases the map of the right half of the s plane by the transformation $w = T(s)$ has a rather complicated appearance, and it is often a difficult matter to determine which portions of the w plane correspond to points in the right half of the s plane and which correspond to points in the left half of the s plane.   The following example provides an illustration.

Example 12.8   Consider the system of Example 12.4 (Fig. 12.1).   The loop transmission is given by

$$T(s) = \frac{1}{s(s + 2)^2}$$

The map of the imaginary axis $\epsilon < |\omega| < \infty$ is shown by the solid line of Fig. 12.6b.

The range of frequencies $-\epsilon < \omega < \epsilon$ requires special attention since $T(s)$ has a pole at $s = 0$, and hence $T(s)$ becomes infinite as $\omega \to 0$. The map of the right half of the s plane cannot be complete unless a contour is chosen around the pole at the origin. In order to accomplish this we must decide whether the neighborhood of the origin is to be regarded as part of the left half plane or part of the right half plane. If we regard the neighborhood of the origin as part of the left half plane by choosing contour 1 in Fig. 12.6, zeros of $1 + KT(s)$ *in the neighborhood of the origin* will not be detected by the map covering the point $-1/K$. If contour 2 is chosen, thereby identifying the neighborhood of the origin with the right half plane, zeros of $1 + KT(s)$ will be detected by the map.

The contours on the $w = T(s)$ plane corresponding to 1 and 2 on the s plane are indicated in Fig. 12.6b. Thus we see that there are two possible maps of the right half plane. In either map, however, it is easy to determine that the portion of the left half w plane lying to the left of the map of the imaginary axis corresponds to the left half of the s plane. Hence we infer that the map of the right half s plane covers $-1/K$ if K is negative or if $K > 16$. Hence the region of stability is $0 < K < 16$, as previously calculated in Example 12.4.

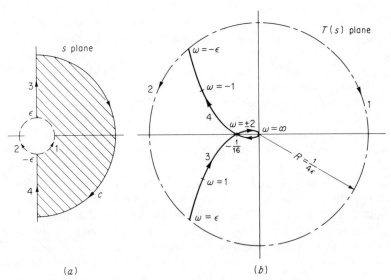

(a)   (b)

FIG. 12.6 *Nyquist diagram for Example 12.8.*

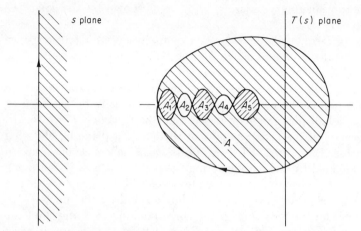

FIG. 12.7   Typical map by $w = T(s)$ of the imaginary axis in high-order systems.

In many instances $T(s)$ will have poles on the imaginary axis (as in Example 12.8).   In such cases these points must be avoided by detours. Since poles on the imaginary axis of $H(s)$ imply that the system is not asymptotically stable, these points should be regarded as portions of the right half plane.   They should therefore be detoured by clockwise arcs of infinitesimal radius, such as contour 2 in Fig. 12.6, if system poles on the imaginary axis are to be excluded.   Often poles at the or gin are desirable or even required, and the origin is usually detoured by an arc extending into the right half plane as shown in Fig. 12.6a.

In cases where $T(s)$ has a numerator or denominator of high degree with both poles and zeros, a typical map of the right half s plane on the $T(s)$ plane could have the appearance shown in Fig. 12.7, where the map of the imaginary axis crosses itself several times.   One must determine to which regions of the s plane the closed regions (indicated by A_i in Fig. 12.7) on the $w = T(s)$ plane correspond.   For this purpose we make use of the fact that the transformation $w = T(s)$ is conformal (except at the poles of $T(s)$ and the zeros of $dT(s)/ds$).   This means that points to the right of the imaginary axis in the s plane map into points to the right of the map of the imaginary axis in the $w = T(s)$ plane.   Thus, by assigning an upward orientation to the imaginary axis so that the right half plane lies to the right of the imaginary axis, the map of the right half plane will lie to the right of the map of the imaginary axis.†   By

† Another viewpoint is to imagine oneself walking along the map of the imaginary axis with the right hand outstretched.   Then any region touched by the right hand

shading the region immediately to the right of the map of the imaginary axis, we establish which regions of the $w = T(s)$ plane correspond to the right half of the s plane. Thus, in Fig. 12.7, the regions labeled A, A_1, A_3, and A_5 correspond to the right half plane, and $-1/K$ must lie in A_2 or A_4 if the system is stable.

The Nyquist diagram, or map of the imaginary axis, is usually obtained by direct calculation. Practical suggestions for constructing this map may be found in most books on feedback control systems.

A difficulty arises when $T(s)$ has one or more poles in the right half plane. In this case, when the right half s plane is enclosed by the contour of Fig. 12.5a, the poles in the right half plane will be enclosed and the preceding reasoning fails to hold. Instead we use the following theorem† for functions of a complex variable:

If $F(s)$ is meromorphic (has poles as its only singularities) inside a closed contour C and is not infinite or zero at any point on the contour,

$$\frac{1}{2\pi j} \oint_C \frac{F'(s)}{F(s)} \, ds = Z - P \tag{12.25}$$

where Z is the number of zeros and P is the number of poles of $F(s)$ within the contour and $F'(s) = dF/ds$. (Note that here C is traversed in the *counterclockwise* direction.)

Let C be the contour which extends along the imaginary axis and goes back along a semicircle of infinite radius, thus enclosing the entire right half plane, as shown in Fig. 12.5a. (Small detours around any poles or zeros are used to satisfy the requirement on the contour.) Also let

$$F(s) = \frac{1}{K} + T(s) = re^{j\theta}$$

Then

$$\log F = \log r + j\theta$$
$$d(\log F) = d(\log r) + j \, d\theta$$

But

$$\frac{F'(s)}{F(s)} = \frac{d(\log F)}{ds}$$

---

corresponds to a point on the right half plane. This means that the right half plane is encircled in the clockwise direction, which is contrary to the convention of complex-variable theory, but standard in engineering, motion being in the direction of increasing frequency along the imaginary axis.

† See E. G. Phillips, "Functions of a Complex Variable with Applications," p. 107, Interscience Publishers, Inc., New York, 1951.

Hence (12.25) can be written

$$\frac{1}{2\pi j} \oint_C d(\log F) = \frac{1}{2\pi j} \oint_C d(\log r) + \frac{1}{2\pi} \oint_C d\theta = Z - P$$

Since C is a closed contour, the first integral on the right-hand side vanishes, and

$$N = \frac{1}{2\pi} \oint_C d\theta = Z - P$$

where N is the number of times the map of the contour C by the transformation $F = (1/K) + T(s)$ goes around the origin of the F plane in the counterclockwise direction as C is traversed in the counterclockwise direction. On making the transformation

$$w = T(s) = F(s) - \frac{1}{K}$$

which shifts the origin to $-1/K$ in the T plane, we obtain the result that the number of zeros of $F(s) = T(s) + 1/K$ in the right half plane is given by

$$Z = N + P \qquad (12.26)$$

where N is the number of times the point $-1/K$ is encircled in the counterclockwise direction as C is traversed in the counterclockwise direction, and P is the number of poles of $T(s)$ in the right half s plane. If $T(s)$ has no poles in the right half plane, the criterion for stability is that the origin must not be encircled in the counterclockwise direction as C is traversed in the same direction. In order for the system to be stable if $T(s)$ has P poles in the right half s plane, however, it is necessary that the point $-1/K$ be encircled $N = P$ times in the clockwise direction ($-P$ times in the counterclockwise direction).

The Nyquist diagram can be used to obtain a qualitative indication of the sensitivity of the system stability to changes in parameters. If instability is evidenced by the Nyquist diagram covering or encircling the point $-1/K$, it is reasonable to expect that the greater the distance of the plot from the point $-1/K$, the less the likelihood of the system becoming unstable as the result of changes in the system parameters.

Root-locus method

In 1950 Evans[†] introduced an alternative graphical method for locating the zeros of $1 + KT(s)$, that is, the roots of $1 + KT(s) = 0$. This

† W. R. Evans, Control System Synthesis by Root Locus Method, *Trans. AIEE*, vol. 69, pp. 66–69, 1950.

method is useful principally when the locations of the zeros and poles of $T(s)$ are already known.   The root locus (or more properly, root loci) are curves in the s plane, with K as the parametric variable, for which $1 + KT(s) = 0$, that is, curves in the s plane for which

$$\frac{N(s)}{D(s)} = T(s) = -\frac{1}{K} \tag{12.27}$$

In effect, these loci are maps of the real axis of the complex K plane onto the s plane by the transformation

$$s = T^{-1}\left(-\frac{1}{K}\right) \tag{12.28}$$

where T^{-1} here denotes the mapping inverse to T.   Clearly, these loci are continuous with the parameter K and symmetrical about the real axis.

The number of loci is equal to the degree of the denominator of $T(s)$ or of the numerator, whichever is greater, as this is the degree of the polynomial $D(s) + KN(s)$.

When the zeros and poles of $T(s)$ are known, $T(s)$ may be written

$$T(s) = A \frac{\prod_{j} (s - z_j)}{\prod_{i} (s - p_i)} \tag{12.29}$$

where z_j and p_i are the zeros and poles, respectively, of $T(s)$, and A is a real constant.   With no loss of generality we may assume that the constant A equals unity by absorbing it in the adjustable parameter K. As $K \to 0$ in (12.27), $s \to p_i$, and as $K \to \infty$ in (12.27), $s \to z_j$.   *Hence the root loci move continuously from the poles of $T(s)$ to the zeros of $T(s)$ as K increases from zero to infinity.*

We denote the factors of (12.29) as follows:

$$\rho_j e^{j\theta_i} = s - z_j$$
$$\delta_i e^{j\phi_i} = s - p_i$$

Then, in order to satisfy (12.27), it is necessary that

$$\frac{\prod_{i} \delta_i}{\prod_{j} \rho_j} = K \tag{12.30}$$

and

$$\sum_{j} \phi_j - \sum_{i} \theta_i = (2n + 1)\pi \qquad n = 0, \pm 1, \pm 2, \ldots, \pm(k - 1) \qquad (12.31)$$

where k is the number of loci.

Example 12.9   Calculate the root loci for

$$T(s) = \frac{1}{s(s + 2)^2}$$

We observe that the poles of $T(s)$ occur at $s = 0$ and (doubly) at $s = -2$ and that the (triple) zero of $T(s)$ occurs at $s = \infty$.   Hence the loci move continuously from the points $s = -2$ and $s = 0$ to $s = \infty$.

For large values of s corresponding to large values of K, $T(s)$ behaves as $1/s^3$.   Hence s^3 must approach a large negative number and s must approach one of the cube roots of $-K$, namely, $K^{\frac{1}{3}}e^{-j\pi}$, $K^{\frac{1}{3}}e^{j\pi/3}$, $K^{\frac{1}{3}}e^{-j\pi/3}$.   Thus we infer that the root loci move as shown in Fig. 12.8a.   The roots are first real, and two become complex.   There must be a point at which there are two equal real roots.   Let these be denoted by $-\alpha$, and the remaining root by $-\beta$.   Then we must have

$$(s + \alpha)^2(s + \beta) = s^3 + 4s^2 + 4s + K$$

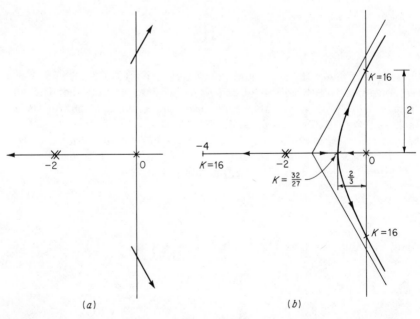

(a)   (b)

FIG. 12.8   Root loci for $T(s) = 1/[s(s + 2)^2]$.   (a) Initial sketch; (b) final loci.

Solving for α, β, and K, we find

$$\alpha = 2 \qquad \beta = 0 \qquad K = 0$$

and

$$\alpha = \tfrac{2}{3} \qquad \beta = \tfrac{8}{3} \qquad K = \tfrac{32}{27}$$

The second solution gives two additional points on the root loci. For larger values of K, the two equal roots move off the real axis. They cross the imaginary axis at $s = \pm j\omega$, and we must have

$$(s^2 + \omega^2)(s + \gamma) = s^3 + 4s^2 + 4s + K$$

from which we calculate $\gamma = 4$, $\omega = 2$, and $K = 16$. This information allows us to sketch the root locus shown in Fig. 12.8b. For negative K, a different set of loci would have to be constructed.

Note that the roots lie in the left half plane for $0 < K < 16$, as previously determined.

The problem of plotting a set of root loci is generally not as simple as Example 12.9 may have made it appear. A number of rules which simplify the construction of such loci have been established.† At the crucial step, i.e., the determination of the points at which the loci cross the imaginary axis, the rules require the use of a Routh-Hurwitz algorithm. It is also possible to plot the root loci by graphical construction with the aid of (12.30) and (12.31).

The root loci also give qualitative information about the nature of the transient response. For example, values of K which result in closed-loop poles (roots of $T(s) + (1/K) = 0$) close to the imaginary axis will cause a transient response containing lightly damped oscillatory components with frequencies approximately equal to the imaginary part of the roots. On the other hand, if K is such that the roots are on the real axis, the transient response will be overdamped (nonoscillatory).

DISCRETE-TIME SYSTEMS

The Nyquist criterion and the root-locus method are directly applicable to discrete-time systems in which the transfer function to be investigated for stability is of the form

$$H(z) = \frac{F(z)}{1 + KT(z)} \tag{12.32}$$

The principal difference is that the unit circle in the z plane plays the role of the imaginary axis in the s plane. Consequently, in the Nyquist method, the *unit circle* of the z plane is mapped by the transformation

† See Truxal, *op. cit.*

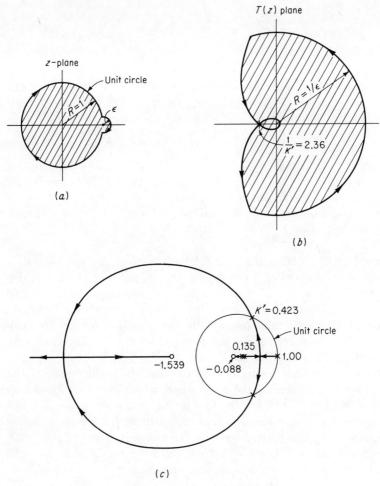

FIG. 12.9   Nyquist diagram and root loci for

$$T(z) = \frac{(z + 1.539)(z + 0.088)}{(z - 1)(z - 0.135)^2}$$

(a) Contour for Nyquist diagram; (b) Nyquist diagram; (c) root loci.

$w = T(z)$ into the w plane.   If the map of the exterior of the unit circle covers the points $-1/K$, then $1 + KT(z)$ has a zero outside the unit circle when $T(z)$ has no poles outside the unit circle.   If $T(z)$ has poles outside the unit circle, (12.26) is employed, with P the number of poles outside the unit circle.   The rule for determining the map of the exterior of the unit circle of the z plane is identical with the rule for determining the map of the right half s plane.

With the root-locus method, the loci must be inside the unit circle in the z plane in order for the system to be stable.

Example 12.10 In the sampled-data system of Example 12.6 we found that

$$T(z) = F(z) = \frac{(z + 1.539)(z + 0.088)}{(z - 1)(z - 0.135)^2}$$

It is readily established that the Nyquist diagram and root loci have the appearance of Fig. 12.9.

PROBLEMS

12.1 Determine by means of a Routh-Hurwitz algorithm which of the following are Hurwitz polynomials:

(a) $s^6 + s^5 + s^4 + s^3 + s^2 + s + 1$.
(b) $s^6 + 2s^5 + 3s^4 + 4s^3 + 5s^2 + 6s + 7$.
(c) $s^4 + 7s^3 + 17s^2 + 17s + 6$.
(d) $s^5 + s^4 + 2s^3 + 2s^2 + 1$.
(e) $s^5 + 5s^4 + 20s^3 + 60s^2 + 120s + 120$.

12.2 Determine the range of K for which the systems of Fig. P 12.2 are stable by using the Hurwitz algorithm.

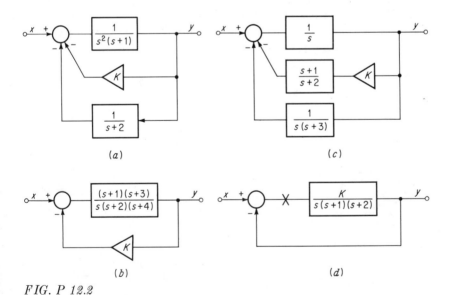

(a)

(c)

(b)

(d)

FIG. P 12.2

12.3   A sampler with the characteristics of Fig. 8.6b with $T = 1$ sec is inserted at point X in Fig. P 12.2d.   Determine the new range of K for which the system is stable.

12.4   The transfer function of the system of Fig. P 12.4 is given by

$$H(s) = \frac{Y(s)}{X(s)} = \frac{K}{K + e^s}$$

(a) Calculate the exact range of K for which the system is stable.

(b) Let the nth-order approximation to e^s be given by

$$A_n(s) = 1 + s + \cdots + \frac{s^n}{n!}$$

Calculate the approximate range of stability by the Hurwitz algorithm, using increasingly better approximations of A_n for e^s, and comment on the result.

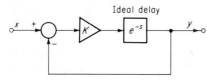

FIG. P 12.4

12.5   Determine the range of K for stability for the systems of Fig. P 12.2 by using the Nyquist diagram.

12.6   Determine the range of K for stability of the systems of Fig. P 12.2 by using the root-locus method.

CHAPTER THIRTEEN

DISTRIBUTED SYSTEMS

13.1 INTRODUCTION

In the foregoing chapters attention was confined to systems governed by *ordinary* differential equations. For linear systems of that type a fairly comprehensive theory was developed; frequency-domain and time-domain behavior were related to the differential equations for the systems. The problems of calculating the response to a specified input or of the determination of the stability of such systems were shown to be algebraic problems, with well-defined (although often tedious) techniques for their solution.

The principal feature which made the techniques of the earlier chapters applicable is the absence of any dynamic dependence of those systems on their spatial configuration. A signal appearing at the output of a component is assumed to be transmitted without delay or distortion to the next component in the system; the distances between the components is not a relevant consideration.

There are many systems, however, in which the spatial configuration is an important factor in their dynamic behavior. Electrical examples include systems containing waveguides, transmission lines, or others in which the "propagation time" is not negligible. Similarly, in thermal and hydraulic systems, in which the time it takes for energy to move through the system is not insignificant, the spatial configuration must be taken into account. Still other examples occur in deflecting beams, vibrating strings, and in chemical processes containing such devices as reactors and heat exchangers.

The systems in which spatial configuration is important are often called distributed-parameter systems, or simply *distributed systems*, and their dynamics, unlike that of the systems treated in the earlier chapters, are mathematically represented by *partial differential equations*.

In contrast to the comprehensive theory which exists for systems governed by ordinary differential equations, the theory of the dynamics of distributed systems is only rudimentary. For this reason our attention will be confined to systems in which only one space coordinate occurs, i.e., to those in which the partial differential equations have only two independent variables, time and distance.

13.2 ELECTRICAL TRANSMISSION LINE

An electrical transmission line is one of the most thoroughly studied distributed systems, and many of its properties are familiar to electrical engineers; it can thus serve as an example to motivate the more general theory to be developed later. Moreover, many other physical systems are exactly analogous to an electrical transmission line (i.e., their differential equations are of identical form) so that an understanding of the behavior of transmission lines can be translated directly to many other problems.

A section of transmission line† of length Δx is shown in Fig. 13.1. The so-called line parameters, or constants, are as follows:

	Symbol	Unit
Series resistance	r	*ohms/meter*
Series inductance	l	*henrys/meter*
Shunt (leakage) conductance	g	*mhos/meter*
Shunt capacitance	c	*farads/meter*

† It is assumed that the operation is in the "transverse electromagnetic mode," i.e., that the electric and magnetic fields are normal to the x axis.

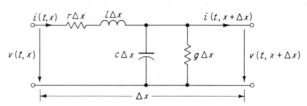

FIG. 13.1   Transmission-line section.

The voltage between the two wires and the current at time t and point x are denoted by $v(t, x)$ and $i(t, x)$, respectively.

The change in voltage between the ends of the section is obtained by Kirchhoff's voltage law and is

$$v(t, x + \Delta x) - v(t, x) = - \left[l \frac{\partial i(t, x)}{\partial t} + ri(t, x) \right] \Delta x$$

On dividing by Δx and passing to the limit as $\Delta x \to 0$, we obtain the partial differential equation

$$\frac{\partial v(t, x)}{\partial x} = -l \frac{\partial i(t, x)}{\partial t} - ri(t, x) \tag{13.1}$$

Likewise, Kirchhoff's current law gives the change of current as

$$i(t, x + \Delta x) - i(t, x) = - \left[c \frac{\partial v(t, x + \Delta x)}{\partial t} + gv(t, x + \Delta x) \right] \Delta x$$

Hence, dividing by Δx and taking the limit, we obtain the partial differential equation

$$\frac{\partial i(t, x)}{\partial x} = -c \frac{\partial v(t, x)}{\partial t} - gv(t, x) \tag{13.2}$$

The partial differential equations can be arranged conveniently in matrix form:

$$\frac{\partial \mathbf{q}}{\partial x} = \mathbf{F}\mathbf{q} + \mathbf{G} \frac{\partial \mathbf{q}}{\partial t} \tag{13.3}$$

where

$$\mathbf{q} = \begin{bmatrix} v \\ i \end{bmatrix} \qquad \mathbf{F} = \begin{bmatrix} 0 & -r \\ -g & 0 \end{bmatrix} \qquad \mathbf{G} = \begin{bmatrix} 0 & -l \\ -c & 0 \end{bmatrix}$$

On the assumption that $v = q_1$ and $i = q_2$ possess Laplace transforms with respect to time denoted by

$$Q_j(s, x) = \mathcal{L}[q_j(t, x)] = \int_0^\infty q_j(t, x)e^{-st}\, dt \qquad j = 1, 2$$

it is evident that their space derivatives $\partial q_j/\partial x$ possess Laplace transforms given by

$$\int_0^\infty \frac{\partial q_j(t,\,x)}{\partial x}\, e^{-st}\, dt = \frac{\partial}{\partial x} \int_0^\infty q_j(t,\,x) e^{-st}\, dt = \frac{\partial Q_j(s,\,x)}{\partial x}$$

Thus, on taking the Laplace transform of (13.3), we obtain

$$\frac{\partial \mathbf{Q}(s,\,x)}{\partial x} = (\mathbf{F} + \mathbf{G}s)\mathbf{Q}(s,\,x) - \mathbf{G}\mathbf{q}(0,\,x) \tag{13.4}$$

where $\mathbf{q}(0,\,x)$ is the initial voltage and current distribution on the line.

Since the derivative with respect to s does not appear in (13.4), we may write the latter as an ordinary differential equation

$$\frac{d\mathbf{Q}}{dx} = (\mathbf{F} + \mathbf{G}s)\mathbf{Q} - \mathbf{G}\mathbf{q}(0,\,x) \tag{13.5}$$

This is a first-order (vector) ordinary differential equation, which in accordance with the theory of Chap. 4 has the complete solution

$$\mathbf{Q}(s,\,x_2) = e^{(\mathbf{F}+\mathbf{G}s)(x_2-x_1)}\, \mathbf{Q}(s,\,x_1) - \mathbf{G} \int_{x_1}^{x_2} e^{(\mathbf{F}+\mathbf{G}s)(x_2-x)}\, \mathbf{q}(0,\,x)\, dx \tag{13.6}$$

Equation (13.6) expresses the relation between the Laplace transforms of the voltage and current at a point x_2 in terms of the Laplace transforms of these quantities at any other point x_1. Most frequently, in considering a transmission line of finite length L, we take $x_1 = 0$, in which case

$$\mathbf{Q}(s,\,x) = e^{(\mathbf{F}+\mathbf{G}s)x}\mathbf{Q}(s,\,0) - \mathbf{G} \int_0^x e^{(\mathbf{F}+\mathbf{G}s)(x-\xi)}\mathbf{q}(0,\,\xi)\, d\xi \tag{13.7}$$

Two relations between $V(s,\,x)$, $I(s,\,x)$, $V(s,\,0)$, $I(s,\,0)$ are expressed by (13.7). In order to obtain a complete solution of a transmission-line problem it is necessary that two additional relations between these quantities be specified. These relations are known as the *termination relations*, which we shall consider shortly.

The expression for the fundamental matrix $e^{(\mathbf{F}+\mathbf{G}s)x}$ can be obtained by evaluating the series

$$e^{(\mathbf{F}+\mathbf{G}s)x} = \mathbf{I} + (\mathbf{F} + \mathbf{G}s)x + (\mathbf{F} + \mathbf{G}s)^2 \frac{x^2}{2!} + \cdots$$

(Prob. 13.1), but it is here more convenient to solve the two equations represented by (13.5) directly. We seek the solution to the *homogeneous* form of (13.5), namely,

$$\begin{aligned}
\frac{dV}{dx} &= -(ls + r)I \\
\frac{dI}{dx} &= -(cs + g)V
\end{aligned} \tag{13.8}$$

where $I \equiv I(s, x)$ and $V \equiv V(s, x)$. Differentiating the second equation with respect to x gives

$$\frac{d^2I}{dx^2} = -(cs + g)\frac{dV}{dx} = (ls + r)(cs + g)I$$

or

$$\frac{d^2I}{dx^2} - (ls + r)(cs + g)I = 0$$

Likewise   (13.9)

$$\frac{d^2V}{dx^2} - (ls + r)(cs + g)V = 0$$

The voltage and current thus satisfy differential equations of identical form, and their solutions also have the same form. Let us define $\Gamma = \sqrt{(ls + r)(cs + g)}$ as that root of $\Gamma^2 - (ls + r)(cs + g) = 0$ with a positive real part for $\mathrm{Re}\ s > 0$. It is readily verified that

$$V(s, x) = A \cosh \Gamma x + B \sinh \Gamma x$$
$$I(s, x) = C \sinh \Gamma x + D \cosh \Gamma x \tag{13.10}$$

where A, B, C, and D are to be obtained from the conditions $V(s, 0)$ and $I(s, 0)$ at the "input" end of the line. Setting $x = 0$ in (13.10) gives

$$A = V(s, 0)$$
$$D = I(s, 0)$$

Differentiating (13.10) with respect to x and employing (13.8), we find

$$-(ls + r)I(s, x) = A\Gamma \sinh \Gamma x + B\Gamma \cosh \Gamma x$$
$$-(cs + g)V(s, x) = C\Gamma \cosh \Gamma x + D\Gamma \sinh \Gamma x$$

Thus by setting $x = 0$ we obtain

$$B = -\frac{ls + r}{\Gamma} I(s, 0) = -\sqrt{\frac{ls + r}{cs + g}}\, I(s, 0)$$

$$C = -\frac{cs + g}{\Gamma} V(s, 0) = -\sqrt{\frac{cs + g}{ls + r}}\, V(s, 0)$$

The quantity

$$Z_0(s) = \sqrt{\frac{ls + r}{cs + g}}$$

which has the dimension of impedance, is known as the *characteristic impedance* of the line; Γ is known as the *propagation constant.*†

---

† There is no ambiguity in the definition of Z_0 once Γ is defined as above, since $Z_0 = (ls + r)/\Gamma = \Gamma/(cs + g)$. Note also that $\mathrm{Re}\ Z_0(s) > 0$ for $\mathrm{Re}\ s > 0$.

Having evaluated A, B, C, and D, we can now proceed to write (13.10) as

$$
\begin{aligned}
V(s, x) &= V(s, 0) \cosh \Gamma x - Z_0(s) I(s, 0) \sinh \Gamma x \\
I(s, x) &= -Z_0^{-1} V(s, 0) \sinh \Gamma x + I(s, 0) \cosh \Gamma x
\end{aligned}
\tag{13.11}
$$

Hence, by comparing (13.11) with (13.7), we have found that

$$
e^{(\mathbf{F} + \mathbf{G}s)x} = \begin{bmatrix} \cosh \Gamma x & -Z_0 \sinh \Gamma x \\ -Z_0^{-1} \sinh \Gamma x & \cosh \Gamma x \end{bmatrix}
\tag{13.12}
$$

where

$$
\Gamma = \sqrt{(ls + r)(cs + g)}
$$

$$
Z_0 = \sqrt{\frac{ls + r}{cs + g}}
$$

It is noted that although Γ and Z_0 both have branch points in the complex-frequency plane, they occur in (13.12) in such a way that each element of $e^{(\mathbf{F} + \mathbf{G}s)x}$ is a single-valued function of s without branch points.

SEMI-INFINITE LINES

The relations (13.11) are valid for a transmission line of any finite length. This relation is not valid, however, when the line is infinitely long if we insist that $v(t, \infty)$ and $i(t, \infty)$ continue to be physical quantities which possess Laplace transforms $V(s, \infty)$ and $I(s, \infty)$, respectively. The difficulty can be avoided by writing (13.10) in the alternative form

$$
\begin{aligned}
V(s, x) &= A' e^{\Gamma x} + B' e^{-\Gamma x} \\
I(x, s) &= C' e^{\Gamma x} + D' e^{-\Gamma x}
\end{aligned}
$$

In the above expression $\pm \Gamma$ denotes the two roots of the equation $\Gamma^2 - (ls + r)(cs + g) = 0$. Recall that $+\Gamma$ is the root with positive real part for $\operatorname{Re} s > 0$. Then $e^{\Gamma x}$ becomes infinite for any s in the right half plane as $x \to \infty$. If $V(s, x)$ and $I(s, x)$ are to be Laplace transforms of some functions, however, they must exist everywhere to the right of some line in the s plane. Therefore $e^{\Gamma x}$ cannot appear in the solution, and A' and C' must be zero. Consequently we are left with

$$
\begin{aligned}
V(s, x) &= B' e^{-\Gamma x} \\
I(s, x) &= D' e^{-\Gamma x}
\end{aligned}
$$

Now substitution of $x = 0$ gives $B' = V(s, 0)$ and $D' = I(s, 0)$ so that

$$
\begin{aligned}
V(s, x) &= V(s, 0) e^{-\Gamma x} \\
I(s, x) &= I(s, 0) e^{-\Gamma x}
\end{aligned}
\tag{13.13}
$$

and consequently the ratio $V(s, x)/I(s, x)$ is independent of position along the line.   This ratio is a property of the transmission line, and is found by noting that

$$\frac{dV}{dx} = -(ls + r)I = -B'\Gamma e^{-\Gamma x}$$

$$\frac{dI}{dx} = -(cs + g)V = -D'\Gamma e^{-\Gamma x}$$

or

$$\frac{ls + r}{cs + g} \frac{I(s, x)}{V(s, x)} = \frac{B'}{D'} = \frac{V(s, x)}{I(s, x)}$$

from which

$$\frac{V(s, x)}{I(s, x)} = \sqrt{\frac{ls + r}{cs + g}} \tag{13.14}$$

It is readily established that the square root must be chosen so that the real part of the ratio in (13.14) is positive for Re $s > 0$ (Prob. 13.2).   We thus conclude that *the ratio of the Laplace transform of the voltage to that of the current along a semi-infinite line is equal to the characteristic impedance $Z_0(s)$.*

Note that the transfer functions from quantities at the end $x = 0$ to the same quantities at a different x are not in general single-valued functions of s.

PROPAGATION AND DIFFUSION

We consider two special cases of interest, namely, (1) $r = g = 0$ and (2) $l = g = 0$.

In the first case the transformed differential equation for the voltage on the transmission line has the form

$$\frac{d^2V}{dx^2} - lcs^2V = 0$$

and this results from the partial differential equation

$$\frac{\partial^2 v}{\partial x^2} - lc\frac{\partial^2 v}{\partial t^2} = 0 \tag{13.15}$$

This is the one-dimensional form of the *wave equation* which governs many physical phenomena, including propagation on transmission lines at high frequencies, the vibrations of a string, longitudinal vibrations of a thin rod, and many other *propagation* phenomena.   The constants Z_0 and Γ

have the following forms in this case:

$$Z_0 = \sqrt{\frac{l}{c}} = R_0 \qquad \text{a positive real number}$$

$$\Gamma = s\sqrt{lc}$$

As a consequence of the above expression for Γ and (13.13), it is seen that, in a semi-infinite line, the transform of the voltage at any point in the line is related to the input voltage by

$$V(s, x) = V(s, 0)e^{-s\sqrt{lc}x}$$

(and similarly for the transform of the current).   Thus in the time domain

$$v(t, x) = v(t - \sqrt{lc}\,x, 0)$$

This means that the voltage (and current) at any point on the line have the same shape as the voltage at $x = 0$, but are delayed by the time

$$\tau_d = \sqrt{lc}\,x$$

Thus the voltage and current propagate without distortion along the line with a propagation velocity

$$v = \frac{1}{\sqrt{lc}}$$

The case in which l instead of r is zero gives rise to an entirely different phenomenon, that of *diffusion*. The transformed differential equation in this case is [see (13.9)]

$$\frac{d^2V}{dx^2} - rcsV = 0$$

which results from the partial differential equation

$$\frac{\partial^2 v}{\partial x^2} - rc\frac{\partial v}{\partial t} = 0 \tag{13.16}$$

This equation is the one-dimensional *diffusion equation* which governs many physical phenomena, one of the most familiar being the one-dimensional conduction of heat in a metallic rod.   The diffusion equation differs from the wave equation (13.15) in that only the first space derivative appears in the former.   In the diffusion equation the constants Z_0 and Γ have the form

$$Z_0 = \sqrt{\frac{r}{cs}}$$

$$\Gamma = \sqrt{rcs}$$

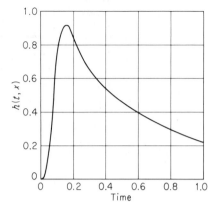

FIG. 13.2 Impulse response of diffusive line ($rcx^2 = 1$).

The use of these relations in (13.13) results in the following relation between $V(s, x)$ and $V(s, 0)$:

$$\frac{V(s, x)}{V(s, 0)} = H(s, x) = e^{-\sqrt{rcs}\,x} \tag{13.17}$$

Since s appears under the radical, the impulse response of the "diffusive" line is not simply an impulse delayed by a time proportional to the distance from the origin, but is given by the inverse Laplace transform of (13.17).

By use of contour integration (as explained in Chap. 6) the response at a point x to an impulse applied at $t = 0$ and $x = 0$ is given by

$$h(t, x) = \mathcal{L}^{-1}[e^{-\sqrt{rcs}\,x}] = \sqrt{\frac{rc}{4\pi t^3}}\, x e^{-rcx^2/4t}$$

This expression has the shape shown in Fig. 13.2.   The peak of the response occurs at $t = rcx^2/6$ and has the amplitude

$$h_{\max} = \frac{1}{rcx^2} \sqrt{\frac{216}{4\pi}}\, e^{-\frac{3}{2}} = \frac{0.920}{rcx^2}$$

It should be noted that the response at any x begins to appear at $t = 0$ and does not return to zero at any finite time.   The transmitted impulse is thus distorted and widened more and more as x increases.

TERMINATION

The semi-infinite lines discussed above are abstractions from physical reality.   In any real case the line will be of finite length and terminated by some combination of lumped elements and sources.   By the use of

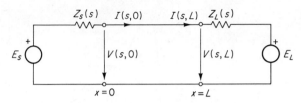

FIG. 13.3   *Representation of terminated line.*

Thévenin's theorem,[†] the relation imposed at the end $x = L$ can be expressed by

$$V(s, L) = Z_L(s)I(s, L) + E_L(s) \qquad (13.18)$$

where $Z_L(s)$ is the impedance of the "load" at $x = L$, and $E_L(s)$ is the Laplace transform of the open-circuit voltage. Similarly, the voltage and current at the end $x = 0$ can be related by

$$V(s, 0) = -Z_S(s)I(s, 0) + E_S(s) \qquad (13.19)$$

where the subscript S refers to quantities at the source end $x = 0$. The terminating relations (13.18) and (13.19), together with (13.11) with x equal to L, completely specify the behavior of the transmission line at both ends, and (13.11) with $0 < x < L$ specifies the behavior at intermediate points.   Figure 13.3 is a schematic representation of a terminated line.   The following examples illustrate how the calculations are performed.

Example 13.1   Short-circuited line   The termination imposed by a short circuit at $x = L$ is expressed by

$$V(s, L) = 0$$

Substitution of this relation into (13.11) gives

$$V(s, 0) \cosh \Gamma L = Z_0(s)I(s, 0) \sinh \Gamma L$$

or

$$V(s, 0) = Z_0(s)I(s, 0) \tanh \Gamma L$$

If $V(s, 0)$ is expressed as in (13.19),

$$-Z_S(s)I(s, 0) + E_S(s) = Z_0(s)I(s, 0) \tanh \Gamma L$$

or

$$I(s, 0) = \frac{E_S(s)}{Z_S(s) + Z_0(s) \tanh \Gamma L}$$

and $\hspace{8cm}$ (13.20)

$$V(s, 0) = \frac{E_S(s)Z_0(s) \tanh \Gamma L}{Z_S(s) + Z_0(s) \tanh \Gamma L}$$

[†] B. Friedland, O. Wing, and R. Ash, "Principles of Linear Networks," chap. 3, p. 52, McGraw-Hill Book Company, New York, 1961.

Substitution of these relations into (13.11) then gives the Laplace transforms of the voltage and current at any other point on the line.

We now consider the calculation of the voltage and current in a few special cases in which the source impedance $Z_S(s)$ is zero. We obtain

$$V(s, 0) = E_S(s)$$
$$I(s, 0) = E_S(s)/[Z_0(s) \tanh \Gamma L]$$

from which

$$V(s, x) = \left[\cosh \Gamma x - \frac{Z_0(s) \sinh \Gamma x}{Z_0(s) \tanh \Gamma L} \right] E_S(s)$$

$$= \frac{\cosh \Gamma x \sinh \Gamma L - \sinh \Gamma x \cosh \Gamma L}{\sinh \Gamma L} E_S(s)$$

$$= \frac{\sinh \Gamma (L - x)}{\sinh \Gamma L} E_S(s)$$

The transfer function relating the voltage at any distance x from the origin to the source voltage is

$$\frac{V(s, x)}{E_S(s)} = H(s, x) = \frac{\sinh \Gamma (L - x)}{\sinh \Gamma L}$$

If the line is governed by the wave equation ($r = g = 0$), the transfer function becomes

$$H(s, x) = \frac{\sinh [\sqrt{lc}\ (L - x)s]}{\sinh (\sqrt{lc}\ Ls)}$$

It is of interest to calculate the corresponding impulse response. We may write

$$H(s, x) = \frac{e^{\sqrt{lc}(L-x)s} - e^{-\sqrt{lc}(L-x)s}}{e^{\sqrt{lc}Ls} - e^{-\sqrt{lc}Ls}}$$

$$= [e^{-\sqrt{lc}xs} - e^{-\sqrt{lc}(2L-x)s}][1 + e^{-2\sqrt{lc}Ls} + e^{-4\sqrt{lc}Ls} + \cdots]$$

$$= e^{-\sqrt{lc}xs} - e^{-\sqrt{lc}(2L-x)s} + e^{-\sqrt{lc}(2L+x)s} - e^{-\sqrt{lc}(4L-x)s} + \cdots$$

Thus the impulse response is given by

$$h(t, x) = \delta\left(t - \frac{x}{v}\right) - \delta\left(t - \frac{2L - x}{v}\right) + \delta\left(t - \frac{2L + x}{v}\right) - \cdots$$

where $v = 1/\sqrt{lc}$. The impulse response has the appearance of Fig. 13.4. The result may be interpreted as follows. The impulse propagates down the line with a *characteristic velocity* v and thus reaches the point x at the time $t = x/v$; it continues to the end $x = L$, which is reached at $t = L/v$. Since the voltage must be zero at $x = L$, another impulse of opposite sign starts out from this end (or the original impulse

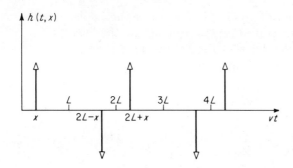

FIG. 13.4   Impulse response of short-circuited transmission line.

is reflected with change of sign).   The new, or reflected, impulse propagates in the opposite direction at the same velocity and reaches the point x at the time $t = (2L - x)/v$, the total distance traversed up to now being $2L - x$.   The impulse continues to the end $x = 0$.   Since the line is now short-circuited, a reflection takes place similar to that at $X = L$. The new pulse now propagates to the right, and the phenomenon repeats indefinitely.

Example 13.2   Short-circuited diffusive line   If the transmission line is diffusive, the transfer function is expressed by

$$\frac{V(s, x)}{E_s(s)} = H(s, x) = \frac{\sinh \sqrt{rcs}\,(L - x)}{\sinh \sqrt{rcs}\,L} \tag{13.21}$$

It appears at first that $H(s, x)$ has a branch point at the origin as a result of the appearance of the factor $\sqrt{s}$.   This is not the case, however; $H(s, x)$ is a meromorphic function, having poles as its only singularities in the finite s plane.   To demonstrate this we need only expand the numerator and denominator in power series:

$$H(s, x) = \frac{(k_1 s)^{\frac{1}{2}} + \dfrac{(k_1 s)^{\frac{3}{2}}}{3!} + \dfrac{(k_1 s)^{\frac{5}{2}}}{5!} + \cdots}{(k_2 s)^{\frac{1}{2}} + \dfrac{(k_2 s)^{\frac{3}{2}}}{3!} + \dfrac{(k_2 s)^{\frac{5}{2}}}{5!} + \cdots}$$

$$= \left(\frac{k_1}{k_2}\right)^{\frac{1}{2}} \left(\frac{1 + \dfrac{k_1 s}{3!} + \dfrac{k_1^2 s^2}{5!} + \cdots}{1 + \dfrac{k_2 s}{3!} + \dfrac{k_2^2 s^2}{5!} + \cdots} \right) \tag{13.22}$$

where $k_1 = rc(L - x)^2$ and $k_2 = rcL^2$.   Since both numerator and denominator are analytic in the finite s plane, $H(s, x)$ is meromorphic.   The poles of $H(s, x)$ are located at the zeros of $\sinh \sqrt{rcs}\,L$, except that there

is no zero at the origin since numerator and denominator both approach zero at equal rates. [This is also evident from (13.22).] These zeros occur when

$$e^{\sqrt{rcsL}} - e^{-\sqrt{rcsL}} = 0$$

or when

$$e^{2\sqrt{rcsL}} = 1 = e^{j2n\pi}$$

$(n = \pm 1, \pm 2, \ldots)$ or when $\sqrt{rcs} = jn\pi/L$, that is, when

$$s = -\frac{n^2\pi^2}{rcL^2}$$

The impulse response can thus be calculated using the expansion formula (6.55), which in this case is

$$H(s, x) = H(0, x) + \sum_{n=1}^{\infty} A_n \left(\frac{1}{s + \dfrac{n^2\pi^2}{rcL^2}} - \frac{1}{\dfrac{n^2\pi^2}{rcL^2}} \right)$$

where

$$A_n = \text{residue of } H(s, x) \text{ at } s = \frac{-n^2\pi^2}{rcL^2}$$

$$= \frac{\sinh \sqrt{rcs}\,(L - x)}{(d/ds) \sinh \sqrt{rcs}\, L} \bigg|_{s = \frac{-n^2\pi^2}{rcL^2}}$$

$$= \frac{2n\pi}{rcL^2} \sin \frac{n\pi x}{L}$$

Thus

$$H(s, x) = \frac{L - x}{L} + \sum_{n=1}^{\infty} \frac{2n\pi}{rcL^2} \sin \frac{n\pi x}{L} \left(\frac{1}{s + \dfrac{n^2\pi^2}{rcL^2}} - \frac{1}{\dfrac{n^2\pi^2}{rcL^2}} \right)$$

which can be written

$$H(s, x) = \frac{L - x}{L} - \sum_{n=1}^{\infty} \frac{2}{n\pi} \sin \frac{n\pi x}{L} + \sum_{n=1}^{\infty} \frac{2n\pi}{rcL^2} \frac{1}{s + \dfrac{n^2\pi^2}{rcL^2}} \sin \frac{n\pi x}{L}$$

The second term on the right is the Fourier series for $-(L - x)/L$ and cancels the first term, thus leaving only the third term. Hence the impulse response is

$$h(t, x) = \sum_{n=1}^{\infty} \frac{2n\pi}{rcL^2} \sin \frac{n\pi x}{L} \exp \left(-\frac{n^2\pi^2 t}{rcL^2} \right) \qquad (13.23)$$

The unit-step response $a(t, x)$ is given by the inverse Laplace transform of

$$A(s, x) = \frac{H(s, x)}{s} = \frac{1}{s}\left(\frac{L - x}{L} - \sum_{n=1}^{\infty} \frac{2}{n\pi} \frac{s}{s + \frac{n^2\pi^2}{rcL^2}} \sin \frac{n\pi x}{L}\right)$$

or   or

$$a(t, x) = \frac{L - x}{L} - \sum_{n=1}^{\infty} \frac{2}{n\pi} \sin \frac{n\pi x}{L} \exp\left(-\frac{n^2\pi^2}{rcL^2} t\right)$$

Upon differentiation of $a(t, x)$ with respect to t we obtain the impulse response of (13.23).

13.3   ANALOGS OF TRANSMISSION LINE

Numerous physical systems can be characterized by a system of differential equations identical in form with (13.3), which, in general terms, can be written

$$\frac{\partial q_1}{\partial x} = -\alpha \frac{\partial q_2}{\partial t} - \beta q_2$$

$$\frac{\partial q_2}{\partial x} = -\gamma \frac{\partial q_1}{\partial t} - \delta q_1 \tag{13.24}$$

where α, β', γ, and δ are *nonnegative*. This system corresponds to a transmission line with†

$$q_1 \sim v \qquad q_2 \sim i \tag{13.25}$$

and

$$\alpha \sim l \qquad \beta \sim r \qquad \gamma \sim c \qquad \delta \sim g$$

or alternatively,

$$q_1 \sim i \qquad q_2 \sim v \tag{13.26}$$

and

$$\alpha \sim c \qquad \beta \sim g \qquad \gamma \sim l \qquad \delta \sim r$$

The expressions for q_1 and q_2 in the frequency domain can be written

$$\begin{bmatrix} Q_1(s, x) \\ Q_2(s, x) \end{bmatrix} = \begin{bmatrix} \cosh \Gamma x & -Z_0 \sinh \Gamma x \\ -Z_0^{-1} \sinh \Gamma x & \cosh \Gamma x \end{bmatrix} \begin{bmatrix} Q_1(s, 0) \\ Q_2(s, 0) \end{bmatrix}$$

where

$$\Gamma = \sqrt{(\alpha s + \beta)(\gamma s + \delta)}$$

† The sign $\sim$ is used here as an abbreviation for "corresponds to."

and

$$Z_0 = \sqrt{\frac{\alpha s + \beta}{\gamma s + \delta}}$$

The quantity Z_0 may be regarded as an "impedance" by analogy with the electrical transmission line.

The following examples are concrete illustrations of these analogies.

Example 13.3   Thermal conduction in a rod   Let $\theta(t, x)$ be the temperature at a point x in an insulated slender rod at a given time t, and $q(t, x)$ be the heat flux through a section of the rod.   The heat flux is related to the temperature by

$$-\sigma A \frac{\partial \theta}{\partial x} = q$$

where A is the cross-sectional area of the rod, and σ is the thermal conductivity of the metal.   The minus sign indicates that heat flows from the higher to the lower temperature.

Now consider a section of rod of length Δx as shown in Fig. 13.5.   The heat which leaves at the end $x + \Delta x$ must be equal to the heat which enters at the end x less the heat lost in the section, which is proportional to the specific heat, volume, and the rate of temperature rise in the section.   Thus

$$q(t, x + \Delta x) = q(t, x) - C\rho A \, \Delta x \frac{\partial \theta(t, x)}{\partial t} \qquad (13.27)$$

where $C =$ specific heat (heat capacity),
$\quad \rho =$ density,
$\quad A =$ cross-sectional area (that is, $A \, \Delta x =$ volume)
On transposing $q(t, x)$ to the left, dividing by Δx, and passing to the limit as $x \rightarrow 0$, we obtain

$$\frac{\partial q}{\partial x} = -C\rho A \frac{\partial \theta}{\partial t}$$

FIG. 13.5   Thermal conduction.

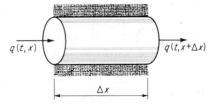

Thus, in the general form of (13.24),

$$\frac{\partial q_1}{\partial x} = -\beta q_2$$

$$\frac{\partial q_2}{\partial x} = -\gamma \frac{\partial q_1}{\partial t} \qquad (13.28)$$

where $q_1 = \theta$
$\qquad q_2 = q$ = heat flux
$\qquad \beta = 1/\sigma A$
$\qquad \gamma = C\rho A$

The thermal impedance is

$$Z_0 = \sqrt{\frac{\beta}{\gamma s}} = \frac{1}{A \sqrt{C\rho\sigma s}}$$

and the "diffusion constant"

$$\Gamma = \sqrt{\beta\gamma s} = \sqrt{\frac{C\rho s}{\sigma}}$$

The two equations relating temperature and heat flux may be used to derive the second-order *diffusion equation*

$$\frac{\partial^2 q}{\partial x^2} - \frac{C\rho}{\sigma}\frac{\partial q}{\partial t} = 0 \qquad (13.29)$$

where q can be either heat flux or temperature.

Typical terminating conditions at one end or another are the following:

1. The end $x = L$ is held at a constant temperature,

$$q_1(t, L) = \text{const}$$

2. The heat flux passing through the cross section at end $x = L$ is constant,

$$q_2(t, L) = \text{const}$$

3. At the end $x = L$, heat is lost due to radiation,†

$$q_2(t, L) = \epsilon k A[q_1{}^4(t, L) - \theta_a{}^4]$$

where ϵ = emissivity
$\qquad k$ = Stefan-Boltzmann constant
$\qquad A$ = surface area
$\qquad \theta_a$ = ambient temperature

---

† See, for example, F. W. Sears, "Principles of Physics," vol. 1, "Mechanics, Heat and Sound," pp. 383–384, Addison-Wesley Publishing Company, Inc., Reading, Mass., 1947.

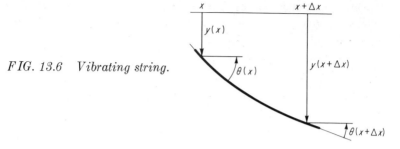

FIG. 13.6   *Vibrating string.*

This relation is nonlinear, but the temperature is measured from absolute zero. Hence, if $q_1(t) \doteq \theta_a$ so that terms of order $(q_1 - \theta_a)^2$ may be neglected and temperatures are measured with respect to θ_a, a reasonable approximation would be

$$q_2(t, L) \doteq 4\epsilon kA\theta_a{}^3\bar{q}_1(t, L)$$

where $\bar{q}_1$ is the difference between the temperature at the end of the rod and the ambient.

If heat were lost along the rod to the surroundings in the absence of insulation, a term would have to be added to (13.28) to account for the loss. If it is again assumed that heat is lost due to radiation with an ambient temperature not far (on an absolute scale) from the temperature along the rod, the heat loss in a length Δx could be approximated by

$$\delta q_1 \, \Delta x = 4\epsilon kp \, \Delta x \, \theta_a{}^3\bar{q}_1(t, x)$$

where p is the perimeter of the cross section. Hence the partial differential equations would be

$$\frac{\partial q_1}{\partial x} = -\beta q_2$$

$$\frac{\partial q_2}{\partial x} = -\gamma \frac{\partial q_1}{\partial t} - \delta q_1$$

Example 13.4   Vibrating string Consider a string under constant tension f; a section of the string is shown in Fig. 13.6. Let $y(x)$ be the vertical (downward) displacement of the string at a point x units from its left end, and let θ be the slope of the string. Clearly,

$$\theta = \frac{\partial y}{\partial x}$$

or, upon differentiating with respect to t and denoting $\partial^2 y/\partial x \partial t$ by $\partial v/\partial x$ (with $v = \partial y/\partial t =$ vertical velocity), we obtain

$$\frac{\partial \theta}{\partial t} = \frac{\partial v}{\partial x}$$

Consider an element of string of length Δx.   The total downward force is $f[\sin\,\theta(x + \Delta x) - \sin\,\theta(x)]$, which must equal the rate of change of momentum of the element; i.e.,

$$f[\sin\,\theta(x + \Delta x) - \sin\,\theta(x)] = \rho\,\Delta x\,\frac{\partial v}{\partial t}$$

where ρ is the mass per unit length of the string.   Assume also that the displacement y is small; then $\sin\,\theta \doteq \theta$, so that

$$\frac{\theta(x + \Delta x) - \theta(x)}{\Delta x} = \frac{\rho}{f}\frac{\partial v}{\partial t}$$

which, on passing to the limit as $\Delta x \to 0$, gives

$$\frac{\partial\theta}{\partial x} = \frac{\rho}{f}\frac{\partial v}{\partial t}$$

Thus identification of v with q_1 and θ with q_2 results in the standard equations

$$\frac{\partial q_1}{\partial x} = \frac{\partial q_2}{\partial t}$$
$$\frac{\partial q_2}{\partial x} = \frac{\rho}{f}\frac{\partial q_1}{\partial t} \qquad (13.30)$$

Hence $\alpha = -1$, $\beta = \delta = 0$, $\gamma = -\rho/f$, and the mechanical "impedance" is given by

$$Z_0 = \sqrt{\frac{f}{\rho}}$$

while the "propagation constant" is given by

$$\Gamma = \sqrt{\frac{\rho}{f}}\,s$$

Note also that the deflection of the string can be represented by the wave equation

$$\frac{\partial^2 q}{\partial x^2} - \frac{\rho}{f}\frac{\partial^2 q}{\partial t^2} = 0$$

where q may be either $q_1 = v$ or $q_2 = \theta$.

In a modern musical string instrument the relevant terminal conditions are

$$v(t, 0) = v(t, L) = 0$$

and vibrations are started by an impulse applied at some intermediate point or by an initial nonzero deflection of the string.

If there were no damping, the string would vibrate indefinitely. To account for the loss of energy due to viscous (air) damping, a force per unit length proportional to the velocity must be added, and thus (13.30) would read

$$\frac{\partial q_1}{\partial x} = \frac{\partial q_2}{\partial t}$$

$$\frac{\partial q_2}{\partial x} = \frac{\rho}{f}\frac{\partial q_1}{\partial t} + \delta q_1$$

where δ is the coefficient of viscous friction.

Example 13.5   Longitudinal vibrations in a bar   Consider a metal bar free to vibrate longitudinally. Let $\sigma(x, t)$ be the stress (force/area). Then a section of length Δx will be accelerated in proportion to the stress differential, namely,

$$[\sigma(x + \Delta x) - \sigma(x)]A = A\rho \Delta x \frac{\partial v}{\partial t}$$

where A = area
ρ = density (mass/volume)
v = velocity of section

Thus

$$\frac{\partial \sigma}{\partial x} = \rho \frac{\partial v}{\partial t}$$

Let Δy denote the elongation of the section Δx. Then, by Hooke's law,

$$\Delta y = \frac{\Delta x\, \sigma}{E}$$

where E is the modulus of elasticity of the bar (stress/strain, with units of force/area), or

$$\frac{\partial y}{\partial x} = \frac{\sigma}{E}$$

Since the velocity at a point x is identical with the rate of elongation, on differentiating the last equation with respect to time, we find

$$\frac{\partial v}{\partial x} = \frac{1}{E}\frac{\partial \sigma}{\partial t}$$

The equations for $-\sigma = q_1$ and $v = q_2$ are in the form of those for a lossless transmission line,

$$\frac{\partial q_1}{\partial x} = -\rho \frac{\partial q_2}{\partial t}$$

$$\frac{\partial q_2}{\partial x} = -\frac{1}{E}\frac{\partial q_1}{\partial t}$$

or in the form of the wave equation

$$\frac{\partial^2 q}{\partial x^2} - \frac{\rho}{E} \frac{\partial^2 q}{\partial t^2} = 0$$

where q can be either velocity (rate of strain) or stress.

13.4 REPRESENTATION OF GENERAL DISTRIBUTED SYSTEMS

A large class of systems may be represented in the general form of a system of linear partial differential equations, of first order in the spatial dimension and of arbitrary order in t. The equations for these systems thus are

$$\frac{\partial q_1}{\partial x} = \left(f_{11}^0 + f_{11}^1 \frac{\partial}{\partial t} + \cdots + f_{11}^r \frac{\partial^r}{\partial t^r} \right) q_1 + \cdots$$
$$+ \left(f_{1n}^0 + f_{1n}^1 \frac{\partial}{\partial t} + \cdots + f_{1n}^r \frac{\partial^r}{\partial t^r} + \cdots \right) q_n$$
$$\cdots\cdots\cdots\cdots\cdots\cdots\cdots\cdots\cdots\cdots\cdots\cdots\cdots\cdots\cdots \quad (13.31)$$
$$\frac{\partial q_n}{\partial x} = \left(f_{n1}^0 + f_{n1}^1 \frac{\partial}{\partial t} + \cdots + f_{n1}^r \frac{\partial^r}{\partial t^r} \right) q_1 + \cdots$$
$$+ \left(f_{nn}^0 + f_{nn}^1 \frac{\partial}{\partial t} + \cdots + f_{nn}^r \frac{\partial^r}{\partial t^r} \right) q_n$$

where $q_i \equiv q_i(t, x)$. The transmission line and all its analogs fall into this category, as do many other systems. In matrix form (13.31) reads

$$\frac{\partial \mathbf{q}}{\partial x} = \mathbf{F}_0 \mathbf{q} + \mathbf{F}_1 \frac{\partial \mathbf{q}}{\partial t} + \mathbf{F}_2 \frac{\partial^2 \mathbf{q}}{\partial t^2} + \cdots + \mathbf{F}_r \frac{\partial^r \mathbf{q}}{\partial t^r} \quad (13.32)$$

The matrices $\mathbf{F}_i = [f_{jk}^i]$ may be constants or, more generally, functions of x. Hereafter we shall terminate the series in (13.32) with the third matrix $\mathbf{F}_2$, since this is sufficient for most systems.

If it is assumed that the solution of (13.31) exists and possesses a Laplace transform with respect to t, (13.32) can be transformed into

$$\frac{d\mathbf{Q}}{dx} = (\mathbf{F}_0 + \mathbf{F}_1 s + \mathbf{F}_2 s^2)\mathbf{Q} - \mathbf{F}_1 \mathbf{q}(0, x) - \mathbf{F}_2[\dot{\mathbf{q}}(0, x) + s\mathbf{q}(0, x)]$$

$$(13.33)$$

where the dot indicates differentiation with respect to time. It is also

possible to include forcing terms in (13.32); i.e.,

$$\frac{\partial \mathbf{q}}{\partial x} = \mathbf{F}_0 \mathbf{q} + \mathbf{F}_1 \frac{\partial \mathbf{q}}{\partial t} + \mathbf{F}_2 \frac{\partial^2 \mathbf{q}}{\partial t^2} + \mathbf{u}(t, x) \tag{13.34}$$

in which case the transformed version would be

$$\frac{d\mathbf{Q}}{dx} = (\mathbf{F}_0 + \mathbf{F}_1 s + \mathbf{F}_2 s^2)\mathbf{Q} + \bar{\mathbf{U}}(s, x) \tag{13.35}$$

where

$$\bar{\mathbf{U}}(s, x) = \mathbf{U}(s, x) - \mathbf{F}_1 \mathbf{q}(0, x) - \mathbf{F}_2[\dot{\mathbf{q}}(0, x) + s\mathbf{q}(0, x)]$$

and

$$\mathbf{U}(s, x) = \mathcal{L}[\mathbf{u}(t, x)]$$

In accordance with the theory developed in Chap. 4 for systems of first-order equations, the solution of (13.35) can be expressed by

$$\mathbf{Q}(s, x) = \mathbf{H}(s, x - x_0)\mathbf{Q}(s, x_0) + \int_{x_0}^{x} \mathbf{H}(s, x - \xi)\bar{\mathbf{U}}(s, \xi)\, d\xi \tag{13.36}$$

where $\mathbf{H}(s, x)$ is the fundamental matrix for the homogeneous form of (13.35). In particular, when $\mathbf{F}_0$, $\mathbf{F}_1$, and $\mathbf{F}_2$ are constant matrices, the fundamental matrix is

$$\begin{aligned}
\mathbf{H}(s, x) &= \exp\left[(\mathbf{F}_0 + \mathbf{F}_1 s + \mathbf{F}_2 s^2)x\right] \\
&= \mathbf{I} + (\mathbf{F}_0 + \mathbf{F}_1 s + \mathbf{F}_2 s^2)x + (\mathbf{F}_0 + \mathbf{F}_1 s + \mathbf{F}_2 s^2)^2 \frac{x^2}{2!} + \cdots
\end{aligned} \tag{13.37}$$

On expansion of the series defining $\mathbf{H}(s, x)$, it will be found that each element of $\mathbf{H}(s, x)$ is a power series in x whose coefficients are polynomials in s. Since the series defining an exponential converges for all finite values of x when s is any finite (complex) number, it is thus necessary for each element in the matrix $\mathbf{H}(s, x)$ to be an entire function[†] of s for all finite values of x. We shall employ this fact subsequently to prove that a system of the form (13.34) with rational terminations has only meromorphic transfer functions.

The basic techniques illustrated by the electrical transmission line and its analogs can be applied to the more general system described by (13.34).

Example 13.6   Transverse vibration of an elastic beam   Consider the motion of an elastic beam of uniform cross section; a section of length Δx is shown in Fig. 13.7.

[†] An entire function of a complex variable s is one which is analytic for all finite values of s. Thus every polynomial is an entire function.

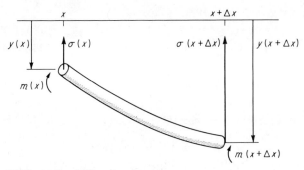

FIG. 13.7   Vibrating beam.

Let $y(t, x)$ = vertical downward displacement at point x, ft
   $\theta(t, x)$ = slope of bar at point x, ft/ft
   $m(t, x)$ = bending moment at point x, ft-lb
   $\sigma(t, x)$ = shear stress at point x, lb/ft^2

Then the partial differential equations governing the motion are

$$\frac{\partial y}{\partial x} = \theta \qquad\qquad \text{definition of slope}$$

$$\frac{\partial \theta}{\partial x} = -\frac{1}{EI}\, m \qquad\qquad \text{simple beam theory}$$

$$\frac{\partial m}{\partial x} = \sigma \qquad\qquad \text{definition of bending moment}$$

$$\frac{\partial \sigma}{\partial x} = \rho\,\frac{\partial^2 y}{\partial t^2} - f(x, t) \qquad \text{Newton's law}$$

where $f(x, t)$ = external (downward) force per unit length (if any)
   I = moment of inertia of area about neutral axis, ft^4
   E = modulus of elasticity, lb/ft^2
   ρ = linear density, slugs/ft = lb-sec^2/ft^2

   The first equation relates the slope to the deflection; the second relates the "spring torque" to the change in slope; the third relates the bending moment to the shear stress; and the fourth is Newton's law of motion for the acceleration of a section of mass $\rho\,\Delta x$ acted upon by a downward force $\sigma(x + \Delta x) - \sigma(x)$ as $\Delta x \to 0$. If the force $f(x, t)$ per unit length results from air damping, it can be expressed as

$$f(x, t) = -K\,\frac{\partial y}{\partial t}$$

and results in a damping term in the differential equations.

It is seen that the above equations are in the standard form of (13.31). If the vector $\mathbf{q}$ is defined by

$$\mathbf{q} = \begin{bmatrix} q_1 \\ q_2 \\ q_3 \\ q_4 \end{bmatrix} = \begin{bmatrix} y \\ \theta \\ m \\ \sigma \end{bmatrix}$$

the matrices $\mathbf{F}_0$, $\mathbf{F}_1$, and $\mathbf{F}_2$ are, in the absence of viscous damping,

$$\mathbf{F}_0 = \begin{bmatrix} 0 & 1 & 0 & 0 \\ 0 & 0 & -\dfrac{1}{EI} & 0 \\ 0 & 0 & 0 & 1 \\ 0 & 0 & 0 & 0 \end{bmatrix} \qquad \mathbf{F}_1 = 0 \qquad \mathbf{F}_2 = \begin{bmatrix} 0 & 0 & 0 & 0 \\ 0 & 0 & 0 & 0 \\ 0 & 0 & 0 & 0 \\ \rho & 0 & 0 & 0 \end{bmatrix}$$

Consequently

$$\mathbf{F}_0 + \mathbf{F}_1 s + \mathbf{F}_2 s^2 = \begin{bmatrix} 0 & 1 & 0 & 0 \\ 0 & 0 & -\dfrac{1}{EI} & 0 \\ 0 & 0 & 0 & 1 \\ \rho s^2 & 0 & 0 & 0 \end{bmatrix}$$

The characteristic equation for this matrix is, according to (7.18),

$$|w\mathbf{I} - \mathbf{F}_0 - \mathbf{F}_1 s - \mathbf{F}_2 s^2| = \begin{vmatrix} w & -1 & 0 & 0 \\ 0 & w & \dfrac{1}{EI} & 0 \\ 0 & 0 & w & -1 \\ -\rho s^2 & 0 & 0 & w \end{vmatrix} = w^4 + \frac{\rho s^2}{EI} = 0$$

$$(13.38)$$

Hence it follows that the terms in the fundamental matrix

$$\mathbf{H}(s, x) = \exp\left[(\mathbf{F}_0 + \mathbf{F}_1 s + \mathbf{F}_2 s^2)x\right]$$

are sums of the form

$$ae^{\lambda x} + be^{j\lambda x} + ce^{-\lambda x} + de^{-j\lambda x}$$

where λ, $-\lambda$, $j\lambda$, and $-j\lambda$ are the four roots of (13.38). In particular,

$$\lambda = (1 + j)\left(\frac{\rho s^2}{4EI}\right)^{\frac{1}{4}}$$

Using this fact, it is a simple although somewhat tedious calculation to

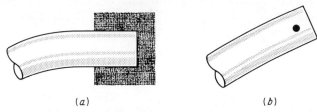

FIG. 13.8 Boundary conditions for vibrating beam.
(a) Built-in end: $y = 0$, $\theta = 0$; (b) pinned end: $y = 0$,
$m = 0$.

obtain the fundamental matrix $\mathbf{H}(s, x)$; (Prob. 13.14a). The result is

$$
\mathbf{H}(s, x) = \begin{bmatrix}
f_1(s, x) & f_2(s, x) & -\dfrac{f_3(s, x)}{EI} & -\dfrac{f_4(s, x)}{EI} \\[2ex]
-\dfrac{\rho s^2 f_4(s, x)}{EI} & f_1(s, x) & -\dfrac{f_2(s, x)}{EI} & -\dfrac{f_3(s, x)}{EI} \\[2ex]
\rho s^2 f_3(s, x) & \rho s^2 f_4(s, x) & f_1(s, x) & f_2(s, x) \\[2ex]
\rho s^2 f_2(s, x) & \rho s^2 f_3(s, x) & -\dfrac{\rho s^2 f_4(s, x)}{EI} & f_1(s, x)
\end{bmatrix}
$$

where

$f_1(s, x) = \frac{1}{2}(\cosh \lambda x + \cos \lambda x) = \cosh \alpha x \cos \alpha x$

$f_2(s, x) = \dfrac{1}{2\lambda}(\sinh \lambda x + \sin \lambda x) = \dfrac{1}{2\alpha}(\sinh \alpha x \cos \alpha x + \cosh \alpha x \sin \alpha x)$

$f_3(s, x) = \dfrac{1}{2\lambda^2}(\cosh \lambda x - \cos \lambda x) = \dfrac{1}{2\alpha^2}\sinh \alpha x \sin \alpha x$

$f_4(s, x) = \dfrac{1}{2\lambda^3}(\sinh \lambda x - \sin \lambda x) = \dfrac{1}{4\alpha^3}(\cosh \alpha x \sin \alpha x - \sinh \alpha x \cos \alpha x)$

$\alpha = \left(\dfrac{\rho s^2}{4EI}\right)^{\frac{1}{4}}$

It may be verified that $f_1, f_2, f_3,$ and f_4 are all entire functions of s and that
there is no branch point at $s = 0$; (Prob. 13.14b).

   Since only four relations are specified between the eight quantities (four
at each end) by (13.36), four boundary conditions must be given in order
to determine the problem completely. Typical terminal or boundary
conditions are the following (Fig. 13.8):

End "built in": $\qquad y(t, X) = 0 \qquad \theta(t, X) = 0$
End fixed (pinned): $\quad y(t, X) = 0 \qquad m(t, X) = 0$ (since pin exerts no
$\qquad\qquad\qquad\qquad\qquad\qquad\qquad\qquad\qquad\qquad$ bending moment in
$\qquad\qquad\qquad\qquad\qquad\qquad\qquad\qquad\qquad\qquad$ ideal case)

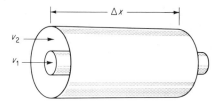

FIG. 13.9   Heat exchanger.

where $X = 0$ or L, depending on the end at which the condition is established.

Example 13.7   Heat exchanger   Consider a section of a heat exchanger as illustrated in Fig. 13.9.   Heat is transferred from the fluid in the outer tube through the wall to the inner tube.

Let $q_1(t, x)$ = average temperature of fluid in inner tube at point x
$q_2(t, x)$ = average temperature of fluid in outer tube at point x
v_1 = velocity of fluid in inner tube
v_2 = velocity of fluid in outer tube

Both v_1 and v_2 are assumed constant.   If ideal transfer takes place in the wall (i.e., the thickness is very small and/or the thermal conductivity is very high), the partial differential equations governing the temperatures in the fluids can be shown to be

$$\frac{dq_1}{dt} = \frac{\partial q_1}{\partial t} + v_1 \frac{\partial q_1}{\partial x} = -k_1(q_1 - q_2)$$

$$\frac{dq_2}{dt} = \frac{\partial q_2}{\partial t} + v_2 \frac{\partial q_2}{\partial x} = -k_2(q_2 - q_1)$$

where k_1 and k_2 are constants, depending on the properties of the fluids.†
These equations may be written

$$\frac{\partial q_1}{\partial x} = -\frac{k_1}{v_1}(q_1 - q_2) - \frac{1}{v_1}\frac{\partial q_1}{\partial t}$$

$$\frac{\partial q_2}{\partial x} = -\frac{k_2}{v_2}(q_2 - q_1) - \frac{1}{v_2}\frac{\partial q_2}{\partial t}$$

The matrices of the standard form are

$$\mathbf{F}_0 = \begin{bmatrix} -\dfrac{k_1}{v_1} & \dfrac{k_1}{v_1} \\ \dfrac{k_2}{v_2} & -\dfrac{k_2}{v_2} \end{bmatrix} \qquad \mathbf{F}_1 = \begin{bmatrix} -\dfrac{1}{v_1} & 0 \\ 0 & -\dfrac{1}{v_2} \end{bmatrix}$$

† D. P. Campbell, "Process Dynamics," pp. 198–200, John Wiley & Sons, Inc., New York, 1958.

Hence

$$\mathbf{H}(s, x) = \exp \begin{pmatrix} -\dfrac{k_1 + s}{v_1} & \dfrac{k_1}{v_1} \\ \dfrac{k_2}{v_2} & -\dfrac{k_2 + s}{v_2} \end{pmatrix} x$$

The characteristic equation of $\mathbf{H}(s, x)$ is

$$\begin{vmatrix} w + \dfrac{k_1 + s}{v_1} & -\dfrac{k_1}{v_1} \\ -\dfrac{k_2}{v_2} & w + \dfrac{k_2 + s}{v_2} \end{vmatrix} = w^2 + w \left[s \left(\frac{1}{v_1} + \frac{1}{v_2} \right) + \frac{k_1}{v_1} + \frac{k_2}{v_2} \right]$$

$$+ \frac{s^2 + s(k_1 + k_2)}{v_1 v_2} = 0$$

The characteristic roots are

$$w_1 = \frac{1}{2} \left[-s \left(\frac{1}{v_1} + \frac{1}{v_2} \right) - \frac{k_1}{v_1} - \frac{k_2}{v_2} + R \right]$$

$$w_2 = \frac{1}{2} \left[-s \left(\frac{1}{v_1} + \frac{1}{v_2} \right) - \frac{k_1}{v_1} - \frac{k_2}{v_2} - R \right]$$

where

$$R = \left[\left(\frac{1}{v_1} - \frac{1}{v_2} \right)^2 s^2 + 2s \left(\frac{k_1}{v_1} - \frac{k_2}{v_2} \right) \left(\frac{1}{v_1} - \frac{1}{v_2} \right) + \left(\frac{k_1}{v_1} + \frac{k_2}{v_2} \right)^2 \right]^{\frac{1}{2}}$$

and the elements of $\mathbf{H}(s, x)$ are of the form

$$ae^{w_1 x} + be^{w_2 x}$$

13.5 THEORY OF FINITE SYSTEMS

The dynamic behavior of a physical distributed system depends not only on the partial differential equation governing its internal behavior, but also on what happens at the ends, or terminals. We have already encountered the matter of termination in the electrical transmission line of Sec. 13.2. In this section we generalize the treatment and derive general expressions for distributed systems with arbitrary lumped termination.
Consider the general system

$$\frac{\partial \mathbf{q}}{\partial x} = \mathbf{F}_0 \mathbf{q} + \mathbf{F}_1 \frac{\partial \mathbf{q}}{\partial t} + \mathbf{F}_2 \frac{\partial^2 \mathbf{q}}{\partial t^2} + \mathbf{u}(t, x)$$

with the general frequency-domain solution (13.36); namely,

$$\mathbf{Q}(s, x) = \mathbf{H}(s, x - x_0)\mathbf{Q}(s, x_0) + \int_{x_0}^{x} \mathbf{H}(s, x - \xi)\bar{\mathbf{U}}(s, \xi)\, d\xi \quad (13.39)$$

If the system is of order k in space (that is, $\mathbf{q}$ and $\mathbf{Q}$ are k-vectors), the last equation gives k relations between the k quantities at a point x and the k quantities at a point x_0. Now suppose the system is of finite length; $0 \leq x \leq L$. Then we have, at $x = L$,

$$\mathbf{Q}(s, L) = \mathbf{H}(s, L)\mathbf{Q}(s, 0) + \int_{0}^{L} \mathbf{H}(s, L - \xi)\bar{\mathbf{U}}(s, \xi)\, d\xi \quad (13.40)$$

To determine $\mathbf{Q}(s, L)$ and $\mathbf{Q}(s, 0)$ (and hence $\mathbf{Q}(s, x)$ for any x between 0 and L), k terminal relations must be specified. These terminal relations can generally be put in the form of k independent *ordinary* differential equations

$$m_{11}(D)q_1(t, 0) + \cdots + m_{1k}(D)q_k(t, 0)$$
$$+ n_{11}(D)q_1(t, L) + \cdots + n_{1k}(D)q_k(t, L) = z_1(t)$$
$$\cdot\ \cdot\ \cdot\ \cdot\ \cdot\ \cdot\ \cdot\ \cdot\ \cdot\ \cdot\ \cdot\ \cdot\ \cdot\ \cdot\ \cdot\ \cdot\ \cdot\ \cdot\ \cdot\ \cdot$$
$$m_{k1}(D)q_1(t, 0) + \cdots + m_{kk}(D)q_k(t, 0)$$
$$+ n_{k1}(D)q_1(t, L) + \cdots + n_{kk}(D)q_k(t, L) = z_k(t) \quad (13.41)$$

where $m_{ij}(D)$ and $n_{ij}(D)$ are linear differential operators, and $z_i(t)$ are external forcing functions (the physical inputs or linear combinations thereof).

In vector-matrix form, (13.41) can be written

$$\mathbf{M}(D)\mathbf{q}(t, 0) + \mathbf{N}(D)\mathbf{q}(t, L) = \mathbf{z}(t) \quad (13.42)$$

Laplace transformation of (13.42) results in the frequency-domain expression for the terminal relations

$$\mathbf{M}(s)\mathbf{Q}(s, 0) + \mathbf{N}(s)\mathbf{Q}(s, L) = \bar{\mathbf{Z}}(s) \quad (13.43)$$

where $\bar{\mathbf{Z}}(s)$ is the sum of the Laplace transform of $\mathbf{z}(t)$ and any initial-condition terms arising in the transformation of (13.42), transposed to the right-hand side. The termination is said to be *homogeneous* if $\bar{\mathbf{Z}}(s) = \mathbf{0}$.

Note that each of the differential equations of (13.41) can involve quantities at *both* ends of the distributed system. This is the type of termination characteristic of a feedback system where quantities at one end are made to depend on quantities at the other. When no feedback is involved, the quantities at each end are governed by differential equations which do not involve any quantities at the other. In particular,

in the frequency domain, (13.43) would become two separate equations

$$\mathbf{A}(s)\mathbf{Q}(s, 0) = \bar{\mathbf{Z}}_1(s)$$
$$\mathbf{B}(s)\mathbf{Q}(s, L) = \bar{\mathbf{Z}}_2(s)$$

where the first represents k_1 independent equations and the second represents $k - k_1$ independent equations.

In order to obtain a complete representation of the system governed by (13.39) and (13.43), we substitute the former into the latter with $x_0 = 0$ and $x = L$; the result is

$$[\mathbf{M}(s) + \mathbf{N}(s)\mathbf{H}(s, L)]\mathbf{Q}(s, 0) = \mathbf{V}(s)$$

where

$$\mathbf{V}(s) = \bar{\mathbf{Z}}(s) - \mathbf{N}(s) \int_0^L \mathbf{H}(s, L - \xi)\bar{\mathbf{U}}(s, \xi)\,d\xi \qquad (13.44)$$

If the relations (13.41) are indeed independent (which is a requirement of a fully specified system), $\mathbf{M}(s) + \mathbf{N}(s)\mathbf{H}(s, L)$ is of rank k and has an inverse. Hence we can write

$$\mathbf{Q}(s, 0) = [\mathbf{M}(s) + \mathbf{N}(s)\mathbf{H}(s, L)]^{-1}\mathbf{V}(s) \qquad (13.45)$$

Thus the "transfer matrix" from the "input" $\mathbf{V}$ to $\mathbf{Q}(s, 0)$ is $[\mathbf{M}(s) + \mathbf{N}(s)\mathbf{H}(s, L)]^{-1}$. More generally, using (13.39) with $x_0 = 0$,

$$\mathbf{Q}(s, x) = \mathbf{H}(s, x)[\mathbf{M}(s) + \mathbf{N}(s)\mathbf{H}(s, L)]^{-1}\mathbf{V}(s)$$
$$+ \int_0^x \mathbf{H}(s, x - \xi)\bar{\mathbf{U}}(s, \xi)\,d\xi \qquad (13.46)$$

In many cases of practical interest, it is simpler to perform the calculations implicit in (13.46) without the use of matrix algebra. The formal expression is convenient for theoretical reasons and as a method of avoiding computational errors. The following result shows the utility of this general formalism.

If there are no distributed forcing terms and initial conditions, (13.46) can be written

$$\mathbf{Q}(s, x) = \mathbf{H}(s, x)[\mathbf{M}(s) + \mathbf{N}(s)\mathbf{H}(s, L)]^{-1}\mathbf{Z}(s) \qquad (13.47)$$

where $\mathbf{Z}(s)$ is the Laplace transform of the external forcing terms in (13.41). Hence the matrix of transfer functions from $\mathbf{Z}$ to $\mathbf{Q}(s, x)$ is given by

$$\mathbf{K}(s, x) = \mathbf{H}(s, x)[\mathbf{M}(s) + \mathbf{N}(s)\mathbf{H}(s, L)]^{-1}$$

Each term in the matrix $\mathbf{M}(s) + \mathbf{N}(s)\mathbf{H}(s, L)$ is a sum of products of entire functions and is thus an entire function. All elements of its adjoint

are also entire functions. Likewise, the determinant

$$|\mathbf{M}(s) + \mathbf{N}(s)\mathbf{H}(s, L)|$$

is a sum of products of entire functions and is thus an entire function. Consequently every term of the matrix $\mathbf{K}(s, x)$ is a ratio of entire functions of s. Since the ratio of entire functions is a meromorphic function, we have the following theorem.

Theorem 13.1 *The transfer function from any input to any dynamic variable in the distributed system* (13.39) *whose terminal relations are given by* (13.41) *is a meromorphic function of s.*

This means that the only singularities which any transfer function may have in the finite s plane are poles.

The following examples will serve to illustrate the application of the formal method.

Example 13.8 Transmission line with general terminations Consider a transmission line terminated at the "receiving end" $x = L$ by an impedance $Z_L(s)$ and excited at the "sending end" $x = 0$ by a voltage source $E(s)$ having an output impedance $Z_S(s)$ as shown in Fig. 13.3.

The terminal relations at $x = 0$ and $x = L$ are expressed by the equations

$$V(s, 0) + Z_S(s)I(s, 0) = E(s)$$
$$V(s, L) - Z_L(s)I(s, L) = 0$$

or in matrix form

$$\begin{bmatrix} 1 & Z_S \\ 0 & 0 \end{bmatrix}\begin{bmatrix} V(s, 0) \\ I(s, 0) \end{bmatrix} + \begin{bmatrix} 0 & 0 \\ 1 & -Z_L \end{bmatrix}\begin{bmatrix} V(s, L) \\ I(s, L) \end{bmatrix} = \begin{bmatrix} E(s) \\ 0 \end{bmatrix}$$

[Note that these are not exactly in the form specified in (13.43) since Z_L and Z_S are not, in general, polynomials, but rational functions. This is no restriction, however, since we can multiply the equations by the denominator of the impedance to obtain the form (13.43).] We obtain by use of (13.12) with $x = L$

$$\mathbf{M}(s) + \mathbf{N}(s)\mathbf{H}(s, L)$$
$$= \begin{bmatrix} 1 & Z_S \\ 0 & 0 \end{bmatrix} + \begin{bmatrix} 0 & 0 \\ 1 & -Z_L \end{bmatrix}\begin{bmatrix} \cosh \Gamma L & -Z_0 \sinh \Gamma L \\ -Z_0^{-1} \sinh \Gamma L & \cosh \Gamma L \end{bmatrix}$$
$$= \begin{bmatrix} 1 & Z_S \\ \cosh \Gamma L + \dfrac{Z_L}{Z_0} \sinh \Gamma L & -Z_0 \sinh \Gamma L - Z_L \cosh \Gamma L \end{bmatrix}$$

and

$$[\mathbf{M}(s) + \mathbf{N}(s)\mathbf{H}(s, L)]^{-1} = \begin{bmatrix} \dfrac{Z_0 \sinh \Gamma L + Z_L \cosh \Gamma L}{\Delta} & \dfrac{Z_S}{\Delta} \\[2ex] \dfrac{\cosh \Gamma L + \dfrac{Z_L}{Z_0} \sinh \Gamma L}{\Delta} & \dfrac{-1}{\Delta} \end{bmatrix} \qquad (13.48)$$

where

$$\Delta = -|\mathbf{M}(s) + \mathbf{N}(s)\mathbf{H}(s, L)|$$
$$= (Z_L + Z_S) \cosh \Gamma L + \left(Z_0 + \frac{Z_S Z_L}{Z_0} \right) \sinh \Gamma L$$

in which

$$\Gamma \equiv \Gamma(s) = \sqrt{(ls + r)(cs + g)}$$
$$Z_0 \equiv Z_0(s) = \sqrt{(ls + r)/(cs + g)}$$

Note that although the expressions in (13.48) contain factors which are not meromorphic, they combine to yield functions which are meromorphic and have poles at the points in the s plane for which

$$\Delta = (Z_L + Z_S) \cosh \Gamma L + \left(Z_0 + \frac{Z_S Z_L}{Z_0} \right) \sinh \Gamma L = 0$$

It is of course a difficult problem to calculate the exact location of the poles, except for special combinations of Z_L, Z_S, Z_0, and Γ, such as already calculated in Sec. 13.1.

Example 13.9 Temperature-control problem Consider the following temperature-control problem. A thin bar (Fig. 13.10) of length L is fully insulated, except at its ends. Assume further that the heat flux at the end $x = L$ is a constant A. The objective is to control the temperature at this end; to accomplish this a thermometer (a thermocouple, for example) is placed on the bar at this end and compared with a reference temperature $f(t)$. The difference is multiplied by a constant and used to control a heater in such a manner that the heat input at $x = 0$ is proportional to the difference between the desired and the actual tem-

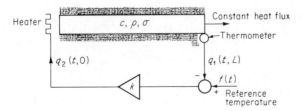

FIG. 13.10 Temperature-control problem.

perature. To simplify matters we assume that the heat input at $x = 0$ can be decreased as well as increased by the heater. Although this cannot be done with a heater of the usual type, the analysis is valid if we assume that a quiescent temperature is established which causes a constant exit flux A and that the quantities referred to subsequently are measured with respect to these quiescent conditions.

As already shown in Example 13.3, the partial differential equations for heat conduction are

$$\frac{\partial q_1}{\partial x} = -\beta q_2$$

$$\frac{\partial q_2}{\partial x} = -\gamma \frac{\partial q_1}{\partial t}$$

where q_1 is temperature deviation, q_2 is heat flux deviation, and β and γ are defined after (13.28). Since these are analogous to the transmission-line equations, we can immediately write

$$\mathbf{H}(s, x) = \begin{bmatrix} \cosh \Gamma x & -Z_0 \sinh \Gamma x \\ -\dfrac{1}{Z_0} \sinh \Gamma x & \cosh \Gamma x \end{bmatrix}$$

$$\Gamma = \sqrt{\beta \gamma s} = \sqrt{\frac{C\rho}{\sigma}} \sqrt{s}$$

$$Z_0 = \sqrt{\frac{\beta}{\gamma s}} = \frac{1}{A} \sqrt{\frac{1}{C\rho\sigma}} \frac{1}{\sqrt{s}}$$

The terminal conditions for this problem are

$$q_2(t, 0) = k[f(t) - q_1(t, L)]$$
$$q_2(t, L) = 0$$

if we keep in mind that we are assuming q_2 to be the change in heat flux from the quiescent value A.

The matrix form of the terminal conditions is

$$\begin{bmatrix} 0 & 1 \\ 0 & 0 \end{bmatrix} \begin{bmatrix} Q_1(s, 0) \\ Q_2(s, 0) \end{bmatrix} + \begin{bmatrix} k & 0 \\ 0 & 1 \end{bmatrix} \begin{bmatrix} Q_1(s, L) \\ Q_2(s, L) \end{bmatrix} = \begin{bmatrix} kF(s) \\ 0 \end{bmatrix}$$

and the transfer matrix is given by

$$\mathbf{K}(s, x) = \mathbf{H}(s, x)[\mathbf{M} + \mathbf{N}\mathbf{H}(s, L)]^{-1} = \begin{bmatrix} K_{11} & K_{12} \\ K_{21} & K_{22} \end{bmatrix}$$

where

$$\mathbf{M} = \begin{bmatrix} 0 & 1 \\ 0 & 0 \end{bmatrix} \qquad \mathbf{N} = \begin{bmatrix} k & 0 \\ 0 & 1 \end{bmatrix}$$

Carrying out the required calculations, we obtain

$$\mathbf{M} + \mathbf{NH}(s, L) = \begin{bmatrix} 0 & 1 \\ 0 & 0 \end{bmatrix} + \begin{bmatrix} k & 0 \\ 0 & 1 \end{bmatrix} \begin{bmatrix} \cosh \Gamma L & -Z_0 \sinh \Gamma L \\ -\dfrac{1}{Z_0} \sinh \Gamma L & \cosh \Gamma L \end{bmatrix}$$

$$= \begin{bmatrix} k \cosh \Gamma L & 1 - kZ_0 \sinh \Gamma L \\ -\dfrac{1}{Z_0} \sinh \Gamma L & \cosh \Gamma L \end{bmatrix}$$

$$[\mathbf{M} + \mathbf{NH}(s, L)]^{-1}$$

$$= \frac{1}{k + \dfrac{1}{Z_0} \sinh \Gamma L} \begin{bmatrix} \cosh \Gamma L & -(1 - kZ_0 \sinh \Gamma L) \\ \dfrac{1}{Z_0} \sinh \Gamma L & k \cosh \Gamma L \end{bmatrix} \tag{13.49}$$

and finally

$$\mathbf{K}(s, x) = \begin{bmatrix} \cosh \Gamma(L - x) & kZ_0 \sinh \Gamma(L - x) - \cosh \Gamma x \\ \dfrac{\sinh \Gamma(L - x)}{Z_0} & \dfrac{1}{Z_0} \sinh \Gamma x + k \cosh \Gamma(L - x) \end{bmatrix} \frac{1}{k + \dfrac{\sinh \Gamma L}{Z_0}} \tag{13.50}$$

(The reader should establish to his satisfaction that every element of $\mathbf{K}(s, x)$ is a meromorphic function.)

From the definition of $\mathbf{K}(s, x)$ the expression for the Laplace transform of the temperature at any point is $Q_1(s, x) = K_{11}(s)kF(s)$, where K_{11} is the (1, 1) element of $\mathbf{K}$. Thus

$$Q_1(s, x) = \frac{k \cosh \Gamma(L - x)}{k + (\sinh \Gamma L)/Z_0} F(s)$$

There is no systematic method for obtaining the inverse Laplace transform $q_1(t, x)$ of $Q_1(s, x)$; one must usually be content with an approximate solution, which can sometimes be obtained by methods to be discussed subsequently.

We shall return to this example in our discussion of stability.

Example 13.10   Vibrating beam   Consider the transverse motion of a flexible beam, fastened to a wall at its right end $x = L$ and with a force $f(t)$ applied at its left end, as shown in Fig. 13.11. The terminal conditions at the left end are expressed by

$$q_3(t, 0) \equiv m(t, 0) = 0 \qquad \text{no bending moment}$$
$$q_4(t, 0) \equiv \sigma(t, 0) = f(t)$$

FIG. 13.11   Vibrating beam.

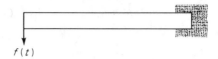

$$f(t)$$

The terminal conditions at the right end are expressed by

$$q_1(t, L) = y(t, L) = 0$$

and either

(1) $q_3(t, L) \equiv m(t, L) = 0$ if end is pinned

or

(2) $q_2(t, L) \equiv \theta(t, L) = 0$ if end is built in

In matrix form the Laplace transforms of these terminal conditions are expressible as

$$\mathbf{M}(s)\mathbf{Q}(s, 0) + \mathbf{N}(s)\mathbf{Q}(s, L) = \mathbf{Z}(s)$$

where

$$\mathbf{M}(s) = \begin{bmatrix} 0 & 0 & 0 & 0 \\ 0 & 0 & 0 & 0 \\ 0 & 0 & 1 & 0 \\ 0 & 0 & 0 & 1 \end{bmatrix} \qquad \mathbf{Z}(s) = \begin{bmatrix} 0 \\ 0 \\ 0 \\ F(s) \end{bmatrix}$$

and

(1) $\mathbf{N}(s) = \begin{bmatrix} 1 & 0 & 0 & 0 \\ 0 & 0 & 1 & 0 \\ 0 & 0 & 0 & 0 \\ 0 & 0 & 0 & 0 \end{bmatrix}$ if end is pinned

or

(2) $\mathbf{N}(s) = \begin{bmatrix} 1 & 0 & 0 & 0 \\ 0 & 1 & 0 & 0 \\ 0 & 0 & 0 & 0 \\ 0 & 0 & 0 & 0 \end{bmatrix}$ if end is built in

For the built-in end we have

$$\mathbf{M}(s) + \mathbf{N}(s)\mathbf{H}(s, L) = \begin{bmatrix} f_1 & f_2 & -\dfrac{f_3}{EI} & -\dfrac{f_4}{EI} \\ -\dfrac{\rho s^2 f_4}{EI} & f_1 & -\dfrac{f_2}{EI} & -\dfrac{f_3}{EI} \\ 0 & 0 & 1 & 0 \\ 0 & 0 & 0 & 1 \end{bmatrix}$$

where the expressions for $f_1, f_2, f_3,$ and f_4 are those given in Example 13.6, evaluated at $x = L$. Then

$$[\mathbf{M}(s) + \mathbf{N}(s)\mathbf{H}(s, x)]^{-1}$$

$$= \begin{bmatrix} \dfrac{f_1}{\Delta} & -\dfrac{f_2}{\Delta} & \dfrac{f_1f_3 - f_2{}^2}{EI\Delta} & \dfrac{f_1f_4 - f_2f_3}{EI\Delta} \\[2ex] \dfrac{\rho s^2 f_4}{EI\Delta} & \dfrac{f_1}{\Delta} & \dfrac{\rho s^2 f_3 f_4/EI + f_1f_2}{EI\Delta} & \dfrac{\rho s^2 f_3 f_4/EI + f_1f_3}{EI\Delta} \\[2ex] 0 & 0 & 1 & 0 \\[1ex] 0 & 0 & 0 & 1 \end{bmatrix}$$

where $\Delta = f_1{}^2 + \rho s^2 f_2 f_4/EI$.

After simplification it is found that

$$\Delta = \tfrac{1}{2}(\cosh^2 \alpha L + \cos^2 \alpha L) = \tfrac{1}{2}\left[\cosh^2 \left(\frac{\rho s^2}{4EI}\right)^{\frac{1}{4}} L + \cos^2 \left(\frac{\rho s^2}{4EI}\right)^{\frac{1}{4}} L \right]$$

As a more specific example we calculate the transfer function from the external force $F(s)$ to the deflection $Y(s, 0)$. This is given by

$$\frac{Y(s, 0)}{F(s)} = K_{14}(s, 0)$$

where

$$\mathbf{K}(s, 0) = [\mathbf{M}(s) + \mathbf{N}(s)\mathbf{H}(s, L)]^{-1}\mathbf{H}(s, 0) = [\mathbf{M}(s) + \mathbf{N}(s)\mathbf{H}(s, L)]^{-1}$$

since $\mathbf{H}(s, 0) = \mathbf{I}$. Now

$$K_{14}(s, 0) = \frac{f_1f_4 - f_2f_3}{EI\Delta}$$

After simplification it is found that

$$f_1f_4 - f_2f_3 = \frac{1}{4\alpha^3} (\sin \alpha L \cos \alpha L - \sinh \alpha L \cosh \alpha L)$$

$$= \frac{1}{8\alpha^3} (\sin 2\alpha L - \sinh 2\alpha L)$$

so that

$$K_{14}(s, 0) = \frac{\sin 2\alpha L - \sinh 2\alpha L}{4EI\alpha^3 (\cosh^2 \alpha L + \cos^2 \alpha L)}$$

where

$$\alpha = \left(\frac{\rho s^2}{4EI}\right)^{\frac{1}{4}}$$

It is noted that $K_{14}(s, 0)$ is a meromorphic function of s.

13.6 CHARACTERISTIC TERMINATION AND SEMI-INFINITE SYSTEMS

The expression for the fundamental matrix given by (13.37) is an entire function of s for all finite x.   It is evident, however, that if x is allowed to become infinite, the series may diverge for all finite values of s.   If this were to happen, the transfer functions would not exist.   If the equations represent the behavior of a physical system which might be semi-infinite, we require that the transfer functions exist as $x \to \infty$, since a finite output is to be expected as $x \to \infty$.   This requires that certain terms in $\exp[(\mathbf{F}_0 + \mathbf{F}_1 s + \mathbf{F}_2 s^2)x]$ vanish as $x \to \infty$ in such a manner that the transfer functions continue to exist.   As we shall subsequently discover, this implies a particular relationship between the dynamic variables at every point in the system.   By analogy with electrical transmission lines, we shall denote this relationship as the *constraint of characteristic termination*.

To approach the problem we transform the matrix $\mathbf{F}_0 + \mathbf{F}_1 s + \mathbf{F}_2 s^2$ to a diagonal matrix by means of a similarity transformation

$$\mathbf{F}_0 + \mathbf{F}_1 s + \mathbf{F}_2 s^2 = \mathbf{T}(s)\mathbf{\Lambda}(s)\mathbf{T}^{-1}(s) \tag{13.51}$$

where $\mathbf{\Lambda}(s)$ is a diagonal matrix, and $\mathbf{T}(s)$ is the matrix of the transformation.

The matrix $\mathbf{T}(s)$ is the matrix of vectors $\mathbf{T}_i(s)$ [the ith column of $\mathbf{T}(s)$] for which

$$\mathbf{F}_0 + \mathbf{F}_1 s + \mathbf{F}_2 s^2 = \lambda_i \mathbf{T}_i \tag{13.52}$$

where the $\lambda_i \equiv \lambda_i(s)$ are the eigenvalues† of the matrix $\mathbf{F}_0 + \mathbf{F}_1 s + \mathbf{F}_2 s^2$, that is, the roots of the characteristic equation

$$|\lambda \mathbf{I} - \mathbf{F}_0 - \mathbf{F}_1 s - \mathbf{F}_2 s^2| = 0 \tag{13.53}$$

We can now write the solution of the homogeneous form of (13.35) as

$$\mathbf{Q}(s, x) = e^{\mathbf{T}(s)\mathbf{\Lambda}(s)\mathbf{T}^{-1}(s)x}\mathbf{Q}(s, 0) \tag{13.54}$$

By expanding the exponential we may write

$$e^{\mathbf{T}(s)\mathbf{\Lambda}(s)\mathbf{T}^{-1}(s)x} = \mathbf{T}(s)\mathbf{T}^{-1}(s) + \mathbf{T}(s)\mathbf{\Lambda}(s)x\mathbf{T}^{-1}(s)$$

$$+ \frac{1}{2!}\mathbf{T}(s)\mathbf{\Lambda}(s)x\mathbf{T}^{-1}(s)\,\mathbf{T}(s)\mathbf{\Lambda}(s)x\mathbf{T}^{-1}(s) + \cdots$$

$$= \mathbf{T}(s)\left[\mathbf{I} + \mathbf{\Lambda}(s)x + \mathbf{\Lambda}^2(s)\frac{x^2}{2!} + \cdots\right]\mathbf{T}^{-1}(s)$$

† These eigenvalues are assumed to be *distinct*.

Hence

$$\mathbf{Q}(s, x) = \mathbf{T}(s)e^{\mathbf{\Lambda}(s)x}\,\mathbf{T}^{-1}(s)\mathbf{Q}(s, 0) \tag{13.55}$$

so that

$$\mathbf{H}(s, x) = \mathbf{T}(s)e^{\mathbf{\Lambda}(s)x}\,\mathbf{T}^{-1}(s) \tag{13.56}$$

If we define a new set of dynamical variables by

$$\mathbf{P}(s, x) = \mathbf{T}^{-1}(s)\mathbf{Q}(s, x) \tag{13.57}$$

(13.55) becomes

$$\mathbf{P}(s, x) = e^{\mathbf{\Lambda}(s)x}\,\mathbf{P}(s, 0)$$

Thus the transfer function from $P_i(s, 0)$ to $P_i(s, x)$ is given by $e^{\lambda_i(s)x}$ since $\mathbf{\Lambda}$ is a diagonal matrix.

If $e^{\lambda_i(s)x}$ is the transfer function of a physical quantity, it must be analytic to the right of some line $\sigma = \sigma_a$ (the abscissa of absolute convergence) in the plane $s = \sigma + j\omega$ for *all* positive (not merely *finite*) values of x. Thus a necessary condition for $e^{\lambda_i(s)x}$ to be a physical transfer function is the existence of a real number σ_a such that $e^{\lambda_i(s)x}$ is analytic for any s with Re $s > \sigma_a$ for *all* (not merely finite) positive values of x. In other words, it is necessary that

$$\lim_{x \to \infty} e^{\lambda_i(s)x}$$

be analytic for $\sigma = $ Re s sufficiently large. This further requires that $\lambda_i(s)$ be nonpositive for real s. Hence those eigenvalues $\lambda_i(s)$ which are positive for large σ cannot appear in the matrix $e^{\mathbf{\Lambda}(s)x}$. Accordingly, the components of $\mathbf{P}$ corresponding to these eigenvalues must be identically zero in the semi-infinite system.

Example 13.11 Transmission line To relate the previous statements to familiar systems we again return to the transmission-line example. We have

$$\mathbf{F} + \mathbf{G}s = \begin{bmatrix} 0 & -(ls + r) \\ -(cs + g) & 0 \end{bmatrix}$$

Hence the characteristic equation $|\lambda\mathbf{I} - \mathbf{F} - \mathbf{G}s| = 0$ is given by

$$\begin{vmatrix} \lambda & ls + r \\ cs + g & \lambda \end{vmatrix} = \lambda^2 - (ls + r)(cs + g) = 0$$

Let $ls + r = z$ and $cs + g = y$. Then

$$\lambda_1 = -\sqrt{(ls + r)(cs + g)} = -\Gamma(s) = -\sqrt{zy}$$
$$\lambda_2 = +\sqrt{(ls + r)(cs + g)} = +\Gamma(s) = +\sqrt{zy}$$

Only $\lambda_1(s)$ is permitted in the transfer matrix which is to be valid in the semi-infinite transmission line, since $\lambda_2(s)$ is positive for $s = \sigma > 0$.

We now calculate the matrix $\mathbf{T}(s)$, using (13.52), which for $i = 1$ gives

$$\begin{bmatrix} 0 & -z \\ -y & 0 \end{bmatrix}\begin{bmatrix} T_{11} \\ T_{21} \end{bmatrix} = -\sqrt{zy}\begin{bmatrix} T_{11} \\ T_{21} \end{bmatrix}$$

so that

$$-zT_{21} = -\sqrt{zy}\, T_{11}$$

or

$$T_{21} = \sqrt{\frac{y}{z}}\, T_{11} = \frac{T_{11}}{Z_0}$$

where $Z_0 = \sqrt{z/y}$.   Also, for $i = 2$,

$$\begin{bmatrix} 0 & -z \\ -y & 0 \end{bmatrix}\begin{bmatrix} T_{12} \\ T_{22} \end{bmatrix} = +\sqrt{zy}\begin{bmatrix} T_{12} \\ T_{22} \end{bmatrix}$$

so that $T_{22} = -T_{12}/Z_0$.   Setting $T_{11} = T_{12} = 1$, we have

$$\mathbf{T} = \begin{bmatrix} 1 & 1 \\ \dfrac{1}{Z_0} & -\dfrac{1}{Z_0} \end{bmatrix}$$

and

$$\mathbf{T}^{-1} = \begin{bmatrix} \dfrac{1}{2} & \dfrac{Z_0}{2} \\ \dfrac{1}{2} & \dfrac{-Z_0}{2} \end{bmatrix}$$

Thus, since $\mathbf{Q} = \mathbf{TP}$ by (13.57), we obtain

$$\begin{bmatrix} V(s, x) \\ I(s, x) \end{bmatrix} = \begin{bmatrix} 1 & 1 \\ \dfrac{1}{Z_0} & -\dfrac{1}{Z_0} \end{bmatrix}\begin{bmatrix} P_1(s, x) \\ P_2(s, x) \end{bmatrix}$$

i.e.,

$$V(s, x) = P_1(s, x) + P_2(s, x)$$
$$I(s, x) = \frac{1}{Z_0} P_1(s, x) - \frac{1}{Z_0} P_2(s, x)$$

Note that P_1 is the well-known voltage V^+ propagating to the right and P_2 is the voltage V^- propagating to the left.   In the semi-infinite line, P_2 (corresponding to $\lambda_2(s) = +\sqrt{zy}$) must be absent; i.e., *there must be no reflected wave.*

The requirement that $P_2 = 0$ for all x means that

$$V(s, x) - Z_0(s)I(s, x) \equiv 0$$

everywhere along the transmission line. This is the *constraint of characteristic termination*.

To generalize the result obtained for the case of transmission lines, let us assume that m eigenvalues $\lambda_1(s)$, $\lambda_2(s)$, . . . , $\lambda_m(s)$ are positive for sufficiently large positive values of s. Then the corresponding components $P_1(s, x)$, . . . , $P_m(s, x)$ must be identically zero. Thus

$$\mathbf{P}(s, x) = \begin{bmatrix} P_1(s, x) \\ \cdot \\ \cdot \\ \cdot \\ P_m(s, x) \\ \hline P_{m+1}(s, x) \\ \cdot \\ \cdot \\ \cdot \\ P_k(s, x) \end{bmatrix} = \begin{bmatrix} \mathbf{0} \\ \hline \bar{\mathbf{P}}(s, x) \end{bmatrix}$$

But

$$\mathbf{P}(s, x) = \mathbf{T}^{-1}(s)\mathbf{Q}(s, x) = \begin{bmatrix} \mathbf{W}_1(s) \\ \hline \mathbf{W}_2(s) \end{bmatrix} \mathbf{Q}(s, x) = \begin{bmatrix} \mathbf{0} \\ \hline \bar{\mathbf{P}}(s, x) \end{bmatrix}$$

where $\mathbf{W}_1(s)$ is the matrix consisting of the first m rows of the inverse of the matrix $\mathbf{T}(s)$, the first m columns of which correspond to the m unallowed eigenvalues.

Hence, in a physical system, it is necessary to have

$$\mathbf{W}_1(s)\mathbf{Q}(s, x) \equiv \mathbf{0} \qquad \text{all } x \tag{13.58}$$

This is the general form of the *equation of characteristic constraint*.

Example 13.12 Vibrating beam In Example 13.6 it was found that the characteristic roots of the system are

$$\lambda_1 = (1 + j)\left(\frac{\rho s^2}{4EI}\right)^{\frac{1}{4}}$$

$$\lambda_2 = (1 - j)\left(\frac{\rho s^2}{4EI}\right)^{\frac{1}{4}}$$

$$\lambda_3 = (-1 + j)\left(\frac{\rho s^2}{4EI}\right)^{\frac{1}{4}}$$

$$\lambda_4 = (-1 - j)\left(\frac{\rho s^2}{4EI}\right)^{\frac{1}{4}}$$

The characteristic roots which must vanish in the semi-infinite beam are thus λ_1 and λ_2. It is readily established that

$$
\mathbf{T} =
\begin{bmatrix}
1 & 1 & 1 & 1 \\
\lambda_1 & \lambda_2 & \lambda_3 & \lambda_4 \\
-EI\lambda_1^2 & -EI\lambda_2^2 & -EI\lambda_3^2 & -EI\lambda_4^2 \\
-EI\lambda_1^3 & -EI\lambda_2^3 & -EI\lambda_3^3 & -EI\lambda_4^3
\end{bmatrix}
$$

$$
=
\begin{bmatrix}
1 & 0 & 0 & 0 \\
0 & 2^{\frac12}k & 0 & 0 \\
0 & 0 & -2k^2EI & 0 \\
0 & 0 & 0 & -2^{\frac12}k^3EI
\end{bmatrix}
\begin{bmatrix}
1 & 1 & 1 & 1 \\
e^{j\pi/4} & e^{-j\pi/4} & e^{j3\pi/4} & e^{-j3\pi/4} \\
e^{j\pi/2} & e^{-j\pi/2} & e^{j3\pi/2} & e^{-j3\pi/2} \\
e^{j3\pi/4} & e^{-j3\pi/4} & e^{j9\pi/4} & e^{-j9\pi/4}
\end{bmatrix}
$$

where $k = (\rho s^2/4EI)^{\frac14}$. Hence

$$
\mathbf{T}^{-1} = \tfrac14
\begin{bmatrix}
1 & e^{-j\pi/4} & e^{-j\pi/2} & e^{-j3\pi/4} \\
1 & e^{j\pi/4} & e^{j\pi/2} & e^{j3\pi/4} \\
1 & e^{-j3\pi/4} & e^{-j3\pi/2} & e^{-j9\pi/4} \\
1 & e^{j3\pi/4} & e^{j3\pi/2} & e^{j9\pi/4}
\end{bmatrix}
\begin{bmatrix}
1 & 0 & 0 & 0 \\
0 & \dfrac{1}{2^{\frac12}k} & 0 & 0 \\
0 & 0 & \dfrac{-1}{2k^2EI} & 0 \\
0 & 0 & 0 & \dfrac{-1}{2^{\frac12}k^3EI}
\end{bmatrix}
$$

$$
= \tfrac14
\begin{bmatrix}
1 & \dfrac{1-j}{2k} & \dfrac{j}{2k^2EI} & \dfrac{1+j}{4k^3EI} \\
1 & \dfrac{1+j}{2k} & \dfrac{-j}{2k^2EI} & \dfrac{1-j}{4k^3EI} \\
1 & \dfrac{-1-j}{2k} & \dfrac{-j}{2k^2EI} & \dfrac{-1+j}{4k^3EI} \\
1 & \dfrac{-1+j}{2k} & \dfrac{j}{2k^2EI} & \dfrac{-1-j}{4k^3EI}
\end{bmatrix}
$$

The characteristic constraints are therefore, according to (13.58),

$$
Y + \frac{1-j}{2k}\,\Theta + \frac{j}{2k^2EI}\,M + \frac{1+j}{4k^3EI}\,\Sigma = 0
$$

$$
Y + \frac{1+j}{2k}\,\Theta - \frac{j}{2k^2EI}\,M + \frac{1-j}{4k^3EI}\,\Sigma = 0
$$

where Y, Θ, M, Σ are the Laplace transforms of $y(t, x)$, $\theta(t, x)$, $m(t, x)$, and $\sigma(t, x)$, respectively. By adding and subtracting these equations, we find

$$
Y + \frac{\Theta}{2k} + \frac{1}{4k^3EI}\,\Sigma = 0
$$

$$
\frac{\Theta}{2k} - \frac{M}{2k^2EI} - \frac{\Sigma}{4k^3EI} = 0
$$

which are two relations between the transforms of the displacement, slope, bending moment, and shear stress which must be satisfied for all x in the semi-infinite beam.

13.7 STABILITY

It is generally impossible to obtain an explicit analytic relation for the time-domain response of a distributed system to a specified input, since the transfer functions involved in the calculation are irrational.   When the system is finite and its terminations are lumped, the transfer functions are meromorphic, but there are still infinitely many poles,† so that a closed-form solution cannot generally be obtained.   In many cases even the location of the poles cannot be established, except by numerical methods.

For many purposes an expression for the response of the system is, fortunately, unnecessary.   It is often adequate to establish the stability of the system (or in design problems, to establish the range of adjustable parameters which leads to stability) and then to obtain an approximate expression for the response.   Methods for accomplishing these tasks are discussed in this section and the following.

For a system represented as described in Sec. 13.5, the transfer functions all have the common denominator

$$|\mathbf{M}(s) + \mathbf{N}(s)\mathbf{H}(s, L)|$$

whose zeros are the poles (the only singularities) of the system.   Thus the impulse response from any input to any output can be expressed as a sum of exponentials

$$h(t) = \sum_{n=1}^{\infty} A_n e^{s_n t} \tag{13.59}$$

where s_n are the roots of the characteristic equation

$$|\mathbf{M}(s) + \mathbf{N}(s)\mathbf{H}(s, L)| = 0 \tag{13.60}$$

It thus follows that $h(t) \to 0$ as $t \to \infty$ if and only if $\mathrm{Re}\, s_n < 0$, $n = 1, 2, \ldots$ (provided that (13.59) converges uniformly in n as $t \to \infty$).   Thus the problem of establishing whether the system is stable is equivalent to the problem of establishing whether the (infinitely many) roots of (13.60) all lie in the left half plane.

† Thus one can regard a finite distributed system as being governed by an ordinary differential equation of denumerably infinite order.

Since the Routh-Hurwitz algorithms discussed in Chap. 12 are useful only for systems with a finite number of poles, they cannot be applied in the present problem.† The graphical techniques (Nyquist diagram and root loci), however, are not restricted to systems of finite order and can often be applied successfully. The application is illustrated in the following example.

Example 13.13   Stability of temperature-control system   In Example 13.9 the characteristic equation was found to be

$$k + \frac{1}{Z_0} \sinh \Gamma L = 0 \tag{13.61}$$

where

$$Z_0 = \frac{1}{A} \sqrt{\frac{1}{C\rho\sigma s}}$$

$$\Gamma = \sqrt{\frac{C\rho s}{\sigma}}$$

To establish the range of stability, it is necessary to determine the range of k for which the roots of (13.61) lie in the left half plane. It is convenient to introduce the normalizing parameters

$$w = \frac{C\rho s L^2}{\sigma}$$

$$a = \frac{kL}{\sigma A}$$

Then (13.61) becomes

$$a + \sqrt{w} \sinh \sqrt{w} = 0 \tag{13.62}$$

The root-locus method is convenient for this problem. The (infinitely many) root loci start at the zeros of $\sqrt{w} \sinh \sqrt{w}$, and all go to infinity with increasing k or a. The zeros occur for $\sqrt{w} = \pm jn\pi, n = 1, 2, \ldots$, or for $w = -n^2\pi^2$. The root loci have the general appearance of Fig. 13.12.

It is observed that our problem becomes that of locating the value of a for which the first crossing of the imaginary axis occurs on any locus. The normalized frequencies v at which the crossings occur are obtained by substituting $w = jv$ into (13.62). This gives

$$a + \sqrt{jv} \sinh \sqrt{jv} = a + (1 + j) \sqrt{\frac{v}{2}} \sinh \left[(1 + j) \sqrt{\frac{v}{2}} \right] = 0$$

† See, however, Sec. 13.8.

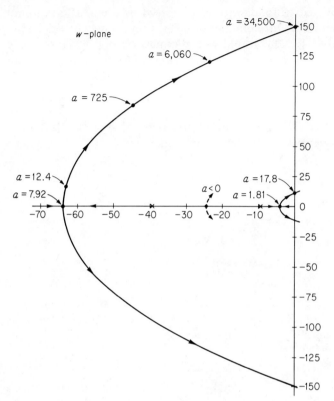

FIG. 13.12   *Loci of roots of* $a + \sqrt{w} \sinh \sqrt{w} = 0$.

Denoting $\sqrt{v/2}$ by λ, we have

$$a + (\lambda + j\lambda)(\sinh \lambda \cos \lambda + j \cosh \lambda \sin \lambda)$$
$$= a + \lambda(\sinh \lambda \cos \lambda - \cosh \lambda \sin \lambda) + j\lambda(\sinh \lambda \cos \lambda + \cosh \lambda \sin \lambda) = 0$$

Since a is real, we require

$$\lambda(\sinh \lambda \cos \lambda - \cosh \lambda \sin \lambda) = -a$$
$$\lambda(\sinh \lambda \cos \lambda + \cosh \lambda \sin \lambda) = 0$$

The values of λ at the required crossings are given by

$$\tanh \lambda = -\tan \lambda$$

These values occur at the intersections of the curves shown in Fig. 13.13a. The values of a at these crossings are given by

$$a = -2\lambda \sinh \lambda \cos \lambda$$

as shown in Fig. 13.13b.   As the value of λ at which the crossing occurs increases, so does the corresponding value of a.   Thus the value of a at only the first crossing needs to be calculated to determine the range of stability.   A numerical solution gives $\lambda_1 = 2.365$, and $a_1 = 17.80$.   Thus

$$k_{max} = 17.80 \frac{\sigma A}{L}$$

This problem was apparently first solved by Turner in 1936, who also demonstrated thermal oscillations in the system by means of an experimental apparatus.†

† L. B. Turner, Self-oscillations in a Retroacting Thermal Conductor, *Proc. Cambridge Phil. Soc.*, vol. 32, pp. 663–675, 1936.

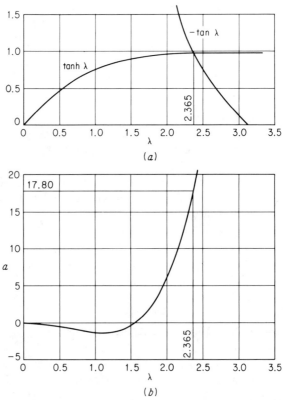

FIG. 13.13   Calculation of maximum gain in temperature-control problem.

13.8 APPROXIMATIONS

The derivation of an explicit expression for the impulse response of a distributed system or, more generally, the response to a given input usually requires a rational approximation to be made. There does not seem to be a technique which is universally valid, but the following approaches are often of value.

PADE APPROXIMANTS

For a finite system with lumped termination, a typical transfer function is a ratio of entire functions; viz.,

$$K(s) = \frac{a_0 + a_1 s + a_2 s^2 + \cdots}{b_0 + b_1 s + b_2 s^2 + \cdots}$$

If the series in the numerator and denominator are terminated after i and j terms, respectively, the resulting approximation is

$$K_{ij}(s) = \frac{a_0 + a_1 s + \cdots + a_i s^i}{b_0 + b_1 s + \cdots + b_j s^j} \tag{13.63}$$

Unfortunately, there does not seem to be a known rule for determining the number of terms to be retained in the series. It is also usually not possible to ascertain whether the truncation of the series after any finite number of terms gives a reasonable approximation in the time domain. In order to establish this fact, one would have to show that, for any $\epsilon > 0$, there exist integers i and j such that

$$\int_0^\infty [h_{ij}(t) - h(t)]^2 \, dt < \epsilon$$

or some equivalent property.

LUMPED-PARAMETER APPROXIMATION

An alternative to the above method which has somewhat better physical justification is to employ the fact that

$$\exp\left[(\mathbf{F}_0 + \mathbf{F}_1 s + \mathbf{F}_2 s^2)L\right] = \lim_{n \to \infty} \left[\mathbf{I} + (\mathbf{F}_0 + \mathbf{F}_1 s + \mathbf{F}_2 s^2)\frac{L}{n}\right]^n$$

The approximation uses a finite n.   This means that the relation between $\mathbf{Q}(s, 0)$ and $\mathbf{Q}(s, L)$ is approximated by

$$\mathbf{Q}(s, L) = \left[\mathbf{I} + (\mathbf{F}_0 + \mathbf{F}_1 s + \mathbf{F}_2 s^2) \frac{L}{n} \right]^n \mathbf{Q}(s, 0)$$

This is equivalent to breaking up the distributed system into n pieces, each piece having a transfer matrix

$$\mathbf{I} + (\mathbf{F}_0 + \mathbf{F}_1 s + \mathbf{F}_2 s^2) \frac{L}{n} \qquad (13.64)$$

Example 13.14 Short-circuited transmission line We found in Example 13.2 that the voltage transfer function for a short-circuited diffusive line is

$$H(s, x) = \left(\frac{k_1}{k_2} \right)^{\frac{1}{2}} \left(\frac{1 + \dfrac{k_1 s}{3!} + \dfrac{k_1^2 s^2}{5!} + \cdots}{1 + \dfrac{k_2 s}{3!} + \dfrac{k_2^2 s^2}{5!} + \cdots} \right)$$

With $k_1 = \frac{1}{4}$ and $k_2 = 1$, this expression becomes

$$H\left(s, \frac{L}{2}\right) = \frac{1}{2} \left(\frac{1 + \dfrac{s}{(4)3!} + \dfrac{s^2}{(16)5!} + \cdots}{1 + \dfrac{s}{3!} + \dfrac{s^2}{5!} + \cdots} \right)$$

The evaluation of the corresponding impulse responses for various degrees of approximation (by terminating the two series) is left to the reader (Prob. 13.4).   It is of interest to compare the locations of the poles of the approximants with the exact locations.   The results are as tabulated.

m	First m approximate poles	First m exact poles
1	-6	$-\pi^2 = -9.87$
2	$-10 \pm j4.48$	$-\pi^2 = -9.87,\ -4\pi^2 = -39.48$
3	$-9.5,\ -16.3 \pm j16.3$	$-9.87,\ -39.48,\ -88.8$

Note that while the exact poles are all real, the approximations may be complex.   The real pole with the smallest real part, however, is not too poorly approximated when $m = 3$.

The lumped-parameter approximation discussed above makes use of

$$\mathbf{H}(s, L) \doteq \left[\mathbf{I} + (\mathbf{F}_0 + \mathbf{F}_1 s)\frac{L}{n} \right]^n$$

$$= \begin{bmatrix} 1 & -\dfrac{rL}{n} \\ -\dfrac{csL}{n} & 1 \end{bmatrix}^n$$

The termination conditions resulting from a short circuit at $x = L$ and a source voltage $E_S(s)$ at $x = 0$ are

$$\begin{bmatrix} 1 & 0 \\ 0 & 0 \end{bmatrix}\begin{bmatrix} V(s, 0) \\ I(s, 0) \end{bmatrix} + \begin{bmatrix} 0 & 0 \\ 1 & 0 \end{bmatrix}\begin{bmatrix} V(s, L) \\ I(s, L) \end{bmatrix} = \begin{bmatrix} E_S(s) \\ 0 \end{bmatrix}$$

The first square matrix is $\mathbf{M}$, and the second is $\mathbf{N}$. Hence the approximate characteristic equation is

$$|\mathbf{M} + \mathbf{NH}(s, L)| = \left| \begin{bmatrix} 1 & 0 \\ 0 & 0 \end{bmatrix} + \begin{bmatrix} 0 & 0 \\ 1 & 0 \end{bmatrix}\begin{bmatrix} H_{11} & H_{12} \\ H_{21} & H_{22} \end{bmatrix} \right|$$

$$= H_{12} = 0$$

The matrices $\mathbf{H}(s, L)$ for $n = 1, 2, 3, 4$ are given below.

n	$\mathbf{H}(s, L)$
1	$\begin{bmatrix} 1 & -rL \\ -csL & 1 \end{bmatrix}$
2	$\begin{bmatrix} 1 + \dfrac{rcsL^2}{4} & -rL \\ -csL & 1 + \dfrac{rcsL^2}{4} \end{bmatrix}$
3	$\begin{bmatrix} 1 + \frac{1}{3}rcsL^2 & -rL - \frac{1}{27}r^2csL^3 \\ -csL - \frac{1}{27}rc^2s^2L^3 & 1 + \frac{1}{3}rcsL^2 \end{bmatrix}$
4	$\begin{bmatrix} 1 + \frac{3}{8}rcsL^2 + \frac{1}{256}r^2c^2s^2L^4 & -rL - \frac{1}{16}r^2csL^3 \\ -csL - \frac{1}{16}rc^2s^2L^3 & 1 + \frac{3}{8}rcsL^2 + \frac{1}{256}r^2c^2s^2L^4 \end{bmatrix}$

The term H_{12} of the first two approximations is not a function of s, and these must be ruled out as valid approximations. The characteristic equation corresponding to the third matrix is

$$1 + \tfrac{1}{27}rcL^2 s = 0$$

which, for $rcL^2 = k_2 = 1$, has the characteristic root $s = -27$, which

is quite far from the first exact root of $-\pi^2 = -9.87$.   The characteristic equation for the third matrix is

$$1 + \tfrac{1}{16} rcL^2 s = 0$$

giving a *single* characteristic root of $s = -16$ for $rcL^2 = k_2 = 1$, which is somewhat closer to the smallest true characteristic root.   For $n = 6$, the characteristic equation is

$$1 + \frac{5}{54} rcL^2 s + \frac{1}{1,296} (rcL^2)^2 s^2 = 0$$

with roots, for $rcL^2 = k_2 = 1$, of $s = -12$ and $s = -108$.   It is evident that reasonable approximations to the exact values of the roots are obtained only for fairly large values of n.   Since the characteristic equation turns out to be of disappointingly low order compared with the order of the approximation, the technique is not very useful in this case.

Example 13.15   Temperature-control problem   We return to the temperature-control problem considered in Example 13.13.   We found the characteristic equation to be

$$a + \sqrt{w} \sinh \sqrt{w} = 0 \qquad w = \frac{sC\rho L^2}{\sigma}$$

In view of the tedious graphical method required to obtain the exact stability region, it is natural to ask how good a result is obtained by applying the Hurwitz criterion (Chap. 12) to the partial sums of $a + \sqrt{w} \sinh \sqrt{w}$.   The general expression for the approximate characteristic equation obtained by terminating the series expansion is

$$a + w + \frac{w^2}{3!} + \frac{w^3}{5!} + \cdots + \frac{w^n}{(2n-1)!} = 0$$

In particular,

For $n = 1$: $a + w = 0$
For $n = 2$: $6a + 6w + w^2 = 0$
For $n = 3$: $120a + 120w + 20w^2 + w^3 = 0$
For $n = 4$: $5{,}040a + 5{,}040w + 840w^2 + 42w^3 + w^4 = 0$

are the characteristic equations.   Evidently $n = 1$ and $n = 2$ are inadequate approximations, since they give the erroneous result that the system is stable for all positive a.   On the other hand, the Hurwitz matrix for $n = 3$ is

$$\mathbf{H} = \begin{bmatrix} 20 & 120a & 0 \\ 1 & 120 & 0 \\ 0 & 20 & 120a \end{bmatrix}$$

and results in the region of apparent stability

$$0 < a < 20$$

The upper limit is not too far from the exact value of 17.80.   The Hurwitz matrix for $n = 4$ is

$$\mathbf{H} = \begin{bmatrix} 42 & 5,040 & 0 & 0 \\ 1 & 840 & 5,040a & 0 \\ 0 & 42 & 5,040 & 0 \\ 0 & 1 & 840 & 5,040a \end{bmatrix}$$

and leads to a stability region of

$$0 < a < 17.14$$

which is an even better estimate.

It appears that as n is increased, we converge upon the true stability region.   While this seems to be a justifiable conclusion on intuitive grounds, there is no theorem which ensures this result.   Moreover, without knowing the exact region of stability, there is no way of determining how closely the estimated region of stability for a given n approximates the true region.

13.9 GENERALIZATIONS

Most of our attention has been confined to systems which upon transformation can be represented by differential equations, in the frequency domain, of the form

$$\frac{d\mathbf{Q}}{dx} = (\mathbf{F}_0 + \mathbf{F}_1 s + \mathbf{F}_2 s^2)\mathbf{Q} + \bar{\mathbf{U}}(s, x) \qquad (13.65)$$

where $\mathbf{F}_0$, $\mathbf{F}_1$, and $\mathbf{F}_2$ are constant matrices.   While a good many systems fall into this category, there are a number of practical ones which do not.   Our objective here is to indicate how the previous results may be applied in some of these cases.

SYSTEMS WITH SPATIAL PARAMETER VARIATION

There are many systems whose parameters are space-dependent.   These parameters form the elements of the matrices $\mathbf{F}_0$, $\mathbf{F}_1$, and $\mathbf{F}_2$ (which must be time-invariant to permit the use of the Laplace transform method).

In this case, (13.65) is a linear system with variable coefficients. The theory of linear time-varying systems applies to (13.65), except that the independent variable of the differential equation is space, not time. In particular, the solution of (13.65) can be written

$$\mathbf{Q}(s, x_1) = \mathbf{H}(s, x_1, x_0)\mathbf{Q}(s, x_0) + \int_{x_0}^{x_1} \mathbf{H}(s, x_1, \xi)\mathbf{\bar{U}}(s, \xi)\, d\xi$$

where $\mathbf{H}(s, x_1, x_0)$ is the fundamental matrix for (13.65). Note that $\mathbf{H}$ is a function of x_1 and x_0 and cannot be expressed as a function of their difference $x_1 - x_0$ as in the case of spatially invariant systems. All the results, however, which have been obtained through the use of $\mathbf{H}(s, x) = \exp\left[(\mathbf{F}_0 + \mathbf{F}_1 s + \mathbf{F}_2 s^2)x\right]$ remain valid when the correct fundamental matrix is employed in place of $\mathbf{H}(s, x)$. For example, the general result (13.47) for the transmission from an external vector source $\mathbf{Z}(s)$ to any point in the system, with the termination expressed by (13.43), can be generalized to read

$$\mathbf{Q}(s, x) = \mathbf{H}(s, x, 0)[\mathbf{M}(s) + \mathbf{N}(s)\mathbf{H}(s, L, 0)]^{-1}\mathbf{Z}(s)$$

The characteristic equation thus remains

$$|\mathbf{M}(s) + \mathbf{N}(s)\mathbf{H}(s, L, 0)| = 0$$

Unfortunately, this generalization is not of much use, since it is usually impossible to obtain an analytic expression for the fundamental matrix $\mathbf{H}(s, x, x_0)$. One important case in which the fundamental matrix can be calculated is that in which all the parameters vary with x in the same way, either by design or through fortuitous circumstances. In this case (13.65) takes the form

$$\frac{d\mathbf{Q}}{dx} = \eta(x)(\mathbf{F}_{00} + \mathbf{F}_{10}s + \mathbf{F}_{20}s^2)\mathbf{Q} + \mathbf{\bar{U}}(s, x) \tag{13.66}$$

where $\eta(x)$ is a scalar function and $\mathbf{F}_i = \eta(x)\mathbf{F}_{i0}$ ($i = 1, 2, 3$). In this case, as discussed in Chap. 4 (pp. 115–118), the required fundamental matrix is given by

$$\mathbf{H}(s, x_1, x_0) = \exp\left[(\mathbf{F}_{00} + \mathbf{F}_{10}s + \mathbf{F}_{20}s^2)\int_{x_0}^{x} \eta(\xi)\, d\xi\right] \tag{13.67}$$

Example 13.16 Tapered transmission line If an electrical transmission line has parameters which vary in the same way along the line, i.e.,

$$r = r_0\eta(x)$$
$$l = l_0\eta(x)$$
$$c = c_0\eta(x)$$
$$g = g_0\eta(x)$$

it follows from the above discussion that

$$\mathbf{H}(s, x_1, x_0) = \begin{bmatrix} \cosh \Gamma\lambda & -Z_0 \sinh \Gamma\lambda \\ -\dfrac{1}{Z_0} \sinh \Gamma\lambda & \cosh \Gamma\lambda \end{bmatrix}$$

where

$$\Gamma = \sqrt{(l_0 s + r_0)(c_0 s + g_0)}$$

$$Z_0 = \sqrt{\frac{l_0 s + r_0}{c_0 s + g_0}}$$

$$\lambda \equiv \lambda(x_1, x_0) = \int_{x_0}^{x_1} \eta(\xi)\, d\xi$$

Note that the characteristic impedance is the same as for a uniform line.

CASCADED SYSTEMS WITH BOUNDARY CONTINUITY

The situation may arise where two or more distributed systems, each with different parameters, are connected together. For simplicity, suppose we have only two systems, without distributed forcing terms, as shown in Fig. 13.14. The first is characterized by †

$$\frac{d\mathbf{Q}_1}{dx} = (\mathbf{F}_0 + \mathbf{F}_1 s + \mathbf{F}_2 s^2)\mathbf{Q}_1$$

Hence

$$\mathbf{Q}_1(s, x) = \mathbf{H}_1(s, x)\mathbf{Q}_1(s, 0) \qquad 0 \le x \le x_1 \qquad (13.68)$$

where

$$\mathbf{H}_1(s, x) = \exp\left[(\mathbf{F}_0 + \mathbf{F}_1 s + \mathbf{F}_2 s^2)x\right]$$

Likewise, the second system is governed by

$$\frac{d\mathbf{Q}_2}{dx} = (\mathbf{G}_0 + \mathbf{G}_1 s + \mathbf{G}_2 s^2)\mathbf{Q}_2(s, 0)$$

with

$$\mathbf{Q}_2(s, x - x_1) = \mathbf{H}_2(s, x - x_1)\mathbf{Q}_2(s, x_1) \qquad x_1 < x < L \qquad (13.69)$$

† The subscript 1 on $\mathbf{Q}_1$ denotes system number 1 and not the first component of a vector.

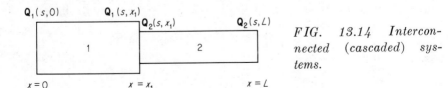

FIG. 13.14 Interconnected (cascaded) systems.

where

$$\boxed{\mathbf{H}_2(s, x) = \exp\left[(\mathbf{G}_0 + \mathbf{G}_1 s + \mathbf{G}_2 s^2)x\right]}$$

If the transition across the boundary is continuous, i.e.,

$$\lim_{\delta \to 0}\left[\mathbf{q}_1(x_1 - \delta) - \mathbf{q}_2(x_1 + \delta)\right] = 0$$

we can write

$$\mathbf{Q}_2(s, x_1) = \mathbf{Q}_1(s, x_1)$$

and it follows from (13.68) and (13.69) that

$$\mathbf{Q}_2(s, x) = \mathbf{H}_2(s, x - x_1)\mathbf{H}_1(s, x_1)\mathbf{Q}_1(s, 0) \qquad (13.70)$$

This result is readily extended to more than two systems.

Example 13.17   Cascaded transmission lines   The transfer matrix of two cascaded transmission lines of length L_1 and L_2, respectively, is

$$\mathbf{H} = \begin{bmatrix} \cosh \Gamma_1 L_1 & -Z_{01} \sinh \Gamma_1 L_1 \\ -\dfrac{1}{Z_{01}} \sinh \Gamma_1 L_1 & \cosh \Gamma_1 L_1 \end{bmatrix} \begin{bmatrix} \cosh \Gamma_2 L_2 & -Z_{02} \sinh \Gamma_2 L_2 \\ -\dfrac{1}{Z_{02}} \sinh \Gamma_2 L_2 & \cosh \Gamma_2 L_2 \end{bmatrix}$$

If the parameters change so that $Z_{01} = Z_{02} = Z_0$,

$$\mathbf{H} = \begin{bmatrix} \cosh (\Gamma_1 L_1 + \Gamma_2 L_2) & -Z_0 \sinh (\Gamma_1 L_1 + \Gamma_2 L_2) \\ -\dfrac{1}{Z_0} \sinh (\Gamma_1 L_1 + \Gamma_2 L_2) & \cosh (\Gamma_1 L_1 + \Gamma_2 L_2) \end{bmatrix}$$

which is of the same form as the transfer matrix for a single system, except that ΓL is replaced by $\Gamma_1 L_1 + \Gamma_2 L_2$ (the weighted sum).

SYSTEMS OF OTHER FORM

There are instances in which the system under investigation cannot be put in the form of (13.65). This usually arises in one of the following situations:

1. The process differential equations contain terms of the form $\partial^2 q_i / \partial x \partial t$.
2. One or more differential equations do not contain a term $\partial q_i / \partial x$.

Case 1 can be reduced to case 2 by the introduction of a new variable q_j and the auxiliary equation $\partial q_i / \partial t - q_j = 0$ by which q_j is defined.

The transform method can be used in such systems, and the results of the previous sections are generally applicable with one important

exception: the transfer matrix of the system terminated with lumped elements usually has an *essential singularity* in the finite part of the s plane.

Example 13.18 Acoustic propagation in viscous medium Consider a pipe filled with an ideal compressible fluid having a mean density ρ, a bulk modulus b, and a coefficient of viscosity μ.

Let p = pressure excess over that at equilibrium
  ξ = displacement

Then it can be shown† that the motion of the fluid for small displacements can be approximated by

$$\frac{\partial p}{\partial x} = -\rho \frac{\partial^2 \xi}{\partial t^2}$$

$$\tfrac{4}{3}\mu \frac{\partial^2 \xi}{\partial x\, \partial t} + b \frac{\partial \xi}{\partial x} = -p$$

Although these equations are not in the standard form, they can be transformed to the frequency domain. Ignoring initial conditions, the result obtained is, with $P(s, x) = \mathcal{L}[p(t, x)]$ and $\Xi(s, x) = \mathcal{L}[\xi(t,x)]$,

$$\frac{dP(s, x)}{dx} = -\rho s^2 \Xi(s, x)$$

$$-(\tfrac{4}{3}\mu s + b)\frac{d\Xi(s, x)}{dx} = P(s, x)$$

or in matrix form

$$\begin{bmatrix} \dfrac{dQ_1}{dx} \\ \dfrac{dQ_2}{dx} \end{bmatrix} = \begin{bmatrix} 0 & -\rho s^2 \\ -\dfrac{1}{\frac{4}{3}\mu s + b} & 0 \end{bmatrix} \begin{bmatrix} Q_1 \\ Q_2 \end{bmatrix}$$

where $Q_1 = P$, $Q_2 = \Xi$.

In the frequency domain the differential equations have the same form as the transmission-line equations (zero on the main diagonal). Hence we can write

$$\mathbf{Q}(s, x) = \mathbf{H}(s, x)\mathbf{Q}(s, 0)$$

where

$$\mathbf{H} = \begin{bmatrix} \cosh \Gamma x & -Z_0 \sinh \Gamma x \\ -\dfrac{1}{Z_0} \sinh \Gamma x & \cosh \Gamma x \end{bmatrix}$$

$$\Gamma = \sqrt{\frac{\rho s^2}{\frac{4}{3}\mu s + b}}$$

$$Z_0 = \sqrt{\rho s^2(\tfrac{4}{3}\mu s + b)}$$

† R. B. Lindsay, "Methods and Concepts of Theoretical Physics," pp. 363–367, D. Van Nostrand Company, Inc., Princeton, N.J., 1951.

When expanded in a power series, each term in $\mathbf{H}(s, x)$ will be a power series in $\rho s^2/(\frac{4}{3}\mu s + b)$. Thus $\mathbf{H}(s, x)$ has an essential singularity at $s = -3b/4\mu$, which will also occur in all transfer functions of the terminated system.

PROBLEMS

13.1   Evaluate $\mathbf{H}(s, x) = \exp(\mathbf{F} + \mathbf{G}s)x$ for the transmission line by use of the series definition for the exponential.

13.2   Show that in a semi-infinite transmission line $\operatorname{Re} V(s)/I(s) > 0$ for $\operatorname{Re} s > 0$.

13.3   Evaluate the inverse Laplace transform of

$$H(s, x) = e^{-\sqrt{rcs}\,x}$$

by contour integration, and thereby obtain the impulse response of a semi-infinite transmission line with negligible inductance and leakage conductance.

13.4   (a) Plot the impulse response of the short-circuited transmission line of Example 13.2 by calculating a sufficient number of terms in the series.   Use $k_1 = \frac{1}{4}$, $k_2 = 1$.

(b) Compare this response with the result obtained by the use of the approximate transfer function

$$H_{ij}(s, x) = \left(\frac{k_1}{k_2}\right)^{\frac{1}{2}} \left(\frac{1 + \dfrac{k_1 s}{3!} + \dfrac{k_1{}^2 s^2}{5!} + \cdots + \dfrac{k_1{}^i s^i}{(2i+1)!}}{1 + \dfrac{k_2 s}{3!} + \dfrac{k_2{}^2 s^2}{5!} + \cdots + \dfrac{k_2{}^j s^j}{(2j+1)!}} \right)$$

Perform the calculation for $i = j = 1, 2, 3$.

13.5   Consider the transmission line terminated as shown in Fig. 13.3. Calculate the transfer function and impulse response from E_S to $V(s, L)$ under the following conditions:

	Z_0	Γ	Z_L	Z_s
1	$\sqrt{lc}\,s$	$\sqrt{l/c}$	∞	Z_0
2	$\sqrt{lc}\,s$	$\sqrt{l/c}$	Z_0	0
3	$\sqrt{lc}\,s$	$\sqrt{l/c}$	$1/Cs$	Z_0
4	$\sqrt{rcs}$	$\sqrt{r/cs}$	∞	0

13.6   A slender rod of length $2L$, having conductivity σ per unit length, specific heat k per unit length, and linear density ρ per unit length, has its right-hand end immersed in freezing water ($0°C$). After the entire rod is brought to equilibrium at $t = 0$, the temperature of the left-hand end is suddenly raised to $100°C$ and kept constant thereafter. Assume that the rod is insulated, except at its ends, and that the temperature distribution through the cross section is uniform.

(a) Find the Laplace transform of the temperature θ in the middle of the rod.

(b) Find the steady-state temperature at this point. Is this reasonable?

13.7   An rc transmission line ($l = g = 0$) of length L is terminated in a resistor $R' = 2rL$ in parallel with a capacitor $C' = cL/2$, where r and c are the resistance and capacitance, respectively, per unit length of the line.

(a) Obtain the voltage transfer function $G(s) = V(s, L)/V(s, 0)$ in terms of $T = rcL^2$.

(b) What is the nature of the singularities of $G(s)$? Where are they located?

(c) Find an approximate expression for the impulse response $g(t)$ for *large* t.

13.8   Consider a flexible rocket in which aerodynamic effects are negligible. Assume that the rocket is propelled by an engine which provides a constant thrust F and that the thrust is along the

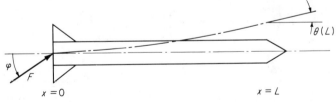

FIG. P 13.8

longitudinal axis of the rocket at $t = 0$. At this time the engine is suddenly rotated through a small angle φ, as shown in Fig. P 13.8. Compare the angle $\theta(L)$ with the angle $\bar{\theta}$ which the rocket would have if it were absolutely rigid. *Hint:* The terminations can be expressed as

$$\sigma(t, L) = m(t, L) = m(t, 0) = 0, \sigma(t, 0) \doteq F\varphi$$

13.9 An lc transmission line is terminated in an rc transmission line as shown in Fig. P 13.9. The voltage input to the lc line is given by

$$V_1(0) = E - kV_2(L)$$

(a) Calculate the transfer function from E to $V_2(L)$.
(b) What is the characteristic equation of the system?
(c) Determine the range of stability as accurately as possible.
(d) Find the approximate range of stability by approximating the characteristic equation by an equation of the third degree. Repeat for an equation of the fourth degree. Compare with result of part c.

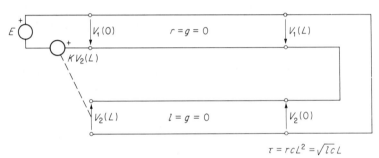

FIG. P 13.9

13.10 A lossless transmission line ($r = g = 0$) is terminated in a resistor $R = Z_0/2$ at each end. The sending-end voltage is made proportional to the receiving-end voltage, thus resulting in the circuit shown in Fig. P 13.10.

(a) Find the characteristic equation of the system.
(b) Find the exact range of K for which the system is stable. Sketch the root loci.
(c) Find the range of K for which the system is stable when the characteristic determinant is approximated by polynomials of degree 1, 2, 3, and 4.

FIG. P 13.10

13.11   Consider an electric network consisting of n identical sections as shown in Fig. P 13.11.

   (a) Compute the transfer matrix $\mathbf{H}_n(s)$ defined by

$$\begin{bmatrix} V_n \\ I_n \end{bmatrix} = \mathbf{H}_n(s) \begin{bmatrix} V_0 \\ I_0 \end{bmatrix}$$

   Hint: Write a difference equation relating V_n and I_n to V_{n-1} and I_{n-1}.

   (b) Show that, if $n \to \infty$ and R, C, L, $G \to 0$ in such a manner that nR, nL, nC, and nG remain constant, $\mathbf{H}_n(s)$ becomes the transfer matrix of a transmission line having the identical *total* resistance, capacitance, inductance, and conductance.

   (c) In view of part b, $\mathbf{H}_n(s)$ is an approximation to $\mathbf{H}(s, L)$ of a transmission line. Compare this approximation with the others used in Examples 13.14 and 13.15. In particular, compare the characteristic-root locations or region of stability for $n = 1, 2, 3, 4$.

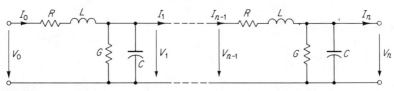

FIG. P 13.11

13.12   In the manner of Prob. 13.11, show that an electric network consisting of n sections, each of which has the structure illustrated in Fig. P 13.12, is a lumped approximation to a vibrating beam, provided that the voltages and currents are appropriately identi-

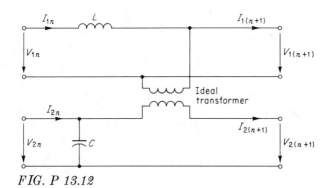

FIG. P 13.12

fied with mechanical quantities.   Can the ideal transformer be omitted?   *Hint:* Use $\dot{y}$ and $\dot{\theta}$ instead of y and θ as variables.

13.13   Consider a pipe of length L filled with a viscous fluid and capped with a bellows at each end (Fig. P 13.13).   The length of the

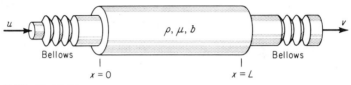

FIG. P 13.13

bellows is negligible with respect to the length of the pipe.   Calculate the transfer matrix of the system thus terminated, where u and v are forces at the ends of the bellows.   *Hint:* The bellows may be described by $p = kx$, where $p = $ pressure and $x = $ displacement.

13.14   (*a*) Show that the matrix $\mathbf{H}(s, x)$ for the beam of Example 13.6 is correctly given on page 458.

(*b*) By expanding the elements of $\mathbf{H}(s, x)$ in series, show that none contains any branch points.

BIBLIOGRAPHY

A. BOOKS

Aitken, A. C., "Theory of Matrices," 9th ed., Interscience Publishers, Inc., New York, 1958.

Beckenbach, E. F. (ed.), "Modern Mathematics for the Engineer," Second Series, McGraw-Hill Book Company, New York, 1961.

Bellman, R., "Introduction to Matrix Analysis," McGraw-Hill Book Company, New York, 1960.

Bendat, J. S., "Principles and Applications of Random Noise Theory," John Wiley & Sons, Inc., New York, 1958.

Bode, H. W., "Network Analysis and Feedback Amplifier Design," D. Van Nostrand Company, Inc., Princeton, N.J., 1945.

Campbell, D. P., "Process Dynamics," John Wiley & Sons, Inc., New York, 1958.

Carslaw, H. S., "Introduction to the Theory of Fourier's Series and Integrals," 3d rev. ed., Dover Publications, Inc., New York, 1930.

Coddington, E. A., and N. Levinson, "Theory of Ordinary Differential Equations," McGraw-Hill Book Company, New York, 1955.

Churchill, R. V., "Operational Mathematics," 2d ed., McGraw-Hill Book Company, New York, 1958.

Cramér, H., "Mathematical Methods of Statistics," Princeton University Press, Princeton, N.J., 1947.

Davenport, W. B., Jr., and W. L. Root, "An Introduction to the Theory of Random Signals and Noise," McGraw-Hill Book Company, New York, 1958.

Derman, C., and M. Klein, "Probability and Statistical Inference for Engineers," Oxford University Press, Fair Lawn, N.J., 1959.

Doetsch, G., "Theory and Application of the Laplace Transform" (in German), Dover Publications, Inc., New York, 1943.

Doob, J. L., "Stochastic Processes," John Wiley & Sons, Inc., New York, 1953.

Faddeeva, V. N., "Computational Methods of Linear Algebra," Dover Publications, Inc., New York, 1959.

Feller, W., "An Introduction to Probability Theory and Its Applications," vol. 1, 2d ed., John Wiley & Sons, Inc., New York, 1957.

Friedland, B. O. Wing, and R. Ash, "Principles of Linear Networks," McGraw-Hill Book Company, New York, 1961.

Gantmacher, F. R., "Theory of Matrices," 2 vols., Chelsea Publishing Company, New York, 1959.

Gardner, M. F., and J. L. Barnes, "Transients in Linear Systems," vol. 1, John Wiley & Sons, Inc., New York, 1942.

Hahn, W., "Theory and Application of Liapunov's Direct Method," (English transl. by H. H. Hosenthien), Prentice-Hall, Inc., Englewood Cliffs, N.J., 1963.

Halmos, P., "Finite-dimensional Vector Spaces," 2d ed., D. Van Nostrand Company, Inc., Princeton, N.J., 1958.

Hildebrand, F. B., "Methods of Applied Mathematics," Prentice-Hall, Inc., Englewood Cliffs, N.J., 1952.

Jordan, C., "Calculus of Finite Differences," 2d ed., Chelsea Publishing Company, New York, 1952.

Jury, E. I., "Sampled-Data Control Systems," John Wiley & Sons, Inc., New York, 1958.

Kaplan, W., "Advanced Calculus," Addison-Wesley Publishing Company, Inc., Reading, Mass., 1952.

———, "Operational Methods for Linear Systems," Addison-Wesley Publishing Company, Inc., Reading, Mass., 1962.

Korn, G. A., and T. M. Korn, "Electronic Analog Computers," 2d ed., McGraw-Hill Book Company, New York, 1956.

Lamb, H., "Higher Mechanics," 2d ed., Cambridge University Press, New York, 1929.

LaSalle, J. P., and S. Lefschetz, "Stability by Liapunov's Direct Method with Applications," Academic Press, Inc., New York, 1961.

Lefschetz, S., "Differential Equations: Geometric Theory," Interscience Publishers, Inc., New York, 1957.

Letov, A. M., "Stability in Nonlinear Control Systems" (English transl. by J. G. Adashko), Princeton University Press, Princeton, N.J., 1961.

Lindsay, R. B., "Methods and Concepts of Theoretical Physics," D. Van Nostrand Company, Inc., Princeton, N.J., 1951.

Loève, M., "Probability Theory," D. Van Nostrand Company, Inc., Princeton, N.J., 1955.

Lur'e, A. I., "Some Nonlinear Problems in the Theory of Automatic Control" (Eng. transl.), H. M. Stationery Office, London, 1957.

Lyapunov, M. A., Le Problème général de la stabilité du mouvement, *Ann. Fac. Sci. Toulouse*, vol. 9, pp. 203–474, 1907 (originally published in Russian in 1892; reprinted as *Annals of Math. Studies*, no. 17, Princeton University Press, Princeton, N.J., 1947).

Marden, M., The Geometry of the Zeros of a Polynomial in a Complex Variable, *Math. Surveys*, no. 3, American Mathematical Society, New York, 1949.

Mason, S. J., and H. J. Zimmerman, "Electronic Circuits, Signals, and Systems," John Wiley & Sons, Inc., New York, 1960.

Middleton, D., "An Introduction to Statistical Communication Theory," McGraw-Hill Book Company, New York, 1960.

Millman, J., "Vacuum Tube and Semiconductor Electronics," McGraw-Hill Book Company, New York, 1958.

Milne-Thomson, L. M., "The Calculus of Finite Differences," St Martin's Press, Inc., New York, 1933; reprinted 1951.

Morse, P. M., and H. Feshbach, "Methods of Theoretical Physics," 2 vols., McGraw-Hill Book Company, New York, 1953.

Parzen, E., "Modern Probability Theory and Its Applications," John Wiley & Sons, Inc., New York, 1960.

Peirce, B. O., "A Short Table of Integrals," Ginn and Company, Boston, 1929.

Phillips, E. G., "Functions of a Complex Variable," Interscience Publishers, Inc., New York, 1951.

Ragazzini, J. R., and G. F. Franklin, "Sampled-data Control Systems," McGraw-Hill Book Company, New York, 1958.

Rogers, A. E., and T. W. Connolly, "Analog Computation in Engineering Design," McGraw-Hill Book Company, New York, 1960.

Routh, E. J., "A Treatise on the Stability of a Given State of Motion," Macmillan and Co., Ltd., London, 1877.

Salvadori, M. G., and R. J. Schwarz, "Differential Equations in Engineering Problems," Prentice-Hall, Inc., Englewood Cliffs, N.J., 1954.

Schwartz, L., "Théorie des distributions," 2 vols., Hermann and Cie., Paris, 1950–1951.

Sears, F. W., "Principles of Physics," vol. 1, "Mechanics, Heat and Sound," Addison-Wesley Publishing Company, Inc., Reading, Mass., 1947.

Sneddon, I. N., "Fourier Transforms," McGraw-Hill Book Company, New York, 1951.

Starkey, B. J., "Laplace Transforms for Electrical Engineers," Philosophical Library, Inc., New York, 1954.

Truxal, J. G., "Automatic Feedback Control System Synthesis," McGraw-Hill Book Company, New York, 1955.

Van der Pol, B., and H. Bremmer, "Operational Calculus Based on the Two-sided Laplace Integral," Cambridge University Press, New York, 1950.

Wax, N. (ed.), "Selected Papers on Noise and Stochastic Processes," Dover Publications, Inc., New York, 1954.

Whittaker, E. T., and G. N. Watson, "A Course of Modern Analysis," Cambridge University Press, New York, 1954.

Whittaker, J. M., "Interpolatory Function Theory," Cambridge Tracts in Mathematics and Mathematical Physics, no. 33, Cambridge University Press, New York, 1935.

Widder, D. V., "The Laplace Transform," Princeton University Press, Princeton, N.J., 1941.

Wiener, N., "The Extrapolation, Interpolation and Smoothing of Stationary Time Series," John Wiley & Sons, Inc., New York, 1949.

Wylie, C. R., Jr., "Advanced Engineering Mathematics," 2d ed., McGraw-Hill Book Company, New York, 1960.

Zadeh, L. A., and C. A. Desoer, "Linear System Theory," McGraw-Hill Book Company, New York, 1963.

B. ARTICLES

Aseltine, J. A., A Transform Method for Linear Time-varying Systems, *J. Appl. Phys.*, vol. 25, pp. 761–764, June, 1954.

Bashkow, T. R., The A Matrix: A New Network Description, *IRE Trans. Circuit Theory*, vol. CT-4, pp. 117–120, September, 1957.

Bates, M. R., D. H. Bock, and F. D., Powell, Analog Computer Applications in Predictor Design, *IRE Trans. Electron. Computers*, vol. EC-6, pp. 143–153, September, 1957.

Bennett, W. R., Methods of Solving Noise Problems, *Proc. IRE*, vol. 44, pp. 609–638, May, 1956.

Bode, H. W., and C. E. Shannon, A Simplified Derivation of Linear Least Square Smoothing and Prediction Theory, *Proc. IRE*, vol. 38, pp. 417–425, April, 1950.

Booton, R. C., Jr., An Optimization Theory for Time-varying Linear Systems with Nonstationary Statistical Inputs, *Proc. IRE*, vol. 40, pp. 977–981, August, 1952.

Bridgland, T. F., Jr., and R. E. Kalman, Some Remarks on the Stability of Linear Systems, *IRE Trans. Circuit Theory*, vol. CT-10, pp. 539–542, December, 1963.

Bryant, P. R., The Explicit Form of Bashkow's *A* Matrix, *IRE Trans. Circuit Theory*, vol. CT-9, pp. 303–306, September, 1962.

Davis, R. C., On the Theory of Prediction of Nonstationary Stochastic Processes, *J. Appl. Phys.*, vol. 23, pp. 1047–1053, September, 1952.

Doob, J. L., The Brownian Movement and Stochastic Equations, *Ann. Math.*, vol. 43, pp. 351–369, April, 1942; reprinted in N. Wax (ed.), "Selected Papers on Noise and Stochastic Processes," Dover Publications, Inc., New York, 1954.

Erdélyi, A., From Delta Functions to Distributions, chap. 1 in E. F. Beckenbach (ed.), "Modern Mathematics for the Engineer," McGraw-Hill Book Company, New York, 1961.

Evans, W. R., Control System Synthesis by Root Locus Method, *Trans. AIEE*, vol. 69, pp. 66-69, 1950.

Frame, J. S., Matrix Functions and Applications, parts I-V, *IEEE Spectrum*, vol. 1, pp. 208–220, March, 1964; pp. 102–108, April, 1964; pp. 100–109, May, 1964; pp. 123–131, June, 1964; pp. 103–109, July, 1964.

Friedland, B., Least Squares Filtering and Prediction of Non-stationary Sampled Data, *Information and Control*, vol. 1, pp. 297–313, December, 1958.

Gabor, D., Theory of Communication, *Proc. IEEE (London)*, vol. 93, pt. III, pp. 429–445, November, 1946.

Ho, E. C., and H. Davis, Generalized Operational Calculus for Time-varying Networks, University of California, Department of Engineering, Report 54-71, Los Angeles, July, 1954.

Hurwitz, A., Ueber die Bedingungen, unter welchen eine Gleichung nur Wurzeln mit negativen reellen Teilen besitzt, *Math. Ann.*, vol. 146, pp. 273–284, 1895.

Jury, E. I., A Simplified Stability Criterion for Linear Discrete Systems, *Proc. IRE*, vol. 50, pp. 1493–1500, June, 1962.

———, On the Roots of a Real Polynomial Inside the Unit Circle and a Stability Criterion for Linear Discrete Systems, in *Proc. Second Intern. Congr. IFAC*, Basle, 1963, paper no. 413 (preprint) [Butterworth & Co., Ltd.-Oldenbourg (Publishers), London-Munich, 1963].

———— and J. Blanchard, A Stability Test for Linear Discrete Systems in Table Form, *Proc. IRE*, vol. 49, pp. 1947–1948, December, 1961.

Kalman, R. E., A New Approach to Linear Filtering and Prediction Problems, *Trans. ASME*, ser. D (*J. Basic Eng.*), vol. 82, pp. 35–45, March, 1960.

————, On the General Theory of Control Systems, in Automatic and Remote Control, *Proc. First Intern. Congr. IFAC, Moscow*, 1960, pp. 481–492 (Butterworth and Co. (Publishers), Ltd., London, 1961).

————, On the Stability of Linear Time-varying Systems, *IRE Trans. Circuit Theory*, vol. CT-9, pp. 420–423, December, 1962.

———— and J. E. Bertram, Control System Analysis and Design via the "Second Method" of Lyapunov, *Trans. ASME*, ser. D (*J. Basic Eng.*), vol. 82, pp. 371–393, June, 1960.

———— and R. S. Bucy, New Results in Linear Filtering and Prediction Theory, *Trans. ASME*, ser. D (*J. Basic Eng.*), vol. 83, pp. 95–108, March, 1961.

————, Y. C. Ho, and K. S. Narendra, Controllability of Linear Dynamical Systems, *Contrib. Differential Equations*, vol. 1, pp. 189–213, 1961.

Lampard, D. G., The Response of Linear Networks to Suddenly Applied Stationary Random Noise, *IRE Trans. Circuit Theory*, vol. CT-2, pp. 49–57, March, 1955.

Liénard and Chipart, Sur le signe de la partie réelle des racines d'une équation algébrique, *J. Math. Pures Appl.*, 6th ser., vol. 10, pp. 291–346, 1914.

Mason, S. J., Feedback Theory: Some Properties of Signal Flow Graphs, *Proc. IRE*, vol. 41, pp. 1144–1156, September, 1953.

————, Feedback Theory: Further Properties of Signal Flow Graphs, *Proc. IRE*, vol. 44, pp. 920–926, July, 1956.

Massera, J. L., Contributions to Stability Theory, *Ann. Math.*, vol. 64, pp. 182–206, 1956.

Nyquist, H., Regeneration Theory, *Bell System Tech. J.*, vol. 11, pp. 126–147, January, 1932.

Parks, P. C., A New Proof of the Routh-Hurwitz Stability Criterion Using the "Second Method" of Lyapunov, *Proc. Cambridge Phil. Soc.*, vol. 58, pt. 4, pp. 694–720, 1962.

Rice, S. O., Mathematical Analysis of Random Noise, *Bell System Tech. J.*, vol. 23, pp. 282–332, July, 1944; vol. 24, pp. 46–156, January, 1945; reprinted in N. Wax (ed.), "Selected Papers on Noise and Stochastic Processes," Dover Publications, Inc., New York, 1954.

Shannon, C. E., Communication in the Presence of Noise, *Proc. IRE*, vol. 37, pp. 10–21, January, 1949.

Souriau, J-M., Une méthode pour la décomposition spectrale à l'inversion des matrices, *Compt. rend.*, vol. 227, pp. 1010–1011, 1948.

Turin, G., An Introduction to Matched Filters, *IRE Trans. Information Theory*, vol. IT-6, pp. 311–329, June, 1960.

Turner, L. B., Self-oscillations in a Retroacting Thermal Conductor, *Proc. Cambridge Phil. Soc.*, vol. 32, pp. 663–675, 1936.

Zadeh, L. A., An Extended Definition of Linearity, *Proc. IRE*, vol. 49, p. 1452, September, 1961; vol. 50, p. 200, February, 1962.

———, Frequency Analysis of Variable Networks, *Proc. IRE*, vol. 38, pp. 291–299, March, 1950.

INDEX